Fundamentals of Criminology

Fundamentals of Criminology

New Dimensions

Kelly Frailing

Dee Wood Harper

CAROLINA ACADEMIC PRESS
Durham, North Carolina

Library of Congress Cataloging-in-Publication Data

Frailing, Kelly.
  Fundamentals of criminology : new dimensions / Kelly Frailing and Dee Wood
Harper.
     pages cm
  Includes bibliographical references and index.
  ISBN 978-1-59460-690-8 (alk. paper)
  1. Criminology. I. Harper, Dee Wood. II. Title.

  HV6025.F73 2013
  364--dc23

                              2013017674

Carolina Academic Press
700 Kent Street
Durham, North Carolina 27701
Telephone (919) 489-7486
Fax (919) 493-5668
www.cap-press.com

Printed in the United States of America

Contents

Part IV • Explanation of Crime Types

List of Tables and Figures

Tables

Figures

Preface

There is a large number of criminology textbooks out there and a smaller yet still sizable number of excellent books, so why add another into the mix and why call it *Fundamentals of Criminology: New Dimensions*?

We believe that this book well captures the fundamentals of criminology through its descriptions of the extent of crime, major theories of crime causation and crime types. While many criminology textbooks do this, there are several things that set *Fundamentals of Criminology: New Dimensions* apart from other criminology texts. First, for each theory of crime, we provide a description of the tenets of the theory as well as a discussion of empirical research that tests the theory in a variety of settings; an evaluation of each theory's strengths and weaknesses; and an explanation of its policy implications. We take care to introduce readers to that empirical research that supports or does not support the theories of crime causation, we include empirical research that attempts to extend the theories of crime in new directions and in both instances, we refer to both past and very current empirical work. We believe this, in combination with a discussion of strengths and weaknesses and policy implications, assists readers in understanding each theory of crime in and of itself and in relation to the others, as well as what these theories mean for the real world. Providing this assistance is all the more important for readers who have had little to no exposure to theories of crime causation prior to opening this book and to that end, we also created a useful Appendix summarizing the details of the major theories of crime.

Second, we provide the most up-to-date information on crime commission in our descriptions of the different types of crime as well as changes in the amounts over time. This assists readers in understanding the extent of the crime problem as a whole and as broken down into specific offenses, as well as the characteristics of people involved in crime both as offenders and as victims. Third, we devote a lengthy chapter to the connection between criminological theory and the criminal justice system, in which we consider the theoretical bases for punishment, prevention and rehabilitation and how they are connected to the criminal justice system. We also consider a handful of lingering issues for criminology and criminal justice that make the connection between these two disciplines explicit and comprehensible for readers. Throughout the book, we attempt to connect relevant concepts in a way that makes it easier for readers to obtain a complete and comprehensive picture of criminology. We also provide some historical context so that readers may draw on what they already know to better understand the concepts in this book.

That explains the *Fundamentals of Criminology*, but what about the *New Dimensions*? There are a number of different concepts we explore in this book that to our knowledge are absent from the majority if not all other introductory criminology texts. We include them not just to be able to subtitle this book *New Dimensions* but to give readers the richest, most complete understanding of what crime is, how much of it there is, what causes it and what we can do to stop it. These new dimensions include but are not limited to research designs in criminology, new theories of crime causation, crime in different contexts, connections between criminology and criminal justice policy and a number of lingering issues for both disciplines. In more detail, the new dimensions of this book include:

Sir Francis Galton

The criminal mind and the concept of *mens rea*

International data sources

Criminologists' commonly used methodological techniques

Crime control through eugenics

The Jukes family

The Grasmick scale for measuring self-control

Green Criminology

The pushes and pulls of crime

Situational action theory

Organized retail crime

Crime and disasters

Active shooter situations

Hate crimes and victims

Tangible and intangible costs of victimization

Homicide-suicide

Cyber vandalism

Pink collar crime

Khaki collar crime

Criminalized lifestyles

Theoretical basis for crime punishment, prevention and rehabilitation

Explanations for changes in the crime rate

Gun control and crime

Wider legalization of prostitution and its effect on crime

Wider legalization of drugs and its effect on crime

Sex offender policies

The death penalty and deterrence

The Organization of This Book

This book is organized into five parts. Naturally, we begin at the beginning. Part I provides introductory material and Chapter 1 addresses what crime is, how society responds to crime and what criminology is. Chapter 2 raises and answers the related questions of how much crime is there and how we study it.

Part II of the book deals with theories and correlates of crime. Here we ask the question why do they do it and we find myriad answers, including psychosocial and biosocial answers (Chapter 3), social structural answers, social process answers (Chapter 5), critical answers (Chapter 6) and a lifetime of answers (Chapter 7). We conclude this section with a thorough treatment of the pushes and pulls of crime (Chapter 8).

Part III ask the questions where, when and to whom does crime happen. Chapter 9 considers the contexts in which choices to offend are made and opportunities for offending are present. In Chapter 10, we cover the nature and extent of criminal victimization as well as consider explanatory theories.

Part IV is an explanation of crime types beginning with violent crimes (Chapter 11), including both traditional and new forms of violence and a discussion of their causes. Our explanation of property crime in Chapter 12 begins with a brief history of stealing and continues with what we know about the many forms of theft and the people who engage in it. Chapter 13 explores white and other collar crime and shows how different positions people hold in the workplace and other organizations, especially the military, give rise to different forms of criminality. In Chapter 14, we discuss public order crimes as well as the criminalization of certain lifestyles.

Finally, Part V connects criminology and criminal justice in a variety of areas such as punishment, crime prevention and rehabilitation. It also explores lingering issues that have implications for both criminology and criminal justice. We conclude in Chapter 15 that these need to be addressed forthrightly lest the criminological enterprise ring hollow. We believe this text will provide those who read it with a thorough understanding of what crime is, what causes it and what can be done about it, as well as the ability and desire to pose important questions for the future of both criminology and criminal justice.

Acknowledgments

To my husband Jay and my daughter Matilda, thank you for your enduring love and support through this seemingly endless process. You are my treasures. I am grateful to Kristian Hernandez for his tireless research assistance as well as to my colleagues and students at Texas A&M International University for their patience and flexibility. Of course this book would not have been possible if not for the good people at Carolina Academic Press, who have our appreciation.

To my wife, Daniele Denis who is forever my bride. I am grateful to the Department of Criminal Justice and my colleagues William E. Thornton, Shauna Rae Taylor, Bethany Brown, Brenda Vollman, Vincenzo Sainato, David Khey and Christian Bolden for their collegiality and the College of Social Sciences at Loyola University New Orleans for continuing to provide me with an office to do my research and writing.

Part I

Introduction

Chapter 1

Introduction

Crime does not exist. Only acts exist, acts often given different meanings within various social frameworks. Acts and the meanings given to them are our data. Our challenge is to follow the destiny of acts through the universe of meanings. Particularly, what are the social conditions that encourage or prevent giving the acts the meaning of being crime? (Christie, 2004, p. 3)

What Is Crime?

Nils Christie's (2004) provocative assertion is an excellent starting point for this introductory chapter where we begin our analysis of this highly complex phenomenon. His thesis is that there is an endless supply of crimes—acts with the potentiality of being defined as crime are like an unlimited natural resource. The often cited definition of crime by criminologist Paul Tappan is considerably narrower, with crime defined as "an intentional act or omission in violation of criminal law (statutory and case law), committed without defense or justification, and sanctioned by the state as a felony or misdemeanor" (1960, p. 10). This legalistic formulation can be a starting point; the preceding sentence contains all of the elements of a definition but begs for elaboration.

What is a crime depends on whose laws are violated. What is a "crime" depends on the laws of the country, state or municipality where the act is committed; it also depends on the time period. This notion is easily observed in the case of underage drinking. In the United Kingdom, the drinking age is 18 while in the United States, it is 21. An 18-year-old having a beer in the United Kingdom today has not committed any crime while the same 18-year-old having a beer in the United States has violated the law. Similarly, until 1984, the drinking age in the United States was 18 years of age. In 1984, the age was upped to the current 21 years of age. An 18 year old having a beer in the United States in 1983 was not violating any law, but an 18 year old having a beer in the United States in 1985 becomes a law breaker due to the change in the drinking age.

While there is commonality in what constitutes a crime according to the law, there is great variability between nation states regarding how consequential certain criminal acts are. For example, the federal government of the United States has 41 offenses prescribing the death penalty as of 2009. Nearly all of these involve murder or other actions that result in death, but espionage and treason are also included on the list of capital offenses (Snell, 2009). Similarly, the death penalty is prescribed in 36 of the 50 United States of America as of 2009, but the crimes that can result in the death penalty vary widely from state to state. For example, Arkansas, California, Colorado, Georgia and Louisiana all allow the death penalty for treason while none of the other 31 states with the death penalty do. Twenty three states limit the crimes for which the death penalty can be applied to aggravated or first degree murder, but as reported in Snell (2009), several states have a laundry list of crimes that can result in the death penalty, including but not limited to California (first degree murder with special circumstances, sabotage, train wreck causing death, treason, perjury causing execution of an innocent person, fatal assault by a prisoner serving a life sentence) and Wyoming (first degree murder, murder during the commission of sexual assault, sexual abuse of a minor, arson, robbery, escape, resisting arrest, kidnapping or abuse of a minor under 16).

This variability in punishment makes defining crime, especially from a punishment perspective, even more difficult because what is considered a serious crime in one place at one time may not be viewed as criminal elsewhere or at other times. This is true for minor crimes as well; see the above mention of the drinking age for a clear illustration. To further elaborate on Christie's (2004) observations, crime is a social construction which depends on the meanings we attach to various acts. As a result what is crime and what is not crime is not consistent across nation states, jurisdictions or time.

Types of Crime

There are four ways in which crimes can be categorized by type. The first of these is *mala in se* and *mala prohibita* crimes. *Mala in se* crimes are inherently bad while *mala prohibita* crimes are bad because they have been designated as such. Examples of *mala in se* crimes include murder, rape, robbery and theft, while examples of *mala prohibita* crimes include drug use and prostitution. There is nothing inherently bad about the latter two activities, but they have been made illegal during certain times and in certain places. *Mala in se* crimes are not time- and culture-bound the way *mala prohibita* crimes are; *mala in se* crimes are universally condemned as wrong and deserving of punishment.

Crimes can also be categorized in terms of seriousness from felonies to misdemeanors. In the Louisiana Criminal Code (R.S. 14:2 (4)) a "felony is any crime for which an offender may be sentenced to death or imprisonment at hard labor"; other states have similar definitions of a felony. A "misdemeanor is any crime other than a felony" (R.S. 14:2 (6)). The length of sentence is also a distinguishing feature, with felonies being those crimes for which a sentence of one year or more is prescribed.

Another axis along which crimes can be defined is violent versus nonviolent. Crimes of violence are those offenses that have as an element the attempted, threatened or actual use of force against a person and by their very nature, involve a substantial risk that physical force will be used against a person in the course of committing the offense that may involve the possession or use of a dangerous weapon. Nonviolent crimes can include both property and public order crimes. The possession and sale of various drugs which have been criminalized by state and federal statutes may be considered nonviolent crimes. However, they are thought by authorities to be serious enough to warrant considerable prison time in some instances and as a result, those convicted of nonviolent crimes make up a large proportion of persons confined to jails and prison or under direct supervision. Nearly 28 percent of all inmates in state prisons in 2010 were incarcerated for drug and public order offenses, compared to 53 percent incarcerated for violent crimes and 18 percent for property crimes. About 40 percent of those incarcerated for drug and public order offenses were African American (Carson and Sabol, 2012), even though African Americans made up only 13.6 percent of the total population of the United States in that year (U.S. Census, 2011).

A fourth axis is the distinction between personal and property crimes. Of course some crimes can be both, for example, aggravated burglary and armed robbery.[1] Personal crimes include murder, rape, robbery, assault and domestic violence and property crimes include those offenses that involve the theft or destruction of property, including larceny-theft, which itself includes shoplifting and theft from motor vehicles, motor vehicle theft, burglary and arson. Obviously and as seen above, property crimes can be serious enough in nature to warrant prison time, but they can be minor as well; one such example is vandalism.

What Is Criminal Law?

Normative Systems

The beginning point of this discussion is not with the emergence of criminal law but the question of what comported the behavior of people before there was such a thing as law. Henry Sumner Maine (1822–1888) the great English jurist, ethnographer, historian and probably the originator of the sociology of law provides us with a useful examination of the emergence of formal law. For Maine (1876), the basic unit of analysis is not the isolated person but the family. Before Maine, most historic treatments of law had focused on the ancient lawgivers such as Hammurabi, Moses and Draco and the ancient codex as if they had suddenly come into existence. According to Maine (1876), the further back we go into the primitive history of thought, the further we get from a conception of law which resembles contemporary jurisprudence. It is certain that, in the dawn of humankind, there was no legislature, nor a single author of the law or a real conception of what law is. In its earliest form it was probably best described, according to Maine (1876), as habit. In his view, in ancient society every person spent the greater part of their lives under a patriarchal despotism, and was controlled in all his or her actions by a regimen not of law but of caprice. And the extent of capriciousness was largely a function of one's status. Primitive societies then were aggregations of families with varying degrees of status and the individual was not identifiable outside of the family.

Another early contributing theorist to what we know about law and social control is William Graham Sumner (1840–1910). For Sumner (1906), what he termed folkways were habits of people and customs of society which come about in the efforts to satisfy basic needs. For primitive societies, folkways are intertwined with notions of demonism

---

1. Burglary and robbery are discussed in more detail in Chapters 12 and 11 respectively.

and primitive fatalistic ideas and take on the character of authority (1906, p. iv). Over time, folkways become regulative for future generations and become a social force. Their force ebbs and flows with time; some lose their power, disappear or become transformed, while at their peak of influence they largely control individual and social behavior.

Folkways are essentially customary ways of doing things. In his wide-ranging treatise Sumner (1906) concludes that the folkways are quite relative; what is polite in one cultural context may be completely abhorrent in another. He cites kissing as an example, noting that it is a custom that carries with it in many cultures special rules of propriety. Sumner (1906, p. 460) notes that kissing is viewed with disgust in China and Japan, while it is unknown in the South Pacific and South America, were rubbing noses, gentle bites and sniffing are the preferred greetings. In the Middle Ages in Europe, kissing was extensively used across a variety of contexts, including greeting newcomers and acknowledging dance partners. Customs associated with politeness, etiquette and manners may rise to the level of mores when they become characteristic features of the behavior of a people and violating them becomes sanctionable behavior for which the society in question cannot tolerate.

Criminal law does not emerge until civilizations come into being and when proper behavior cannot be left to chance. When society has an interest in proscribing or prescribing and punishing certain acts, formal law comes into existence. The administration of early law largely depended on the status of the victim and the accused. The ancient roots of modern law find a more or less direct lineage to the Law of the Twelve Tables which were promulgated in Rome in 450 B.C.

In more modern times, we can look to those with the power to make laws and the effect their lawmaking has on crime commission. Violation of the law (i.e., crime) is dependent on the law making process or what is codified into the criminal law. Chambliss (1974) has observed that acts that are prohibited by law may come about as a result of the desire of special interests to protect and bolster their position in the social order and may not reflect the value consensus of society as a whole. From this perspective, law violation is the result of the imposition of laws often favoring one interest group over another.

Chambliss (1974) proposed a model of how the law changes that is based on the reality of conflict in society. His starting point is the observation that modern societies are comprised of many social classes and interest groups who compete for favors from the state. Stratification and the unequal distribution of wealth, influence and prestige inevitably leads to conflict between and among classes and interest groups. It is through these struggles and working with inherent competing interests that the content of law takes its form and it is out of the conflict that the definition of crime and delinquency emerges.

So long as those outside the halls of economic and political power remain docile, those in power can influence the bureaucratic, legislative and judicial structures to manipulate existing law or create new laws to suit their own purposes. Only when class conflict breaks out (e.g., the Civil Rights Movement of the 1960s which led to the Civil Rights Act of 1964 and the Voting Rights Act of 1965) does the state enact new legislation or reinterpret existing laws so as to provide what is perceived to be solutions to the conflict. Thus, defining what is crime is a political process; it is this process that makes behavior and actors either criminal or noncriminal. Recall in the opening of this chapter the assertion that nothing is inherently criminal; it is only the law that makes it so.

Those social groups that hold the balance of power in societies are the most likely to influence the form and content of the law.

Changing Times, Changing Laws?

Laws often remain on the books long after the agencies of law enforcement have lost interest in enforcing them or the consensus that made certain actions crimes in the first place is no longer present. Consider sodomy. Laws against certain sexual acts have been around for a long time and probably have not been comprehensively enforced for an equally long time especially for heterosexual couples. Why? Because the so-called criminal act is preformed in the privacy of the bedroom and those involved are highly unlikely to report what they have done to the authorities. The Louisiana Criminal Code proscribes such behavior and describes it as sodomy, a crime against nature (R.S. 14:89) or the unnatural carnal copulation between members of the same sex or opposite sex and includes solicitation to engage in unnatural carnal copulation for compensation. The penalty includes a fine of not more than $2,000 and imprisonment, with or without hard labor for not more than five years, or both. The lack of enforcement may also be a function of the draconian quality of the penalty. This also holds true, for example, in the case of three other crimes in the Louisiana criminal code: treason, misprision of treason and criminal anarchy. They have received scant attention from law enforcement, yet they remain in the criminal statutes (R.S. 14:113, 114, 115). Once an act has been criminalized, legislators are reluctant to remove it from the code for fear of being labeled soft on crime. The passage of new laws by state legislatures in combination with retaining old, usually unenforced laws results in an increase in the number of activities that are considered criminal.

The United States Constitution mentions only three federal crimes that can be committed by citizens: treason, piracy and counterfeiting. According to Fields and Emshwiller (2011), there were an estimated 4,500 crimes in federal statutes in 2008. What explains the incredible growth in federal criminal statutes? Fields and Emshwiller (2011) note that the increase is partly in response to hot button issues, including damage to the environment, child kidnapping, harm to consumers and financial misdeeds. Some federal statutes are inarguably beneficial such as those helping to secure civil rights for African Americans and those addressing political corruption and violent crimes. However, the recent expanse of federal statutes has contributed to an eight-fold increase in the number of people serving time in federal prison in the last 30 years, with the number of people serving time for nonviolent offenses doubling in the last 20 years.

What Is Criminology?

Simply, and most generally, criminology is the scientific study of crime. Criminologists take a variety of different approaches to studying crime, including focusing on what causes crime, how and why crime rates change, why some people and groups engage in more crime than others, why some activities are criminalized while others are not and how to prevent crime. We delve deeply into each of these areas of concern for criminologists throughout the book. Regardless of which of these questions a particular criminologist is interested in, he or she uses the scientific method to study it rather than simply theorizing about the answer. Indeed, criminology has reached a stage where it is both possible and desirable go beyond mere observation and to embed experimental elements into studies so that the evidence we find is more robust and instructive than ever before (Sherman, 2005).

The Evolution of Criminology

Codified Laws and Prescribed Punishments

The link between law and prescribed punishment can be found in many ancient legal codes. The laws that shape Western society find their sources in the religious legacies of Christianity and classical Greece and Rome. This is where we can trace the emergence of the origins of the content and rule of law, crime and punishment. The darker side of early civilization is that these societies were often ruled by exceptionally cruel and despotic tyrants such as the Greek tyrants Phalarus (570–554 B.C.) and Nabis (207–192 B.C.) and the Romans Caligula (12–41 A.D.) and Nero (37–68 A.D.). They did not rely on consensus to rule but fear by treating any opposition or rebellion with violent suppression through quick resort to torture and execution.

The Old Testament Jehovah was not a particularly sympathetic character. According to Kiernan (2007), there are many references in the Old Testament in which Jehovah commands his people to hate and visit gratuitous violence on competing ethnic groups. For example, in Deuteronomy (7:2, 16), God commands, "[T]hou shall smite them, and utterly destroy them; thou shall make no covenant with them, nor show mercy unto them.... Thou shalt consume all the people which the Lord thy God shall deliver thee; thine eye shall have no pity upon." The Old Testament book of Judges chronicles the lack of sympathy God shows his own people when they are unfaithful (Soggin, 1981).

According to the story in Exodus in the Old Testament of the Hebrew Bible, God inscribed on two stone tablets the Ten Commandments, which are a set of rules of conduct that followers of God must obey. As the story goes, at some point in Moses' leading the children of Israel out of Egyptian bondage, they stopped at Mount Sinai. While Moses was on the mountain he received the Ten Commandments from God; the first four concern the relationship between God and humans, while the next six concern the relationships between people. These six provide the Biblical basis for civil relationships:

- Honor your father and mother—the greatest intergenerational obligation.
- Do not murder—a prohibition against the greatest injury.
- Do not commit adultery—a prohibition against the greatest injury to the family bond.
- Do not steal—a prohibition against the greatest injury to personal property.
- Do not lie—a prohibition against the greatest injury against the law and commerce.
- Do not covet the property of your neighbor—a prohibition against the greatest injury to community.

Calhoun (1999[1927]) points out that in ancient Greece, civil law preceded criminal law. Attention was given over to the maintenance of private rights before any conception of crime as an offense against the social order was established or punishments for transgressions were formulated. Customary procedures for adjudicating private disputes even existed in the Homeric period (700–800 B.C.). It would be at least 200 years before anything resembling criminal law appeared. The decisive move toward what is recognizable as criminal laws occurred at the beginning of the sixth century when Solon granted every citizen the right in the prosecution against certain offenses including offences against the state. According to Calhoun (1999[1927], p. 7), we can see the fusion of two primitive methods of punishing acts we now regard as crime in this period of Greek history. Intrusions on an individual's right which had earlier been dealt with as a tort[2] but had now come to be regarded as crime gave the community as a whole a right of action.

A universal precursor to criminal law revolved around murder in the form of *lex talionis* or the law of injury for injury (retribution). The loss of a family member to murder was seen as a threat to the survival of that family and must be compensated through the payment of the blood price (the reason for the murder was not always at issue). Adjudication focused on the amount of the blood price. In the case of murder, if the offender himself could not pay the blood price, it would fall on his relatives to help him pay. Most scholars argue that this system was designed to avoid blood feuds which could ultimately destroy a whole community (Hartland, 1924, p. 155).

In Barbarian Europe (400–900 A.D.), the blood price was largely set by the status of the person in these highly stratified kingdoms with slaves and semi-free persons at the bottom and aristocracy and royalty at the top. A free Anglo Saxon was worth 200 shillings and an aristocrat was worth three or more times that amount. Blood prices were paid by the murderer to the victim's kin (James, 1988, p. 77). Again, the whole system was designed in this manner in order to avoid the depredations that would be attendant to an all out blood feud.

The Emergence of Classical Criminology (1700s)

Classical criminology is a designation mainly for the writings of judicial reformers Cesare Beccaria in Italy and Jeremy Bentham in England during the 1700s. Both were well-educated aristocrats who were responding to the excesses of the judicial and penal systems in their respective countries. The legal systems of most European countries at that time could be characterized as cruel, arbitrary and usually biased in favor of elites. Their goal was to reform the criminal justice system to make it more rational and fair; to this end they were successful. Their efforts aligned well with the interest of an emerging merchant class and an economic philosophy that promoted the rise of industrialism. Given the content of the United States Constitution and the accompanying Bill of Rights, it appears the Founding Fathers were familiar with the works of both Beccaria and Bentham.

---

2. A tort is a civil wrong that unfairly causes someone to suffer loss or harm and for which repair of some kind must be made.

Cesare Beccaria (1738–1794) is considered the father of classical criminology. The reason he is included in a criminology text is his most noted essay *On Crimes and Punishments* published in 1764. The influence of the Enlightenment on his work is quite evident; he also received assistance of two close friends, the brothers Alessandro and Pietro Verri. The work was initially published anonymously and only when it was well received by the government did Beccaria attach his name to it (Maestro and Morris, 1973).

In his masterwork, Beccaria was principally concerned with crime and how to control it. Operating from the position that human beings are rational and acted in their own interests, choosing courses of actions that would maximize pleasure and minimize pain, Beccaria theorized that punishment could be used to control crime because punishment could be used to make the pains of crime outweigh its pleasures, but only if punishment was applied in a certain way. At the time of his writing, punishment was utilized in a cruel and irregular manner. He did not challenge the right of the state to punish, but believed that punishment must arise from absolute necessity. To punish without absolute necessity is tyranny. His treatise contains a number of influential principles for his time and these principles form the basis of the classical school of criminology:

- Punishment should not be for retribution but be a deterrent (Beccaria, 1764[1819], p. 47)
- Punishment should be proportionate to the crime committed (Beccaria, 1764[1819], p. 33)
- Certainty and promptness of punishment—not severity—will achieve the greatest deterrent effect (Beccaria, 1764[1819], p. 74)
- Criminal procedures should be public (Beccaria, 1764[1819], p. 52) and
- The state does not have a right to kill a person and moreover, punishment by death has no utility (Beccaria, 1764[1819], p. 98).

In essence, Beccaria believed that crime could be deterred (i.e., prevented) through punishment, but only punishment applied in a very specific way would achieve the desired deterrent effect. Punishment should be appropriate for the crime committed; severe punishments should be reserved for severe crimes. Punishment should also be applied swiftly and with certainty. In other words, punishment should come as soon as possible after the commission of a crime and there should be no doubt, either among the person committing the crime or the general public, that punishment will follow commission of a crime in order for punishment to serve as an effective deterrent. The certain application of punishment is the most important feature in achieving deterrence. Beccaria's work has a great deal of influence even today. As we will see in Chapters 9 and 15, his ideas are at the foundation of the criminal justice system in the United States.

Jeremy Bentham (1748–1832) was also concerned with the purpose of punishment and was even more intently focused on its utility. In his work *The Rationale of Punishment*[3] he writes:

---

3. Etienne Dumont translated this work of Bentham into French and subsequently back into English because Bentham himself always had difficulty getting his writings, which were voluminous, into print. The difficulty did not lie in their publishability. Rather, Bentham never seemed to know when his work was good enough.

> Pain and pleasure are the great springs of human action. When a man perceives or supposes pain to be the consequence of an act, he will withdraw himself from committing the act. If the … magnitude of that pain be greater than … the pleasure or good he expects to be a consequence … he will be absolutely prevented from performing it. The recurrence of an offense by any given individual may be prevented in three ways: 1. By taking from him the physical power of offending. 2. By taking away the desire of offending. 3. By making him afraid of offending. In the first case, the individual can no more commit the offense; in the second, he no longer desires to commit it; in the third, he may still wish to commit it, but he no longer dares to do it. In the first case there is a physical incapacity, in the second, a moral reformation; in the third, there is intimidation or terror of the law. (1830[1811], p. 20)

Punishment can be used to prevent people from engaging in criminal activity because it prevents them from daring to engage in crime. Bentham elaborates on the utility of punishment by noting that it can be used to prevent future law breaking of the current offender and it can be used to prevent law breaking among the general public. Bentham referred to these concepts as "particular prevention" and "general prevention" (1830[1811], p. 19); we recognize these concepts today as specific and general deterrence and they are covered in more detail in Chapter 9.

General prevention, or general deterrence, according to Bentham ought to be the real justification for punishment. In many cases, a delinquent's offense is an isolated occurrence that may never recur, but it cannot be ignored because in doing so, the message would be sent to both the offender and the public that offending is tolerable. The punishment that is inflicted serves as a source of security to all, not as an act of wrath or vengeance against the guilty, "but as an indispensable sacrifice to the common safety" (Bentham, 1811[1830], p. 21).

With respect to individual delinquents, Bentham believed punishment had two important purposes, incapacitation and reformation. If the crime committed is heinous and outrageous and suggests a crime prone disposition in the offender, it becomes necessary to take from the delinquent the power of committing it again (incapacitation). If the crime is less serious and the offender less dangerous it would be appropriate for the punishment to be tailored around his or her rehabilitation (reformation). In a sense, Bentham was an early advocate of restorative justice in that he advocated for the perpetrator compensating his victim—giving a good equal to the evil suffered. The injured party is compensated for his injury and the perpetrator is punished at the same time.

John Howard (1726–1790) also weighed in on the control of behavior with his work on jails and prisons in England and Wales. Upon becoming sheriff of the county of Bedford in England, he grew appalled at jail and prison conditions. He observed that people were still confined even after they had been found not guilty because they could not pay the jailer (jails were run on a fee system at this time in which inmates had to pay for their own room and board). He campaigned to change the fee system to one in which jailers were paid by the government. In order to amass evidence for the proposed changes, he visited a large number of county jails in England. These visits left him horrified at the deplorable conditions in many English jails. Many inmates had smallpox and in such close quarters, this highly communicable disease killed many more inmates awaiting release than did the executioner. Howard (1777) made direct reference to Beccaria and his ideas when he noted that jail conditions should not be overly harsh or severe in order to serve their purpose. Howard's (1777) work is a comprehensive, empirical and comparative assessment of the policies, laws, management, staffing and conditions of jails and prisons throughout England and Wales and some of the changes he suggested are still with us today, including chaplains and medical personnel being made available to inmates.

The Emergence of Positive Criminology (1800s)

While classical criminology focuses on the rationality of offenders, their ability to make choices that maximize their pleasure and minimize their pain and the ways punishment can be used to minimize the pleasure of crime, positive criminology is concerned with factors that are outside the control of the individual that may facilitate crime. Some early positive criminologists considered facial features, body type and shape of the skull to be among these factors.

The notion that a person's character or personality can be known by what they look like, especially the appearance of the face, is the underlying premise of physiognomy. The idea of physiognomy has been around for a few thousand years. In some ways, the physiognomists can be viewed as precursors of criminologists. The principal figure in promoting physiognomy in the late 1700s was Johann Kaspar Lavater (1741–1801), who published a collection of essays on the subject in German in 1772. But the ideas that he promoted were not original with him for he was influenced substantially by the writings on the subject by Gianbattista Della Porta (1535–1615) and English physician Sir Thomas Browne (1605–1682). Both of these writers argued for the possibility of detecting inner qualities from the appearance of the face. Their preoccupation with this linkage was more moralistic than scientific.

Box 1.1. Sir Francis Galton: Overlooked in Criminology?

While physiognomy is now dismissed as pseudoscience, it gained some additional scientific traction in the late 1800s with the work of Sir Francis Galton (1822–1911). Galton was a jack of many trades, including geography, meteorology, psychology, physical identification, statistical correlation and regression, heredity and genetics. His work in physiognomy is quite fascinating. Using composite photographs of various groups of convicts with the negatives overlaid, he discovered the resulting face, a composite in which individual peculiarities disappear "and the common humanity of a low type is all that is left" (Galton, 1904, p. 11). Individual portraits depicted the criminal subjects, according to Galton, all of whom appeared villainous in different ways, but when combined in the overlay, individual peculiarities disappear.

From the perspective of his contribution to modern criminology and crime detection, his invention of fingerprinting and the development of correlation and regression cannot be overlooked. Galton perhaps, has been largely ignored in the linage of mainstream criminology because of his views on eugenics. In fact he invented the term. "Eugenics is the science which deals with all influences that improve the inborn qualities of a race; also with those that develop them to the utmost advantage" (Galton, 1904, p. 1). In the rejoinders to his paper, it is clear that a great deal of skepticism greeted his thesis. Nevertheless, until his death in 1911, eugenics was his all-consuming preoccupation. Had he never broached this controversial topic, he would likely have been treated with more respect as a founder of modern social science.

A practice related to physiognomy is phrenology. The father of phrenology was Franz Joseph Gall (1758–1828) and he believed that the brain had certain localized and specific parts that control specific functions. He further believed that people had certain behavioral tendencies based on the size of certain parts of the brain and that behavior and character could be determined by feeling the shape and surface of the skull. The practice of phrenology was further popularized by Gall's assistant and colleague Johann Spurzheim. It even became a wildly popular parlor game during much of the first half of the 1800s in Europe and the United States (Simpson, 2005). Gall suggested that the brain was divided into 27 separate organs and each organ supposedly corresponded to a discrete faculty. Gall identified 19 of these faculties as being shared with other animal species, with the remaining eight being specific to humans (van Wyhe, 2011). Phrenology has been completely discredited since its heyday, with scientists agreeing that it is not possible to determine character or predict behavior based on the shape of the skull. However, the idea that there are certain areas of the brain responsible for specific functions has been borne out by neuroscience and is central to our understanding of how the brain works (van Wyhe, 2011a).

John Martyn Harlow (1819–1907), a physician remembered for treating the railroad worker Phineas Gage who experienced severe brain trauma in 1848, was one of the first to associate certain regions of the brain with behavior outside the confines of phrenology. Gage was involved in an accident in which a large iron rod was driven completely through his head, destroying much of his brain's left frontal lobe. Harlow published his first paper about Gage in 1848, but perhaps more important was his follow up publication in 1868, eight years after the death of his patient. This follow-up recounts what Harlow had learned about behavioral and psychological changes in Gage, which he attributed to the damaging effects of the accident on parts of his brain. Harlow reported that prior to Gage's injury, he was a highly responsible, hard working man but that after the injury, Gage became fitful, profane, obstinate and capricious (Macmillan, 2000).

The belief that biology is destiny has been around for quite some time (e.g., Lange, 1929). The idea that criminals might somehow be biologically different in a defective and abnormal way has also been a persistent proposition that is familiar to most of us. As criminologists, we owe much for the idea of being born criminal to Cesare Lombroso (1835–1909), an Italian physician and the father of positive criminology. The ideas in Lombroso's book *L'Uomo Delinquente (The Criminal Man)*, which was published in 1876, appear to have been influenced by Charles Darwin's seminal *Descent of Man*, which was published in 1871. Lombroso asserted that certain physical stigmata indicated an atavistic or throwback to a primitive earlier man or born criminal. He had an extensive

14 1 · INTRODUCTION

list of stigmata that he made while dissecting cadavers in the prisons and asylums of Pavia, Italy. Many of these stigmata focused on primitive or ape-like features such as ears, nose, chin, hair, wrinkles and excessive length of arms. Lomborso's notion of atavism was based on an unproved and unprovable notion that prehistoric or even contemporary primitives were biologically prone to criminal conduct.

In his later research, Lombroso compared Italian criminals and noncriminal Italian soldiers and concluded that only a very small proportion of criminals, perhaps a third, were truly atavistic. Lombroso added to his typology what he described as a criminaloid, a description resembling what we refer to now as an antisocial personality—compulsive law-breakers with no sense of right or wrong or empathy for others. While criminaloids did not exhibit the stigmata of the atavistic type, they exhibited the same antisocial and vicious behavior (Vold and Bernard, 1986).

With Guglielmo Ferrero, Lombroso also wrote *Criminal Woman, The Prostitute, and The Normal Woman*, which was originally published in 1893. In this book, he and his co-author argued that female deviations are usually sexual in nature and often expressed through prostitution. In instances when women are involved in the crimes that are more typically male, the female perpetrator will likely have distinctly masculine traits. They also contended that women were not typically criminal because they were less intelligent and also because their jealous and cruel temperaments were mitigated by their maternal instincts. This notion of women being less criminal because they are less intelligent than males seems to run counter to the atavistic criminal proposition in Lombroso's earlier work where the atavistic criminal was certainly not intelligent.

Responding to a great deal of criticism, Lombroso modified his views in *Crime: Its Causes and Remedies* (1911). In this later work, he acknowledged that there are many other factors related to crime ranging from climate and the economy to sex and marriage customs. Atavism was relegated to a single chapter at the end of the book. This work, published after his death in 1909, was not influential outside of his native country.[4]

Lombroso's followers took up a substantially modified version of his theory, yet were still committed to the notion of a biologic basis for criminal behavior. For example, Raffaele Garofalo (1914) emphasized psychological factors and argued that criminals lacked proper development of altruistic sensibility, which Garofalo believed had a physical basis. His contemporary, Enrico Ferri, argued in his 1917 book *Criminal Sociology* that Lombroso gave too much weight to skull measurement and measurements of other parts of the body and should have given greater weight to social, political and economic factors. Ferri proposed five types of criminals: criminal lunatics, born criminals (incorrigibles), habitual criminals, occasional criminals and emotional criminals. In spite of the implication in the typology of distinctiveness for each type, Ferri concluded that all criminals are abnormal and possess aberrant organic and psychological characteristics. Garofalo and Ferri are the most famous members of what is known as the Italian school of criminology. Their beliefs about the nature of offenders informed their propositions about punishment. In contrast to Beccaria, who believed the punishment should fit the crime, Garofalo believed the punishment should fit the criminal and be

---

4. For a fascinating review of this period in criminology, see Becker and Wetzell (2005).

tailored to his or her peculiarities. Ferri believed the only acceptable rationale for punishment was social defense, the protection of society from those who were born and would always remain dangerous (Walsh and Hemmens, 2011).

Lombroso's ideas about the biologic causes of crime made their way across the Atlantic to the United States, thanks in large part to Arthur MacDonald (1893) and their arrival and popularity is obvious in the work of some scholars, such as Harvard anthropologist Ernest Hooton. He argued in his 1931 book *Crime and the Man* that criminals were organically inferior and that the inferiority was genetically inheritable. To solve the problem of crime, a program of eugenics (sterilization of criminals) was necessary. Based on measurements of more than 17,000 people from all walks of life, he concluded that 19 of the 35 measurements he made showed significant differences between offenders and nonoffenders. Hooton (1931) claimed that criminals had low foreheads, high pinched nasal roots, crooked noses, compressed faces, narrow jaws, small ears, long necks and stooped shoulders. He believed physical inferiority was linked to mental inferiority, making the problem of crime all the more serious. Scientists' interest in eugenics in the United States began to wane in the later 1930s after Hooton's work was severely critiqued both methodologically (inadequate controls and sampling bias) and conceptually (failing to link physical deviations with criminality in a causal way).

We noted above that Lombroso is the father of the positive school of criminology and we note here that the positive school of criminology is the dominant perspective in the field today. Does that mean we blindly adhere to Lombroso's ideas about a born criminal being recognizable by his or her physical features? Of course not. Rather, when we say the positive school is dominant, what we mean is that the idea of looking to factors outside the individual's control to find the causes of crime is dominant. As we will see in subsequent chapters, there are many factors that have been proposed as causes of crime, especially when they are present in combination with one another.

Box 1.2. The Criminal Mind

As we contemplate factors outside the control of the individual that may be partially responsible for crime, we may think of one's mental state at the time of the criminal action. Interestingly, this idea is one that has occupied the attention of legal scholars more than it has criminologists. The importance of the mental state at the time of a criminal action has long been recognized. In the 1200s, the English jurist Henry Bracton asserted a culpable mental state, a *mens rea*, was necessary for criminal culpability. The test to determine whether someone was lacking *mens rea* at the time of a crime and therefore could not be held criminally responsible for it has taken on many forms. The wild beast test was utilized in England until the early 1700s. The wild beast test held that if someone did "not know what he was doing, no more than an infant, than a brute or wild beast," he or she could not be held criminally responsible for his or her actions (Appelbaum, 1994, p. 165). Beginning in the 1700s in England, a new test was utilized that focused on whether the defendant was able to distinguish between good and evil at the time of his or her crime. In 1843, Daniel M'Naghten tried to kill the Prime Minister of England, Sir Robert Peel. It appeared that M'Naghten did know that trying to kill someone was wrong, so he would have been culpable under the good and evil test. However, his lawyers argued that a broader test for *mens rea* was necessary because M'Naghten was operating under a delusional belief system. A special panel of judges in the case formulated the core of the *M'Naghten* standard for determining *mens rea*: "at the time of the committing of the act, the party accused was laboring under such a defect of reason, from disease of the mind, as to not know the nature and quality of the act he was doing; or, if he did know it, that he did not know he was doing what was wrong" (Appelbam, 1994, p. 167).

The *M'Naghten* test was the standard for determining *mens rea* in the United States for many years. About a third of states added an irresistible impulse test to their *M'Naghten* tests at the end of the 1800s so that individuals who could not control their actions could not be held responsible for them. Between 1955 and 1975, about half the states adopted the substantial capacity test, which held that a defendant did not have *mens rea* if he or she did not possess "substantial capacity either to appreciate the criminality of his conduct or to conform to the requirements of the law" (Slate and Johnson, 2008, p. 328). In 1982, John Hinckley, Jr. was found not guilty by reason of insanity for attempting to assassinate then President Ronald Reagan. The verdict was hugely unpopular and a number of states reverted to the more restrictive *M'Naghten* rule (Appelbaum, 1994; Slate and Johnson, 2008). When the tests by which we determine *mens rea* change, our legal standards for criminal culpability change with them, even though we may have our own, deeply ingrained ideas about who can possess a criminal mind and who cannot.

The Precursors of Sociological Criminology (1800s)

In order to better understand how sociological criminology came to be the dominant perspective in the field, it is instructive to first look at some influential social reformers of the 1800s. And to better understand these influential social reformers, it is instructive to consider the times in which they lived.

In 1801, the population of Paris, France was 546,856. By 1846, it was well over a million, meaning it had nearly doubled in just 45 years (Cox, 2003). In 1801 the population of London, England was 1,096,784 and by 1850, it had more than doubled to approximately 2.6 million people (Cox, 2001). This rapid population growth was responsible for what one writer of the period coined the term the dangerous classes (Fregier, 1840). Fregier's position was that rural peasants migrating into Paris brought with them few skills and thus contributed to a burgeoning lower class. This growing lower class that lived in fetid conditions was the major contributor to the growing social problems of crime, drunkenness and prostitution that were plaguing the city and that were a serious affront to bourgeois' sensibilities. Policing the poor and improving their lot, most felt, would decrease the crime problem. Parallel concerns were raised at the same time in London by the likes of Patrick Colquhoun (1745–1820), William Augustus Miles (1796–1851) and Edwin Chadwick (1800–1890). Like Fregier, these men were social reformers and sounded the alarm concerning the dangerous classes and the need to control them and, if possible, make them less dangerous.

This early 19th century crime wave and the public fascination and outcry set the stage for intellectuals and governments to begin to try to understand the exact nature of the crime problem and begin to devise ways to solve it. Two of the central figures in early efforts to measure crime were Adolphe Quetelet (1796–1874) and Andre-Michel Guerry (1802–1866). Quetelet was a pioneer in introducing the use of statistical methods to the social sciences. Trained as a mathematician, his first statistical work published in 1826 utilized Belgium birth and mortality tables as a means of defining insurance rates. During the same period, he published works in physics, astronomy, mathematics, a commentary on Dutch demographic policies, a development of plans for a national census for Belgium and the collection of crime statistics (Beirne, 1987). In these works, Quetelet reasoned that the same law-like regularity that exists in the heavens and the natural world also exists in the world of social facts. The identification of these regularities in the social world was dependent on statistical calculation. Initially he termed his project social mechanics, later, social physics (preempting Auguste Comte, who had to settle for inventing the term "sociology" to label his science of society).

Also catching Quetelet's interest as a statistician was the publication of the *Compte general de l' administration de la justice criminelle en France* in 1827. The *Compte* was created in response to the increase in crime in France, especially in Paris, that accompanied the rapid increase in population there. It was a quarterly compilation prepared by the public prosecutors of all personal and property crimes recorded and the punishments handed down to those convicted. Additionally, the document began to record the time of year of the offense and the age, sex, occupation and education of both accused and convicted. Eventually, the *Compte* began to include information about repeat offenders and presented tables showing relationships between type of offence and characteristics of the accused (Beirne, 1987).

Guerry was trained in the law and employed by the Ministry in Justice in Paris in the late 1820s. It was at the Ministry of Justice that he became fascinated with the huge amount of data the Ministry was collecting. Going beyond simply producing tables and going beyond a cross sectional look at one area, Guerry used maps to present the crime rate in France and England for crimes against persons and property over time in his masterwork. With this approach, it was possible for readers to see not just how much crime there was, but where it took place (Friendly, 2007). What began in Guerry's time as thematic cartography and the first instances of modern statistical maps has progressed to what is now called geovisualization (e.g., Dykes, MacEachren and Kraak, 2005) and exploratory spatial data analysis (ESDA), which can provide multiple linked univariate views of geospatial data.

The latter part of the1800s and the early 1900s saw the emergence of academic sociology. Arguably, Emile Durkheim (1858–1917) was one of the most important figures of this time. His theorizing and research laid part of the foundation for the development of sociological criminology. In establishing sociology as a discipline in its own right, Durkheim rejected biological and psychological interpretations of social behavior. In fact his master work *Suicide* (Durkheim, 1951[1897]) was a conscious critique of a psychological interpretation of this highly personal act. If suicide was purely a psychological phenomenon then rates should be stable across social groups. Empirically, this was not the case. From official statistics gathered by the French government, Durkheim found that rates of suicide were fairly stable over time but varied by social groups. For example, rural rates of suicide were consistently lower than urban rates and suicide was more prevalent among Protestants than Catholics. Durkheim argued that the difference had to do with the level of cohesiveness and integration of social groups.

Durkheim begins with the assertion that human beings are in possession of insatiable desires that if left unchecked would result in worse than anarchy. Durkheim argued that social phenomena are social facts, concrete things that are not amenable to be reduced to biological or psychological explanation. Moreover, these social facts are external to any individual, meaning simply that these social facts existed before and will still exist long after any individual. They are more than external to individuals — they exercise coercive power independent of the desires of the individual (Durkheim, 1951[1897]). These constraints take the form of customs and laws whose violation invokes sanctions which tend to direct the desires and proclivities of people.

In *The Rules of the Sociological Method*, Durkheim (1953[1895]) stressed the exteriority and constraining power of social facts. However, in his later work his position on this idea was somewhat nuanced. In *Sociology and Philosophy*, he asserted that social facts such as moral rules become guides and controls over peoples' behavior to the extent that they are internalized in the consciousness of individuals while remaining external and independent of individuals. From this perspective, society is within us but at the same time beyond us (Durkheim, 1953[1904]).

Durkheim was more concerned with group characteristics than individuals. Group properties exist independent of individual characteristics. He was focused on rates of behavior in groups and not incidences of individual attributes. Thus in his analysis he was not concerned with a single suicide but with the rate of suicide within a specific group. If suicides increased significantly in a particular group, it would indicate weakened social cohesion with the members no longer sufficiently protected experiencing the kind of crises that might lead to suicide. Examining rates of behavior in social groups had the added advantage of allowing Durkheim to compare different groups. A comparative analysis of social groups on rates of suicide, for example, allowed Durkheim to arrive at an overall generalization concerning the role that social cohesion or integration played. Durkheim (1951[1897]) demonstrated that there was an inverse relationship between rates of suicide and the degree of integration for social groups.

Moreover, Durkheim viewed criminal behavior as not inherently illegitimate in and of itself. Rather, certain types of behavior are labeled criminal by the collective decisions of the group. Durkheim said, for example, "We must not say that an action shocks the common conscience because it is criminal, but rather that it is criminal because it shocks the common conscience" (1960[1893], p. 81). Durkheim uses killing to illustrate his point: The act of taking the life of another human being receives many responses depending on the social context and may lead to different responses to perpetrators or victims: In the context of a social role, a police officer may legitimately kill someone; a social situation in which a person kills defending one's life or the life of another and certain events or conditions such as warfare legitimize killing the enemy, for example.

Durkheim further claims that no known society is without crime. "Assuming that this condition [a society without crime] could actually be realized, crime would not thereby disappear; it would only change its form, for the very cause which would thus dry up the sources of criminality would immediately open up new ones" (1953[1895], p. 67). Durkheim here is referring to acts defined as criminal in the collective conscious. However, once a particular behavior is no longer socially defined as criminal, another may take its place. Durkheim suggests that behavior that would be normal under ordinary circumstances in ordinary society might be repugnant and intolerable in another.

The Emergence of Criminology as Its Own Discipline

In the early part of the 1900s, we see criminology remaining rooted in sociology and nowhere is this clearer than in the development of what is known as the Chicago School. The research of Shaw and McKay (1942) was focused on delinquency in the city of Chicago, not only who was committing it, but where it was being committed and what characteristics of place might be criminogenic. One of the major findings of their research was what they called the gradient tendency; delinquency declined with increasing distance from the city core. They relied on a general concept of social disorganization which for them had to do with a disruption of normal communal social controls. Shaw and McKay's (1942) work was very influential, but this does not mean their ideas about what causes crime went unchallenged (if they had, there would be no need for such a lengthy and multifaceted textbook) or that criminology remained neatly tucked into sociology. A multitude of academic answers have been put forth to the question of what causes crime and these answers implicate psychological and biological factors, the experience of strain, learning from others, the deficient exercise of control, conflict among groups, the presence of risk factors over the lifetime, rational decision making and opportunities for crime. With all of these different ideas about what causes crime, criminology has come into its own as a discipline, informed by not just sociology, but biology, psychology, economics and ecology as well.

A Word about Theory

Much of this book is concerned with theories of crime. As such, it is prudent to say a bit about what theories are and the criteria on which they are judged here. A theory can be understood as a set of logically connected ideas that purport to explain some phenomena we observe in the world. In the case of this textbook, the phenomena with which we are concerned is crime. Hypotheses are statements about the relationships we expect to find within the phenomena of interest based on the logic of a theory. For example, if we theorize that crime is caused by weak bonds to social institutions and the people in them (as Hirschi (1969) did), we would hypothesize that weak bonds as measured by things like quality of relationship with parents and performance in school are associated with greater involvement in crime. As we will see throughout the course of this book, a number of theories have been put forth to explain crime, but as of yet, criminologists have not uncovered what is called a necessary cause of crime, a factor which must be present to cause crime. We routinely see offenders with a number of risk factors for crime, but empirical work has not revealed even one of these risk factors

Box 1.3. A Timeline of Criminology

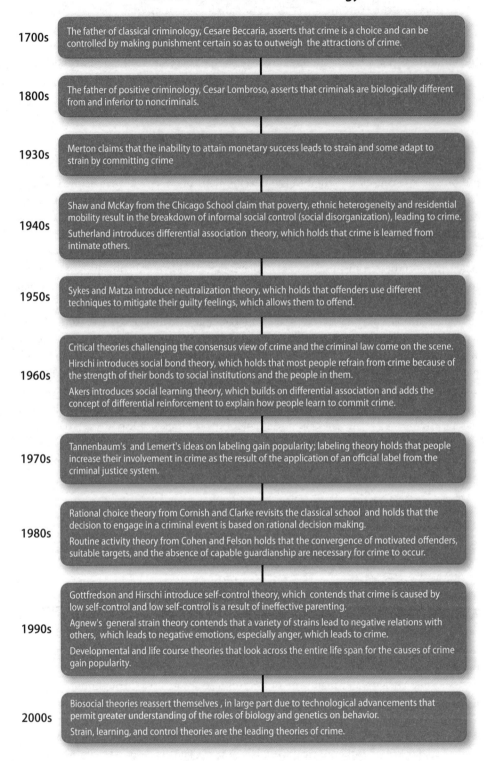

1700s — The father of classical criminology, Cesare Beccaria, asserts that crime is a choice and can be controlled by making punishment certain so as to outweigh the attractions of crime.

1800s — The father of positive criminology, Cesar Lombroso, asserts that criminals are biologically different from and inferior to noncriminals.

1930s — Merton claims that the inability to attain monetary success leads to strain and some adapt to strain by committing crime

1940s — Shaw and McKay from the Chicago School claim that poverty, ethnic heterogeneity and residential mobility result in the breakdown of informal social control (social disorganization), leading to crime.
Sutherland introduces differential association theory, which holds that crime is learned from intimate others.

1950s — Sykes and Matza introduce neutralization theory, which holds that offenders use different techniques to mitigate their guilty feelings, which allows them to offend.

1960s — Critical theories challenging the consensus view of crime and the criminal law come on the scene.
Hirschi introduces social bond theory, which holds that most people refrain from crime because of the strength of their bonds to social institutions and the people in them.
Akers introduces social learning theory, which builds on differential association and adds the concept of differential reinforcement to explain how people learn to commit crime.

1970s — Tannenbaum's and Lemert's ideas on labeling gain popularity; labeling theory holds that people increase their involvement in crime as the result of the application of an official label from the criminal justice system.

1980s — Rational choice theory from Cornish and Clarke revisits the classical school and holds that the decision to engage in a criminal event is based on rational decision making.
Routine activity theory from Cohen and Felson holds that the convergence of motivated offenders, suitable targets, and the absence of capable guardianship are necessary for crime to occur.

1990s — Gottfredson and Hirschi introduce self-control theory, which contends that crime is caused by low self-control and low self-control is a result of ineffective parenting.
Agnew's general strain theory contends that a variety of strains lead to negative relations with others, which leads to negative emotions, especially anger, which leads to crime.
Developmental and life course theories that look across the entire life span for the causes of crime gain popularity.

2000s — Biosocial theories reassert themselves, in large part due to technological advancements that permit greater understanding of the roles of biology and genetics on behavior.
Strain, learning, and control theories are the leading theories of crime.

to be a necessary cause of crime. We are also still on the search for a sufficient cause of crime, a factor that can produce criminal behavior without any other factor being present (Walsh and Hemmens, 2011).

To determine whether or not a theory is a meritorious one, we examine it using several different criteria. The first of these is predictive accuracy. This is the most important criterion on which to judge a theory and it refers to the extent that a theory can predict what is observed. The second criterion is predictive scope. Predictive scope refers to how much of what is observed can be explained by the theory. The third criterion is parsimony or simplicity. All other things being equal, the more parsimonious and less complicated a theory is, the better. The fourth criterion is falsifiability. A theory may never be proven correct (especially in criminology), but it must be able to be falsified or disproven, which means it must be empirically testable. The fifth criterion is usefulness and policy implications, which refers to the extent to which the theory can provide feasible guidelines for programs and policies that reduce or prevent crime (Akers and Sellers, 2009; Walsh and Hemmens, 2011). We encourage readers to think back to these criteria as they make their way through the book and discover the different theories of crime causation.

Conclusion

This chapter was designed to introduce readers to the concepts of crime, the criminal law and criminology and how they have changed over time. As we proceed with learning about theories of crime through much of the remainder of this book, we believe it is important to present a set of facts that theories of crime should be able to explain:

1. Crime is committed disproportionately by males.
2. Crime is perpetrated disproportionately by 15–25 year olds.
3. Crime is committed disproportionately by unmarried people.
4. Crime is committed disproportionately by people living in large cities.
5. Crime is committed disproportionately by people who have experienced high residential mobility and who live in areas characterized by high residential mobility.
6. Young people who are strongly attached to their school are less likely to engage in crime.
7. Young people who have high educational and occupational aspirations are less likely to engage in crime.
8. Young people who do poorly at school are more likely to engage in crime.
9. Young people who are strongly attached to their parents are less likely to engage in crime.
10. Young people who have friendships with criminals are more likely to engage in crime themselves.
11. People who believe strongly in complying with the law are less likely to violate the law.

12. For both men and women, being at the bottom of the class structure—whether measured by personal socioeconomic status, socioeconomic status of the area of residence, being unemployed or belonging to an oppressed racial minority—increases rates of offending for all types of crime apart from those for which opportunities are systematically less available to the poor.

13. Crime rates have been increasing since the Second World War in most countries, developed and developing. The only case of a country which has been clearly shown to have had a falling crime rate in this period is Japan (Braithwaite, 1989, pp. 44–49).

These facts were first published over two decades ago but they remain true today. In addition to providing a basic understanding of who is more likely to be involved in crime and some ideas as to why, it is also a set of facts by which to judge the quality of a theory of crime. If a given theory can explain all or most of these facts about crime, it is likely that theory has merit. We encourage readers to return to these facts as they discover each of the theories of crime and determine how many (if any) of the facts each theory is able to explain.

Websites to Visit

Cesare Beccaria: http://www.criminology.fsu.edu/crimtheory/beccaria.htm
Jeremy Bentham: http://www.criminology.fsu.edu/crimtheory/bentham.htm
Classical School of Criminology: http://www.criminology.fsu.edu/crimtheory/week3.htm
Positive School of Criminology: http://www.criminology.fsu.edu/crimtheory/week4.htm
Earnest Hooton: http://www.criminology.fsu.edu/crimtheory/hooton.html
Emile Durkheim: http://durkheim.uchicago.edu/Biography.html
Criminological Theories: http://www.criminology.fsu.edu/crimtheory/lectures.htm,
   http://www.drtomoconnor.com/criminology.htm

Discussion Questions

1. Do you agree that there is such a thing as a *mala in se* crime?
2. Do you agree with Chambliss (1974) that laws are created by powerful groups to preserve their interests and position, or do laws reflect a consensus among people about what behavior should be criminalized?
3. Can you think of any law that appears to have little utility? Conversely, can you think of some form of behavior that is currently not criminalized but should be?
4. To what extent do you think crime is a choice, consistent with the classical school of criminology? To what extent do you think crime is the result of forces outside an individual's control, consistent with the positive school of criminology?
5. Should punishment fit the crime or the criminal? Why?
6. Without looking ahead to the rest of the book, what do you think causes crime and why?

References

Akers, Ronald and Christine Sellers. (2009). *Criminological theories: Introduction, evaluation, and application.* 5th ed. Los Angeles, CA: Roxbury.

Appelbaum, Paul. (1994). *Almost a revolution: Mental health law and the limits of change.* New York, NY: Oxford University Press.

Beccaria, Cesare. (1819[1764]). *An essay on crimes and punishments.* 2nd ed. Trans. M. D. Voltaire. Philadelphia, PA: Philip H. Nicklin.

Becker, Peter and Richard Wetzell (Eds.). (2005). *Criminals and their scientists: The history of criminology in international perspective.* Cambridge, England: Cambridge University Press.

Beirne, Piers. (1987). Adolphe Quetelet and the origins of positivist criminology. *American Journal of Sociology, 92,* 1140–1169.

Bentham, Jeremy. (1811[1830]). *The rationale of punishment.* London, England: Robert Heward.

Braithwaite, John. (1989). *Crime, shame and reintegration.* New York, NY: Cambridge University Press.

Calhoun, George. (1999[1927]). *The growth of criminal law in ancient Greece.* Union, New Jersey: The Lawbook Exhange, LTD.

Carson, E. Ann and William Sabol. (2012). *Prisoners in 2011.* Bureau of Justice Statistics. Retrieved from: http://bjs.gov/content/pub/pdf/p11.pdf.

Chambliss, William. (1974). The state, the law, and the definition of behavior as criminal or delinquent. In D. Glaser (Ed.), *Handbook of criminology* (pp. 7–43). Chicago, IL: Rand McNally.

Christie, Nils. (2004). *A suitable amount of crime.* London, England: Routledge.

Cox, Wendell. (2001). Greater London, inner London and outer London population and density history. Retrieved from: http://www.demographia.com/dm-lon31.htm.

Cox, Wendell. (2003). Ville de Paris: Population and density from 1600. Retrieved from: http://www.demographia.com/dm-par90.htm.

Darwin, Charles. (1871). *Descent of man and selection in relation to sex.* London, England: John Murray.

Durkheim, Emile. (1960[1983]). *The division of labor in society.* Trans. G. Simpson. Glencoe, IL: Free Press.

Durkheim, Emile. (1953[1895]). *The rules of sociological method.* New York: The Free Press.

Durkheim, Emile. (1951[1897]). *Suicide.* New York, NY: The Free Press.

Durkheim, Emile. (1953[1904]). *Sociology and philosophy.* New York, NY: The Free Press.

Dykes, Jason, Alan MacEachren and Menno-Jan Kraak. (2005). *Exploring geovisualization.* Amsterdam, Netherlands: Pergavon.

Fields, Gary and John Emshwiller. (2011). As criminal laws proliferate, more are ensnared. *The Wall Street Journal,* July 24. Retrieved from: http://online.wsj.com/article/SB10001424052748703749504576172714184601654.html.

Fregier, Honore Antoine. (1840). *Des classes dangereuses de la population dans les grandes villes.* Paris, France: Chez J.-B. Bailliere.

Friendly, Michael. (2007). A. M. Guerry's moral statistics of France: Challenges for multivariable spatial analysis. *Statistical Science, 22*, 368–399.

Galton, Francis. (1904). Eugenics: Its definition, scope, and aims. *The American Journal of Sociology, 10*, 1–6.

Hartland, Edwin Sidney. (1924). *Primitive law.* London: Methuen & Co.

Hirschi, Travis. (1969). *The causes of delinquency.* Berkeley, CA: University of California Press.

Hooton, Ernest. (1931). *Crime and the man.* Cambridge, MA: Harvard University Press.

Howard, John. (1777). *The state of the prisons in England and Wales with preliminary observations, and an account of some foreign prisons.* London, England: William Eyres.

James, Edward. (1988). The northern world in the dark ages, 400–900. In G. Holmes (Ed.), *The Oxford history of medieval Europe* (pp. 59–108). Oxford, England: Oxford University Press.

Kiernan, Ben. (2007). *Blood and soil: A world history of genocide and extermination from Sparta to Darfur.* New Haven, CT: Yale University Press.

Lange, Johaness. (1929). *Crime and destiny.* Leipzig: Georg Thieme Verlag.

Lombroso, Cesare. (2006[1876]). *The Criminal Man (L'Uomo delinquente).* Trans. M. Gibson and N. Hahn Rafter. Durham, NC: Duke University Press.

Lombroso, Cesare. (1911). *Crime: Its causes and remedies.* Trans. H. P. Horton. Boston, MA: Little Brown.

Lombroso, Cesare and Guglielmo Ferrero. (2004[1893]). *Criminal woman, the prostitute, and the normal woman.* Trans. N. Hahn Rafter and M. Gibson. Durham, NC: Duke University Press.

Louisiana Criminal Code (R.S. 14:2 (4)). Definitions, felony. Retrieved from: http://www.legis.state.la.us/lss/lss.asp?doc=78337.

Louisiana Criminal Code (R.S. 14:2 (6)). Definitions, misdemeanor. Retrieved from: http://www.legis.state.la.us/lss/lss.asp?doc=78337.

Louisiana Criminal Code (R.S. 14:89). Crime against nature. Retrieved from: http://www.legis.state.la.us/lss/lss.asp?doc=78695.

Louisiana Criminal Code (R.S. 14:113). Treason. Retrieved from: http://www.legis.state.la.us/lss/lss.asp?doc=78274.

Louisiana Criminal Code (R.S. 14:114). Misprision of treason. Retrieved from: http://www.legis.state.la.us/lss/lss.asp?doc=78275.

Louisiana Criminal Code (R.S. 14:115). Criminal anarchy. Retrieved from: http://www.legis.state.la.us/lss/lss.asp?doc=78276.

Macmillan, Malcolm. (2000). *An odd kind of fame: Stories of Phineas Gage.* Cambridge, MA: MIT Press.

Maestro, Marcello and Norval Morris. (1973). *Cesare Beccaria and the origins of penal reform.* Philadelphia, PA: Temple University Press.

MacDonald, Arthur. (1893). *Criminology.* New York, NY: Funk & Wagnalls Company.

Maine, Henry Sumner. (1876). *Village-communities in the east and west.* Oxford, England: John Murray.

Shaw, Clifford and Henry McKay. (1942). *Juvenile delinquency and urban areas.* Chicago, IL: University of Chicago Press.

Sherman, Lawrence. (2005). The use and usefulness of criminology, 1751–2005: Enlightened justice and its failures. *The ANNALS of the American Academy of Political and Social Science, 600,* 115–135.

Simpson, Donald. (2005). Phrenology and the neurosciences: contributions of F. J. Gall and J. G. Spurzheim. *ANZ Journal of Surgery, 75,* 475–482.

Slate, Risdon and Wesley Johnson. (2008). *The criminalization of mental illness.* Durham, NC: Carolina Academic Press.

Snell, Tracy. (2009). *Capital punishment, 2009—Statistical tables.* Bureau of Justice Statistics. Retrieved from: http://bjs.gov/content/pub/pdf/cp09st.pdf.

Soggin, J. Alberto. (1981). *Judges: A commentary.* Trans. J. Bowden. Philadelphia, PA: The Westminster Press.

Sumner, William Graham. (1906). *Folkways.* Boston, MA: Ginn and Company.

Tappan, Paul. (1960). *Crime, justice and correction.* New York, NY: McGraw-Hill.

U.S. Census. (2011). *The black population: 2010.* Retrieved from: http://www.census.gov/prod/cen2010/briefs/c2010br-06.pdf.

van Wyhe, John. (2011). The phrenological organs. Retrieved from: http://www.historyofphrenology.org.uk/organs.html.

van Wyhe, John. (2011a). The history of phrenology on the web. Retrieved from: http://www.historyofphrenology.org.uk/overview.htm.

Vold, George and Thomas Bernard. (1986). *Theoretical Criminology.* New York, NY: Oxford University Press.

Walsh, Anthony and Craig Hemmens. (2011). *Introduction to criminology: A text/reader.* 2nd ed. Los Angeles, CA: Sage.

Chapter 2

How Much Crime Is There, and How Do We Study It?

Introduction

In this chapter, we explore the extent of crime and the different ways we become aware of its extent and its features. We cover official crime statistics including the Uniform Crime Reports (UCR) and the National Incident Based Reporting System (NIBRS), victimization statistics, including the National Crime Victimization Survey (NCVS), self-report surveys and data from international sources. We also describe the different research techniques that criminologists commonly employ, including examination of previously gathered data, surveys, field research, longitudinal studies and meta-analyses. As we will see, certain sources of information and techniques are better suited to investigating certain issues. A multifaceted approach to studying crime aids in understanding its extent and moves us closer to understanding what to do about it.

Official Crime Statistics

The Uniform Crime Reports (UCR)

Each year, the Federal Bureau of Investigation (FBI) publishes the most widely used source of official crime statistics, the Uniform Crime Reports (UCR). The Uniform Crime Reports traces its origin to the formation of the National Chiefs of Police Union in 1893 when police chiefs from all parts of the United States assembled in Chicago; this organization later became the International Association of Chiefs of Police (IACP). Their main concern at that time was to devise a way to apprehend persons wanted for crimes who had fled from local jurisdictions. By 1897, the association had formed a National Bureau of Criminal Identification. In 1922, work began on a uniform crime records reporting system and in 1924, the IACP files were used to create the Federal Bureau of Investigation's (FBI) Identification Division. In 1930, the IACP uniform records system was transferred over to the FBI (ICAP, 2013).

The FBI was formed during the presidency of Theodore Roosevelt. It grew out of an assemblage of special agents brought together by then United States Attorney General Charles Bonaparte. Since its beginning in 1870, the Department of Justice (DOJ) hired private detectives and later investigators from other agencies to investigate federal crimes. In 1907, the DOJ frequently used Secret Service operatives to conduct investigations. While these agents were well-trained professionals, they reported to the chief of the Secret Service. Bonaparte wanted complete control of investigations under his jurisdiction. With Roosevelt's blessing, Bonaparte hired 34 agents, 10 of whom were former Secret Service employees. On July 26, 1908, Bonaparte ordered them to report to Chief Examiner Stanley W. Finch. This action is celebrated as the beginning of the FBI. Attorney General Bonaparte and President Theodore Roosevelt recommended that the force become a permanent part of the Department of Justice. Attorney General George Wickersham, Bonaparte's successor, named the force the Bureau of Investigation in 1909 (FBI, n.d.).

The scope of work that the FBI does has expanded exponentially since its founding. However, our main concern here is with the evolution of the UCR. The UCR was first published in 1930 and is published annually to this day. The UCR contains information on offenses known to the police. The way the FBI obtains information on offenses known to the police is through reports from police departments. Every year, law enforcement agencies gather the data on the crimes that were reported to them and submit it in a standardized way to the FBI. Participation in the UCR is voluntary, but most law enforcement agencies do participate; as of 2007, law enforcement agencies active in the UCR program represented 94.6 percent of the United States population (FBI UCR, 2009). The UCR divides crimes into Part I and Part II offenses. Table 2.1 describes

Table 2.1. Uniform Crime Reports Part I and II offenses

Part I Offenses	Part II Offenses*	
Murder and nonnegligent manslaughter	Simple assaults	Offenses against the family and children
Forcible rape	Forgery and counterfeiting	Driving under the influence
Robbery	Fraud	Liquor laws
Aggravated assault	Embezzlement	Drunkenness
Burglary	Stolen property	Disorderly conduct
Larceny-theft	Vandalism	Vagrancy
Motor Vehicle Theft	Weapons	All other offenses
Arson	Prostitution and commercialized vice	Suspicion
	Other sex offenses	Curfew/loitering
	Drug abuse violations	Runaways
	Gambling	

* The FBI only collects arrest data on Part II offenses.   Source: Adapted from FBI UCR, 2011.

the Part I and II offenses; in large part, criminologists are concerned with the more serious Part I offenses. Beyond simply summing the number of different crimes committed in the United States by year, the UCR provides data on crime types by region, state and city as well as trends over time. The UCR also collects data on those crimes that are cleared by arrest or exceptional means; these data provide information on the demographic characteristics of the persons arrested. The UCR also contains information on hate crimes and law enforcement officers killed and assaulted in action.

As alluded to above, the UCR is a wealth of information on crimes reported to the police. To give just some examples of the kinds of information in the UCR, both violent and property crime have been on a steady decline in the United States since 2007. Nearly half of violent crimes but less than 20 percent of property crimes were cleared by arrest in the United States in 2011. Firearms were used in 68 percent of murders, 41 percent of robberies and 21 percent of aggravated assaults in the United States in 2011. The financial losses due to property crimes in 2011 were estimated at $15.6 billion (FBI UCR, 2011a, 2011b, 2011c).[1]

The UCR, as with all data sources, has several strengths and weaknesses. The chief strength of the UCR is that it is the premier source of official crime statistics. It is the most accurate source of data on murder in particular. The data are stable and standard enough to permit comparisons across time and place. Among the disadvantages are hierarchical reporting, unreported crime and skewed reporting by local agencies due to varying definitions of crime. The hierarchy rule refers to a reporting method in which only the most serious crime in a criminal incident is recorded in the UCR. For example, in an incident involving an offender who trespasses, falsely imprisons and murders, the only crime recorded in the UCR is murder. The report given by the police agency to the FBI will not reflect the two other serious offenses and therefore they will not be reflected in annual violent crime totals and rates. The unreported crime problem is also known as the dark figure of crime and is based on crimes that are never reported to the police and do not appear in the UCR statistics; it also includes those crimes that are reported to but never recorded by the police. The dark figure is known to be especially problematic with certain crimes, such as rape, assault and robbery. This is most easily observed by comparing UCR data to National Crime Victimization Survey (NCVS) data; the NCVS is described in more detail below. For example, the UCR reports 84,767 cases of forcible rape in 2010 (FBI UCR, 2010) whereas the NCVS reports 188,380 cases of rape in the United States in 2010 (Truman, 2011), for a difference of more than 100,000. Cases of assault, robbery and rape in particular are underreported for a number of reasons, including but not limited to distrust in the criminal justice system, a belief that nothing can be done and embarrassment upon experiencing victimization.

Cross-jurisdictional definitions of a crime, in spite of the FBI's efforts at standardization, remain a problem. What one jurisdiction or country calls rape or attempted rape, another may not. This issue is present at all jurisdictional levels. Moreover, some agencies may be tempted to classify a crime as less serious than what actually occurred—calling an aggravated assault a simple assault, for exam-

---

1. We make much use of UCR data in Chapters 11 and 12 especially.

ple — in order to downplay the dangerousness of that area as reflected in the UCR's tally of Part I offenses. The UCR also fails to collect data on white collar offenses, which can have a larger impact on society than do the statistically rare incidents of violent crime.

Box 2.1. The Crime Rate

Astute readers may already be questioning the use of raw numbers in comparing the crime that is committed in one place to another. Does it mean anything to say that New York City, with its population of 8.2 million had more murders (515 in 2011) than New Orleans, which had a population of 346,974 and 200 murders in 2011? Not really, because it makes sense to expect more murders in places with more people. Rather than relying on raw numbers to make comparisons about crime from place to place, criminologists use the crime rate, which is the number of crimes divided by the population and standardized by some unit, usually 100,000. When we use this formula:

Crime rate = Number of crimes/population of area x unit of standardization

we can easily see that in fact New Orleans had a much higher murder rate, 57.6 per 100,000 people, than did the much bigger New York City, which had a murder rate of 6.3 per 100,000 in 2011 (FBI UCR, 2011d).

The National Incident-Based Reporting System (NIBRS)

In 1982, the FBI and the Bureau of Justice Statistics (BJS) funded a five-year project to revise the UCR and to expand upon the data it collects. This project became known as the National Incident-Based Reporting System (NIBRS). NIBRS collects data on 46 different offenses, including those listed in the UCR. NIBRS collects more detailed data on criminal incidents than does the UCR, including the nature and type of each offense within a criminal incident, the demographic characteristics of victims and offenders, the type and value of any property stolen and demographic characteristics of anyone arrested for any offense within a criminal incident (NACJD, 2010). Importantly, the way the NIBRS counts crimes, by tallying each offense within a criminal incident, eliminates the hierarchy rule that stands out as one of the weaknesses of the UCR. Returning to the example above, in an incident involving an offender who trespasses, falsely imprisons and murders, the NIBRS records all three of these offenses, not just the most serious one. Table 2.2 reveals the NIBRS Group A and Group B offenses.

The main strength of NIBRS data is that it is comprehensive and it allows criminologists and others working on criminal justice policy an opportunity to enhance our understanding of crime and the contexts surrounding those who offend and those who are victimized. As noted, it also eliminates the hierarchy rule. However, only 19 states and just three large cities were participating in NIBRS data collection and reporting as of 2004 (Finkelhor and Ormrod, 2004), which raises issues about the generalizability

Table 2.2. NIBRS Group A and B offenses

Group A Offenses		Group B Offenses
Arson	Homicide offenses including murder and nonnegligent manslaughter, negligent manslaughter and justifiable homicide	Bad checks
Assault offenses, including aggravated assault, simple assault and intimidation	Kidnapping, abduction	Curfew, loitering, vagrancy violations
Bribery	Larceny-theft offenses including pocket picking, purse snatching, shoplifting, theft from building, theft from coin operated machine or device, theft from motor vehicle, theft of motor vehicle parts or accessories and all other larceny	Disorderly conduct
Burglary, breaking and entering	Motor vehicle theft	Driving under the influence
Counterfeiting, forgery	Pornography and obscene material	Drunkenness
Destruction, damage, vandalism of property	Prostitution offenses including prostitution and assisting or promoting prostitution	Nonviolent family offenses
Drug and narcotic offenses, including drug/narcotic violations and drug equipment violations	Robbery	Liquor law violations
Embezzlement	Forcible sex offenses including forcible rape, forcible sodomy, sexual assault with an object and forcible fondling	Peeping Tom
Extortion, blackmail	Nonforcible sex offenses including incest and statutory rape	Runaway
Fraud offenses, including false pretenses, swindle or confidence game, credit card and AMT fraud, impersonation, welfare fraud and wire fraud	Stolen property offenses including receiving	Trespass of real property
Gambling offenses including betting and wagering, operating, promoting and assisting gambling, gambling equipment violations and sports tampering	Weapons law violations	All other offenses

Source: Adapted from NACJD, 2010b.

of findings based on NIBRS data. Many law enforcement agencies appear to be reluctant to participate in NIBRS because of the technical training needed to be able to comply with reporting demands and the extra time required to summarize each criminal incident as fully as the NIBRS requires (Dunworth, 2000).

Victimization Statistics

The National Crime Victimization Survey (NCVS)

A number of precursors to the National Crime Victimization Survey (NCVS) were commissioned by the President's Commission on Law Enforcement and the Administration of Justice in 1965. Recognizing that police crime reports at that time did not provide an adequate picture of the nature and extent of the crime problem, the Commission funded three crime surveys carried out by the National Opinion Research Center of the University of Chicago in 1967. The thrust of the survey of 10,000 households was to discover experiences as crime victims. Those responding to the survey were asked whether they or any members of their household had been a victim of an index crime in the past year and whether or not the crime had been reported and if not reported, why (President's Commission, 1967).

Beginning in 1973, the U.S. Census Bureau began administering the National Crime Victimization Survey (NCVS) on behalf of the Bureau of Justice Statistics (BJS). Data on victimization by crime are collected twice a year from a nationally representative sample of about 49,000 households, which corresponds to approximately 100,000 in- dividuals. Household remain in the sample for three years, after which time they are rotated out and new, representative households are rotated in. The survey is administered to people in the household who are 12 and over and is designed to gather information on the victims and consequences of crime and to provide estimates of crime not reported to the police (NACJD, 2010a).

The NCVS has produced important findings. Sixty seven percent of crimes committed against individuals do not involve the use of any weapon, and in cases of violent crime, non-stranger relationships account for 40 percent of all cases (Truman, 2011). These findings have been impactful, but most importantly give specific contextual information about crime. The statistics are antithetical to the public fear of innately violent strangers roaming the streets just waiting for an unsuspecting victim. Moreover, the event of violent victimization is statistically rare; the NCVS reports 2011 violent victimization at a rate of 22.5 incidents per 1,000 individuals (Truman and Planty, 2012).

The BJS redesigned the NCVS survey in 1993 to better discover crimes and broaden the scope of crimes measured. The new survey collects detailed data on the frequency and nature of the crimes of rape, sexual assault, personal robbery and aggravated and simple assault, as well as property crimes such as household burglary, theft and motor vehicle theft. Because it is a self-report survey, it does not measure homicide. The following are some highlights of the 2010 NCVS (Truman, 2011):

- Between 2001 and 2010, about 6 percent to 9 percent of all violent victimization was committed with firearms. This percentage has remained stable since 2004.
- About half (50 percent) of all violent crimes were reported to the police in 2010.
- Males (15.7 per 1,000) and females (14.2 per 1,000) had similar rates of victimization during 2010.
- Strangers were offenders in about 40 percent of all violent victimizations in 2010, a percentage that has declined from 44 percent in 2001. When offenders are known to their victims, they are most often friends or acquaintances.

- The percentage of female victims (22 percent) of intimate partner violence was about 4 times that of male victims (5 percent).

The redesign of the NCVS means that longitudinal comparisons must be taken with a grain of salt. For example, the previous version of the NCVS asked questions about whether respondents had been attacked in any way or whether someone had tried to attack them while the redesigned NCVS asks specific questions about attacks of a sexual nature and make reference in the question to possible victimization by a partner, family member, friend or acquaintance. The redesign of these questions has resulted in more people reporting violence, including sexual violence, at the hands of people they know, but it is important to note that these questions may be better designed to measure what is happening in the real world and not necessarily that there is more sexual violence by intimates and acquaintances than there was before the redesign (Maxfield and Babbie, 2011).

The greatest strength of the NCVS is that it aids us in seeing how much crime was not reported to the police and obtain a truer picture of the crime problem. It also reveals information on the relationship between offenders and victims. However, the NCVS is not without its weaknesses. First, it does not measure victimless crimes, such as drug dealing and gambling. As noted above, it cannot measure murder and because it is a household survey, it does not measure crimes against commercial establishments and does not well capture victimization of the homeless. And because it is a survey, it is subject to the same pitfalls that all surveys of past experiences are, namely inaccurate reporting, willful or otherwise. Some people may underreport their experiences with victimization because of embarrassment and some people may overreport due to mis-remembered incidents or deliberate dishonesty, so the NCVS is far from a perfect measure of victimization.

Self-Report Surveys

Self-report surveys are designed to measure the behavior of the respondents and their use in academia goes back decades (e.g., Porterfield, 1943; Wallerstein and Wylie, 1947). For criminologists, self-report surveys are a way of measuring criminal behavior that does not require reliance on official statistics, which have their own pitfalls as we have seen. Much of self-report research in criminology has attempted to gauge the volume of criminal activity that never comes to the attention of the authorities; this is distinct from the NCVS, which measures victimization. Self-report surveys are concerned with respondents' commission of crimes, not their victimization by crime.

One of the most well-known surveys of this type is the Monitoring the Future (MTF) survey, an ongoing study of the attitudes, values and behaviors, including drug use, of American middle and high school students, college students and young adults. Each year since 1975, a total sample of about 50,000 8th, 10th and 12th grade students have been surveyed. Follow up surveys are mailed annually to a sample of each participating high school's graduating class (MTF, 2013). The way the survey is administered permits

Figure 2.1. Percent of 8th, 10th and 12th graders who used marijuana in the last year

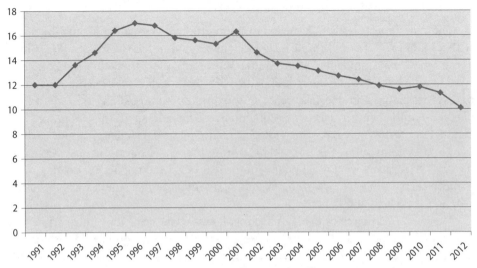

Source: Adapted from Johnston, O'Malley, Bachman and Schulenberg, 2012.

researchers to examine drug use by secondary schoolers over time. For example, Figure 2.1 reveals the percent of 8th, 10th and 12th graders who used marijuana in the last year between 1991 and 2012.

Another nationwide longitudinal survey on social environments and behaviors in adolescence and their relationship to outcomes in adulthood is the National Longitudinal Study of Adolescent Health (Add Health for short). Add Health was administered to students in a sample of 80 high schools and 52 middle schools in the 1994–1995 school year and that group of students has been followed ever since; in 2008, the students who initially filled out the survey were between 24 and 32 years of age. Add Health data have been utilized in thousands of social science studies, many of which focus on factors in adolescence that are associated with criminal and other negative outcomes later in life (for a list of these studies, see Add Health, 2013).

The greatest strength of self-report surveys such as Monitoring the Future is that they provide information on law breaking behavior, such as drug use, that is not typically captured by official statistics. However, self-report surveys have a number of weaknesses, including reliance on convenience samples (which as their name implies are handy but may not be representative of the population at large or even of the population of interest), failure to capture information on the commission of more serious crimes and misrepresentation of involvement in crime. We should not reasonably expect to find seriously criminally involved young people among convenience samples of middle school, high school and college students. Moreover, administration of the survey in the school setting may not capture information on more serious law breaking by those students who do not routinely attend class. Self-report surveys are generally focused on involvement in minor crimes such as shoplifting, drug use, fighting and truancy than they are on more serious crimes and so self-report surveys are typically a poor measure of more serious criminal involvement.

Much like victimization surveys, self-report surveys are also subject to over and underreporting. As Nettler states, "asking people questions about their behavior is a poor way of observing it" (1978, p. 107). Self-report survey respondents may willfully or otherwise misrepresent their criminal involvement. Hindelang, Hirschi and Weis (1981) found that most people have a very minor criminal history and those with a more serious criminal history tend to be the ones who underreport involvement in crime. As the number of crimes a respondent has committed increases (as verified through criminal records), the number of offenses reported on the survey drops (Farrington, 1982) and reporting by the same respondent may be inconsistent from one self-report survey to the next (Farrington, 1973). As alluded to, the validity of self-report surveys can be significantly improved with the use of creative methodology. For example, checks against official data sources such as police reports and field observation of known groups can improve the reliability and validity of self-report surveys, as can the use of standardized scales available to measure veracity, measures of internal consistency and retests (Thornberry and Krohn, 2000).

International Crime Data Sources

The United Nations Office of Drugs and Crime (UNODC) collects a variety of information on drugs throughout the world and its annual World Drug Report summarizes information on drug consumption, production and trafficking provided by 194 UN member states as well as 15 territories. In 2009, it was estimated that between 3 and 6 percent of the world's population aged 15–64 used illegal drugs at least once in the last year. Marijuana is by far the most commonly used illegal drug and it is the most commonly seized drug, as well. Both opioid and cocaine production were on the decline in 2011, but they remained lucrative markets, with the former valued at $68 billion and the latter at $85 billion; almost all the profits from these markets goes to drug traffickers (WDR, 2011).

The UNODC is also concerned with international crime and criminal justice statistics and collects this information through its Surveys on Crime Trends and Operations of Criminal Justice Systems (CTS). The CTS is administered to UN member states and though it is designed to measure crime in a standard way across countries to allow for comparisons, different definitions of crimes from country to country and multiple data sources complicate the ease with which this can be accomplished. Nevertheless, the UNODC's Global Study on Homicide reveals some comparative information on homicides for 2010 for the 207 countries surveyed. Homicide rates tend to be higher in developing countries, such as those in southern Africa, Central and South America and the Caribbean, than in developed countries such as in western, northern and southern Europe and in eastern Asia. The high homicide rate in Central and South American and the Caribbean appears to be driven up by organized drug trafficking groups' use of lethal violence in those areas. Young men are at the greatest risk for being murdered the world over, indicating that older men and women are less involved in high risk activities such as gang membership. However, women are at greater risk for injury and death as a result of intimate partner and family violence (GSH, 2011).

The World Health Organization (WHO), a component of the United Nations, investigates violence from a public health perspective. Its 2002 report on violence and health defines violence as "the intentional use of physical force or power, threatened or actual, against oneself, another person, or against a group or community, that either results in or has a high likelihood of resulting in injury, death, psychological harm, maldevelopment or deprivation" (WHO, 2002, p. 5). Importantly, this definition encompasses self-directed, interpersonal and collective forms of violence. Data on the use of violence were collected from a variety of sources for the report, beginning with mortality data, which includes death certificates and coroners' reports. However, violence is much more often nonlethal than lethal, so additional types of information were collected from a variety of different sources, including health data, mortality data, community data, crime data, economic data and policy and legislative data. In 2000, interpersonal violence took the lives of an estimated 520,000 people worldwide for a rate of 8.8 per 100,000.[2] Of these 520,000, nearly 200,000 were young people and for every young person killed by interpersonal violence, another 20–40 received injuries severe enough to require hospitalization. Surveys conducted around the world reveal that anywhere from 10 to 69 percent of women were physically assaulted by an intimate partner at least once over the lifetime. In some countries, as many as one in four women have been sexually assaulted by an intimate partner (WHO, 2002).

The greatest strength of international sources of data is that they permit us to observe the extent of a problem (e.g., drugs, crime, violence) throughout the world as well as across geographic and cultural places and to investigate features of those places that may contribute to a given problem. The main weakness of international data sources has already been alluded to, namely that the information of interest may not be defined, collected and reported in a standardized way from place to place, which means comparisons and worldwide totals must always be taken with a grain of salt.

Research Designs in Criminology

The type of questions one is interested in answering helps dictate what sources of data will be most helpful and should be utilized, as well as what research design should be followed. There are a number of different techniques that criminologists use to conduct their research. Happily, this is not a research methods textbook, so we will not belabor our descriptions of those techniques here. However, as readers make their way through the book, they will see that we have made reference to the different ways that criminologists have conducted research and been able to conclude something about crime. For that reason, we believe it is important to touch briefly on secondary analysis

---

2. However, the report points out that there are known instances of misattribution of death which means this finding is not perfectly accurate. For example, the deaths of women who are set on fire by their husbands or family members in India for some transgression are sometimes recorded as accidental burning (WHO, 2002).

and record reviews, surveys, field research and case studies, cohort and longitudinal studies and meta-analysis. Again, the research question at hand generally dictates the methodological strategy and the statistical techniques that are appropriate.

Secondary Analysis and Record Reviews

Secondary analysis, sometimes also called record reviews, refers to data that were originally collected for other purposes that are reused for new research. Secondary analysis is possible with data found in the UCR, NCVS, most of the data files of the Interuniversity Consortium for Political and Social Research (ICPSR), already published academic articles, letters, memoirs and personal documents. The advantages to secondary analysis sources are numerous. They offer quick (usually electronic) access to already accumulated information, reducing the time necessary for data collection. Secondary analysis saves money so that research grants and funding can be better used elsewhere. They are also unobtrusive and nonreactive, meaning there is no possibility of the researcher influencing responses or actions on the part of study participants. However, a disadvantage of secondary analysis is that the original data collection was perhaps for another purpose and may present some level of inflexibility in reanalysis. For instance, some data is summary in nature and cannot be disaggregated in order to address the present research question and its contextual underpinnings.

A study by Spohn (1990) also illustrates the use of secondary analysis. In comparing the sentencing decisions of white and African American sitting judges, she reused data on the sentencing decisions for 3,283 defendants charged with violent felonies. The data on the defendants were made available by the ICPSR and were originally collected by Loftin, Heumann and McDowall (1983). Spohn's (1990) study would have proven more difficult if she collected her own data for comparison, especially considering the difficulties of finding a comparable group of white and African American sitting judges in one jurisdiction in 1990.

The results of the study were remarkable. Spohn (1990) found that judicial decisions from judge to judge were remarkably similar and that the race of the judge had little predictive power in the sentencing outcome. Perhaps most intriguing was the finding that both white and African American judges sentenced African American defendants more harshly than white defendants. The results of this study raise serious questions about the appropriate interpretation of racial disparity in incarceration rates. Moreover, the harsher treatment of African American offenders cannot be solely attributed to the racism of white judges.

Spohn (1990) also found that even after relevant legal and extralegal factors were taken into account, African American defendants still were sentenced to prison more often than white defendants. Further analysis revealed that the discriminatory treatment of African American defendants was not conditioned by the race of the victim. African American defendants were more likely than white defendants to be sentenced to prison, regardless of whether the victim was white or African American. Unless other variables can account for this difference, Spohn (1990) contends the difference suggests an overt discrimination against African American felony defendants with respect to the decision to incarcerate. Of course, sentencing decision by itself says nothing about the possibility of pervasive discrimination at other stages in the criminal justice process.

Spohn's (1990) study is an excellent example of secondary analysis, but it is important to note foreseeable challenges for those readers who might one day wish to use this technique in their own work. The first such challenge is reliability. Repeated observations of the same phenomena should yield similar or the same results, but if measurements change over time, this can impact results. For example, if data on drug use by probationers is initially measured by drug test results and later by self-reports, this can have an adverse effect on reliability. Validity problems can also occur when doing secondary analysis of existing data. Validity becomes an issue when the concepts the researcher wishes to investigate are not well captured by the existing data. For example, if a researcher wants to investigate the sexual assault of adult males, the UCR would be a poor choice for data on this topic because the FBI's definition of forcible rape only includes females. This means that when law enforcement agencies supply their data to the FBI to include in the UCR, no adult males who were sexually assaulted are included in those tallies of rape.[3] Researchers utilizing second analysis of existing data must also be mindful of missing data, which can adversely affect the conclusions they are able to draw from their analyses.

Surveys

Survey research is widely used today by criminologists; to give just one example, the Monitoring the Future Survey seen above measures drug use by middle and high schoolers. The Monitoring the Future survey is an example of a survey that utilizes closed-ended questions, in which respondents are forced to pick from a number of answers that are determined by the researcher. Other surveys utilize open-ended questions in which respondents are asked to provide their own answers and are unconstrained by choices provided by the researcher. Open-ended questions are designed to elicit descriptive or contextual information. While surveys using closed-ended questions yield quantitative summary data, surveys using open-ended questions yield narrative and contextual data that are qualitative in nature. The type of survey utilized will depend on what questions the researcher wants to answer. If the researcher wants to know how often college students shoplift, he or she will use closed-ended questions. However, if the researcher wants to know about how shoplifters construct the experience of shoplifting, as Katz (1988)[4] did, he or she will use open-ended questions.

Some of the challenges of conducting quality survey research include using appropriate sampling techniques and creating valid questions (see e.g., Maxfield and Babbie, 2011 for more on these issues). Other challenges include the reactivity of respondents, who may give inaccurate responses due to being observed by the researcher. For example, a respondent might be hesitant to report involvement in criminal activity, especially serious criminal activity, sitting across the table from a stranger who is taking down his or her responses; a desire to please the researcher on the part of the respondent may also impact responses. One way that criminologists and other social science researchers

---

3. For more on how the FBI defines rape and the changes that definition is undergoing, see Chapter 11.

4. Katz's (1988) work is discussed in more detail in Chapters 8 and 12.

have aimed to address this problem is to provide self-report surveys to respondents that do not require administration by a researcher. As seen above, the very real possibility of inaccurate reporting, willful or otherwise, means that survey research results are always taken with a grain of salt.

Field Research

Field research falls along a continuum. In complete participation at the one end, the researcher becomes a part of the culture or group being studied. The researcher participates just as any other member and records observations at a later point. This method yields rich contextual data but places the researcher in a position of being less dispassionate about the objects of the research. This kind of in-depth research yields few if any generalizable results. In complete observation at the other end, researchers have little if any direct interaction with or emotional attachment to the culture or group under investigation. Complete observation eliminates an inability to see the culture or group objectively as can happen with complete participation, but complete observation means it is less likely that the researcher will grasp the meanings attached to the behaviors of the culture or group. Most researchers who employ field studies fall in the middle of the continuum and use what is called participant observation, wherein the group being observed is aware of the researcher's presence and his or her role as an investigator.

One very famous example of a field study using participation is Humphreys' (1975[1970]) investigation of the "tearoom trade." Humphreys was interested in men who identified as heterosexual yet engaged in homosexual activity of a casual nature with other men in the bathrooms at public parks. In order to identify these men, Humphreys agreed to serve as a lookout, called the watchqueen in this setting, during the sexual encounter. The watchqueen was permitted to observe the sexual encounter in exchange for his services as a lookout. Once the sexual encounter had concluded, Humphreys made a note of the license plate numbers of participants, then tracked down their names and addresses through the police. Humphreys went to the homes of the men who had participated in these casual, often anonymous sexual encounters (in disguise, lest he be recognized as the watchqueen) and conducted a survey; the ethics of this approach are still debated to this day.

Another well-known but less controversial field research study in criminology is Baumer and Rosenbaum's (1982) study of shoplifting. They set out to determine the prevalence of shoplifting at a large department store by assigning field workers to subtly follow around a systematic sample of shoppers at that store and record the instances of shoplifting that occurred. They also assigned field workers as faux shoplifters to ensure that the field workers tasked with recording the instances of shoplifting were making accurate observations.

A more recent example of field research is Anderson's (1999) study of life circumstances and values of the inner city poor in Philadelphia.[5] Lack of jobs or jobs that pay low wages, the stigma of race, open displays of violence associated with drug

---

5. Anderson's (1999) work is covered in more detail in Chapter 4.

use and trafficking, alienation and lack of hope for the future, which typically characterize living in inner city environments, place young people at especial risk of crime and deviant behavior. Anderson's (1999) field study identifies two cultural forces running through the neighborhood that shape the residents' value sets and associated patterns of interactions and especially reactions to conflicts, decent values and street values. Decent values can be thought of as middle class values and include hard work, self-reliance, sacrifice for children and a commitment to faith and education. Street values, on the other hand, revolve around respect. Respect is hard earned and easily lost, so when respect is challenged, it is acceptable to meet that challenge in aggressive, even violent ways. Anderson (1999) claims that these two orientations socially organize the community. Their coexistence means that youngsters who are brought up in decent homes must be able to successfully navigate the demands of street culture. Even decent parents recognize that the code must be obeyed or at the very least negotiated and must not be ignored. Pattillo-McCoy (1999) draws many of the same conclusions as Anderson (1999) in her study of a neighborhood on the south side of Chicago. Both Anderson (1999) and Pattillo (1999) draw attention to the fact that the majority of people living in areas of concentrated socioeconomic disadvantage and high levels of crime are law abiding citizens committed to mainstream norms and values and do not advocate use of violence.

As alluded to in the research using field studies described above, it is unlikely that this type of in depth, contextually rich information could have been obtained any other way, certainly not by secondary analysis or surveys. The great strength of field research is that it provides a comprehensive look at one phenomenon, but this is also the source of its greatest weakness, namely that the findings of one study utilizing field research are unlikely to be able to be generalized to other groups, other places or other times.

Longitudinal Studies

Longitudinal studies involve following a group of people over time, taking measurements of various concepts of interest at different points during their lives. There are some famous longitudinal studies in criminology that deserve brief description here. In their classic study, Wolfgang, Figlio and Sellin (1972) gathered a variety of demographic, family, school and criminal information on nearly 10,000 boys born in Philadelphia in 1945 until they turned 18 in 1963. They found that about a third of the boys had no contact with the police during the first 18 years of their lives. Of the 3,475 that had any contact with the police, 1,862 had repeated contact with the police and of the nearly 10,000 boys in the sample, 627 (six percent of the sample) had five or more police contacts. This six percent was responsible for nearly 52 percent of all the offenses committed by the entire group. Moreover, this group was heavily involved in the most serious delinquency; it was responsible for 70 percent or more of all the homicides, rapes, robberies and aggravated assaults committed by the entire group.

In another famous longitudinal study, Sheldon and Eleanor Glueck compared 500 institutionalized delinquents to 500 controls on a variety of measures over time. Though their work is remembered today for their focus on body type and the correlation between physical build and delinquent involvement (Glueck and Glueck, 1930), the Gluecks actually collected a huge amount and variety of information on each of the boys at each data collection point. They were able to determine that delinquency begins long before children become adolescents; signs are often visible by the time children are between three and six, and almost always before they are 11 years old. "The onset of persistent misbehavior tendencies was at the early age of seven years or younger among 48 per cent of our delinquents, and from eight to ten in an additional 39 per cent; thus a total of almost nine-tenths of the entire group showed clear delinquent tendencies before the time when boys generally become members of organized boys' gangs" (Glueck and Glueck, 1964, p. 285). Despite the considerable gravitas provided by the Gluecks' long association with the Harvard Law School, their research received little support from other criminologists. Critics continued to note serious methodological flaws (Clinard, 1974).

In one of the lucky turn of events in criminology, John Laub stumbled upon the Gluecks' original data gathering dust in a basement at Harvard in the 1980s. He and colleague Robert Sampson recreated the original data set and were able to follow up with many of the delinquents in the original study and find out what factors were associated with their persistence in and desistance from delinquency. In other words, Sampson and Laub (1993) were able to conduct a true life course study in criminology and their work is covered in more detail in Chapter 7.

Wolfgang, Figlio, and Sellin (1972) note many advantages to longitudinal studies. Among these advantages are a better understanding of causal order of events over time, the dynamics of repeat offending and generational and cultural influences. Understanding causal order is of paramount importance in empirical validity testing because without knowing the proper temporal order of variables, causation cannot really be inferred. Moreover, longitudinal analysis allows for a better understanding of offender recidivism. Longitudinal studies allow for richer data on generational and culturally nuanced factors in offending. Wolfgang, Figlio and Sellin's choice of the 1945 birth year was purposeful because at the end of World War II, "social variables of significance to delinquency that may be due to wartime did not intervene directly in a cohort that grew up between 1945 and 1963" (1972, p. 29). However, longitudinal studies are not without their challenges, which include the time and money necessary to execute them, as well as difficulties with retaining participants.

Meta-Analysis

Meta-analysis research is a quantitative analysis of past research and its findings. This method is essentially an integrative literature review in quantitative form with emphasis on comparing research reports with a focus on the variables studied and the methodology and statistical techniques employed. Glass (1976) calls this type of research an analysis of analysis. Wells (1991) notes that meta-analysis has been used mostly in medico-psychological research studies, rather than criminological-theoretical applications. Presently, the power of meta-analysis is being recognized and its use in criminology is becoming more commonplace.

Meta-analyses have been highly persuasive in the public opinion and policy arena. A watershed meta-analysis in criminology and criminal justice was published in 1974 by Robert Martinson, who was working with two associates, Douglas Lipton and Judith Wilks. Unknown to Lipton and Wilks, Martinson published the now famous article peremptorily and without their specific consent (Sarre, 1999). In the mid 1970s, many researchers and practitioners in the field of corrections embraced the rehabilitation model and believed prison inmates could be reformed. Martinson (1974) conducted a meta-analysis of 231 evaluations of prison rehabilitation programs conducted from 1945 to 1967 and concluded that no program or type of program was particularly useful for reducing recidivism. Though he never said as much, his article came to be known as the Nothing Works Report. Nothing works became the mantra of those in favor of punishment and who viewed rehabilitative efforts as a waste of money. Martinson's conclusions were soon treated as fact (Lipton, 1998, p. 2). In part as a result of Martinson's paper, the paradigm in American corrections shifted away from a rehabilitation model to a punishment model which still tends to hold sway.[6]

Martinson's (1974) article may be the most famous meta-analysis in criminology but there are others that focus on a variety of different topics. To detail just two examples, Land, McCall and Cohen (1990) conducted a review of 21 studies with 11 overlapping structural covariates that are typically hypothesized to be related to the ecological clustering of homicides. The studies they analyzed in their meta-analysis varied by time and by unit of analysis (cities, metropolitan areas or SMSAs, and states). The overlapping covariates for these studies consist of population size, population density, percent of population age 15–29, percent of male population 15 years and older, percent divorced, percent of children under the age of 18 years not living with both parents, median family income, percentage of families living below the official poverty line, the GINI index of family income inequality, percent unemployment and a variable indicating southern/non-southern location of cities, metropolitan areas or states. What is most striking about their findings is that no covariates exhibit consistent statistically significant estimates across all studies. These data raise serious doubts about developing a general theory of variation in homicide rates that is more than context specific. According to the authors, this limits the prospect for developing a general theory of homicide rate variation particularly across time and social space (Land, McCall and Cohen, 1990).

Gottfredson and Hirschi (1990) made the bold claim in 1990 that the singular cause of crime was low self-control and unsurprisingly, criminological researchers rushed out to empirically test this notion. Pratt and Cullen (2000) conducted a meta-analysis of 21 studies that measured the relationship between the level of self-control and crime. These studies were both cross-sectional and longitudinal in nature and they measured self-control using both questions about attitudes and about behavior. Among the approximately 50,000 participants in this study, self-control explained 19 percent of the

---

6. For more on the criminal justice system's focus on both punishment and rehabilitation as well as the use of meta-analyses in rehabilitation research, see Chapter 15.

variance in delinquent and criminal behavior. Pratt and Cullen (2000) conclude that low self-control is one of the strongest predictors of crime, but that does not mean it is the sole cause of crime.

Among the strengths of meta-analyses is that they permit researchers to gather a large amount of data on one subject fairly easily and inexpensively and to draw broader conclusions than studies which are necessarily limited in focus (on one city at one point in time or on one sample of high schoolers, for example). However, a challenge of this technique is that a meta-analysis is only as good as the studies it includes, so studies that have serious flaws can affect the quality of the meta-analysis; this is known as the garbage in, garbage out problem. The ability to discern what is high quality empirical research as well as a good deal of training in sophisticated statistical analyses are also necessary to competently execute a meta-analysis.

Conclusion

In this chapter, we described the different types of data sources that criminologists typically use when trying to better understand the extent of and reasons for crime. We also described the typical methodological techniques that criminologists employ in their work. It is important to understand not only how criminologists go about measuring crime but also the strengths and weaknesses of various data sources and techniques, as this is helpful in determining the predictive accuracy and scope of the theories of crime detailed in this book. If a theory has been empirically tested using the best data sources and methodological techniques for the research question of interest and the empirical tests revealed support for the theory, it is robust evidence that the theory is able to explain the origins of criminal behavior. If, on the other hand, empirical tests of a theory use inappropriate data sources or questionable methodological techniques, the conclusions we can draw about the theory's ability to explain crime are much less strong. The data and methods criminologists use are at the heart of understanding how the concepts of each theory of crime operate in the real world.

Websites to Visit

FBI's Uniform Crime Reports (for 2011): http://www.fbi.gov/about-us/cjis/ucr/crime-in-the-u.s/2011/crime-in-the-u.s.-2011
NIBRS: http://www.icpsr.umich.edu/icpsrweb/NACJD/NIBRS/
NCVS: http://www.icpsr.umich.edu/icpsrweb/NACJD/NCVS/, http://bjs.gov/index.cfm?ty=dcdetail&iid=245
Monitoring the Future: http://www.monitoringthefuture.org/
Add Health: http://www.cpc.unc.edu/projects/addhealth
World Drug Report: http://www.unodc.org/documents/data-and-analysis/WDR2011/WDR2011-ExSum.pdf

Global Study on Homicide: http://www.unodc.org/documents/data-and-analysis/ statistics/Homicide/Globa_study_on_homicide_2011_web.pdf

WHO World Report on Violence and Health: http://www.who.int/violence_injury_prevention/violence/world_report/en/summary_en.pdf

Discussion Questions

1. Examine the most recent UCR data for your hometown or current city. What are some of the crime trends and how do they compare to national averages? How can you account for any differences?
2. What are some ways to improve victimization and self-report surveys so that they do not have to rely so much on respondents' recall of events?
3. Think of a criminal phenomenon you are interested in learning more about. What methodological technique would be best suited to studying this phenomenon and why?
4. Are the potential ethical difficulties in conducting field research worth the contribution to knowledge? Why or why not?

References

Add Health. (2013). Publications. Retrieved from: http://www.cpc.unc.edu/projects/ addhealth/publications.

Anderson, Elijah. (1999). *Code of the streets: Decency, violence and the moral life of the inner city*. New York, NY: W.W. Norton and Company.

Baumer, Terry and Dennis Rosenbaum. (1982). *Combatting retail theft: Programs and strategies*. Boston, MA: Butterworth.

Clinard, Marshall. (1974). *Sociology of deviant behavior*. 4th ed. New York, NY: Holt, Rinehart and Winston.

Dunworth, Terence. (2000). Criminal justice and the IT revolution. In W. Reed and L. Winterfield (Eds.), *Criminal Justice 2000, Vol. 3: Policies, processes and decision of the criminal justice system* (pp. 371–426). National Institute of Justice. Retrieved from: https://www.ncjrs.gov/criminal_justice2000/vol_3/03h.pdf.

Farrington, David. (1973). Self reports of deviant behavior: Predictive and stable? *Journal of Criminal Law and Criminology, 64*, 99–110.

Farrington, David. (1982). Longitudinal analyses of criminal violence. In M. Wolfgang and N. Weiner (Eds.), *Criminal violence* (pp. 171–200). Beverly Hills, CA: Sage.

FBI. (N.d.). A brief history of the FBI. Retrieved from: http://www.fbi.gov/about-us/ history/brief-history.

FBI UCR. (2009). UCR Frequently asked questions. Retrieved from: http://www.fbi.gov/ about-us/cjis/ucr/frequently-asked-questions/ucr_faqs08.pdf.

FBI UCR. (2010). Crime in the United States 2010: Crime in the United States by volume and rate, 1991–2010. Retrieved from: http://www.fbi.gov/about-us/cjis/ucr/ crime-in-the-u.s/2010/crime-in-the-u.s.-2010/tables/10tbl01.xls

FBI UCR. (2011). Crime in the United States: Offense definitions. Retrieved from: http://www.fbi.gov/about-us/cjis/ucr/crime-in-the-u.s/2011/crime-in-the-u.s.-2011/offense-definitions.

FBI UCR. (2011a). Crime in the United States: Violent crime. Retrieved from: http://www.fbi.gov/about-us/cjis/ucr/crime-in-the-u.s/2011/crime-in-the-u.s.-2011/violent-crime/violent-crime.

FBI UCR. (2011b). Crime in the United States: Property crime. Retrieved from: http://www.fbi.gov/about-us/cjis/ucr/crime-in-the-u.s/2011/crime-in-the-u.s.-2011/property-crime/property-crime.

FBI UCR. (2011c). Crime in the United States: Clearances. Retrieved from: http://www.fbi.gov/about-us/cjis/ucr/crime-in-the-u.s/2011/crime-in-the-u.s.-2011/clearances.

FBI UCR. (2011d). Offenses known to law enforcement: By state by city, 2011. Retrieved from: http://www.fbi.gov/about-us/cjis/ucr/crime-in-the-u.s/2011/crime-in-the-u.s.-2011/tables/table_8_offenses_known_to_law_enforcement_by_state_by_city_2011.xls/view.

Finkelhor, David and Richard Ormrod. (2004). *Prostitution of juveniles: Patterns from NIBRS*. Office of Juvenile Justice and Delinquency Prevention. Retrieved from: https://www.ncjrs.gov/pdffiles1/ojjdp/203946.pdf.

Glass, Gene. (1976). Primary, secondary, and meta-analysis of research. *Educational Researcher, 5*, 3–8.

Glueck, Sheldon and Eleanor Glueck. (1930). *Five hundred criminal careers*. New York, NY: Knopf.

Glueck, Sheldon and Eleanor Glueck. (1964).*Ventures in criminology: Collected Recent Papers*. London, England: Tavistock Publications.

GSH. (2011). *Global study on homicide, 2011*. United Nations Office on Drugs and Crime. Retrieved from: http://www.unodc.org/documents/data-and-analysis/statistics/Homicide/Globa_study_on_homicide_2011_web.pdf.

Gottfredson, Michael and Travis Hirschi. (1990). *A general theory of crime*. Palo Alto, CA: Stanford University Press.

Hindelang, Michael, Travis Hirschi and Joseph Weis. (1981). *Measuring delinquency*. Beverly Hills, CA: Sage.

Humphreys, Laud. (1975[1970]). *The tearoom trade*. Chicago, IL: Aldine.

ICAP. (2013). ICAP timeline. Retrieved from: http://www.theiacp.org/About/History/Timeline/tabid/101/Default.aspx.

Johnston, Lloyd, Patrick O'Malley, Jerald Bachman and John Schulenberg. (2012). *Monitoring the Future national results on drug use*. Retrieved from: http://www.monitoringthefuture.org//pubs/monographs/mtf-overview2012.pdf.

Katz, Jack. (1988). *Seductions of crime: Moral and sensual attractions of doing evil*. New York, NY: Basic Books.

Land, Kenneth, Patricia McCall and Lawrence Cohen. (1990). Structural covariates of homicide rates: Are there any invariances across time and social space? *American Journal of Sociology, 95*, 922–963.

LaPiere, Richard T. (1934). Attitudes vs. actions. *Social Forces, 13*, 230–237.

Lipton, Douglas. (1998). The effectiveness of correctional treatment revisited thirty years later: Preliminary meta-analytic findings from the CDATE study. Unpublished paper presented to the 12th International Congress on Criminology, Seoul Korea, August.

Loftin, Colin, Milton Heumann and David McDowall. (1983). Mandatory sentencing and firearms violence: Evaluating an alternative to gun control, *Law & Society Review, 17*, 287–318.

Martinson, Robert. (1974). What works? Questions and answers about prison reform. *The Public Interest, 35*, 22–54.

Maxfield, Michael and Earl Babbie. (2011). *Research methods for criminal justice and criminology.* 6th ed. Belmont, CA: Wadsworth.

MTF. (2013). Monitoring the Future. Retrieved from: http://www.monitoringthe future.org/.

NACJD. (2010). National Incident-Based Reporting System resource guide. Retrieved from: http://www.icpsr.umich.edu/icpsrweb/NACJD/NIBRS/.

NACJD. (2010a). National Crime Victimization Survey resource guide. Retrieved from: http://www.icpsr.umich.edu/icpsrweb/NACJD/NCVS/.

NACJD. (2010b). NIBRS concepts. Retrieved from: http://www.icpsr.umich.edu/icpsrweb/NACJD/NIBRS/concepts.jsp.

Nettler, Gwynn. (1978). *Explaining crime.* New York, NY: McGraw-Hill.

Pattillo-McCoy, Mary. (1999). *Black picket fences: Privilege and peril among the black middle class.* Chicago, IL: University of Chicago Press.

Porterfield, Austin. (1943). Delinquency and its outcome in court and college. *American Journal of Sociology, 49*, 199–208.

Pratt, Travis and Francis Cullen. (2000). The empirical status of Gottfredson and Hirschi's general theory of crime: A meta-analysis. *Criminology, 38*, 931–964.

President's Commission. (1967). *The Challenge of crime in a free society.* President's Commission on Law Enforcement and the Administration of Justice. Washington, D.C.: U.S. Government Printing Office.

Sampson, Robert and John Laub. (1993). *Crime in the making: Pathways and turning points through life.* Cambridge, MA: Harvard University Press.

Sarre, Rick. (2009). *Beyond "what works?" A 25 year jubilee retrospective on Robert Martinson.* Presentation at the Australian Institute of Criminology meeting in Canberra. Retrieved from: http://www.aic.gov.au/media_library/conferences/hcpp/sarre.pdf.

Spohn, Cassia. (1990). The sentencing decisions of black and white judges: Expected and unexpected similarities. *Law & Society Review, 24*, 1197–1216.

Thornberry, Terrence and Marvin Krohn. (2000).The self-report method for measuring delinquency and crime. In D. Duffee (Ed.), *Measurement and analysis of crime and justice* (pp. 33–84). Washington, D.C.: National Institute of Justice.

Truman, Jennifer. (2011). *Criminal victimizations, 2010.* Bureau of Justice Statistics. Retrieved from: http://bjs.ojp.usdoj.gov/content/pub/pdf/cv10.pdf.

Truman, Jennifer and Michael Planty. (2012). *Criminal victimizations, 2011.* Bureau of Justice Statistics. Retrieved from: http://www.bjs.gov/content/pub/pdf/cv11.pdf.

Wallerstein, James and Clement Wyle. (1947). Our law-abiding law breakers. *Probation, 25*, 107–112.

WDR. (2011). *World drug report, 2011.* United Nations Office on Drugs and Crime. Retrieved from: http://www.unodc.org/documents/data-and-analysis/WDR2011/WDR2011-ExSum.pdf.

Wells, Edward. (1991). The utility of meta-analysis in criminal justice research. Paper presented at the Academy of Criminal Justice Sciences meeting, Nashville, TN.

WHO. (2002). *World report on violence and health: Summary.* World Health Organization. Retrieved from: http://www.who.int/violence_injury_prevention/violence/world_report/en/summary_en.pdf.

Wolfgang, Marvin, Robert Figlio and Thorsten Sellin. (1972). *Delinquency in a birth cohort.* Chicago, IL: University of Chicago Press.

Part II

Theories and Correlates of Crime

Chapter 3

Why Do They Do It?
Psychosocial and Biosocial Answers

Introduction

Remember back to Chapter 1 and the position of the positive school of criminology, which holds that crime is caused by forces outside an individual's control. This idea has longstanding roots and one of its earliest manifestations is the demonic perspective, which held that crime and other antisocial behavior was caused by demonic possession. This idea was widespread among the ancients, from Sumerians to the earliest Christians and beyond. A variant on the theory of demonic possession was the notion that the devil or a demon could possess a person and give them powers to harm others. In fact most of Europe was in the grip of a witchcraft hysteria from the 1300s to the end of the 1600s. Much of this probably had to do with trying to explain why so many were dying from the bubonic plague (Black Death) that gripped Europe from 1347 until about 1400. The tail end of the witch hysteria even reached the New England colonies. The Salem witch trials occurred in colonial Massachusetts between 1692 and 1693. More than 200 people were accused of practicing witchcraft—the devil's magic—and 20 were executed (Blumberg, 2007). This ancient proclivity to look for the causes of bad behavior within the person has been recognized in attribution theory in social psychology as a normal response when people try to understand others' behavior (Kelley, 1967).

In this chapter, we will explore both psychosocial and biosocial theories of crime. We begin with psychosocial theories of crime, which focus on the interaction of the individual with his or her environment and how that interaction develops certain traits. We continue with biosocial theories of crime, which examine biologic and genetic factors that may predispose people to behave in criminal ways.

Psychosocial Theories of Crime

Intelligence and Crime

Early ideas about the connection between individual psychological differences and how they might be connected to crime focused primarily on intelligence. Wechsler (1944, p. 3) defines intelligence as "the aggregate or global capacity of the individual to act purposefully, to think rationally and to deal effectively with his environment." Early 20th century researchers such as Goddard (1914) believed there to be a direct connection between mental deficiencies, such as low intelligence, and crime. More recent work has found the connection between lower intelligence, especially lower verbal intelligence, and crime to be robust (Lynam, Moffitt and Stouthamer-Loeber, 1993; Walsh, 2003; Ellis and Walsh, 2003). Does having low intelligence cause crime? If it did, there would no reason to keep reading this book. Rather, low intelligence appears to be a risk factor for crime (see Chapter 7 for more on risk factors) and moreover, its effects on crime do not appear to be direct. Lower intelligence probably acts on crime through the mechanism of school, where those who are lower in intelligence do not perform well in school, which may facilitate their dropping out and starting to associate with other dropouts (Ward and Tittle, 1994). They may also drop out due to negative interactions with peers at school, who target their lower intelligence for teasing or bullying. As seen in Walsh and Hemmens (2011), lower intelligence can negatively impact other life areas as well, such as employment, socioeconomic status and family stability.

Box 3.1. The Heritability of Antisocial Behavior and Eugenics

Remember Goddard (1914) and his ideas about the link between what he termed feeble-mindedness and crime. Many of Goddard's ideas on this subject were informed by his study of the Kallikak family. In investigating members of the family over generations, he concluded that a variety of traits were hereditary and predisposed people to a variety of behaviors, including criminal behavior. He also embraced the position that society could limit these traits through eugenics (sterilization) of the mentally deficient. Goddard's (1912) work on the Kallikak family was part of a growing number of studies at that time that focused on the heritability of undesirable traits and fueled the eugenics movement in the United States.

Another such study was Dugdale's (1877) study on the Jukes family.[1] In 1874, Dugdale was serving as a volunteer inspector for the New York Prison Association. While at the Ulster

---

1. In a high school sociology class taken by the second author in 1956–1957, the textbook used was Landis and Landis' *Social Living*. This textbook treated as factual the main thesis of both Goddard and Dugdale. "There is but one remedy for criminality caused by heredity—eugenics, the breeding of a better race of human beings. We should sort out the criminal and forbid his marriage, permitting him to leave no offspring" (Landis and Landis, 1938, p. 353). While Landis and Landis (1938) were definitely pro-eugenics, they did point out that environmental factors also play a role in the social production of crime. To put things in temporal perspective, the first author of this book's mother was just three years old when the second author was taking his high school sociology class.

County Jail, he discovered that six people being held there were blood relatives. He did some research and found that of 29 males who were blood relatives of the six, 17 had been arrested and 15 had been convicted of crimes. He claimed the Jukes family was beset by many social ills going back to the early 1700s and that they had cost the state over $1 million (nearly $21 million today) in a variety of services including medical, welfare and criminal justice (Christianson, 2003).

Though Dugdale acknowledged that the Jukeses were a composition of 42 families and that only 540 of the 709 subjects in his study were blood relatives, his work was misrepresented as being focused solely on heredity and its role in the production of these social ills. A follow up study of the Jukeses by Estabrook in 1915 contained information on 2,820 Jukeses and though Estabrook's data revealed a decrease in problems over time, the Eugenics Record Office pronounced the Jukeses irredeemable. Importantly, because the study subjects were deidentified, there was no way for other researchers to verify either Dugdale's or Estabrook's findings (Christianson, 2003).

At the height of the eugenics movement in the United States, compulsory sterilization was the law in 33 states; 65,000 people are estimated to have been sterilized (Kevles, 1985). Eugenics and compulsory sterilization laws were rapidly discredited following the *Skinner* v. *Oklahoma* decision in 1942, in which the Supreme Court ruled that compulsory sterilization could not be imposed as a punishment for a crime on the grounds that the relevant Oklahoma law excluded some crimes from carrying sterilization penalties. Eugenics also came under attack by the scientific community primarily on its research methods and theoretical assumptions (Zucchino, 2012). The moral bankruptcy of eugenics was confirmed in the United States after World War II when the full horror of the Holocaust became clear.

Traits and Crime

In large part, modern psychosocial theories of crime are built around the psychological concept of the personality and the traits that make it up, so it behooves us to begin with a definition of both personality and traits. Personality can be thought of as a person's habitual ways of thinking, feeling and behaving that develop over the course of the lifetime as a result of the interaction of genetic and biologic factors and the environment. Traits can be thought of as the building blocks of personality. Psychologists have identified a number of discrete traits that compose the personality and we will see below how some of these traits may be associated with crime.

Before the 1990s, criminologists paid relatively little attention to insights from research on personality that was conducted within the discipline of psychology. However, that all changed with the publication of *A General Theory of Crime* by Michael Gottfredson and Travis Hirschi in 1990. Gottfredson and Hirschi (1990) claimed that crime is the result of being low on the trait for self-control and that low self-control results from ineffective parenting.[2] Miller and Lynam (2001) believe that understanding the

---

2. Though Gottfredson and Hirschi (1990) identify self-control as a trait, we discuss their groundbreaking theory not here in Chapter 3, but in Chapter 5 alongside other social process theories, in large part because they identified low self-control as resulting from interaction between parents and children.

relationships between basic dimensions of personality and antisocial behavior can make a substantial contribution to criminology and they examined the relationships between antisocial behavior and the four most widely used structural models of personality: the five-factor model (FFM; McCrae and Costa, 1990), the PEN model (Eysenck, 1977), Tellegen's three factor model (1985) and Cloninger's temperament and character model (Cloninger, Svrakic and Przybeck, 1993). These models differ from each other in terms of their derivation and the number and composition of the basic dimensions they include; these models are summarized in Table 3.1. Despite differences, Miller and Lynam (2001) conclude that there is a great deal of conceptual overlap among the personality models and that because these are the most popular and empirically well supported, they should have some relevance to understanding the link between personality and antisocial behavior.

To varying degrees, all of the above models have been used to examine antisocial behavior. In fact, both Eysenck (1973) and Cloninger and colleagues (1993) have hypothesized specific links between their personality models and antisocial behavior. For example, Eysenck (1973) argued that the personality profile of the typical criminal would be one marked by elevations on all three of his dimensions of personality. Cloninger, Svrakic and Przybek (1993) hypothesized that criminality would be associated with high novelty seeking, low harm avoidance and low reward dependence. From looking at the models in tandem, Miller and Lynam (2001, p. 780) describe the personality traits of those who tend to be involved in crime: "Individuals who commit crimes tend to be hostile, self-centered, spiteful, jealous, and indifferent to others (i.e., low in Agreeableness). They tend to lack ambition, motivation, and perseverance, have difficulty controlling their impulses, and hold nontraditional and unconventional values and beliefs (i.e., are low in Conscientiousness)."

Remember that Gottfredon and Hirschi (1990) claim that low self-control is responsible for crime. On the basis of their analysis, Miller and Lynam (2001, p. 780) disagree with this contention. The personality characteristics of criminals, they believe, cannot be subsumed under the single rubric of low self-control; personality dimensions of criminals "are better understood as coming from two distinct and separate basic dimensions of personality Agreeableness and Conscientiousness. Much basic research in the area of personality supports this conclusion."

Miller and Lynam (2001) believe that personality constructs deserve a broader application in criminology and that they complement many extant criminological theories. For example, control theories (see Chapter 5) that suggest that delinquency results from a lack of connection to others and a lack of commitment to conventional norms pairs well with personality traits including Agreeableness and Constraint. On another level, personality theories may help us understand the relative stability of antisocial behavior over time which has been observed in longitudinal studies (e.g., Sampson and Laub, 1993 and see Chapter 7). Personality stability over time is axiomatic in research on personality. Therefore, antisocial behavior may be stable over time because personality, a contributor to antisocial behavior, is also stable over time. A certain personality predisposition is not going to help us understand why someone commits a specific crime. However, it should aid us in understanding how certain dispositions toward thinking, feeling and acting in certain characteristic ways may predispose a person toward some criminal behaviors.

Table 3.1. A summary of Miller and Lynam's (2001) personality models and dimensions

Model and Dimensions	Definitions
Five Factor Model (McCrae and Costa, 1990)	
1. Neuroticism	Emotional stability and adjustment v. emotional instability and maladjustment
2. Extraversion	Sociability and agency
3. Openness to experience	Interest and willingness to consider or try new activities, ideas and beliefs, also intellectual curiosity
4. Agreeableness	Interpersonal strategies; agreeableness v. antagonism
5. Conscientiousness	Ability to control impulses, perform tasks and carry out plans, organizational skills follow the internal moral code
PEN Model (Eysenck, 1977)	
1. Psychoticism	Egocentricity, interpersonal coldness and disconnectedness, lack of empathy and impulsiveness
2. Extraversion	Sociability and agency
3. Neuroticism	Emotional stability and adjustment v. emotional instability and maladjustment
Three Factor Model (Tellegen, 1985)	
1. Positive emotionality	Sociability, tendency to experience positive emotions, assertiveness, achievement orientation
2. Negative emotionality	Tendency to experience negative emotions and to experience situations as aversive
3. Constraint	Ability to control impulses, avoid potentially dangerous situations and endorse traditional values and standards
Temperament and Character Model (Cloninger, Svrakic and Przybeck, 1993)	
1. Novelty seeking	Tendency toward intense exhilaration or excitement in response to novel stimuli
2. Harm avoidance	Tendency to respond intensely to aversive stimuli
3. Reward Dependence	Tendency to respond intensely to signals of reward
4. Persistence	Perseverance despite frustration and fatigue
5. Self-directedness	Self-determination and willpower
6. Cooperativeness	Tendency to be agreeable versus antagonistic and hostile
7. Self-transcendence	Involvement with spirituality

Source: Adapted from Miller and Lynam, 2001.

Caspi, Moffitt, Silva, Stouthamer-Loebre, Krueger and Schmutte (1994) begin their work on personality traits and crime by questioning whether some people are crime prone and whether there is a criminal personality. In order to find out, they administered a personality questionnaire to a group of teenagers and measured their involvement in delinquent and criminal behavior. The group of teenagers in question was a complete cohort of all those born in Dunedin, New Zealand between April 1, 1972 and March 31, 1973. The representative sample (N=1,037) has been repeatedly assessed on a battery of psychological, medical and sociological measures beginning when the children were 3 years of age. Data were collected for 991 subjects at age 5, 954 at age 7, 955 at age 9, 925 at age 11, 850 at age 13, 976 at age 15, and 1,008 at age 18 (Krueger, Schmutte, Caspi, Moffitt, Campbell and Silva, 1994, p. 330).

The personality questionnaire that Caspi and colleagues (1994) administered to members of the cohort at age 18 was Tellegen and Waller's (1982) Multidimensional Personality Questionnaire (MPQ). Caspi and colleagues (1994) chose the MPQ for a number of reasons. First, it provides a comprehensive description of individual personality differences. Second, it was not designed to distinguish between those who had offended and those who had not. Third, it measures a number of personality traits, allowing researchers to see which if any are associated with delinquency and crime. Fourth, the ten scales on the MPQ can be put into just three higher order categories, Constraint, Negative Emotionality and Positive Emotionality. The measures of delinquency and crime that Caspi and colleagues (1994) chose were designed to overcome the problems with the various measures of crime that we saw in Chapter 2. They employed self-reports of delinquency and crime, as well as a secondary analysis of both police and court records as well as reports from informants, those who knew the teenagers in the sample and could confirm or augment information on delinquency and crime gathered in other ways. Table 3.2 describes the 10 MPQ scales and their higher order categories.

Upon reading the descriptions of those people who tend to score high on the various scales and higher order categories, it will likely come as little surprise that people who are low in constraint and high in negative emotionality are the ones who tend to be involved in delinquency and crime. This was true in Caspi and colleagues' (1994) New Zealand sample, as well as for a sample of American inner city youths at ages 12 and 13 (Caspi, Moffitt, Silva, Stouthamer-Loebre, Krueger and Schmutte, 1994) and true for both males and females (Krueger, Schmutte, Caspi, Moffitt, Campbell and Silva, 1994). The negative correlations with the Constraint factor suggest that delinquent adolescents were likely to be impulsive, danger seeking and rejecting of conventional values. The positive correlations with the Negative Emotionality factor suggest that these delinquent adolescents were prone to respond to frustrating events with strong negative emotions, to feel stressed or harassed and to approach interpersonal relationships with an adversarial attitude. And as would be expected, Positive Emotionality was not significantly associated with any measure of delinquent or criminal behavior.

The researchers went a step further and examined the personality basis of non-normative delinquency. Non-normative delinquent behavior (i.e., complete abstention or extensive participation) could be associated with a unique personality profile. Krueger

Table 3.2. Description of MPQ scales and higher order categories

MPQ Higher Order Categories and Scales	Description of a High Scorer
CONSTRAINT	
— Traditionalism	Likes a conservative social environment, has high moral standards
— Harm avoidance	Prefers safe activities, avoids danger and excitement
— Control	Is cautious, careful, planful, rational and reflective
NEGATIVE EMOTIONALITY	
— Aggression	Hurts, frightens or causes discomfort to others for own advantage
— Alienation	Feels victimized, betrayed, mistreated
— Stress reaction	Is worrisome, nervous, vulnerable, sensitive
POSITIVE EMOTIONALITY	
— Achievement	Enjoys demanding projects and hours of work
— Social potency	Likes to lead and influence others, forceful and decisive
— Well-being	Is happy and cheerful, feels good about self
— Social closeness	Likes others, seeks them out, is sociable

Source: Adapted from Caspi, Moffitt, Silva, Stouthamer-Loebre, Krueger and Schmutte, 1994.

and colleagues (1994) identified three sub-groups: those who reported that they had never engaged in delinquency, those who engaged in a wide variety of delinquent acts and those who engaged in normative levels of delinquency (the vast majority of teenagers in the sample) and compared each group's results of the MPQ. Those who engaged in a wide variety of delinquent acts, the versatile delinquents, scored significantly higher than their normative counterparts on the Aggression, Alienation, and Stress Reaction scales and significantly lower on the Traditionalism, Control, and Social Closeness scales, meaning their personality profile was significantly different than the profile those who engaged in normative delinquency. The personality profile of versatile delinquents was characterized by a rejection of traditional values, thrill seeking, impulsivity, aggressive behavior, lack of sociability and feelings of alienation.

Caspi and colleagues (1994) echo Miller and Lynam's (2001) conclusion that when it comes to explaining crime through personality traits, namely, we should not rely on just Gottfredson and Hirschi's (1990) concept of self-control. Instead, there are multiple psychological components of crime. Though they do not claim to be the final authority on the origins of Constraint and Negative Emotionality, Caspi and colleagues (1994) implicate both the home environment and genetic underpinnings in the development of these traits. An aversive environment replete with harsh or erratic parent-child interactions in combination with a genetic disposition for low serotonin levels (see below for more on this concept) may be the primary culprits in the development of these two

Table 3.3. Summary of personality traits associated with crime

Personality Trait and Brief Description	How Associated with Crime?	Supportive Empirical Findings
Impulsiveness, acting without thinking about the consequences	Positively correlated*	Ellis and Walsh, 2000
Negative Emotionality, experiencing many situations as aversive and reacting with irritation and anger	Positively correlated	Caspi and colleagues, 1994; Agnew, 2005; Veenstra, Lindenberg, Oldehinkel, De Winter and Ormel, 2006
Sensation Seeking, the desire for varied and dangerous experiences	Positively correlated	Ellis and Walsh, 2000
Empathy, the ability to understand and feel the distress someone else is in	Negatively correlated**	Covell and Scalora, 2002
Altruism, acting to alleviate someone else's distress	Negatively correlated	Fishbein, 2001; Ellis and Walsh, 2000
Conscientiousness, well organized, responsible, reliable and disciplined	Negatively correlated	Miller and Lynam, 2001
Agreeableness, friendly, courteous, considerate, helpful	Negatively correlated	Miller and Lynam, 2001
Constraint, preference for traditional values and safety, planful, cautious, careful, rational	Negatively correlated	Caspi and colleagues, 1994; Miller and Lynam, 2001; Veenstra, Lindenberg, Oldehinkel, De Winter and Ormel, 2006

* Where positive correlation means that as the level of the trait increases, so does the likelihood of criminal involvement.
** Where negative correlation means that as the level of the trait increases, the likelihood of criminal involvement decreases.

traits that are associated with crime. Table 3.3 summarizes the personality traits known to be associated with crime, including and beyond those detailed above.

Psychopathy and Crime

We can think of psychopathy as a syndrome characterized by selfishness, manipulation, deceit, a lack of guilt or remorse and an inability to experience empathy with others and colloquially, this is a catch all term that we use to describe the most serious offenders. Psychiatrists use the latest versions of the *Diagnostic and Statistical Manual of Mental Disorders (DSM)* to apply the label of antisocial personality disorder to many of these offenders. Table 3.4 shows the different diagnostic criteria for antisocial personality disorder from two recent versions of the DSM.

Table 3.4. Diagnostic criteria for antisocial personality disorder
from two recent versions of the DSM

DSM-IV Antisocial Personality Disorder (from 1994)	DSM-5 Antisocial Personality Disorder (Revised April, 2012)
A. Pervasive pattern of disregard for and violation of the rights of others occurring since the age of 15 and as indicated by having hurt, mistreated or stolen from another	**A. Significant impairments in personality functioning manifest themselves by:**
— 1. **Failure to conform to social norms** with respect to law abiding behavior, repeated commission of acts that are grounds for arrest	— 1. **Impairments in self functioning**, either in **identity** (egocentrism, self-esteem build on personal gain, power or pleasure) or in **self-direction** (goal setting based on personal gratification, absence of prosocial internal standards, failure to conform to the law and other normative behavior
— 2. **Deceitfulness**, including repeated lying, use of aliases or conning others for profit or pleasure	— 2. **Impairments in interpersonal functioning**, either in **empathy** (lack of concern about the feelings, needs or suffering of others, lack of remorse) or in **intimacy** (exploitation is the primary way to relate to others, so there is an incapacity for mutually intimate relationships, use of dominance to intimidate or control others)
— 3. **Impulsivity** or failure to plan ahead	**B. Pathological personality traits in the following domains:**
— 4. **Irritability and aggressiveness**, repeated physical fights or assaults	— 1. **Antagonism**, characterized by manipulativeness, deceitfulness, callousness and hostility
— 5. **Reckless disregard for others' safety**	— 2. **Disinhibition**, characterized by irresponsibility, impulsivity and risk taking
— 6. **Consistent irresponsibility**, repeated failure to sustain work or honor financial obligations	**C. Impairments in personality functioning and trait expression are consistent across time and situations**
— 7. **Lack of remorse**	**D. Impairments in personality functioning and trait expression cannot be better understood by referencing his/her culture**
B. 18 years of age or older	**E. Impairments in personality functioning and trait expression are not the sole result of drug ingestion or a medical condition**
C. Evidence of conduct disorder before the age of 15	**F. 18 years of age or older**
D. Antisocial behavior is not confined to symptoms of schizophrenia or bipolar disorder	

Source: Adapted from DSM, 2012.

However, the world's leading expert on psychopathy, Robert Hare, takes great umbrage with the idea that psychopathy and antisocial personality disorder are the same thing. He notes that while many offenders probably have antisocial personality disorder, very few offenders with antisocial personality disorder are psychopaths as measured by Hare's widely used checklist. This may seem like unnecessary hair splitting,[3] but Hare (1996) notes that because antisocial personality disorder is so common among the criminal population, a diagnosis of antisocial personality disorder has limited utility for predicting behavior while incarcerated, amenability to treatment and the likelihood of recidivism once released. The proper identification of someone as a psychopath using Hare's checklist is quite useful in predicting behavior while incarcerated, amenability to treatment and the likelihood of recidivism. The checklist is completed by a trained clinician who conducts an interview with the potential psychopath and reviews his or her case history. Items are scored on a scale from zero to one to two, for a maximum possible score of 40. Approximately 15–20 percent of offenders receive a score of 30 or higher; 30 is the low threshold for a psychopathy diagnosis. By way of comparison, the mean scores for all offenders and for nonoffenders are approximately 22 and five, respectively (Hare, 1996). Figure 3.1 provides the details of Hare's checklist.

How do people become psychopaths? One possible answer to this question is arousal theory. Arousal theory holds that psychopaths have a low level of autonomic nervous system arousal, which means the stimuli that most of us find thrilling are not sufficient to result in a desirable level of autonomic arousal for them. Psychopaths, then, have to seek out novel, intense and even dangerous stimuli, including crime, in order to attain optimum arousal level. A variety of research has found support for arousal theory (Raine, Venables and Williams, 1990; Blair, Jones, Clark and Smith, 1997, Raine, 1997); the inability to achieve autonomic arousal has even been linked to the inability to form

Figure 3.1. Hare's Psychopathy Checklist Revised (PCL-R)

1. Glibness, superficial charm	11. Promiscuous sexual behavior
2. Grandiose sense of self-worth	12. Early behavioral problems
3. Need for stimulation, prone to boredom	13. Lack of realistic and long term goals
4. Pathological lying	14. Impulsivity
5. Manipulation and/or conning	15. Irresponsibility
6. Lack of guilt or remorse	16. Fail to accept responsibility for actions
7. Shallow affect	17. Many short-term marriages
8. Callous, lacking empathy	18. Juvenile delinquency
9. Parasitic lifestyle	19. Revocation of conditional release
10. Poor behavioral controls	20. Criminal versatility

Source: Adapted from Hare, 2003.*

* Hare (1999) prefers the term psychopath to sociopath because he believes that biological, psychological and genetic factors play a role in the development of psychopathy; to call it sociopathy would imply that social forces are entirely at the root of this personality type, though others (e.g., Lykken, 1995) do make a distinction between the two.

---

3. No pun intended.

a conscience (Kochanska, 1991). Another culprit in the development of psychopathy is amygdala dysfunction. The amygdala is the part of the brain responsible for emotional memories as well as the experience of strong emotions including anger, fear and sexual feelings. Many psychopathy researchers agree that amygdala dysfunction means that psychopaths are unable to be properly conditioned by aversive experiences and unable to modulate their aggression (Vien and Beech, 2006); these ideas are discussed in more detail below.

Vien and Beech (2006) note that psychopaths present huge challenges to the criminal justice system in terms of the number of crimes they commit and in terms of how difficult they are to treat while incarcerated. Their frequent disruption of traditional treatment settings in prison has been attributed to their glibness and grandiose sense of self-worth. However, both Skeem, Monahan and Mulvey (2002) and Wong and Hare (2005) point out that treating psychopaths is not necessarily a lost cause. Increased provision of treatment can be useful as can treatment that focuses on helping psychopaths develop insights into their condition, rather than attempting to cure them. Little research has been done on psychopharmacological treatments for psychopathy, but medicines that have demonstrated the ability to control aggression and impulsivity in people with other psychiatric disorders could be useful with psychopaths (Vien and Beech, 2006).

Box 3.2. Is Psychopathy a Mental Illness?

Unfortunately, it is unlikely that this text box will be able to fully allay the reader's confusion on this point. Insofar as psychopathy and antisocial personality disorder are the same thing (and remember there is disagreement on this issue), we can say that psychopathy is a mental illness because antisocial personality disorder is included in the fourth version of the DSM, the *Diagnostic and Statistical Manual of Mental Disorders*. However, it is found on Axis II in the manual. Axis II disorders such as personality disorders and mental retardation are distinct from Axis I disorders such as schizophrenia, bipolar disorder and major depression by their enduring and inflexible natures. Axis II disorders are much less amenable to typical psychiatric treatments than are Axis I disorders, raising the question of whether personality disorders, including antisocial personality disorder, can be effectively treated even if they do qualify as mental illnesses. Muddying the water further is the release of the new version of the manual, the *DSM 5*. The *DSM 5* has done away with the multiaxial system, opting instead to put separate disorders into chapters. Does the new version of the DSM mean that personality disorders such as antisocial personality are now as treatable using standard techniques as disorders such as schizophrenia and bipolar disorder? Of course not. People with antisocial personality disorder will continue to pose a great many challenges to both clinicians and the criminal justice system.

Biosocial Theories of Crime

In this section of the chapter, we investigate a number of different biological approaches to explaining crime causation. These approaches include body type, brain dysfunction, arousal, neurochemistry and genetics.

Body Type and Appearance

One of the early efforts to link biology and behavior was the work of William Sheldon (1949), who attempted to connect body type to personality traits and eventually to delinquency. Sheldon borrowed and quantified Ernst Kretschmer's (1925) typology of body types and associated personality traits and renamed them *ectomorphs* (thin body types), *mesomorphs* (athletic body types) and *endomorphs* (heavy or obese body types). Sheldon then devised a quantitative scale based on one used to grade poultry and dogs to classify people into one of the three types.

Sheldon's position was that specific personality types or temperaments accompanied each body type. Ectomorphs, according to Sheldon (1949), are cerebrotonic (meaning restrained, self-conscious and hypersensitive) while endomorphs are viscerotonic (meaning relaxed, food-oriented and even-tempered) and mesomorphs are somatotonic (meaning dominating, assertive, competitive and unrestrained). While temperament alone is not viewed as criminal, Sheldon felt that physique in combination with corresponding temperament and certain other social factors could be criminogenic.

To test his theory, Sheldon (1949) compared 200 delinquent boys with a control group of 200 nondelinquents. From extensive measurements taken from photographs of each youth, Sheldon concluded that boys classified as mesomorphs possessed the physical and psychological characteristics most suitable for delinquency. Sheldon's (1949) research came under intense criticism by Edwin Sutherland (1951), an eminent criminologist of the time, who took issue with Sheldon's (1949) operational definition of delinquency, his method of classification of delinquents and his sampling design. In spite of these criticisms, Sheldon (1949) continued to work on this project until his death in 1977. His major finding was that within the delinquent group, 60 percent had the mesomorphic body type. However, follow up studies revealed that only seven percent of mesomorphs in the delinquent group went on to commit crime in adulthood (Hartl, Monnelly and Elderkin, 1982).

Even though we have largely cast off the Lombrosian ideas of determining criminal involvement by assessing physical appearance, some recent research has revealed that people may be able to accurately determine criminality based on a quick look at faces. Valla, Ceci and Williams (2011) conducted a study in which they presented participants with 32 pictures of faces, 16 of which were convicted of a certain crime (rape, assault, drug dealing or arson) and 16 of which were noncriminal. The faces were all Caucasian with no scars, tattoos or other marks, between the ages of 20 and 29 and rated equally attractive by independent raters. They found that participants were able to correctly determine who had committed a crime and who had not just based on a quick look at their faces. Interestingly, the (large majority female) participants were least successful at correctly identifying rapists and rapists were rated as more attractive, though not significantly more attractive, than all other categories of faces.

Brain Dysfunction

Remember back to Chapter 1 and the story of Phineas Gage, whose personality was completely altered after he sustained a serious head injury. The idea of localization of brain function that Gage's case helped to bring about laid the groundwork for investigations into brain anatomy as it may be related to the expression of violence and antisocial behavior. In the present day, studies attempt to find associations between structural brain damage and behavioral patterns. While there is no violence center in the brain, the limbic system and the frontal lobes are areas thought to be involved in the expression of violence. The limbic system is the most primitive region of the brain and is the anatomic substrate for emotion. Within the limbic system, the structure most often implicated in violent behavior is the amygdala; violence has been observed in those with abnormal electrical activity in this region (Miller, Collins and Kent, 2008; we saw above how amygdala dysfunction might be implicated in psychopathy, as well). The frontal lobes are regarded as the location of the cognitive and intellectual functions of the brain. In particular, part of the prefrontal cortex known as the orbitofrontal cortices are thought to inhibit aggression. Individuals with injury to this area have displayed antisocial traits, including disinhibition, impulsivity and lack of empathy, and some are at increased risk of violent behavior (Miller, Collins and Kent, 2008). Bufkin and Luttrell (2005) conducted a meta-analysis on 17 studies that utilized neuroimaging to try to determine deficits in brain function and the effect of those deficits on aggression and violence. Their results echo those of Miller, Collins and Kent (2008); across the 17 studies, both prefrontal cortex dysfunction and temporal lobe dysfunction were associated with a history of aggressive or violent behavior; the temporal lobe includes the amygdala. Without damage or injury, there is a balance between the potential for impulsive aggression mediated by the limbic region of the brain and the control exerted by the orbitofrontal regions (Siever, 2008). With injury to either or both areas, however, the likelihood of aggression can increase.

Arousal

We mentioned the ability to achieve psychological arousal via the autonomic nervous system above in our discussion of psychopaths, but research on the role of the autonomic nervous system and arousal is not limited to this small group. In a longitudinal study by Raine, Venables and Williams (1990), the relationship between both central nervous system and autonomic nervous system measures of arousal at age 15 and criminality at age 24 were examined. Raine and colleagues (1990) used heart rate, skin conductivity and electroencephalographic activity as their three independent measures of arousal and measured these with a sample of 15 year olds. It was predicted that those who would eventually go on to commit crime would have a lower resting heart rate, less skin conductivity and slower electroencephalographic activity (brain waves) than those who would not break the law later in life. A lower resting heart rate, less skin conductivity and slower brain waves are all indicative of autonomic nervous system underarousal. The researchers found that these three independent indicators of arousal measured at age 15 correctly predicted nearly three quarters of those who were criminally involved by age 24. In other words, a low resting heart rate, less skin conductivity and slower brain waves in the teen years can accurately predict crime commission in early adulthood. Moreover, differences in social class, academic ability and residence did not mediate the link between underarousal and antisocial behavior. A low resting heart rate has subsequently been shown to be strongly associated with antisocial behavior (Raine and Portnoy, 2012). In fact, in the famous Cambridge Study in Delinquent Development, resting heart rate was one of only two factors of the 48 investigated that was independently related to violence (Farrington, 1997).

Even with much evidence for the relationship between low resting heart rate and antisocial behavior, it is still unclear why a low resting heart rate predisposes people to crime and delinquency. One theory as to why involves sensation seeking. Those who are underaroused as measured by resting heart rate find underarousal unpleasant and seek stimulation in order to achieve an optimal level of arousal. As seen above, the stimulation they seek may be novel, intense or even dangerous. A meta-analysis by Wilson and Scarpa (2011) found that stimulation seeking and aggression are positively related, which lends some support to the sensation seeking theory.

Another theory as to why a low resting heart rate predisposes people to crime and delinquency has to do with fearlessness. A low resting heart rate may be indicative of fearlessness. Low levels of fear are required to engage in antisocial behavior. Moreover, children who have low levels of fear are less responsive to socializing punishments (those punishments that help them learn proper behavior), which may contribute to poor fear conditioning and eventual lack of conscience development (Raine, 1993). More recent research on fearlessness echoes these sentiments. Low skin conductivity measured in infancy accurately predicts the parent-reported level of antisocial behavior and aggression in toddlers two years later; infants with low skin conductivity engaged in more antisocial and aggressive behavior as toddlers than those with higher skin conductivity (Baker, Shelton, Baibazarova, Hay and van Goozen, 2013). Gao, Raine, Venables, Dawson and Mednick (2010) investigated the role of poor fear conditioning in the production of crime, using skin conductivity as a measure of the level of fear conditioning. They measured skin conductivity in nearly 1,800 three year olds and criminals offending 20 years later. One hundred thirty seven members of the sample who had criminal records were matched to 274 members of the sample who did not have criminal records and then the researchers looked back at the measures of skin conductivity for those individuals. Gao and colleagues (2010) found that measured skin conductivity at age three predisposes individuals to crime in early adulthood and that poor fear condition implicates amygdala dysfunction; remember the amygdala is the part of the brain responsible for strong emotions. They suggest that amygdala dysfunction reduces individuals' ability to recognize threat, making them relatively fearless, less sensitive to the negative consequences of their behavior and more available to engage in antisocial behavior.[4]

A third theory as to why a low resting heart rates predisposes people to crime and delinquency has to do with the connection between a low resting heart rate and other processes more directly implicated in antisocial behavior. One such process may be

---

4. For a fascinating look at the role of the amygdala and other factors in producing mass murders, see the PBS Nova documentary *Mind of a Rampage Killer*.

lower noradrenergic functioning. The most important neurotransmitter in noradrenergic functioning is norepinephrine and low levels of norepinephrine are associated with antisocial behavior. Research has found that children with conduct disorder have both low resting heart rates and low levels of norepinephrine (Rogeness, Cepeda, Macedo, Fischer and Harris, 1990; Rogeness, Javors, Mass and Macedo, 1990).

Neurochemistry

The neurochemistry of violence is another area of interest to brain researchers and (some) criminologists alike. Neurotransmitters are chemicals in the brain that facilitate the movement of information from one nerve cell or network to the next. The neurotransmitters dopamine and serotonin have received the most attention in efforts to explain crime from a neurochemical basis; dopamine facilitates pleasure seeking while serotonin inhibits behavior (Depue and Collins, 1999).

Dopamine and serotonin have been implicated in a biologic theory of crime known as reward dominance. This theory holds that when the behavioral systems associated with these two neurotransmitters are imbalanced, antisocial behavior, including crime, is more likely to occur. Dopamine is associated with the behavioral activating system (BAS). This system motivates us to seek rewarding stimuli. Serotonin, on the other hand, is associated with the behavioral inhibition system (BIS). This system motivates us to cease our pleasure seeking behavior and is sensitive to the threat of punishment. These systems are in balance in most people most of the time. For someone with a dominant BAS, though, he or she continues to seek rewarding stimuli with no (or ignorable) input from the BIS that might inhibit such behavior (Day and Carelli, 2007). It is easy to imagine how constant pleasure seeking with little regard for the threat of punishment might be associated with antisocial behavior, including crime.

As mentioned, serotonin serves to inhibit behavior. One type of behavior in which serotonin has been strongly implicated is impulsive aggression (Krakowski, 2003). When serotonin levels in the brain are normal, this neurotransmitter inhibits the use of aggression or violence on impulse. However, when serotonin levels are low, especially in those areas of the brain that regulate emotion such as the prefrontal cortex and anterior cingulate cortex, impulsive aggression is more likely to occur (see e.g., Seo and Patrick, 2008). Low levels of serotonin have also been observed in conjunction with an excess of dopamine, which serves to further promote impulsive aggression, in accord with the reward dominance theory seen above. Seo and Patrick (2008) note that pharmacological treatment can be effective in raising serotonin levels to reduce the likelihood of impulsive aggression, as can making positive changes in the environment, training and support for parents, social skills acquisition training and dietary changes.

Box 3.3. What about Testosterone?

It may be easy to connect the idea of hormones and crime in our minds, especially testosterone. Testosterone is the male hormone (though women have it too) and we need only think of those using testosterone supplements in the course of physical training and flying into a rage at the slightest provocation. Less colorfully, we can look to the fact that men are so much more crime involved than women to see an easy link between testosterone and crime. However, the latest research shows only a weak connection between testosterone levels and aggression and that connection practically disappears when aggression is more narrowly defined as violence. Testosterone appears to be a necessary but not sufficient cause for violence (Mims, 2007); other factors must be considered when we try to explain violence.

Genetics

Some of the most interesting recent work on the connection between biology and crime focuses on genetics. Before we go further, let us disabuse readers of the notion that a crime gene exists. There is no such thing. If there was, there would be no point in reading this book further. Indeed, genes do not make us behave in a certain way; they simply facilitate our behavior through their effects on the development of traits. All traits are heritable to some degree and the degree of heritability can tell us how much variance of a given trait is explained by genetics and how much is explained by the environment. Some of the biologic factors we have already seen associated with crime in this chapter are heritable. Zahn-Waxler and McBride (1998) contend that psychophysiological measures of arousal are heritable, meaning they have a genetic basis. Seo and Patrick (2008) claim that low levels of serotonin are also heritable.

Though there is wide agreement about the notion that genes can affect antisocial behavior (Ellis and Walsh, 2000), it appears that genetic influences on behavior are quite modest for most offenders. Lyons, et al. (1995) conducted a study on over 3,200 twin pairs and found that genes accounted for just 7 percent of the variance in antisocial behavior among juveniles, but 43 percent of the variance in antisocial behavior among adults. The strongest genetic effects on antisocial behavior are most likely to be found in those who begin offending early in life, during elementary school, and continue to offend over the rest of their lives (Moffitt and Walsh, 2003); more recent research by Barnes and Boutwell (2012) finds that nearly all of the stability in offending over the lifetime is explained by genetic factors, while changes in offending over the life course are better explained by environmental factors.

Though genotyping makes it possible to start to determine which genes may be implicated, however modestly, in antisocial behavior, it is important to reiterate that there is no such thing as a crime gene and that the effects individual genes have on behavior are always indirect through the effect they have on the development of traits. With that said (again), one gene that has been associated with antisocial behavior is the dopamine transporter gene. Beaver, Wright and Walsh (2008) believe a version of this gene to be implicated in the relationship between the number of sex partners and involvement in criminal activity. Those involved in criminal activity tend to have more sexual partners than those not involved in crime and Beaver, Wright and Walsh (2008) found that those who had a certain allele (or version) of the dopamine transporter gene were more likely to have both higher numbers of sexual partners and greater involvement in criminal activity. This allele quickly and thoroughly clears dopamine out of the brain once it has activated subsequent neurons. With the dopamine cleared out, the pleasurable sensation does not linger, which may mean that people with this allele are motivated to seek additional activity (sex, in this case) to feel the effects of dopamine anew.

Another gene that may be implicated in the production of antisocial behavior is called monoamine oxidase A (MAOA). When the MAOA gene is functioning properly, it helps to activate an enzyme that controls neurotransmitters in the brain and keeps them in balance. Most people have the normal MAOA allele, also called high activity MAOA, but some people have a different allele of the gene that is shorter and does not function properly, meaning it is unable to regulate neurotransmitters in the brain; this is called low activity MAOA. High activity MAOA is thought to protect against antisocial behavior while low activity MAOA is thought to be a risk factor for antisocial behavior.[5] In a longitudinal study of children, some of whom experienced abuse and neglect and some of whom did not and some of whom had high activity MAOA and some of whom had low activity MAOA, Caspi, et al. (2002) found that those with low activity MAOA and in an abusive or neglectful environment were nearly 10 times more likely to have an arrest for a violent crime than those who had high activity MAOA and were in a supportive environment. These findings underscore the important idea that whatever effects genes have on criminal behavior through traits, the environment remains an important contributor to criminal behavior. The idea that those with genes that predispose to antisocial behavior who are reared in aversive environments are going to be at the greatest risk for crime is known as the dual hazard hypothesis and it has received support in the literature (see e.g., Barnes and Jacobs, 2013).

Strengths and Weaknesses of Psychosocial and Biosocial Theories of Crime

Both psychosocial and biosocial theories of crime have a number of strengths. They are particularly useful in explaining why some individuals in aversive environments do not commit crime and why some individuals in supportive environments do; many of the theories we are going to learn about in the remainder of this book make predictions about all the people in certain circumstances and what about those circumstances is criminogenic. Psychosocial and biosocial theories of crime also provide substantial insight into the etiology of violent behavior and the origins of the most chronic and serious offending. We can think of psychosocial and biosocial theories of crime as complementing some of the leading theories of crime we are going to learn about in the remaining chapters; in the instances where those leading theories cannot explain crime, psychosocial and biosocial theories can provide useful explanations of the causes of crime and vice versa.

Psychosocial and biosocial theories of crime are not without their weaknesses. Many criminologists view them as too individualistic and ignorant of social structural and social process variables that appear to have a great deal of effect on crime causation.

---

5. For a real world example of the connection between the MAOA gene and criminal behavior, see Spiegel (2012).

While psychosocial and biosocial theories of crime may shed light on individuals' involvement in crime, they cannot explain fluctuations in crime rates over time, nor do they do a particularly good job of explaining desistance from crime. While young people commit the bulk of offending, it is clear that the vast majority of these offenders do not continue committing crime into adulthood. Psychosocial and biosocial theories of crime imply a good deal of stability in behavior and therefore are not well equipped to explain changes. It is also quite difficult and often very expensive to conduct the sort of research described in this chapter and while the trend is toward longitudinal studies with larger sample sizes, past studies with small sample sizes are limited in generalizability.

Conclusion: Policy Implications of Psychosocial and Biosocial Theories

If the causes of crime are psychosocial or biosocial in nature, what can be done to reduce or prevent crime? With the belief that therapy and counseling might be useful in reducing criminal involvement, a number of programs were designed to provide these and other supportive services to delinquent youth. These programs include the Wayne County Clinic in Detroit from the 1920s through the 1940s, the Cambridge-Somerville Youth Study in New Jersey from 1937 to 1945, the New York Youth Consultation Service Project from 1955 to 1960, the New York Youth Board Project in 1952, the Maximum Benefits Project in Washington, D.C. from 1954–1957, the Pilot Intensive Counseling Organization (PICO) Project in California from 1955–1960 and the Community Treatment Project in California from 1961 to 1969. However, evaluations of these programs reveal that they did not produce a reduction in delinquency. Psychological counseling, at least as delivered in these programs, appears to be ineffective at reducing criminal involvement (Akers and Sellers, 2009).

However, the disappointing results for these programs do not mean that no attempt should be made to address the root causes of offending that are psychosocial or biosocial in nature. In fact, some research (Andrews, 1995) points to antisocial attitudes, values and cognitions, association with antisocial others and antisocial personality characteristics as major predictors of recidivism that can be addressed with a properly designed, implemented and run program, even in the prison setting. The best programs designed to address these issues utilize cognitive behavioral treatment in which dysfunctional cognitions, emotions and behaviors are addressed and reoriented through techniques such as modeling, practice, reinforcement and concrete verbal suggestions (Andrews, 1995).[6] Meta-analyses of programs that utilize cognitive behavioral therapy and are delivered in a way consistent with the Canadian theory of offender rehabilitation revealed a 26 percentage point difference in the recidivism rate between those who participated in the programs and those who did not (Andrews and Bonta, 2006), indicating that

---

6. Determining the risk factors most strongly associated with recidivism, devising effective treatment programs to target those risk factors and then testing the efficacy of the programs is all part of the Canadian theory of offender rehabilitation (see Cullen and Jonson, 2011).

effectively targeting antisocial personality characteristics among others strongly associated with recidivism can noticeably reduce future law breaking.

Though we see pharmacological treatments as a unique policy implication for biosocial theories of crime, especially as those psychopharmacological treatments can bring neurotransmitters into balance, biosocial theories have other policy implications that are not dissimilar from those suggested by other theories, as we will see. Remember Seo and Patrick (2008) note that making positive changes in the environment, training and support for parents, social skills acquisition training and dietary changes may all help to reduce impulsive aggression. School and community programs may also help ameliorate any genetic or biologic risk of crime (Pagani, Tremblay, Vitaro and Parent, 1998; Fishbein, 2001, 2006).

Websites to Visit

Robert Hare: http://www.hare.org/welcome/
Antisocial Personality Disorder: http://www.mentalhealth.com/dis/p20-pe04.html
Biological Perspectives on Crime: http://www.criminology.fsu.edu/crimtheory/week5.htm
Biosocial Factors and Crime: http://www.crimetimes.org/

Discussion Questions

1. Would you rate yourself high on any of the traits associated with criminal involvement? Would others rate you high on these traits? What consequences if any do you believe your traits have had for you in life?
2. Look at Hare's (2003) PCL-R adapted above. Do you know anyone who might score a 2 on some or many of these items? If so, what are your impressions of that person?
3. Do you agree that psychopaths and people with antisocial personality disorder are different groups, as Hare (1996) does? Why or why not?
4. What should we do when we discover a child has a low resting heart rate or low skin conductivity, which are indicative of underarousal and poor fear conditioning and are associated with later criminal involvement?
5. Should having one of the genes described above be a defense to or excuse for crime? Why or why not?
6. What are some of the benefits and drawbacks of using psychopharmacological treatments to change behavior?
7. Which of the perspectives introduced in this chapter makes the most sense to you and why?
8. Which of the perspectives introduced in this chapter makes the least sense to you and why?

References

Agnew, Robert. (2005). *Why do criminals offend? A general theory of crime and delinquency.* Los Angeles, CA: Roxbury.

Akers, Ronald and Christine Sellers. (2009). *Criminological theories: Introduction, evaluation, and application.* 5th ed. Los Angeles, CA: Roxbury.

Andrews, Donald. (1995). The psychology of criminal conduct and effective treatment. In J. McGuire (Ed.), *What works: Reducing offending* (pp. 35–62). West Sussex, England: John Wiley.

Andrews, Donald and James Bonta. (2006). *The psychology of criminal conduct.* 4th ed. Cincinnati, OH: Anderson.

Baker, Erika, Katherine Shelton, Eugenia Baibazarova, Dale Hay and Stephanie van Goozen. (2013). Low skin conductance activity in infancy predicts aggression in toddlers 2 years later. Psychological Science. Retrieved from DOI: 10.1177/0956797612465198.

Barnes, J.C. and Brian Boutwell. (2012). On the relationship of past to future involvement in crime and delinquency: A behavior genetic analysis. *Journal of Criminal Justice, 40*, 94–102.

Barnes, J.C. and Bruce Jacobs. (2013). Genetic risk for violent behavior and environmental exposure to disadvantage and violent crime. *Journal of Interpersonal Violence, 28*, 92–120.

Beaver, Kevin, John Wright and Anthony Walsh. (2008). A gene-based evolutionary explanation for the association between criminal involvement and number of sex partners. *Biodemography and Social Biology, 54*, 47–55.

Blair, Robert, Lawrence Jones, Fiona Clark and Margaret Smith. (1997). The psychopathic individual: A lack of responsiveness to distress cues? *Psychophysiology, 34*, 192–198.

Blumberg, Jess. (2007). *A brief history of the Salem witch trials: One town's strange journey from paranoia to pardon.* Smithsonian. Retrieved from: http://www.smithsonianmag.com/history-archaeology/brief-salem.html?c=y&page=1.

Bufkin, Jana and Vickie Luttrell. (2005). Neuroimaging studies of aggressive and violent behavior: Current findings and implications for criminology and criminal justice. *Trauma, Violence, and Abuse, 6*, 176–191.

Caspi, Avshalom, Terrie Moffitt, Phil Silva, Magda Stouthamer-Loeber, Robert Krueger and Pamela Schmutte. (1994). Personality and crime: Are some people crime prone? Replication of the personality-crime relationship across countries, genders, races, and methods. *Criminology, 32*, 163–195.

Caspi, Avshalom, Joseph McClay, Terrie Moffitt, Jonathan Mill, Judy Martin, Ian Craig, Alan Taylor and Richie Poulton. (2002). Role of genotype in the cycle of violence in maltreated children. *Science, 297*, 851–854.

Christianson, Scott. (2003). Bad seed or bad science? The story of the notorious Jukes family. *The New York Times*, February 8. Retrieved from: http://www.albany.edu/~scifraud/data/sci_fraud_4751.html.

Cloninger, Robert, Dragan Svrakic and Thomas Przybeck.(1993). A psychobiological model of temperament and character. *Archives of General Psychiatry 50*, 975–990.

Costa, Paul and Robert McCrae. (1995). Primary traits of Eysenck's P-E-N model: Three- and five-factor solutions. *Journal of Personality and Social Psychology, 69*, 308–317.

Covell, Christmas and Mario Scalora. (2002). Empathetic deficits in sexual offenders: An integration of affective, social, and cognitive constructs. *Aggression and Violent Behavior, 37*, 251–270.

Cullen, Francis and Cheryl Jonson. (2011). Rehabilitation and treatment programs. In J. Wilson and J. Petersilia (Eds.), *Crime and public policy* (pp. 293–344). New York, NY: Oxford University Press.

Day, Jeremy and Regina Carelli. (2007). The nucleus accumbens and Pavlovian reward learning. *The Neuroscientist, 13*, 148–159.

Depue, Richard and Paul Collins. (1999). Neurobiology of the structure of personality: Dopamine, facilitation of incentive motivation, and extraversion. *Behavior and Brain Sciences, 22*, 491–569.

DSM. (2012). DSM-IV and DSM-5 criteria for the personality disorders. Retrieved from: http://www.dsm5.org/Documents/Personality%20Disorders/DSM-IV%20and%20 DSM-5%20Criteria%20for%20the%20Personality%20Disorders%205-1-12.pdf.

Dugdale, Richard. (1877). *The Jukes: A study of crime, pauperism, disease and heredity.* New York, NY: G.P. Putnam Sons.

Ellis, Lee and Anthony Walsh. (2000). *Criminology: A global perspective.* Boston, MA: Allyn & Bacon.

Ellis, Lee and Anthony Walsh. (2003). Crime, delinquency and intelligence: A review of the worldwide literature. In H. Nybord (Ed.), *The scientific study of general intelligence: A tribute to Arthur Jensen* (pp. 343–365). Amsterdam, The Netherlands: Pergamon.

Farrington, David. (1997). The relationship between low resting heart rate and violence. In A. Raine, P. Brennan, D. Farrington and S. Mednick (Eds.), *Biosocial bases of violence* (pp. 89–106). New York, NY: Plenum.

Fishbein, Diana. (2001). *Biobehavioral perspectives in criminology.* Belmont, CA: Wadsworth.

Fishbein, Diana. (2006). Integrating findings from neurobiology into criminological thought. In S. Henry and M. Lanier (Eds.), *The essential criminology reader* (pp. 43–68). Boulder, CO: Westview.

Gao, Yu, Adrian Raine, Peter Venables, Michael Dawson and Sarnoff Mednick. (2010). Association of poor childhood fear conditioning and adult crime. *American Journal of Psychiatry 167*, 56–60.

Goddard, Henry Herbert. (1912). *The Kallikak family: A study in the heredity of feeble-mindedness.* New York, NY: The Macmillan Company.

Goddard, Henry. (1914). *Feeble-mindedness: Its causes and consequences.* New York, NY: MacMillan.

Gottfredson, Michael and Travis Hirschi (1990). *A general theory of crime.* Stanford, CA: Stanford University Press.

Hare, Robert. (1996). Psychopathy and antisocial personality disorder: A case of diagnostic confusion. *Psychiatric Times, 13*, 1–6.

Hare, Robert. (1999). *Without conscience: The disturbing world of the psychopaths among us.* New York, NY: Guilford.

Hare, Robert. (2003). *The Hare psychopathy checklist-revised.* 2nd ed. Toronto, Canada: Multi-Health Systems.

Hartl, Emil, Edward Monnelly and Roland Elderkin. (1982). *Physique and delinquent behavior: A thirty-year follow-up of William H. Sheldon's Varieties of Delinquent Youth.* New York, NY: Academic Press.

Kevles, Daniel. (1985). *In the name of eugenics: Genetics and the uses of human heredity* New York, NY: Knopf.

Kelley, Harold. (1967). Attribution theory in social psychology. In D. Levine (Ed.), *Nebraska symposium on motivation,* pp. 192–238). Lincoln, NE: University of Nebraska Press.

Kochanska, Grazyna. (1991). Socialization and temperament in the development of guilt and conscience. *Child Development, 62,* 1379–1392.

Kretschmer, Ernst. (1925). *Physique and character.* London, England: Kegan Paul.

Krueger, Robert, Pamela Schmutte, Avshalom Caspi, Terrie Moffitt, Kathleen Campbell and Phil Silva. (1994). Personality traits are linked to crime among men and women: Evidence from a birth cohort. *Journal of Abnormal Psychology, 103,* 328–328.

Krakowski, Menahem. (2003). Violence and serotonin: Influence of impulse control, affect regulation, and social functioning. *The Journal of Neuropsychiatry and Clinical Neurosciences, 15,* 294–305.

Landis, Paul and Judson Landis. (1938). *Social living: Principles and problems in introductory sociology.* Boston, MA: Ginn and Company.

Lykken, David. (1995). *The antisocial personalities.* Hillsdale, NJ: Lawrence Erlbaum.

Lyons, Michael, William True, Seth Eisen, Jack Goldberg, Joanne Meyer, Stephen Faraone, Lindon Eaves and Ming Tsuang. (1995). Differential heritability of adult and juvenile antisocial traits. *Archives of General Psychiatry, 53,* 906–915.

Lynam, Douglas, Terrie Moffitt and Magda Stouthamer-Loeber. (1993). Explaining the relation between IQ and delinquency: Class, race, test motivation, school failure or self control? *Journal of Abnormal Psychology, 102,* 187–196.

McCrae, Robert and Paul Costa. (1990). *Personality in adulthood: A six-year longitudinal study of self reports and spouse ratings on the NEO personality inventory.* New York, NY: Guilford Press.

Miller, Joshua and Donald Lynam. (2001). Structural models of personality and their relation to antisocial behavior: A meta-analytic review. *Criminology, 39,* 765–795.

Miller, Lisa, Robert Collins and Thomas Kent. (2008). Language and the modulation of impulsive aggression. *The Journal of Neuropsychiatry and Clinical Neurosciences, 20,* 261–273.

Mims, Christopher. (2007). Strange but true: Testosterone alone does not cause violence. *Scientific American,* July 5. Retrieved from: http://www.scientificamerican.com/article.cfm?id=strange-but-true-testosterone-alone-doesnt-cause-violence.

Moffitt, Terrie and Anthony Walsh. (2003). The adolescent-limited/life-course persistent theory and antisocial behavior: What have we learned? In A. Walsh and L. Ellis (Eds.), *Biosocial criminology: Challenging environmentalism's supremacy* (pp. 125–144). Hauppauge, NY: Nova Science.

Pagani, Linda, Richard Tremblay, Frank Vitaro and Sophie Parent. (1998). Does preschool help prevent delinquency in boys with a history of perinatal complications? *Criminology, 36*, 245–267.

Raine, Adrian. (1993). *The psychopathology of crime: Criminal behavior as a clinical disorder*. San Diego, CA: Academic Press.

Raine, Adrian. (1997). Antisocial behavior and psychophysiology: A biosocial perspective and a prefrontal dysfunction hypothesis. In D. Stoff, J. Breiling and J. Maser (Eds.), *Handbook of antisocial behavior* (pp. 289–304). New York, NY: John Wiley.

Raine, Adrian, Peter Venables and Mark Williams. (1990). Relationships between central and autonomic measure of arousal at age 15 years and criminality at age 24 years. *Archives of General Psychiatry, 47*, 1003–1007.

Raine, Adrian and Jill Portnoy. (2012). Biology of crime. In R. Loeber and B. Welsh (Eds.), *The future of criminology* (pp. 30–39). New York, NY: Oxford University Press.

Rogeness, Graham, Claudio Cepeda, Carlos Macedo, Charles Fischer and William Harris. (1990). Difference in heart rate and blood pressure in children with conduct disorder, major depression, and separation anxiety. *Psychiatry Research, 33*, 199–206.

Rogeness, Graham, Martin Javors, James Mass and Carlos Macedo. (1990). Catecholamines and diagnoses in children. *Journal of the American Academy of Child and Adolescent Psychiatry, 29*, 234–241.

Sampson, Robert and John Laub. (1993). *Crime in the making*. Cambridge, MA.: Harvard University Press.

Seo, Dongju and Christopher Patrick. (2008). Role of serotonin and dopamine system interaction in the neurobiology of impulsive aggression and its comorbidity with other clinical disorders. *Aggressive and Violent Behavior, 13*, 383–395.

Sheldon, William. (1949). *Varieties of delinquent youth: An introduction to constitutional psychiatry*. New York, NY: Harper.

Siever, Larry. (2008) Neurobiology of aggression and violence. *American Journal of Psychiatry, 165*, 429–442.

Skeem, Jennifer, John Monahan and Edward Mulvey. (2002). Psychopathy, treatment involvement, and subsequent violence among civil psychiatric patients. *Law and Human Behavior, 26*, 577–603.

Skinner v. *Oklahoma*. 316 U.S. 535 (1944).

Spiegel, Alix. (2012). Would judge give psychopath with genetic defect lighter sentence? *National Public Radio*, August 17. Retrieved from: http://www.npr.org/blogs/health/ 2012/08/17/158944525/would-judge-give-psychopath-with-genetic-defect-lighter- sentence.

Sutherland, Edward. (1951). Critique of Sheldon's Varieties of Delinquent Youth. *American Sociological Review, 16*, 10–14.

Tellegen, Auke. (1985). Structures of mood and personality and their relevance to assessing anxiety with an emphasis on self-report. In A. Hussain Tuma and J. Maser (Eds.), *Anxiety and the anxiety disorders* (pp. 681–706). Hillsdale, NJ: Lawrence Erlbaum Associates.

Tellegen, Auke and Niels Waller. (1982). Exploring personality through test construction: Development of the multidimensional personality questionnaire. In G. Boyle, G.

Mathews and D. Saklofske (Eds.), *The Sage handbook of personality theory and assessment, Vol. 2* (pp. 261–292). Thousand Oaks, CA: Sage Publications.

Valla, Jeffrey, Stephen Ceci and Wendy Williams. (2011). The accuracy of inferences about criminality based on facial appearance. *Journal of Social, Evolutionary, and Cultural Psychology, 5,* 6–91.

Veenstra, Rene, Siegwart Lindenberg, Albertine Oldehinkel, Andrea De Winter and Johan Ormel. (2006). Temperament, environment, and antisocial behavior in a population of preadolescent boys and girls. *International Journal of Behavioral Development, 30,* 422–432.

Vien, Anh and Anthony Beech. (2006). Psychopathy: Theory, measurement, and treatment. *Trauma, violence, and abuse, 7,* 155–174.

Walsh, Anthony. (2003). Intelligence and antisocial behavior. In A. Walsh and L. Ellis (Eds.), *Biosocial criminology: Challenging environmentalism's supremacy* (pp. 105–124). Hauppauge, NY: Nova Science.

Walsh, Anthony and Craig Hemmens. (2011). *Introduction to criminology: A text/reader.* 2nd ed. Los Angeles, CA: Sage.

Ward, David and Charles Tittle. (1994). IQ and delinquency: A test of two competing explanations. *Journal of Quantitative Criminology, 10,* 189–212.

Wechsler, David. (1944). *The measurement of adult intelligence.* 3rd ed. Baltimore, MD: Williams & Wilkins.

Wilson, Lauren and Angela Scarpa. (2011). The link between sensation seeking and aggression: A meta-analytic review. *Aggressive Behavior, 37,* 81–90.

Wong, Steven and Robert Hare. (2005). *Guidelines for a psychopathy treatment program.* Toronto, Canada: Multi-Health Systems.

Zahn-Waxler, Carolyn and Angela McBride. (1998). Current perspectives on social and emotional development. In J. Adair, D. Belanger and K. Dion (Eds.), *Advances in psychological science, Vol. 1: Social, cultural and personal aspects* (pp. 513–546). Hove, England: Psychology Press/Erlbaum.

Zucchino, David. (2012). Sterilized by North Carolina, she felt raped once more. *The Los Angeles Times,* January 25. Retrieved from: http://articles.latimes.com/2012/jan/25/nation/la-na-forced-sterilization-20120126.

Chapter 4

Why Do They Do It?
Social Structural Answers

Introduction

When we try to answer the question of why people commit crime from the social structural perspective, we are talking about the structures that serve to organize society (families, educational institutions, religion, politics and the economy) and how they might contribute to crime. In this chapter, we will examine three social structural perspectives, including social disorganization, anomie/strain and subcultural theories of crime.

Social Disorganization

The first truly American theory of crime causation was developed in the city of Chicago. During the early part of the 20th century, the United States in general and Chicago in particular were undergoing major changes. The Industrial Revolution was underway and manufacturing jobs became widely available in major American cities. Not only was population in Chicago exploding, from just under 4,500 in 1840 to 2.7 million in 1920 (Gibson, 1998),[1] its composition was changing dramatically, with the Windy City becoming the new home of African Americans from the south and immigrants from all over Europe. People flocked to Chicago in search of work and the changes the city was undergoing made it something of a living laboratory for social scientists. Among the most famous of these social scientists were Clifford Shaw and Henry McKay. Shaw and McKay built on the work of Ernest Burgess (1925), who postulated that cities grow outward from an inner core. As they do, various zones

---

1. Remember from Chapter 1, both Paris and London underwent massive changes that preceded an increase in crime and increased concern with crime, as well.

Figure 4.1. Burgess' concentric zone concept

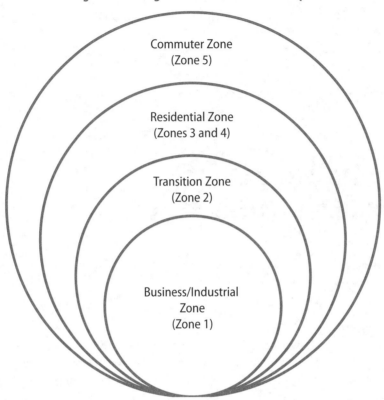

Commuter Zone
(Zone 5)

Residential Zone
(Zones 3 and 4)

Transition Zone
(Zone 2)

Business/Industrial
Zone
(Zone 1)

Source: Adapted from Burgess, 1925.

develop in which people live and work. The inner core serves as the center of business and industry. The zone immediately next to the inner core is comprised of inexpensive housing for those, particularly new arrivals, looking for work in the inner core. The third, fourth and fifth zones out from the inner core are comprised of housing for those who have acclimated to city life and have the resources to leave the zone adjacent to the inner core; by implication, the zone immediately next to the inner core is transitory. Figure 4.1 illustrates Burgess' concentric zone concept.

Burgess' ideas were central to Shaw and McKay's (1942) investigation of juvenile delinquency in Chicago in the first third of the 20th century. Shaw and McKay hypothesized that the transition zone, characterized as it was by poverty, heterogeneity (people of many different races, ethnicities and nationalities) and transiency (people frequently moving in and out), would have higher rates of juvenile delinquency than the other zones. Using a variety of indicators of juvenile delinquency, including referrals to juvenile court, truancy and recidivism, and then mapping the addresses of confirmed delinquents, Shaw and McKay found that, over time, rates of juvenile delinquency tended to remain stable by area. Rates of juvenile delinquency in the transition zone were higher than those of any of the other zones over time, regardless of who lived there. Shaw and McKay called the transition zone socially disorganized, contending that poverty, heterogeneity and transiency undermined the organizing effects of social structures such as the family and educational and religious institutions (and giving us the name of the theory). With these structures undermined, the ability of adults to control children is diminished and the opportunities for children to consort with older delinquents increase (as we will see in Chapter 5, associating with delinquent peers appears to be an important part of crime causation).

Shaw and McKay (1942) accomplished something major with their study. They effectively turned attention away from the Lombrosian idea that criminals are born inferior (see Chapter 1) and put it on the idea that place matters in the origin of criminal and delinquent behavior. Put another way, they turned collective attention to the ecology of crime. However, they neglected to elaborate much further on social disorganization and it was not until the mid-1980s that Shaw and McKay's ideas were reexamined and extended. Robert Sampson (1986) claimed that crime resulted from the inability of residents in some neighborhoods to exercise informal social control over children. The inability to exercise informal social control over children is in part a consequence of the state of families in these neighborhoods. Adults in families that are broken (e.g., upended by death, divorce, incarceration or abandonment) simply do not have the resources necessary to exercise informal social control over children and to intervene in some meaningful way when delinquent behavior is observed. Sampson and Groves (1989) later endeavored to find support for this idea in the British Crime Survey (BCS). Prior to Sampson and Groves' (1989) work, few studies on social disorganization had attempted to measure how organized or disorganized a neighborhood was, opting instead to examine the amounts of key variables (i.e. poverty, residential instability, heterogeneity and family disruption) and what amounts were associated with higher crime rates. BCS data were very useful in overcoming this shortfall, as they included questions on whether adults were willing to supervise youth and intervene when necessary, on whether adults had nearby friends and if so, how many and whether adults participated in voluntary organizations. Sampson and Groves (1989) found that these indicators of social organization were correlated with crime rates. That is, those neighborhoods that appeared to be more organized as measured by the BCS questions had less crime while those that appeared less organized had more crime. These results support Shaw and McKay's (1942) and importantly, provide a more concrete idea of what constitutes social organization and disorganization. Bursik and Grasmick's (1993) work echoes these findings.

By now, readers may have a general concept of the characteristics of a socially disorganized neighborhood, including what it looks like physically and who the residents are. Perhaps surprisingly, it was not until the mid-1990s that scholars attempted to link social disorganization theory to the uniquely American composition of inner city neighborhoods. Sampson and Wilson (1995) took umbrage with the old idea from the Chicago school of criminology that disorganization was part of the development of cities and that it happened as cities grew and changed. Rather, Sampson and Wilson (1995) postulated that disorganization was inextricably linked to the racial inequality that plagued large American cities. African Americans, they noted, were much more likely to reside in neighborhoods that could accurately be called disorganized and the reasons for this were rooted in economic and political policies. These policies resulted in the disappearance of manufacturing jobs, dense and dilapidated inner city housing, the migration of middle class African Americans out of inner city neighborhoods and concomitant disruption of existing neighborhoods and social networks. The consequences of these policies were that many African Americans live in severe isolation, all but cut off from middle class culture. New values emerge as a result of this isolation and in conjunction with the emergence of new values, crime is viewed as an unavoidable part of life in these neighborhoods.

Building on this extension of social disorganization theory to include race, Sampson, Raudenbush and Earls (1997) examined violence in 343 Chicago neighborhoods. In so doing, they created an index of concentrated disadvantage, comprised of poverty, race and age characteristics and family disruption and found that the greater the concentrated disadvantage, the greater the violence, even when controlling for individual characteristics. Using surveys of residents in these neighborhoods, they further found that concentrated disadvantage was mediated by a concept they called collective efficacy. Collective efficacy is the ability of residents of a neighborhood to maintain public order by exercising informal social control when needed. At the root of exerting informal social control as necessary is a mutual trust and support among residents of neighborhoods. Where collective efficacy is high, crime is low and vice versa. In addition to pointing out the root of collective efficacy, Sampson, Raudenbush and Earls (1997) used their study to make another important claim. They postulated that collective efficacy is not a static but a dynamic process that is built on the social bonds among individuals and families and utilized as necessary to maintain order in the neighborhood. A major question left unanswered by these scholars is how residents of neighborhoods, particularly those afflicted with poverty, heterogeneity, transiency and family disruption, can create the requisite trust and support in the first place.

Figure 4.2 provides a graphic illustration of social disorganization theory.

Figure 4.2. Social disorganization theory

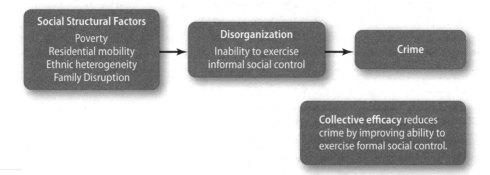

Sources: Adapted from Shaw and McKay, 1942; Sampson and Groves, 1986; Sampson, Raudenbush and Earls, 1997.

Research on Social Disorganization

Social disorganization had its heyday in the 1940s and a revival in the 1980s and 1990s, but there has been research conducted on this theory in recent years. Steenbeek and Hipp (2011) were interested in the direct and indirect effects of neighborhood conditions on disorder, where indirect effects are mediated by social cohesion and social control. They were also interested in the feedback effects of disorder on neighborhood characteristics, cohesion and control. They examined 74 neighborhoods in Utrecht in the Netherlands over the course of 10 years by combining neighborhood-level data with individual-level survey data on cohesion and control, including both feelings of responsibility and actions taken to protect the neighborhood. They found that taking action is more important to combating disorder and improving the neighborhood than feelings of responsibility. Moreover, neighborhoods with high levels of disorder cause people to move away and the resulting higher residential instability causes fewer people to take action and exert informal social control when it is needed. Disorder, then, has direct effects on residential instability and indirect effects on social control.

Cancino, Martinez and Stowell (2009) wanted to know if the social structure of neighborhoods is important in the variation in both intragroup and intergroup robbery by Latinos and African Americans in San Antonio. Residential instability was found to be positively associated with all robberies, consistent with social disorganization theory. Disadvantage (including poverty and female-headed households) was a stronger predictor of African American victimization than of Latino victimization, whereas increased heterogeneity and recent immigration were stronger predictors of Latino victimization. The authors conclude that the social structure may affect some groups differently and that a more nuanced look is needed to better understand social disorganization in modern contexts.

Fagan and Wright (2012) took an approach similar to that of Cancino and colleagues, but instead of inquiring about race and ethnicity, they wanted to know about the effects of structural and social features of neighborhoods on boys' and girls' delinquency. Fagan and Wright (2012) used data from the Project on Human Development in Chicago Neighborhoods, including interviews, self-report surveys and census information, in order to determine feelings of collective efficacy, amount of delinquency and violence and neighborhood disadvantage in 80 neighborhoods. Their results revealed that neither collective efficacy nor neighborhood disadvantage were related to boys' delinquency but that collective efficacy increased the amount of delinquency reported by females. Moreover, neighborhood disadvantage reduced the likelihood that females self-reported violence. These findings are the opposite of those predicted by social disorganization theory and the authors conclude that neighborhood features may impact individual offending in complicated ways.

Though social disorganization as a theory tends to focus on street crime, Akyuz and Armstrong (2011) believe that it is useful in explaining terrorism. They measured poverty, heterogeneity and residential mobility in 81 Turkish provinces alongside terrorist attacks, including bombings, armed assault and arson carried out in those provinces. The authors found that poverty and residential mobility were able to predict terrorist attacks (meaning that provinces with high poverty and high residential mobility had high numbers of terrorist attacks) and that this predictive power held when ethnic heterogeneity was taken into account. This research indicates a new direction for social disorganization theory.

Strengths and Weaknesses of Social Disorganization

Among the strengths of social disorganization theory is its focus on the circumstances in which people live as important in the genesis of crime. As mentioned, social disorganization took attention away from the idea that criminals are born as such and focused on the interaction of people and places. Another strength of social disorganization is its ability to explain high crime rates in certain neighborhoods. It can predict crime rates by taking a variety of neighborhood characteristics, especially poverty, heterogeneity, transiency, family disruption and degree of organization into account. It can also explain how deviant values that acknowledge that violence is a part of life are transmitted from generation to generation.

As with all theories of crime in this book, social disorganization is not without its weaknesses. Of course, it does a poor job of explaining crime outside of high crime neighborhoods. It is particularly weak for explaining white collar crime. It also does a poor job of explaining why a vast majority of people who live in high crime neighborhoods are actually law abiding and that it is a small number of residents of these neighborhoods who are responsible for a vast majority of crime (as we will see in Chapter 7, offenders who start offending early and continue to offend over the lifetime are responsible for a great deal of crime). Social disorganization theory also lacks the power to explain hot spots of crime. Research on hot spots (e.g., Sherman, Gartin and Buerger, 1989) reveals that much crime is concentrated in very small geographic areas, such as individual convenience stores. With its focus on neighborhoods, social disorganization is ill equipped to explain this phenomenon. All these weaknesses are rooted to some degree in the idea of the ecological fallacy, which holds it is inappropriate to draw conclusions about individual people on the basis of characteristics of groups to which they happen to belong.

Anomie/Strain

This subsection focuses on three manifestations of anomie/strain theories, including classic strain theory, institutional anomie theory and general strain theory. All three manifestations are rooted in some way in the concept of anomie. The person most closely associated with the concept of anomie is French sociologist Emile Durkheim. Durkheim was born in 1858 and wrote prolifically on a number of topics, among them religion, labor, suicide and methodological techniques in the social sciences (see Chapter 1). At the time of his writing, the Western world was undergoing a great upheaval, with people moving en masse from rural, agrarian societies to urban cities as industrialization took hold. Durkheim noted that the values and norms that had been endemic to agricultural societies and served to hold them together were no longer viable. Instead, what characterized newly emerging urban areas was anomie, a state of normlessness in which old values are no longer tenable and new ones have yet to emerge (Jones, 2011).

Durkheim (1982[1895]) believed that crime was a part of all societies, contending that crime did not decrease as societies became more civilized, but rather increased.

For him, crime was both a normal and a useful part of society. That is not to say that criminals are normal (indeed, Durkheim took the opposite position) or that some individual crimes, heinous as they may be, are normal. It is the existence of the phenomenon that we call crime that is normal. It may seem odd to think of crime as useful, but to Durkheim, crime reveals the bounds of acceptable behavior. If all deviant behavior was repressed, so too would creativity, innovation and personal freedom be repressed (Jones, 2011).

Institutional Anomie Theory

The scholars most responsible for the development of institutional anomie theory, the current leading version of anomie theory, are Steven Messner and Richard Rosenfeld. Messner and Rosenfeld (2012)[2] believe that the unrelenting pursuit of monetary success, in other words the American Dream, is at the root of the high crime rate in the United States. They note that all other social institutions, including the family, schools, religion and politics are subjugated to the economy. The legitimate goals of these other institutions, such as raising decent children, gaining knowledge and benevolent public service become devalued. For example, most new parents must rush back to work soon after the birth of a baby and may struggle to find childcare in order to remain employed. Moreover, norms endemic to the economic system and the acquisition of the American Dream have become embedded in other institutions. For example, schools encourage competition for rewards among even very young children in the same way the economic system encourages competition for monetary rewards. With this singular focus on achieving monetary rewards running pervasively through all institutions, these social institutions that are supposed to insulate against deviant behavior become less able to do so effectively. To continue the above example, parents who are constantly at work and struggling to find affordable daycare are likely to be less able to effectively socialize their children.

Messner and Rosenfeld (2012) see the solution to the many problems created by the dominance of the economic system in a process called decommodification. Decommodification involves eliminating the dominance of the economy and its focus on competition for rewards over other social institutions. Policies that permit this elimination (or reduction) would liberate families, schools, religion and politics to function as intended. Families would be stronger, students would pursue knowledge for its sake and religion and politics would be positive forces. Allowing people to live free from economic forces would reduce fierce competition which in turn would reduce crime. Some research has found support for the notion that crime is lower in societies in which social institutions other than the economy are stronger. Moreover, economic stressors such as poverty and income inequality have less of an effect on crime in societies in which noneconomic institutions are stronger (Cullen and Agnew, 2011).

---

2. This is the latest edition of Messner and Rosenfeld's work. They have been developing this theory since the mid-1990s.

Classic Strain Theory

Sociologist Robert Merton utilized Durkheim's concept of anomie as the basis of his explanation of crime, which came to be called strain theory. Merton (1938) noted that American culture supports monetary success as a legitimate goal toward which we should all strive. Some people are able to attain monetary success through legitimate means, such as working hard, but some are not. The inability to achieve monetary success through legitimate means is a major source of strain and that strain may lead to crime. In other words, Merton (1938) believed the strain created by the inability to achieve monetary success through legitimate means was caused by American culture's unrelenting focus on the importance of this one goal.

Merton (1938) contended that people adopt one of five strategies, what he called modes of adaptation, in order to cope with this strain. The five strategies he proposed are:

1. *Conformity*: Conformity involves striving toward monetary success through legitimate means, such as legal work, and according to Merton (1938), this is the most widely adopted strategy.

2. *Ritualism*: This strategy involves a denial of the goal of monetary success as being attainable. However, people who are ritualistic are committed to the means of trying to attain that success. We might think of someone who is ritualistic as going to the same job every day and punching a clock, not because he or she expects to get rich but because that is what is done.

3. *Innovation*: This strategy may be thought of as the opposite of ritualism and stands out as the criminal adaptation. That is, the goal of monetary success is accepted, but legitimate means for attaining it are not. Instead, the innovator adopts deviant or criminal means (such as drug dealing, for example) in order to attain monetary success.

4. *Retreatism*: This strategy involves rejecting both the goals of monetary success and legitimate means of attaining them. Retreatists drop out of society, living on its margins and often using drugs and alcohol.

5. *Rebellion*: This strategy, like retreatism, also involves rejecting both the goals of American society and the means of attaining them. Unlike retreatism, however, new goals and means of attainment are substituted. Those who adopt the strategy of rebellion may be committed to an alternative political and economic system, such as communism or socialism.

Table 4.1 graphically illustrates each of the strategies and responses to both goals and means.

A recent modification to classic strain theory comes from Murphy and Robinson (2008), who propose a new strategy to cope with strain called maximization. Maximization combines conformity and innovation so that maximizers pursue both legitimate and illegitimate means to achieve culturally desirable goals, most especially wealth. Murphy and Robinson (2008) proposed this new strategy because they believe Merton's (1938) strategies are insufficient for explaining white collar crime; white collar crime is discussed in more detail in Chapter 13.

Table 4.1. Merton's strategies and responses to goals and means

Strategy	Cultural Goals	Legitimate Means
1. Conformity	Accept	Accept
2. Ritualism	Reject	Accept
3. Innovation	Accept	Reject
4. Retreatism	Reject	Reject
5. Rebellion	Reject and substitute	Reject and substitute

Source: Adapted from Merton, 1938.

General Strain Theory

Remember that in classic strain theory, the major source of strain is inability to achieve monetary success through legitimate means. Robert Agnew has extended and refined this basic idea in a related yet distinct theory he calls general strain theory or GST, the leading version of strain theory. Agnew (1997)[3] finds Merton's (1938) assertions a useful starting point, but observes a major problem. If Merton (1938) is correct, crime and delinquency should skyrocket when young people enter the workforce and come to the realization that legitimate employment may not result in achieving monetary success. Upon this realization, some will employ the strategy of innovation, using illegitimate means to attain wealth. However, data bears out the opposite: as young people enter the workforce, delinquency decreases sharply. With this problem exposed, Agnew worked to extend and refine the basic idea that strain leads to crime.

One of the important ways in which GST is different from classic strain theory is that GST identifies a variety of strains. For Agnew (2002), these strains are not limited to the inability to achieve monetary success through legitimate means, though the failure to achieve positively valued goals is one of the strains Agnew identifies. Strains also come from the removal of stimuli that are positively valued, such as breaking up with a significant other and from the presentation of stimuli that are negatively valued, such as abuse and failure in school. Agnew (2002) maintains that an abundance of strains over time may lead to a negative view of others, followed by negative emotions, principally anger, and the tendency to respond to affronts with aggression. Figure 4.3 provides a graphic illustration of GST.

Everyone experiences strain in life, but strain may lead to delinquency when the strain is perceived to be unjust, perceived to be high in magnitude, associated with low self-control and when it creates an incentive for criminal coping. But if everyone experiences strains and some experience a multitude of serious, unfair, persistent strains, why is it that not everyone engages in criminal coping? Agnew (2002) maintains that people differ on important traits that are associated with the ability to cope with strains in legitimate ways. Among the traits Agnew (2002) considers important are even tem-

---

3. Agnew has been developing his GST since the mid-1980s.

Figure 4.3. Graphic illustration of GST

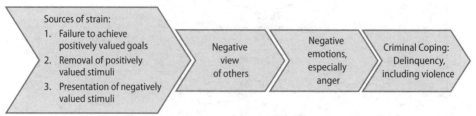

Source: Adapted from Agnew, 2002.

perament, higher intelligence, the ability to think creatively and solve problems, the ability to have positive interactions with others and a belief in one's abilities. People who possess these traits are often able to choose legitimate, noncriminal coping strategies while those who do not possess them are more likely to cope with strains in a criminal fashion. The development of these traits is a two-way street as far as Agnew is concerned; some strains may contribute to the development of certain traits that may be conducive to crime commission. Moreover, some strains can reduce social control and facilitate the learning of crime (Agnew, 2006).

Agnew continues to refine GST, working to determine the effects of strain on different people and what specific strains are likely to lead to criminal coping. For example, Broidy and Agnew (1997) believe GST is useful in explaining males' and females' different rates of crime commission.[4] They hypothesize that females, when they are unable to achieve positively valued goals, turn the negative emotions that result from this strain inward and engage in self-destructive behaviors, such as eating disorders. Males, on the other hand, turn the negative emotions that results from the inability to achieve positively valued goals outward in the form of anger and engage in crime.[5] Other research supports the notion that there is a gendered response to strain (e.g. Sharp, Terling-Watt, Atkins, Gilliam and Sanders, 2001; Jang, 2007).

In addition to testing the applicability of his theory to males and females, Agnew (2001, 2010) attempted to clarify what strains, of the thousands of strains that can fall under Agnew's three broad categories seen above, are more likely to lead to crime. Among those on the list are: failure to achieve valued goals when those goals are easily achieved through crime, parental rejection including child neglect, strict, erratic or harsh discipline including child abuse, negative experiences in elementary school, low wage work or no work, homelessness especially while young, abusive relationships with peers especially while young, abusive romantic relationships, poverty, the experience of criminal victimization and the experience of prejudice or discrimination. Moreover,

---

4. Agnew's work to refine GST goes beyond gender. Research has also tested the utility of GST in explaining the relationship between race and crime (Kaufman, 2005; Kaufman, Rebellon, Thaxton and Agnew, 2008), age and crime (Agnew, 1997; Slocum, Simpson and Smith, 2005), community characteristics and crime (Agnew, 1999) and offending over the life course (Agnew, 1999; Slocum, Simpson and Smith, 2005).

5. For more on the generalizability of traditional theories to both men's and women's crime, see the Feminist Criminology section in Chapter 6.

these strains need not be directly experienced to lead to criminal coping. Agnew (2002a) notes that vicarious and anticipated strains may also lead to criminal coping, where vicarious strains are those experienced by those to whom one is close and anticipated strains are those that one believes will be experienced in the future.

Research on Anomie/Strain

It should come as little surprise that much recent research on anomie and strain theories is focused on GST. Blevins, Listwan, Cullen and Jonson (2010)[6] propose that GST can provide insight into deviant behavior across contexts, including the prison. Research on prison violence and misconduct reveals three competing models, deprivation, importation and coping. Blevins and colleagues (2010) believe all of these models can be subsumed under GST. In accord with the deprivation model, which holds that prison deprives prisoners of desirable situations, GST maintains that prison environment will result in the three categories of strain, failure to achieve positively valued goals, removal of positively valued stimuli and presentation of negatively valued stimuli. In accord with the importation model, which holds that prison misconduct and violence results from individual attributes including personal values, GST maintains that reactions to strain are contingent upon individual attributes, especially traits. In accord with the coping model, which holds that prison limits the coping strategies available to prisoners, GST maintains that responses to strain are contingent upon ability to cope with them. GST is therefore a useful theory in explaining prison misconduct and violence.

Another area to which GST has been recently applied is bullying. In their study on traditional school bullying in South Korea, Moon, Morash and McCluskey (2010) found some support for GST. In more detail, young people who are victimized by peers and those who experience conflict with their parents are more likely to engage in bullying. However, attachment to parents and positive relationships with teachers do not reduce the effects of strains, nor does anger serve as a mediating variable, as GST would predict. Hay, Meldrum and Mann (2010) examined both traditional and cyber bullying in the United States. They found that victimization by either kind of bullying was associated with delinquency and moreover, that they were associated with external delinquency, such as harm to people and property, as well as with internal delinquency, such as self-injury and suicidal thoughts. Interestingly, the effects of both types of bullying on self-injury and suicidal thoughts were greater for boys than girls, which is the opposite of what GST would predict.

Remember that one of the kinds of strains identified by GST is the removal of positively valued stimuli. One example of the removal of positive stimuli is the dissolution of a romantic relationship. Most romantic relationships end and may cause strain when they do. Larson and Sweeten (2012) examined data on over 2,500 high school and college age youth and found that breakups were associated with increases in offending and alcohol and drug use. For those who entered into a new relationship after the breakup, there were no changes in offending or in drug use, though alcohol use still

---

6. The entire issue of the journal in which this article appears is dedicated to GST.

increased. The effects of a breakup were more negative for males than for females. Males experienced increases in offending and alcohol and drug use after a breakup, but females only experienced increase in alcohol and marijuana consumption and not in offending. These results are consistent with GST and indicate that the dissolution of romantic relationships have far reaching consequences.

Another area to which GST has been recently applied is drug use among Native American youth. Native American youth are at greater risk of using illegal substances than the population at large but there is little in the way of tests of theories of crime that aim to explain this fact. Using data from the Add Health survey, McNulty-Eitle, Eitle and Johnson-Jennings (2013) found that recent exposure to stressful life events was strongly correlated with illegal substance use as GST would predict. The connection between exposure to stress and substance abuse was mediated by parental and self-control factors, religiosity and association with illegal substance using peers in the expected directions, but in more nuanced ways than GST would predict. However, the proposition that negative affect, especially anger, mediates the connection between strain and illegal substance use was not well supported, opposite of what GST would predict.

Finally and in contrast to Akyuz and Armstrong (2011) above, Agnew (2010) believes that although GST is commonly used to explain rather ordinary street crimes, it can be useful to explain the crime of terrorism. The strains most likely to contribute to terrorism are those that are high in magnitude involving civilian victims, those that are unjust and those caused by powerful others. Agnew believes these strains lead to negative emotional states, including anger, humiliation and hopelessness while simultaneously reducing noncriminal coping abilities. These strains also reduce social controls that prevent terrorism, they provide models for and encourage the belief that terrorism is acceptable and they foster a collective mentality and a collective response to the strain. Terrorist groups then tend to promote terrorism as a way to alleviate strains that are experienced both individually and collectively. Of course, not everyone under these types of strain becomes involved in terrorism and Agnew (2010) points out that certain factors condition the effect of strains on terrorism. These factors include ability to cope, possession of skills and available opportunities, extent of social support, extent of social control, presence of certain individual traits (negative emotionality, low constraint and cognitive inflexibility in particular are associated with terroristic coping), association with others who favor terrorism, harboring beliefs that favor terrorism and perceiving greater benefits of terrorism than costs.

Strengths and Weaknesses of Anomie/Strain

One of the great strengths of anomie/strain theories is that they put focus on the role that an inability to achieve valued goals and the frustration that follows plays in producing crime. Messner and Rosenfeld's (2012) institutional anomie theory is able to explain why crime rates are so high in the United States relative to other capitalistic countries and they propose a solution to the crime problem. Merton's (1938) strain theory is able to explain high crime rates among those who are disadvantaged and describes a number of strategies people employ in adapting to strain. Agnew (2002) recognized that there are several sources of strain and continues to work to reveal which strains are most relevant for which people and what combination of strains and individual characteristics are most likely to lead to criminal coping.

Anomie/strain theories are not without their weaknesses. First, if anomie/strain theories are correct, the rates for instrumental crimes, those crimes committed for money, material or status gain, should be higher than the rates for expressive crimes, those crimes committed out of rage, anger or frustration. Those who cannot achieve desired goals through legitimate means who turn to crime should commit instrumental crime in higher numbers, say anomie/strain theories. However, the expressive crime rate in the United States is higher and the instrumental crime rate is lower than in other comparable countries, such as England (van Kesteren, Mayhew and Nieuwbeerta, 2000; Langan and Farrington, 1998). Messner and Rosenfeld (2012) propose only one cause of crime that does not take into account factors from some of the leading theories of crime causation. Merton (1938) did not attempt to explain why some people employ the innovation strategy of adaptation and turn to crime while others do not. Agnew's GST (2002) has been criticized for taking strains as a given and not making enough explicit effort to explore the sources of strain that are rooted in the social structure.

Subcultural Theories[7]

As their name implies, subcultural theories of crime focus on the development of cultures that are distinct from the mainstream. Subcultural theories have their roots in the concepts of anomie and strain and at their essence, hold that some groups have values that approve of or justify crime. These values permit commission of crime at high rates within these groups. A number of theorists have proposed subcultural explanations of crime, among them Albert Cohen, Richard Cloward and Lloyd Ohlin, Walter Miller and Elijah Anderson. We will examine each of these theorists' ideas in turn.

Albert Cohen (1955) postulated that young people from the lower socioeconomic classes have limited legitimate opportunities available to them in order to achieve middle class success. These youth are frustrated by their inability to achieve (in Cohen's terms, they experience status frustration as a result of blocked opportunities) and form a subculture as a result that shuns middle class values. Cohen believes that the subculture substitutes its own values that are easier for its members to attain, values such as appearing to be a tough guy who does not hesitate to use aggression and even violence. Cohen contends that much of the crime committed by lower class youths is expressive and not instrumental in nature. That is, the crime is committed in accordance with the subcultural values (of appearing tough, et cetera) and not strictly for monetary gain. Cohen notes that this type of crime is meant to fly in the face of middle class values.

Richard Cloward and Lloyd Ohlin (1960) devised a subcultural theory called opportunity structure theory. Like Cohen (1955), they recognized that young people from

---

7. Other authors, notably Cullen and Agnew (2011), cover subcultural theories alongside learning theories of crime, referring to them as macro-level learning theories. While a valid placement for them, we consider them here because of their roots in the anomie/strain tradition.

the lower socioeconomic classes have limited legitimate opportunities to attain middle class success and may form a subculture that values the luxuries of life, including cars, clothes and romantic partners and engaging in criminal activity to obtain them. However, they recognized the existence of several delinquent subcultures that are predicated on the illegitimate opportunities available in a given neighborhood. Cloward and Ohlin (1960) believed that just as opportunities for success through legitimate means may be blocked, so too can opportunities for success through illegitimate means be blocked. That is, just as it takes talent, opportunity and connections to do well in legitimate occupations, it also takes talent, opportunity and connections to do well in illegitimate (criminal) occupations and not everyone is successful in these occupations.

There are three types of specialized delinquent subcultures according to Cloward and Ohlin (1960), the first of which is known as criminal. The criminal delinquent subculture is characterized by gangs involved mainly in economic offenses such as theft and fraud. Moreover, criminal gangs are stable and run by adults, meaning that they provide criminal role models and values over time. Those who come into the world as part of a criminal delinquent subculture have a leg up on those outsiders who wish to join. Someone wishing to join a criminal delinquent subculture must have someone in that enterprise who will vouch for him or her. The second type of specialized delinquent subculture is known as conflict. Conflict gangs form in areas of poverty, transience and general instability, the kinds of areas we might now recognize as characterized by social disorganization. Conflict gangs commit criminal acts that are both expressive and instrumental, but in a much less organized, much more individualized fashion than criminal gangs do. The third type of specialized delinquent subculture is known as retreatist. Retreatist gang members, as their name implies, retreat from the pressures of daily life through the use of drugs and alcohol. In contrast to the actions of criminal gangs, the actions of both conflict and retreatist gangs are focused on immediate gratification.

Walter Miller (1958) took a different tack in his approach to subcultural theorizing. In contrast to Cohen (1955), Miller (1958) believed that values characteristic of the middle class, including hard work, perseverance, responsible life choices and efforts at stability are not attractive to members of the lower classes. Rather, the lower class has its own set of inherent values that are not formed as a reaction to those of the middle class. Miller's theory is based on a large study he conducted for the National Institutes of Health (NIH) that involved daily contact with members of the lower class.

Through this daily contact, Miller identified six focal concerns, issues that are a part of living life in the lower class.

1. *Trouble*: Trouble should be avoided if possible, but trouble may provide an opportunity to prove one can handle him or herself and thereby confer desirable status.

2. *Toughness*: This focal concern is of great import to people, especially males, in the lower class. It includes bravery, machismo, sexual aggression and cold heartedness.

3. *Smartness*: Smartness refers not to a traditional idea of a high IQ, but rather street smart and using one's wits to survive as well as the ability to outsmart others.

4. *Excitement*: Excitement involves the search for fun. Fun may manifest itself in many different forms for members of the lower class, including sex, drugs, alcohol and gambling.

5. *Fatalism*: This is a belief that one has no control over what happens to him or her.

6. *Autonomy*: Autonomy refers to the ability to make one's own decisions and to do what one wants to do outside the control of authority figures (parents, teachers, employers, law enforcement officers, et cetera).

Taken together, the focal concerns of the lower class practically ensure the commission of crime and deviance. If trouble comes along, for example, one may prove one's toughness by engaging in aggression or even violence. The search for excitement may result in unprotected sex and eventual parental absence in the interest of autonomy. On this point, Miller (1958) expressed concern that many lower class youth grow up without fathers or other male role models, which has a dual effect. First, these youth go largely unsupervised and second, they seek out other, possibly delinquent or criminal male youth in order to establish their male identities. Research by Bellair, Roscigno and Velez (2003) bears out the importance of positive role models.

Miller's (1958) idea that there is a lower class subculture with values inherent to the class and not formed in opposition to middle class values is supported by both Wolfgang and Ferracuti (1982) and Elijah Anderson (1994, 1999). Wolfgang and Ferracuti (1982) proposed that what they called a subculture of violence explained high rates of homicide among inner city African Americans. Members of this subculture view violence as an appropriate and even mandatory way to respond to a number of affronts. Anderson (1994, 1999) provides an account of the subculture of violence from his observations of American neighborhoods in Philadelphia.[8] He concluded that in the neighborhoods he observed, there are two orientations toward the world. The first is a decent orientation in which strong, loving families embrace middle class values. The second is a street orientation, the values of which directly oppose those of the middle class. For children growing up in these neighborhoods, they must be able to adopt the street values as needed (in Anderson's terms, they must learn to code switch). The code of the street provides a set of rules that governs interpersonal interactions and even decent families reluctantly encourage children to learn the code so that they may survive on the street.

According to Anderson (1994, 1999), the person who can take care of him or herself is afforded respect, but respect is very elusive and easily challenged. When respect (or juice, in Anderson's terms) is challenged, walking away from the situation is not an option, as to do so would destroy self-esteem and reputation. Rather, what is prescribed by the code of the street is answering challenges to respect with aggression and violence, either in the moment or in the form of later revenge. Underlying these actions is a particularly dangerous fearlessness—not being afraid to die or to kill. Within this oppositional culture, members are not failures because of poor school performance or unemployment. Rather, they can be successful by obtaining and keeping respect through displays of aggression and violence. While Anderson's (1994, 1999) thesis was developed

---

8. Anderson's (1999) work is also discussed in Chapter 1.

largely around young males, Nowacki (2012) provides evidence that girls embrace street codes as well and act in accordance with them.

While the work of Wolfgang and Ferracuti (1982) and Anderson (1994, 1999) focuses on African Americans, it is important to note that the subculture of violence in the terms of the former researchers or the code of the street in the terms of the latter may be more related to residing in disadvantaged neighborhoods than to race (Sampson and Bartusch, 1999; Wilkinson, 2003; Brezina, Agnew, Cullen and Wright, 2004; Stewart and Simons, 2006; Mullins, 2006). Remember that Sampson and Wilson (1995) pointed out that African Americans are more likely to live in these disadvantaged areas than whites, accounting for their disproportional participation in these subcultures.

Gangs[9]

The preceding paragraphs on subcultural theories inevitably turn our attention to the phenomenon of gangs. As reported by Howell and Moore (2010), gang formation has been influenced by both poverty and immigration in the United States. In the Northeast and Midwest, poor, mostly white families from Europe came to the United States in huge numbers between the period following the Revolution and about 1860. People with shared nationalities and languages clustered together in urban areas in the United States. When discriminated against by native born Anglo Americans, conflict developed and gangs started to form. At this same time, Mexican migration and immigration was fueling gang development in the West. After the Civil War, African Americans from the South flocked to all three regions. These migrations also fueled gang development and the result was a mix of gangs comprised of whites, of Mexicans and of African Americans (gangs in the southern United States did not emerge until much later, in part because unlike in the other regions, one city did not emerge as the main urban center in the South).

In the 1960s, immigration to the United States shifted from European points of origin to Central and South American and Asian points of origin. New Asian and Latin American immigrants settled in urban areas and some formed gangs, much in the same way earlier waves of immigrants did. The move away from an industrial economy in the United States at the same time meant fewer legitimate job opportunities for those wishing to earn a living wage, further disadvantaging some, especially those who were un- or undereducated (Moore and Hagedorn, 2001; Wilson, 1997; Frailing and Harper, 2010). Another important factor influencing gang formation, especially in recent decades, is the loosening of the tight control the Italian Mafia once had over the illegal drug market (Sanchez-Jankowski, 2003).

Theorists seem to agree that young people join gangs to gain status, to obtain power, for excitement, to make money from illegal activities or trades and to have new experiences. At the root of these reasons for joining, though, is the idea that gangs provide security to its members and a set of rules that must be followed and a set of punishments for breaking the rules. In other words, gangs serve as a source of

---

9. Gangs, including organized criminal enterprises, are discussed in more detail in Chapter 9.

Figure 4.4. Some currently active gangs in the United States by region

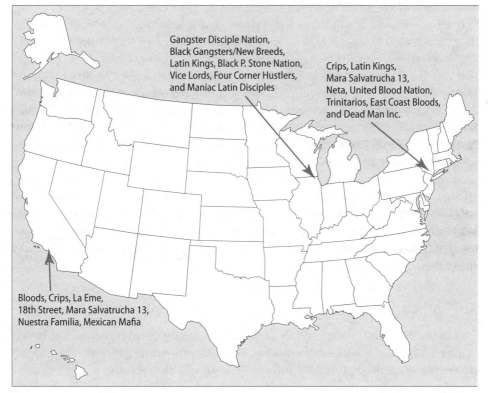

Gangster Disciple Nation,
Black Gangsters/New Breeds,
Latin Kings, Black P. Stone Nation,
Vice Lords, Four Corner Hustlers,
and Maniac Latin Disciples

Crips, Latin Kings,
Mara Salvatrucha 13,
Neta, United Blood Nation,
Trinitarios, East Coast Bloods,
and Dead Man Inc.

Bloods, Crips, La Eme,
18th Street, Mara Salvatrucha 13,
Nuestra Familia, Mexican Mafia

Sources: U.S. Census Bureau, n.d.; Howell and Moore, 2010.

employment, education, friendship and family (Spergel, 1995; Walsh and Hemmens, 2011). Figure 4.4 names some of the gangs currently active in different regions of the United States by region.

Research on Subcultural Theories[10]

Perhaps some of the best known subcultural research besides that described above focuses on the culture of honor among Southerners in the United States. Cohen, Nisbett, Bowdle and Schwarz (1996) conducted an experiment in which male students from the North and the South were subjected to an insult. Northern students were relatively unaffected by the insult (being called an "asshole"), but Southern students were affected in a number of ways. They perceived their masculine reputation to be under threat, got upset and were prepared for aggressive reaction (as measured by cortisol and testosterone levels, respectively) and they were more likely to actually engage in aggressive and dominant behavior than their Northern counterparts. Nisbett and Cohen (1996) went on to explain the development of a Southern culture of honor, in which aggressive

---

10. Subcultures of violence in particular are discussed in more detail in Chapter 11.

and even violent responses to affronts were acceptable, lay in the need of Scottish and Irish settlers to the region to protect their livestock. Adherents of this idea point to data that show that even Southerners who migrate north have higher violent crime rates than native Northerners (Lee, Bankston, Hayes and Thomas, 2007; Butterfield, 1995).

However, more recent evaluations of Nisbett and Cohen's (1996) work, including that by Chu, Rivera and Loftin (2000) do not bear out the same conclusions and on some points, come to opposite conclusions. Moreover, Andreescu, Shutt and Vito (2011) found that religiosity was strongly associated with homicide rates, even when controlling for structural factors. Areas in Appalachian counties with more conservative Protestants had more homicides and areas with more mainstream Protestants and more Roman Catholics had fewer homicides. Belief in a more conservative religion is probably associated with more conservative beliefs, including the use of violence when honor is at stake (Barber, 2009); Lee and Ousey (2012) note that there are likely both ethnic/national and religious factors at the root of the Southern subculture of violence. The South consistently has higher homicide rates than any other region of the country and it appears that Southerners are more likely to be involved in argument-precipitated (i.e., expressive) homicides than others. Findings such as these keep the Southern subculture of violence alive.

Strengths and Weaknesses of Subcultural Theories

One of the main strengths of all the subcultural theories covered here is that they extend the scope of anomie/strain theories. Moreover, they integrate aspects of anomie/strain and social disorganization theories, recognizing that features of both of these theories may be important in explaining crime. Subcultural theories bring new focus to the ways in which members of the lower class, especially youth, adapt to their inability to attain goals. Subcultural theories also explain intergenerational patterns of value transmission that serve to maintain deviant and criminal behavior. The main weakness of subcultural theories is that they only explain crime and delinquency among a given subculture. They do not well explain middle class or white collar crime. Moreover, debate exists as to whether there exists a subculture that is defined by values that condone antisocial behavior (Walsh and Hemmens, 2011).

Conclusion: Policy Implications of Social Structural Perspectives

Social Disorganization

If the causes of crime are socially disorganized neighborhoods, what can be done to help organize these neighborhoods and assist residents in developing a sense of collective efficacy that will be useful in the exercise of informal social control? Some attempts have come in the form of programs designed to give youth a number of legitimate opportunities outside of school and work. Indeed one such program was devised by one of the architects of social disorganization theory, Clifford Shaw. His Chicago Area Project (CAP) aimed to increase informal social control and social organization and to overcome the influences of delinquent peers by providing conventional ones. Local clubs and groups run by prosocial adults were provided and they organized camps, athletics, recreational programs and other activities for young people. Social workers on the street helped resolve conflicts among gang members and intercede during contact with the police; the Project also encouraged residents to form neighborhood groups to address problems together in an effort to promote collective efficacy. Evaluations of CAP decades after its implementation have revealed mixed success (Kobrin, 1959; Finestone, 1976; Schlossman and Sedlak, 1983; Schlossman, Shavelson, Sedlak and Cobb, 1984). For example, delinquency was reduced in some neighborhoods where CAP was strong, but it is unclear if CAP was the main reason for the reduction and there was a great deal of variation in the way that CAP was implemented across the city and in its most disorganized neighborhoods.

Anomie/Strain

If the root cause of crime is the domination of the economy over all other institutions as institutional anomie theory says, what can be done to reduce it? Rosenfeld and Messner (2010) point to the robust economy in the 1990s in the United States as one of the reasons for the precipitous crime drop during that time. They also point to the mass incarceration in the United States between 1980 and 2000 as a factor in the crime drop. During those two decades, the prison population in the United States quadrupled. Rosenfeld and Messner (2010) maintain that the strong economy and the concomitant crime drop is consistent with institutional anomie theory—there were plenty of legitimate opportunities to earn a living, so less need to commit crime. However, mass incarceration is only a superficial solution to the American crime problem and one that does not address the underlying causes of criminality. Rather, the solution to the crime problem proposed by institutional anomie includes decommodification as described above, as well as social welfare programs that protect people against the ebb and flow of the economy.

If the root cause of crime is strain, what can be done to reduce it? In fact, the ideas of anomie/strain theory have informed major policy implementations in the United States. President Johnson's War on Poverty of 1964 was born out of the idea that poverty is a major strain and reducing poverty and equalizing opportunities for success would reduce crime. War on Poverty programs included Head Start, Job Corps and the Community Action Program. In fact, the models for these programs were created by none other than Richard Cloward and Lloyd Ohlin, who devised the Mobilization for Youth program in New York. Their program attempted to increase legitimate employment and educational opportunities for young people. While many young people had increased access to legitimate opportunities between the 1960s and the 1990s thanks to these programs and others like them, the United States underwent a substantial increase in crime during these decades, causing conservatives to decry social welfare as ineffectual in preventing crime (Walsh and Hemmens, 2011; for more on the way conservatism fueled changes in criminal justice policy, see Chapter 15).

Remember that Agnew (2002) believes that there are not just one but several sources of strain. To reduce or eliminate crime, we need to reduce strains and we can do that,

Agnew (2010a) says, in three different ways. First, we can alter the environment that includes the family, peers, work, school and community. Altering the environment can take several different forms. First, we can try to eliminate strains. Programs that are designed to eliminate child abuse and bullying, for example, aim to change a strain-producing environment. We can also alter strains to make them less conducive to crime. Efforts here might include raising the minimum wage and providing benefits through jobs, providing job training programs, ensuring that those subject to sanctions (from parents, teachers or the criminal justice system) have a chance to voice their opinions and that sanctions are applied fairly and consistently and lastly, targeting those who appear to be at risk of criminal coping for extra monitoring and support. We can also make it easier for people to avoid strains. Practices that make the consequences of rule breaking well known are promising, as are providing adolescents with mechanisms for changing classes to avoid teachers or peers with whom they have difficulty. We can also remove individuals from strains, such as abusive environments, where appropriate. In addition to the programs, policies and practices alluded to above, Agnew (2010a) advocates two other ways to alter the environment to reduce strains that have not yet been tried, namely the creation of strain responders and social support centers.

The second way that Agnew (2010a) maintains we can reduce strains is to alter the characteristics of the individual. For those young people who have the traits of low constraint and negative emotionality, programs in which they learn anger management, problem solving and social skills and how to exercise greater self-control may be useful in helping them avoid strains. We might also teach people to interpret the environment in a way that minimizes strain. Programs that help individuals, especially those with negative emotionality, change the way in which they perceive the actions of others may be helpful here. The third and final way in which Agnew (2010a) believes we can reduce strain is to reduce the likelihood that people will use crime to cope with the strains they do experience. One obvious way to do this is to improve people's coping skills so that they might be able to effectively handle a wide variety of situations. Programs that increase individuals' levels of social support and social control, such as mentoring and school-based programs, as well as those programs that help young people resist peer pressure are promising.

Subcultural

If subcultural theories explain gang formation and gangs commit crime, what can be done to reduce the allure of gangs for young people? One obvious policy implication here is to provide employment opportunities to young people that are not tied to extensive schooling and that permit them to earn a living wage. However, for some young people, the draw of the gang, with its provision of economic opportunities as well as friendship and family, may prove too strong even in the face of increased legitimate employment opportunities.

One attempt to combat delinquency on the part of gangs came in the form of the Boston Mid-City Project. Based on Miller's (1958) ideas, the project ultimately involved detached workers, mostly graduate students in the social sciences, who identified a number of gangs and gang members. The workers arranged prosocial activities for the gang members and served as conventional role models with whom the gang members could have regular contact. The project was not implemented as initially planned and data collected by project staff did not reveal a reduction in deviance or crime on the part of gang members who participated (Miller, 1958, 1962; Lundman, 1993).

More modern-day programs such as G.R.E.A.T. (Gang Resistance Education and Training) are designed to promote anti-gang and anti-drug attitudes as well as reduce gang involvement and improve relations with law enforcement. While participation in G.R.E.A.T. appeared to be associated with pro-police attitudes, anti-gang attitudes, less victimization, less risk taking and more association with prosocial peers, it did not appear to reduce gang membership or delinquent behavior (Esbensen, Osgood, Taylor, Peterson and Freng 2001; Esbensen, 2004). Though redesigned in part because of these disappointing results, G.R.E.A.T. does not appear to be based on the principles of any criminological theory. Akers (2010) maintains G.R.E.A.T. implicitly acknowledges that social learning is important in explaining how and why young people join gangs but confusingly, utilizes practices, such as having a police officer deliver presentations to students and occasionally parents, that are not in accord with the theory. Akers (2010) levels similar criticisms against Drug Abuse Resistance Education, the D.A.R.E. program, and many robust evaluations of the D.A.R.E. reveal the program has no long term impact on drug use among youth (see especially Rosenbaum and Hanson, 1998; Rosenbaum, 2007 and also Berman and Fox, 2009).[11]

One of the lingering challenges in solving the gang problem is that there has been very little deliberate effort to link theories of gang formation with gang policy. That is, what we know about the reasons for and mechanisms behind gang formation and membership at individual, group and macro levels have not been explicitly referred to when designing anti-gang policies. The exceptions to this generality lie at the macro level; one intervention, the Boston Gun Project and its operational component, Operation CeaseFire, serves as an example. This operation recognized the individual, group and macro level factors that facilitate gang membership and function and derived policies focused on each level. For example, law enforcement made it clear to gangs that if one member engaged in a violent offense, both the individual and the gang as a whole would then receive a great deal of unrelenting attention from law enforcement. This individual level focus fostered group accountability within the gang, which wanted to avoid such scrutiny by law enforcement and eventually made the gang as an organization a partner in the effort to reduce violence (McGloin and Decker, 2010). Maxson (2011) points out an even more fundamental problem, that many anti-gang programs, whether they are focused on prevention, intervention or suppression, do not take into account the context in which gangs are formed and operate, nor do they take into account the processes and structures of particular gangs. Many programs focus on targeting individuals in gangs and even with this singular strategy, fail to differentiate between core and fringe members, stable and intermittent members and former and current members, which diminishes their ability to be effective.

---

11. For more on G.R.E.A.T. and D.A.R.E., see Chapter 15.

Websites to Visit

Social Disorganization Theory: http://www.drtomoconnor.com/1060/1060lect05a.htm,
    https://www.criminology.fsu.edu/crimtheory/week6.htm
Emile Durkheim: http://durkheim.uchicago.edu/
Strain Theories: http://www.drtomoconnor.com/1060/1060lect06.htm
Robert Agnew: http://www.criminology.fsu.edu/crimtheory/agnew.htm

Discussion Questions

1. Would you characterize the neighborhood where you live (or where you grew up) as socially disorganized? Why or why not?
2. Are there any factors besides poverty, ethnic heterogeneity, residential mobility and family disruption that you think are indicative of social disorganization? If so, what and why?
3. Do you agree with Agnew about the strains that are most likely to lead to crime? Why or why not? If not, how would you revise his list?
4. Is Cohen (1955) right that delinquent subcultures form values in response to the middle class or is Miller (1958) right that subcultures' values are not created as a response to the middle class but instead as a consequence of living in the lower class?
5. Which of the theories introduced in this chapter makes the most sense to you and why?
6. Which of the theories introduced in this chapter makes the least sense to you and why?

References

Agnew, Robert. (1997). Stability and change in crime over the life-course: A strain theory explanation. In T. Thornberry (Ed.), *Developmental theories of crime and delinquency* (pp. 101–132). New Brunswick, NJ: Transaction.

Agnew, Robert. (1999). A general strain theory of community differences in crime rates. *Journal of Research in Crime and Delinquency, 36,* 123–155.

Agnew, Robert. (2001). Building on the foundation of general strain theory: Specifying the types of strain most likely to lead to crime and delinquency. *Journal of Research in Crime and Delinquency, 38,* 319–361.

Agnew, Robert. (2002). Foundation for a general strain theory of crime. In S. Cote (Ed.), *Criminological theories: Bridging the past to the future* (pp. 113–124). Thousand Oaks, CA: Sage.

Agnew, Robert. (2002a). Experienced, vicarious, and anticipated strain: An exploratory study on physical victimization and delinquency. *Justice Quarterly, 19,* 603–632.

Agnew, Robert. (2006). *Pressured into crime: An overview of general strain theory.* Los Angeles, CA: Roxbury.

Agnew, Robert. (2010). A general strain theory of terrorism. *Theoretical Criminology, 14*(2), 131–153.

Agnew, Robert. (2010a). Controlling crime: Recommendations from general strain theory. In H. Barlow and S. Decker (Eds.), *Criminology and public policy* (pp. 25–44). Philadelphia, PA: Temple University Press.

Akers, Ronald. (2010). Nothing is as practical as a good theory: Social learning theory and the treatment and prevention of delinquency. In H. Barlow and S. Decker (Eds.), *Criminology and public policy* (pp. 84–105). Philadelphia, PA: Temple University Press.

Akyuz, Kadir and Todd Armstrong. (2011). Understanding the sociostructural correlates of terrorism in Turkey. *International Criminal Justice Review, 21*(2), 134–155.

Anderson, Elijah. (1994). The code of the streets. *The Atlantic Monthly, 5*, 81–94.

Anderson, Elijah. (1999). *Code of the street.* New York, NY: W.W. Norton.

Andreescu, Viviana, John E. Shutt and Gennaro Vito. (2011). The violent south: Culture of honor, social disorganization, and murder in Appalachia. *Criminal Justice Review, 36*(1), 76–103.

Barber, Nigel. (2009). Is southern violence due to a culture of honor? *Psychology Today.* Retrieved from: http://www.psychologytoday.com/blog/the-human-beast/200904/is-southern-violence-due-culture-honor.

Bellair, Paul, Vincent Roscigno and Marcia Velez. (2003). Occupational structure, social learning, and adolescent violence. In R. Akers and G. Jensen (Eds.), *Social learning theory and the explanation of crime* (pp. 197–225). New Brunswick, NJ: Transition.

Berman, Greg and Aubrey Fox. (2009). *Lessons from the battle over D.A.R.E.* Center for Court Innovation. Retrieved from: http://www.courtinnovation.org/sites/default/files/DARE.pdf.

Blevins, Kristie, Shelley Johnson Listwan, Francis T. Cullen and Cheryl Jonson. (2010). A general strain theory of prison violence and misconduct: An integrated model of inmate behavior. *Journal of Contemporary Criminal Justice, 26*, 148–166.

Brezina, Timothy, Robert Agnew, Francis Cullen and John Paul Wright. (2004). The code of the street. *Youth Violence and Juvenile Justice, 2*, 303–328.

Broidy, Lisa and Robert Agnew. (1997). Gender and crime: A general strain theory perspective. *Journal of Research in Crime and Delinquency, 34*(3), 275–306.

Burgess, Ernest W. (1925). The growth of the city: An introduction to a research project. In Robert E. Park, Ernest W. Burgess and Roderick D. McKenzie (Eds.), *The city* (pp. 47–62). Chicago, IL: University of Chicago Press.

Bursik, Robert and Harold Grasmick. (1993). *Neighborhoods and crime: The dimensions of effective community control.* New York, NY: Lexington Books.

Butterfield, Fox. (1995). *All God's children: The Boskett family and the American tradition of violence.* New York, NY: HarperCollins Publishers.

Cancino, Jeffrey M., Ramiro Martinez and Jacob Stowell. (2009). The impact of neighborhood context on intragroup and intergroup robbery: The San Antonio experience. *The ANNALS of the American Academy of Political and Social Science, 623*(12), 12–25.

Chu, Rebekah, Craig Rivera and Colin Loftin. (2000). Herding and homicide: An examination of the Nisbett-Reaves hypothesis. *Social Forces, 78*, 971–987.

Cohen, Albert. (1955). *Delinquent boys.* New York, NY: Free Press.

Cohen, Dov, Richard Nisbett, Brian Bowdle and Norbert Schwarz. (1996). Insult, aggression, and the southern culture of honor: An "experimental ethnography." *Journal of Personality and Social Psychology, 70,* 945–960.

Cullen, Francis T. and Robert Agnew. (2011). *Criminological theory: Past to present.* 4th ed. New York, NY: Oxford University Press.

Durkheim, Emile. (1982 [1895]). *The rules of sociological method.* New York, NY: Free Press.

Esbensen, Finn, D. Wayne Osgood, Terrance Taylor, Dana Peterson and Adrienne Freng. (2001). How great is G.R.E.A.T.? Results from a longitudinal quasi-experimental design. *Criminology & Public Policy, 1,* 87–118.

Esbensen, Finn. (2004). *Evaluating G.R.E.A.T.: A school-based gang prevention program.* Washington, D.C.: U.S. Department of Justice, Office of Justice Programs. Retrieved from: https://www.ncjrs.gov/pdffiles1/nij/198604.pdf.

Fagan, Abigail A. and Emily M. Wright. (2012). The effects of neighborhood context on youth violence and delinquency: Does gender matter? *Youth Violence and Juvenile Justice, 10*(1), 64–82.

Finestone, Harold. (1976). *Victims of change.* Westport, CT: Greenwood.

Ford, Jason. (2009). Nonmedical prescription drug use among adolescents: The influence of bonds to family and school. *Youth and Society, 40,* 336–352.

Frailing, Kelly and Dee Wood Harper. (2010). School kids and oil rigs: Two more pieces of the post-Katrina puzzle in New Orleans. *American Journal of Economics and Sociology, 69,* 717–735.

Gibson, Campbell. (1998). Population of the 100 largest cities and other urban places in the United States: 1790–1990. U.S. Census Bureau. Retrieved from: http://www.census.gov/population/www/documentation/twps0027/twps0027.html.

Hay, Carter, Ryan Meldrum and Karen Mann. (2010). Traditional bullying, cyber bullying, and deviance: A general strain theory approach. *Journal of Contemporary Criminal Justice, 26,* 130–147.

Howell, James and John Moore. (2010). History of street gangs in the United States. National Gang Center Bulletin. Retrieved from: http://www.nationalgangcenter.gov/Content/Documents/History-of-Street-Gangs.pdf.

Huang, Bu, Rick Kosterman, Richard Catalano, J. David Hawkins and Robert Abbott. (2001). Modeling mediation in the etiology of violent behavior in adolescence: A test of the social development model. *Criminology, 39,* 75–108.

Jang, Sung Joon. (2002). The effects of family, school, peers, and attitudes on adolescents' drug use: Do they vary with age? *Justice Quarterly, 19,* 97–126.

Jang, Sung Joon. (2007). Gender differences in strain, negative emotions, and coping behaviors: A general strain theory approach. *Justice Quarterly, 24,* 523–553.

Jones, Robert A. (2011). The Durkheim pages. Retrieved from: http://durkheim.uchicago.edu/.

Kaufman, Joanne. (2005). Explaining the race/ethnicity-violence relationship: Neighborhood context and social psychological processes. *Justice Quarterly, 22,* 224–251.

Kaufman, Joanne, Ceasr Rebellon, Sherod Thaxton and Robert Agnew. (2008). A general strain theory of racial differences in offending. *The Australian and New Zealand Journal of Criminology, 41,* 421–437.

Kobrin, Solomon. (1959). The Chicago Area Project—25 year assessment. *Annals of the American Academy of Political and Social Science, 322*, 19–29.

Langan, Patrick and David Farrington. (1998). *Crime and justice in the United States and in England and Wales, 1981–1996: Executive summary*. Bureau of Justice Statistics. Retrieved from: http://bjs.gov/content/pub/pdf/cjusew96.pdf.

Larson, Matthew and Gary Sweeten. (2012). Breaking up is hard to do: Romantic dissolution, offending, and substance use during the transition to adulthood. *Criminology, 50*, 605–636.

Lee, Matthew, William Bankson, Timothy Hayes and Shaun Thomas. (2007). Revisiting the Southern culture of violence. *The Sociological Quarterly, 48*, 253–275.

Lee, Matthew and Graham Ousey. (2012). Southern violence: A contemporary overview. In D. Harper, L. Voigt and W. Thornton (Eds.), *Violence: Do we know it when we see it?* (pp. 115–127). Durham, NC: Carolina Academic Press.

Lundman, Richard. (1993). *Prevention and control of juvenile delinquency*. 2nd ed. New York, NY: Oxford University Press.

Maxson, Cheryl. (2011). Street gangs: How research can inform policy. In J. Wilson and J. Petersilia (Eds.), *Crime and public policy* (pp. 158–182). New York, NY: Oxford University Press.

McGloin, Jean, Travis Pratt and Jeff Maahs. (2004). Rethinking the IQ-delinquency relationship: A longitudinal analysis of multiple theoretical models. *Justice Quarterly, 21*, 603–631.

McGloin, Jean and Scott Decker. (2010). Theories of gang behavior and public policy. In H. Barlow and S. Decker (Eds.), *Criminology and public policy* (pp. 150–165). Philadelphia, PA: Temple University Press.

McNulty-Eitle, Tamela, David Eitle and Michelle Johnson-Jennings. (2013). General strain theory and substance use among American Indian adolescents. *Race and Justice, 3*, 3–30.

Merton, Robert K. (1938). Social structure and anomie. *American Sociological Review, 3*, 672–682.

Messner, Steven F. and Richard Rosenfeld. (2012). *Crime and the American dream*. Independence, KY: Cengage Learning.

Miller, Walter. (1958). Lower-class culture as a generating milieu of gang delinquency. *Journal of Social Issues, 14*, 5–9.

Miller, Walter. (1962). The impact of a "total community" delinquency control project. *Social Problems, 10*, 168–191.

Moon, Byongook, Merry Morash and John McClusky. (2010). General strain theory and school bullying: An empirical test in South Korea. *Crime and Delinquency, 20*, 1–29.

Moore, Joan and John Hagedorn. (2001). *Female gangs: Focus on research*. OJJDP Juvenile Justice Bulletin. Retrieved from: http://www.west.asu.edu/ckatz/gangclass/Section_1/female.pdf.

Mullins, Christopher. (2006). *Holding your square: Masculinities, streetlife, and violence*. Portland, OR: Willan.

Murphy, Daniel and Matthew Robinson. (2008). The maximizer: Clarifying Merton's theories of anomie and strain. *Theoretical Criminology, 12*, 501–521.

Nisbett, Richard and Dov Cohen. (1996). *Culture of honor*. Boulder, CO: Westview Press.

Nowacki, Jeffrey. (2012). Sugar, spice, and street codes: The influences of gender and family attachment on street code adoption. *Deviant Behavior, 33*, 831–844.

Rankin, Joseph and Roger Kern. (1994). Parental attachments and delinquency. *Criminology, 32*, 495–516.

Rebellon, Cesar. (2002). Reconsidering the broken homes/delinquency relationship and exploring its mediating mechanism(s). *Criminology, 40*, 103–136.

Rosenbaum, Dennis. (2007). Just say no to D.A.R.E. *Criminology & Public Policy, 6*, 815–824.

Rosenbaum, Dennis and Gordon Hanson. (1998). Assessing the effects of school-based drug education: A six-year multi-level analysis of Project D.A.R.E. *Journal of Research in Crime and Delinquency, 35*, 381–412.

Rosenfeld, Richard and Steven Messner. (2010). The normal crime rate, the economy, and mass incarceration: An institutional anomie perspective on crime control policy. In H. Barlow and S. Decker (Eds.), *Criminology and public policy* (pp. 45–65). Philadelphia, PA: Temple University Press.

Sampson, Robert. (1986). Crime in cities: The effects of formal and informal social control. In A. Reiss, Jr. and M. Tonry (Eds.), *Communities and crime* (pp. 271–311). Chicago, IL: University of Chicago Press.

Sampson, Robert and Dawn Bartusch. (1999). *Attitudes toward crime, police and the law: Individual and neighborhood differences.* Washington, D.C.: U.S. Department of Justice. Summary retrieved from: https://www.ncjrs.gov/pdffiles1/fs000240.pdf.

Sampson, Robert and W. Byron Groves. (1989). Community structure and crime: Testing social disorganization theory. *American Journal of Sociology, 94*, 774–802.

Sampson, Robert, Stephen W. Raudenbush and Felton Earls. (1997). Neighborhoods and violent crime: A multilevel study of collective efficacy. *Science, 277*, 918–924.

Sampson, Robert and William J. Wilson. (1995). Toward a theory of race, crime, and urban inequality. In J. Hagan and R. Peterson (Eds.), *Crime and inequality* (pp. 36–54). Stanford, CA: Stanford University Press.

Sanchez-Jankowski, Martin. (2003). Gangs and social change. *Theoretical Criminology, 7*, 191–216.

Schlossman, Steven and Michael Sedlak. (1983). The Chicago Area Project revisited. *Crime and Delinquency, 29*, 398–462.

Schlossman, Steven, Richard Shavelson, Michael Sedlak and Jane Cobb. (1984). *Delinquency prevention in south Chicago: A fifty year assessment of the Chicago Area Project.* Santa Monica, CA: RAND Corporation.

Sharp, Susan, Toni Terling-Watt, Leslie Atkins, Jay Gilliam and Anna Sanders. (2001). Purging behavior in a sample of college females: A research note on general strain theory and female deviance. *Deviant Behavior, 22*, 171–188.

Shaw, Clifford and Henry D. McKay. (1942). *Juvenile delinquency and urban areas.* Chicago, IL: University of Chicago Press.

Sherman, Lawrence, Patrick Gartin and Michael Buerger. (1989). Hot spots of predatory crime: Routine activities and the criminology of place. *Criminology, 27*, 27–55.

Slocum, Lee Ann, Sally Simpson and David Smith. (2005). Strained lives and crime: Examining intra-individual variation in strain and offending in a sample of incarcerated women. *Criminology, 43*, 827–854.

Spergel, Irving. (1995). *The youth gang problem: A community approach.* New York, NY: Oxford University Press.

Steenbeek, Wouter and John Hipp. (2011). A longitudinal test of social disorganization theory: Feedback effects among cohesion, social control, and disorder. *Criminology, 49*(3), 833–871.

Stewart, Eric. (2003). School, social bonds, school climate, and school misbehavior: A multilevel analysis. *Justice Quarterly, 20,* 575–604.

Stewart, Eric and Ronald Simons. (2006). Structure and culture in African American adolescent violence: A partial test of the "code of the street" thesis. *Justice Quarterly, 23,* 1–33.

United States Census Bureau. (n.d.). State and county quickfacts: Map of the United States. Retrieved from: http://quickfacts.census.gov/qfd/index.html.

van Kesteren, John, Mayhew, Paul and Nieuwbeerta, Paul. (2000). *Criminal victimization in seventeen industrialized countries: Key findings from the 2000 international crime victims survey.* The Hague, NL: Ministry of Justice.

Walsh, Anthony and Craig Hemmens. (2011). *Introduction to criminology: A text/reader.* 2nd ed. Los Angeles, CA: Sage.

Wilkinson, Deanna. (2003). *Guns, violence, and identity among African American and Latino youth.* New York, NY: LFB Scholarly Publishing.

Wilson, William J. (1997). *When work disappears: The world of the new urban poor.* New York, NY: Vintage.

Wolfgang, Marvin and Franco Ferracuti. (1982). *The subculture of violence: Towards and integrated theory of criminology.* Beverly Hills, CA: Sage.

Chapter 5

Why Do They Do It?
Social Process Answers

Introduction

Remember that one of the criticisms of social structural theories, social disorganization in particular, is that they cannot explain why everyone in a high crime area does not commit crime. The social process theories examined here attempt to remedy this shortfall, focusing on the processes by which we interact with one another and social institutions or entities. Five social process perspectives are examined, differential association/social learning, social control, self-control, labeling and neutralization.

Differential Association/Social Learning

The theorist most responsible for differential association theory is Edwin Sutherland.[1] Sutherland (1947; Sutherland and Cressey, 1978) set out to devise a theory that could explain both individual and aggregate rates of offending, one that elucidated more clearly how factors such as social disorganization (differential social organization in Sutherland's terms) caused crime. The result of his efforts is differential association theory.

Sutherland (1947; Sutherland and Cressey, 1978) explains differential association theory with the following nine propositions:

1. *Criminal behavior is learned.* Sutherland believes people learn how to commit crime the same way they learn anything else. As we will see, learning is not limited to criminal techniques, but extends to the attitudes that permit crime.

---

1. As we will see in Chapter 13, Sutherland was also instrumental in theorizing about white collar crime; his esteemed position among criminologists is well earned.

2. *Criminal behavior is learned in interaction with other persons in a process of communication.* This communication is mostly verbal, but may include body language as well. This proposition supports the first proposition, as well as the idea that people do not become criminal on their own.

3. *The principal part of the learning of criminal behavior occurs within intimate personal groups.* With this proposition, Sutherland is implying that the media plays a relatively unimportant role in learning criminal behavior.[2]

4. *When criminal behavior is learned, the learning includes (a) techniques of committing the crime, which are sometimes very complicated, sometimes very simple, and (b) the specific direction of motives, drives, rationalizations, and attitudes.* As noted above, learning includes both techniques of crime and attitudes that favor it. Importantly, Sutherland notes that the techniques of crime must be learned from others. They cannot be learned from books, for example.

5. *The specific direction of motives and drives is learned from definitions of the legal codes as favorable or unfavorable.* Sutherland believes the United States has definitions both favorable and unfavorable to following the law, producing a cultural conflict.

6. *A person becomes delinquent because of an excess of definitions favorable to violation of law over definitions unfavorable to violation of law.* This is the key proposition of differential association theory. People become criminal when they acquire an excess of definitions (attitudes) that favor law breaking.

7. *Differential associations may vary in frequency, duration, priority, and intensity.* This is another very important proposition in which Sutherland is saying that the earlier we are exposed to definitions (or attitudes) that favor crime, the more often we are exposed to such definitions, the longer that exposure lasts and the more strongly we are attached to those who provide criminal definitions, the more likely we are to become criminal.

8. *The process of learning criminal behavior by association with criminal and anticriminal patterns involves all of the mechanisms that are involved in any other learning.* Here, Sutherland is reaffirming the idea that crime is learned just like any other behavior and implying that, in contrast to the ideas of psychologists at the time, there is nothing psychologically abnormal about criminal behaviors, though they are regrettable.

9. *While criminal behavior is an expression of general needs and values, it is not explained by those general needs and values, since noncriminal behavior is an expression of the same needs and values.* In other words, crime cannot be satisfactorily explained by the need for money, because other activities, such as legitimate work, meet that need.

Social learning theory can be thought of as an extension of differential association theory and the theorist most responsible for social learning theory is Ronald Akers. Wanting to go beyond an examination of attitudes favorable to criminal activity, Akers

---

2. Debate rages in psychology over whether violent media, violent video games in particular, increase aggression and decrease positive behaviors and emotions, such as helping and empathy. For both sides of this debate, see Bushman and Anderson (2009) and Ferguson and Dyck (2012).

(1997, 2002)[3] has proposed a way to better understand how individuals both persist in and desist from crime and delinquency. In so doing, Akers relies on the principles of operant psychology. At its most basic, operant psychology holds that behavior is governed by consequences. When behavior has positive consequences for the actor, he or she is more likely to repeat it. When behavior has negative consequences for the actor, he or she is less likely to repeat it. Burgess and Akers (1966) maintain that the differential reinforcement of criminal behavior either increases or decreases it, the same as it does for any other type of behavior.

In more detail, operant psychology holds that behavior that is reinforced is more likely to be repeated. Reinforcement can be either positive or negative in nature. Positive reinforcement from a crime might be the money gained in a robbery. Negative reinforcement involves removal of some aversive condition; using the robbery example again, commission of this crime might remove a status as weak or cowardly. Punishment diminishes or extinguishes behavior and can also be positive or negative. Positive punishment is the application of something aversive, such as prison. Negative punishment is the removal of something positive, such as tough guy status among peers. Another component of social learning theory that is rooted in operant psychology is discrimination. Both reinforcement and punishment follow behavior, but discrimination precedes it. Discriminative stimuli give the actor clues as to whether the behavior he or she is about to engage in is likely to be followed by reinforcement or punishment; understanding these stimuli are based on prior experience with them and others like them. Akers (1997, 2002) points out that what is reinforcing for some may be punishing for others and vice versa. For an honors student who seeks the approval of parents and teachers, an arrest is a punishment. For a gang member who seeks approval of others in the gang, an arrest may be reinforcing. Social context is therefore of the utmost importance in social learning theory.

There are four major concepts in social learning theory. The first of these concepts is differential association. Differential association is taken directly from Sutherland's theory of this name and it holds that the group with which one is in greatest contact (that is, the group with which one differentially associates) provides the context in which social learning takes place. The second concept is that of definitions. Definitions are, similar to what Sutherland thought, attitudes or meanings that are attached to specific behaviors. Both general and specific definitions exist; general definitions are attitudes and beliefs from religious or moral sources that favor conventional behavior while specific definitions center on certain actions. Someone may hold the general definition that theft is wrong under all circumstances but hold the specific definition that occasional drug use is just fine. The stronger the attitudes are that favor a certain behavior, the more likely one is to engage in it and vice versa (Akers and Sellers, 2009).

The third major concept of social learning theory is differential reinforcement and it is within this concept that we see the principles of operant psychology at work. Differential reinforcement refers to the rewards and punishments that follow or are expected to follow certain behaviors. The commission of crime is based on rewards and

---

3. Akers has been developing this theory over the course of several decades.

punishments that followed past commission of crime and the anticipated rewards or punishments of doing it this time around. As alluded to above, what is reinforcing and punishing may vary from person to person and what constitutes a reward or punishment may vary as well. Certainly money or material gain may be thought of as rewarding, but so too may esteem from peers. The fourth major concept is imitation. Imitation is defined as engaging in the same or similar behavior of others upon observing that behavior. Imitation is more important in the initial acquisition of a certain behavior, but appears to play a role in maintaining it, as well (Akers and Sellers, 2009).

While maintaining that social learning is a complex process, Akers (1998; Akers and Sellers, 2009) proposes the typical process by which crime occurs. Learned definitions, imitation and anticipated reinforcement, either positive or negative, precede and produce the initial criminal action. Whether the initial act is repeated depends on the rewards and punishment that follow. Definitions may also be affected by the consequences of the initial criminal act; they may become stronger or weaken and undergo revision. Differential association with both conforming and delinquent peers also precedes the initial criminal action and not the other way around, meaning that association with delinquent peers is important in causing delinquency, not just intensifying it.

Research on Differential Association/Social Learning

Testing differential association and social learning theories usually involves examining the relationship between delinquency and association with delinquent peers because it is believed that delinquent peers are the major source of learned delinquency. Dozens of studies by Akers and a host of others that directly test one or more of the four concepts of social learning theory, differential association, imitation, definitions and differential reinforcement, have found support for the theory's hypotheses (see e.g., Haynie, 2001; Batton and Ogle, 2003; Sellers, Cochran and Winfree, 2003; Brezina and Piquero, 2003; Chappell and Piquero, 2004; McGloin, Pratt and Maahs, 2004; Osgood and Anderson, 2004; Triplett and Payne, 2004; Durkin, Wolfe and Clark, 2005; Matsueda, Kreager and Huizinga, 2006; Church, Wharton and Taylor, 2009 for some recent work). This is true of studies conducted in the United States as well as overseas (Junger-Tas, 1992; Bruinsma, 1992; Zhang and Messner, 1995; Hwang and Akers, 2003, 2006; Wang and Jensen, 2003). When put to a test against other theories of crime, social learning is usually found to better explain crime than those other theories and when integrated into other theories of crime, social learning concepts are typically the most important in terms of ability to explain criminal involvement (Huang, Kosterman, Catalano, Hawkins and Abbott, 2001; Jang, 2002; Rebellon, 2002; Hwang and Akers, 2003, 2006; Preston, 2006; Neff and Waite, 2007; but importantly, see Pratt and Cullen, 2000). Moreover, the relationship between social learning variables and delinquency ranges from moderate to strong across these studies and there is very little evidence reported in the literature that runs contrary to the theory (Akers and Sellers, 2009).

Many of the studies mentioned above reveal that association with delinquent peers is the variable most strongly correlated with delinquency. However, the meaning of this correlation is debatable. It may be that association with delinquent peers causes delinquency, as differential association and social learning theories predict. It may also be that already-delinquent peers seek one another out for association. In this case, delinquent peers might increase delinquency, but do not cause it. Studies that examine young people over time indicate that association with delinquent peers causes delinquency and that delinquency increases the likelihood of associating with delinquent peers (Cullen and Agnew, 2011), leaving the issue at least partially unresolved at this time.

Strengths and Weaknesses of Differential Association/Social Learning

One of the strengths of differential association theory is that it explains how those in lower class neighborhoods who are exposed to an onslaught of antisocial definitions come to commit crime. That is, it explains the onset of criminal behavior. The same can be said of social learning theory. In fact, Akers (1998) has worked to extend social learning theory to a social structural social learning (SSSL) model, which holds that the criminogenic effects of social structures are mediated by social learning variables. Recent research has found support for the SSSL model; Gibson, Poles and Akers (2012) revealed that neighborhood disadvantage influences both the amount of delinquency in which children engage as well as the number of delinquent peers that they have at one point in time but that only number of delinquent peers and not neighborhood disadvantage influenced involvement in delinquency two years later. This suggests that neighborhood disadvantage mediates association with delinquent peers as predicted by the SSSL model. Differential association theory also focuses attention on the power of peer pressure. As we will see in Chapter 7, young people are responsible for much of the crime committed and it cannot be a coincidence that the commission of crime is happening during the years in which young people spend more time with friends than with others they know. Relationships with peers are therefore very important. One of the great strengths of social learning theory is that it seeks to explain exactly how people learn criminal definitions and the mechanisms by which criminal behavior persists and desists. Social learning theory in particular is highly regarded by criminologists and is frequently rated as one of the strongest and most important theories of crime.

The main weakness of differential association theory is that it neglects the idea that birds of a feather may flock together. As alluded to above, it does not satisfactorily address the notion that delinquents may seek one another out for peer groups and while those groups may serve to amplify delinquency, they do not cause it. If the point of a criminological theory is to explain crime causation, this is a potentially serious blow to differential association theory. Gottfredson (2006) claims that most evidence points to already similar peers associating with one another, though Akers addresses (1999, p. 480) the birds of a feather problem by noting that "if you lie down with dogs, you get up with fleas." Another weakness of differential association theory as pointed out by Warr (2000) is that it does not distinguish between those who wholeheartedly accept criminal definitions and engage in crime and those who engage in criminal activity but do not accept those definitions as right or correct. One weakness of social learning theory is that it appears to assume that everyone has the same capacity for learning and ability to respond with their future behavior to the consequences of their past behavior (Cao, 2004).

Social Control

Many of the theories we have described thus far ask and attempt to answer the question why do people commit crime. Social control theory, especially its most famous version devised by Travis Hirschi, social bond theory, takes the opposite approach. Instead of asking why people commit crime, social bond theory starts from the proposition that our natural inclination as human beings is the pursuit of pleasure and the avoidance of pain. If this natural inclination is common to all human beings, the question is no longer why do people commit crime because the clear answer is that crime provides immediate gratification. Instead, the question becomes why do people refrain from crime commission. Hirschi (1969) attempts to answer this question with his social bond theory.

At its essence, social bond theory holds that it is our bonds to various social institutions and entities that prevent us from committing crime. Among the institutions and entities implicated in social bond theory are families, schools, jobs and peers. Hirschi (1969) proposes four elements of the social bond; people who have these elements are bonded to social institutions and entities and will refrain from crime while those who lack the elements have little stopping them from committing crime. When one element is strong, the others will be strong as well. When one element is weak, the others will be weak, as well.

1. *Attachment*: This can be thought of as the emotional part of the bond to various social institutions and entities and it serves as the foundation for the other elements. Attachment is the degree to which we have close ties to others, affection for them and care about what they think. Much of what we do involves seeking approval from parents, teachers, friends and bosses and demonstrating a commitment to shared norms and values. For those lacking attachment, the informal social control exerted by the desire for approval and to be looked upon favorably by others is absent.

2. *Commitment*: This can be thought of as the rational part of the bond and refers to longtime investment in a law abiding career and lifestyle. Those who have spent years or decades committed to lawful living are unlikely to engage in crime because to do so might ruin everything they have worked for. In contrast, people who drop out of school or who are unemployed have not demonstrated a long term commitment to social institutions and entities and for them, the risk of crime is greater.

3. *Involvement*: This can be thought of as time spent in conventional activities. People who go to school, work and spend time with law abiding peers have very little time and probably very little opportunity to commit crime. Those who are not involved in conventional activities such as these have more time and resources to devote to criminal activity.

4. *Belief*: This can be thought of as the acceptance of conventional values and norms and the ways in which these values and norms serve to regulate conduct. People who have the elements of attachment, commitment and involvement are likely to believe in conventional morality. In contrast, those lacking attachment, commitment and involvement are less likely to believe in conventional morality and more likely to act in their self-interest.

Research on Social Control

When Hirschi (1969) proposed his social bond theory for the first time, one of the most important things he did was to make his concepts, notably the four elements of the social bond, measurable. In so doing, he set a precedent for future theorists to operationalize their concepts as well. Research on social bond theory has found support for the tenets of the theory. For example, Junger-Tas (1992) found that bonds to family, school and peers were inversely related to self-reported and officially recorded frequency of offending over time; strong bonds were associated with less offending and if bonds weaken, offending increases. Attachment to both parents in a two parent home insulates against delinquency (Rankin and Kern, 1994). Lieber, Mack and Featherstone (2009) found that the level of maternal attachment predicted delinquent behavior for whites, African Americans and Hispanics; those with greater maternal attachment self-reported less delinquency. Greater attachment and commitment to school is associated with lower levels of misbehavior in school (Stewart, 2003) and with lower levels of delinquency for both white and African American children (Cernkovich and Giordano, 1992). Strong bonds to both family and school predict low levels of illegal use of prescription drugs among a large sample of both whites and minorities (Ford, 2009). However, Peguero, Popp, Latimore, Shekarkhar and Koo (2011) found that while attachment and commitment were associated with less misbehavior in school for white students, attachment and commitment were not associated with less school misbehavior for African Americans, as social bond theory would predict. The authors suggest that that misbehavior among African American students may be a way to avoid or reduce the chances of victimization while at school. In fact, victimization while at school may serve to undermine the social bond to school (Popp and Peguero, 2012).

Strengths and Weaknesses of Social Control

One of the major strengths of social bond theory is that it emphasizes the importance of the family in preventing crime and delinquency. Parents and caregivers who can foster attachment in children are setting them on a course for strong social bonds that will reduce the likelihood that they become involved in crime. It also provides policy implications that are actually feasible, including programs that help young children start to establish elements of the social bond; there policy implications are discussed in more detail below. Social bond theory also has support in the literature, with the strength of the relationship between social bonds and delinquency ranging from low to moderate across the many studies on this theory (Akers and Sellers, 2009).

One of the major weaknesses of social bond theory is that while it focuses on the family, it neglects the social structure in which families exist and function and the factors that cause them to become weak and ineffectual in the first place (Grasmick, Tittle, Bursik and Arneklev, 1993); this is similar to one of the criticisms of Agnew's GST as seen in Chapter 4. Another serious weakness is that social bond theory predicts that bonds to friends insulate against delinquency and that by extension, delinquents will be isolated loners. However, research has shown that attachment to friends is associated with criminal behavior (e.g., Alarid, Burton and Cullen, 2000; see also the above section on differential association/social learning). Social bond theory also fails to address individual differences in the attachment process. Some children may attach more easily than others. Those who have difficulty attaching may be difficult to parent effectively, creating a potentially vicious cycle. Finally, social bond theory does not address religious beliefs, which clearly represent conventional values. Research has shown that religiosity insulates against delinquent behavior, indicating social bond theory may be overlooking an important component (Johnson, Spencer, Larson and McCullough, 2000; Baier and Wright, 2001).

Self-Control

Self-control theory starts with the same premise as social bond theory, namely that it is in our nature as human beings to seek pleasure and avoid pain. The pursuit of pleasure may lead to criminal activity. While social bond theory focuses on bonds to social institutions and entities and the strength of these bonds in preventing crime, self-control theory focuses on our own level of control over our behavior. Self-control is the extent to which we are susceptible to momentary enticements; those with high self-control are able to pass on tempting situations while those with low self-control are more vulnerable to those temptations.

The most famous self-control theorists are Michael Gottfredson and Travis Hirschi, the same Travis Hirschi who developed social bond theory. Gottfredson and Hirschi (1990) maintain there are key personality differences between people with high and low self-control; these differences and how they may affect crime commission are summarized in Table 5.1.

According to Gottfredson and Hirschi (1990), low self-control is necessary for the commission of crime, but it alone is not sufficient for crime commission. What is necessary in conjunction with low self-control is an opportunity to commit crime. Some people are surrounded by criminal opportunities but for those with low self-control who have few criminal opportunities, their lack of self-control manifests itself in other ways. These other ways include analogous behaviors such as smoking, drinking, taking drugs, driving recklessly and having unprotected sex. While not necessarily criminal behaviors, they reflect the level of self-control a person has.

Gottfredson and Hirschi (1990) contend that low self-control can be traced back to parenting. It is necessary for parents to be warm and nurturing, of course, but they also need to monitor their children's behavior, recognize deviant behavior and punish that behavior to help children learn self-control. Monitoring behavior and recognizing and punishing deviant behavior helps children learn to delay gratification, helps them to focus on others instead of just themselves, helps them to understand that there are constraints on their activities and helps them to understand that violence is an unacceptable form of conflict resolution. This is a difficult enough task in and of itself (ask any parent), but some factors may make it more difficult for children to learn self-control. Among these factors are criminal involvement of parents, large family size, single parent families and working mothers where no acceptable substitute caregiver is

Table 5.1. Characteristics of high and low self-control individuals

High Self-Control	Low Self-Control	Effect on Crime Commission
Oriented toward the future	Oriented toward the present	Crime provides immediate gratification
Cautious and thoughtful	Risk-taking and physical	Crime provides exciting adventures
Patient, persistent, diligent	Lacking patience, persistence and diligence	Crime is a quick and easy way of obtaining things (money, sex, status, et cetera)
Focused on others and sensitive	Self-focused and insensitive	Crime commission produces little guilt about others' suffering

Source: Adapted from Gottfredson and Hirschi, 1990.

present. Once low self-control develops, during the first 10 years of life according to Hirschi and Gottfredson (2001), it is a stable trait that cannot be changed by external sources of social control. Consequently, people with low self-control are likely to fail at endeavors in later life that require commitment, including schooling, work, marriage and parenting.

Because they have a theorist in common and start from the same assumptions about human nature, astute readers will have asked themselves whether Hirschi's (1969) social bond and Gottfredson and Hirschi's (1990) self-control theories are compatible. While the former puts the origin of crime on weak bonds to societal institutions and entities and the resulting lack of informal social control exercised by these institutions and entities and the people in them, the latter puts the origin of crime on the amount of self-control, an individual trait that is present and persistent with or without social bonds. Put another way, the source of the control of behavior as described by each of these theories is fundamentally different. Hirschi (2004) himself has attempted to integrate the two theories. He claims that self-control and the informal social control exerted by bonds with societal institutions and entities mutually affect one another over the course of the lifetime.

Research on Self-Control

When Gottfredson and Hirschi (1990) first proposed their theory, it generated and has continued to generate a great deal of interest and testing. Empirical evidence tends to support the tenets of self-control theory. In fact, a meta-analysis of 21 studies investigating self-control by Pratt and Cullen (2000) found that among the nearly 50,000 participants in those studies, low self-control as measured by both attitudes and behavior was the strongest correlate of crime commission. However, they challenge Gottfredson and Hirschi's (1990) claim that social learning variables can be wholly disregarded on the strength of their theory.

Box 5.1. How Is Self-Control Measured?

When studies such as those included in the Pratt and Cullen (2000) meta-analysis find that low self-control is strongly associated with delinquency and crime, how do the researchers know? In other words, how is the level of self-control actually measured? One very popular tool for measuring a person's level of self-control is known as the Grasmick scale, which was published by Grasmick, Tittle, Bursik and Arneklev in 1993. The scale consists of 24 items across six components of self-control. Examples of the items from each of the six components are as follows:

Impulsivity
—I often act on the spur of the moment without stopping to think.
—I often do whatever brings me pleasure here and now, even at the cost of some distant goal.
Simple Tasks
—When things get complicated, I tend to quit or withdraw.
—I frequently try to avoid projects that I know will be difficult.
Risk Seeking
—Sometimes I will take a risk just for the fun of it.
—I sometimes find it exciting to do things for which I might get in trouble.
Physical Activities
—If I had a choice, I would almost always rather do something physical than something mental.
—I like to get out and do things more than I like to read or contemplate ideas.
Self-Centered
—If things I do upset people, it's their problem not mine.
—I will try to get the things I want even when I know it's causing problems for other people.
Temper
—I lose my temper pretty easily.
—When I'm really angry, other people better stay away from me (Grasmick Tittle, Bursik and Arneklev, 1993, pp. 14–15).

Respondents are presented with a Likert scale from one to four for each item on the scale where one is strongly disagree and four is strongly agree so that a higher score is indicative of low self-control. The Grasmick scale has become a standard measure of self-control in studies designed to test the theory (e.g., Pratt and Cullen, 2000; DeLisi, Hochstettler and Murphy, 2003), though not all researchers agree it is the best way to measure the concept (Higgins, 2007).

Another area of research on self-control theory focuses on the stability and origin of self-control over the lifetime. Gottfredson and Hirschi (1990) maintain that once a person's level of self-control is established in the first decade of life, it does not change. Moffitt (2012) found that low self-control in childhood was associated with higher crime and substance abuse as well as lower wealth and physical health in adulthood. Hay and Forest (2006) found that the level of self-control is stable for most people from childhood to adolescence, but that it changes for some as well. More recently, Na and Paternoster (2012) examined differences in self-control from childhood to adolescence for two groups. The caregivers of one group, the treatment group, received training in effective childrearing practices. The caregivers of the second group, the control group, received no such training. The children of the caregivers who received effectiveness training showed greater gains in self-control that the children of those in the control group, revealing that self-control is malleable and responsive to deliberate attempts to raise its level; for more on the notion that self-control can change, see LeBlanc (2012).

On the specific point that low self-control results from inadequate parenting, Teasdale and Silver (2009) found that in contrast to what self-control theory would predict, neighborhood disadvantage significantly predicts the level of self-control of adolescents when other variables, including demographics, family characteristics and social integration are controlled for. Moreover, some recent research points to a genetic component of self-control; Gottfredson and Hirschi (1990) famously denied a genetic component of both self-control and delinquency. Using data from the Add Health survey, Boisvert, Wright, Knopik and Vaske (2012) found that a moderate 33 to 45 percent of the variance in low self-control was attributed to genetic influences and that about a third to a half of the variance in overall delinquency, nonviolent delinquency and violent delinquency was attributed to genetic influences. The remaining variance in delinquency was attributed to nonshared environmental factors. These results are in line with hundreds of other studies (Moffitt, 2005) that show genetic factors are important in explaining variation in antisocial behavior. Boisvert and colleagues' (2012) work indicates that a closer inspection of the role of genetics in the development of low self-control is warranted.

Strengths and Weaknesses of Self-Control

One of the great strengths of self-control theory is its parsimony. It proposes that a single, measurable trait is largely responsible for criminal behavior. The idea that low self-control is at the root of crime is in accord with what appears to be the impulsivity that characterizes most crime. Self-control theory has received a great deal of support in the literature (see, e.g., Pratt and Cullen, 2000 for a domestic support and Vazsonyi, Pickering, Junger, Hessing, 2001for international support). These strengths are impressive and self-control is a very highly regarded theory, but self-control theory does have its weaknesses. The same criticism that Grasmick and colleagues (1993) leveled against social bond theory, namely that it ignores the causes of the weakening of families and focuses only on the consequences, can be similarly leveled against self-control theory. Self-control theory purports to be a general theory of crime causation, meaning it should apply equally well to all kinds of crime. Some crimes, though, such as white collar crime and serial murder, have extensive planning periods. Moreover, the people who commit these crimes tend to be highly specialized in these specific crimes; self-control theory predicts that criminals tend to be generalists. Another weakness of self-control theory is that it appears to neglect the difficulty involved in instilling self-control in some children. This difficulty, which may have a genetic basis, may cause even the most well-intentioned parents to be less diligent about monitoring, recognizing and punishing certain behaviors (Walsh and Hemmens, 2011). And as we have seen, there is some evidence that self-control has a genetic basis and that it can be altered through deliberate effort, neither of which the theory predicts.

Labeling

Most of the theories covered thus far are focused on the individual actor and possible reasons why he or she may commit crime. Labeling theory (also called social reaction theory) focuses instead on the reactor, the criminal justice system, and is concerned with the power of labels that it applies. There are two theorists closely associated with labeling theory. The first is Frank Tannenbaum (1938), who maintained that if we want to better understand how a person becomes criminal, we need to investigate the process of being identified and labeled a criminal. Tannenbaum believed that identifying someone as criminal creates a self-fulfilling prophecy for that person, in which the person who has been so labeled starts to believe that he or she is a criminal and starts acting like one. Involvement with the criminal justice system, instead of functioning as a possible deterrent, actually serves to further ingratiate people into a criminal lifestyle.

The second theorist closely associated with labeling theory is Edwin Lemert. Lemert's (1952) main contribution to labeling theory was to distinguish between primary and secondary deviance. Primary deviance is a criminal action that results in initial contact with the criminal justice system. Though many theories of crime are concerned with this initial law breaking, labeling theory is not because at that point, engaging in criminal activity is not part of the self-concept. Labeling theory is concerned with what happens after criminal activity is detected and officially labeled as such. Secondary deviance results from societal reaction to primary deviance. The stigma of being labeled a criminal may increase criminal behavior beyond what would have occurred without the label. There are two ways in which this may occur. First, people may internalize the label put on them by the criminal justice system ("They say I'm a criminal, so I'm going to act like one."). Second, the label itself may block opportunities for legitimate success, including in education and employment (on the latter point, see Pager, 2003; Western, 2002, 2006) as well as diminish contact with law abiding friends and family members. Inability to secure legitimate employment and spend time with law abiding peers may steer people who have been labeled toward criminal careers and toward other criminals. Figure 5.1 shows the labeling process and its outcomes.

Research on Labeling

Labeling theory enjoyed a great deal of popularity in the 1960s and early 1970s. One of the reasons for this is that the theory was novel, putting the focus on the criminal justice system and its role in crime causation. A second reason was the coincidental publication of Howard Becker's *Outsiders* (1963). Becker's widely read work claimed neither people nor their actions are inherently deviant. Rather people and actions become deviant when they are labeled as such by powerful groups. A third reason was the zeitgeist of the times. Several examples of abuses of power by the state, including the poor execution of the Vietnam War, state reaction against the Civil Rights movement and the killing of students at Kent State and of inmates at Attica around this time resulted in a precipitous decline in faith and trust in the state to care for citizens. Rather, the state came to be seen as a harmful agent and labeling theory and its core message that the criminal justice system is responsible for the amplification of delinquency fit

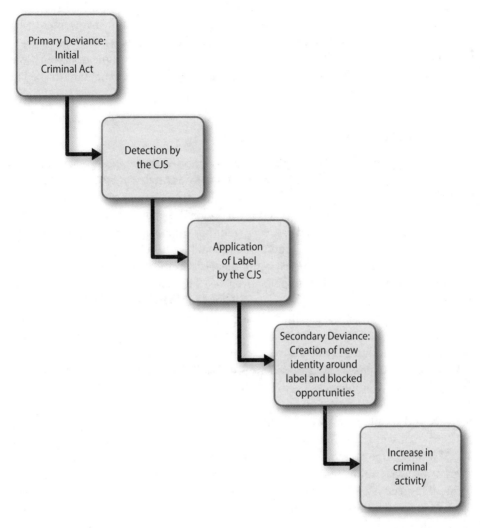

Source: Adapted from Lemert, 1952.

nicely with this revised perspective. The popularity of labeling theory waned beginning in the mid-1970s, in large part because there was little empirical support found for it (Cullen and Agnew, 2011). In fact, one study found that juveniles who were officially labeled by the criminal justice system went on to engage in more crime, but that those juveniles who received the label were at greater risk for crime before its application than the comparison group of lower risk juveniles who were not so labeled. In short, it is unclear that the label resulted in more crime; rather, risk factors present before the label may the culprit (Smith and Paternoster, 1990). Nevertheless, recent research on labeling is supportive of the theory. Chiricos, Barrick, Bales and Bontrager (2007) found that among their sample of nearly 20,000, those officially labeled by the criminal justice system were significantly more likely to recidivate in two years than those who had the label withheld. Bernburg, Krohn and Rivera (2006) found that young people whose actions are brought to the attention of the juvenile justice system had increased delinquency in the future and that increase was largely mediated by involvement with delinquent peer groups. Moreover, Lopes, Krohn, Lizotte, Schmidt, Vasquez and Bernburg (2012) found that early police intervention, occurring in the mid-teens, was indirectly associated with drug use, unemployment and receipt of welfare in the late 20s and early 30s.

Strengths and Weaknesses of Labeling

One of the strengths of labeling theory is that it brought theretofore new focus on the role of the criminal justice system in creating crime and deviance. It drew attention to the effects a criminal label could have on future employment and educational opportunities (ask anyone who has a drug conviction and is applying for a federal student loan if a label from the criminal justice system has impacted their opportunities). It also drew attention to the effects a criminal label could have on family and peer networks. Finally, labeling theory also spurred some theorists to think about how involvement with the criminal justice system might actively be used as an opportunity to reintegrate offenders into society. One such theorist is John Braithwaite (2003), who devised the concept of restorative justice[4] and the process of reintegrative shaming, in which offenders and victims meet in order to shame the offender's actions (importantly, not the offender him or herself) and to provide forgiveness.

The main weakness of labeling theory is its lack of concern with primary deviance. If the point of a criminological theory is to explain why people commit crime, neglecting initial law breaking is problematic. Moreover, if we are not concerned with primary deviance and simultaneously believe that the label of criminal applied by the criminal justice system will result in more crime and deviance, it follows that no intervention should be taken upon discovery of primary deviance. This may be appropriate for minor crimes, but what about major ones? Labeling theory advocates treatment instead of criminal justice system intervention for those who engage in primary deviance, but it also fails to find anything intrinsically bad about primary deviance, begging the question of what there is to treat (Walsh and Hemmens, 2011).

Neutralization

The final social process theory to be addressed here is neutralization theory. Neutralization theory takes umbrage with some of the implications of both differential association theory and subcultural theories, namely that once committed to it, people are always fully committed to delinquency. Neutralization theory holds instead that criminals know on some level that crime is wrong and employ a number of techniques to mitigate the guilt they feel when they commit criminal acts. It also runs contrary to

---

4. Restorative justice and reintegrative shaming are discussed in more detail in Chapter 6.

one implication of labeling theory, namely that people passively accept the labels put upon them. The theorists mostly closely associated with neutralization theory are Gresham Sykes and David Matza. Sykes and Matza (1957) proposed a number of techniques of neutralization that criminals employ to mitigate their culpability as well as their guilt and to reject attempts to label them as criminal or deviant. These five techniques of neutralization are:

1. *Denial of responsibility*: deflecting blame away from the actor ("It wasn't my fault.")
2. *Denial of injury*: claiming that no real harm occurred as the result of the crime ("It's no big thing. That rich dude won't miss the money.")
3. *Denial of the victim*: maintaining that the victim deserved the criminal action taken against him or her ("She deserved it!")
4. *Condemnation of the condemners*: asserting that the behavior of authority figures, including parents, teachers and law enforcement officials, is just as bad as that of the offender ("You did much worse stuff when you were my age.")
5. *Appeal to higher loyalties*: claiming altruistic motives ("I had to stand up for my friend.")

Research on Neutralization

Research shows that offenders do neutralize their criminal actions using the techniques proposed by Sykes and Matza, as well as some other techniques (Maruna and Copes, 2005). Some recent research on techniques of neutralization has focused on illegal downloading. Interestingly, some people who would never steal something like an unattended backpack or purse have no problem with downloading songs, movies and software and neutralization theory may provide some insight as to why. Harris and Dumas (2009) found that those who engage in peer-to-peer file sharing employ a number of techniques of neutralization both before and after their acts of digital piracy. Morris and Higgins (2009) surveyed hundreds of undergraduate students to ask about digital piracy as well as several theories of crime. Techniques of neutralization was supported as an explanatory theory for this crime, as was social learning, indicating that this crime may be better explained by considering more than one theory. Shigihara (2013) found that restaurant workers utilized the previously identified techniques of neutralization to explain their theft, as well as two new ones, denial of excess and no one cares.

Strengths and Weaknesses of Neutralization

One of the main strengths of neutralization theory is that it provides some explanation as to how people can commit to both prosocial and antisocial values and how they can move (drift, in Sykes and Matza's terms) into and out of delinquent behavior by neutralizing responsibility and guilt and repudiating the attempt to apply labels. The main weakness of neutralization theory, and the reason it has never gained a great amount of popularity among criminologists, is that it is unclear whether criminals use techniques of neutralization in advance of committing a crime or whether they use them after a crime to deny responsibility, injury, the victim, et cetera. If techniques of neutralization are employed before the fact, it would give some insight into the causes of offending, or at least into what permits offending to occur. If however, the techniques are employed after the fact, it does little to explain the causes of crime.

Conclusion: Policy Implications of Social Process Perspectives

Differential Association/Social Learning

If the cause of crime is learning criminal techniques and attitudes from others, what can be done to reduce or prevent crime? One obvious policy implication here is to try to replace antisocial peers with prosocial ones, but this is much easier said than done. Programs designed to bring youth together in prosocial settings, such as sports, civic organizations and service clubs are also policy implications in accord with learning theories, especially when they include a mentoring component as is found in programs such as Big Brothers Big Sisters and the Buddy System. Greenwood and Turner (2011) go so far as to call Big Brothers Big Sisters a proven program for reducing antisocial behavior. And a recent longitudinal study of the effects of participation in the Buddy System revealed that for those with an arrest prior to participating in the program, subsequent arrest rates decreased as compared to a non-participating control group (O'Donnell and Williams, 2012).

Some programs have been explicitly designed around the idea that young people learn how to be criminals from their peers. Early attempts to provide youth at risk for delinquency with prosocial peer groups in Highfields and Essexfield in England (Weeks, 1958) as well as in Provo and Silverlake in Utah (Empey and Erickson, 1972) were moderately successful. The Teaching Family Model attempted to connect at risk youth with two prosocial adults who served as surrogate parents to at risk youth. The model reduced delinquent behavior while the at risk youth live with the prosocial teaching family, but did not appear to do so afterward (Braukmann and Wolf, 1987).

The Oregon Social Learning Center provides several programs for youth based on social learning principles. The first, the Adolescent Transition Program (ATP), provides parents of at risk youth with training on effective discipline and socialization skills and on the maintenance of prosocial behavior in the home. Peer groups designed to help youth learn prosocial definitions and behavior from other youth were also part of the program. Parents who participated developed improved parenting skills and antisocial behavior in the home was reduced, but delinquency among those participating in the peer groups actually increased (Dishion, Patterson and Kavanagh, 1992; Dishion, McCord and Poulin, 1999). The second, the Multidimensional Treatment Foster Care (MTFC) program, connects already-delinquent youth with competent foster parents as well as with therapists and participation in this program was associated with reduced recidivism (Chamberlain, Fisher and Moore, 2002). In fact, Greenwood and Turner

(2011) go so far as to call MTFC a proven strategy for reducing recidivism. The third, the Linking the Interests of Families and Teachers (LIFT) program, helps to modify and improve children's social interactions at home, at school and with peers. Those participating in LIFT had fewer arrests, less drug use and fewer delinquent peers than those who did not (Reid and Eddy, 2002). Greenwood and Turner (2011) note that while it does not rise to the level of being a proven program like MTFC, LIFT is nevertheless a promising program for reducing antisocial behavior. Generally speaking, a promising practice for crime prevention programs is to incorporate a cognitive-behavioral component designed to reorient offenders' thinking and actions in a prosocial direction (Sherman, Gottfredson, MacKenzie, Eck, Retuer and Bushway, 1998; Cullen, Wright, Gendreau and Andrews, 2003; Losel, 2007; Cullen and Jonson, 2011).

Social Control

If the causes of crime are rooted in a lack of control, whether the informal social control exerted by social institutions and entities or the control exerted by the self, what can be done to reduce or prevent crime? Both social bond and self-control theories implicate the family in crime reduction. Assisting parents and caregivers with fostering attachment and helping their children gain self-control in the early years of life are seen as important. Social bond theory further suggests children's involvement in prosocial programs run by or in conjunction with schools; vocational programs offered through schools may help to keep older children who do not thrive in the traditional classroom bonded to this institution. The Social Development Model (SDM) combines elements of social bond and social learning theories in an effort to strengthen bonds to the family and to school as well as to facilitate the learning of prosocial skills and attitudes and the avoidance of delinquent learning patterns. SDM was implemented in Seattle classrooms and through families who volunteered. Participants were compared to non-participants at ages 10 and 18 and results reveal some support for the model. Those who participated in SDM performed better in school and were more attached to school than those who did not. There was no difference between participants and non-participants on arrests, self-reported nonviolent delinquency, drinking and drug use but the SDM group had less self-reported violence, less heavy drinking and less sexual activity, especially with multiple partners (Hawkins, Catalano, Kosterman, Abbott and Hill, 1999). Subsequent research on SDM reveals that this model is robust across different populations, suggesting that the provision of prosocial opportunities to youth leads to increasingly prosocial interactions, which strengthens bonds to conventional others, which reduces involvement in delinquency (Sullivan and Hirschfield, 2011) and Greenwood and Turner (2011) call it a promising program for delinquency and recidivism reduction.

Self-Control

Remember that self-control theory maintains a criminal opportunity is necessary for crime and so it advocates the reduction of criminal opportunities by hardening targets and making them less attractive to criminals. However, this acknowledgement and adoption of rational choice principles (see Chapter 9) does not extend to advocating harsh punishment for offenders. On the contrary, Gottfredson and Hirschi believe incarceration will have much less effect on the crime rate than hardening targets (Piquero, 2010).

Self-control theory's main focus is on parents' and caregivers' ability to instill self-control in their children by monitoring behavior and recognizing and punishing deviant behavior; helping parents and caregivers develop this ability is paramount if we want to reduce crime. In fact, Gottfredson and Hirschi (1997) make the bold claim that postponing pregnancy among young, unmarried girls until they are older, with a partner and better able to instill self-control in their children could do more to reduce crime over time than all criminal justice programs put together; Maynard and Garry (1997) echo this view. Short of delaying pregnancy on a large scale, some early childhood intervention programs have shown promise in helping children develop prosocial behavior (Tremblay, Masse, Pagani and Vitaro, 1996; Olds, et al., 1998; Schweinhart, Montie, Xiang, Barnett, Belfield and Nores 2005) and external sources of social control, including schools, neighborhoods, treatment programs and even correctional facilities appear to have an effect on self-control, as well (Piquero, 2010). There is also evidence that programs designed to provide caregivers with specialized training to improve their childrearing practices can raise the level of self-control (Na and Paternoster, 2012).

Labeling and Neutralization

Labeling and neutralization theories have opposite policy implications. Labeling theory suggests that primary deviance should be ignored if possible in the interest of avoiding secondary deviance. Juveniles in particular should be protected from labeling and diversion programs have been instituted to permit juveniles as well as some adults with specific issues such as drug addiction, mental illness and homelessness to receive treatment in lieu of traditional criminal justice processing with the hope that the treatment will reduce if not eliminate future contact with the criminal justice system. Another policy implication of labeling theory is the implementation of restorative justice practices in which offenders and victims come together in order to shame the offenders' actions, bestow forgiveness and determine a plan for the offender to repair the harm caused by his or her actions (Akers and Sellers, 2009).

Neutralization theory suggests that officials should challenge criminals' attempts to neutralize their law breaking and to resist the application of a label. If offenders start to believe these neutralizations and fail to understand the negative consequences of their actions, rehabilitation will be more difficult (Walsh and Hemmens, 2011).

Websites to Visit

Learning Theories: http://www.drtomoconnor.com/1060/1060lect06a.htm, https://www.criminology.fsu.edu/crimtheory/learning.htm
Edwin Sutherland: http://criminology.fsu.edu/crimtheory/sutherland.html
Ronald Akers: http://www.criminology.fsu.edu/crimtheory/akers.htm
Control Theories: http://www.drtomoconnor.com/1060/1060lect06b.htm
Labeling theories: http://www.drtomoconnor.com/1060/1060lect07.htm, http://www.criminology.fsu.edu/crimtheory/blomberg/thefuture.html
David Matza: http://www.criminology.fsu.edu/crimtheory/matza.htm

Discussion Questions

1. Do you think Sutherland is right that media plays a relatively unimportant role in learning crime?
2. Is Akers' claim that association with delinquent peers precedes (and therefore causes) crime correct or do you believe involvement in crime precedes association with delinquent peers?
3. Do you believe social bonds, once established, have the same strength or can the strength of those bonds be altered?
4. Rate yourself on the Grasmick scale. Does your score indicate you have a high or low level of self-control? Do you see your score reflected in your behavior and attitudes?
5. What are some potential drawbacks to being officially labeled by the criminal justice system? Can you imagine any benefits of being so labeled?
6. Are there any other techniques of neutralization that you can think of besides the five proposed by Sykes and Matza (1957)?
7. Which of the theories introduced in this chapter makes the most sense to you and why?
8. Which of the theories introduced in this chapter makes the least sense to you and why?

References

Akers, Ronald. (1997). *Criminological theories: Introduction and evaluation.* 2nd ed. Los Angeles, CA: Roxbury.
Akers, Ronald. (1998). *Social learning and social structure.* Boston, MA: Northeastern University Press.
Akers. Ronald. (1999). Social learning and social structure: Reply to Sampson, Morash, and Krohn. *Theoretical Criminology, 3,* 477–493.
Akers, Ronald. (2002). A social learning theory of crime. In S. Cote (Ed.), *Criminological theories: Bridging the past to the future* (pp. 135–143). Thousand Oaks, CA: Sage.

Akers, Ronald and Christine Sellers. (2009). *Criminological theories: Introduction, evaluation, and application.* 5th ed. Los Angeles, CA: Roxbury.

Akers, Ronald. (2010). Nothing is as practical as a good theory: Social learning theory and the treatment and prevention of delinquency. In H. Barlow and S. Decker (Eds.), *Criminology and public policy* (pp. 84–105). Philadelphia, PA: Temple University Press.

Alarid, Leanne F., Velmer S. Burton and Francis T. Cullen. (2000). Gender and crime among felony offenders: Assessing the generality of social control and differential association theories. *Journal of Research in Crime and Delinquency, 37*(2), 171–199.

Baier, Colin and Bradley Wright. (2001). "If you love me, keep my commandments:" A meta-analysis of the effect of religion on crime. *Journal of Research in Crime and Delinquency, 38,* 3–21.

Batton, Candice and Robbin Ogle. (2003). Who's it gonna be — you or me? The potential of social learning for integrated homicide-suicide theory. In R. Akers and G. Jensen (Eds.), *Social learning theory and the explanation of crime: A guide for the new century. Advances in criminological theory, Vol. 11* (pp. 85–108). New Brunswick, NJ: Transaction.

Becker. Howard. (1963). *Outsiders: Studies in the sociology of deviance.* New York, NY: Free Press.

Bernburg, Jon G., Marvin Krohn and Craig Rivera. (2006). Official labeling, criminal embeddedness, and subsequent delinquency: A longitudinal test of labeling theory. *Journal of Research in Crime and Delinquency, 67,* 67–88.

Boisvert, Danielle, John Paul Wright, Valerie Knopik and Jamie Vaske. (2012). Genetic and environmental overlap between low self-control and delinquency. *Journal of Quantitative Criminology, 28,* 477–507.

Braithwaite, John. (2003). Principles of restorative justice. In A. von Hirsch, J.V. Roberts, A.E. Bottoms, K. Roach and M. Schiff (Eds.), *Restorative justice and criminal justice: Competing or reconcilable paradigms?* (pp. 1–20). Oxford: Hart Publishing.

Braukmann, Curtis and Montrose Wolf. (1987). Behaviorally based group homes for juvenile offenders. In E. Morris and C. Braukmann (Eds.), *Behavioral approaches to crime and delinquency: A handbook of application, research, and concepts* (pp. 135–159). New York, NY: Plenum.

Brezina, Timothy and Alex Piquero. (2003). Exploring the relationship between social and non-social reinforcement in the context of social learning theory. In R. Akers and G. Jensen (Eds.), *Social learning theory and the explanation of crime: A guide for the new century. Advances in criminological theory, Vol. 11* (pp. 265–288). New Brunswick, NJ: Transaction.

Bruinsma, Gerben. (1992). Differential association theory reconsidered: An extension and its empirical test. *Journal of Quantitative Criminology, 8,* 29–49.

Burgess, Robert and Ronald Akers. (1966). A differential association-reinforcement theory of criminal behavior. *Social Problems, 14,* 128–147.

Bushman, Brad and Craig Anderson. (2009). Comfortably numb: Desensitizing effects of violent media on helping others. *Psychological Science, 20,* 273–277.

Cernkovich, Stephen and Peggy Giordano. (1992). School bonding, race, and delinquency. *Criminology, 30*, 261–291.

Chamberlain, Patricia, Phillip Fisher and Kevin Moore. (2002). Multidimensional treatment foster care: Applications of the OSLC intervention model to high risk youth and their families. In J. Reid, G. Patterson and J. Snyder (Eds.), *Antisocial behavior in children and adolescents: A developmental analysis and model for intervention* (pp. 203–218). Washington, D.C.: American Psychological Association.

Chappell, Allison and Alex Piquero. (2004). Applying social learning theory to police misconduct. *Deviant Behavior, 25*, 89–108.

Chiricos, Ted, Kelle Barrick, William Bales and Stephanie Bontrager. (2007). The labeling of convicted felons and its consequences for recidivism. *Criminology, 45*(3), 547–581.

Church, Wesley, Tracy Wharton and Julie Taylor. (2009). An examination of differential association and social control theory. *Youth Violence and Juvenile Justice, 7*, 3–15.

Cullen, Francis, John Paul Wright, Paul Gendreau and D. A. Andrews. (2003). What correctional treatment can tell us about criminological theory: Implications for social learning theory. In R. Akers and G. Jensen (Eds.), *Social learning theory and the explanation of crime: A guide for the new century. Advances in criminological theory, Vol. 11* (pp. 339–362). New Brunswick, NJ: Transaction.

Cullen, Francis T. and Robert Agnew. (2011). *Criminological theory: Past to present.* 4th ed. New York, NY: Oxford University Press.

Cullen, Francis T. and Cheryl Jonson. (2011). Rehabilitation and treatment programs. In J. Wilson and J. Petersilia (Eds.), *Crime and public policy* (pp. 293–344). New York, NY: Oxford University Press.

DeLisi, Matt, Andy Hochstettler and Daniel Murphy. (2003). Self-control behind bars: A validation study of the Grasmick et al. scale. *Justice Quarterly, 20*, 240–264.

Dishion, Thomas, Gerald Patterson, and Kathryn Kavanagh. (1992). An experimental test of the coercion model: Linking theory, measurement, and intervention. In J. McCord and R. E. Tremblay (Eds.), *Preventing antisocial behavior: Interventions from birth through adolescence* (pp. 253–282). New York, NY: Guilford Press.

Dishion, Thomas, Joan McCord and Francois Poulin. (1999). When interventions harm: Peer groups and problem behavior. *American Psychologist, 54*, 755–764.

Durkin, Keith, Timothy Wolfe and Gregory Clark. (2005). College students and binge drinking: An evaluation of social learning theory. *Sociological Spectrum, 25*, 255–272.

Empey, LaMar and Maynard Erickson. (1972). *The Provo experiment: Evaluating community control of delinquency.* Lexington, MA: Lexington.

Ferguson, Christopher and Dominic Dyck. (2012). Paradigm change in aggression research: The time has come to retire the General Aggression Model. *Aggression and Violent Behavior, 17*, 220–228.

Gibson, Chris, Traci Poles and Ronald Akers. (2012). A partial test of social structure social learning: Neighborhood disadvantage, differential association with delinquent peers, and delinquency. In M. DeLisi and K. Beaver (Eds.), *Criminological theory: A life-course approach.* 2nd ed (pp. 187–200). Burlington, MA: Jones and Bartlett.

Gottfredson, Michael. (2006). The empirical status of control theory in criminology. In F. Cullen, J. Wright and K. Blevins (Eds.), *Taking stock: The status of criminological theory* (pp. 77–100). New Brunswick, NJ: Transaction.

Gottfredson, Michael and Travis Hirschi. (1990). *A general theory of crime.* Palo Alto, CA: Stanford University Press.

Gottfredson, Michael and Travis Hirschi. (1997). National crime control policies. In M. Fisch (Ed.), *Criminology 97/98* (pp. 27–33). Guilford, CT: Dushkin.

Grasmick, Harold G., Charles R. Tittle, Robert J. Bursik, and Bruce J. Arneklev. (1993). Testing the core empirical implications of Gottfredson and Hirschi's general theory of crime. *Journal of Research in Crime and Delinquency 30,* 5–29.

Greenwood, Peter and Susan Turner. (2011). Juvenile crime and juvenile justice. In J. Wilson and J. Petersilia (Eds.), *Crime and public policy* (pp. 88–129). New York, NY: Oxford University Press.

Harris, Lloyd and Alexia Dumas. (2009). Online consumer misbehavior: An application of neutralization theory. *Marketing Theory, 9*(4), 379–402.

Hawkins, J. David, Richard Catalano, Rick Kosterman, Robert Abbott and Karl Hill. (1999). Preventing adolescent health-risk behaviors by strengthening protection during childhood. *Archives of Pediatric and Adolescent Medicine, 153,* 226–234.

Hay, Carter and Walter Forrest. (2006). The development of self-control: Examining self-control theory's stability thesis. *Criminology, 44,* 739–774.

Haynie, Dana. (2001). Delinquent peers revisited: Does network structure matter? *American Journal of Sociology, 106,* 1013–1057.

Higgins, George. (2007). Examining the original Grasmick scale: A Rasch model approach. *Criminal Justice and Behavior, 34,* 157–179.

Hirschi, Travis. (1969). *The causes of delinquency.* Berkeley, CA: University of California Press.

Hirschi, Travis. (2004). Self-control and crime. In R. Baumeister and K. Vohs (Eds.), *Handbook of self-regulation research, theory, and applications* (pp. 537–552). New York, NY: Guilford Press.

Hirschi, Travis and Michael R. Gottfredson. (2001). Self-control theory. In R. Paternoster and R. Bachman (Eds.), *Explaining criminals and crime.* Los Angeles, CA: Roxbury.

Huang, Bu, Rick Kosterman, Richard Catalano, J. David Hawkins and Robert Abbott. (2001). Modeling mediation in the etiology of violent behavior in adolescence: A test of the social development model. *Criminology, 39,* 75–108.

Hwang, Sunghyun and Ronald Akers. (2003). Substance abuse by Korean adolescents: A cross-cultural test of social learning, social bond and self-control theories. In R. Akers and G. Jensen (Eds.), *Social learning theory and the explanation of crime: A guide for the new century. Advances in criminological theory, Vol. 11* (pp. 39–64). New Brunswick, NJ: Transaction.

Hwang, Sunghyun and Ronald Akers. (2006). Parental and peer influences on adolescent drug use in Korea. *Asian Journal of Criminology, 1,* 59–69.

Johnson, Byron, De Li Spencer, David Larson and Michael McCullough. (2000). A systematic review of the religiosity and delinquency literature. *Journal of Contemporary Criminal Justice, 16,* 32–52.

Junger-Tas, Josine. (1992). An empirical test of social control theory. *Journal of Quantitative Criminology, 8,* 9–28.

LeBlanc, Marc. (2012). Twenty-five years of developmental criminology: What we know, what we need to know. In R. Loeber and B. Welsh (Eds.), *The future of criminology* (pp. 124–133). New York, NY: Oxford University Press.

Lemert, Edwin. (1952). Primary and secondary deviance. In *Social Pathology*. New York, NY: McGraw Hill.

Lieber, Michael, Kristin Mack and Richard Featherstone. (2009). Family structure, family processes, economic factors, and delinquency: Similarities and differences by race and ethnicity. *Youth Violence and Juvenile Justice, 7*(2), 79–99.

Lopes, Giza, Marvin Krohn, Alan Lizotte, Nicole Schmidt, Bob Vasquez and Jon Bernburg. (2012). Labeling and cumulative disadvantage: The impact of formal police intervention on life chances and crime during emerging adulthood. *Crime and Delinquency, 58,* 456–488.

Losel, Friedrich. (2007). It's never too early and never too late: Toward an integrated science of developmental intervention in criminology. *The Criminologist, 32*(5), 3–8.

Maruna, Shadd and Heith Copes. (2005). What have we learned from five decades of neutralization research? In M. Tonry (Ed.), *Crime and justice: A review of research, Vol. 32* (pp. 221–320). Chicago, IL: University of Chicago Press.

Matsueda, Ross, Derek Kreager and David Huizinga. (2006). Deterring delinquents: A rational choice model of theft and violence. *American Sociological Review, 71,* 95–122.

Maynard, Rebecca and Eileen Garry. (1997). *Adolescent motherhood: Implications for the juvenile justice system*. U.S. Department of Justice. Retrieved from: https://www.ncjrs.gov/pdffiles/fs9750.pdf.

McGloin, Jean, Travis Pratt and Jeff Maahs. (2004). Rethinking the IQ-delinquency relationship: A longitudinal analysis of multiple theoretical models. *Justice Quarterly, 21,* 603–631.

Moffitt, Terrie. (2005). Genetic and environmental influences on antisocial behaviors: Evidence from behavioral-genetic research. *Advances in Genetics, 55,* 41–104.

Moffitt, Terrie. (2012). Self-control, then and now. In R. Loeber and B. Welsh (Eds.), *The future of criminology* (pp. 40–45). New York, NY: Oxford University Press.

Morris, Robert and George Higgins. (2009). Neutralizing potential and self-reported digital piracy: A multi theoretical explanation among college undergraduates. *Criminal Justice Review, 34*(2), 173–195.

Na, Chongmin and Raymond Paternoster. (2012). Can self-control change substantially over time? Rethinking the relationship between self and social control. *Criminology, 50*(2), 427–462.

Neff, Joan and Dennis Waite. (2007). Male versus female substance abuse patterns among incarcerated juvenile offenders: Comparing strain and social learning variables. *Justice Quarterly, 24,* 106–132.

O'Donnell, Clifford and Izaak Williams. (2012). The Buddy System: A 35-year follow-up of criminal offenses. *Clinical Psychological Science*. Retrieved from DOI: 10.1177/2167702612456907.

Olds, David, Charles Henderson, Robert Cole, John, Eckenrode, Harriet Kitzman, Dennis Luckey, Lisa Pettitt, Kimberly Sidora, Pamela Morris and James Powers.

(1998). Long-term effects of nurse home visitation on children's criminal and antisocial behavior: 15-year follow-up of a randomized controlled trial. *JAMA: Journal of the American Medical Association 280*, 1238–1244.

Osgood, Wayne and Amy Anderson. (2004). Unstructured socializing and rates of delinquency. *Criminology, 42*, 519–549.

Pager, Devah. (2003). The mark of a criminal record. *The American Journal of Sociology, 108*, 937–975.

Peguero, Anthony, Ann Popp, Lorraine Latimore, Zahra Shekarkhar and Dixie J. Koo. (2011). Social control theory and school misbehavior: Examining the role of race and ethnicity. *Youth Violence and Juvenile Justice, 9*(3), 259–275.

Piquero, Alex. (2010). A general theory of crime and public policy. In H. Barlow and S. Decker (Eds.), *Criminology and public policy* (pp. 66–83). Philadelphia, PA: Temple University Press.

Popp, Ann and Anthony Peguero. (2013). Social bonds and the role of school-based victimization. *Journal of Interpersonal Violence, 27*, 3366–3388.

Pratt, Travis and Francis Cullen. (2000). The empirical status of Gottfredson and Hirschi's general theory of crime: A meta-analysis. *Criminology, 38*, 931–964.

Preston, Pamela. (2006). Marijuana use as a coping response to psychological strain: Racial, ethnic, and gender difference among young adults. *Deviant Behavior, 27*, 397–422.

Reid, John and J. Mark Eddy. (2002). Preventive efforts during the elementary school years: The Linking of the Interests of Families and Teachers (LIFT) project. In J. Reid, G. Patterson and J. Snyder (Eds.), *Antisocial behavior in children and adolescents: A developmental analysis and model for intervention* (pp. 219–233). Washington, D.C.: American Psychological Association.

Schweinhart, Lawrence, Jeanne Montie, Zongping Xiang, W. Steven Barnett, Clive Belfield and Milagros Nores. (2005). *Lifetime effects: The High/Scope Perry Preschool study through age 40.* Ypsilanti, MI: High/Scope Press.

Sellers, Christine, John Cochran and Thomas Winfree. (2003). Social learning theory and courtship violence: An empirical test. In R. Akers and G. Jensen (Eds.), *Social learning theory and the explanation of crime: A guide for the new century. Advances in criminological theory, Vol. 11* (pp. 109–129). New Brunswick, NJ: Transaction.

Sherman, Lawrence, Denise Gottfredson, Doris MacKenzie, John Eck, Peter Retuer and Shawn Bushway. (1998). *Preventing crime: What works, what doesn't, what's promising. Research in brief.* Washington, D.C.: National Institute of Justice.

Shigihara, Amanda. (2013). It's only stealing a little a lot: Techniques of neutralization for theft among restaurant workers. *Deviant Behavior, 34*, 494–512.

Smith, Douglas and Raymond Paternoster. (1990). Formal processing and future delinquency: Deviance amplification as selection artifact. *Law & Society Review, 24*, 1109–1131.

Sullivan, Christopher and Paul Hirschfield. (2011). Problem behavior in the middle school years: An assessment of the social development model. *Journal of Research in Crime and Delinquency, 48*, 566–593.

Sutherland, Edwin. (1947). *Principles of criminology.* 4th ed. Philadelphia, PA: J.B. Lippincott Company.

Sutherland, Edwin H. and Donald R. Cressey. 1978. *Criminology*. Philadelphia, PA: J.B. Lippincott Company.

Sykes, Gresham and David Matza. (1957). Techniques of neutralization: A theory of delinquency. *American Sociological Review, 22*, 664–670.

Tannenbaum, Frank. (1938). *Crime and community*. New York, NY: Columbia University Press.

Teasdale, Brent and Eric Silver. (2009). Neighborhoods and self-control: Toward and expanded view of socialization. *Social Problems, 56*(1), 205–222.

Tremblay, Richard, Louise Masse, Linda Pagani and Frank Vitaro. (1996). From childhood physical aggression to adolescent maladjustment: The Montreal Prevention Experiment. In R. D. Peters and R. J. McMahon (Eds.), *Preventing childhood disorders, substance use, and delinquency* (pp. 168–298). Thousand Oaks, CA: Sage.

Triplett, Ruth and Brian Payne. (2004). Problem solving as reinforcement in adolescent drug use: Implications for theory and policy. *Journal of Criminal Justice, 32*, 617–630.

Walsh, Anthony and Craig Hemmens. (2011). *Introduction to criminology: A text/reader*. 2nd ed. Los Angeles, CA: Sage.

Wang, Shu-Neu and Gary Jensen. (2003). Explaining delinquency in Taiwan: A test of social learning theory. In R. Akers and G. Jensen (Eds.), *Social learning theory and the explanation of crime: A guide for the new century. Advances in criminological theory, Vol. 11* (pp. 65–84). New Brunswick, NJ: Transaction.

Warr, Mark. (2000). *Companions in crime: The social aspects of criminal conduct*. New York, NY: Cambridge University Press.

Weeks, H. Ashley. (1958). *Youthful offenders at Highfields*. Ann Arbor, MI: University of Michigan Press.

Western, Bruce. (2002). The impact of incarceration on wage mobility and inequality. *American Sociological Review, 67*, 526–546.

Western, Bruce. (2006). *Punishment and inequality in America*. New York, NY: Russell Sage Foundation.

Zhang, Lening and Steven Messner. (1995). Family deviance and delinquency in China. *Criminology, 33*, 359–388.

Chapter 6

Why Do They Do It?
Critical Answers

Introduction

More than anything else, critical theories of crime center on how power creates conflict. They are focused on the ways in which those in the upper strata of society use the laws themselves to maintain their power as well as on the ways in which those in the lower strata violate those laws to improve their position. While all the sociological theories of crime focus in some way on inequality, critical theories focus on the sources of inequality and the ways in which inequality (to the exclusion of anything else) breeds crime. They also call for a major reorganization of society in order to increase equality; they are the most political of the criminological theories. Four critical theories will be examined in turn in this chapter: Marxist, conflict, peacemaking and feminist.

Marxist Criminology

The philosopher, journalist and revolutionary behind Marxist criminology, is, of course, Karl Marx. Marx was born in Germany in 1818. His family was Jewish, but converted to Christianity so his father could work as a lawyer. Marx earned his doctorate in philosophy in 1841, but when it came time to look for a job, he had already demonstrated political leanings prospective employers deemed too radical. He found work as a journalist and became involved in political and social issues through his writing (Wolff, 2010). In one of his most famous works, the *Communist Manifesto* (1948), he and co-author Friedrich Engels explain the concept of the class struggle, in which the oppressors and those oppressed are in constant conflict. Marx and Engels called the oppressors the bourgeoisie and the oppressed the proletariat. The bourgeoisie own the means of production (from factories to manufacturing plants to companies and corporations) and do what they can to keep the cost of labor low. The proletariat does what they can to demand the highest price for their labor. Working at these cross-purposes keeps these two groups in a constant struggle in which the bourgeoisie are usually ahead. Though the proletariat wants the highest price for their labor, they often have little leverage to get it because of high unemployment and desperation for work at any price.

Marx and Engels (1948) thought of criminals as the lowest of the low. In fact, they believed criminals comprised part of a third class of society called the lumpenproletariat. As a consequence, they did not develop a detailed theory of crime, but they did contend that crime was a product of the unequal and alienating conditions created by capitalism. Marx (1967) believed many people living in capitalist societies were alienated from their work and from one another. When alienation from all facets of society like this occurs, those who are alienated and who have been objectified by the capitalist system may then treat others as objects, including through criminal victimization. However, because Marx and Engels (1948) said so relatively little about crime, they leave the door open for an interpretation of crime that involves a desire to rebel against the political and economic structure.

Early Marxist Criminology

Writing at the turn of the 20th century, the first Marxist criminologist, Willem Bonger (1969[1905]), believed the exploitation and alienation of capitalism were root causes of crime. He further believed that some people were more at risk for crime than others because they differed in the social sentiments of altruism and egoism. People who are altruistic are concerned with the welfare of others. People who are egoistic, on the other hand, are only concerned with their own welfare and not that of others. Because the capitalistic system is based on competition that pits person against person, we see an abundance of egoism and a scarcity of altruism. Bonger maintained that poverty was the main cause of crime, but pointed out that poverty also affected the family structure, the ability to supervise children and educational attainment; as we saw in Chapter 4, these three factors have been implicated in crime causation as well.

Modern Marxist Criminology

Modern day Marxist criminologists differ from their earlier counterpart Bonger in two principal ways. First, modern day Marxists have a tendency to excuse or justify criminals and criminal behavior. While Marx and Engels (1948) saw criminals as occupying the bottom rung of society, modern day Marxist criminologists see crime as appropriate and acceptable behavior arising from the economic relationships that characterize our society (Chambliss, 1975). Second, modern day Marxists call their earlier counterparts, especially Bonger, on the carpet for including family, supervision and educational factors (that is, individual or non-structural) in his ideas of crime causation. They believe that the class struggle is the only cause of all crime and for Bonger to include individual rather than structural factors in his explanation strays from a purely Marxist explanation of crime and does the field a disservice as a result (Taylor, Walton and Young, 1973).

In his work, Richard Quinney spoke directly to the connection between class struggle and the criminal justice system. Quinney (1974, 1974a, 1979, 1980) believed that while there may appear to be a number of sources of conflict in society, there is in reality only one, that between the proletariat and the bourgeoisie that lies at the heart of capitalism. Even in modern day America, those who do not own the means of production are members of the oppressed working class. Moreover, all power lies with the bourgeoisie and in an effort to retain this power, the ruling class imposes its will on the working class in the form of laws. The laws created by the ruling class serve to criminalize the activities of the working class and the criminal justice system is then used against the proletariat, especially to incarcerate members of this class. Incarceration is used as a tool to suppress those members of the proletariat who cannot find work and may be considering the need for revolution or, in other words, the overthrow of the capitalistic system (Rusche, 1978[1933]; Rusche and Kirchheimer, 2003).

By now, astute readers will have thought back to Messner and Rosenfeld's (2012) institutional anomie theory. With its focus on the dominance of the economy, the pervasiveness of the goal of monetary success and the inability of other societal institutions to regulate deviant behavior in pursuit of monetary success, institutional anomie theory seems a natural fit with Marxist criminology. Sims (1997) believes institutional anomie and Marxist criminology are indeed a natural fit but that Messner and Rosenfeld do not do enough to explicitly acknowledge the reason for the economy's dominance, which is of course the capitalistic system. Capitalism has created a system of workers who sell their labor to the owners of the means of production. However, these workers are also consumers and while they do not earn enough to afford many consumable goods, they are taught to want these goods and measure their success in life by how many they can attain. People may engage in crime in order to attain these goods illegitimately or they may engage in crime because they are frustrated with the system that has created their inability to attain these goods legitimately.

Currie (1997) also acknowledges the connection between institutional anomie theory and Marxist criminology. He implicates a market society as the culprit in crime creation. This market society is characterized by the centrality of economic attainment in all aspects of life, similar to what institutional anomie theory says. However, he recognizes that the capitalistic system is not unique to the United States. It is a nearly global phenomenon but importantly, it does not appear in the same form everywhere. Some countries, especially advanced industrial nations, embrace what Currie (1997) calls a compassionate capitalism that includes safety nets for those who struggle to survive in the system, as well as steps to ensure that inequality does not spread too widely. The United States, on the other hand, embraces a harsh capitalism that includes few cushions for those struggling to survive. The rich in the United States are richer than the rich in other capitalistic countries, but the poor in the United States are also poorer than the poor in other comparable countries. This great distance between rich and poor is a consequence of harsh capitalism and crime is an inevitable consequence of this brand of capitalism, with its inequality, deprivation, absence of social supports, diminished informal social controls, materialistic culture and technology focused on violence.

Colvin (2000) proposes an alternative mechanism for how capitalism creates crime. He believes there is a connection between the way workers are treated in the capitalistic system and the way those workers then treat their children. According to Colvin (2000), those employed in the secondary labor market (in dead end jobs, in Colvin's terms) are subject to coercive sanctions in the workplace. These sanctions include yelling, harsh discipline and termination and they are often applied erratically. With limited alternative opportunities available, workers must stay in these demoralizing situations. The workers in jobs that utilize tactics such as these then use the same tactics with their children in order to produce conforming behavior. However, the use of coercive sanctions in an erratic way actually produces alienation from and weak bonds to parents that create problems later in childhood, such as difficulty in school and association with delinquent peers. Colvin (2000) notes that it is inner city youths who are more likely to experience these conditions and become involved in crime.

Some modern day Marxist criminologists started re-branding themselves as left realists in the 1980s. At this time, violent and property crime rates were on the rise and Marxist criminologists were recognizing that members of the working class ran a real risk of being victimized by crime. They similarly recognized the need for pragmatic and realistic solutions to the crime problem. Recasting themselves in this way, left realists moved away from thinking about the political economic system as the sole source of crime and toward a view that embraced the roles of the offender, the victim, the community and the state. The orientation of left realists is unabashedly socialistic. Nevertheless, they have been criticized by more traditional Marxist criminologists for looking for solutions to the problem of crime outside of the exclusive context of capitalism (Bohm, 2001; Walsh and Hemmens, 2011). For example, left realists recognize that economic policies that allow corporations to move factories and jobs overseas where labor is cheaper and regulations not as strict have disadvantaged many North American workers. This is especially true of young male workers who experience challenges to their masculine identities when unable to find work. They are discontent because of unemployment and because of the relative wealth of other social classes and experience a status frustration that increases their risk of grouping together with others also experiencing status frustration and reasserting their masculinity through violent means (DeKeseredy, 2011).

Research on Marxist Criminology

One of the ideas of Marxist criminology that has been subject to empirical testing is the notion that imprisonment rates will go up in difficult economic times when many people are unemployed. During the Great Depression, imprisonment rates in the United States were indeed quite high, but they were also high during the economic expansion of recent decades. In fact, during this recent economic expansion, the United States experienced the greatest increase in the prison population in its history (Akers and Sellers, 2009). Though studies have shown the unemployment rate and the imprisonment rate are correlated, the apparent effects of the unemployment rate on the imprisonment rate are greatly diminished when other variables, such as political conservatism and family disorganization are taken into account (D'Alessio and Stolzenberg, 1995; Jacobs and Helms, 1996; Sutton, 2000; Jacobs and Helms, 2001; Jacobs and Carmichael, 2001).

Research has shown that crime in capitalist societies tends to be higher than that in socialist countries and this fact is something Marxist criminologists take as evidence that supports their theoretical perspective. However, Akers and Sellers (2009) point out that Marxist criminologists are reluctant to draw comparisons on crime between actual countries that are identified as either capitalistic or socialistic and instead compare and contrast capitalistic countries to hypothetical socialistic utopias. This is no way to test a theory of crime. Akers and Sellers (2009) contend that many countries that identify as socialist are actually totalitarian regimes in which one leader or a small group of people retains all the power and actively represses the vast majority of the people. Though crime rates in countries like this appear to be relatively low (with the important caveat that crime statistics from these countries may be highly controlled by their governments), the fact these countries are identified as socialist is not the reason their crime rates are relatively low. Rather, it is the widespread oppression of the people there that tightly controls all aspects of their lives, including crime. For example, while Marxist criminologists would consider the escalation in crime in many former Eastern bloc countries, especially those that were once part of the Soviet Union a result of their move away from communism into capitalism, critics maintain that it is more likely the economic and social upheaval, combined with the absence of oppressive law enforcement that accounts for this rise in crime (Akers and Sellers, 2009).

Strengths and Weaknesses of Marxist Criminology

Perhaps the greatest strength of Marxist criminology is that it focused attention on the role of power in the creation of conflict. It brought attention to the notion that our very economic system and its inherent class conflict may have a role in crime causation and Marxist criminologists point out that capitalist countries tend to have much higher crime rates than their socialist counterparts. It is easy to draw to mind realistic hypothetical examples of crime that Marxist criminologists can easily explain: the young man unable to survive on minimum wage burglarizes homes to obtain additional cash and valued goods, the single mother with two children who embezzles from her job as a bank teller to help make ends meet and so on.

As with all theories of crime, Marxist criminology also has its weaknesses. First of all, Marxist criminology has been criticized for not bringing anything new to the discipline. Second, Marxist criminologists prefer historical analyses to empirical research, which makes it difficult to measure the extent of support for the theory. Third, especially the first generation of modern day Marxist criminologists tended to romanticize criminals. Referring back to the hypothetical examples above, the burglar and the embezzler are fairly easy to sentimentalize, but what about a murderer, rapist or robber? Fourth and as alluded to above, while the fact that crime in capitalist countries far outpaces that in socialist countries, it is unclear that the reason for this is the difference in political economic systems. That is, it cannot be definitively said that socialism is the reason crime is lower in socialist countries. Fifth and finally, Marxist criminologists (with the possible exception of left realists) have been slow to recognize that the capitalism of today is not the same as it was during Marx's time. Specifically, capitalist countries today tend to have more respect for human rights than they once did (Walsh and Hemmens, 2011).

Conflict Criminology

Inherent in Marxist criminology is the idea of conflict. In Marx's case, the main source of conflict was the economic system itself, which pitted the proletariat against the bourgeoisie in a class struggle. However, others have recognized additional sources of conflict, including Max Weber, a German lawyer and sociologist born in 1864. Unlike Marx, who believed capitalism was such an insidious force that it shaped our very ideas, Weber believed that our ideas shape our cultural and economic systems. Weber also differed from Marx in his beliefs on the origins of conflict. As alluded to above, Marx believed in a single source of conflict, where Weber believed there were multiple sources of conflict. Marx also maintained that conflict would only resolve with a revolution that destroyed the capitalistic system. Weber believed conflict is an inherent part of society and will exist regardless of the political, social and economic systems in place (Walsh and Hemmens, 2011).

Conflict theory, with which Weber is most closely associated, offers explanations for both the law and criminal behavior. With regard to the former, conflict theory challenges the long held notion, most famously stated by Sumner (1906), that laws are the product of consensus among members of society. That is, the law reflects norms and values to which we all subscribe and it is very slow to change because norms and values are slow to change. Conflict theorists challenge the notion that the law is a product of consensus (see especially on this point Vold, 1958). As conflict theory gained popularity in the 1960s, theorists in this tradition began to turn their attention from questions about why people commit crime to those about why certain acts are criminalized and others are not (Chambliss, 1975). Conflict theorists believe, as Weber did, that society is characterized by continuous conflict among various groups (Ritzer, 1992) and that the groups with power are able to enact laws that protect their interest while at the same time criminalizing the behavior of those in other, less powerful groups whose actions may pose a threat to the retention of power by those groups who have it. Characteristics such as class, race, ethnicity, gender and age that indicate one's place in society help to determine who is punished by the criminal justice system. Those who are disadvantaged in life, then, particularly young, lower class minorities and women will be similarly disadvantaged within the criminal justice system (Akers and Sellers, 2009). One set of laws that illustrates the conflict theory perspective quite clearly is that on powder and crack cocaine; crack cocaine is a smokable form of power cocaine that is mixed with baking soda and water and heated until it forms rocks. Until recently, there was a 100-to-1 disparity between the amounts of powder cocaine and crack cocaine needed to trigger mandatory minimum sentences. That is, while possession with intent to distribute five grams of crack cocaine would trigger the mandatory minimum five-year sentence, it would take possession with intent to distribute 500 grams of powder cocaine to trigger the same sentence. Thanks to the Fair Sentencing Act (2010), the disparity has been reduced to 18-to-1 and it now takes possession with intent to distribute 28 grams of crack cocaine to trigger the mandatory minimum five-year sentence. Consider the people who are associated with the use of these two different types of cocaine (inner city African Americans and crack, upper class whites and powder cocaine) and it should be easy to see how conflict criminologists could claim that one group is much more criminalized than the other for the use of the same drug.[1]

On the second point above, conflict theorists see criminal behavior as rooted in conflict among groups. Crime occurs when people, acting as members of groups, act in accord with the norms and values of that group. Their actions violate the norms and rules of another group, which happen to have been enacted into law. Recent immigrants acting in accord with their group's norms may inadvertently violate law. Protesters seeking to right a perceived wrong may deliberately violate the laws they see as unjust. Should the protesters succeed in their quest, their norms and values become law and the previously held norms and values become criminal. This process is probably most easily understood within the context of the American Civil Rights Movement of the 1950s and 1960s (Akers and Sellers, 2009).

Research on Conflict Criminology

Research on conflict criminology takes a number of different forms. Some research is focused on the process of creating laws, in which special interest groups, from farmers to laborers to businesses, can use their resources to attempt to influence legislators to create laws that favor their interests. In their study of the law creation process, McGarrell and Castellano (1991) found that most crime control legislation is targeted at the urban poor. Other research from the conflict theory perspective examines the degree to which there is public consensus on the seriousness of certain kinds of criminal behavior. Probably not surprisingly, violent crimes against people, such as murder, rape and robbery, are judged as more serious than either property or public order crimes, with the latter being judged the least serious (Wolfgang, Figlio, Tracy and Singer, 1985). Another area of research for conflict theorists is the examination of extra-legal variables in criminal justice decision making. Extra-legal variables are those such as race, class and gender that should have no influence on criminal justice decision making. It appears that for serious crimes, legal variables, such as seriousness of current offense and criminal history, make much more of a difference for criminal justice system decisions about whether to arrest, prosecute, convict and what sentence to give than extra-legal variables do. Yet it appears that extra-legal variables play a subtle and complicated role in the criminal justice system. Research has shown that extra-legal variables make a difference when it comes to the death penalty, but not on when it comes to the race of the offender. Rather, the race of the victim seems to be of greater importance, with the murderers of white victims more likely to be sentenced to death (Radelet, 1981; Radelet and Pierce, 1991). If extra-legal variables make relatively little difference in criminal justice system decision making, how is it that there are so many poor African American males in prison? Some research has shown that lower class African Americans are overrepresented

---

1. There is still a great disparity in sentencing crack defendants by race. African Americans are significantly more likely to be convicted of crack offenses than white or Hispanic defendants (Tellis, Rodriguez and Spohn, 2010). Though just 13 percent of the people who use crack cocaine in the United States are African American, 90 percent of the crack defendants at the federal level are African American (Jarecki, 2012).

in the small group of offenders who persist in offending from adolescence into adulthood (Wolfgang, Figlio and Sellin, 1972; Wolfgang, Thornberry and Figlio, 1987). The behavior, lifestyle and circumstances of these chronic persisters (in the terms of Blumstein, Farrington and Moitra, 1985) put them at risk for greater criminal justice system attention, but more research is needed to determine whether other mechanisms are at work in producing this reality.[2]

In contrast to research on the creation of laws from a conflict perspective, there is little research on whether and if so how conflict among groups creates crime. Work in this area tends to center around applying conflict explanations to crime after the fact. Only some crimes, such as those committed by protesters in furtherance of their cause, seem to easily fit with this perspective. Moreover, one heralded conflict theorist, Vold (1958), acknowledged that conflict theory could not explain impulsive criminal acts that appeared unrelated to any group conflict.

Box 6.1. Green Criminology and the Ecocidal Tendencies of Late Modernity

A critical green criminology has emerged in the last two decades whose focus is on environmental issues that result in social harm. Green criminology finds its theoretical roots in the modern world systems theory of Immanuel Wallerstein (1974) who proposed an explanation and comprehensive understanding of the modernization process. According to Wallerstein (1974), the present capitalist world system reflects an international division of labor that determines relationships not just between worker and owner, but between different regions, their labor conditions, their political systems and their location within the world economy. The capitalist core regions of the world grow at the expense of the peripheral or less developed regions of the world. The capitalist core has expropriated much of the capital surplus generated by the periphery through unequal trade relations. According to green criminology, this process contains ecocidal tendencies (Smith, 2010).

Ecocide is the destruction of the natural environment to the extent that it cannot support life. Smith (2010) contends that it is an important task for natural and social scientists to raise awareness of the late modern tendencies toward ecocidal behavior. These tendencies are particularly manifest in transnational crime (e.g., trade and smuggling of rare animals and body parts such as rhinoceros tusks) which could bring about the extinction of many animal species. A green criminology brings a new academic way of looking at the world that includes a political perspective committed to environmentalism and environmental justice that goes beyond the narrow boundaries of traditional criminology. Smith feels this is important because "it is the health of the environment globally that needs to be preserved and protected from the violence and violations of ecocide" (2010, p. 243).

---

2. For more on the connection between race and the criminal justice system, especially the corrections portion, see Tonry (2011).

Strengths and Weaknesses of Conflict Criminology

Probably the greatest strength of conflict criminology is that it recognizes the importance of the power relationships in society. In particular, it focuses our attention on how laws are created that support the interests of a small number of powerful groups. In so doing, it encourages us to ask not just what causes crime but why certain behaviors are designated as criminal. However and as alluded to above, the main weakness of conflict criminology is that it does not explicitly attempt to explain the origins of crime. Rather, it identifies the existence of conflict and cites that conflict as a source of discrimination for some (Adler, Mueller and Laufer, 2001). Moreover, the conflict theory position that laws are created and certain acts are criminalized solely in the interests of the powerful can serve to minimize the very real suffering that victims of violence have experienced (Walsh and Hemmens, 2011). As seen above, there is a great deal of consensus about the seriousness of violent crimes and it is very unlikely that laws which criminalize murder, for example, are created in the interests of those with power.

Peacemaking Criminology

Peacemaking criminology starts with the idea that punitiveness begets violence and no place is more punitive than the United States. The prison population in the United States increased by more than 700 percent between 1972 and 2011. In fact, it doubled between 1990 and 2010 alone. In 2008, it was estimated that one in every 100 American was behind bars, for a total of 2.3 million (Pew Center on the States, 2012). It is no coincidence that in addition to being so punitive, the United States is one of the most violent countries in the world (DeKeseredy, 2011). Many criminologists contend that the United States' experiment with extremely harsh punishment has failed in many respects, including in reducing violence,[3] and it is time to devise another solution to the crime problem.

The most famous peacemaking criminologist is Richard Quinney. This is the same Richard Quinney discussed above in the section on Marxist criminology. Over the course of his career, Quinney's thinking on crime and how to stop it underwent a dramatic transformation. In his peacemaking work, Quinney (1991) contends that crime is suffering and the only way to end crime is to alleviate suffering. Crime and suffering can only be alleviated by peace and peace can only be achieved through human transformation, which itself requires major changes to the social, economic and political structure. Peacemaking criminologists believe our current criminal justice system is rooted in the very problem it is supposed to solve—violence. The War on Drugs and the War on Crime imply in their very names that we should use some sort of violent action to stop criminal activity. This mentality leads to harsher punishments, even for nonviolent crimes, and when those harsh punishments fail to stop crime, we make the punishments harsher still. Peacemaking criminologists believe we cannot end violence

---

3. For more on punishment and the crime rate in the United States, see Chapter 15.

by perpetrating violence (Pepinsky, 2008; DeKeseredy, 2011). The only way we can end violence is by perpetrating peace.

These are nice ideas, but what do they mean in practice? In their rejection of harsh punishments, especially prison, peacemaking criminologists call for the embrace of community-based strategies including alternative dispute resolution, mediation and reconciliation. One such practice that stems from peacemaking principles is that of restorative justice.[4] Restorative justice is a system of mediation and conflict resolution that is aimed at repairing the damage done by the offender and his or her crime to both the victim and the community. Restorative justice programs are focused on modifying behavior, attitudes and cognition of offenders and promoting acquisition of values that support kindness, respect for others, honesty and integrity, all in the interest of reducing recidivism (Cullen, Sundt and Wozniak, 2001). In so doing, restorative justice programs provide an opportunity for the victims to confront the offender and delineate the full consequences of the crime, an opportunity for the offender to tell his or her side of the story, an opportunity for the offender's loved ones (and sometimes victims) to counter the notion that he or she is a bad person and an opportunity for offenders to apologize and for victims to forgive. These interactions start to repair and restore relationships that have been harmed as a result of the offender's criminal actions and in so doing, demonstrate a commitment to reintegration of the offender into the community (Braithwaite, Ahmed and Braithwaite, 2006).

The main theorist associated with restorative justice is John Braithwaite (2002), an Australian criminologist. He does not accept retribution and deservedness as legitimate goals of criminal justice. Instead, he endorses universal human rights, such as those set down by the United Nations (1948) along with respectful listening, mercy, apology and forgiveness as key components of restorative justice. That is not to say that Braithwaite (2002) does not believe in the necessity of traditional criminal justice punishments. He understands that where offenders do not support prosocial values, they cannot participate meaningfully in the restoration process and punishment is necessary as a fallback measure where attempts at restoration are ineffective. Braithwaite (2002) points out that restorative justice principles have been used for millennia and all over the world and though programs employing restorative justice principles have, in their formal iterations, been mostly focused on juveniles and those who have committed minor offenses, they are appropriate for a variety of other crimes, including serious crimes committed by adults, organized crime, corporate crime, political crimes and even war crimes.[5] Restorative justice programs take several forms, including victim-offender mediation (VOM), reparative probation, such as that practiced throughout the state of Vermont, peacemaking courts, sentencing circles, restorative conferences, victim advocacy, victim empathy groups and neighborhood accountability boards (Schiff,

---

4. We touched on restorative justice in our discussion of labeling theory in Chapter 5.

5. As pointed out by Akers and Sellers (2009), the tenets of restorative justice appear to mirror those of the Judeo-Christian tradition (e.g. "Do unto others as you would have them do unto you") and many faith-based programs designed to reorient values in a prosocial direction in order to reduce recidivism share both underlying rationales and guiding principles with secular restorative justice programs.

1998; Bazemore and Umbreit, 1998; Bazemore and Schiff, 2001; Braithwaite, 2002; Van Ness and Strong, 2006; Schiff, Bazemore and Brown, 2011).

One important component of some restorative justice programs and one that Braithwaite (1989) himself devised is known as reintegrative shaming. Shaming as a general concept is designed to invoke remorse in the person being shamed as well as condemnation by others. The traditional labeling done by the criminal justice system is known as disintegrative shaming or stigmatization. This type of shaming, in which the offender's actions and the offender him or herself are shamed, gives the offender no opportunity to repair the harm caused by his or her actions or to reintegrate him or herself into the community. In fact, disintegrative shaming may serve to distance the offender from the community and prosocial opportunities it may provide and lead to greater delinquency, as labeling theory predicts. Reintegrative shaming, on the other hand, provides victims with an opportunity to shame the offenders' actions, but importantly, not the offender him or herself ("You did a terrible thing that had profoundly negative effects on my life," and not, "You are a terrible person who is beyond redemption."). The shame experienced by the offender as a result of these interactions that are ultimately characterized by social approval of the offender him or herself should serve to insulate them against further criminal behavior.

Research on Peacemaking Criminology

Not surprisingly, the bulk of research on peacemaking criminology is focused on its natural outgrowth, restorative justice. Even though Braithwaite (1989) himself proposes that reintegrative shaming (a component of some restorative justice programs) should reduce recidivism, much research on restorative justice is not focused on reduction in recidivism but instead on measures such as participants' satisfaction with the process, participants' perception of fairness, different programs' adherence to restorative justice principles, the degree to which victims experienced restoration and compliance by program participants (Akers and Sellers, 2009).

Nevertheless, there are some studies that address restorative justice and its impact on recidivism. The restorative justice approach is somewhat effective at reducing recidivism and support for reintegrative shaming's effectiveness at reducing recidivism is mixed but modest (Braithwaite, 2002; Braithwaite, Ahmed and Braithwaite, 2006). Rodriguez (2005) found that young offenders diverted into a restorative justice program had lower rates of recidivism than those diverted to other types of programs. A study of one faith-based program that employs restorative justice principles, InnerChange Faith Initiative, revealed that participants who were the most active in the program, especially the Bible study component, were significantly less likely to be arrested up to three years after release from prison. By eight years after release, there was no difference in likelihood of arrest for those who most actively and least actively participated in the program (Johnson, 2004). Agnew (2010) claims that restorative justice can reduce the magnitude of sanctions handed down by the criminal justice system, increase perceived procedural justice, enhance social control and reduce the likelihood of associating with delinquent peers. In other words, restorative justice can reduce strains that lead to crime.

One new area of research on reintegrative shaming is within the context of mental health courts. Mental health courts are specialty courts designed to divert offenders with mental illness away from traditional justice processing and toward mental health and related treatment with the hope that treatment will ameliorate symptoms of the mental illness and reduce or eliminate future contact with the criminal justice system. Ray, Dollar and Thames (2011) found that the mental health court, with its focus on getting participants engaged in treatment, is more likely to utilize reintegrative rather than disintegrative or stigmatizing shaming. They also found that those who participate in the mental health court and thereby experience reintegrative shaming are less likely to recidivate than those who have a stigmatizing experience in traditional court.

Strengths and Weaknesses of Peacemaking Criminology

Probably the greatest strength of peacemaking criminology is that it focuses our attention on the effects of a system of harsh punishment and proposes a different way to approach the crime problem. Restorative justice programs have been widely implemented and while findings do not indicate that these programs solve the crime problem once and for all, they may have some positive effects. If nothing else, it is very unlikely that even the most poorly planned and implemented restorative justice programs worsen the crime problem (Braithwaite, 2002) and with that, peacemaking criminology has given us one more tool to use in reducing or eliminating crime. Restorative justice programs and reintegrative shaming have a practical advantage, as well, in that they can be used in a variety of criminal justice settings, including police interactions (on this setting, see for example O'Mahony and Doak, 2004, 2009), as well as diversion programs, specialty courts, community-based corrections and incarceration, all as described above. Among the weaknesses of peacemaking criminology is that, beyond restorative justice, it offers little in the way of helping us reorient our position from a violent one, with our wars on crime and drugs, to a peaceful one. Reducing suffering for all members of society would likely reduce crime, but peacemaking criminology does not specifically prescribe how to accomplish this, especially outside the confines of the criminal justice system. Moreover, some critics of the perspective maintain that simple kindness will not keep people from engaging in crime (Lanier and Henry, 1998). Peacemaking is also a historically difficult theory to test empirically, though Fuller and Wozniak (2006) have developed 17 propositions of peacemaking that might help to overcome this particular weakness, should scholars choose to investigate those propositions.

Feminist Criminology

For many years, men occupied a central place in criminology in more ways than one. First, the vast majority of crime is committed by men (refer back to Braithwaite's list of facts in Chapter 1), so criminologists were much more concerned with the criminality of males. The theories of crime that have been described in this book so far were developed with males in mind and empirically tested using mostly male populations. Moreover,

Figure 6.1. Number of men and women arrested for Part I UCR crimes in the U.S. in 2010

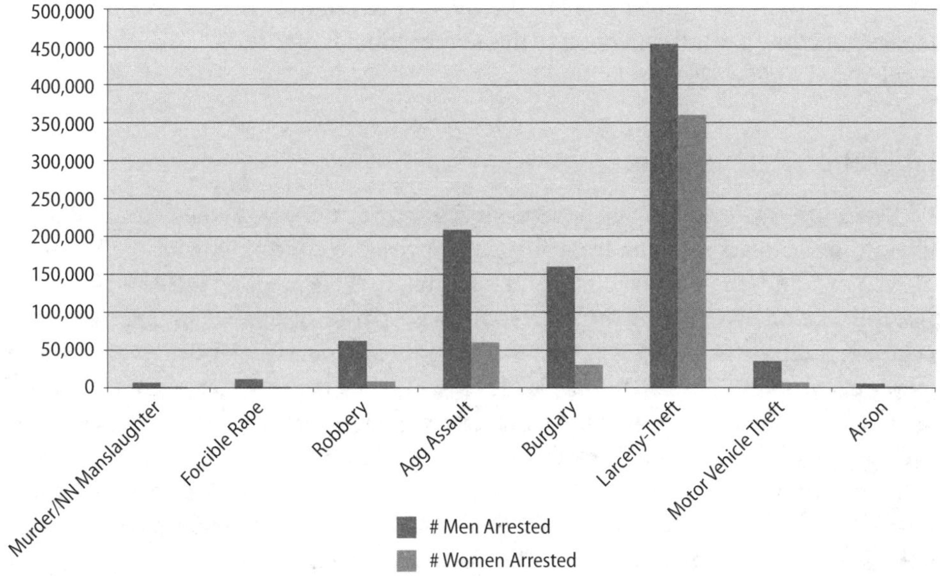

Men Arrested
Women Arrested

Source: FBI UCR, 2010.

crime committed by women was seen as totally aberrant and a result of psychopathology, given that women were supposed to be caring, gentle and passive (Klein, 1973; Smart, 1977). Second, until recent decades, a majority of criminologists were men and as such, were operating from a male perspective on the causes and cures of crime. Since the 1970s, feminist criminologists have been challenging the notion that gender is unimportant in crime. The rise of feminist criminology occurred, coincidentally, with the Women's Movement in the 1970s. During this time, women were joining the workforce and seeking higher education in larger numbers than ever before and as a result, there was a new focus on gender-based inequalities and for feminist criminologists, how gender relations influence crime (Cullen and Agnew, 2011).

Feminist criminology is concerned with a number of key questions. First is the explanation or explanations for female crime. Can we explain crime committed by females the same way we explain crime committed by males? That is, are the traditional theories of crime generalizable to men and women (Daly and Chesney-Lind, 1988)? Some (e.g., Smith and Paternoster, 1987) have argued that traditional theories of crime such as those covered in this book explain male and female criminality equally well, but feminist criminologists argue that new theories or revisions of older theories that place gender at the center are needed in order to solve the generalizability problem. Second, men are much more involved in crime than women. Males commit many times more serious crimes than females (Steffensmeier and Allan, 2000; Chesney-Lind and Shelden, 2004) and though women are closing in on men in terms of the commission of certain crimes (Heimer, 2000), this may be in part a result of changing law enforcement practices (Steffensmeier, Schwartz, Zhong and Ackerman, 2005; Chesney-Lind, 2006) and not necessarily a true increase in crime among women. Figure 6.1 graphically reveals the gender gap in crime as measured by arrests for Part I UCR offenses in 2010 for the United States as a whole.

Third is what role gender plays in the creation of crime by males. Even traditional theories of crime pay little attention to this matter and it is one deserving of investigation (Cullen and Agnew, 2011).

Liberation Perspective

There are two primary perspectives in feminist criminology, the first of which is liberation. Scholars working from this perspective are concerned with the Women's Movement and the social changes it facilitated. Freda Adler (1975) posed the masculinization hypothesis to explain women's greater involvement in crime. The masculinization hypothesis suggests that as women began to experience greater equality with men as a result of the Women's Movement, they began to shrug off traditional roles of mother and homemaker and take on roles traditionally viewed as more masculine, such as breadwinner or breadearner. In adopting these new, masculine roles, some women would turn to crime, just like their male counterparts. Rita Simon (1975) proposed a different explanation for women's increasing involvement in crime, what she called the emancipation hypothesis. Simon believed that as equality for women increased and they joined the workforce in greater numbers, they would have more opportunities for crime, especially occupational crime that were absent in their more traditional roles of mother and homemaker. Simon (1975) proposed her hypothesis in contrast to Adler (1975), who predicted an increase in all types of crime among females as a consequence of greater equality. Simon (1975) believed that the unique opportunities afforded by the workplace would result in an increase in very specific types of crime among women.

A third hypothesis within the liberation perspective is the economic marginalization hypothesis and it was proposed in contrast to both the masculinization and emancipation hypotheses. Both the masculinization and emancipation hypotheses state that as women become more involved in the workforce, they will become more criminal. However, most female criminals are impoverished and un- or underemployed. Crime may very well be the only way they can support themselves and their children or any other dependents (Crites, 1976; Chapman, 1980; Box and Hale, 1984). Freedom to join the workforce is not what is causing crime among women. Rather it is the difficult economic situations in which some women find themselves (though on the point of compatibility between economic marginality and increased participation in the workforce, see Hunnicutt and Broidy, 2004). Fourth and finally in this perspective, Anne Campbell (1999) has developed the staying alive hypothesis, which draws heavily on evolutionary theory. The staying alive hypothesis argues that women engage in less crime than men because they are more heavily invested in the parenting effort than are men. Investment in the parenting effort means that they are less likely to engage in risky behaviors that would endanger their survival and that of their children. When women do engage in crime, it is largely instrumental in nature and designed to increase the chance of survival.

Patriarchy Perspective

The second perspective in feminist criminology is the role of patriarchy. Scholars working within this perspective have been called radical feminist criminologists and currently, this is the dominant perspective in feminist criminology (Cullen and Agnew, 2011). These scholars believe there is a need to develop gender-specific theories that incorporate patriarchy and its role in the subordination of women in explaining the production of crime. Probably the most well-known theorist here is Meda Chesney-Lind. Chesney-Lind (1989) delineated the ways in which patriarchy may contribute to female delinquency. She starts by pointing out the fact that girls are frequent targets of violence and sexual abuse in the home; patriarchy facilitates sexual abuse of girls because it facilitates the view of girls as objects whose sexuality is for the taking by any interested man. Running away from home does not solve the problem of abuse. Rather, runaways are returned to their homes by the police, which does nothing to stop the abuse, or they must live on the streets. Once on the streets, they have to resort to crime, including prostitution, in order to survive. With this seminal work, Chesney-Lind (1989) highlights a prominent theme in this feminist criminological perspective, namely that the criminal victimization of women is a key factor in their offending.

Maleness and Crime

Though liberation and patriarchy are the two main perspectives in feminist criminology, some research has actively rejected the patriarchal perspective and focused instead on how being male facilitates participation in crime. Messerschmidt (1993) contends that men are constantly placed in situations in which they must establish their maleness. In order to establish their maleness, men engage in behavior that has been sanctioned by society as demonstrating masculinity, including seeking independence, pursuing, sexual gratification, dominating women and so on. For white middle class boys, demonstrating maleness (or doing gender, in Messerschmidt's terms) might come in the form of occasional petty theft, but they have other ways to do gender, such as success in school and at work. For minority lower class boys, on the other hand, demonstrating maleness cannot be done in the context of school or a job. Rather, they do gender through repeated commission of violent crimes. With his ideas on masculinity and crime, Messerschmidt (1993) provides an explanation for why men engage in so much more crime than women and why minority members of the lower class engage in relatively more crime than other groups.

Research on Feminist Criminology

Research on the liberation perspective of feminist criminology has generally not been supportive. For example, though the masculinization and emancipation hypotheses in particular are predicated on females' increasing equality with males, there is little evidence that females were experiencing more equality at the time when female crime rates started to increase. Moreover, Steffensmeier (1980) contends that the increase in female crime started to occur before the Women's Movement. The gender gap has remained fairly consistent over time, with men committing much more crime than women and there appears to be no relationship between feminist attitudes and female crime (Chesney-Lind and Shelden, 2004). What increases in female crime there have been are not confined to occupational crime, but extend to other offenses such as shoplifting, contrary to what Simon's (1975) emancipation hypothesis predicts (Datesman and Scarpitti, 1980). Research on victimization and its association with crime as discussed by Chesney-Lind (1989) reveals that people who have been subjected to victimization are more likely to become criminal offenders than those who have not been victimized (Brezina, 1998; Widom and Maxfield, 2001). However, Widom's (1989) robust study found that both male and female victims of abuse went on to have equal likelihoods of offending, undermining the notion of a special pathway to offending for women that is predicated on victimization. Moreover, traditional theories of crime, particularly social learning, social bond and self-control, appear to be able to explain both why a small number of women engage in crime and why so many more men engage in crime than women (Akers and Sellers, 2009).

Nevertheless, some research has revealed that it is useful to examine gendered pathways to offending largely for a practical reason, namely being better able to predict recidivism. The Level of Supervision Inventory—Revised (LSI-R) is a tool used to determine recidivism risk and it is supposed to be gender-neutral. That is, it should be able to predict recidivism for men and women equally well. Reiseg, Holtfreter and Morash (2006) believe that understanding women's life experiences, the contexts in which their offending took place and their social location are important in predicting female recidivism. Using Daly's (1992, 1994) framework, they recognize several pathways to offending that are specific to women, the street women pathway, the drug-connected pathway, the harmed and harming pathway, the battered women pathway and the economically motivated pathway. Women who come to offending through these pathways have very different risks and needs. In order to determine if the LSI-R could predict reoffending for women who come to their offending through these different pathways, the researchers interviewed 402 women about to go into community supervision. They administered the LSI-R during the interview and followed up with the women to see if they had recidivated and if so, whether the LSI-R had predicted they would. The LSI-R correctly predicted the recidivism of those women who followed the economically motivated pathway into offending, but not the recidivism of women who followed the other pathways, especially the drug connected and harmed and harming pathways, calling into question the LSI-R's gender neutrality. Careful investigation is needed to ensure the LSI-R, as well as other supposedly gender-neutral instruments, can take into account women's unique pathways into crime and make accurate predictions based on the needs and risks associated with those pathways (Holtfreter and Cupp, 2007).

Strengths and Weaknesses of Feminist Criminology

Perhaps the greatest strength of feminist criminology is that it turned collective attention toward how social changes have the potential to influence women's involvement in crime and, more recently, how women's subjugation under patriarchy may lead to their victimization and their eventual criminality. In short, feminist criminology convincingly emphasized the need to examine gender as not just a demographic variable but as a way to understand human experiences and behavior. As seen above, consideration and appreciation of the importance of gender-based experiences may lead to better assessments of needs and predictions about future behavior. Feminist criminology is not without its weaknesses. As yet, there is no gender-specific theory of crime. The different perspectives discussed above have not received a great deal of empirical support. As mentioned, predictions from both the liberation and patriarchy perspectives are not supported by data. In addition to the studies noted above that challenge the various perspectives, Campbell's (1999) staying alive hypothesis does little to explain why women are involved in crime, instead focusing on why they are not. Messerschmidt's (1993) work cannot explain why if men, especially low class minority males, are always doing gender, they do not always engage in crime.

Conclusion: Policy Implications of Critical Theories

Marxist Criminology

If the causes of crime are rooted in the class struggle between the proletariat and the bourgeoisie, what can be done to ameliorate this struggle? Marxist criminologists offer one answer: the overthrow of capitalism. The destruction of the capitalist system would eliminate the source of the conflict that causes crime. However, Marxist criminologists recognize that the overthrow of capitalism is very unlikely and they have devised some more practical policy implications as a result. The policy implications that Marxist criminologists, particularly left realists suggest are similar to those suggested by other theories of crime, especially social disorganization and routine activity, and include the provision of community activities, the creation of neighborhood watches, the introduction of both community policing and dispute resolution centers and reducing target suitability (Walsh and Hemmens, 2011).

Conflict Criminology

If the causes of crime are rooted in the conflicts among different groups, what can we do to solve these conflicts and reduce or eliminate crime? Because the existence of groups with varying levels of power is a given in conflict criminology, it is difficult to point to specific policy implications from this theory. That is, if there are always groups that are in constant conflict, crime is going to be a fact of life. Nonetheless, we can surmise from conflict criminology that efforts to more equally distribute power throughout different groups in society should reduce crime. Conflict criminologists tend to endorse policies that are designed to more equally distribute power, such as increasing the minimum wage, implementing progressive taxation policies, developing a comprehensive health care system and the creation of family support policies, including the provision of maternal and paternal leave (Currie, 1989; Walsh and Hemmens, 2011).

Drawing on Black's (1983) work, Jacques and Wright (2010) point out that people with the lowest status in society are subject to the greatest amount of control by the law. That may come as no surprise in the context of conflict criminology, but the great amount of control that the law exerts over these lower status individuals also means that they are less able to access the legal system to solve disputes. With reduced access to the legal system, many turn to violence to solve interpersonal problems, including those that result in some way from involvement in drugs. Another policy implication from conflict criminology for violence reduction, then, is to provide those with the lowest status and the least amount of power with better access to legal channels in order to resolve disputes.

Peacemaking Criminology

If crime results from the harsh punishments meted out by the criminal justice system, what can be done to change the way we punish and therefore reduce crime? As detailed above, one idea stemming from peacemaking criminology that has taken hold in our contemporary criminal justice system is restorative justice. Restorative justice, especially the programs that employ reintegrative shaming, are designed to use the opportunity of involvement with the criminal justice system to help offenders understand the true harms their crimes have caused, thereby making punishment simultaneously less harsh and more effective. As we have seen, research on restorative justice programs reveals that they have modest effects on recidivism. However, Bazemore and Boba (2010) argue that if restorative justice is to have a greater impact on recidivism, we need to move toward greater adoption of restorative practices. That does not mean simply introducing more restorative justice programs. Rather, it means that restorative practices need to be utilized to solve longer standing problems in the community and within the criminal justice system itself.

Feminist Criminology

What does feminist criminology have to say about reducing or eliminating crime? One of the problems feminist criminologists see as producing crime is the patriarchal structure of society. Changing the patriarchal system so that there are fewer inequalities between men and women when it comes to the criminal justice system sounds like an insurmountable challenge, but there are some practical measures that can be taken. Chesney-Lind and Pasko (2004) have suggested that prevention and treatment programs may be preferred over harsh punishments, especially when these programs are equipped to address the unique issues of women who have come into contact with the criminal justice system, including a history of sexual abuse, early motherhood, drug involvement and domestic violence victimization. These issues that are unique to women create a unique path to criminality for them and must be recognized as such. Griffin (2010) makes a compelling case for reentry programs in particular to be modified with special attention to women's circumstances. Other criminal justice reforms that were spurred on by the ideas of feminist criminologists are mandatory arrests in domestic violence incidents (though this may be a double edged sword for some women, as mandatory arrest policies may involve more female victims of domestic violence becoming ensnared in the criminal justice system) and changes in laws regarding rape. Until the 1980s, for example, it was not legally possible for a man to rape his wife within the context of their marriage. Though a very real phenomenon, marital rape was not recognized in the law until quite recently and its legal recognition was due in part to the work of feminist criminologists (Walsh and Hemmens, 2011).

Websites to Visit

Conflict Criminology: http://www.drtomoconnor.com/1060/1060lect07a.htm, https://www.criminology.fsu.edu/crimtheory/conflict.htm
Feminist Criminology: http://www.drtomoconnor.com/1060/1060lect07b.htm

Discussion Questions

1. Between Currie (1997) and Colvin (2000), who do you think is right about how capitalism might contribute to crime?
2. Can you think of any other laws (besides the sentencing disparity between crack and powder cocaine) that appear to illustrate the principles of conflict theory?
3. Do you think there are any contexts other than the criminal justice system in which peacemaking principles, including restorative justice, might be successfully employed?
4. Does peacemaking criminology have a future in the United States, considering how punitive the country is?
5. Does Messerschmidt's (1993) theory resonate with you? If so, why? If not, why not?
6. Of the many circumstances that are unique to women and may be found along their pathway to offending, do you think they are all equally important in criminal involvement?
7. Which of the theories introduced in this chapter makes the most sense to you and why?
8. Which of the theories introduced in this chapter makes the least sense to you and why?

References

Adler, Freda. (1975). *Sisters in crime: The rise of the new female criminal*. New York, NY: McGraw-Hill.

Adler, Freda, Gerhard Mueller and William Laufer. (2001). *Criminology and the criminal justice system*. Boston, MA: McGraw-Hill.

Agnew, Robert. (2010). Controlling crime: Recommendations from general strain theory. In H. Barlow and S. Decker (Eds.), *Criminology and public policy* (pp. 25–44). Philadelphia, PA: Temple University Press.

Akers, Ronald and Christine Sellers. (2009). *Criminological theories: Introduction, evaluation, and application*. 5th ed. Los Angeles, CA: Roxbury.

Bazemore, Gordon and Mark Umbreit. (1998). *Guide for implementing the balanced and restorative justice model*. Washington, D.C.: Office of Juvenile Justice and Delinquency Prevention, U.S. Department of Justice. Retrieved from: https://www.ncjrs.gov/pdffiles/167887.pdf.

Bazemore, Gordon and Mara Schiff (Eds.). (2001). *Restorative community justice: Repairing harm and transforming communities*. Cincinnati, OH: Anderson.

Bazemore, Gordon and Rachel Boba. (2010). Problem solving restorative justice: From incidents and cases to community building and collective outcomes in a new response to youth crime. In H. Barlow and S. Decker (Eds.), *Criminology and public policy* (pp. 254–276). Philadelphia, PA: Temple University Press.

Black, Donald. (1983). Crime as social control. *American Sociological Review, 48*, 34–45.

Blumstein, Alfred, David Farrington and Soumyo Moitra. (1985). Delinquency careers: Innocents, desisters, and persisters. In M. Tonry and N. Morris (Eds.), *Crime and justice, Vol. 6* (pp. 137–168). Chicago, IL: University of Chicago Press.

Bohm, Robert. (2001). *A primer on crime and delinquency*. 2nd ed. Belmont, CA: Wadsworth.

Bonger, Willem. (1969[1905]). *Criminality and economic conditions*. Bloomington, IN: Indiana University Press.

Box, Steven and Chris Hale. (1984). Liberation/emancipation, economic marginalization, or less chivalry. *Criminology, 22*, 473–498.

Braithwaite, John. (1989). *Crime, shame, and reintegration*. Cambridge, England: Cambridge University Press.

Braithwaite, John. (2002). *Restorative justice and responsive regulation*. New York, NY: Oxford University Press.

Braithwaite, John, Eliza Ahmed and Valerie Braithwaite. (2006). Shame, restorative justice and crime. In F. Cullen, J. Wright and K. Blevins (Eds.), *Taking stock: The status of criminological theory. Advances in criminological theory, Vol. 15* (pp. 397–412). New Brunswick, NJ: Transaction.

Brezina, Timothy. (1998). Adolescent maltreatment and delinquency: The question of intervening processes. *Journal of Research in Crime and Delinquency, 35*, 71–99.

Campbell, Anne. (1999). Staying alive: Evolution, culture, and women's intrasexual aggression. *Behavioral and Brain Sciences, 22*, 203–214.

Chambliss, William. (1975). *Criminal law in action*. Santa Barbara, CA: Hamilton.

Chapman, Jane. (1980). *Economic realities and the female offender*. Lexington, MA: Lexington.

Chesney-Lind, Meda. (1989). Girls' crime and woman's place: Toward a feminist model of female delinquency. *Crime and Delinquency, 35*, 5–29.

Chesney-Lind, Meda. (2006). Patriarchy, crime, and justice. *Feminist Criminology, 1*, 6–26.

Chesney-Lind, Meda and Lisa Pasko. (2004). *The female offender: Girls, women, and crime*. 2nd ed. Thousand Oaks, CA: Sage.

Chesney-Lind, Meda and Randall Shelden. (2004). *Girls, delinquency, and juvenile justice*. 3rd ed. Belmont, CA: Wadsworth.

Colvin, Mark. (2000). *Crime and coercion: An integrated approach to chronic criminality*. New York, NY: Palgrave.

Crites, Laura (Ed.). (1976). *The female offender.* Lexington, MA: Lexington.

Cullen, Francis and Robert Agnew. (2011). *Criminological theory: Past to present.* 4th ed. New York, NY: Oxford University Press.

Cullen, Francis, Jody Sundt and John Wozniak. (2001). The virtuous prison: Toward a restorative rehabilitation. In H. Pontell and D. Shichor (Eds.), *Contemporary issues in crime and criminal justice: Essay in honor of Gilbert Geis* (pp. 265–286). Upper Saddle River, NJ: Prentice Hall.

Currie, Elliot. (1989). Confronting crime: Looking toward the twenty-first century. *Justice Quarterly, 6,* 5–25.

Currie, Elliott. (1997). Market, crime and community: Toward a mid-range theory of post-industrial violence. *Theoretical Criminology, 1,* 147–172.

D'Alessio, Stewart and Lisa Stolzenberg. (1995). Unemployment and incarceration of pretrial defendants. *American Sociological Review, 60,* 350–359.

Daly, Kathleen. (1992). Women's pathways to felony court: Feminist theories of lawbreaking and problems of representation. *Southern California Review of Law and Women's Studies, 2,* 11–52.

Daly, Kathleen. (1994). *Gender, crime, and punishment.* New Haven, CT: Yale University Press.

Daly, Kathleen and Meda Chesney-Lind. (1988). Feminism and criminology. *Justice Quarterly, 5,* 497–535.

Datesman, Susan and Frank Scarpitti (Eds.). (1980). *Women, crime, and justice.* New York, NY: Oxford University Press.

DeKeseredy, Walter. (2011). *Contemporary critical criminology.* New York, NY: Routledge.

Fair Sentencing Act. (2010). Fair sentencing act of 2010. Public law 111–220. Retrieved from: http://www.gpo.gov/fdsys/pkg/PLAW-111publ220/pdf/PLAW-111publ220.pdf.

FBI UCR. (2010). Uniform Crime Report Ten Year Arrest Trends by Sex. Retrieved from: http://www.fbi.gov/about-us/cjis/ucr/crime-in-the-u.s/2010/crime-in-the-u.s.-2010/tables/10tbl33.xls.

Fuller, John and John Wozniak. (2006). Peacemaking criminology: Past, present, and future. In F. Cullen, J. Wright and K. Blevins (Eds.), *Taking stock: The status of criminological theory. Advances in criminological theory, Vol. 15* (pp. 251–273). New Brunswick, NJ: Transaction.

Griffin, Marie. (2010). Feminist criminology: Beyond the slaying of demons. In H. Barlow and S. Decker (Eds.), *Criminology and public policy* (pp. 215–232). Philadelphia, PA: Temple University Press.

Heimer, Karen. (2000). Changes in the gender gap in crime and women's economic marginalization. In G. LaFree (Ed.), *The nature of crime, continuity and change, criminal justice 2000, Vol. 1* (pp. 427–485). Washington, D.C.: Office of Justice Programs, U.S. Department of Justice.

Holtfreter, Kristy and Rhonda Cupp. (2007). Gender and risk assessment: The empirical status of the LSI-R for women. *Journal of Contemporary Criminal Justice, 23,* 363–382.

Hunnicutt, Gwen and Lisa Broidy. (2004). Liberation and economic marginalization: A reformulation and test of (formerly?) competing models. *Journal of Research in Crime and Delinquency, 41,* 130–155.

Jacobs, David and Jason Carmichael. (2001). The politics of punishment across time and space: A pooled time-series analysis of imprisonment rates. *Social Forces, 80,* 61–89.

Jacques, Scott and Richard Wright. (2010). Drug law and violent retaliation. In H. Barlow and S. Decker (Eds.), *Criminology and public policy* (pp. 201–214). Philadelphia, PA: Temple University Press.

Jacobs, David and Ronald Helms. (1996). Toward a political model of incarceration: A time-series examination of multiple explanations for prison admission rates. *American Journal of Sociology, 102,* 323–357.

Jacobs, David and Ronald Helms. (2001). Toward a political sociology of punishment: Politics and changes in the incarcerated population. *Social Science Research, 30,* 171–194.

Jarecki, Eugene. (2012). Director, *The House I Live In.*

Johnson, Byron. (2004). Religious programs and recidivism among former inmates in prison fellowship programs: A long-term follow-up study. *Justice Quarterly, 21,* 359–354.

Klein, Dorie. (1973). The etiology of female crime: A review of the literature. *Issues in Criminology, 8,* 3–30.

Lainer, Mark and Stuart Henry. (1998). *Essential criminology.* Boulder, CO: Westview.

Marx, Karl. (1967). *The economic and philosophic manuscripts of 1844.* 3rd printing. New York, NY: International.

Marx, Karl and Friedrich Engels. (1948). *The communist manifesto.* New York, NY: International.

McGarrell, Edmund and Thomas Castellano. (1991). An integrative conflict model of the incarceration rate. *Justice Quarterly, 10,* 7–28.

Messerschmidt, James. (1993). *Masculinities and crime: Critique and reconceptualization of theory.* Lanham, MD: Rowman and Littlefield.

Messner, Steven F. and Richard Rosenfeld. (2012). *Crime and the American dream.* Independence, KY: Cengage Learning.

O'Mahony, David and Jonathan Doak. (2004). Restorative justice—is more better? The experience of police-led restorative cautioning pilots in Northern Ireland. *Howard Journal of Criminal Justice, 43,* 484–505.

O'Mahony, David and Jonathan Doak. (2009). Restorative justice and police-led cautioning practice: Tensions in theory and practice. *Journal of Police Studies, 2,* 139–158.

Pepinsky, Harold. (2008). Empathy and restoration. In D. Sullivan and L. Tift (Eds.), *Handbook of restorative justice* (pp. 188–197). London: Routledge.

Pew Center on the States. (2012). *Time served: The high cost, low return of longer prison terms.* Retrieved from: http://www.pewstates.org/uploadedFiles/PCS_Assets/2012/Prison_Time_Served.pdf.

Quinney, Richard. (1974). *Critique of the legal order.* Boston, MA: Little, Brown.

Quinney, Richard (Ed.). (1974a). *Criminal justice in America: A critical understanding.* Boston, MA: Little, Brown.

Quinney, Richard. (1979). The production of criminology. *Criminology, 16,* 445–458.

Quinney, Richard. (1980). *Class, state, and crime.* 2nd ed. New York, NY: Longman.

Quinney, Richard. (1991). The way of peace: On crime, suffering, and service. In H. Pepinsky and R. Quinney (Eds.), *Criminology as peacemaking* (pp. 3–13). Bloomington, IN: Indiana University Press.

Radelet, Michael. (1981). Racial characteristics and the imposition of the death penalty. *American Sociological Review, 46,* 918–927.

Radelet, Michael and Glenn Pierce. (1991). Choosing those who will die: Race and the death penalty in Florida. *Florida Law Review, 43,* 1–43.

Ray, Bradley, Cindy Dollar and Kelly Thames. (2011). Observations of reintegrative shaming in mental health court. *International Journal of Law and Psychiatry, 34,* 49–55.

Reiseg, Michael, Kristy Holtfreter and Merry Morash. (2006). Assessing recidivism risk across female pathways to crime. *Justice Quarterly, 23,* 384–405.

Ritzer, George. (1992). *Sociological theory.* 3rd ed. New York, NY: McGraw-Hill.

Rodriguez, Nancy. (2005). Restorative justice, communities and delinquency: Whom do we reintegrate? *Criminology & Public Policy, 4,* 103–130.

Rusche, Georg. (1978 [1933]) Labor market and penal sanction: Thoughts on the sociology of criminal justice. *Crime and Social Justice, 10,* 2–8. Trans. G. Dinwiddie.

Rusche, Georg and Otto Kirchheimer. (2003). *Punishment and social structure.* Piscataway, NJ: Transaction.

Schiff, Mara. (1998). Restorative justice interventions for juvenile offenders: A research agenda for the next decade. *Western Criminological Review, 1.* Retrieved from: http://wcr.sonoma.edu/v1n1/schiff.html.

Schiff, Mara, Gordon Bazemore and Martha Brown. (2011). Neighborhood accountability boards: The strength of weak practices and prospects for a "community building" restorative model. *Washington University Journal of Law, 36,* 17–46.

Sims, Barbara. (1997). Crime, punishment and the American dream: Toward a Marxist integration. *Journal of Research in Crime and Delinquency, 34,* 5–24.

Smart, Carol. (1977). *Women, crime, and criminology: A feminist critique.* London, England: Routledge and Kegan Paul.

Smith, Douglas and Raymond Paternoster. (1987). The gender gap in theories of deviance: Issues and evidence. *Journal of Research in Crime and Delinquency, 24,* 140–172.

Smith, Nigel. (2010). The ecocidal tendencies of late modernity: Transnational crime, social exclusion, victims and rights. In R. White (Ed.), *Global environmental harm: Criminological perspectives* (pp. 228–241). Portland, OR: Willan Publishing.

Steffensmeier, Darrell. (1980). Sex differences in patterns of adult crime, 1965–77. *Social Forces, 58,* 1080–1109.

Steffensmeier, Darrell and Emile Allan. (2000). Looking for patterns: Gender, age, and crime. In J. Sheley (ed.), *Criminology: A contemporary handbook.* 2nd ed (pp. 84–127). Belmont, CA: Wadsworth.

Steffensmeier, Darrell, Jennifer Schwartz, Hua Zhong and Jeff Ackerman. (2005). An assessment of recent trends in girls' violence using diverse longitudinal sources: Is the gender gap closing? *Criminology, 43,* 355–406.

Sumner, William. (1906). *Folkways.* Boston, MA: Ginn and Company

Sutton, John. (2000). Imprisonment and social classification in five common-law democracies, 1955–1985. *American Journal of Sociology, 106,* 350–386.

Taylor, Ian, Paul Walton and Jock Young. (1973). *The new criminology: For a social theory of deviance.* New York, NY: Harper & Row.

Tellis, Katharine, Nancy Rodriguez and Cassia Spohn. (2010). Critical race perspectives: Explaining the differential treatment of racial minorities by the criminal justice system. In H. Barlow and S. Decker (Eds.), *Criminology and public policy* (pp. 233–253). Philadelphia, PA: Temple University Press.

Tonry, Michael. (2011). *Punishing race: A continuing American dilemma.* New York, NY: Oxford University Press.

United Nations. (1948). *The universal declaration of human rights.* Retrieved from: http://www.un.org/en/documents/udhr/index.shtml.

Van Ness, Daniel and Karen Strong. (2006). *Restoring justice: An introduction to restorative justice.* Cincinnati, OH: Anderson.

Vold, George. (1958). *Theoretical criminology.* New York, NY: Oxford University Press.

Wallerstein, Immanuel. (1974). *The modern world system: Capitalist agriculture and the origins of the European world economy in the sixteenth century.* New York, NY: Academic Press.

Walsh, Anthony and Craig Hemmens. (2011). *Introduction to criminology: A text/reader.* 2nd ed. Los Angeles, CA: Sage.

Widom, Cathy. (1989). The cycle of violence. *Science, 244,* 160–166.

Widom, Cathy and Michael Maxfield. (2001). *An update on the "cycle of violence."* Washington, D.C.: U.S. National Institute of Justice.

Wolff, Jonathan. (2010). Karl Marx. *Stanford encyclopedia of philosophy.* Retrieved from: http://plato.stanford.edu/entries/marx/.

Wolfgang, Marvin, Robert Figlio and Thorsten Sellin. (1972). *Delinquency in a birth cohort.* Chicago, IL: University of Chicago Press.

Wolfgang, Marvin, Robert Figlio, Paul Tracy and Simon Singer. (1985). *The national survey of crime severity.* Washington, D.C.: Bureau of Justice Statistics, U.S. Department of Justice. Retrieved from: https://www.ncjrs.gov/pdffiles1/Digitization/96017NCJRS.pdf.

Wolfgang, Marvin, Terrence Thornberry and Robert Figlio. (1987). *From boy to man, from delinquency to crime.* Chicago, IL: University of Chicago Press.

Chapter 7

Why Do They Do It?
A Lifetime of Answers[1]

Introduction

In this chapter, we will consider a variety of developmental theories of crime. Developmental theories are distinguished from their more traditional counterparts by their focus on what happens over the course of the lifetime that may facilitate persistence in and desistance from crime. The theories we have considered thus far, especially those in Chapters 4 and 5, tend to focus on what happens when certain individuals find themselves in certain social contexts. In other words, they are static, while developmental theories of crime are dynamic. There are several reasons why criminologists, prior to the last 20 years or so, did not deliberately focus on what happens from childhood forward that may be associated with crime. The first is that crime peaks in the teen years (see e.g., Caspi and Moffitt, 1995). Criminologists thus concerned themselves with individuals at this time in their lives and the social contexts in which they lived. The second reason is that it is much more practical for any researcher, criminologists included, to take a cross sectional view and examine what is currently happening that may be associated with crime; an added bonus for criminological researchers is that people in the age group in which they are most interested gather daily at school, making data collection via a survey distributed during class a preferred method. However, some criminologists have begun to take a longer view, employing longitudinal studies and examining what happens over the lifetime that may be associated with commission or cessation of crime (Cullen and Agnew, 2011). The developmental theories that will be

---

1. It is difficult in a book of this nature to comprehensively introduce readers to all developmental theories of crime that have been advanced, particularly since the 1990s, so this chapter focuses on the most important of these theories. For additional reading on developmental theories, see Farrington (2008) and DeLisi and Beaver (2012).

covered in this chapter include Robert Agnew's general theory of crime and delinquency, David Farrington's integrated cognitive antisocial potential (ICAP) theory, Terrie Moffitt's dual pathway developmental theory and Robert Sampson and John Laub's life-course theory.[2]

Before turning to the first of these four theories, it is important to note that developmental theories recognize a variety of risk factors at various stages and in various domains of life.[3] Risk factors increase the likelihood of engaging in crime and as seen in Table 7.1, there are a number of risk factors in childhood and in adolescence across life domains; there are also a number of protective factors that help to insulate against involvement in criminal activity. Some of these risk factors have been explored in our discussion of other theories of crime.

Readers may be examining this table and wondering how, with so many risk and protective factors, we could ever make predictions on their basis. That is, with so many things that put one at greater or less risk for criminal involvement, which of these are the most important and where should our crime prevention resources be directed as a result? Recent longitudinal research on this very topic using Add Health data attempted to determine risk and protective factors for violence at ages 14 and ages 18–20. Bernat, Oakes, Pettingell and Resnick (2012)[4] found that 12 percent of 14 year olds and eight percent of those ages 18–20 were involved in serious violence in year prior to the administration of the survey. Risk factors for violence at age 14 included early onset attention deficit/hyperactivity disorder (ADHD) symptoms, weak bond to school, low school performance and high delinquency by peers. Protective factors for violence at age 14 included low or no symptoms of ADHD, low emotional distress, high educational aspirations and high school performance; note how these risk and protective factors seem to mirror one another. Bernat and colleagues (2012) also found a lower risk for violence at ages 18–20 for those who had low peer delinquency when they were 13.

Risk factors tend to cluster together so that people who have one tend to have others. For example, children who are abused or neglected by their parents tend to live in single parent households in poor neighborhoods that are beset by violence and drugs. Moreover, research has shown that risk factors have additive effects so that people with more risk factors are at far greater risk for crime, especially violence, than those with fewer or none. Herrenkohl, Maguin, Hill, Hawkins, Abbot and Catalano (2000) found that a 10-year-old who is exposed to six or more risk factors is 10 times more likely to be violent at age 18 than a 10-year-old who is exposed to only one risk factor. As Table 7.1 implies, developmental theorists are concerned with risk factors at various stages and domains of life, recognizing that risk factors for young children are somewhat different

---

2. Closely related to but distinct from developmental theories are integrated theories of crime. For a fine treatment of these theories that seek to put criminological concepts together in innovative ways, see Cullen and Agnew (2011) and Akers and Sellers (2009).

3. We recognize that these risk factors are associated with crime, but how long do risk factors last? Decades? Years? Months? Weeks? Days? Hours or even minutes? For an intriguing classification of risk factors based on their duration, see Agnew (2011).

4. The entire issue of the journal in which this study is found focuses on protective factors for violence.

Table 7.1. Risk and protective factors across life stages and domains

Life Domain	Risk Factor		Protective Factor
	Early Onset (ages 6–11)	**Late Onset (ages 12–14)**	
Individual	– General offenses – Substance use – Being male – Aggression* – Psychological condition – Hyperactivity (ADHD) – Antisocial, problem behavior – Exposure to TV violence – Medical and physical problems – Low intelligence (IQ) – Antisocial attitudes, beliefs – Dishonesty*	– General offenses – Psychological condition – Restlessness – Difficulty concentrating* – Risk taking – Aggression* – Being male – Physical violence – Antisocial attitudes, beliefs – Crimes against persons – Antisocial, problem behavior – Physical violence – Low IQ – Substance abuse	– Intolerant attitude toward deviance – High IQ – Being female – Positive social orientation – Perceived sanctions for transgressions
Family	– Low SES/poverty – Antisocial parents – Poor parent/child relations – Harsh, lax, inconsistent parenting – Broken home – Separation from parents – Abusive parents – Neglect	– Poor parent/child relations – Harsh, lax discipline – Poor parental monitoring, supervision – Low parental involvement – Antisocial parents – Broken home – Low SES/poverty – Abusive parents – Family conflict*	– Warm, supportive relationships with parents, other adults – Parents' positive evaluation of peers – Parental monitoring
School	– Poor performance, attitude	– Poor performance, attitude – Academic failure	– Commitment to school – Recognition for involvement in conventional activities
Peer Group	– Weak social ties – Antisocial peers	– Weak social ties – Antisocial, delinquent peers – Gang membership	– Friends who engage in conventional behavior
Community	– N/A	– Neighborhood crime, drugs – Neighborhood disorganization	– N/A

* males only   Source: Adapted from OSGUS, 2001.

from those for adolescents. These risk factors appear to be most relevant for children and adolescents in Western countries, but they may not be universal; on this point, see Eisner and Nivette (2012).

Robert Agnew's General Theory of Crime and Delinquency[5]

The same Robert Agnew who developed general strain theory (see Chapter 4) has also developed a general theory of crime and delinquency. He begins with the proposition that crime is most likely when motivations for it are high and constraints against it are low. Motivations for crime include reinforcements for criminal activity, exposure to successful criminal models, learning beliefs favorable to crime as well as a variety of strains (all in accord with social learning and general strain theories; see Chapters 4 and 5). Constraints against crime include external controls exerted by parents, teachers, peers, employers and criminal justice officials, having a stake in conformity and conforming behavior and internal (or self) control. From there, Agnew (2005) identifies a host of variables[6] across five life domains that have a moderate to strong direct effect on crime. These five life domains are the self, the family, the school, peers and work. The variables in the self domain that have the strongest direct effect on crime are low self-control and high irritability.[7] The variables in the family domain that have the strongest direct effect on crime are poor parental supervision and/or discipline of children, negative bonding between parents and children, absence of positive parenting, family conflict, child abuse, criminal parents and/or siblings and failure to marry and/or bad marriages. The variables in the school domain that have the strongest direct effect on crime are negative bonding to teachers and/or school, negative relationships with teachers, the absence of positive teaching, poor academic performance, little time spent on homework and low level educational and/or occupational goals. The variables in the peer domain that have the strongest direct effect on crime are peer delinquency, conflict and/or abuse among peers and unstructured and/or unsupervised time spent with peers. Finally, the variables in the work domain that have the strongest direct effect on crime are unemployment, poor work performance, poor supervision and/or discipline, negative bonding to work, poor working conditions and criminal coworkers. All of these variables serve to increase motivations for and decrease constraints against crime.

Agnew (2005) points out that while some of these variables have their strong direct effects on crime across the lifetime, some are more salient at different life stages and

---

5. Some, notably Cullen and Agnew (2011), classify Agnew's general theory of crime and delinquency as an integrated rather than a developmental theory of crime. We choose to discuss it here as a developmental theory because it implicates several domains across the life course as important in crime causation; Walsh and Hemmens (2011) do the same.

6. Agnew (2005) introduces these as variables and throughout the course of his work, goes on to call them causes. Here, we alternately refer to them as variables, causes and (most commonly) risk factors.

7. Irritability is analogous to the trait of negative emotionality seen in Chapter 3.

with this revelation, it is easier to see this theory of crime as developmental in nature. In childhood, the most important causes of crime are poor parenting practices and irritability and low self-control (in the family and self domains, respectively). In adolescence, the most important causes of crime are peer delinquency and irritability and low self-control (in the peer and self domains, respectively). In adulthood, the most important causes of crime are peer delinquency, no marriages or poor marriage, unemployment or undesirable jobs and irritability and low self-control (in the peer, family, work and self domains, respectively). We clearly see irritability and low self-control running through the stages of life as important causes of crime. Not only do these variables have a strong and direct effect on crime causation, they facilitate other causes of crime as well. It is very likely that people with irritability and low self-control will engage in poor parenting practices, will fail to marry and to have bad marriages when they do, to have negative experiences in school, to have low levels of educational attainment, to associate with delinquent peers and to be unemployed and to have bad jobs when they are working. That is, they are more likely than those without these traits to find themselves with other, demonstrated risk factors for crime across the domains and here we see the notion that risk factors for crime tend to cluster together clearly illustrated.

According to Agnew (2005), there are several reasons that irritability and low self-control tend to have a greater number of risk factors for crime than those without these traits. People with these two traits tend not to devote much time to conventional pursuits such as marriage, family, school and work and when they try to do so, they often fail at these pursuits. Moreover, they tend to elicit negative responses from others (think, for example of how difficult it might be to effectively parent a child with low self-control, or how unpleasant it might be to have a friendship with someone who is irritable). The negative responses they elicit may foster the creation of environments that are conducive to criminal activity. Finally, people with low self-control and irritability are more likely than those without these traits to perceive environments as conducive to crime. Figure 7.1 illustrates the salient risk factors in each domain and how each domain has an effect, not only on crime, but on the other domains as well. The two-headed arrows are no accident; the effects of the risk factors on one another are reciprocal so that irritability and low self-control, for example, affects and is affected by poor parenting.

Prior experience with crime also plays a role in Agnew's (2005) theory. Prior crime has a direct effect on future crime. It may reduce the fear of formal sanctions, particularly for those whose crime goes undetected. It may also increase the motivation for engaging in future crime by increasing strain and by providing short term benefits of both a tangible and intangible nature. Prior experience with crime also has an indirect effect on future crime through the five domains. Engagement in crime may facilitate negative family, school, work and peer relationships by helping to create a preference for environments that are conducive to crime, by affecting performance in life domains and by forcing people into crime-conducive environments. For example, the use of drugs may start a chain reaction of negative relationships with family, poor school performance, association with delinquent peers, unemployment and future crime to support a drug habit.

Figure 7.1. Effects of life domains on one another and on crime

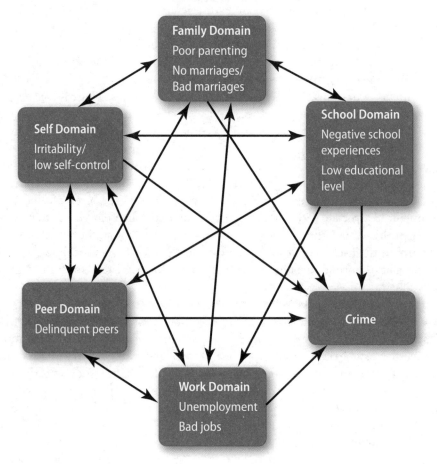

Source: Adapted from Agnew, 2005.

At this stage in Agnew's (2005) theory, he is claiming that crime is caused by risk factors across five life domains and that these risk factors work to reduce constraints against and increase motivations for crime. Each domain affects not just crime, but the other domains as well, as does prior criminal activity. He goes on to assert that any one of the causes he identifies is more likely to lead to crime when other causes are present. As mentioned, risk factors tend to cluster together and so someone who is high on irritability and low self-control, suffers poor parenting and abuse, does poorly in school, associates with delinquent peers and has no job or a bad job is more likely to engage in crime than someone with only one of these risk factors. Similarly, problems in any one domain increase the likelihood of problems in other domains. Agnew (2005) further claims that the effects of risk factors on crime are contemporaneous, meaning that they occur close together in time. The risk factors an individual is experiencing at the moment are the most important in determining whether or not he or she will engage in crime, much more important than risk factors he or she may have experienced in the past. Similarly, the effects of domains on one another are also contemporaneous; what is happening in one domain right now affects what happens in the others. Agnew (2005) proposes that the effects of risk factors on crime and on other domains have a nonlinear effect, so that as the amount of a risk factor increases, the increase in crime is exponential. Agnew (2005) looks to strain and social learning theories to explain this phenomenon. One may experience moderate strains that do not lead to crime, but once a threshold or tipping point is passed, strains start to generate anger which may lead to criminal coping. Similarly, one may learn some criminal definitions from a few others and not engage in crime. But the more definitions they learn and the more people (especially intimate others) they learn them from, those definitions start to outweigh conventional definitions.

Agnew (2005) recognizes that risk factors do not come into existence in a vacuum and explains that outside factors have effects on each of the life domains. He puts most of his focus on age, sex, race/ethnicity, parents' socioeconomic status and community characteristics (with the exception of the self domain, in which he acknowledges the influence of both genetic and non-genetic biological factors on irritability and low self-control). These sociodemographic characteristics have large, direct effect on all the life domains. On the back of this claim, Agnew (2005) is confident that his general theory can explain not only why some individuals become involved and stay involved in crime, but also why there are group differences in rates of offending, among groups of people of different ages, races/ethnicities, genders and classes. For example, we know that males offend more than females. In accord with his theory, Agnew (2005) maintains that males are more likely to have low self-control and high irritability, to experience poor parenting, to have weak ties to family as adults and to associate with delinquent peers, which explains why this group as a whole engages in more crime than females.

Research on Robert Agnew's General Theory of Crime and Delinquency

As astute readers will have surmised by now, there is a good deal of indirect support for Agnew's (2005) theory because it is based on empirically supported propositions. However, direct tests of the theory are not numerous, probably in part because the theory was so recently developed. One direct test of the theory aimed to examine whether each of the variables in the five domains are associated with recidivism, whether there is a nonlinear relationship between domains and recidivism and whether the domains interact with each other in causing recidivism, all as Agnew (2005) proposes. Ngo, Paternoster, Cullen and Mackenzie (2011) utilized baseline data from 238 adult offenders who were randomly assigned to a boot camp or to a traditional correctional facility in order to determine the presence of risk factors. In order to determine the amount of recidivism, they followed up with survey respondents in the Maryland Department of Public Safety database to determine whether respondents were rearrested in the two years after their release. The authors found that traditional risk factors, including age and extensive criminal history were significantly related to rearrest. However, they found that only two risk factors within the domains Agnew identifies, having a bad job and dropping out of high school, were significantly related to recidivism. Moreover, with the exception of the peer domain, there was little evidence for a nonlinear relationship between domains and their effects on crime and there was little evidence for the interaction of domains in producing recidivism, especially as higher level statistical analyses were employed. Despite this weak showing for Agnew's general theory of crime and delinquency, Ngo, Paternoster, Cullen and Mackenzie (2011) contend that they may not have been able to find support for the theory because of limitations of their data.

Strengths and Weaknesses of Robert Agnew's General Theory of Crime and Delinquency

Perhaps the greatest strength of Agnew's (2005) general theory of crime and delinquency is that it draws attention to various life domains and how they may be important to crime causation over the lifetime. So instead of an exclusive focus on learning from peers, for example, or on bonds formed during adolescence, Agnew's (2005) general theory looks across five domains over the lifetime to determine how risk factors in each domain may cause crime during childhood, adolescence and adulthood. The theory also recognizes the reciprocal relationship that crime has with domains and that the domains have with one another, so that poor performance in school, for example, may lead to poor jobs. Moreover, Agnew's (2005) theory is built on empirically supported notions so it makes sense and is in accord with our observations of what is associated with crime. Among the theory's weaknesses is a lack of empirical support to date, though further testing may reveal it to be stronger than it appears now. In particular, longitudinal testing is necessary to reveal whether the domains Agnew (2005) identifies are indeed important in crime causation over the lifetime. It would be particularly interesting to follow a group of children with low self-control and irritability over decades to determine precisely how these risk factors from the self domain interact with and amplify risk factors from other domains and when during the lifetime they do so. Another weakness of Agnew's (2005) theory is that it implicates so many risk factors in crime causation. That is, it lacks parsimony. And as alluded to above, if we say crime has so many different causes, what on earth are we to do to control it?

David Farrington's Integrated Cognitive Antisocial Potential (ICAP) Theory

In 2003, as part of his address upon winning the American Society of Criminology's Sutherland Award, which recognizes outstanding contributions to criminological theory and understanding of the etiology of crime, David Farrington presented a developmental theory he had been working on since the early 1990s. The name of his developmental theory is the integrated cognitive antisocial potential (ICAP) theory and in presenting its tenets, Farrington (2003, p. 230) began by asking a series of questions that any developmental theory should be able to answer. These questions include:

1. Why do people start offending?
2. How can we explain the onset of offending?

3. Why is there continuity in offending?
4. Why do people stop offending?
5. Why does the prevalence of offending peak in the teenage years?
6. Why does early onset of offending predict a long criminal career?
7. Why is there versatility in offending?
8. Why does co-offending (committing an offense in conjunction with one or more people) decrease from adolescence to adulthood?
9. Why are there between-individual differences in offending?
10. What are the risk factors for onset of and desistance from offending and how can their effects be explained?
11. Why are there within-individual differences in offending?
12. What are the main motivations and reasons for offending?
13. What are the effects of life events on offending?

These questions that any developmental theory should be able to answer are born out of empirical realities. That is, research has shown that offending does peak in the teen years (Caspi and Moffitt, 1995; Wolfgang, Figlio and Sellin, 1987; Farrington, 1986). The early onset of offending does predict a long criminal career (LeBlanc and Frechette, 1989; Farrington, Lambert and West, 1998). Most offenses up through the teenage years are committed with others and co-offending does drop off after the age of 20 (McCord and Conway, 2002; Reiss and Farrington, 1991), to give just a few examples of the research.

Farrington's (2003) ICAP theory was designed to explain offending by lower class males and draws on concepts from other theories, including strain, control, learning, labeling and rational choice. The central construct of ICAP is what Farrington (2003) called antisocial potential and the theory holds that antisocial potential becomes antisocial behavior when certain cognitive processes are employed that take into account both criminal opportunities and potential victims. There are two types of antisocial potential, long and short term. For those with a large number of risk factors, antisocial potential may be long term and those with long term antisocial potential may be ranked on a continuum from low to high. Only a few people in the population have a high level of long term antisocial potential and these people, when antisocial potential becomes antisocial behavior through the mechanisms described above, commit a wide variety of offenses over the course of the lifetime. Crime peaks in the teenage years because the level of antisocial potential is higher at this time, particularly with the increasing influence of peers and the decreasing influence of parents. In particular, there may be an increase in short term antisocial potential at this time that is associated with offending. Short term variations in antisocial potential depend on the situation in which one finds him or herself at any given moment. For example, being angry, bored, frustrated, encouraged by peers or drunk or high may increase short term antisocial potential.

According to Farrington (2003), various strains lead to high levels of long term antisocial potential, including the desire for material goods, for status, for excitement and for sex. Everyone has these desires, though, and Farrington (2003) points out that these motivations only contribute to high levels of long term antisocial potential when the chosen ways of satisfying them are antisocial in nature. Those who choose antisocial methods have difficulty meeting their needs in legitimate ways, including those with low income, routine unemployment and failure at school. Antisocial potential also depends on attachment and socialization; those children who are not well attached to prosocial parents or who come from broken homes are more likely to have high long term antisocial potential. These children may also have low levels of anxiety, which implies that they are not concerned with negative consequences for their behavior. Exposure to antisocial models, including parents, peers and siblings, will also increase the level of long term antisocial potential, as will a low level of impulse control. Additive effects may be present, as well, meaning that those who experience strains as well as exposure to antisocial models are even more likely to develop high long term antisocial potential. Whether a person commits a given crime depends on his or her level of antisocial potential and the given social environment and whether a person with a certain level of antisocial potential commits a crime in that given social environment depends on a cost benefit analysis of the situation as well as the outcomes of experiences with previous, similar situations. The contributions of ideas from other theories of crime in Farrington's (2003) ICAP theory are clear; Figure 7.2 provides a graphic illustration of ICAP theory.

In addition to claiming ICAP theory can answer to satisfaction all of the aforementioned questions that are central to developmental theories, Farrington (2003) contends that his theory effectively grapples with the theoretical questions that must be addressed by any developmental theory of crime. It specifies short term risk factors (boredom, anger, frustration, intoxication, influence of male peers) and long term risk factors (strains, antisocial models and impulsiveness) that encourage offending and implies that those factors opposite of risk factors serve as protectors or insulators. It specifies not one but two learning processes, that involved in the socialization of children by parents and that involved in learning from the consequences of offending. It sets forth an operational definition of the key construct underlying offending, antisocial potential as antisocial behavior or antisocial attitude. It can explain the empirical findings on crime over the life course and it makes predictions somewhat different from those of other developmental theories, thereby making it a necessary addition to this group.

Research on David Farrington's Integrated Cognitive Antisocial Potential (ICAP) Theory

There is very little empirical research on ICAP theory, in part because it was first articulated so recently and in part because the most robust research on developmental theories is longitudinal in nature; it takes time to determine the predictive accuracy of developmental theories. One of the most important contributions of the ICAP theory is that it considers both short and long term risk factors, where the former refer to factors that help to determine a person's behavior in a given situation (Farrington, 2005). At least one study has attempted to study both short and long term risk factors for offending. Van der Laan, Blom and Kleemans (2009) obtained a variety of information on 1,460 adolescents between the ages of 10 and 17 who were randomly selected to participate in a Dutch survey on youth delinquency. The survey inquired about both more and less serious offenses committed in the previous 12 months, as well as about long

Figure 7.2. Integrated Cognitive Antisocial Potential (ICAP) theory

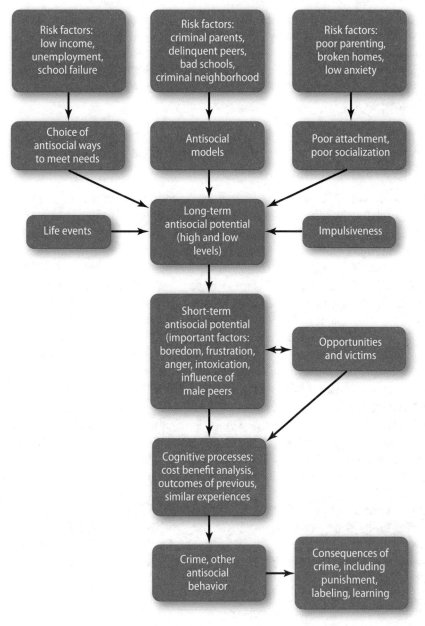

Source: Adapted from Farrington, 2003.

term risk factors, including antisocial behavior, hyperactivity and attention disorders, emotional problems, relationship with parents, parenting styles, performance at school and attachment to school; and about short term risk factors, including the presence of co-offenders, limited risk of detection, absence of guardians and intoxication. The authors found that long term risk factors retain their importance in predicting who will engage in crime and the more long term risk factors a person has, the more likely he or she will engage in crime, as has been shown elsewhere. However, when long term risk factors were controlled for, short term risk factors played a role in the commission of serious juvenile delinquency. Moreover, it appears that the circumstances that encourage offending by serious delinquents are different from those that encourage offending for more moderate delinquents. These results support Farrington's (2005) ICAP theory by demonstrating that short term, situational factors have an effect on the commission of crime apart from long term risk factors.

Strengths and Weaknesses of David Farrington's Integrated Cognitive Antisocial Potential (ICAP) Theory

One of the principal strengths of Farrington's (2003, 2005) ICAP theory has been described in the above section, namely that it considers both long term and short term risk factors. In so doing, it helps to elucidate what it is about potential offenders and the situations they are in at the moment that encourages offending beyond the experience with long term risk factors that they may have. It can explain offending between individuals, that is, from one individual to another, as well as within-individual offending, that is, offending by one individual at different points in his or her life. It is also capable of explaining the empirically demonstrated facts about crime over the life course and satisfactorily answering the list of 13 questions noted above. Moreover, the theory clearly operationalizes concepts and has been designed with empirical testing in mind so that whether its predictions are correct can be demonstrated through research. Among the weaknesses of ICAP theory are that it does not well explain variations in crime rates over place or over time (from country to country, for example), nor does it well explain individual development in different neighborhoods; these weaknesses can also be ascribed to the bulk of developmental theories of crime. ICAP is not designed to explain gang crime, nor is it specifically designed to explain variations in offending among different demographic groups. Moreover, ICAP theory also does not give very much attention to factors that promote resistance to or desistance from offending. Farrington (2003) notes that some future empirical findings may challenge the ICAP theory, including those that show early behavior is a stepping stone to later behavior; ICAP theory maintains that there are different behavioral manifestations of antisocial potential over time, not that one behavior leads to another.

Terrie Moffitt's Dual Pathway Developmental Theory

Terrie Moffitt (1993) postulates that while many juveniles engage in antisocial behavior, their delinquency hides two qualitatively different groups of offenders, those whose delinquency is temporary and situational and those whose delinquency is consistent over time and situation. Moffitt (1993) calls those who engage in temporary and situational antisocial behavior adolescent limited offenders and discontinuity in behavior over the lifetime is the hallmark of this very large group She calls those whose antisocial behavior is consistent over time and situation life course persistent offenders and continuity of behavior over the lifetime is the hallmark of this rather small group. As implied in their names, adolescent limited offenders engage in some delinquency during the adolescent years and cease antisocial behavior as they enter adulthood.[8] Life course persistent offenders, on the other hand, engage in a variety of antisocial behaviors over the lifetime, from childhood to adolescence to adulthood and do so across situations, for example, at home, at school and at work.

A vast majority of offenders are adolescent limited. For those small number of life course persistent offenders, what causes their distinct behavior? Moffitt (1993) points first to disruptions in normal neural development that may lead to deficits in neuropsychological abilities. These disruptions may include maternal drug use, poor nutrition, exposure to toxic agents and later abuse and neglect. There are two particular neuropsychological deficits that are strongly empirically linked to antisocial behavior, verbal and executive functions. Deficits in verbal functions include reduce ability to listen and read receptively, to problem solve, to express oneself in speech and writing and to remember. Deficits in executive functions include inattentiveness and impulsivity. Moffitt (1993) points out that those infants who have the disruptions to normal neural development that can lead to neuropsychological deficits that are later associated with antisocial behavior tend not to be born into environments that are warm, nurturing and potentially ameliorative of these conditions. Rather, they tend to be born into environments in which their families are disadvantaged or deviant. These environments are ones in which the parents or caregivers of children are unlikely to have the resources necessary to parent effectively. When a difficult child (one who has deficits in verbal and executive functioning) finds him or herself in an aversive environment (one in which parents or caregivers do not effectively care for their child), the seeds of life course persistent offending are sown.

Moreover, the interaction between difficult children and ineffective parents is a two way street, where difficult children evoke negative responses from their ineffective parents and not just once, but over the course of childhood and adolescence. As

---

8. Life course persistent offenders are often labeled LCP offenders in the literature and adolescent limited offenders are often labeled AL offenders. We imagine that this is most readers' first exposure to Moffitt's (1993) ideas and as such, we have chosen to spell out each use the terminology here to aid in clarity.

implied, there is a person-environment interaction at work in the development of life course persistent offenders. Moffitt (1993) identifies two other types of interaction (in addition to evocative) that may explain how deviant behavior, once demonstrated, persists over the lifetime. The first of these is reactive interaction, in which different children exposed to the same environment experience that environment, interpret it and react to it in accord with their personalities. Proactive interaction is when people seek out or create environments that are supportive of their personalities. These three types of interactions may lead to cumulative consequences or contemporary consequences. Cumulative consequences are those in which early childhood experiences lead to continuity in behavior over the lifetime while contemporary consequences are those in which the traits of childhood are present in and have similar negative effects in adolescence and in adulthood.

Both cumulative and contemporary consequences mean that life course persistent offenders have little opportunity to learn how to react to situations in prosocial rather than antisocial ways. Difficult children are often rejected by parents and peers and they come to expect rejection, even striking out at prosocial peers who offer acceptance. Moreover, those who do poorly in school due to deficits in verbal and executive functioning and fail to achieve basic levels of reading and math will have very few if any lucrative job opportunities and may turn to crime as a result. As time goes by, there are increasingly limited opportunities for prosocial behavior. Moffitt (1993) believes that even opportunities offered to life course persistent offenders to help them strike out on a prosocial path are transformed by these offenders into situations that suit their personalities. For example, placement in a supervised residential setting becomes a place to learn tips and tricks from other offenders, a new job is a new place from which to steal and a new spouse is someone new to abuse. Moffitt (1993) maintains that antisocial styles are set sometime after childhood but well before late adolescence.

Up to this point, we have been talking about only one of Moffitt's (1993) two types of offenders, the life course persistent offenders. As mentioned, these offenders start offending early and persist in offending from childhood through adolescence into adulthood. Adolescent limited offenders, on the other hand, do exactly what their name implies: they limit their offending to adolescence. Empirical studies demonstrate that for adolescent limited offenders, there is little continuity in their antisocial behavior, including across situations. This flexibility in antisocial behavior that sets adolescent limited offenders very much apart from life course persistent offenders suggests that for adolescent limited offenders, reward and punishment may play a large role in whether they persist in short lived delinquency. When delinquency is profitable, adolescent limited offenders may engage in it, but when prosocial behavior becomes more attractive, they abandon delinquent behavior in a way that their life course persistent peers will not or cannot.

A great number of adolescents engage in delinquent behavior. In an attempt to explain why, Moffitt (1993) looks to the effects of the developmental period of puberty, which include increasing importance of peers and decreasing importance of parents, biological changes and formation of values, attitudes and aspirations. Moffitt (1993) maintains that adolescent limited offenders who engage in delinquency first do so because they are mimicking the behavior of their life course persistent peers. Mimicking delinquency confers maturity that adolescents do not otherwise have. The current long period of adolescence means that teenagers are biologically mature but socially immature (the maturity gap in Moffitt's terms), unable to hold a job or drive until they reach a certain age, thus denying them the independence that comes with adulthood. As young people enter the maturity gap and have the motivation to engage in delinquency, they also enter high school where they will meet older adolescents, some of whom have dealt with the gap by engaging in delinquency. Young people thus gain delinquent role models and social mimicry of delinquency can happen when adolescent limited offenders are recruited into delinquency by life course persistent offenders or when adolescent limited offenders merely observe the delinquency of life course persistent offenders and imitate it.

As mentioned, Moffitt (1993) believes that reinforcement and punishment are important in the delinquency of adolescent limited offenders. Reinforcements for adolescents may include earning the ire of parents and teachers through their defiant actions. As adolescents age out of the maturity gap into adulthood, the consequences of delinquency are no longer attractive in their view. That is, what was reinforcing for them as adolescents is no longer reinforcing for them as adults. Astute readers may be asking themselves why the same does not apply to life course persistent offenders. To explain this important difference, Moffitt (1993) returns to the notions of cumulative and contemporary continuity. Unlike their life course persistent counterparts, adolescent limited offenders do not have a long history of antisocial behavior. As such, they have opportunities to foster prosocial relationships and behavior. Also unlike their life course persistent counterparts, adolescent limited offenders do not begin life with a host of neuropsychological deficits that lead to antisocial behavior that persists over time and situation.

Finally, while many adolescents, be they adolescent limited or life course persistent offenders, engage in delinquency, not every young person does. To explain this phenomenon, Moffitt (1993) points first to the maturity gap. She maintains that some youth may not enter the maturity gap because of either late puberty or early adoption of adult roles. Another reason some adolescents may not engage in delinquency is that they lack opportunities to model the antisocial behavior of life course persistent offenders. For example, those who live in rural areas may have fewer or no life course persistent offenders to imitate and those who have some characteristics that make them unappealing to other adolescents may not be accepted by groups, even delinquent ones. Figure 7.3 provides a graphic illustration of Moffitt's (1993) dual pathway developmental theory (for more detail on this theory, see Moffitt, 1994, 1997, 2003, 2006).

Research on Terrie Moffitt's Dual Pathway Developmental Theory

Shortly after Moffitt (1993) first published her dual pathway developmental theory of crime, researchers began testing its predictions. Moffitt and Walsh (2003) summarize the results of some of these tests. First, Moffitt's (1993) theory predicts that there is a greater genetic basis for the behavior of life course persistent offenders than there is for adolescent limited offenders and research has revealed this prediction to be accurate. Moreover, the antisocial behavior of life course persistent offenders may be transmitted

Figure 7.3. Dual pathway developmental theory

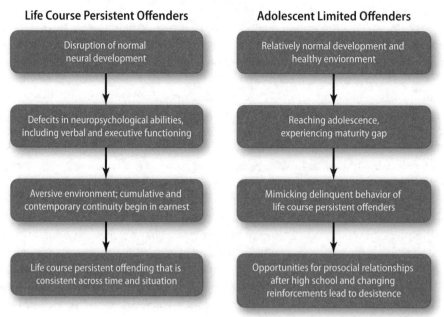

Source: Adapted from Moffitt, 1993.

intergenerationally because of the tendency of like to seek like. People with antisocial behavior select one another for mating and produce children that not only have inherited tendencies for antisocial behavior but who are also raised in aversive environments by antisocial parents, setting them on the course for life course persistent offending (Moffitt and Walsh, 2003). Moffitt's (1993) theory also predicts that neurodevelopmental factors are important in the creation of life course persistent offenders and research has shown this prediction to be accurate, as well. Some individual risk factors for becoming a life course persistent offender include an undercontrolled temperament, lower intelligence, difficulty with reading and memory and hyperactivity. Environmental risk factors include having a young single parent, experiencing abuse and neglect, low socioeconomic status and rejection by peers; children with both individual and environmental risk factors are at great risk of becoming life course persistent offenders (Tibbetts and Piquero, 1999; Moffitt and Caspi, 2001; Moffitt and Walsh, 2003).

Moffitt's theory (1993) predicts that adolescent limited offenders are drawn into delinquency as they enter the maturity gap and begin imitating the behavior of their life course persistent peers and research has shown this prediction to be accurate. Peer influence is very important in the onset of delinquency in adolescence, but because adolescent limited offenders have relatively normal development and environments, they are able to resume prosocial behavior as they age into adulthood. Resuming prosocial behavior may be delayed for those who experience relatively serious and negative consequences as a result of their adolescent delinquency (snares, in Moffitt's terms), such as a criminal record, drug addition, et cetera (Moffitt and Walsh, 2003). Moffitt's theory also predicts that the personality structures of adolescent limited and life course persistent offenders will be quite different and research has shown this prediction to be accurate, as well. Life course persistent offenders rate themselves and others rate them higher on negative emotionality and lower on agreeableness than adolescent limited offenders and this is true over time (Moffitt and Walsh, 2003). Moffitt's (1993) theory predicts that life course persistent offenders engage in a wider variety of offenses than adolescent limited offenders and research has shown this prediction to be accurate. Piquero and Brezina (2001) found that adolescent limited offenders tended to engage in what they called rebellious rather than aggressive delinquency. Life course persistent offenders engage in much more violence than their adolescent limited offender counterparts (Moffitt and Walsh, 2003) and they are more likely to force or coerce sex than non life course persistent offenders (Boutwell, Barnes and Beaver, 2013).

Though Moffitt and Walsh (2003) find support for Moffitt's (1993) theory, they acknowledge that some of the theory's key predictions remained unexamined even 10 years after its initial publication. Some of these predictions concern reactions to turning point opportunities, the need for peer support in criminal activity and the stability of measures of antisocial behavior from childhood to adolescence to adulthood (Moffitt and Walsh, 2003). Some support was found for this last prediction, that childhood measures of antisocial behavior should be more highly correlated with adult measures than with adolescent measures (Stattin, Kerr and Bergman, 2010). This prediction was also thoroughly examined by Donker, Smeenk, van der Laan and Verhulst (2003), who measured instances of overt behavior, especially violence and aggression, covert behavior, especially theft and fraud and status violations, among 6–11 year old children (by surveying their parents), among 12–17 year old children (by surveying their parents and via a self-report from the children) and among 20–25 year olds (via an administered survey and a self-report). They began research with this group of 631 children in 1983 and followed them for 20 years. The researchers found that overt behavior was more stable from childhood to adulthood than from childhood to adolescence, in accord with Moffitt's (1993) theory. However, the authors found that covert behavior continues in adulthood at about the same rate as it exists in adolescence, which does not support Moffitt's (1993) theory. Donker, Smeenk, van der Laan and Verhulst (2003) suggest that the adolescent limited label may be most appropriate for overt rather than covert behaviors.

Though Moffitt's dual pathway developmental theory is quite influential, some researchers have been critical of it. One such researcher is Skardhamar (2009), who questions whether offenders can be divided into two and only two types and that individuals who fall into these types are in fact qualitatively different. He also questions whether life course persistent offenders have their behavior reinforced in the same way that adolescent limited offenders do and whether life course persistent offenders lack a maturity gap as Moffitt (1993) implies that they do. In summarizing the literature on attempts to find evidence of Moffitt's (1993) two and only two types of offenders, Skardhamar (2009) notes that other studies have found from three to seven types of offenders (see for example Blokland, Nagin and Nieuwbeerta (2005), who found four groups of offenders in their longitudinal study of convicted Dutch offenders, including sporadic offenders, low-rate desisters, moderate-rate desisters and high-rate persisters; both Kratzer and Hodgins (1999) and Stattin, Kerr and Bergman (2010) also found four distinct groups of offenders). Other studies have also found a different peak age of offending, from as young as 13 to as old as 37; it is important to note that many of these studies use a particular statistical technique that Moffitt herself endorses. Skardhamar (2009) concludes that these two types might be better thought of as points on a continuum, with abstainers at one end, then adolescent limited, high rate adolescent limited, low rate life course persistent and finally true life course persistent offenders at the other end. A 26 year follow up of life course persistent and adolescent limited offenders by Moffitt herself and colleagues revealed strong evidence for the distinction between these two types of offenders as well as the existence of a third group, those who are aggressive in childhood but who do not engage in much delinquency in adolescence and who are low level chronic offenders in adulthood, suggesting the possible need for modification of this theory (Moffitt, Caspi, Harrington and Milne, 2002).

Though Barnes, Beaver and Piquero (2011) did find support for Moffitt's prediction that skipping the maturity gap by being socially isolated would result in abstention from delinquency, Chen and Adams (2010) did not find support for the claim that those who abstain from delinquent behavior are unpopular and isolated. Rather, much more complex mechanisms appear to be at work with regard to social networks and delinquency and Moffitt's (1993) theory may need further modification as a result. Even with these challenges, Moffitt's (1993) theory has garnered a great deal of academic interest and influence since its first publication. In fact, an entire panel at the 2012 American Society of Criminology meeting was dedicated to research on it.

Strengths and Weaknesses of Terrie Moffitt's Dual Pathway Developmental Theory

One of the greatest strengths of Moffitt's (1993) dual pathway developmental theory is that it identifies two pathways to offending instead of assuming that everyone in similar circumstances acts similarly. The theory is clear about what causes life course persistent versus adolescent limited offending and it is clear about what causes desistance for adolescent limited offenders. It is based on comprehensive data collected on a large cohort in New Zealand that has been followed for decades, so it has its foundation in empirical reality. Moffitt's (1993) theory has a particularly good explanation for why the rate of offending is so high among adolescents. Generally speaking, it has the same strengths as other developmental theories, including consideration of biological, psychological and sociological factors in crime causation, the use of longitudinal studies so that the temporal order of causes and effects can be correctly established, reliance on broader and usually larger samples and identification of those factors associated with onset, persistence and desistance from crime (Walsh and Hemmens, 2011). The weaknesses of Moffitt's (1993) theory have been alluded to above. Some of the theory's key propositions have yet to be empirically tested and some of those that have been tested have not received unqualified support. For example, consistency of behavior for life course persistent offenders from childhood to adulthood is much more pronounced when overt (i.e. violent) acts are being considered. The two pathway typology may not be comprehensive enough and further study may necessitate modification on this point and on delinquent abstainers, as well.

Robert Sampson[9] and John Laub's Life-Course Theory

To thoroughly understand Sampson and Laub's life-course theory, we need to first look back to the 1950s and the work of Sheldon and Eleanor Glueck. As noted in Chapter 2, the Gluecks gathered a wide variety of data on 500 white, male juvenile delinquents in reformatories in Massachusetts and a matched sample of 500 non-delinquent boys from the Boston area. The Gluecks collected data on biological, psychological and sociological factors, as they believed all of these factors were potentially important in causing or at least contributing to delinquency, and followed up their sample, which was initially between the ages of 10 and 17, at ages 25 and 32 as well. Glueck and Glueck (1950) found that the delinquent boys tended to be mesomorphs (muscular and solid) as compared their non-delinquent counterparts. Delinquent boys were also more extroverted, impulsive, hostile, destructive and exhibited less self-control than the non-delinquents. The delinquents tended to be concrete rather than abstract thinkers. They also had lower school achievement than the non-delinquents, poorer attitudes toward school and exhibited more misbehavior in school. The delinquents in Glueck and Glueck's (1950) study also spent far more unstructured, unsupervised time with equally delinquent peers than did non-delinquents and they were more likely to have parents with serious biosocial deficits that rendered them unable to attach with and properly rear their children.

Their research was an impressive achievement for its time (and would be today, as well), but Glueck and Glueck's (1950) findings were criticized by other scholars, most notably Edwin Sutherland, in large part because in trying to explain the causes of delinquency, the Gluecks focused on biological and psychological causes. Astute readers will have noticed that the Gluecks published their findings at a time when sociological theories dominated criminology and focusing on biology and psychology as they did won them few fans. In fact, their research was largely ignored for decades in favor of research espousing more sociological causes of crime (Cullen and Agnew, 2011). In one of the more incredible moments in criminological history, John Laub found the Gluecks' raw data collecting dust in a basement at Harvard in the 1980s. He and Robert Sampson spent years recreating the data set from the raw information in the files and decided to try to follow up with the delinquents in the Gluecks' original sample. The results of their efforts were two seminal criminological texts.

In the first, Sampson and Laub (1993) concluded that a complicated set of factors is responsible for a lifetime of offending. These factors include difficult temperament and conduct problems early in life; as we have seen, these factors make effective childrearing challenging for even the most capable, dedicated parents. For those parents or caregivers with deficits of their own, forming meaningful bonds with their children is increasingly difficult and when structural conditions such as poverty, disorganization

---

9. This is the same Robert Sampson from Chapter 4, who has also conducted much research on social disorganization and other social structural factors that contribute to crime.

and a variety of strains are also in play, the chances that children will have meaningful bonds with and do well in school decrease. Lack of attachment to school decreases the likelihood of legitimate and lucrative work and increases the likelihood of association with delinquent peers, which in turn increases the likelihood of delinquency. A criminal record, especially one that includes incarceration, makes connecting to conventional society and conventional others more difficult (in Sampson and Laub's terms, these opportunities for conventional living are knifed off the life trajectory, elevating the likelihood of a criminal career). A key component of this first book is the idea of social capital. As people continue in an offending trajectory, they have increasingly few legitimate sources of support and trust upon which they can draw when they run afoul of the law or otherwise get into trouble. The lack of social capital also increases the likelihood of continued criminal activity. Astute readers will have observed the influence of Hirschi (1969) and his ideas on social bonds in Sampson and Laub's (1993) work. A key difference between Hirschi (1969) and Sampson and Laub (1993) is that the latter consider the importance of social bonds and the informal social control they are able to exert over the course of the lifetime, emphasizing that different bonds carry different weight at different points in the lifetime. Bonds to school, for example, are more important for younger people, while bonds to a spouse or to a job are more important for those who are older (on this point, see especially Sampson and Laub, 1990).

In the second text, Laub and Sampson (2003) reported on the 500 delinquents from the Gluecks' study with whom they had followed up until the age of 70, including the in depth interviews they were able to conduct with 52 of them. This book focuses primarily on the changes that can result in the end of a criminal career and the start of a law abiding existence. Laub and Sampson (2003) found that all of the offenders in their sample eventually desisted from crime by age 70 and that for many, desistance did not seem to be a deliberate choice. Rather, it was an outcome of encountering turning points, such as marriage to a supportive spouse, acquiring a good job or military service, and investing by default in a legitimate life (on the importance of marriage as a turning point, see Sampson, Laub and Wimer, 2006 and Laub, Nagin and Sampson, 1998; on the importance of military service, see Sampson and Laub, 1996; on the importance of military service for females, see Craig and Foster, 2013). Moving forward from these turning points, the former offenders were able to build up social capital and did not want to risk their investment in their law abiding lives by returning to crime.

Upon further reflection on their work, Sampson and Laub (2005) emphasized the importance of choice (human agency, in their terms), the decisions that offenders made during their lives that led them to stay criminally involved or to desist from crime. This is not to say that Sampson and Laub (2005) simply tacked on a rational choice component (see Chapter 9) to their theory. Rather, Sampson and Laub (2005) believed that both actions and preferences are chosen, leading people, offenders included, to make decisions that are embedded in their social structures and relationships (in their terms, these are situated choices). Sampson and Laub (2005) conclude that involvement in crime has to be more than just weak social bonds and desistance has to be more than acquiring social bonds. The choices offenders make, whether to continue in crime or go straight and the contexts in which these decisions are made are crucial in understanding crime

Figure 7.4. Life-course theory

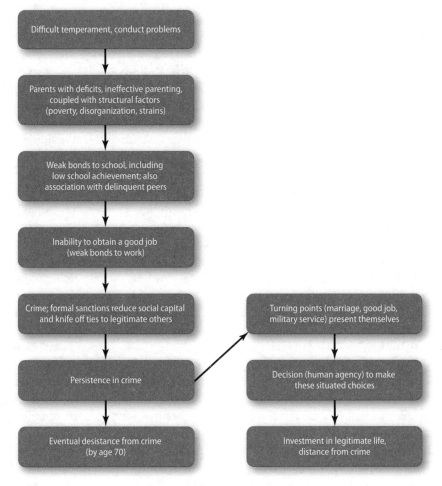

Source: Adapted from Sampson and Laub, 1993, 2005; Laub and Sampson, 2003.

over the life course (for more on offenders' choices and their transformations to law abiding citizens, see Giordano, Cernkovich and Rudolph, 2002). We need to devise ways to study and better comprehend offenders' choices if we are to fully grasp how people become involved in crime, stay involved in crime and eventually desist from crime. Figure 7.4 is a graphic representation of life-course theory.

Notice how different Figure 7.4 is from Figure 7.3 above. In Moffitt's (1993) theory, there are two distinct pathways to offending and once on one trajectory, offenders stay on that trajectory. However, Sampson and Laub (2003) believe that offenders start out on one trajectory or pathway and diverge from it when they encounter turning points. It is no coincidence that their 2003 book is called *Shared Beginnings, Divergent Lives*.

Research on Robert Sampson and John Laub's Life-Course Theory

Perhaps unsurprisingly, research that replicates Sampson and Laub's findings is rarely encountered. The reason for this is that they took a truly life course approach, examining the same offenders from childhood into late adulthood. It takes a great deal of planning, money and importantly, time to conduct such a study. Rather, research on the life course theory focuses on clarifying it, further developing it and more thoroughly explaining its predictions. For example, Laub and Sampson (1993) explicitly connected the idea of social capital to social bonds, contending that social bonds are important because they foster the accumulation of social capital. It also appears that residential change may serve as a turning point. Kirk (2012) found that parolees who were unable to return to their former residences in New Orleans due to the damage from Hurricane Katrina and had to move to new locations were significantly less likely than those parolees who returned to their old neighborhoods to be reincarcerated for the first three years after their location change.

In their theory, Sampson and Laub imply that desistance is a gradual process and research has shown that desistance is usually a gradual process (DeLisi, Kosloski, Drury, Vaughn, Beaver, Trulson and Wright, 2012), but there are those who instantaneously desist from crime as well (Kurlycheck, Bushway and Brame, 2012). Sampson and Laub (1990) also suggested that marriage and a good job are the most important turning points in desisting from a life of crime, but they did not let this suggestion go unexamined. Using a sophisticated statistical technique to analyze the importance of marriage to a law abiding, supportive partner, Laub, Nagin and Sampson (1998) found that a good marriage does influence desistance from crime and that the effects of a good marriage on desistance are both gradual and cumulative. Using another advanced analytic technique, Sampson, Laub and Wimer (2006) found that marriage is not just associated with desistance from crime, but is a causal factor in desistance. In fact, marriage resulted in a 35 percent reduction in the odds of crime commission for the same man. That is, a man's marriage caused a reduction in the likelihood that he would engage in crime, compared to that same man had he not wed. Sampson and Laub (1996) similarly found that World War II-era military service and subsequent assistance provided by the G.I. Bill was an important turning point for the delinquents in the Gluecks' data set and more recent military service is an important turning point for females (Craig and Foster, 2013).

Sampson and Laub claim in their theory that everyone eventually desists from crime. However, DeLisi, Kosloski, Drury, Vaughn, Beaver, Trulson and Wright (2012) contend that a focus on arrests may indicate desistance has occurred when in fact offending is still taking place. In their study, they found that the lifelong offenders continued to offend late into life, far beyond the peak ages of offending normally observed. Moreover, these offenders continued to commit serious and often violent offenses against people. The number of arrests for these serious crimes declined as the offenders got older, but this was in comparison to their own previous criminal histories, which were extensive and violence-filled. Lifelong offenders were increasingly arrested for less serious crimes as they aged, indicating they were still involved in crime, even if that crime was not as serious as the crime they committed when they were younger. DeLisi and colleagues

(2012) maintain that measuring arrests for serious crimes may indicate that desistance has occurred when it has not and they take issue with the notion that everyone desists as Sampson and Laub's theory predicts.

Strengths and Weaknesses of Robert Sampson and John Laub's Life-Course Theory

The greatest strength of life course theory is that it is a true life course theory of crime. That is, it not just theoretically but empirically examines the factors associated with persistence in and desistance from crime over the entire lifetime. It shares some strengths with other developmental theories, especially Moffitt's (1993) theory: it considers biological, psychological and sociological factors in crime causation, it relies on longitudinal studies to clarify the temporal ordering of cause and effect and it definitely attempts to identify those factors associated with desistance from crime (Walsh and Hemmens, 2011). Life course theory also makes a convincing case for the importance of human agency in choosing to persist in and desist from crime. It is refreshing to think that once on a trajectory of criminal activity, offenders need not remain on that pathway for the rest of their lives.

Perhaps the principal weakness of life-course theory is its generalizability or lack thereof. As mentioned above, the Gluecks' data set, on which life-course theory is directly based, included only white, male non-delinquents and white, male institutionalized delinquents who grew up in Massachusetts during the Great Depression. It is entirely possible that the reasons this group persisted in and desisted from crime are different from the reasons members of other races and ethnic groups would, are different from the reasons girls and women would, are different from the reasons delinquents who were never institutionalized would or are different from the reasons delinquents of a different generation would. Of course, it makes intuitive sense that marriage to a supportive partner would influence if not cause desistance from crime, but is the effect present for criminally involved women who marry law abiding men, for example? Are any of the factors associated with persistence in and desistance from crime the same for men and women and if so, to what degree? Only more empirical study will bear this and other generalizability issues out (for more on the applicability of life-course theory to different ethnic groups, see Nielsen, 1999; for more on the criminal pathways of women, see Blokland and van Os, 2010[10]). Another weakness of life-course theory is that it reveals relatively little about the onset of crime and its causes, focusing to a large extent instead on desistance. In fact, while Akers (2005), Farrington (2003) and Moffitt (1993) focus on the causes of offending that are present in childhood and adolescence and while Sampson and Laub (1993) focus on desistance from crime in adulthood, these theories offer little insight into those who begin offending in adulthood and how they are similar to and different from those who begin offending earlier in life (see Zara, 2012 for more on adult onset offending).

---

10. The entire volume of the journal in which this research was published was devoted to criminal careers.

Conclusion: Policy Implications of Developmental Theories

With the possible exception of Sampson and Laub's life-course theory, all of the theories covered in this chapter start with many of the same factors that put people at risk for offending over the lifetime. As such, policy implications of many if not all developmental theories of crime focus on addressing these risk factors. In his introduction of ICAP theory, Farrington (2003) chose not to expound on policy implications of his theory, instead using the space in the article to describe it in detail. Four years later, Farrington and Welsh (2007) devoted an entire book to policy implications that are widely applicable to most developmental theories.

In this book, Farrington and Welsh (2007) describe those programs that have been rigorously evaluated and shown to be effective crime, delinquency and antisocial behavior preventive programs. In fact, they are only interested in those programs that have undergone the most robust evaluations, especially those that contain a key element of outstanding experimental design, random assignment to groups. Random assignment to groups helps to ensure that the experimental condition is what results in the outcomes being measured. In the cases Farrington and Welsh (2007) describe, the experimental condition is participation in programs designed to prevent criminal, delinquent or antisocial activity (the control condition, of course, is no participation in these programs) and the outcomes being measured are involvement in crime, delinquency or antisocial activity.

Farrington and Welsh (2007) begin their work by describing (and for our purposes, reiterating) the risk factors that predict involvement in crime and they do so by domains. In the individual domain, the risk factors that predict criminal involvement are low intelligence, difficult personality and temperament, low empathy and high impulsiveness. In the family domain, the risk factors that predict criminal involvement are criminal or antisocial parents, a large family, ineffective parenting, conflict between parents and broken families. In the environmental domain, the risk factors that predict criminal involvement are low socioeconomic status, having delinquent friends, attending a school with high rates of delinquency among students and residence in deprived neighborhoods.

The Individual Domain

According to Farrington and Welsh (2007), preschool intellectual enrichment and child skills training programs have been shown to prevent crime and delinquency in the individual domain. Preschool intellectual enrichment programs provide very young students with cognitively and socially enriching experiences that their parents or caregivers are unlikely to provide them with at home. One example of an effective preschool intellectual enrichment program is the Perry Preschool project in Ypsilanti, Michigan (this is not the only successful preschool intellectual enrichment program, but there is a good deal of follow up data on participants, which is why it is described in some detail here). A follow up study on children who went through the Perry Preschool program revealed that at age 19, they were more likely to have jobs, to have high school diplomas and some post-secondary education or training and were less likely to have been arrested

(Berrueta-Clement, Schweinhart, Barnett, Epstein and Weikart, 1984). At age 27, those who went through Perry Preschool had half as many arrests as those who did not participate in the program (Schweinhart, Barnes and Weikart, 1993). At age 40, those who went through Perry Preschool had fewer arrests for violent crime, property crime and drug crime and were less likely to be chronic offenders than those who did not participate in the program (Schweinhart, Montie, Xiang, Barnett, Belfield and Nores, 2005; Kirp, 2004).

Child skills training programs attempt to teach children a variety of competencies across cognitive, social and emotional domains by providing them with social skills, problem solving skills, anger management skills and the ability to use emotional language. One example of a successful child skills training program (again, not the only example) is the Montreal Longitudinal-Experimental Study. Children at high risk for aggression at age six were identified and between the ages of seven and nine, received training in social skills and self-control. The parents of these high risk children were taught how to be consistent disciplinarians and manage family crises effectively. By age 12, those who participated in the Montreal experiment engaged in less property crime, less alcohol use, less fighting and had higher school achievement than those who did not (McCord, Tremblay, Vitaro and Desmarais-Gervais, 1994; Tremblay, Tremblay, Vitaro, Bertrand, LeBlanc, Beauchensne, Boileau and David, 1992). By age 15, those who participated in the Montreal experiment were less likely to be gang involved and less likely to use intoxicants than those who did not (Tremblay, Pagani-Kurtz, Masse, Vitaro and Pihl, 1995; Tremblay, Masse, Pagani and Vitaro, 1996). The benefits of both preschool intellectual enrichment and child skills training programs go beyond the prevention of crime in later life. These programs also have important and positive effects on other life areas, including educational attainment, job acquisition, income level, substance abuse and stability of family and there is some evidence that they produce a cost savings to communities, even after their start up and maintenance costs are accounted for (Farrington and Welsh, 2007).

The Family Domain

Farrington and Welsh (2007) explain that general parent education and parent management programs have been shown to prevent crime and delinquency in the family domain. Parental education includes home visitation programs, in which nurses visit new mothers and provide them with an array of education on how to care for newborns and young children and how to prevent abuse and neglect, as well as links to community resources for help with education, job and sobriety acquisition. An example of a successful home visitation program is the Prenatal/Early Intervention Project, also called the Nurse-Family Partnership in Elmira, New York. New mothers who participated in this program were less likely to abuse or neglect their children through age two (Olds, Henderson, Chamberlin, and Tatelbaum, 1986) and through age 13 (Olds, et al., 1997); child abuse is associated with violent offending in later life (Widom, 1989). Moreover, the children of those mothers who participated in the program had significantly fewer arrests at age 15 than the children of those mothers who did not participate (Olds, et al., 1998; Olds, Sadler and Kitzman, 2007). Greenwood and Turner (2011) go so far as to call the Nurse Family Partnership a proven program for reducing recidivism in both mothers and children who participate. Parental education also includes parent education plus daycare programs, in which daycare is provided to the children of the parents who participate in the educational component. Daycare has its own positive effects for the children who attend, including interaction with other children and skill acquisition across the sensory, cognitive and motor domains. One example of a parent education plus daycare program is the Syracuse University Family Development Research Project in Syracuse, New York. Expectant and new mothers were given weekly training on a variety of topics important to child rearing while their children went to daycare through the age of five. At age 15, those children who participated in the program had significantly fewer referrals to juvenile court than those who did not participate. Moreover, those who did not participate had a much higher number of and much more serious offenses than those who did (Lally, Mangione and Honig, 1988). Both types of parental education programs, home visitation and parent education plus daycare, have been shown to prevent later criminal involvement (Farrington and Welsh, 2003, 2002; Welsh and Farrington, 2004; Welsh, 2012).

Parent management programs, on the other hand, are those in which parents are trained to effectively manage their children's behavior. Effective management includes monitoring behavior closely, rewarding good behavior and consistently and appropriately punishing negative behavior.[11] One example of a parent management training program that has undergone long term evaluation is that created by Patricia Long. The children of those parents who received management training exhibited less deviant behavior and more compliance at the conclusion of their participation in the program. A follow up study done 14 years after program completion revealed that those children whose parents participated in the program were similar on measures of delinquency, school achievement and emotional adjustment to those children whose parents did not participate (Long, Forehand, Wierson and Morgan, 1994). However, taken together, parent management programs have been shown to be somewhat effective at preventing later crime for the children of parents who participate (Farrington and Welsh, 2003; Welsh, 2012).

The Environmental Domain

Of the three environments under consideration here, peer, school and community, the greatest amount of robust research has been conducted on school-based programs. The effectiveness of a school-based program is generally determined by assessing delinquency, alcohol and drug use, dropping out and other problem behavior. A meta-analysis by Wilson, Gottfredson and Najaka (2001) revealed that four types of school-based programs are effective when measured in this way, those that use cognitive behavioral or behavioral instructional methods to develop self-control and social competence, those that reorganize grades or classes, those that involve school and discipline management and those that rely on classroom or instructional management.

---

11. Astute readers will be thinking back to Gottfredson and Hirschi (1990) and their thoughts on the development of self-control in children (see Chapter 5).

One example of a program designed to increase self-control or social competency using cognitive behavioral or behavioral instructional methods is Responding in Peaceful and Positive Ways (RIPP), a semester-long violence prevention program targeted at sixth graders, who learn how to build trust, respect differences, and manage anger, and the consequences of fighting and alternatives to doing so. Those who participated in RIPP had a reduction in violent violations of the school disciplinary code a year after their participation ended (Farrell, Meyer, Sullivan and Kung, 2003). One example of a program designed to reorganize grades or classes is Student Training Through Urban Strategies (STATUS), in which high-risk students spend two hours a day learning a combined social studies and English curriculum in a setting that emphasizes student participation. Those who participated had lower rates of criminal activity, use of intoxicants, school dropout and antisocial behavior than those who did not (Gottfredson, Wilson and Najaka, 2002). One example of a program that involves school and discipline management is the Positive Action Through Holistic Education (PATHE), which was designed to increase shared decision making across schools, teacher competence and student achievement as well as to improve the school climate. An evaluation of this program revealed that it reduces criminal activity, use of intoxicants and antisocial behavior among students in the schools in which it was implemented (Gottfredson, Wilson and Najaka, 2002). One example of a program that involves classroom or instructional management is the Seattle Social Development Project, which combines training for parents and teachers with skills training for students. The students who participate are trained in problem solving skills and their parents are trained in reinforcing good behavior. A follow up of the students who participated in the program in first through sixth grades revealed that at age 18, they committed less violence, abused alcohol less and had fewer sexual partners than those who did not participate (Hawkins, Catalano, Kosterman, Abbott and Hill, 1999). Greenwood and Turner (2011) call the Seattle Social Development Project a promising program for reducing delinquency and recidivism.

There is little evidence on peer-based programs that are designed to prevent delinquency, though there is some research that reveals placement of antisocial adolescents in social groups dominated by prosocial adolescents reduces their antisocial behavior (Feldman, Wodarski and Caplinger, 1983). There is a bit more evidence on community-based programs that are designed to prevent delinquency. Community-based programs include after school programs and community-based mentoring. An example of an after school program is the Boys and Girls Club of America (BGC); BGC provides young people with a variety of programs designed to improve physical health, develop leadership skills, increase school achievement and enhance social skills. In addition to the usual compliment of reading classes, help with homework and sports, some BGCs offer substance abuse resistance training. Research on the impact of BGCs reveals that those housing developments with BGCs (those with and without the substance abuse resistance training component) had less criminal activity by juveniles, lower rates of substance abuse, less drug trafficking and less property damage (Schinke, Orlandi and Cole, 1992). An example of a community-based mentoring program is Big Brothers Big Sisters of America (BBBS). BBBS is designed to pair youth with prosocial adult mentors who spend about 60 hours a week per year together. Research on the impact of BBBS reveals that those youth who participated in the mentoring program were less likely to commit

Table 7.2. Selected interventions that prevent crime

Program (and domain)	Ranking
Parent management training (family)	1
Preschool intellectual enrichment (individual)	2
Home visiting (family)	3
School-based programs (environmental)	4

Source: Adapted from Farrington and Welsh, 2007.

assault, to have used drugs or alcohol and to have been truant from school and they were more likely to have higher school achievement and more positive relationships with parents and friends (Grossman and Tierney, 1998).[12] Greenwood and Turner (2011) note that Big Brothers Big Sisters is a proven program for reducing antisocial behavior.

Table 7.2 ranks each of the interventions discussed by Farrington and Welsh (2007) in order of the preventive effect they have on crime, delinquency and antisocial behavior. Note that the most effective interventions are those that take place within the individual and family domains and are designed to target very young children; it bears repeating that claims of their effectiveness are based on the most robust evaluations conducted over long follow up periods with randomly assigned experimental and control groups. It is fascinating that these successful interventions have little to nothing to do with the criminal justice system. Perhaps it is time to rethink the way we deal with crime causation. Farrington and Walsh (2007) agree, calling for a national crime prevention strategy for America that is focused on addressing risk factors, evidence based, situated within the Department of Health and Human Services and effectively executed at the local level, as each community has different needs and resources at its disposal.

Though a majority of policy implications for developmental theories have to do with ameliorating risk factors early in life, this does not mean there are no policy implications for Sampson and Laub's life-course theory. The theory maintains that a good marriage, a good job and military service can be turning points that result in desistance from crime (for more on desistance, see Maruna, 2001). Programs that increase the chances of offenders encountering one or more of these turning points would be useful here, including job acquisition programs for those returning from incarceration. Latessa (2012) contends that employment programs which target and improve offenders' attitudes about work as well as help them learn marketable skills are likely to be the most effective at reducing recidivism and helping offenders get on and stay on a law abiding path.

---

12. Astute readers will be thinking back to the policy implications of social learning theory discussed in Chapter 5.

Summary of Criminological Theories So Far

Throughout Chapters 3, 4, 5, 6 and 7, we have explained many of the leading criminological theories. Psychosocial and biosocial theories were examined in Chapter 3, social structural theories were examined in Chapter 4, social process theories were examined in Chapter 5, critical theories were examined in Chapter 6 and developmental theories were examined in Chapter 7. Especially for the newcomer to criminology, the number and content of these theories can seem overwhelming. Table 7.3 summarizes the main tenets of the theories covered thus far.

While all the theories described to this point have their merits, some are more meritorious than others. The current leading criminological theories are control, strain and leaning theories. More specifically, this means Hirschi's (1969) social control (social bond) theory, Gottfredson and Hirschi's (1990) self-control theory, Agnew's (2002) general strain theory and Akers' (1997, 2002) social learning theory. These are the most empirically supported theories of crime and the ones held in highest esteem by many criminologists (Agnew, 2005; Cullen and Agnew, 2011).

What does this mean for the future? Will control, strain and learning theories retain their places at the top of the heap? Recall that other theories of crime have ascended to prominence in the past. Lombroso's ideas about the atavistic criminal were very popular at their time, as were Shaw and McKay's ideas on social disorganization. Even labeling theory enjoyed some time as one of the most popular theories of crime, so it is reasonable to think that theories other than control, strain and learning will one day be among the leading theories of crime. Though criminologists have been very reluctant to accept them in the past, at least two scholars think biosocial theories will soon be among the leading criminological theories, in large part because the techniques used to investigate the biological and genetic influences on crime are becoming more sophisticated by the day (Walsh and Hemmens, 2011). Other contenders for future leading theories of crime include developmental theories. As we have seen, developmental theories are able to consider biological, psychological and sociological risk factors for crime, they are able to determine the temporal order of causes and effects, in large part due to the longitudinal studies that characterize them, they rely on very large samples followed for years if not decades and they are able to address the onset, persistence in and desistance from crime (Walsh and Hemmens, 2011). In 2012, the American Society of Criminology formed a Division of Developmental and Life Course Criminology, chaired and founded by none other than David Farrington.[13] This founding is indicative of the importance of these theories in explaining crime.

---

13. For an invigorating look at some of the issues that scholars believe are most relevant to the future of criminology, see Loeber and Welsh (2012).

Table 7.3. Brief summary of criminological theories

	Tenets	Theorists
Chapter 3		
Psychosocial theories	Certain traits, especially high levels of negative emotionality and impulsiveness and low levels of constraint and agreeability are associated with crime; trait development is influenced by both biologic and environmental factors	Caspi, et al.; Miller and Lynam; Ellis and Walsh
Biosocial theories	Crime may be rooted in a number of biological factors, such as brain dysfunction, deficits in arousal, problems with neurochemistry and genetics; biological factors interact with environmental factors to produce crime	Bufkin and Luttrell; Raine, Venables and Williams; Day and Carelli; Seo and Patrick; Beaver, Wright and Walsh; Caspi, et al.
Chapter 4		
Social Disorganization	Poverty, residential mobility, heterogeneity and family disruption lead to inability to exert informal social control, which leads to crime	Shaw and McKay, Sampson, Wilson
Anomie	Normlessness and an unclear sense of what is right and wrong leads to crime	Durkheim
Institutional Anomie	Subjugation of all other social institutions to the economy means those social institutions cannot regulate criminal behavior, especially that done in pursuit of money	Messner and Rosenfeld
Classic Strain	Belief in culturally accepted goals but rejection of legitimate means to attain them leads to innovation (criminal adaptation to strain)	Merton
General Strain	Failure to achieve positively valued goals, removal of positively valued stimuli and presentation of negatively valued stimuli lead to a negative view of others leads to negative emotions, especially anger leads to criminal coping	Agnew
Subcultural Theories	Criminal groups reject middle class values and/or develop their own, easier to attain goals; there are limits to criminal as well as legitimate opportunities	Cohen, Miller, Cloward and Ohlin, Anderson
Chapter 5		
Differential Association	Association with delinquent others leads to crime	Sutherland
Social Learning	Definitions, anticipated reinforcement and imitation of delinquent peers leads to initial crime, differential reinforcement for criminal activity leads to persistence in crime	Akers
Social Control	The strength of bonds to social institutions and the people in them determines criminal involvement; stronger bonds mean less crime	Hirschi
Self-Control	Low self-control causes crime and is a result of ineffective parenting	Gottfredson and Hirschi
Labeling	Formal labeling by the criminal justice system leads to an increase in crime, called secondary deviance	Tannenbaum, Lemert
Neutralization	Offenders use a variety of techniques to ameliorate their guilty feelings and thereby engage in crime	Sykes and Matza

Chapter 6		
Marxist Criminology	Crime is the result of the struggle between the classes; the harsh capitalism in the United States is particularly criminogenic	Marx, Bonger, Currie, Colvin
Conflict Criminology	Crime is an inevitable result of conflict among groups vying for power; the groups with more power will criminalize the actions of those with less	Weber, Vold
Peacemaking Criminology	Harsh punishments beget violence; restorative justice is the solution to crime	Quinney, Braithwaite
Feminist Criminology	Liberation perspective says that as women take on masculine roles, they will commit more crime; patriarchy perspective says women's victimization by men causes their criminal activity; crime is a way for men to do gender	Adler, Simon, Chesney-Lind, Messerschmidt
Chapter 7		
General Theory of Crime and Delinquency	Risk factors in various life domains have an effect on crime and on one another; the more risk factors, the greater the likelihood of crime	Agnew
Integrated Cognitive Antisocial Potential (ICAP) Theory	Long term antisocial potential that results from risk factors in combination with short term antisocial potential leads to crime	Farrington
Dual Pathway Developmental Theory	Offenders are either adolescent limited or life course persistent offenders; the latter start life with a host of risk factors while the former age out of offending in adulthood	Moffitt
Life-Course Theory	Even offenders who persist in crime well into adulthood can lead legitimate lives if they encounter and choose important turning points, such as marriage	Sampson and Laub

Websites to Visit

ASC Division of Developmental and Life Course Criminology: http://www.dlccrim.org/
Office of Juvenile Justice and Delinquency Prevention: http://www.ojjdp.gov/
Ex-Offender Employment Resources: http://www.bop.gov/inmate_programs/itb_references.jsp

Discussion Questions

1. Do you have any of the risk factors for crime mentioned in Table 7.1? If so, which ones? Have they impacted your involvement in crime?
2. Which risk factors in which life domains as explained in Agnew's (2005) theory do you think are most important in producing crime? Why?

3. Are there any programs or policies you can conceive of to address the short term risk factors in Farrington's (2003) ICAP theory?
4. Do you think Moffitt (1993) is right when she says that offenders are on one path from early childhood forward with no deviation from it, or do you think Laub and Sampson (2003) are right when they say offenders can move to a law abiding path when they encounter turning points? Why?
5. Implied in Farrington and Welsh's (2007) explanation of policy implications for developmental theories of crime is that prevention is better than rehabilitation. Do you agree and why or why not?
6. Which of the theories introduced in this chapter makes the most sense to you and why?
7. Which of the theories introduced in this chapter makes the least sense to you and why?

References

Agnew, Robert. (2002). Foundation for a general strain theory of crime. In S. Cote (Ed.), *Criminological theories: Bridging the past to the future* (pp. 113–124). Thousand Oaks, CA: Sage.

Agnew, Robert. (2005). *Why do criminals offend? A general theory of crime and delinquency.* Los Angeles, CA: Roxbury.

Agnew, Robert. (2011). Crime and time: The temporal patterning of causal variables. *Theoretical Criminology, 15,* 115–140.

Akers, Ronald. (1997). *Criminological theories: Introduction and evaluation.* 2nd ed. Los Angeles, CA: Roxbury.

Akers, Ronald. (2002). A social learning theory of crime. In S. Cote (Ed.), *Criminological theories: Bridging the past to the future* (pp. 135–143). Thousand Oaks, CA: Sage.

Akers, Ronald and Christine Sellers. (2009). *Criminological theories: Introduction, evaluation, and application.* 5th ed. Los Angeles, CA: Roxbury.

Barnes, J.C., Kevin Beaver and Alex Piquero. (2011). A test of Moffitt's hypothesis of delinquency abstention. *Criminal Justice and Behavior, 38,* 690–709.

Bernat, Debra, J. Michael Oakes, Sandra Pettingell and Michael Resnick. (2012). Risk and direct protective factors for youth violence: Results from the National Longitudinal Study of Adolescent Health. *American Journal of Preventive Medicine, 43,* S57–S66.

Berrueta-Clement, John, Lawrence Schweinhart, W. Steven Barnett, Ann Epstein and David Weikart. (1984). *Changed lives: The effects of the Perry Preschool program on youths through age 19.* Ypsilanti, MI: High/Scope Press.

Blokland, Arjan, Daniel Nagin and Paul Nieuwbeerta. (2005). Life span offending trajectories of a Dutch conviction cohort. *Criminology, 43,* 919–954.

Blokland, Arjan and Riann van Os. (2010). Life span offending trajectories of convicted Dutch women. *International Criminal Justice Review, 20,* 169–187.

Boutwell, Brian, J.C. Barnes and Kevin Beaver. (2013). Life-course persistent offenders and the propensity to commit sexual assault. *Sexual Abuse, 25,* 69–81.

Caspi, Avshalom and Terrie Moffitt. (1995). The continuity of maladaptive behavior: From description to understanding the study of antisocial behavior. In D. Cicchetti and D. Cohen (Eds.), *Manual of developmental psychology* (pp. 472–511). New York, NY: John Wiley.

Chen, Xiaojin and Michele Adams. (2010). Are teen delinquency abstainers social introverts? A test of Moffitt's theory. *Journal of Research in Crime and Delinquency*, 47(4), 439–468.

Craig, Jessica and Holly Foster. (2013). Desistance in the transition to adulthood: The roles of marriage, military, and gender. *Deviant Behavior, 34*, 208–223.

Cullen, Francis T. and Robert Agnew. (2011). *Criminological theory: Past to present.* 4th ed. New York, NY: Oxford University Press.

DeLisi, Michael and Kevin Beaver (Eds.). *Criminological theory: A life-course approach.* 2nd ed. Burlington, MA: Jones and Bartlett.

DeLisi, Matt, Anna Kosloski, Alan Drury, Michael Vaughn, Kevin Beaver, Chad Trulson and John Paul Wright. (2012). Never-desisters: A descriptive study of the life-course-persistent offender. In M. DeLisi and K. Beaver (Eds.), *Criminological theory: A life-course approach*. 2nd ed (pp. 297–310). Burlington, MA: Jones and Bartlett.

Donker, Andrea, Wilma Smeenk, Peter van der Laan and Frank Verhulst. (2003). Individual stability of antisocial behavior from childhood to adulthood: Testing the stability postulate of Moffitt's developmental theory. *Criminology, 41*, 593–610.

Eisner, Manuel and Amy Nivette. (2012). How to reduce the global homicide rate to 2 per 100,000 by 2060. In R. Loeber and B. Welsh (Eds.), *The future of criminology* (pp. 219–225). New York, NY: Oxford University Press.

Farrell, Albert, Aleta Meyer, Terri Sullivan and Eva Kung. (2003). Evaluation of the Responding in Peaceful and Positive Ways (RIPP) seventh grade violence prevention curriculum. *Journal of Child and Family Studies, 12*, 101–120.

Farrington, David. (1986). Age and crime. In M. Tonry and N. Morris (Eds.), *Crime and justice, Vol. 7* (pp. 189–250). Chicago, IL: University of Chicago Press.

Farrington, David. (2003). Developmental and life-course criminology: Key theoretical and empirical issues—The 2002 Sutherland Award address. *Criminology, 41*, 221–256.

Farrington, David. (2005). The integrated cognitive antisocial potential (ICAP) theory. In D. Farrington (Ed.), *Integrated developmental and life-course theories of offending* (pp. 73–92). New Brunswick, NJ: Transaction Publishers.

Farrington, David (Ed.). (2008). *Integrated development and life-course theories of offending: Advances in criminological theory. Vol. 14.* New Brunswick, NJ: Transaction Publishers.

Farrington, David, Sandra Lambert and Donald West. (1998). Criminal careers of two generations of family members in the Cambridge Study in Delinquent Development. *Studies on Crime and Crime Prevention, 7*, 85–106.

Farrington, David and Brandon Welsh. (2002). Family-based crime prevention. In L. Sherman, D. Farrington, B. Welsh and D. MacKenzie (Eds.), *Evidence-based crime prevention* (pp. 22–55). New York, NY: Routledge.

Farrington, David and Brandon Welsh. (2003). Family-based prevention of offending: A meta-analysis. *Australian and New Zealand Journal of Criminology, 36*, 127–151.

Farrington, David and Brandon Welsh. (2007). *Saving children from a life of crime*. New York, NY: Oxford University Press.

Feldman, Ronald, John Wodarski and Timothy Caplinger. (1983). *St. Louis conundrum: The effective treatment of antisocial youth*. Englewood Cliffs, NJ: Prentice-Hall.

Giordano, Peggy, Stephen Cernkovich and Jennifer Rudolph. (2002). Gender, crime, and desistance: Toward a theory of cognitive transformation. *American Journal of Sociology, 107*, 990–1064.

Glueck, Sheldon and Eleanor Glueck. (1950). *Unraveling juvenile delinquency*. New York, NY: The Commonwealth Fund.

Gottfredson, Denise, David Wilson and Stacy Najaka. (2002). School-based crime prevention. In L. Sherman, D. Farrington, B. Welsh and D. MacKenzie (Eds.), *Evidence-based crime prevention* (pp. 56–154). New York, NY: Routledge.

Gottfredson, Michael and Travis Hirschi. (1990). *A general theory of crime*. Palo Alto, CA: Stanford University Press.

Grossman, Jean and Joseph Tierney. (1998). Does mentoring work? An impact study of the Big Brothers Big Sisters program. *Evaluation Review, 22*, 403–426.

Hawkins, David, Richard Catalano, Rick Kosterman, Robert Abbott and Karl Hill. (1999). Preventing adolescent health risk behaviors by strengthening prevention during childhood. *Archives of Pediatric and Adolescent Medicine, 153*, 226–234.

Herrenkohl, Todd, Eugene Maguin, Karl Hill, J. David Hawkins, Robert Abbot and Richard Catalano. Developmental risk factors for youth violence. *Journal of Adolescent Health, 26*, 176–186.

Hirschi, Travis. (1969). *The causes of delinquency*. Berkeley, CA: University of California Press.

Kirk, David. (2012). Residential change as a turning point in the life course of crime: Desistance or temporary cessation? *Criminology, 50*, 329–358.

Kirp, David. (2004). Life way after Head Start. *New York Times Magazine*, November 21, 32–38.

Kratzer, Lynn and Sheilagh Hodgins. (1999). A typology of offenders: A test of Moffitt's theory among males and females from childhood to age 30. *Criminal Behavior and Mental Health, 9*, 57–73.

Kurlycheck, Megan, Shawn Bushway and Robert Brame. (2012). Long-term crime desistance and recidivism patterns — Evidence from the Essex County convicted felon study. *Criminology, 50*, 71–104.

Lally, Ronald, Peter Mangione and Alice Honig. (1988). The Syracuse University Family Development Research Program: Long-range impact of an early intervention with low-income children and their families. In D. Powell (Ed.), *Parent education as early childhood intervention: Emerging direction in theory, research and practice* (pp. 79–104). Norwood, NJ: Ablex.

Latessa, Edward. (2012). Why work is important and how to improve the effectiveness of correctional reentry programs that target employment. *Criminology & Public Policy, 11*, 87–91.

Laub, John, Daniel Nagin and Robert Sampson. (1998). Trajectories of change in criminal offending: Good marriages and the desistance process. *American Sociological Review, 63*, 225–238.

Laub, John and Robert Sampson. (2003). Turning points in the life course: Why change matters to the study of crime. *Criminology, 31*, 301–325.

Laub, John and Robert Sampson. (2003). *Shared beginnings, divergent lives: Delinquent boys to age 70.* Cambridge, MA: Harvard University Press.

LeBlanc, Marc and Marcel Frechette. (1989). *Male criminal activity from childhood through youth.* New York, NY: Springer-Verlag.

Loeber, Rolf and Brandon Welsh (Eds.). (2012). *The future of criminology.* New York, NY: Oxford University Press.

Long, Patricia, Rex Forehand, Michelle Wierson and Allison Morgan. (1994). Does parent training with young noncompliant children have long-term effects? *Behavior Research and Therapy, 32*, 101–107.

Maruna, Shadd. (2001). *Making good: How ex-convicts reform and rebuild their lives.* Washington, DC: American Psychological Association.

McCord, Joan, Richard Tremblay, Frank Vitaro and Lyse Desmarais-Gervais. (1994). Boys, disruptive behaviour, school adjustment, and delinquency: The Montreal Prevention Experiment. *International Journal of Behavioral Development, 17*, 739–752.

McCord, Joan and Kevin Conway. (2002). Patters of juvenile delinquency and co-offending. In E. Warning and D. Weisburd (Eds.), *Advances in criminological theory, Vol. 10: Crime and social disorganization* (pp. 15–30). New Brunswick, NJ: Transaction.

Moffitt, Terrie. (1993). Adolescent-limited and life-course persistent antisocial behavior: A developmental taxonomy. *Psychological Review, 100*, 674–701.

Moffitt, Terrie. (1994). Natural histories of delinquency. In E.G.M. Weitekamp and H.-J. Kerner (Eds.), *Cross-national longitudinal research on human development and criminal behavior* (pp. 3–66). Dordrecht: Kluwer Academic Publishers.

Moffitt, Terrie. (1997). Adolescent-limited and life-course persistent offending: A complementary pair of developmental theories. In T.P. Thornberry (Ed.), *Developmental theories of crime and delinquency, Vol. 7* (pp. 11–54). New Brunswick, NJ: Transaction Publishers.

Moffitt, Terrie. (2003). Life-course persistent and adolescent-limited antisocial behavior: A ten-year research review and a research agenda. In B.B. Lahey, T.E. Moffitt and A. Caspi (Eds.), *Causes of conduct disorder and juvenile delinquency* (pp. 49–75). New York, NY: The Guilford Press.

Moffitt, Terrie. (2006). Life-course persistent versus adolescent-limited antisocial behavior. In D. Cicchetti and D.J. Cohen (Eds.), *Developmental psychopathology, Vol. 3* (pp. 570–598). New York, NY: John Wiley.

Moffitt, Terrie and Avshalom Caspi. (2001). Childhood predictors differentiate life-course persistent and adolescent-limited antisocial pathways among males and females. *Development and Psychopathology, 13*, 355–375.

Moffitt, Terrie and Avshalom Caspi. (2002). Males on the life-course-persistent and adolescent-limited antisocial pathways: Follow-up at age 26 years. *Development and Psychopathology, 14*, 179–207.

Moffitt, Terrie and Anthony Walsh. (2003). The adolescence-limited/life-course persistence theory of antisocial behavior: What have we learned? In A. Walsh and L Ellis (Eds.), *Biosocial criminology: Challenging environmentalism's supremacy* (pp. 125–144). Happauge, NY: Nova Science Publishers.

Ngo, Fawn, Raymond Paternoster, Francis Cullen and Doris Layton Mackenzie. (2011). Life domains and crime: A test of Agnew's general theory of crime and delinquency. *Journal of Criminal Justice, 39*, 302–311.

Nielsen, Aime. (1999). Testing Sampson and Laub's life course theory: Age, race/ethnicity and drunkenness. *Deviant Behavior, 20*, 129–151.

Olds, David, Charles Henderson, Robert Chamberlin and Robert Tatelbaum. (1986). Preventing child abuse and neglect: A randomized trial of nurse home visitation. *Pediatrics, 78*, 65–78.

Olds, David, John Eckenrode, Charles Henderson, Harriet Kitzman, Jane Powers, Robert Cole, Kimberly Sidora, Pamela Morris, Lisa Pettitt and Dennis Luckey. (1997). Long-term effects of home visitation on maternal life course and child abuse and neglect: Fifteen-year follow-up of a randomized trial. *JAMA: Journal of the American Medical Association, 278*, 637–643.

Olds, David, Charles Henderson, Robert Cole, John, Eckenrode, Harriet Kitzman, Dennis Luckey, Lisa Pettitt, Kimberly Sidora, Pamela Morris and James Powers. (1998). Long-term effects of nurse home visitation on children's criminal and antisocial behavior: 15-year follow-up of a randomized controlled trial. *JAMA: Journal of the American Medical Association 280*, 1238–1244.

Olds, David, Lois Sadler and Harriet Kitzman. (2007). Programs for parents of infants and toddlers: Recent evidence from randomized trials. *Journal of Child Psychology and Psychiatry, 48*, 355–391.

OSGUS. (2001). *Youth violence: A report of the surgeon general.* Chapter 4: Risk factors for youth violence. Retrieved from: http://www.ncbi.nlm.nih.gov/books/NBK44293/#A12590.

Piquero, Alex and Timothy Brezina. (2001). Testing Moffitt's account of adolescence-limited delinquency. *Criminology, 39*, 353–370.

Reiss, Albert and David Farrington. (1991). Advancing knowledge about co-offending: Results from a prospective longitudinal survey of London males. *Journal of Criminal Law and Criminology, 82*, 360–395.

Sampson, Robert and John Laub. (1990). Crime and deviance over the life course: The salience of adult social bonds. *American Sociological Review, 55*, 609–627.

Sampson, Robert and John Laub. (1993). *Crime in the making: Pathways and turning points through life.* Cambridge, MA: Harvard University Press.

Sampson, Robert and John Laub. (1996). Socioeconomic achievement in the life course of disadvantaged men: Military service as a turning point, circa 1940–1965. *American Sociological Review, 61*, 347–367.

Sampson, Robert and John Laub. (2005). A life-course view of the development of crime. *ANNALS of the American Academy of Political and Social Science, 602*, 12–45 and 73–79.

Sampson, Robert, John Laub and Christopher Wimer. (2006). Does marriage reduce crime? A counterfactual approach to within-individual causal effects. *Criminology, 44*, 465–508.

Schinke, Steven, Mario Orlandi and Kristin Cole. (1992). Boys and Girls Clubs in public housing developments: Prevention services for youth at risk. *Journal of Community Psychology*, OSAP special issue, 118–128.

Schweinhart, Lawrence, Helen Barnes and David Weikart. (1993). *Significant benefits: The High/Scope Perry Preschool study through age 27.* Ypsilanti, MI: High/Scope Press.

Schweinhart, Lawrence, Jeanne Montie, Zongping Xiang, W. Steven Barnett, Clive Belfield and Milagros Nores. (2005). *Lifetime effects: The High/Scope Perry Preschool study through age 40.* Ypsilanti, MI: High/Scope Press.

Skardhamar, Torbjorn. (2009). Reconsidering the theory on adolescent-limited and life-course persistent anti-social behaviour. *British Journal of Criminology, 49,* 863–878.

Stattin, Hakan, Margaret Kerr and Lars Bergman. (2010). On the utility of Moffitt's typology trajectories in long-term perspective. *European Journal of Criminology, 7,* 521–545.

Tibbets, Stephen and Alex Piquero. (1999). The influence of gender, low birth weight, and disadvantaged environment in predicting early onset of offending: A test of Moffitt's interactional hypothesis. *Criminology, 37,* 843–878.

Tremblay, Richard, Frank Vitaro, Lucie Bertrand, Marc LeBlanc, Helene Beauchensne, Helene Boileau and Lucille David. (1992). Parent and child training to prevent early onset delinquency: The Montreal Longitudinal-Experimental Study. In J. McCord and R. Tremblay (Eds.), *Preventing antisocial behavior: Interventions from birth through adolescence* (pp. 117–138). New York, NY: Guilford Press.

Tremblay, Richard, Linda Pagani-Kurtz, Louise Masse, Frank Vitaro and Robert Pihl. (1995). A bimodal preventive intervention for disruptive kindergarten boys: Its impact through mid-adolescence. *Journal of Consulting and Clinical Psychology, 63,* 560–568.

Tremblay, Richard, Louise Masse, Linda Pagani and Frank Vitaro. (1996). From childhood physical aggression to adolescent maladjustment: The Montreal Prevention Experiment. In R.D. Peters and R.J. McMahon (Eds.), *Preventing childhood disorders, substance use, and delinquency* (pp. 168–298). Thousand Oaks, CA: Sage.

Van der Laan, Andre, Martine Blom and Edward Kleemans. (2009). Exploring long-term and short-term risk factors for serious delinquency. *European Journal of Criminology, 6,* 419–438.

Walsh, Anthony and Craig Hemmens. (2011). *Introduction to criminology: A text/reader.* 2nd ed. Los Angeles, CA: Sage.

Welsh, Brandon. (2012). Preventing delinquency by putting families first. In R. Loeber and B. Welsh (Eds.), *The future of criminology* (pp. 1153–158). New York, NY: Oxford University Press.

Welsh, Brandon and David Farrington. (2004). Effective programmes to prevent delinquency. In J. Adler (Ed.), *Forensic psychology: Concepts, debates and practice* (pp. 378–403). Cullompton, England: Willan.

Widom, Cathy. (1989). The cycle of violence. *Science, 244,* 160–166.

Wilson, David, Denise Gottfredson and Stacy Najaka. (2001). School-based prevention of problem behaviors: A meta-analysis. *Journal of Quantitative Criminology, 17,* 247–272.

Wolfgang, Marvin, Robert Figlio and Thorsten Sellin. (1972). *Delinquency in a birth cohort.* Chicago, IL: University of Chicago Press.

Zara, Georgia. (2012). Adult onset offending: Perspectives for future research. In R. Loeber and B. Welsh (Eds.), *The future of criminology* (pp. 85–93). New York, NY: Oxford University Press.

Chapter 8

The Pushes and Pulls of Crime

Introduction

This chapter describes various factors that play a role in determining the prevalence of crime in society from a sociological perspective. While the push factors we will examine cannot be referred to as causes of crime in a scientific sense, they often influence the presence or absence of it. The push factors dovetail very nicely with the risk factors for crime we explored in Chapter 7. We begin by looking at how social class is implicated in crime and discover that violent crime including murder, rape, robbery and assault is heavily skewed toward the lower classes in society. We also look at how gender is implicated in crime and discover that males are predominant in crime but females seem to be catching up and consider the reasons for this. With regard to race in the United States, African Americans predominate in violent crimes such as homicide, robbery, rape and assault and we consider the reasons for this. Conflict over drugs and drug dealing are implicated in violent crime both in the United States and elsewhere and we consider the reasons for this. We also consider the role mental illness might play in causing crime. Finally, we treat guns as an important variable in explaining prevalence of violent crime and homicide in particular. The United States has the highest rate and volume of gun ownership of any country in the world. We will show that this fact in itself contributes to our extraordinarily high homicide rate.

The most dangerous parts of any city are also the poorest. It does not follow, however, that being poor, that being male, African American or drug involved makes one necessarily crime prone; most people fitting these characteristics are not violent or criminal at all. In the latter part of this chapter, we will also explore some theoretical perspectives that offer insight into how people may be drawn to crime. What is it about criminal behavior that is compelling?

Here we examine the seductions of crime, the gratifications associated with doing evil. We also look at monetary motivations associated with crime and how crime within certain subcultures can be viewed as a path toward bolstering one's manhood and gaining respect among one's peers.

The Pushes: Covariates of Crime

Social Class

The perceived linkage between poverty and crime is perhaps as old as our capacity as social beings to define a person as poor. When we speak of poverty and its relationship to crime, we do so in the narrow sense of economic poverty. Historically, the poor have been equated with the dangerous underclass (see Chapter 1). These stereotypes contain a grain of truth in a bushel of ignorance: though a majority of the poor are not involved in violent and other forms of crime, criminologists often include poverty as a covariate of crime. In this section, we will look at how poverty in effect defines the poor as outsiders, as well as how poverty leaves people prone to all manner of deviance, including violent crime.

The unit of analysis in the study of poverty and crime is typically the neighborhood where the actors live. Sociologists of the Chicago school in the 1930s and 1940s were convinced that the ecology of place shaped the social life of the people in that area for good or bad (Shaw and McKay, 1931, 1942). Their focus on the roles of neighborhood and neighborhood organization on crime is referred to as the theory of social disorganization (see Chapter 4). Borrowing from social ecologists/urban sociologists Park and Burgess' concentric zone hypothesis (1925), Shaw and McKay observed fairly stable and high levels of juvenile crime in transitional zones (areas of land use available to poor immigrants) over three time periods between 1900 and 1933. These stable and high levels of juvenile crime were found in the same social areas no matter who lived there. Shaw and McKay's (1942) explanation for this correlation was what they would eventually term social disorganization and it is no coincidence that poverty figures heavily into social disorganization theory, as we saw in Chapter 4.

Social disorganization theory as an explanation of violence and crime has been the theoretical basis for studying variable rates of homicide at the neighborhood level of analysis. This level of analysis is more efficacious because the main processes linking social environments and violence depends, to some degree, on interaction with contiguous others (Sampson, 1986). Poverty, measured variously as unemployment, low income or percent below the federal poverty line, is inevitably a component of the model of social disorganization used to explain variation in the incidents of homicide across neighborhoods. As a correlate of homicide, poverty is usually found to be significant by criminologists, that is, the poorer the neighborhood, the higher the incidence of homicide (Sampson, 1986). However, Harper, Voigt and Thornton (2004) have noted that the linkage is not a direct one. Rather, poverty works to support a culture of violence that in turn contributes to a high rate of neighborhood levels of homicide.

Another theoretical approach to understanding the link between poverty and violent crime is the formation of a culture of poverty. The concept culture figures prominently in the literatures of anthropology, sociology and criminology. In criminology it has, for the most part, been treated as a residual idea to account for variance when more traditional structural variables do not account for the predicted outcomes. The concept itself is not without controversy. Culture is exogenous, an *a priori* social fact that is external and constrains behavior. In this sense, culture has to do with norms (rules governing social behavior), values (what is good or bad in the world) and traditions embodied in our social institutions (family, religion, polity, education, economy) and is identifiable as, for example, American or Japanese. From a different perspective, culture flows from economic and structural conditions. For example, William Julius Wilson (1987) argues that social isolation (concentrated poverty and concentrated race/ethnicity) influences cultural orientation, an orientation that is shaped by the lack of opportunity and a scarcity of conventional role models. These conditions shape the way people respond to their circumstances and in some instances, this response may be criminal and violent.

Box 8.1. The Culture of Poverty: A Double Edged Sword?

Anthropologist Oscar Lewis coined the term culture of poverty in 1959. With this compelling social theory, Lewis postulated that poverty was systemic and so harsh that it led to a subculture of attitudes and mores that future generations of children born into poverty, and knowing little else about the non-poor world, were socialized into a culture of poverty that perpetuated their inability to escape it. Lewis' formulation began a debate that is still going on even today. Just six years after he coined the term, it was used by Daniel Patrick Moynihan, a sociologist by training and at that time, an assistant labor secretary in President Johnson's administration. Moynihan (1965) described the urban African American family as being trapped in an inescapable tangle of pathology of unwed mothers and dependence on welfare and other social programs. The Moynihan Report perpetuated stereotypical assumptions and blamed the poor African American community for its state of economic inequality, essentially castigating them for moral failings.

Since Moynihan's report, was published certain myths have gained traction; that poor people are unmotivated, lack strong work ethics, they do not value education and are therefore unconcerned about the education of their children. Poor people do not know how to talk and spend their days laying about doing drugs and drinking alcohol. However, it appears that in large part, a classist culture is responsible for these stereotypes about the poor. Belief in these stereotypes requires accepting the notion that the poor want to remain poor. Granted there are elements of our culture and economy that seems to condemn a portion of our population to poverty, but there is nothing to be gained by treating poverty as a character flaw.

Violent crime in the context of poverty not only occurs but its occurrence may be condoned. The subculture of violence thesis (Wolfgang and Ferracuti, 1967) holds that physical aggression is required, expected and condoned under certain circumstances. At the time of Wolfgang and Ferracuti's research, African Americans were the "carriers of a ghetto tradition" and were the "recipients of urban deterioration and the social-psychological forces leading to deviance from the law ... Relative deprivation and social disqualification are thus dramatically chained to despair and delinquency" (Wolfgang, 1982, p. 298). Remember Anderson (1999) from Chapters 2 and 4 found evidence for a subculture of violence among the street families he observed in Philadelphia, consistent of course with subcultural theories of crime.

Gender

There are few things that get sociologists' ire up more than invoking a biological explanation for human interaction or social structure (Freese, Li and Wade, 2003). This aversion to the role that biology might play in sociological inquiry, particularly scholarship addressing deviant and antisocial behavior, appears to be linked to the scathing critiques of the now largely discredited works of Lombroso (2006[1876], 2004[1893], 1911; see Chapter 1), those of his intellectual heirs in the Italian school (Garofalo, 1914; Ferri, 1917; see Chapter 1) and those of Sheldon (1949) and the Gluecks (1930, 1964; see Chapters 2 and 7). Moreover, there is a palpable fear on the part of sociologists that biological explanations are a slippery slope that could lead to speculation concerning the role biology might play in explanations of racial and class inequality. The result is that many sociologists are loath to concede any role biology might play in sociological explanation.[1] Some have argued that this position will make sociology increasingly irrelevant, viewed with suspicion and dismissed as politically motivated (Thornhill and Palmer, 2000). As a discipline, sociology should be focused on sociological explanation without dismissing the possibility of other explanations of the same phenomena (Udry, 1995). To borrow an old cliché, dismissing the role of biology in social behavior is to toss the baby out with the bathwater.

One line of research that looks at a biological explanation for behavior has attempted to understand why males predominate in antisocial behavior. The focus of this research is on the role of the hormone testosterone. Higher levels of testosterone have been associated with the commission of more violent crimes in both juvenile and adult incarcerated samples (Dabbs, 1991; Dabbs, 1987). Dabbs and Morris (1990) suggest that two hypotheses have been advanced to explain the link between testosterone and antisocial behavior in delinquent and criminal populations. The first is that testosterone leads directly to antisocial behavior and the second is that testosterone is related to a constellation of dominance, competitiveness and sensation seeking that leads to either antisocial or prosocial behavior depending upon an individual's resources and background. In their study, they analyzed archival data on 4,462 military veterans for level of testosterone, social class and delinquent behavior. Dabbs and Morris (1990) found that high testosterone was associated with delinquent behavior for those in the lower social class but not for those in the higher social class, which provides some support for their second hypothesis. Remember from Chapter 3, testosterone appears to be a necessary but not a sufficient cause for violence.

If testosterone is only part of the answer, how can we fully explain why males are so much more involved in crime than women? To answer this question, Hagan (1988) introduced his power-control theory, which attempts to explain why males are so much more involved in crime and delinquency than females. Hagan (1988) claims that patriarchy tends to reproduce typical gender roles and relations in families. In

---

1. Obviously, sociologists are profoundly influenced by one of the discipline's principal founders, Emile Durkheim, who famously asserted the explanation of social facts should be sought in the social facts preceding them (1938[1895]).

patriarchal families, the father's focus is on his responsibilities as breadwinner while the mother's focus is on childcare. Boys born into patriarchal families are granted greater freedom and encouraged to take risks as they prepare for a future role as father and breadwinner; this risk taking may manifest itself as delinquent behavior. Girls are subject to more control from their mothers and more closely supervised so that delinquent activity is less likely. In egalitarian families, on the other hand, in which the responsibility for childcare is equally shared, boys and girls are both subject to lower levels of control and encouraged to take risks. Boys and girls in egalitarian families are at equal risk for involvement in delinquency and this pattern is observed in single parent households, as well.

We can also think back to Chapter 6 and our discussion of James Messerschmidt. Messerschmidt (1993) theorized that crime could be a way of demonstrating masculinity for boys (in his terms, a way to do gender). White middle class boys typically have more legitimate ways to demonstrate gender available to them such as success at school, at sports and at work; for minority lower class boys, the number of ways to do gender outside repeated commission of violent crime is limited. We can also look back to Chapter 4 and Broidy and Agnew's (1997) research on the gendered response to strain. They claim that while both boys and girls are subject to strains, boys turn the negative emotions that result from failure to achieve positively valued goals outward in the form of anger and engage in crime, while girls turn them inward and engage in more self-destructive behaviors. And in Chapter 7, we saw that Agnew (2005) claims that boys are more likely to have low self-control and irritability, as well as aversive family environments in childhood, weak bonds to family as adults and association with delinquent peers, all of which put boys at greater risk for delinquency and crime than girls.

What about girls and women and crime? Zahn, et al. (2010) note that between 1980 and 2006, the arrest rate for boys for simple assault doubled but the arrest rate for girls for simple assault quadrupled. Are girls getting more violent? The relatively simple answer is no. As Steffensmeier, Zhong, Ackerman, Schwartz and Agha (2006) point out, UCR data reflect a rise in assaults on the part of girls, but this trend is not observed in the NCVS. Victimization data do not show the gender gap closing with respect to assault, but the UCR does. What appears to be happening is that law enforcement agencies are making more arrests of females than they used to and this has the appearance of closing the gender gap. In short, it is not behavior changes on the part of girls and women but rather policy changes on the part of law enforcement that account for the change.

Zahn, et al. (2010) note there are risk factors for criminal involvement that are specific for girls, among them sexual abuse and assault, depression, anxiety and post-traumatic stress disorder (PTSD), ineffective parenting including harsh or inconsistent discipline, inability to leave disadvantaged neighborhoods, weak attachment to school, and early puberty, especially as it fosters negative family relations and association with older males. Sexual victimization as a risk factor for crime was seen in Chapter 6 in our discussion of Chesney-Lind's (1989) work. She contends that girls are frequent targets of violence and sexual abuse in the home. Running away from home does not solve the problem of abuse. Rather, runaways are returned to their homes by the police, which does nothing to stop the abuse, or they must live on the streets. Once on the streets, they have to resort to crime, including prostitution, in order to survive.[2]

Race

"With the exception of poverty, violent crime may be the most important issue in the study of race in American society" (Greene and Gabbidon, 2012, p. 138). The role of race in violent crime is taken on directly with a great deal of apprehension by many criminologists because of the sensitive nature of the subject and perhaps the fear of being labeled racist. However, criminologists, for the most part, when researching or discussing the structural covariates of violent crime invariably consider race. If their focus is on crime rates in social areas, for example, percent African American will be one of the variables in the mix. So race is implicitly considered a predictor variable in explaining violent crime.

Why is race a variable in trying to explain violent crime? Perhaps it is because African Americans are disproportionately represented in violent crime statistics. The July 1, 2009 United States estimate for the male population was 151,449,490. African American males totaled 18,936,457 or 12.5 percent of the population (U.S. Census Bureau, 2010). In 2008, 50.1 percent of those arrested for murder and non-negligent manslaughter, 32.2 percent of those arrested for forcible rape, 56.7 percent of those arrested for robberies and 34.2 percent of those arrested for aggravated assaults were African American. In each category of violent crime, African American males are significantly overrepresented (FBI UCR, 2008). These distributions do not reflect a recent trend; comparable data for 2000 shows 48.8 percent of those arrested for murder and non-negligent manslaughter, 34.1 percent of those arrested for forcible rapes, 53.9 percent of those arrested for robberies and 34 percent of those arrested for aggravated assault arrests were African American (FBI UCR, 2000).

How is this disproportionality accounted for? There is no genetic or biological basis to suggest a proclivity to violent crime by any racial or ethnic group. There is every reason to believe that certain social and cultural conditions apparently support and under certain circumstances condone violence. Elijah Anderson (1994, p. 1) argues that "the inclination to violence springs from the circumstances of life among the ghetto poor—the lack of jobs that pay a living wage, the stigma of race, the fallout from rampant drug use and drug trafficking, and the resulting alienation and lack of hope for the future." The despair produced by these circumstances gives rise to an oppositional street culture, a set of informal rules governing interpersonal public behavior, including violence, which Anderson (1994) refers to as the code of the street. The code has a lot to do with the management of self in the street context. Put another way, it is all about respect and managing that respect through appearances and behaviors. The reality of the code suggests for Anderson (1994) a profound sense of alienation from the mainstream experienced by many poor, inner city African Americans, especially the young. This alienation is the result of social isolation (Wilson, 1987, 1996) and a violent subculture (Wolfgang, 1982).

Darnell Hawkins (1990) has argued that economic inequality and the historical context in which the inequality came about largely accounts for the inordinately high

---

2. For research on those factors that protect girls from delinquency and crime, see Hawkins, Graham, Williams and Zahn (2009).

rates of African American homicide. No other group of people were enslaved and brought to the Americas by force. The conditions of slavery are more comparable to a colonialist model rather than an immigrant analogy. Hawkins (1990) finds the colonialist model useful in conceptualizing African American-white relations. Furthermore, he asserts that slavery set into motion structural, social psychological and economic forces that partially account for the disproportionate involvement of African Americans in violent crime including homicide, even over 150 years after the Emancipation Proclamation.

Violence, physically harming someone, involves personal confrontation. The perpetrator of violence is likely to have strong concerns about the reaction of the person they intend to harm; their attack could have serious or fatal consequences (Tedeschi and Felson, 1994). Knowing this, the attacker is more likely to go into battle armed. In communities where guns are prevalent and revenge or retaliatory killing is a commonplace motive, such as in New Orleans where almost all of the victims and perpetrators of homicide are African American, the victims of lethal violence often suffer multiple gunshot wounds (Levitov and Harper, 2010). Homicide is accomplished in this manner because if the perpetrator does not kill his victim, he will have to deal with him again. From the perspective of young African American males, the circumstances of many poor and extremely racially isolated neighborhoods in New Orleans require carrying firearms for protection from these types of confrontations on the chance that soon-to-be victims might be armed as well (Wright and Rossi, 1986).

Another perspective on this issue is contained in Jack Katz' (1988) analysis of African American overrepresentation in robbery statistics. Katz (1988) argues that the overrepresentation of African Americans in robbery is a result of being close to the seductions of the stickup, that is, quick money, the excitement of power over the victim and the social construction of the hardman as a street robber. Moreover, at an emotional level, within the modern poor urban African American community, being a hardman and being bad are often a collectively celebrated way of being that transcends good and evil.

As we have seen, African Americans are overrepresented in arrests for violent crimes. They are also overrepresented in prison; one in nine African Americans ages 20 to 34 are in prison (Pew Center on the States, 2008). Could this reflect differential arrest and sentencing practices? On the first point, D'Alessio and Stolzenberg (2003) examined NIBRS data on a total of 335,619 arrests for rape, robbery and both simple and aggravated assault from 17 states to determine the effect of the offenders' race on the likelihood of arrest. They found that the likelihood of arrest for robbery, simple assault and aggravated assault was significantly greater for white offenders than for African American offenders and that the likelihood of arrest for rape was equal for both whites and African Americans. D'Alessio and Stolzenberg (2003) conclude that the overrepresentation of African Americans in arrests is probably due to their disproportionately greater involvement in crime, though they do not rule out the possibility of bias on the part of individual law enforcement officers. In a review of the literature on racial disparity and sentencing, Kansal (2005) finds that young African American and Latino defendants are subject to harsher sentences than other groups, especially if they are unemployed. Kansal (2005) also finds that African American and Latino defendants receive harsher sentences than white defendants with similar backgrounds, especially for drug and property crimes.

Age

Crime is a young man's game. In 2011, 74.1 percent of those arrested were male (FBI UCR, 2011). Those under 25 years of age accounted for 41.7 percent of arrests for violent crime and 51.2 percent of arrests for property crime. Among the violent crimes, this age group accounted for 45.9 percent of arrests for murder and 62.5 percent of arrests for robbery. Among the property crimes, this age group accounted for 55.4 percent of arrests for burglary and 61.9 percent of arrests for arson. What accounts for this disproportionately high level of involvement in crime for this age group?

As we saw in Chapter 7, the vast majority of adolescents engage in some delinquent behavior, suggesting that for most teenagers, delinquency is more normative than deviant. A number of theories have been proposed to explain why so many young people engage in delinquency. David Matza[3] (1964) proposed the idea of drift to contest the notion that youthful delinquency would inevitably lead to adult crime. For Matza (1964), drift was the experience of adolescents who were both constrained by the conventional norms of society and free from them. Drifting amounted to behaving in a framework of loosened social controls with no position or inclination to possess agency. As a result, drifters move between delinquent and conventional involvement and while doing so tend to experience what he termed maturational reform as they transition into adulthood.

Hagan (1991) suggests that adolescent subcultural preferences, including delinquency, are in part adaptations to the pressures associated with the passage to adulthood. The subculture of adolescents, which is in many ways oppositional to adult norms, is characterized by an emphasis on having fun, particularly with the opposite sex, and seeking out risk and excitement. These transitional cultural experiences along with other experienced contingencies may set in place life course trajectories for both the directed as well as the drifting adolescent. He hypothesized that adolescents would engage in distinct types of activities they perceive to be fun, some of which would be more deviant than others. He further hypothesized that preferences for these activities would be negatively related to educational commitment and parents' efforts to control children. Hagan (1991) surveyed 693 students in the eighth through twelfth grades near Toronto, Canada in 1976 and followed up with a telephone survey with 490 respondents in 1989. As he hypothesized, Hagan (1991) found evidence for two types of delinquent subcultures, a subculture of delinquency and a party subculture. The former involved theft, vandalism, fighting and running from the police, while the latter involved activities that only edge toward the illegal, e.g., underage drinking; those who identified with this subculture were chiefly concerned with having fun and engaging with the opposite sex. He also found that the less control by parents and the less involved or committed to school, the more likely adolescents were to drift into the subculture of delinquency and the party subculture. During follow up, Hagan (1991) found that drifting into the more serious deviant subculture and not the party subculture created a lasting cultural deficiency, particularly among male respondents.

We have already seen what is probably the most famous explanation of the age-crime connection, that proposed by Moffitt (1993) and detailed in Chapter 7. Moffitt (1993)

---

3. This is the same David Matza from neutralization theory in Chapter 5.

also believes that delinquency in the teenage years is normative and proposes that the vast majority of offenders, adolescent limited offenders, become involved in delinquency because of the maturity gap. The maturity gap is the time between puberty and adulthood in which adolescents are physically mature but are not yet granted any of the freedoms that come with adulthood. During this time, peers also come to have greater influence over adolescents than parents. Adolescent limited offenders may mimic the delinquent behavior of life course persistent offender peers (who started offending well before adolescence) in order to express independence not yet granted to them by the status of adulthood. Certain types of reinforcement keep adolescent limited offenders engaging in delinquency, such as earning the ire of parents and teachers. However, as adolescent limited offenders age out of adolescence and into adulthood, these reactions are no longer reinforcing. Instead, a variety of rewards for hard work and proper behavior, including obeying the law, become reinforcing and they are able to develop prosocial relationships going forward. They also gain the freedoms of adulthood at this time. Taken as a whole, Moffitt (1993) contends this explanation accounts for the high number of juvenile offenders and why delinquency and crime decreases as adolescents age into adulthood and this part of her theory has received empirical support (e.g., Moffitt and Walsh, 2003).

Drugs

It is frankly simple to find a connection between drugs and violence. Levitov and Harper (2012) note that in New Orleans, those neighborhoods that experience high rates of murder also experience high rates of drug arrests, as well as a high volume of murders that the police classify as drug related (Harper, Voigt and Thornton, 2004). Lots of murder on the one hand, lots of drug arrests and drug related murders on the other. But is this the whole story? In order to better understand the link between drugs

Table 8.1. Percent of arrestees testing positive for any of 10 drugs,* 2009

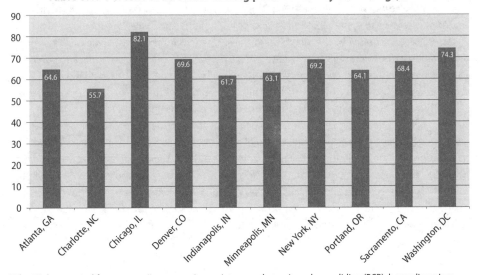

* The 10 drugs tested for were marijuana, cocaine, opiates, amphetamine, phencyclidine (PCP), benzodiazepines, propoxyphene, methadone, barbiturates and oxycodone.

Source: ADAM II, 2010.

and crime, we examine the issue from a variety of perspectives. First, let us explore the notion of whether there is a link between drugs and crime in the first place. Table 8.1 shows the percent of arrestees in 10 cities who tested positive for any of 10 drugs at the time of their arrest in 2009.

From these data, it is clear that there is a link between drug use and crime. Moreover, the use of more than one drug is associated with more serious involvement in crime (Bennett and Holloway, 2005). A great deal of literature bears out the connection between drug use and criminal behavior (see Roman, Rossman and Rempel, 2011 for a review).

Drug use may increase criminal involvement in several ways and we turn here to Goldstein's (1985) tripartite framework. Goldstein (1985) describes three ways in which drugs are linked to violence, namely, pharmacological, economic compulsive and systemic. Pharmacological violence is that violence which is linked to the pharmacological properties of the drug itself. Economic compulsive violence is that done in an effort to obtain money to buy drugs. Systemic violence is the violence committed to gain and keep control of drug markets, both small and large. As drug markets destabilize, they tend to become more violent and as they stabilize, they tend to become less violent. For example, the expansion of crack drug markets in certain social areas in New York City occurred during a period when legitimate economic opportunities were declining. The expansion provided lucrative opportunities for some but the instability of the markets driven by the presence of new players exacerbated violence. However, as the market stabilized, drug related homicides tended to decline (Blumstein, 1995).

Box 8.2. What Are Drug Related Homicides, Anyway?

Drug-related homicides are defined as those murders which occur as a direct result of the use, sale and distribution of narcotics and other illegal drugs. According to Gerberth (1996), this type of homicide can be further broken down into four specific categories, drug hits, in-terpersonal drug disputes, killing of innocent bystanders and drug assassinations. The most common of all drug homicides are drug hits. These types of narcotic murders are premeditated murders intended to eliminate competition or implement power over members of the drug organization. Alternatively, the victim might have been murdered because he or she offered information to the authorities or may have been a potential witness in a drug trial and was con-sidered a risk to the drug community.[4] Murders in which the perpetrator was ripped off also constitute drug hits. Interpersonal drug disputes are homicides that occur spontaneously, usu-ally without any premeditation. These murders take place during drug related quarrels and hostile circumstances among and between persons who are under the influence of drugs and/ or involved in illicit drug activity. The killing of innocent bystanders in drug related homicides is basically the murder of innocent civilians who are caught in the crossfire during drug related disputes. Drug assassinations are premeditated murders that are directed toward government officials, law enforcement and civilians. These types of murders are intended to show the dom-inance the drug world has over the authorities. Drug assassinations are the least frequent type of drug related homicides, at least in the United States.

---

4. In the case of premeditated narcotic homicides, which a majority of these homicides seem to be, investigators must first investigate the homicide case, then the narcotic aspect. A majority of these

With all that said, it is still unclear whether drug use causes crime. The jury is still out on this question to some degree; prevailing academic thought on the matter is that drug use and abuse, while strongly associated with crime, does not cause criminal activity. Drug abuse does appear to lengthen criminal careers and make them more serious in nature (McBride and McCoy, 1993; Menard, Mihalic and Huizinga, 2001). Instead of saying that drug use causes crime or crime causes drug use, it may be most accurate to say that drug use and crime are both part of a deeper propensity for antisocial behavior (McDermott, Alterman, Cacciola, Rutherford, Newman and Mulholland, 2000; Fishbein, 2003).

Mental Illness

Does mental illness cause crime? We may think of past and recent mass shootings, such as those in Columbine, Blacksburg, Aurora and Sandy Hook and wonder how someone could do something so terrible and automatically assume the answer is yes. However, the issue is much more complicated than that. James and Glaze (2006) note that over half of jail and prison inmates have mental health problems, which certainly indicates a link between mental illness and crime as measured by incarceration. However, Steadman, Osher, Robbins, Case and Samuels (2009) took issue with the definition of mental health problem in the James and Glaze (2006) study and conducted their own investigation into the prevalence of serious mental illness. They found that 15 percent of male and 31 percent of female jail inmates have serious mental illnesses. Their findings still indicate a link between mental illness and crime.[5]

With this link established, we must next ask whether offenders with mental illness are violent. Stuart (2003) notes that if major mental illness was eradicated, it would result in about a five percent reduction in violence; Friedman (2006) concurs with this finding. Offenders with mental illness are most likely to perpetrate violence against people they know and love rather than strangers and are much more likely to engage in violence when under the influence of drugs or alcohol. The most important conclusion that Stuart (2003) draws is that the mentally ill are at much greater risk of being victimized by violence than they are for perpetration, which begs the question if offenders with mental illness are not violent in very large part, how are there so many offenders with mental illness in jails and prisons? The answer to this question lies in deinstitutionalization, the mid 20th century practice of emptying out psychiatric hospitals in order to save money but providing no community based services and support for those exiting these institution. With no help to manage what were serious enough mental illnesses to land them in the hospital, many of those returning to the community quickly found themselves on the streets or in jail (Slate and Johnson, 2008). Mental illness, then, cannot accurately be called a push of crime, at least not to the same degree that age, gender and social class can (Stuart, 2003).

---

cases are solved through intelligence and/or informant information, but witnesses in drug related homicides are often reluctant to come forward, thus making investigations difficult. In many of these cases, murder is utilized in order to show authority and control over others in the drug world. Because dealing, using and associating with drugs are deviant practices, formal justice systems are not called upon when needed to resolve disputes.

5. For a fascinating look at offenders with mental illness in jail and prisons, see the PBS Frontline documentaries *The New Asylums* and *The Released*.

Box 8.3. What about Veterans and PTSD?

Increasing media attention has been paid to the deleterious effects that military service can have on mental health, including the connection between posttraumatic stress disorder (PTSD) and violence and suicide. Sontag and Alvarez (2008) uncovered 121 cases in which veterans of Iraq and Afghanistan committed a killing in the United States or were charged with one after they returned from the wars. Seventy-nine had been charged with murder and 14 either committed suicide or were killed by the police. Because the military does not keep track of this kind of information, Sontag and Alvarez (2008) depended on newspaper reports where the perpetrator's military experience was a part of the story. They rightly conclude that the number of military members involved in homicide after their return home is probably much higher.

What was consistent across many cases is captured in the refrain of friends and relatives who described defendants as coming back different, irritable, detached, volatile, sleepless, drinking and drugging excessively and keeping a gun handy. Sontag and Alvarez (2008) described one case where a Marine gunnery sergeant returned from a job handling dead bodies in Iraq. He became increasingly paranoid, jumpy and fearful, moving into his garage, eating military issue meals, wearing his camouflage uniform, drinking heavily and carrying a gun at all times, even to answer the doorbell. On the eve of his second deployment to Iraq in 2004, he fatally shot his mistress after she threatened to kill his family while he was gone.

Suicide after active military service is now recognized by the U.S. Department of Defense as a serious problem. In 2011, 301 military service members committed suicide and another 915 attempts were recorded. Young, white, male service members who were divorced and who had been deployed to Iraq or Afghanistan were at greatest risk for suicide. Interestingly, over half of those who committed suicide did not have a history of mental illness, but PTSD appears to have played a role in 30 percent of these suicides (Luxton, Osenbach, Reger, Smolenski, Skopp, Bush and Gahm, 2012).

Guns

To suggest that guns can be treated as an independent variable or cause of some criminal outcome contradicts the old adage that guns don't kill people, people kill people. People in fact do kill people, but without a gun in their hands the likelihood of killing is greatly diminished. A counterargument might demand the outlawing of baseball bats, because of course baseball bats can be used to kill. Human beings, of course, can be creative when they really want to kill someone. However, there is little creativity required when a gun is present.

In a recent study, Miller, Hemenway and Azrael (2007) looked at the role of firearm ownership in homicide victimization in all 50 states. Data from a state level survey of household firearm ownership and homicide prevalence for each state were aggregated over a three-year study period, from 2001 to 2003. The researchers controlled for state level rates of aggravated assault, robbery, unemployment, urbanization, per capita alcohol consumption and resource deprivation. What they found was that states with higher rates of household firearm ownership had significantly higher homicide victimization rates of men, women and children. The association between firearm prevalence and homicide victimization in the study, they conclude, was driven by gun-related homicide victimization rates. States within the highest quartile of firearm prevalence had firearm homicide rates 114 percent higher than states within the lowest quartile of firearm prevalence. These results suggest that it may be easier for potential perpetrators of a homicide to obtain a gun in states where guns are more prevalent. These results further suggest that in the United States, household firearms may be an important source of guns used to kill people on the street and in homes.

This topic is covered in much more detail in Chapter 15. Suffice it to say here the most robust research indicates that a greater number of guns leads to a greater number of homicides. This relationship is driven by the connection between the prevalence of guns and homicides by guns. Gun prevalence appears to have little effect on robbery and assault rates (Cook, 1979; Kleck and Patterson, 1993) and overall, there is little connection between the number of guns and non-gun homicides or other crimes (Duggan, 2001; Cook and Ludwig, 2006). The amount of violence in the United States cannot be fully explained by the number of guns, but the fact that so many violent crimes in the United States are lethal ones is connected inexorably to the availability of guns (Zimring and Hawkins, 1997).

The Pulls: Seductions of Crime

In the introduction to this section, we borrow from the title of a book by Jack Katz (1988) whose thesis is that crime can also be understood by the compelling nature of many criminal activities. In effect, Katz (1988) argues that most criminologists focus on background forces (in our terminology, the pushes) of crime and by doing so, ignore the fact that many of those subject to these pushes do not commit crime or if they do, the pushes cannot predict with any precision when those crimes will take place. Most criminologists recognize and agree with this argument. What Katz (1988) proposes is that to understand crime, we need to focus on the foreground. In other words, we also need to focus on what draws someone to commit the act; what is it that is so compelling about crime that people commit it even when a rational cost benefit analysis would not support doing so? His point is that material reward is not sufficient in understanding certain crimes because the crime carries a sensual component, something more than money that draws offenders to and into the act, not just once but repeatedly. The shoplifter does not steal for material reasons but in order to experience the thrill of having outsmarted the system. With the armed robber, it is the transcendent joy of dominating an adversary. With the impassioned killer, it is to vent the rage triggered by humiliation or by a threat to some cherished moral value.[6]

The value of Katz's (1988) contribution to understanding the pulls of crime is his grasp of the experiential elements of crime whether it is murder or shoplifting or robbery. The causes of crime are constructed by the offenders themselves and the causes they construct are lures and pressures (pushes, in other words) that move them toward the crime. Katz's (1988) understanding of crime is in stark contrast to the way conventional

---

6. Shoplifting is discussed in more detail in Chapter 12; robbery and murder are discussed in more detail in Chapter 11.

criminology understands it. He takes issue with the correlation between pushes and crime and contends a person's lack of material well being will not determine their intent to commit acquisitive crime even when they are aware of their circumstances.

Looking in the foreground, Katz (1988, p. 312) calls our attention to common or homogeneous criminal projects and explains the necessary and sufficient steps through which people construct different forms of crime. "If we take as our primary research commitment exploration of the distinctive phenomena of crime, we may produce not just ad hoc bits of description or a collection of provocative anecdotes but a systematic empirical theory of crime—one that explains at the individual level the causal process of committing a crime and that accounts at the aggregate level for recurrently documented correlations with biographical and ecological background factors."

Enriching Oneself in the Short Term

Earning and burning money clearly sums up the short term hedonism characteristic of the persistent robbers that Katz (1988) discusses. The pressing need for cash was identified by Richard Wright and Scott Decker (1997) as the primary motivation to commit robbery. Eighty of 81 offenders in their sample spoke directly to the need for cash as the primary motivator. Wright and Decker's (1997) work is fascinating because it is based on interviews with active robbers—a somewhat bold strategy that most criminological researchers would be reluctant to undertake.

Their work is a comprehensive description and interpretation of the lives of a mostly African American snowball sample[7] of active street robbers, their daily lives and their crimes. Historically, most ethnographic research on criminal offenders has been conducted with those under the control of criminal justice managers (jailers, probation and parole officers). This has always raised an important issue—is a caught criminal different from an active criminal? This is why Wright and Decker's (1997) work is important. They completed a fascinating study of decision making by active robbers and found, as noted above, that quick cash was an important motive. However, there is more to it than this. The offenders that Wright and Decker (1997, p. 36) interviewed "implied that the connection between armed robber and other sorts of illicit action often was more subtle. Their motivation to commit a stickup emerged during a period of intense self-indulgence and from a growing sense of frustration and anger because they felt themselves to be locked into a cycle of events that was leading nowhere." They also felt their engagement in robbery tended to isolate and encapsulate from the influence of others so that they believed they had little choice but to continue with robbery (even though over 40 percent of their sample had served time for robbery).

Wright and Decker (1997, p. 37) found an explanation as to why robbers in their sample persisted in the open-ended pursuit of illicit action. "The answer lies in their strong attachment to street culture." Street culture revolves around having good times.

---

7. A snowball sample is a nonprobability sample in which researchers find an initial participant who meets their criteria of interest and then ask if that participant knows and can refer others who meet the criteria to the researcher. Snowball sampling is particularly useful for studies of active offenders.

"To be hip on the street, one must demonstrate an ability to make something happen now. There is no reputational mileage to be gained through deferred gratification. The offenders are easily seduced by street culture at least in part because they view their future prospects as bleak and see little point in long-range planning" (Wright and Decker, 1997, p. 37). Fulfilling the imperatives of street culture requires money. Street culture is the relentless pursuit of action, including heavy drinking, drug use and gambling, all of which require a great deal of money. The offenders in their sample rarely had enough to sustain such activities for long.

"Even when the offenders had a substantial sum of money, their disdain for long-range planning coupled with their desire to live for the present often encouraged them to spend with reckless abandon. The result was that they were under almost constant pressure to generate additional funds. That pressure, in turn, often led them to decide to commit an armed robbery" (Wright and Decker, 1997, p. 39). To the extent that the robbery solved the problem, it supported the offenders' view that robbery was a reliable method of dealing with money pressures in the future and supporting their continuation in the street culture lifestyle. These findings have been supported by other similarly executed studies of street life and crime (Cornwell, Olson and Avary 1991; Shover and Honaker, 1992; Wright and Decker, 1994; Anderson, 1999). To conclude, enriching oneself in the short term through criminal activity and then using the cash to support a fast lifestyle seems to be a powerful pull toward these types of crimes.

Proving Manhood

The research tradition on gender and crime has for the most part conceptualized gender as a package of traits, beliefs and life experiences conditioned on whether the person is biologically male or female.[8] Moreover, much of the work relies on the theoretical tradition of criminology with insights borrowed from recent feminist literature and gender studies. This has led some, Messerschmidt (1993) for example, to propose a reconceptualization of what he calls the masculinist character of criminology. In his work, he scrutinizes gender roles along with social class and race to demonstrate how these variables influence the occurrence and types of crime in society.

Messerschmidt (1993) suggests that an opposition masculinity accounts for the disproportionate number of marginalized racial minority boys being involved in crime. As we have seen above and in Chapter 6, he argues that crime is a means of expressing their masculinity and it flows from their disconcerting school experiences and their life experiences with poverty, racism, negated futures and the power (or lack thereof) accorded them. He argues that because of these conditions, young racial and ethnic minority boys are more likely to commit certain types of street crime and in the process, construct a different type of masculinity outside the school. Robbery provides an ideal opportunity for them to act tough and male. According to Messerschmidt (1993), robbery for them becomes a rational way to demonstrate masculinity or in his terms,

---

8. At least that is the case today. Remember from Chapter 6, gender used to be treated as just another variable in criminological research.

to do gender. This may be viewed as an avenue for validating and affirming manhood where other avenues of more conventional means may not be available to them.

Manhood is a big deal for many inner city youth. On the streets, being distinguished as a man implies physicality and a certain level of ruthlessness and in public, manhood becomes associated with respect. "In other words, an existential link has been created between the idea of manhood and one's self esteem ... Manhood and respect are two sides of the same coin; physical and psychological well-being are inseparable, and both require a sense of control, of being in charge" (Anderson, 1999, p. 91). Respect is extremely valuable on the street and is a risk in every interaction, particularly with strangers who may be unfamiliar with the code of the street. This hyper concern for respect in ordinary interactions can be scary and incomprehensible. "But for those invested in the code, the clear object of their demeanor is to discourage strangers from even thinking about testing their manhood, and the sense of power that comes with the ability to deter others can be alluring" (Anderson, 1999, p. 92).

Anderson (1999, p. 92) argues that central to the issue of manhood is gaining respect through manifesting nerve. "A man shows nerve by taking another person's possessions, messing with someone's woman, throwing the first punch, 'getting into someone's face,' or pulling a trigger. Its proper display helps check others who would violate one's person, and it also helps build a reputation that works to prevent future challenges." The show of nerve is a forceful show of disrespect toward the person to whom it is directed. The receiver is likely to be offended and may retaliate with equal or greater force. The possible provocation of a life-threatening response is what defines the concept of nerve. Possessing true nerve is an expression of lack of fear of death. Possessing true nerve is to possess a willingness to die over an issue of respect. Proving manhood becomes a compelling project for not only inner city youth but is often implicated in a variety of violent contexts.

Demanding Respect

As we saw in Chapter 4, respect on the street is a valuable commodity in the inner city. In Anderson's (1999) view, respect is a form of social capital in an environment where other forms have been denied or are unavailable. Respect is at the core of a person's self esteem. In the most isolated parts of the inner city, a culture emerges that gives rise to an informal system of social control, "a perversion of the Golden Rule, whose by-product in this case is respect and whose caveat is vengeance, or payback. Given its value and its practical implications, respect is fought for and held and challenged as much as honor was in the age of chivalry ... Much of the code has to do with achieving and holding respect" (Anderson, 1999, pp. 66–67).

Schools and the areas around them are often staging areas or hangouts for a wide mix of people—it is here that campaigns for respect are often waged. Large crowds of young people gather at various staging areas to meet the opposite sex, smoke, drink and use drugs. Their presentation of self in this situation often appears as a dare and communicates through joking or direct taunts that they are ready for anything. Any slight can be interpreted as a show of disrespect and challenging this slight creates a beef which can lead to a confrontation in which neither party can back down without a significant loss of respect. The confrontation then can lead to a fight beginning with shouting, name-calling, shoving and fisticuffs (Anderson, 1999). Contemporarily, handguns are often present and serve as behavioral cues leading to a gun battle. If one of the parties to the beef comes to a gun battle armed with a knife or unarmed they are likely to end up dead.[9]

Conclusion

In this chapter, we have reviewed the role that seven pushes play in crime. In reality, these seven often converge in our accounts of the covariates of violent crime and this is something we have seen in our discussion of the various theories of crime. For example, young African-American males from poor neighborhoods, engaged in the drug trade are frequently killed with handguns. A disproportionate amount of violent crime in urban America is perpetrated by poor, young African-American males. In drawing these conclusions, we must always avoid the ecological fallacy, making an inference about individuals based the group characteristics to which they belong. Put another way, the category or group to which one belongs does not preordain his or her behavior. However and as mentioned above, while these push factors cannot be accurately referred to as causes of crime in a scientific sense, they are strong covariates, which means they are deserving of our continued attention.

That the pushes of crime cannot be viewed as the sole causes of crime is even clearer when we examine the pulls of crime. There are elements of criminal activity that appear to be very seductive for the actors. Understanding that robbery is active robbers' preferred way of enriching themselves in the short term in order to remain embedded in the street culture and that crime is not just preferred but sometimes a necessary way to prove manhood and demand respect give us greater insight into the causes of crime than could just measuring the amount of crime and the amount of covariates. The more thoroughly we understand all the pushes and pulls of crime, the better equipped we are to try to prevent it.

Websites to Visit

Drugs and Crime Facts: http://bjs.gov/content/dcf/contents.cfm

How Criminals Get Guns: http://www.pbs.org/wgbh/pages/frontline/shows/guns/procon/guns.html

Jack Katz and the Seductions of Crime: http://www.criminology.fsu.edu/crimtheory/week12.htm, http://www.criminology.fsu.edu/crimtheory/week13.htm, http://www.criminology.fsu.edu/crimtheory/week14.htm

Anderson's (1994) *Code of the Streets*: http://www.theatlantic.com/magazine/archive/1994/05/the-code-of-the-streets/306601/

---

9. The above pattern of confrontation and consequent death is the most common pattern of murder in New Orleans at the present time.

Discussion Questions

1. Were any of the covariates of crime discussed above surprising to you? Why or why not?
2. Of the covariates, which do you think is the strongest and why?
3. Do you think pushes or pulls matter more in causing crime? Why?
4. Can you think of any crimes that do not appear to have a seductive element?
5. What do you think some of the crimes are that people use to prove manhood or demand respect and why?

References

ADAM II. (2010). *ADAM II 2009 annual report*. Retrieved from: http://www.whitehouse.gov/sites/default/files/ondcp/policy-and-research/adam2009.pdf#page=65.

Agnew, Robert. (2005). *Why do criminals offend? A general theory of crime and delinquency*. Los Angeles, CA: Roxbury.

Anderson, Elijah. (1994). The code of the streets. *Atlantic Monthly, 273*, 81–94.

Anderson, Elijah. (1999). *The code of the street: Decency, violence, and the moral life of the inner city*. New York, NY: W.W. Norton & Company, Inc.

Bennett, Trevor and Katy Holloway. (2005). The association between multiple drug misuse and crime. *International Journal of Offender Therapy and Comparative Criminology, 49*, 63–81.

Blumstein, Alfred. (1995). Youth violence, guns and the illicit-drug industry. *Journal of Criminal Law and Criminology, 86*, 10–36.

Broidy, Lisa and Robert Agnew. (1997). Gender and crime: A general strain theory perspective. *Journal of Research in Crime and Delinquency, 34*(3), 275–306.

Chesney-Lind, Meda. (1989). Girls' crime and woman's place: Toward a feminist model of female delinquency. *Crime and Delinquency, 35*, 5–29.

Cook, Philip. (1979). The effect of gun availability on robbery and robbery murder: A cross-section study of fifty cities. In R. Haverman and B. Zellner (Eds.), *Policy Studies Review Annual, Vol. 3* (pp. 743–781). Beverly Hills, CA: Sage.

Cook, Philip and Jens Ludwig. (2006). Aiming for evidence-based gun policy. *Journal of Policy Analysis and Management, 25*, 691–735.

Cromwell, Paul, James Olson, and D'Aunn Avary. (1991). *Breaking and entering: An ethnographic analysis of burglary*. Newbury Park, CA: Sage.

D'Alessio, Stewart and Lisa Stolzenberg. (2003). Race and the probability of arrest. *Social Forces, 81*, 1381–1397.

Dabbs, James, Robert Frady, Timothy Carr and Norma Besch. (1987). Saliva testosterone and criminal violence in young adult prison inmates. *Psychosomatic Medicine 49*, 174–182.

Dabbs, James and Robin Morris. (1990) Testosterone, social class and antisocial behavior in a sample of 4,462 men. *Psychological Science, 1*, 209–211.

Dabbs, James, Gregory Jurkovic and Robert Frady. (1991). Salivary testosterone and cortisol among late adolescent male offenders. *Journal of Abnormal Child Psychology, 19*, 469–478.

Duggan, Mark. (1991). More guns, more crime. *Journal of Political Economy, 109*, 1086–1114.

Durkheim, Emile. (1938[1895]). *The rules of the sociological method.* Chicago, IL: University of Chicago Press.

FBI UCR. (2000). Crime in the United States 2000: Persons arrested. Retrieved from http://www.fbi.gov/about-us/cjis/ucr/crime-in-the-u.s/00crime4.pdf.

FBI UCR. (2008). Crime in the United States 2008: Persons arrested. Retrieved from: http://www2.fbi.gov/ucr/cius2008/arrests/index.html.

FBI UCR. (2011). Crime in the United States 2011: Persons arrested. Retrieved from: http://www.fbi.gov/about-us/cjis/ucr/crime-in-the-u.s/2011/crime-in-the-u.s.-2011/persons-arrested/persons-arrested.

Ferri, Enrico. (1917). *Criminal sociology.* Trans. J. Kellet and J. Lisle. Boston, MA: Little Brown.

Fishbein, Diana. (2001). Neuropsychological and emotional regulatory processes in antisocial behavior. In A. Walsh and L. Ellis (Eds.), *Biosocial criminology: Challenging environmentalism's supremacy* (pp. 185–208). Hauppauge, NY: Nova Science.

Freese, Jeremy, Jui-Chung Allen Li and Lisa Wade. (2003). The potential relevances of biology to social inquiry. *Annual Review of Sociology, 29*, 233–256.

Friedman, Richard. (2006). Violence and mental illness — How strong is the link? *New England Journal of Medicine, 355*, 2064–2066.

Garofalo, Raffaele. (1914). *Criminology.* Trans. R. Wyness. Boston, MA: Little Brown.

Gerberth, Vernon. (1996). *Practical homicide investigation: Tactics, procedures, and forensic techniques.* Boca Raton, FL: CRC Press.

Glueck, Sheldon and Eleanor Glueck. (1930). *Five hundred criminal careers.* New York, NY: Knopf.

Glueck, Sheldon, and Eleanor Glueck. (1964). *Ventures in criminology: Collected recent papers.* London, England: Tavistock Publications.

Goldstein, Paul. (1985). The drug/violence nexus. *Crime, 4*, 493–506.

Greene, Helen Taylor and Shaun Gabbidon. (2012). *Race and crime: A text/reader.* Thousand Oaks, CA: Sage.

Hagan, John. (1988). *Structural Criminology.* Oxford, England: Polity Press.

Hagan, John. (1991). Destiny and drift: Subcultural preferences, status attainment, and the risk and rewards of youth. *American Sociological Review, 56*, 567–582.

Harper, Dee Wood, Lydia Voigt and William Thornton. (2004). Murder in the city: Do we have a witness? American Society of Criminology presentation in Nashville, TN, November.

Hawkins, Darnell. (1990). Explaining the black homicide rate. *Journal of Interpersonal Violence, 5*, 151–163.

Hawkins, Stephanie. Phillip Graham, Jason Williams and Margaret Zahn. (2009). *Resilient girls — Factors that protect against delinquency.* Office of Juvenile Justice and Delinquency Prevention. Retrieved from: https://www.ncjrs.gov/pdffiles1/ojjdp/220124.pdf.

James, Doris and Lauren Glaze. (2006). *Mental health problems of prison and jail inmates.* Bureau of Justice Statistics. Retrieved from: http://www.bjs.gov/content/pub/pdf/mhppji.pdf.

Kansal, Tushar. (2005). *Racial disparity in sentencing: A review of the literature.* The Sentencing Project. Retrieved from: http://www.sentencingproject.org/doc/publications/rd_sentencing_review.pdf.

Katz, Jack. (1988). *Seductions of crime.* New York, NY: Basic Books.

Kleck, Gary and E. Britt Patterson. (1993). The impact of gun control and gun ownership levels on violence rates. *Journal of Quantitative Criminology, 9,* 249–287.

Levitov, Jana and Dee Wood Harper. (2010). Motive for murder: Does the level of neighborhood isolation make a difference? *Proceedings of the 2010 Homicide Research Working Group.* Baltimore, MD.

Levitov, Jana and Dee Wood Harper (2012). You can't do crack on credit: Drug and retaliatory murder. In D.W. Harper, W. Thornton and L. Voigt (Eds.), *Violence: Do we know it when we see it?* (pp. 129–146). Durham, NC: Carolina Academic Press.

Lewis, Oscar. (1959). *Five families: Mexican case studies in the culture of poverty.* New York, NY: Basic Books.

Lombroso, Cesare. (1911). *Crime: Its causes and remedies.* Trans. H. P. Horton. Boston, MA: Little Brown.

Lombroso, Cesare, and Guglielmo Ferrero. (2004[1893]). *Criminal woman, the prostitute, and the normal woman.* Trans. N. Hahn Rafter and M. Gibson. Durham, NC: Duke University Press.

Lombroso, Cesare. (2006[1876]). *The criminal man (L'Uomo delinquente).* Trans. M. Gibson and N. Hahn Rafter. Durham, NC: Duke University Press.

Luxton, David, Janyce Osenbach, Mark Reger, Derek Smolenski, Nancy Skopp, Nigel Bush and Gregory Gahm (2012). *Department of Defense suicide event report: Calendar year 2011 annual report.* United States Department of Defense. Retrieved from: http://t2health.org/sites/default/files/dodser/DoDSER_2011_Annual_Report.pdf.

Matza, David. (1964). *Delinquency and drift.* New York, NY: Wiley.

McBride, Duane and Clyde McCoy. (1993). The drugs-crime relationship: An analytical framework. *The Prison Journal, 73,* 257–278.

McDermott, Paul, Arthur Alterman, John Cacciola, Megan Rutherford, Jospeh Newman and Ellen Mulholland. (2000). Generality of Psychopathy Checklist-Revised factors over prisoners and substance-dependent patients. *Journal of Consulting and Clinical Psychology, 68,* 181–186.

Menard, Scott, Sharon Mihalic and David Huizinga. (2001). Drugs and crime revisited. *Justice Quarterly, 18,* 269–299.

Messerschmidt, James. (1993). *Masculinities and crime: Critique and reconceptualization of theory.* Lanham, MD: Rowman and Littlefield.

Miller, Matthew, David Hemenway and Deborah Azrael. (2007). State-level homicide victimization rates in the U.S. in relation to survey measures of household firearm ownership, 2001–2003. *Social Science and Medicine, 64,* 656–664.

Moffitt, Terrie. (1993). Adolescent-limited and life-course persistent antisocial behavior: A developmental taxonomy. *Psychological Review, 100,* 674–701.

Moffitt, Terrie and Anthony Walsh. (2003). The adolescence-limited/life-course persistence theory of antisocial behavior: What have we learned? In A. Walsh and L Ellis (Eds.), *Biosocial criminology: Challenging environmentalism's supremacy* (pp. 125–144). Happauge, NY: Nova Science Publishers.

Moynihan, Daniel Patrick. (1965). *The negro family: A case for national action.* Washington, D.C.: Office of Policy Planning and Research, U.S. Department of Labor. Cambridge, MA: MIT Press.

Park, Robert and Ernest W. Burgess. (1925). *The city.* Chicago, IL: University of Chicago Press.

Pew Center on the States. (2008). *One in 100: Behind bars in America 2008.* Retrieved from: http://www.pewtrusts.org/uploadedFiles/wwwpewtrustsorg/Reports/sentencing_and_corrections/one_in_100.pdf.

Roman, John, Shelli Rossman and Michael Rempel. (2011). *The multi-site adult drug court evaluation. Volume 1, chapter 2: Review of the literature.* Center for Court Innovation. Retrieved from: http://www.courtinnovation.org/sites/default/files/documents/MADCE_1.pdf.

Sampson, Robert. (1986). Crime in cities: The effects of formal and informal social control. In A. Reiss, Jr. and M. Tonry (Eds.), *Communities and crime* (pp. 271–311). Chicago, IL: University of Chicago Press

Shaw, Clifford and Henry McKay. (1931). *Social factors in delinquency.* Chicago, IL: University of Chicago Press.

Shaw, Clifford, and Henry McKay. (1942). *Juvenile delinquency in urban areas.* Chicago, IL: University of Chicago Press.

Sheldon, William Herbert. (1949). *Varieties of delinquent youth: An introduction to constitutional psychiatry.* New York, NY: Harper.

Shover, Neal, and David Honaker. (1992). The socially-bounded decision making of persistent property offenders. *Howard Journal of Criminal Justice, 31,* 276–293.

Slate, Risdon and Wesley Johnson. (2008). *The criminalization of mental illness.* Durham, NC: Carolina Academic Press.

Sontag, Deborah and Lizette Alvarez. (2008). Across America, deadly echoes of foreign battles. *The New York Times,* January 13. Retrieved from: http://www.nytimes.com/2008/01/13/us/13vets.html?pagewanted=all&_r=0.

Steadman, Henry, Fred Osher, Pamela Robbins, Brian Case and Steven Samuels. (2009). Prevalence of serious mental illness among jail inmates. *Psychiatric Services, 60,* 761–765.

Steffensmeier, Darrell, Hua Zhong, Jeff Ackerman, Jennifer Schwartz and Suzanne Agha. (2006). Gender gap trends for violent crimes, 1980–2003: A UCR-NCVS comparison. *Feminist Criminology, 1,* 72–98.

Stuart, Heather. (2003). Violence and mental illness: An overview. *World Psychiatry, 2,* 121–124.

Tedeschi, James, and Richard Felson. (1994). *Violence, aggression, and coercive actions.* Washington, D.C.: American Psychological Association.

Thornhill, Randy and Craig Palmer. (2000). *The natural history of rape: Biological bases of sexual coercion.* Cambridge, MA: MIT Press.

U.S. Census Bureau. (2010). Annual estimates of the resident population by sex, race, and Hispanic origin for the United States, April 1, 2000 to July 1, 2009. Retrieved from: http://www.census.gov/popest/data/national/asrh/2009/index.html.

Udry, Richard. (1995). Sociology and biology: What biology do sociologists need to know? *Social Forces, 73,* 1267–1278.

Wilson, William Julius. (1987). *The truly disadvantaged: The inner city, the underclass and public policy.* Chicago, IL: University of Chicago Press.

Wilson, William Julius. (1996). *When work disappears: The world of the new urban poor.* New York, NY: Knopf.

Wolfgang, Marvin and Franco Ferracuti. (1967). *The subculture of violence: Towards an integrated theory of criminology.* London, England: Tavistock.

Wolfgang, Marvin Eugene. (1982). *Subculture of violence.* New York, NY: Sage Publications.

Wright, James and Peter Rossi (1986). *Armed and considered dangerous: A survey of felons and their firearms.* New York, NY: Aldine de Gruyter.

Wright, Richard, and Scott Decker (1994). *Burglars on the job: Street life and residential break-ins.* Boston, MA: Northeastern University Press.

Wright, Richard, and Scott Decker. (1997). *Armed robbers in action: Stickups and street culture.* Boston, MA: Northeastern University Press.

Zahn, Margaret A., Robert Agnew, Diana Fishbein, Shari Miller, Donna-Marie Winn, Gayle Dakoff, and Candace Kruttschnitt (2010). *Causes and correlates of girls' delinquency.* Office of Juvenile Justice and Delinquency Prevention. Retrieved from: https://www.ncjrs.gov/pdffiles1/ojjdp/226358.pdf.

Zimring, Franklin and Gordon Hawkins. (1997). *Crime is not the problem: Lethal violence in the United States.* New York, NY: Oxford University Press.

Part III

Where, When and to Whom Does Crime Happen?

Chapter 9

Crime in Context: Choices and Opportunities to Offend

Introduction

In Chapters 3–7 of this book, we explored a variety of theories that imply crime is outside the control of the individual. From biological influences to disorganized neighborhoods to strains to delinquent peers to social bonds to developmental trajectories, readers may come away with the impression that criminologists have neglected the role of choice in crime commission since the early 1900s or so (Cullen and Agnew, 2011). But that is simply not the case and in this chapter, we will be exploring the role of choice as well as the role of opportunity in crime commission. We begin with a discussion of deterrence and rational choice theories and continue with explanations of routine activity theory, situational crime prevention, situational action theory, the spatial distribution of crime and we conclude with an investigation of various criminal opportunities.

Deterrence Theory:
Setting the Stage for Rational Choice

To more fully understand deterrence theory, think back to the discussion of Cesare Beccaria in Chapter 1. Remember that Beccaria specifically and the classical school of criminology more generally believed that people choose to act in ways that will maximize their pleasure and minimize their pain. In their pursuit of pleasure, they may act in criminal ways. The classical school focused on the role of punishment and its ability to deter crime. In order to deter crime, classical theorists believed, punishment must be severe but proportional to the crime committed, swift and above all, certain.

There are two types of deterrence with which modern day deterrence theory is concerned: specific and general. Specific deterrence is the notion that punishment will reduce criminal involvement for those who experience said punishment. There is little if any empirical evidence that severe punishments are more effective at reducing future criminal behavior than less severe punishments and in fact, experiencing punishment, including more severe punishment, may actually increase future criminal involvement (Cullen, Wright and Applegate, 1996; Sherman, Gottfredson, MacKenzie, Eck, Reuter and Bushway, 1998; Huizinga, Weiher, Espiritu and Esbensen, 2003; Pogarsky and Piquero, 2003; Kovandzic, Sloan and Vieraitis, 2004; Bernburg, Krohn and Rivera, 2006; Agnew, 2009; Baay, Liem and Nieuwbeerta, 2012). Specific deterrence may be ineffective for several reasons. Many offenders may continue to be subjected to the conditions that brought them into crime after they experience punishment, thereby reducing the punishment's deterrent effect. Punishment may also increase the severity of the conditions that offenders experienced before they were punished; and having a criminal label (see Chapter 5 for more on labeling theory) may reduce the ability to get funding for education or to secure employment (see Apel and Nagin, 2011 for a review of the literature on this topic). And although the United States has based its criminal justice system on the principles of deterrence, punishment is actually very uncertain (Cullen and Agnew, 2011; for more on the theoretical basis of the American criminal justice system, see Chapter 15). As noted above and in Chapter 1, certainty is the most important element of effective punishment. At least one study places the likelihood of prison or jail time for burglary at less than three percent. That is, for every 100 burglaries committed, fewer than three people will be incarcerated (Reynolds, 1995). It is far more certain that burglary will go unpunished than that it will be punished. Similarly, Dunford and Elliot (1984) found that for youth who self-reported committing between 101 and 200 delinquent acts in the span of two years, only seven percent were arrested. Only 19 percent of those who self-reported committing over 200 delinquent acts in a two-year period were arrested, revealing that punishment is far from certain even for those engaged in nearly daily delinquency. When punishment is certain, it can be a powerful incentive to obey the law. For example, Weisburd, Einat and Kowalski (2008) found that the imminent (i.e., certain) threat of incarceration serves as a powerful motivator to pay court-ordered fees and fines.

The second type of deterrence is general deterrence. General deterrence is the notion that punishment will deter crime among the population as a whole. When scholarly research on general deterrence began in earnest in the 1970s, most work was focused on trying to determine the deterrent effect of the death penalty by comparing states that use capital punishment and those that do not on their homicide rates. A great deal of this research concludes that the death penalty is not an effective deterrent against homicide (Akers and Sellers, 2009).[1]

More recent studies on general deterrence are focused on whether increasing the severity and certainty of punishment for some crimes and some offenders deters crime among the general public. On the topic of severity, most studies that examine whether increasing the severity of punishment produces a general deterrent effect find that it

---

1. For more on the deterrent effect of capital punishment, see Chapter 15.

does not (Cullen and Agnew, 2011). On the topic of certainty, one difficulty with conducting research of this nature is that people do a poor job of estimating the likelihood of punishment (Kleck, Sever, Li and Gertz, 2005). If they think that punishment for a particular crime is always a certainty, for example, they will (or should) always be deterred from committing that crime, regardless of what real world changes are implemented to increase the actual likelihood of punishment. Therefore, perceptions of the likelihood of punishment are much more important to deterrence researchers than the objective level of certainty of punishment. Some research reveals that increasing the certainty of punishment may produce a modest deterrent effect in some circumstances, with the caveat that the certainty of punishment is much less important than other factors that influence crime, including an individual's beliefs about crime and perceptions of informal sanctions from family and friends (Nagin, 1998; D'Alessio and Stolzenberg, 1998; Paternoster and Bachman, 2001; Levitt, 2002; Matsueda, Keager and Huizinga, 2006; Pratt, Cullen, Blevins, Daigle and Madensen, 2006; Wikstrom, 2008; Tonry, 2008; Agnew, 2009).

Research on general deterrence has also focused on the power of the police to deter crime. A host of studies from the 1990s forward find that a greater police presence, either in terms of larger numbers of officers or officers on the street for longer periods of time, serves as a deterrent against crime. In more detail, a 10 percent increase in officers appears to result in a three percent decrease in crime, a finding that is consistent across the aforementioned studies (Apel and Nagin, 2011). Other scholars have focused on not just police presence, but police deployment. Braga (2008) reviewed a number of studies on hot spots policing, a concept which is addressed in more detail below. Briefly, hot spots are those places in which a great deal of crime in a given area is concentrated. Braga (2008) found that in seven out of the nine studies he reviewed, deploying police to these hot spots resulted in significant drops in crime. Moreover, it appears as though that crime, which might have occurred at the hot spots had the police not been there, was not displaced to other locations, providing some further support for the notion of police-based deterrence.

Specific deterrence is focused on people's direct experience with punishment and its effect on their future criminal behavior while general deterrence is focused on people's indirect experience with punishment and its effect on their future criminal behavior. However, perhaps the distinction between specific and general deterrence need not be so sharp. Stafford and Warr (1993) argue that some people are subject to both types of deterrence and that a more nuanced and more informative way to examine deterrent effects of punishment is to investigate direct and indirect experience with both punishment and punishment avoidance. Those who have experienced punishment, for example, have lower estimates of the certainty of punishment than those who have not been punished (Paternoster, 1985). In fact, punishment appears to embolden some to commit future crimes (Piquero and Pogarsky, 2002). These findings run contrary to what deterrence theory would predict but indicate that direct experience or lack thereof with punishment is important in future estimates of the certainty of punishment and important in future criminal behavior. Moreover, informal sanctions, such as the disapproval of family and friends, may be more important in deterring crime than the formal sanctions meted out by the criminal justice system (Green, 1989; Grasmick and Bursik, 1990,

Pratt, Cullen, Blevins, Daigle and Madensen, 2006), though these informal sanctions are not included in the current conception of deterrence or deterrence theory.

Choice and Crime: Rational Choice Theory

The notion of rational choice has its home in economic theory (e.g., Becker, 1968). It was not until the mid-1980s that rational choice principles were brought to bear on the study of crime. Nevertheless, it is clear how rational choice fits with both the classical school and deterrence theory. Rational choice theory as conceived of by Derek Cornish and Ronald Clarke (1986) holds that people make calculated, i.e., rational, choices that are designed to maximize their benefits and minimize their costs. An important element of the theory is that before engaging in a specific criminal action, potential offenders must decide that they are going to become involved in crime. Once they have chosen to become involved in crime, offenders decide which crime to commit by determining the costs and benefits of a particular criminal action (in Cornish and Clarke's terms, the theory distinguishes between criminal involvement and criminal events). If a criminal action is high in benefits and low in costs, people will engage in this action to meet their needs. Conversely, if a criminal action is high in costs and low in benefits, people will refrain from taking this action. Of course, one of the potential costs of engaging in any criminal action is punishment and this is where deterrence and rational choice theories are connected.

Though rational choice has its roots in the classical school of crime, it is a distinct theory. One way in which Cornish and Clarke's (1986) rational choice theory differs from the classical school of criminology is that the former does not assume people (including offenders) are perfectly rational all the time. Cornish and Clarke (1986) recognize that when they choose to engage in criminal activity, offenders may have incomplete or inaccurate information about the situation or they may be limited in their ability to be rational by low intelligence or ingestion of various intoxicants. Nevertheless, Cornish and Clarke (1986) maintain that offenders still act rationally when they choose to engage in crime, operating within a bound or limited rationality.

Another way in which rational choice theory differs from the classical school is that the former considers a wide variety of potential costs and benefits of crime. Remember that the classical school focused almost exclusively on formal punishment as the cost of crime; rational choice theory recognizes that the potential costs of crime go beyond formal sanctions to include disapproval from family and friends, loss of job and feelings of shame. They may also include features of the criminal action itself. A high level of effort, skill and time needed to commit a specific crime may all be perceived as costs to the offender. The potential benefits of crime are not limited to monetary or material gain. They may also include increased status among peers and thrills and features of the criminal action may also function as benefits for the offender. A low level of effort, skill and time needed to commit a specific crime may all be perceived as benefits to the offender.

A third way in which rational choice theory differs from the classical school is that the former recognizes that a variety of factors influence the decision to engage in crime and in specific criminal actions. We are already familiar with these factors, as they are

Figure 9.1. A rational choice explanation for a specific crime

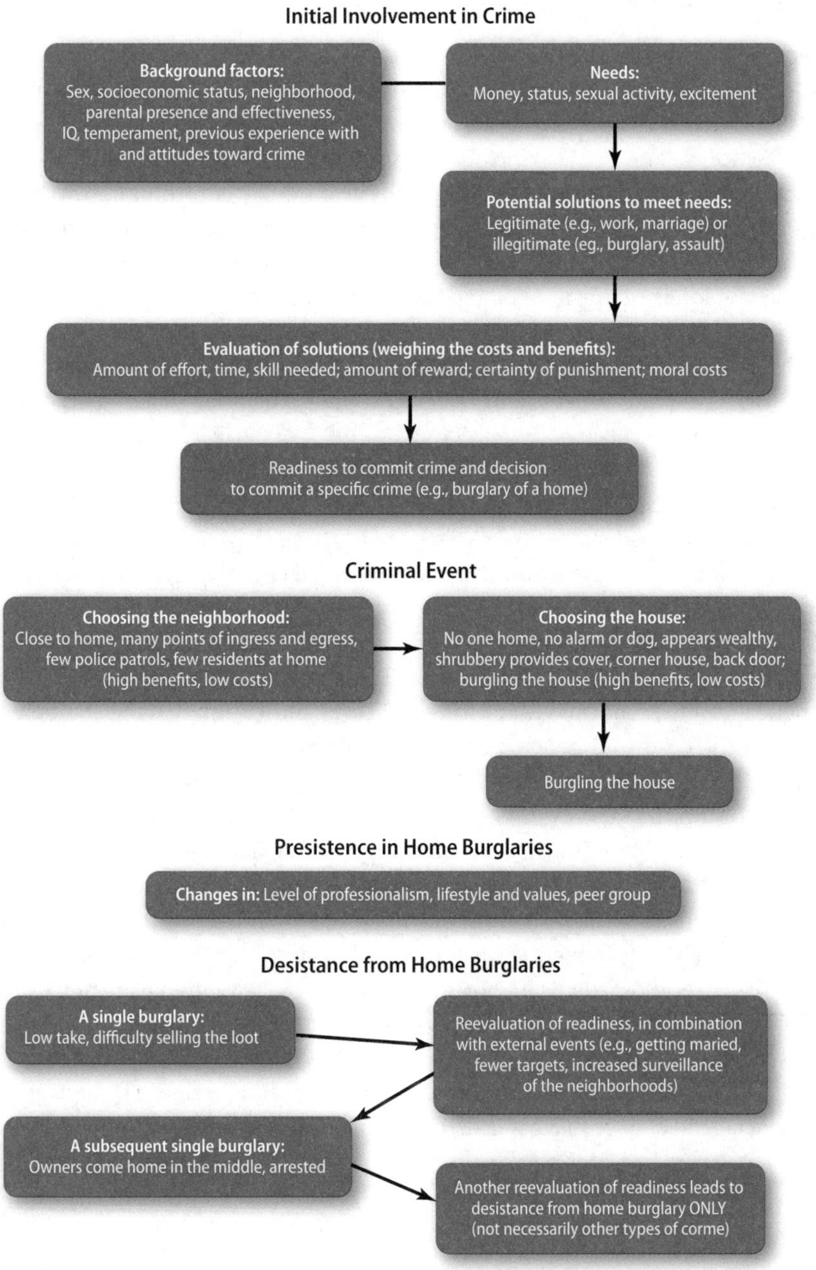

Initial Involvement in Crime

Background factors:
Sex, socioeconomic status, neighborhood, parental presence and effectiveness, IQ, temperament, previous experience with and attitudes toward crime

Needs:
Money, status, sexual activity, excitement

Potential solutions to meet needs:
Legitimate (e.g., work, marriage) or illegitimate (eg., burglary, assault)

Evaluation of solutions (weighing the costs and benefits):
Amount of effort, time, skill needed; amount of reward; certainty of punishment; moral costs

Readiness to commit crime and decision to commit a specific crime (e.g., burglary of a home)

Criminal Event

Choosing the neighborhood:
Close to home, many points of ingress and egress, few police patrols, few residents at home (high benefits, low costs)

Choosing the house:
No one home, no alarm or dog, appears wealthy, shrubbery provides cover, corner house, back door; burgling the house (high benefits, low costs)

Burgling the house

Presistence in Home Burglaries

Changes in: Level of professionalism, lifestyle and values, peer group

Desistance from Home Burglaries

A single burglary:
Low take, difficulty selling the loot

Reevaluation of readiness, in combination with external events (e.g., getting maried, fewer targets, increased surveillance of the neighborhoods)

A subsequent single burglary:
Owners come home in the middle, arrested

Another reevaluation of readiness leads to desistance from home burglary ONLY (not necessarily other types of corme)

Source: Adapted from Cornish and Clarke, 1985.

featured prominently in other theories of crime, including low self-control, experience with strains and association with delinquent peers (Cornish and Clarke, 1986; Cullen and Agnew, 2011). Figure 9.1 graphically illustrates rational choice theory, from the initial involvement to the event to continuing involvement to desistance.

Research on Rational Choice Theory

Much of the research that seeks to test rational choice theory as a valuable explanation of crime focuses on the perceived costs and benefits of engaging in crime. As alluded to above, the potential costs of crime are not limited to formal sanctions meted out by the criminal justice system, but also include costs such as high levels of effort, skill and time needed to commit the crime, high risk of physical injury, confrontation with victim, feelings of guilt or shame, and loss of economic security or status among peers and/or relatives. Similarly, the potential benefits of crime go beyond monetary or material gain to include low levels of effort, skill and time needed to commit the crime, low risk of physical injury, little or no confrontation with victim, thrills and status among peers and/ or relatives. Many of these studies reveal that crime is more likely to occur when costs are perceived as low and benefits are perceived as high (Bachman, Paternoster and Ward, 1992; Nagin and Paternoster, 1993; McCarthy, 1995, 2002; Paternoster and Bachman, 2001; Piquero and Tibbets, 2002; Tittle and Botchkovar, 2005; McCarthy and Hagan, 2005; Tittle and Botchkovar, 2005; Matsueda, Keager and Huizinga, 2006; Pratt, Cullen, Blevins, Daigle and Madensen, 2006; Ward, Stafford and Gray, 2006; Fagan and Piquero, 2007), providing some support for the role of rational choice in crime causation.

An interesting twist on rational choice theory research involves expanding the list of costs and benefits that potential offenders consider when deciding to enter into a criminal action. In a survey of 212 students, Bouffard (2007) presented them with three hypothetical crime scenarios, shoplifting, fighting and drunk driving. Students were asked to list the costs and benefits of engaging in each of those crimes. Importantly, the respondents were not constrained by any costs or benefits of crime provided by the researcher. Bouffard (2007) found that the costs and benefits the respondents listed included but went beyond the usual legal, moral and social costs and benefits thought to be important in determining whether to engage in a criminal action. For example, one of the benefits nearly half the respondents listed for engaging in drunk driving was a rather practical one, having the car for later. This research serves as a reminder that the potential costs and benefits of engaging in a criminal action may be much wider in scope than rational choice theory or previous research on it considers.

A fascinating addition to rational choice theory research involves interviews with active offenders. In these interviews, offenders are asked a variety of questions about how they decide to engage in a particular criminal action. In the case of home burglary, burglars appear to consider a variety of information when deciding which house to target. For example, when assessing what the monetary and material gain from burglarizing a particular house might be, one active offender noted:

> It don't take no Einstein to know [what's in a house]. I can look at a neighborhood and almost tell you what's in every house there. Poor neighborhoods got poor stuff. Rich neighborhoods got rich stuff (Cromwell and Olson, 2010, p. 31).

Another said:

> I'm always looking for signs that they got something worthwhile. Big, expensive houses, rich cars, stuff like that (Cromwell and Olson, 2010, p. 31).

A third offered the following:

> These people mostly have gardeners and other people doing their work for them. When I see somebody mowing that ain't the owners and a gardener truck parked in the street and lots of expensive trees and flowers, I know these people got money. Top of that, if I go on the property, people next door and passing by probably goin' to think I work there (Cromwell and Olson, 2010, p. 32).

When assessing the accessibility of a potential target home, burglars appear to consider a variety of factors, including but not limited to the visibility of the house, the layout of the neighborhood, the presence of an alarm and the presence of a dog. On the topic of the visibility of the house, one active burglar observed:

> Notice how that picture window looks out onto the street. The curtains stay open all the time and both houses across the street can see straight into the living room. I wouldn't do [burglarize] that place (Cromwell and Olson, 2010, p. 34).

On the topic of the layout of the neighborhood, one active burglar reported:

> I don't like to go too deep inside a neighborhood. You kinda get lost once you get in those winding streets and stuff. I like to stay close to the main road so I can find my way out and escape fast (Cromwell and Olson, 2010, p. 38).

Another said:

> I don't do cul-de-sacs. Or dead end streets. Always gotta have an escape route (Cromwell and Olson, 2010, p. 38).

On the topic of alarm systems, one active burglar noted:

> Most houses got a sign, like "This house protected by Westinghouse Security" or one of those other security companies. I just pass them by. People stupid to hit a house with an alarm system. Just go to one without it. That's common sense, you know ... Sometimes you see this blue sign that just says something like "This house protected by an electronic alarm system" without no company name on it. That's not real ... They just trying to scam you. You can get those signs at Radio Shack. Don't mean nothing (Cromwell and Olson, 2010, p. 39).

And on the topic of dogs, one active burglar said:

> I don't mess with no dogs. If they got dogs I go someplace else (Cromwell and Olson, 2010, p. 42).

Taken together, these insights from active burglars on what goes into their estimations of costs and benefits in the face of a potential criminal action appears to provide some anecdotal support for rational choice theory.[2]

---

2. Note that not one of these accounts of rational decision making by active burglars makes any reference to the threat of punishment; the threat of punishment does not appear to be a part of the decision making process for a specific criminal action, in this case burglary (Shover and Copes, 2010).

Strengths and Weaknesses of Rational Choice Theory

One of the great strengths of rational choice theory is that it differentiates between involvement and crime and involvement in a specific criminal action, and in so doing, encourages us to think about the costs and benefits of each criminal action or event. When we consider the costs and benefits of criminal events in this way, we can observe some built in prescriptions for deterring crime that are separate from manipulating punishment, including increasing the effort, skill and time necessary to engage in criminal actions. Continuing with the example of home burglary seen in Figure 9.1, some of the steps that the homeowner can take to increase the effort, skill and time necessary to commit the crime include installing an alarm system, installing extra locks and having a dog; similar measures can be taken to avoid automobile theft or theft from the workplace. On the topic of costs and benefits, another strength of rational choice theory is that research on it reveals what factors offenders take into account when they decide to engage in a specific criminal action.

Among the weaknesses of rational choice theory is the presumption that offenders are rational. Not a little empirical research reveals that offends regularly commit crimes with what appears to be little planning and without taking the time to estimate costs and benefits (Birkbeck and LaFree, 1993; Meier and Miethe, 1993; Tittle, 1995; Newman, Clarke and Shoman, 1997; Pogarsky, 2002; Tunnel, 2002; Exum, 2002; Carmichael and Piquero, 2004). Of course, Cornish and Clarke would respond to the notion that offenders are impulsive, often drunk or high or under the influence of peers by saying that they act rationally, but do so within their limits; remember the notion of bounded rationality. Social learning theory architect Ronald Akers is famously critical of rational choice theory, maintaining that if we presume offenders are acting with a limited ability to be rational, they are in essence the same as the irrational or non-rational offenders with which the other theories of crime are concerned. Moreover, the background factors that influence the decision to become involved in crime (see Figure 9.1) draw on those from other theories, notably control and learning theories, suggesting these factors are at the core of engaging in crime and rational choice theory does not provide us with any great insights as to what causes crime (Akers and Sellers, 2009). In fact, Akers maintains rational choice theory can be easily subsumed under his social learning theory (Cullen and Agnew, 2011).

Opportunity and Crime: Routine Activity Theory

Routine activity theory, as conceived of by Lawrence Cohen and Marcus Felson (1979), maintains that the convergence of three elements: motivated offenders, suitable targets and the absence of capable guardianship, is essential in producing crime. The likelihood of crime increases when a motivated offender encounters a suitable target when capable guardianship is lacking in the same time and space. Cohen and Felson (1979) take motivated offenders as a given and focus most closely on changes in the number of suitable targets and the lack of capable guardianship in producing crime;

Figure 9.2. Routine activity theory

Source: Adapted from Cohen and Felson, 1979.

capable guardianship is not limited to the formal version supplied by law enforcement, but includes informal guardianship provided by ordinary citizens (on this point, see Felson, 1994, 1998, 2002). As evidence for their theory, Cohen and Felson (1979) look to the changes in people's routine activities in the United States after World War II. During this period, people spent more time away from home than they did before, at work, at school and in leisure activities. This had the effect of increasing the likelihood of their victimization in two ways. First, being out of the home makes people more vulnerable to criminal victimization than they would have been had they stayed home. Put another way, they become more suitable targets. Second, being away from home leaves homes and their contents unprotected by the homeowners. Put another way, there is an absence of capable guardianship for homes and their contents, which Cohen and Felson (1979) point out started to get much lighter (i.e., more portable) after the war and into the second half of the 20th century. Cohen and Felson (1979) claim that the increasing crime rates in the United States after World War II, particularly beginning in the 1960s, provide empirical support for their theory. Figure 9.2 provides a graphic depiction of routine activity theory.[3]

---

3. This is the classic conception and depiction of routine activity theory. Later work by Felson (1986) added a concept known as handlers. These are people such as parents, family members, teachers, friends and partners who may prevent the offender from engaging in crime. Eck (1994) suggests a second modification—people who regulate places, such as store clerks, bar staff, parking lot attendants, door persons and maintenance workers among others, who may also serve to prevent crime.

Research on Routine Activity Theory

Researchers have found support for routine activity theory. In their study of hot spots of crime, which are mentioned above and discussed in more detail below, Sherman, Gartin and Buerger (1989) found that 50 percent of calls for service to the police in Minneapolis, Minnesota came from just three percent of locations in the city and that serious crimes were concentrated in a very small number of locations. The researchers concluded that these hot spots involve the confluence of motivated offenders, potential victims (i.e., suitable targets) and a lack of capable guardianship in the same time and space. In a telephone survey, Kennedy and Forde (1990) found that the frequency with which people stayed at home or went out predicted the amount of victimization they experienced. Those who went out more often made themselves suitable targets for crime outside the home and removed capable guardianship of their homes while out, consistent with routine activity theory. Mustaine and Tewksbury (1998) found that for college students, both legal activities taking place outside the home as well as involvement in illegal activities predicted criminal victimization. With this study, Mustaine and Tewksbury (1998) were able to overcome one of the barriers to fully understanding people's routine activities as articulated by Jensen and Brownfield (1986), namely, consideration of both the legal and the illegal things they may do that constitute their routine activities.

More recently, Miller (2012) found that different types of routine activities were associated with different types of offending among teenagers. Involvement in sports and clubs was associated with assault offenses, involvement in nightlife was associated with assault and drug offenses and socializing with friends was associated with assault, vandalism and shoplifting offenses, indicating that different routine activities put people at risk for specific types of offending and of victimization. Routine activity theory may have some utility in explaining sex offenders' choice of victims. Varin and Beauregard (2010) found that sex offenders followed a variety of scripts to complete their assaults and that the specific script that was employed, either home, outdoor or social, was predicated on the routine activities of their victims. Routine activity theory has also been expanded to include non-contact offenses such as those that occur online. Yar (2005) found that the concepts of routine activity theory, motivated offenders, suitable targets and absence of capable guardians, appear to be valid for the study of online crime, but that the convergence of these elements in time and space in the virtual world is problematic. Nevertheless, there is some support for routine activity theory's ability to explain online crime. Reyns (2011) found that those who use the Internet for banking, shopping and e-mail were more likely to be victims of identity theft than those who did not and both online shopping and downloading increased the risk of victimization (see Kigerl, 2011 for a macro-level analysis of this phenomenon).

Some of the more interesting recent research on routine activity theory comes from the study of agent-based models in simulated environments. In one of the first studies in this vein, Groff (2007) established a virtual environment based on the tenets of routine activity theory and observed whether the agents in that virtual world behaved in accordance with what the theory would predict. She found that an increase in activities outside the home was associated with an increase in street robberies and that those robberies tended to cluster in certain locations in the virtual setting. In a more sophisticated analysis, Groff (2007a) found that varying the schedules of the virtual agents while they were away from home, that is, putting time constraints on them, caused a change in the spatial distribution of street robberies. When spatial in addition to temporal constraints were included, the incidents of robberies also increased in the virtual setting, though not significantly (Groff, 2008). It appears that it is not just the total amount of time spent away from home but the type of constraints on routine activity that influence victimization. Moreover, the manner in which this research was conducted may hold promise for empirically testing other choice- and opportunity-based theories of crime (on this point, see Birks, Townsley and Stewart, 2012).

Strengths and Weaknesses of Routine Activity Theory

Among the strengths of routine activity theory are that it furthers our understanding of the spatial and temporal distributions of crime and that it brings our attention to the features of our everyday lives that may constitute opportunities for criminal victimization. Moreover, it has built-in prescriptions for decreasing that risk of victimization. We can make ourselves and our property less suitable targets by locking our doors and vehicles, remaining aware of our surroundings while out and safeguarding our personal information and we can increase capable guardianship by forming neighborhood watches.

Among the weaknesses of routine activity theory are that its three key elements have rarely been properly operationalized and measured. For example, what is a capable guardian? Consider McEvoy's (2013) research on inmate gambling. Even though inmates are constantly supervised by ostensibly capable guardians, inmate gambling, which is prohibited, is fairly common. When capable guardians turn a blind eye to prohibited activity, do they still qualify as capable guardians? In addition, some scholars are troubled by the lack of attention to offenders' motivations. It remains unclear in the tenets of the theory who qualifies as a motivated offender and how they get to be that way. As Wortley (2002) points out, a situation rife with criminal opportunities may turn a person who is not otherwise motivated to offend into a motivated offender in that moment. Is it simply the opportunity to commit crime that motivates the offender in that moment, or are there other factors at work? If the point of a theory of crime is to explain why crime occurs, this is a serious lapse. In fact, Akers and Sellers (2009) contend that routine activity theory is primarily a theory of victimization and not of crime causation. Around the same time that Cohen and Felson (1979) were developing routine activity theory, other scholars were developing an influential theory of victimization called lifestyle theory, which holds that people's lifestyles, their routine activities in other words, may put them at greater risk for victimization (Hindelang, Gottfredson and Garofalo, 1978; Garofalo, 1987; see also Chapter 10).

Settings and Crime: Situational Crime Prevention

As its name implies, situational crime prevention is focused on situational features that serve to facilitate or impede criminal activity. The architect of situational crime prevention, whose name readers already know, Ronald Clarke (1980), begins his seminal work by pointing out the preoccupation of other theories of crime with offenders' dispositions. Clarke (1980) argues that while a focus on criminal dispositions may be interesting, it does little to help us devise any actionable crime prevention solutions. Instead, our focus should be on the immediate choices available to potential offenders in order to develop crime prevention strategies. That is, our focus should be on the situational features that serve to promote or restrict criminal actions. Clarke (1980) highlights some simple solutions to specific types of crime employed in western Europe, including the reinforcement of coin boxes in pay phone booths in England that all but eliminated theft from phone booths and the steering column locks that were mandated on all old and new cars in West Germany that reduced car theft in that country by 60 percent.[4] We can easily draw to mind more modern day examples of efforts to reduce the opportunities for crime, such as requiring swipe cards to enter building doors or security tags on merchandise in stores (Clarke, 1997).

Increasing the risks of detection may also serve to prevent crime. Importantly, Clarke (1980) does not put all of his eggs in the policing basket here. Rather, he focuses on features of the everyday environment that may be manipulated to prevent crime, such as an apartment building with a door person, a paid parking lot with an attendant present and stores with greeters or clerks to assist customers. Devices that aid in surveillance and thereby increase the risks of detection, such as closed circuit television cameras (CCTV) are also of use in crime prevention. Astute readers should be thinking back here to rational choice theory and its focus on the perceived costs and benefits of engaging in a specific criminal action. It is no coincidence that Ronald Clarke was instrumental in the development of both rational choice theory and the notion of situational crime prevention.

Research on Situational Crime Prevention

A great deal of research on situational crime prevention has focused on efforts to make crime more difficult to commit in specific locations. Gated communities experience less burglary than their non-gated counterparts, though it remains unclear whether gates have any reductive effect on other crimes, such as domestic violence and vandalism (Addington and Rennison, 2013). Some of the efforts suggested by Felson (2002) that are particularly applicable for convenience stores include locating cash registers in the front rather than the back of the store, limiting employee access to safes, advertising through signs that there is little cash on hand and keeping the view in and out of the store unobstructed. Other efforts include the installation of security cameras, outside lighting and burglar alarms (Clarke, 1997). These crime prevention through

---

4. For younger readers, a pay phone is a landline telephone made available for public use in exchange for coin payments. Also, for a period in the 20th century, Germany was two countries, communist East and democratic West Germany.

environmental design (CPTED) efforts are taken to make it more difficult or unattractive for potential offenders to commit crimes against specific places (Newman, 1972; Jeffery, 1977), but one of the great difficulties of determining how effective these measures are in preventing crime is that stores may choose to implement more than one CPTED effort at a time. This makes it very difficult if not impossible to determine which single CPTED effort is effective at preventing crime (Hendricks, Landsittel, Amandus, Malcan and Bell, 1999; Felson and Clarke, 2010).

While much research on situational crime prevention is focused on convenience stores because as a location, they have a relatively high crime rate, some more recent research has sought to examine whether the CPTED efforts typically employed at convenience stores are effective at fast food restaurants as well. Exum, Kuhns, Koch and Johnson (2010) found that the factors that predicted robbery for convenience stores were different from those that predicted robbery for fast food restaurants and point out that CPTED efforts should be very business-specific (see also Eck and Guerette, 2012). Other research has attempted to expand the scope of situational crime prevention to go beyond store robberies and to include organized crime, noting that the utility of situational crime prevention is predicated on how applicable it is across places and offenses (von Lampe, 2011).

Strengths and Weaknesses of Situational Crime Prevention

Similar to both rational choice and routine activity theories, one of the greatest strengths of situational crime prevention is that it contains prescriptions for preventing crime that ordinary citizens and business owners can take. Moreover, these are relatively simple measures that do not concern themselves with the enormous tasks of raising a person's level of self-control, for example, or providing a young person with prosocial peers. Rather, these measures involve installing additional locks, alarms, lights and fences. Among the weaknesses of situational crime prevention is one alluded to above, namely that CPTED efforts that are useful for one type of location may not be for others and those useful for one type of crime may not be for others. There is also the issue of displacement. If one convenience store on a street has been fortified with outdoor lighting, security cameras, a time-access safe and other CPTED measures to make it less attractive to robbers, robberies may be displaced to another convenience store on the same street with fewer or none of these CPTED efforts. In the case of displacement, it can be argued that CPTED measures have not really done anything to prevent crime in general, as only crime at that first convenience store has been prevented, though at least one researcher has found that CPTED efforts may be able to prevent crime without a great displacement effect (Weisburd, 1997). Moreover, there is little that CPTED efforts can do to address the areas in which businesses and homes are situated. The convenience store in a socially disorganized neighborhood, even if a variety of CPTED efforts have been taken at that store, is still more likely to be robbed than one located in a more organized neighborhood (D'Alessio and Stolzenberg, 1990; Hendricks, Landsittel, Amandus, Malcan and Bell, 1999). This indicates that CPTED efforts can only go so far in preventing crime.

Situational Action Theory[5]

An intriguing and recent addition to criminological theory has attempted to meld the importance of both offenders and settings. This perspective, known as situational action theory, was developed by Per-Olof Wikstrom, Dietrich Oberwittler, Kyle Treiber and Beth Hardie (2012) and focuses on the person-environment interaction in producing crime, i.e., violations of the law. The factor that is most important on the person side of the interaction is a person's propensity for crime. This propensity is comprised of a person's morality and ability to exercise self-control. The factor that is most important on the environment side of the interaction is the status of a setting as criminogenic. Whether a setting is criminogenic is determined by its moral norms and the degree to which they are enforced; settings themselves are comprised of environments and circumstances. In developing their theory, Wikstrom, Oberwittler, Treiber and Hardie (2012) examined 700 young people in the English city of Peterborough over the course of five years. This middle sized city was chosen in part because it allowed for an in depth examination of not only how much crime young people are involved in, but how they spend their time, with whom and where.

About 70 percent of participants reported committing at least one crime between the ages of 12 and 16 and a very small percentage of participants were responsible for the majority of crimes over these five years. These participants tended to start offending early, before age 12, and to be versatile in their crimes. There was a strong correlation between offending and crime propensity, providing support for this aspect of the theory. In the same way that only a few participants engaged in a great deal of crime, only a few participants were frequently exposed to criminogenic settings, where exposure is defined as the settings themselves and the circumstances in which young people interacted with those settings. The most criminogenic environments include those in the city center and those with low levels of collective efficacy, as these features are thought to indicate lax morals and/or enforcement thereof. The most criminogenic circumstances include those in which young people spend unsupervised, unstructured time with peers outside of the work and school settings. There is a significant relationship between exposure to criminogenic settings and offending, but this relationship is not as strong as the one between crime propensity and offending. Moreover, participants whose peers were frequently involved in crime were more involved in crime themselves and this was true across levels of exposure to criminogenic settings.

In the final analysis, Wikstrom, Oberwittler, Treiber and Hardie (2012) found that their data supported the presumptions of their theory. Taken together, levels of crime propensity and levels of criminogenic exposure are able to accurately predict the amount of crime young people are involved in. Those with low crime propensity and low levels of criminogenic exposure commit small or no amounts of crime, while those with high crime propensity and high levels of criminogenic exposure commit large amounts of crime. Using scenarios that they asked participants to respond to, the researchers were

---

5. General consensus among criminologists may one day place situational action theory among integrated theories of crime, but we consider it as an opportunity theory.

also able to determine that participants with a high crime propensity perceived violence as an alternative more often and had more violent intentions than those with a low criminal propensity; the participants with a high crime propensity also engaged in more real world violence.

Wikstrom, Oberwittler, Treiber and Hardie (2012) have done criminology a great service by connecting person-oriented and environment-oriented approaches of crime causation and focusing on the importance of both in a logical, comprehensive and empirically supported way. It will be interesting to see if other research on situational action theory is as supportive as that detailed above; future research directions for this theory might include but are not limited to exploring the role of biological factors in the development of criminal propensity, whether situational action theory can explain other types of crime such as white collar crime and whether the theory is supported by tests that are conducted in other cities and countries.

Spatial Distribution of Crime: Hot Spots and Broken Windows

Hot Spots

The idea that crime occurs in certain places more than others is nothing new. Think back to Andre Michel-Guerry and Adolphe Quetelet from Chapter 1. However, the modern day investigation of this phenomenon has led some criminologists to focus on the hot spots of crime. As noted above, a hot spot of crime is a very small location where a great deal of crime occurs. In fact, not only is crime highly concentrated in hot spots, it is also predictable over the course of a one year period (Sherman, 1995). These locations may be single businesses or residences or they may be intersections. The existence of these hot spots was emphatically confirmed by Sherman, Gartin and Buerger (1989). They reviewed calls for service to the Minneapolis Police Department and found that 50 percent of the calls for service came from just three percent of the city's addresses and that calls for service for violent crimes were even more concentrated. Subsequent research on hot spots found that 20 percent of disorder crime and 14 percent of personal crime was concentrated in 56 drug hot spots in Jersey City, New Jersey (Weisburd and Green, 1995). Weisburd, Bushway, Lum and Yang (2004) found that 50 percent of crime in Seattle over a 14 year period was concentrated in four to five percent of street segments in that city. Other research is similarly supportive of the notion of hot spots and the concentration of crime (Trickett, Osborn, Seymour and Pease, 1992; Trickett, Osborn and Ellingworth, 1995; Bennett, 1995; Farrell, 1995; Pease and Laycock, 1996; Bennett and Durie, 1996; Guidi, Homel and Townsley, 1997; Pease, 1998; Brantingham and Brantingham, 1999; Roncek, 2000; Eck, Gersh and Taylor, 2000).

With the evidence for hot spots of crime established, researchers in this area have begun to take a more nuanced view, examining among other things the criminal careers of places. On this topic, Sherman (1995) begins by pointing out that the concentration of crime in places is greater than it is in people, about six times greater. While we may not be able to very accurately predict who will continue involvement in crime, we may be able to do a better job of predicting where it will occur. Sherman (1995) explains that to better understand the criminal careers of places, that is, how they get to be hot spots, we can ask the same questions of places as we would of people. Among these questions are when does the onset of crime occur in that place and in what circumstances (onset), how often does crime occur there and under what circumstances (recurrence), how often in a year does crime occur at that place (frequency), how long does that place continue to be a hot spot and under what circumstances does it stop being one (career length and desistance), how intermittent is crime at that place (intermittency) and finally, does that place specialize in any crime types (crime type specialization).

Sherman (1995) provides examples from his research to make each of these questions we should be asking not just about offenders but about places more meaningful. For example, the removal of an elevator operator may serve as the change in guardianship necessary for the onset of a place's criminal career. Poor guardianship in combination with very suitable victims, such as cash businesses that never close, may explain recurrence. The frequency of crime in a place may be explained by a high concentration of motivated offenders, suitable targets and the absence of capable guardianship as routine activity theory predicts; Sherman (1995) mentions a very hot spot from his Minneapolis study, a bar[6] frequented by drug dealers and prostitutes and often full of intoxicated patrons where some of the staff were dealing drugs, as well. That bar had a long criminal career until it was torn down. Unlike with people, many of whom desist from crime after late adolescence, desistance for criminal places usually comes in the form of destruction of the place, planned or otherwise. Intermittency in crime at a place may be affected by changes around that place, such as different vehicle and foot traffic patterns, changes in the population of the neighborhood and different weather patterns. Finally, the evidence is mixed on whether certain places specialize in certain types of crime. Of course, domestic violence is concentrated in residences, but in Minneapolis, shoplifting was common at cash businesses where robbery was also common. Future research on the criminal careers of places should focus on certain types of places, such as bars, and the results of this research should be used to formulate and implement useful crime prevention policies that are place-based (Sherman, 1995).

What can we do about hot spots? After the formal discovery of hot spots, the police departments of at least two cities experimented with increasing patrols to hot spots. Unsurprisingly, one of the two cities is Minneapolis. As Sherman and Weisburd (1995) describe, the Minneapolis police department sent extra patrols to 55 randomly selected hot spots of the 110 identified, with no change in patrol to the other 55. The extra patrols went to the 55 randomly selected hot spots between 7pm and 3am, the time when crime had been identified as being most likely to occur, every day for a year. The amount of time the police actually spent in the experimental and control hot spots was measured by a researcher with a stopwatch. The number of calls for service from the hot spots receiving extra police patrols was about two thirds less than the number from the hot spots not receiving the extra patrols. The researchers measuring the amount of

---

6. A single location or address in a larger hot spot has been referred to as a hot dot (see e.g., Weisel, Clarke and Stedman, 1999).

time the police spent in the hot spots confirmed this finding, noting that there were about half as many disorder events, such as prostitution and drug dealing, in the experimental hot spots. Applying extra patrols to known hot spots co-occurred with the remarkable crime drop in New York in the 1990s (Sherman, 2011) and other research reveals the benefits of extra patrols to hot spots in terms of both crime prevention and disorder reduction (Braga, 2007).

The second city that has undertaken such an experiment is Jersey City, New Jersey. Though the true experimental conditions that were utilized in Minneapolis were not replicated in Jersey City, extra police patrols that were deployed to some hot spots there over the course of 15 months were associated with a reduction in calls for service for disorder issues as compared to the hot spots that received no extra patrols (Weisburd and Green, 1995). Importantly, Weisburd and Green (1995) found no displacement effect in those hot spots receiving extra patrols. That is, crime did not go up in the areas adjacent to those receiving extra patrols and other research on displacement has borne out this finding (Guerette and Bowers, 2009). Sorg, Haberman, Ratcliffe and Groff (2013) found that foot patrols can be effective in reducing crime in hot spots, but that a shorter rather than longer duration as well as random application of these foot patrols to different hot spots may be more effective for preventing both displacement and offenders' return to the initial hot spot.

Broken Windows

The policy implications that stem from many (but not all) of the theories discussed in this chapter have little to do with law enforcement. As we have seen, the policy implications involve everyday citizens making changes to the environments over which they have control that make crime less of a rational choice or make a target less suitable. Broken windows theory as advanced by Wilson and Kelling (1982) is also concerned with the places in which crime occurs, but contends that law enforcement can play an active role in reducing crime.

Wilson and Kelling (1982) reject the notion of root causes of crime that have been proposed by other criminologists and propose instead that crime is caused by disreputable people and the disorder they create. Importantly, the disreputable people, including the homeless, the mentally ill and the substance addicted, may not necessarily be involved in crime. However, if they are allowed to take over public spaces and create disorder that goes unchecked, it sends the message to others, including others who live in that community, that no one cares enough about it to do something. This first central idea of broken windows is where the theory gets its name: imagine two houses, each of which has a broken window. In the first house, the owner rushes to replace the glass and repair any other damage to the home; in essence, order is restored to the house quickly. In the second house, though, the owner neglects to fix the window, perhaps even neglecting to cover the hole. The owner's inaction in the case of the second house sends the message to passersby that no one cares enough about that house (or its contents) to do something as simple as fix a window, so it becomes permissible to break more. And the message that no one cares serves as a signal to more serious criminals to begin engaging in crime at that location because there is little risk of being apprehended by or even reported to the police.

Wilson and Kelling (1982) maintain that when disreputable people are allowed to take over public spaces, law abiding people become fearful of those spaces and go to great lengths to avoid being near them. The withdrawal of the law abiding removes a layer of informal social control over people in the neighborhood and with that layer removed, the disorder created by the disreputable is allowed to spread. Referring back to the broken windows metaphor, the spreading disorder in a neighborhood is akin to breaking more windows in that second house, after which criminals view the places in the community where disorder goes unchecked as prime locations to commit very serious crime. For Wilson and Kelling (1982), disorder leads to a breakdown of control, which leads to high crime rates.

The key to reducing crime, then, is to reduce disorder, or in the theory's terms, to repair the broken windows. Wilson and Kelling's (1982) solution to the problem of disorder comes in the form of law enforcement and this is where they differ from many other criminologists, who typically do not see any portion of the criminal justice system as effective at reducing crime. Wilson and Kelling (1982) believe that the police can be effective in reducing the disorder that they see as the cause of serious crime. To do this, police officers need to intervene and make arrests when they observe signs of disorder, such as drinking, urinating in public, jaywalking, panhandling and the like. When police officers engage in this type of policing, which has also been called quality of life policing or zero tolerance (Harcourt, 2001; Eck and Maguire, 2000), they send the message to criminals that disorder is not tolerated and that someone does care about the neighborhood enough to punish those who create the disorder. This emboldens the law abiding residents of the neighborhood to reassert the informal social control that is necessary for the prevention of future disorder (Wilson and Kelling, 1982).

Does this type of policing serve to reduce crime? Put another way, is broken windows theory valid? Kelling and Coles (1986) claim that this style of law enforcement is responsible for the astonishing reduction in both violent crime as a whole and homicides in particular in New York in the 1990s (for more on the crime decline in New York during this time, see Zimring, 2007). However, there may have been other factors at work in New York's crime decline, including the robust economy of the 1990s, the waning of the crack epidemic and other policing initiatives. Moreover, the drop in crime in New York appears to have begun before this style of law enforcement was implemented there (Harcourt, 2001), and more fundamentally, it may be the case that crime actually causes disorder and not the other way around, which is a potentially serious blow to broken windows theory (Cullen and Agnew, 2011).

Criminal Opportunity in Context: Disasters

As we have seen, opportunities for crime are present in the everyday environment. But sometimes opportunities for crime present themselves in extraordinary circumstances, such as in the wake of disasters. The disaster literature is replete with examples of disaster survivors engaging in prosocial behavior — rescuing one another, providing necessities such as food and shelter and assisting with recovering from physical devastation, which serves to strengthen connections among survivors and forge a new sense of community. However, there are well documented instances of crime in the wake of disasters. Importantly, the disasters provide the opportunities for the different types of crime detailed below. That is, it is very unlikely that these crimes would have occurred absent the disaster and if they did, certainly not to the same scale.

9/11

In the wake of the September 11, 2001 terrorist attacks on the United States, there was a palpable sentiment among those both directly and indirectly affected by the attacks that the country was standing together for the first time in recent memory. Nevertheless, this manmade disaster presented opportunities for crime that might not have otherwise been apparent. As detailed by Peek and Lueck (2012), hate crimes against Muslims in the United States increased from six in the month before 9/11 to 350 in the month after and from 40 in the year before to 567 in the year after. This sudden and dramatic increase was not limited to the year after the 9/11 attacks. For each of the eight years after the attacks, hate crimes against Muslims were at least five times higher (average of 134 per year) than they were in each of the eight years before the attacks (average of 24.3 per year). Importantly, while both personal and property crimes are counted among hate crimes, Muslims were subjected to more personal hate crimes than property hate crimes. Perhaps surprisingly, hate crimes against Muslims were not limited to New York and Washington, D.C., where the terrorist attacks occurred. Hate crimes against Muslims were widely dispersed throughout the country, meaning that Muslims everywhere were at risk for retaliatory hate crimes in the wake of 9/11. To reiterate, it was the terrorist attacks that provided the opportunity for this type of theretofore very unusual crime to occur.

Hurricane Katrina

Hurricane Katrina, which devastated the Gulf Coast states and especially the city of New Orleans in 2005, created opportunities for a number of different crimes to occur. One such crime was rape. As detailed by Thornton and Voigt (2012), rape occurred against women in all phases of the disaster. For those readers not familiar with disaster phases, Table 9.1 provides a brief summary.

During the warning phase of Katrina, many people attempted to evacuate the city. As the calls for evacuation became more urgent and people became more desperate to leave, opportunities for the sexual assault of women were created. Thornton and Voigt (2012) detail the case of a woman who was gang raped by two men from whom she accepted a ride out of town. During the impact phase, the chaos and the need for survival created opportunities for the sexual assault of women. Thornton and Voigt (2012) describe another women who was gang raped in a convenience store while trying to get food for her children and medicine for her mother. Thornton and Voigt (2012) also detail the cases of women who were raped during the emergency, recovery and reconstruction phases. The lack of electricity and reliable communication in the city in

Table 9.1. Disaster phases

Phase Name	Characteristics
Warning	There is knowledge of the imminent disaster but it has not struck
Impact	The disaster strikes
Emergency	Lifesaving efforts taken, including rescues, evacuations, provision of food and water, administration of medical care
Recovery	Restoration of essential infrastructure, including water, roads, electricity, communication
Reconstruction	Massive rebuilding, stabilization of the ecosystem

Source: Adapted from Thornton and Voigt, 2012a.

the immediate aftermath of the storm made women particularly vulnerable to sexual assault. Those in shelters found themselves among strangers and unsure who to trust, as did those who had to stay in makeshift Federal Emergency Management Agency (FEMA) trailer parks because their homes had been destroyed; there are cases of women being raped in both of these settings. And there are cases of women who came to New Orleans, either as volunteers or in search of work to assist with the recovery, being raped; in the case of undocumented women, they felt they had few options in terms of reporting their rapes.

Another crime for which Katrina created an opportunity is looting. Though many people evacuated in advance of the storm, many chose to or had to stay. Most of those who remained in the city resorted to obtaining survival items from stores but some also engaged in looting of nonessential goods. Using burglary as a proxy for looting,[7] Frailing and Harper (2012) examined the amount of looting in New Orleans in the wake of Katrina and compared it to the amount of looting in the wake of other storms that have directly impacted the city. They found that the burglary rate in the month after Katrina per 100,000 people increased by nearly 200 percent in the month after the storm as compared to the month before.

The burglary rate in the month after the unnamed 1947 storm increased by 94.2 percent as compared to the month before and the burglary rate in the month after Hurricane Betsy in 1965 only increased by 15.4 percent as compared to the month before. Frailing and Harper (2012) claim that what accounts for the difference between looting in Katrina and the two other storms are the socioeconomic conditions in New Orleans prior to Katrina. Over the four decades leading up to Katrina, high wage manufacturing jobs disappeared and were replaced by low wage service jobs. Public schools worsened, oil companies moved to other southern cities and those who could move

---

7. Frailing and Harper (2012) used burglary as a proxy for looting for two reasons. First, there was no looting statute in Louisiana until 1993; using burglary allowed comparisons over time. Second, they believed that people would be unlikely to report the loss of essential survival items such as food and water to the police, so burglary reflects the taking of nonessential items. In other words, it is a reasonable measure of opportunistic looting that permits longitudinal comparison.

out of the city, white and African American, did so, leaving behind a largely African American, impoverished, underemployed and undereducated population.

Interestingly, the socioeconomic conditions in the city were very similar in the lead up to Katrina and the 2008 storm Hurricane Gustav, yet there was much less looting after Gustav than after Katrina, just a 92 percent increase in burglary in the month after as compared to the month before. Frailing and Harper (2012) contend that, in accord with Cohen and Felson's (1979) routine activity theory, the increased capable guardianship in the form of law enforcement that was present in New Orleans immediately after Gustav hit kept the burglary level relatively low. Other research on crime in the wake of disasters has borne out the importance of the capable guardian aspect of routine activity theory. Cromwell, Dunham, Akers and Lanza-Kaduce (1995) found that informal guardianship in the form of neighbors working together to recover from Hurricane Andrew in Florida and watching out for each other and each other's property served to deter crime. Zahran, Shelley, Peek and Brody (2009) found similar results, excepting the case of domestic violence; informal guardianship does not appear to deter this particular crime.

A third broad category of crime for which Katrina created opportunity was fraud. Frailing (2012) examined the amount of disaster benefit fraud, defined as obtaining or attempting to obtain disaster benefits, such as those from FEMA or the Red Cross, to which one is not entitled. She found that disaster benefit fraud was committed after a variety of disasters, including 9/11, Hurricane Katrina and the BP oil spill in the Gulf of Mexico in 2010. Those who had family members killed in 9/11 were able to apply for benefits from the Victim Compensation Fund (VCF); the average award for a death was $1.44 million. A variety of official documentation was necessary to obtain these benefits, including a death certificate, official documentation of the victim's presence at one of the attack sites on 9/11, a court document designating the claimant as the recipient of the money, official documentation that other interested parties had been notified of the claim and proof of assets at the time of death. Moreover, those who made claims on the VCF underwent criminal and other background checks. In contrast, it was rather easy to obtain disaster benefits from FEMA after Hurricane Katrina. All one needed was a working phone and some patience. After about a half an hour of providing (unverified) basic information to a representative from FEMA, emergency assistance in the amount of $2,000 was directly deposited into the claimant's bank account. It was also relatively easy to obtain benefits after the BP oil spill. Those whose livelihoods had been adversely affected by the spill, from fishermen to shrimpers to oystermen to hoteliers and those in related professions could apply to the Gulf Coast Claims Facility to recover their losses. A quick turnaround time was promised, a few days for individuals and about a week for businesses, meaning that it was unlikely claims could be thoroughly checked for accuracy.

The amount of benefit fraud after each of these disasters varied greatly. Table 9.2 summarizes the amount of benefit fraud after each of these disasters.

Frailing (2012) believes that rational choice theory is a good explanatory theory for disaster benefit crime. Consider what an easy target FEMA benefit fraud was in the wake of Katrina. Half an hour on the phone for a $2,000 payday is a pretty good deal. Put another way, the amount of time, effort and skill needed to commit this crime is

Table 9.2. Instances of fraud after three disasters

Disaster	Amount of benefit fraud
9/11	Approximately 20 cases (17 by 2003)
Hurricane Katrina	1,360 cases (by September, 2010)
BP oil spill	Approximately 7,000 claims suspected of being fraudulent (by January, 2011)

Source: Adapted from Frailing, 2012.

very low. The Gulf Coast Claims Facility was a similarly easy target in part because the quick turnaround time was widely publicized. In contrast, consider what a hard target the VCF was. The amount of time, effort and skill needed to commit fraud against the VCF was high, turning off most potential fraudsters, even with the big payday; this analysis is consistent with Cornish and Clarke's (1986) rational choice theory. Rational choice theory contains prescriptions for preventing crime, including making targets harder. In the case of disaster benefit fraud, hardening targets includes establishing a database before the next disaster strikes that agencies such as the United States Postal Service, Social Security Administration and FEMA are able to access and quickly check claimants' details.

Other Disasters

Frailing and Harper (2012a) detail the criminal opportunity that other disasters have created. Looting followed in the wakes of Hurricane Hugo of 1989, the San Francisco earthquake of 1906, the Tangshan earthquake of 1976, the Haiti earthquake of 2010, the Chile earthquake of 2010, the Wilkes-Barre flood of 1972, the Buffalo Creek flood of 1972, and the Boxing Day tsunami of 2004. Some of these and other disasters also created opportunities for violent crime. In the wake of the Kanto earthquake in Japan in 1923, Koreans living in Japan at the time made a convenient scapegoat for the inability to recover quickly from the devastation. The Japanese government and military called on civilians to enact vigilante justice and approximately 6,000 Koreans were killed with whatever weapons were handy. In the wake of the Haiti earthquake, reports of men using of violence and sexual intimidation against women to obtain their food vouchers were not uncommon. Gang violence also occurred in Haiti after the earthquake, in part because the prison housing some of the most dangerous gang members was felled by the quake and they were freed. Both women and children made homeless and vulnerable by the Boxing Day tsunami were raped. Interpersonal violence, including assault, sexual assault, domestic violence and robbery were reported in the wake of the BP oil spill, especially as throngs of cleanup workers descended into Gulf Coast towns and cities. Interestingly, the type of property and personal crime seen rather commonly after disasters do not appear to have occurred in the wake of the Tohoku earthquake and tsunami that devastated Japan in 2011. One reason postulated for the low level of looting in the wake of this disaster is the presence of the Yakuza. The Yakuza is an organized criminal enterprise in Japan that in the aftermath of the earthquake and tsunami, served as informal guardians against looting; even in ordinary times, theft is considered verboten among the Yakuza and grounds for expulsion from the group (the Yakuza are discussed in more detail below). Frailing and Harper (2012a) conclude that disasters interrupt the normal flow of social life and that this disruption may allow both new norms and new forms of innovative behavior to emerge. New norms that permit crime in combination with innovative action that is antisocial in nature may be part of a rapid decivilizing process that results in actual criminal activity.

Other Criminal Opportunity

Perhaps surprisingly, theories of crime that deal with choice and opportunity are focused primarily on our traditional notions of crime, that which occurs on the street between a single offender and a single victim. However, similar to the way in which disasters can create criminal opportunity, some occupations and activities, legal or otherwise, also create opportunities for crime. These are not necessarily the offenses that spring to mind when we think of crime, but they are against the law nonetheless.

White Collar Crime

The first of these other criminal opportunities is white collar crime. Edwin Sutherland coined the term white collar crime in 1940 and described it as crime committed by respectable people in the course of their professions. Today we recognize white collar crime as illegal acts committed by non-physical means in the interest of obtaining money, property or some personal or corporate advantage (Weisburd, Wheeler, Waring and Bode, 1991). Both Clinard and Quinney (1973) and Rosoff, Pontell and Tillman (1998) provide a useful distinction between occupational crime and corporate crime. Occupational crime is that committed in the course of employment for one's personal advantage. An example of occupational crime is a bank teller taking the occasional $20 bill out of the drawer. The teller's job creates the opportunity for this type of crime to occur. Professional occupational crime is a subset of occupational crime that involves the crime committed by professionals such as doctors or lawyers in the course of their work. An example of professional occupational crime is a doctor filing an insurance claim for a procedure that he or she never performed or for a patient he or she never treated. Again, the profession creates the opportunity for crime. Corporate crime, on the other hand, is that done to benefit the corporation. One example of recent corporate crime includes the Enron scandal of 2001. Enron was at the top of the corporate heap for years, but the reason the company appeared so successful is that its managers engaged in carefully planned and carefully executed accounting fraud that made the company look much more profitable to investors than it actually was. To reiterate, this crime could not have happened without the company providing the opportunity for it; a serious lack of regulation over the savings and loan industry in the 1980s and over subprime mortgage lending practices in 2008 almost certainly broadened the opportunity for corporate crime in these circumstances. White collar crime is discussed in more detail in Chapter 13.

Political Crime

While a definition of what constitutes political crime defies consensus, a good working definition for our purposes is engaging in ideologically motivated actions that are defined as illegal (Helfgott, 2008; Hagan, 2013). There are two types of political crime, oppositional crime, which is crime against the government and state crime, which is crime by the government. Oppositional crime can include dissent or protest, sedition, espionage, treason, assassination and terrorism offenses and state crime can include domestic espionage and illegal surveillance, political repression, human rights violations, and state violence, including genocide (Helfgott, 2008; Hagan, 2013). Importantly, it is the existence of a government that creates these opportunities for crime.

Those who engage in oppositional crime have strong ideological positions that conflict with those of the government. On the less serious end of the spectrum, oppositional crime includes picketing, sit-ins, blocking roads, protesting, burning flags and engaging in civil disobedience, such as Rosa Parks did. Sedition is the communication of information for the purposes of treason or defamation, treason is actions taken to try to overthrow the government and espionage is spying; these are more serious forms of oppositional crime. Very few cases of treason have been prosecuted in the United States since its inception, in large part because the charge is so difficult to prove. One famous case of espionage and treason involved Julius and Ethel Rosenberg, who were tried, convicted and executed for spying for the Soviet Union in 1953 (Helfgott, 2008). Assassination or attempted assassination of political figures is another serious type of oppositional crime. Assassins may believe their actions are selfless and done in the public interest, they may have a deep need for recognition, they may have a mental illness or they may not fit neatly into any of these categories (Clarke, 1982; Hagan, 2013). Table 9.3 summarizes some famous assassins and their targets as well as the category into which they fall.

On the most serious end of the spectrum of oppositional crime is terrorism, which is covered in some detail in Chapter 11. Briefly, while we principally associate terrorism with 9/11 in this country, there have been many other instances of international terrorism

Table 9.3. Assassins, targets and categories

Assassin	Target	Category
John Wilkes Booth	Abraham Lincoln	Selfless/public interest
Sirhan Sirhan	Robert Kennedy	Selfless/public interest
Lee Harvey Oswald	John Kennedy	Need for recognition
Lynette "Squeaky" Fromme	Gerald Ford	Need for recognition
Daniel M'Naghten*	Robert Peel	Mentally ill
John Hinckley Jr.*	Ronald Reagan	Mentally ill
James Earl Ray	Martin Luther King	No real fit

* M'Naghten and Hinckley are discussed in Chapter 1.   Source: Adapted from Hagan, 2013.

and even instances of domestic terrorism. In fact, domestic terrorist attacks account for nearly three quarters of terrorist attacks in the United States and most of these involve environmental or animal rights groups destroying property in furtherance of their goals (Helfgott, 2008).

State crime is crime committed by the state or by some agency on its behalf. On the less serious end of the spectrum, state crimes include domestic espionage and illegal surveillance. Domestic espionage is defined as the state or agents thereof spying and gathering information on individuals and groups it considers to be dissident. The most common domestic espionage technique is wiretapping and while legal in some cases, surveillance that violates civil rights is a version of state crime. Many groups working for social change in the 1960s and 1970s in the United States were subjected to illegal surveillance, such as the Black Panther Party, the Weather Underground and the Students for a Democratic Society (Helfgott, 2008). On the more serious end of the spectrum of state crime is political repression, which may be achieved through both human rights violations and state violence,[8] including genocide. Among political repression tactics that some states have used are disenfranchisement, discrimination, commitment or confinement, kidnapping, slavery, disappearances, torture and death squads. Of course, the most extreme form of state violence is genocide, which is the purposeful extermination of a group of people based on some characteristic, such as race, ethnicity or religion. We think of the Holocaust as the standout example of genocide in the 20th century, but there are other examples as well, from Bosnia-Herzegovina to Rwanda to the Sudan (Helfgott, 2008; Hagan, 2013).

Cybercrime

Cybercrime can be thought of as the use of computer technology to victimize others. The criminal opportunity in this case is created by going online. Those who never enter cyberspace cannot be victimized by cybercrime, but those who do (and that is many if not all of us these days) increase their risk of victimization. Of course, it stands to reason that people who spend more time in a variety of online activities are at greater risk of criminal victimization and research has borne this out (see Reyns, 2011 above). One example of cybercrime is identity theft, which involves the use of someone's personal information without his or her permission to obtain money, goods or services. Businesses store vast amounts of personal information about their customers, including names, dates of birth, bank account numbers, credit card numbers and Social Security numbers, which is typically used for legitimate purposes. However, should a criminal get access to that information, either by buying it, stealing it or hacking[9] into the databases that contain it, they may be able to take out loans, open lines of credit and make extravagant purchases with this information, which can be disastrous for victims, who may find

---

8. The sometimes-related topic of military crime is covered in more detail in Chapter 13.

9. A hacker can be understood as someone who accesses someone else's computer system without permission. For more on hackers, see Power (2000), Voiskounsky and Smyslova (2003), Kshetri (2006) and Holt (2010).

their credit ruined and themselves indebted (Walsh and Hemmens, 2011).[10] Identity theft was at the top of the Federal Trade Commission's (FTC's) consumer compliant list for the thirteenth year in a row in 2012. Eighteen percent of the over 2 million complaints made to the FTC were related to identity theft (FTC, 2013).

Another example of cybercrime is phishing, which involves sending thousands of fraudulent e-mails requesting or demanding that recipients reply to the message with sensitive information such as that listed above in order to rectify a nonexistent problem with an account. Phishers then wait for people to respond with personal details that they can use for criminal purposes. Phishing appears to be getting more sophisticated, with the fraudulent e-mails mimicking those from legitimate businesses more closely. Many readers have likely received a phishing e-mail in the past and may have even received one or more that originated in Nigeria. These phishing scams involve the sender notifying the recipient that there is a large amount of cash tied up but available if the sender will advance a small amount of money, usually several hundred dollars, to cover the costs of releasing the cash. Once the recipient sends the money, the sender demands more as difficulties with freeing the money arise (Walsh and Hemmens, 2011).

Phishing is one type of an attack on a computer system. Others include a denial of service attack, in which a computer is programmed to send fake messages to a server. These fake messages overload the server and prohibit legitimate users from accessing it. Trojan horse attacks involve hiding a virus in an otherwise harmless program, which is sent as an attachment in an e-mail. Once the recipient opens and runs the program, the virus steals information from the computer and sends it back to the original sender. Web spoof attacks involve the creation of a fake version of a legitimate website. The creators of the fake version can collect information entered into the site by unsuspecting users who think they have accessed the legitimate version of the site.[11] Many of these types of attacks can be utilized in cyberterrorism, which includes but is not limited to attempts to damage or destroy vital infrastructure, theft of information for use in planning future terrorist attacks and taking vast amounts of data hostage (Walsh and Hemmens, 2011; Hagan, 2013).

The computer age has also given pedophiles new avenues of access, i.e., new opportunities, to access their victims. Internet chat rooms provide pedophiles with ways to find potential victims and to build up a relationship with them that may lead to a physical meeting in which sexual contact occurs. The Internet also provides pedophiles with an easy way to share child pornography across international boundaries. In 2007, law enforcement in Great Britain, the United States and Canada busted a pedophile ring whose chat room contained pictures and live videos of the sexual abuse of children, some under a year old. Twenty-two victims of child sexual abuse were rescued as a result of this bust (Hagan, 2013).

---

10. For an intriguing look at the motives, risk perceptions and strategies of those who commit identity theft, see Copes and Vieraitis (2010).

11. Web spoof attacks are of particular concern after disasters, when many people are inclined to donate money to the relief effort online. Thornton and Voigt (2012) refer to this as cyberlooting or online looting.

Organized Criminal Enterprises

Remember back to Chapter 4 and our discussion of Cloward and Ohlin (1960), who recognized that there were opportunities for both legitimate and illegitimate success. One opportunity for illegitimate success comes in the form of organized criminal enterprises. Organized crime is crime committed by structural criminal enterprises that use intimidation, fear and corruption to sustain their illegal activities. The most famous example of an organized criminal enterprise is La Cosa Nostra (LCN; our thing in Italian), which is otherwise known as the Mafia. The Mafia creates an opportunity for illegitimate success for males of Italian descent who have demonstrated their criminal skills, as membership is restricted to this group. The structure of the Mafia is much like that of a corporation, with the boss or don at the helm and an underboss underneath him who is in charge of a handful of lieutenants, who supervise a group of soldiers who themselves have associates working underneath them; associates are not full members (Walsh and Hemmens, 2011). Though the subject of much popular media, the Mafia today is a shell of what it once was. There were five Mafia families in New York from the time of the end of Prohibition forward, but the concerted effort to prosecute those in the Mafia in the 1980s effectively dismantled the families and their organization (Walsh and Hemmens, 2011).

Organized crime is not limited to the Mafia and in fact, the decomposition of the Mafia was one of the factors that allowed other organized crime groups to flourish in the United States (Sanchez-Jankowski, 2003). The Russian Mafiya is considered one of if not the most dangerous organized crime group in the world today. The Mafiya is extremely active in Russia and has been since the breakup of the Soviet Union. Moreover, Russian organized crime took hold in the United States when thousands of Russians emigrated in the 1970s and 1980s (Rush and Scarpitti, 2001).

The Vietnam War allowed African Americans to establish their own connections with Asian drug suppliers for the first time, putting them in a position to form organized crime groups that would rival those comprised of whites (Adamson, 2000). One such group is the Gangster Disciples. Out of the many African American organized crime groups (e.g., the Crips and the Bloods), it is the Gangster Disciples that most closely mimics the Mafia in terms of structure, function and relationships with other organized crime groups (Knox and Fuller, 1995; Abadinsky, 2003), though this group appears to be more violent and dangerous than its Italian counterparts (Cureton, 2009).

Connection with drug supplies in Central and South America led to the rise of Latino organized crime groups, as well. The Marielitos, a group comprised of dissidents who were exiled from Cuba by Fidel Castro and sent to Florida, engage in drug trafficking (Lyman and Potter, 2004). Another Latino organized crime group is Mara Salvatrucha 13 (MS-13). Believed to be an outgrowth of Salvadoran street gangs, members of which began coming to the United States in the 1980s to escape the civil wars in Central America, MS-13 has become one of the most widespread and violent gangs in the United States. MS-13 is especially active in human trafficking (Logan, 2009). Organized crime groups abound in Mexico as well in the form of cartels that have become much more powerful since the dismantling of Colombian drug cartels in the 1990s. These cartels, among them the Sinaloas, Los Zetas, La Familia and Juarez, make it a practice to pay off politicians and law enforcement officials so they may continue their enterprise; lethal violence is also a typical tactic of these groups (Abadinsky, 2003).

As alluded to, the United States is not the only country where organized crime exists. Japanese organized crime groups are probably the largest and oldest in the world. Members of Japanese organized crime groups, including the Yakuza, are largely recruited from two groups, the descendants of those who worked in trades that made them outcasts and from Japanese-born Koreans. While the Yakuza engage in drug trafficking, extortion and prostitution, stealing is absolutely verboten, as it would bring great dishonor to the organization. In part because the Yakuza provide informal guardianship for some neighborhoods, they are well regarded in Japanese society (Johnson, 1990; Lyman and Potter, 2004). In China, criminal organizations called triads by the British because of the organizations' reverence for the number three, were and are involved in trafficking drugs, especially heroin, from the Golden Triangle, as well as in prostitution, gambling, extortion, money laundering and motor vehicle theft. The Sun Yee On triad is particularly active in the latter, supplying stolen cars from Hong Kong to mainland China (Hagan, 2013).

How do the opportunities for organized criminal groups arise? As alluded to above, one of the principal factors in the formation of organized crime groups is prohibition of some intoxicating substance. One of the most famous organized crime figures of all time, Al Capone, made his fortune selling bootleg alcohol during Prohibition (Abadinsky, 2003). Similarly, Mexican drug cartels take in billions of dollars trafficking and selling illegal drugs in the United States. Sanchez-Jankowski (2003) contends that poverty and worsening opportunities for social mobility are important factors in gang formation and have been since the 1800s, especially in the United States. Sung (2004) found that the lack of an independent judiciary and a flourishing black market economy are also important factors in the formation and maintenance of organized crime groups. Albanese (2000) maintains that environmental factors such as governmental regulation, law enforcement effectiveness and technological and social changes intersect with the presence of criminals and criminal groups to produce organized criminal activity. To put it in the terms of this section of the chapter, these factors create the opportunity for organized crime to occur.[12]

Box 9.1. Organized Retail Crime? What's That?

As we have seen, organized criminal enterprises engage in a variety of illegal activities, such as drug trafficking and dealing, human trafficking, prostitution, weapons trafficking, gambling, extortion, money laundering and motor vehicle theft. However, there is another type of illegal activity in which organized criminal enterprises are increasingly involved, organized retail crime. As reported by Montgomery (2012), organized retail crime is the theft of mass quantities of retail merchandise in order to help fund other illegal activities including the aforementioned, as well as terrorism. Large retail markets that have easy access to national transportation net-

---

12. See Chapter 4 for a discussion of policy implications that are specific to gangs.

works such as those in New York, Las Vegas, Miami, Chicago, Los Angeles and Phoenix are the most attractive targets. In Phoenix, retailers and law enforcement have teamed up to create the Arizona Organized Retail Crime Alliance (AZORCA) that allows retailers and law enforcement to share information about suspected organized retail crime in real time in the interest of both detection and prevention. Montgomery (2012) notes that the public's interest in finding a good bargain helps create a market for merchandise stolen on a massive scale.

Conclusion: Policy Implications of Choice and Opportunity Theories of Crime

In this chapter, we have focused on choice and opportunity in the production of crime. The policy implications that come out of most of these theories, whether they are concerned with choice or opportunity, are quite similar. As alluded to above, there are myriad things that ordinary citizens can do to make crime less of a rational choice or to make themselves and their property less suitable targets, such as locking their homes and cars, safeguarding their valuables, installing alarm systems, bars on windows and outside lighting, avoiding unsafe areas of town, avoid drinking or using drugs to excess and getting a dog. Businesses can take similar steps to make crime less of a rational choice or to make themselves and their property less suitable targets, including the installation of CCTV cameras, keeping lines of sight clear, limiting routes of ingress and egress and keeping smaller amounts of cash on hand. Felson and Clarke (2010) provide a useful categorization for these and other precautions against crime. The five categories are formal social control (setting curfews for juveniles and closing times for bars), informal supervision (family and friends looking out for one another and reminding each other about useful precautions), signage and instructions (reminders to lock doors, to safeguard one's things and to deposit valuables for safekeeping), product design (an audible tone when keys are left in a car's ignition, spring mounted doors that automatically shut on apartment buildings, bank customers choosing their own PINs) and environmental design to improve surveillance (adding street lights, trimming hedges).

Interestingly, only hot spots and broken windows directly implicate the actions of law enforcement as useful in preventing crime. Astute readers will have also noticed how few of the theories of crime in Chapters 3–7 have implications for crime prevention that are rooted in the criminal justice system, calling into question whether we are dealing with crime in the most effective way possible.

Websites to Visit

Choice Theories of Crime: http://www.drtomoconnor.com/1060/1060lect02.htm
Rational Choice and Deterrence theory: http://www.umsl.edu/~keelr/200/ratchoc.html
Ronald Clarke: http://www.criminology.fsu.edu/crimtheory/clarke.htm
White Collar Crime: http://www.fbi.gov/about-us/investigate/white_collar

FBI's Innocent Images National Initiative: http://www.fbi.gov/about-us/investigate/vc_
   majorthefts/innocent/innocent
National Gang Crime Research Center: http://www.ngcrc.com/

Discussion Questions

1. Do you believe that offenders engage in the rational decision making that rational choice theory assumes?
2. Do you agree with Akers that rational choice theory can be subsumed under his social learning theory? Why or why not?
3. What are some of your routine activities that could put you at risk for crime? Why do you engage in these activities?
4. Do you believe that routine activity theory is right to disregard offenders' motivations and focus instead on targets and guardianship? Could a deeper understanding of offender motivation strengthen routine activity theory?
5. Describe some situational crime prevention techniques that you are aware of from your own life in addition to those mentioned above. Are these effective in your estimation?
6. Because situational action theory relies so heavily on the concept of self-control as a root cause of crime, do you believe this theory adds anything to the study of crime?
7. Do you or have you ever lived in a crime hot spot? If so, what measures were taken to reduce crime in that area?
8. Do you believe that disorder precedes crime or that crime precedes disorder? Explain your answer.
9. What can be done to minimize the creation of criminal opportunity after disasters?
10. Which of the theories or concepts introduced in this chapter makes the most sense to you and why?
11. Which of the theories or concepts introduced in this chapter makes the least sense to you and why?

References

Abadinsky, Howard. (2003). *Organized crime*. 7th ed. Belmont, CA: Wadsworth.
Adamson, Christopher. (2000). Defensive localism in black and white: A comparative history of European-American and African-American youth gangs. *Ethnic and Racial Studies, 23*, 272–298.
Addington, Lynn and Callie Rennison. (2013). Keeping the barbarians outside the gate? Comparing burglary victimization in gated and non-gated communities. *Justice Quarterly*. DOI: 10.1080/07418825.2012.760644.
Agnew, Robert. (2009). *Juvenile delinquency: Causes and control*. New York: Oxford University Press.
Akers, Ronald and Christine Sellers. (2009). *Criminological theories: Introduction, evaluation, and application*. 5th ed. Los Angeles, CA: Roxbury.

Albanese, Jay. (2000). The causes of organized crime: Do criminals organize around opportunities for crime or do criminal opportunities create new offenders? *Journal of Contemporary Criminal Justice, 16,* 409–423.

Apel, Robert and Daniel Nagin. (2011). General deterrence: A review of recent evidence. In J. Wilson and J. Petersilia (Eds.), *Crime and public policy* (pp. 411–436). New York, NY: Oxford University Press.

Baay, Pieter, Marieke Liem and Paul Nieuwbeerta. (2012). Ex-imprisoned homicide offenders: Once bitten, twice shy? The effects of the length of imprisonment on recidivism for homicide offenders. *Homicide Studies, 16,* 259–279.

Bachman, Ronet, Raymond Paternoster and Sally Ward. (1992). The rationality of sexual offending: Testing a deterrence/rational choice conception of sexual assault. *Law & Society Review, 26,* 343–372.

Becker, Gary. (1968). Crime and punishment: An economic approach. *Journal of Political Economy, 76,* 169–217.

Bennett, Trevor. (1995). Identifying, explaining, and targeting burglary "hot spots." *European Journal on Criminal Policy and Research, 3,* 113–123.

Bennett, Trevor and Linda Durie. (1996). Domestic burglary task force: Cambridge. *Focus on Police Research and Development, No. 8* (December). London, England: Home Office.

Bernburg, Jon, Marvin Krohn and Craig Rivera. (2006). Official labeling, criminal embeddedness, and subsequent delinquency. *Journal of Research in Crime and Delinquency, 43,* 67–88.

Birkbeck, Christopher and Gary LaFree. (1993). The situational analysis of crime and deviance. *Annual Review of Sociology, 19,* 113–137.

Birks, Daniel, Michael Townsley and Anna Stewart. (2012). Generative explanations of crime: Using simulation to test criminological theory. *Criminology, 50,* 221–254.

Bouffard, Jeffrey. (2007). Predicting differences in the perceived relevance of crime's costs and benefits in a test of rational choice theory. *International Journal of Offender Therapy and Comparative Criminology, 51,* 461–485.

Braga, Anthony. (2007). *The effects of hot spots policing on crime.* A Campbell Collaboration Systematic Review. Retrieved from: http://www.campbellcollaboration.org/library.php.

Braga, Anthony. (2008). *Police enforcement strategies to prevent crime in hot spot areas.* Washington, D.C.: Office of Community Oriented Policing Services, U.S. Department of Justice.

Brantingham Patricia and Paul Brantingham. (1999). Theoretical model of crime hot spot generation. *Studies on Crime and Crime Prevention, 8,* 7–26.

Carmichael, Stephanie and Alex Piquero. (2004). Sanctions, perceived anger, and criminal offending. *Journal of Quantitative Criminology, 20,* 371–393.

Clarke, James. (1982). *American assassins: The darker side of politics.* Princeton, NJ: Princeton University Press.

Clarke, Ronald. (1980). Situational crime prevention theory and practice. *British Journal of Criminology, 20,* 136–147.

Clarke, Ronald (Ed.). (1997). *Situational crime prevention: Successful case studies.* Albany, NY: Harrow and Heston.

Clinard, Marshall and Richard Quinney. (1973). Reflections of a typologic, corporate, comparative criminologist. *The Criminologist, 14*, 1, 6, 11, 14–15.

Cloward, Richard and Lloyd Ohlin. (1960). *Delinquency and opportunity.* New York, NY: Free press.

Cohen, Lawrence and Marcus Felson. (1979). Social change and crime rate trends: A routine activity approach. *American Sociological Review, 44*, 588–607.

Copes, Heith and Lynne Vieraitis. (2010). Identity theft: Assessing offenders' motivations and strategies. In P. Cromwell (Ed.), *In their own words: Criminals on crime.* 5th ed (pp. 124–138). New York, NY: Oxford University Press.

Cornish, Derek and Ronald Clarke. (1985). Modeling offenders' decision: A framework for research and policy. In M. Tonry and N. Morris (Eds.), *Crime and justice: An annual review of research, Vol. 6* (pp. 147–185). Chicago, IL: University of Chicago Press.

Cornish, Derek and Ronald Clarke. (1986). *The reasoning criminal.* New York, NY: Springer-Verlag.

Cromwell, Paul, Roger Dunham, Ronald Akers and Lonn Lanza-Kaduce. (1995). Routine activities and social control in the aftermath of a natural catastrophe. *European Journal on Criminal Policy and Research, 3*, 56–69.

Cromwell, Paul and James Olson. (2010). The reasoning offender: Motives and decision-making strategies. In P. Cromwell (Ed.), *In their own words: Criminals on crime.* 5th ed (pp. 22–45). New York, NY: Oxford University Press.

Cuerton, Steven. (2009). Something wicked this way comes: A historical account of black gangsterism offers wisdom and warning for African American leadership. *Journal of Black Studies, 40*, 347–361.

Cullen, Francis, John Paul Wright and Brandon Applegate. (1996). Control in the community: The limits of reform. In A. Harland (Ed.), *Choosing correctional options that work* (pp. 69–116). Thousand Oaks, CA: Sage.

Cullen, Francis and Robert Agnew. (2011). *Criminological theory: Past to present.* 4th ed. New York, NY: Oxford University Press.

D'Alessio, Stewart and Lisa Stolzenberg. (1998). Crime, arrests, and pretrial jail incarceration: An examination of the deterrence thesis. *Criminology, 36*, 735–762.

Dunford, Franklyn and Delbert Elliott. (1984). Identifying career offenders using self-report data. *Journal of Research in Crime and Delinquency, 21*, 57–86.

Eck, John. (1994). *Drug markets and drug places: A case-control study of the spatial structure of illicit drug dealing.* Doctoral dissertation, University of Maryland, College Park.

Eck, John, Jeffrey Gersh and Charlene Taylor. (2000). Finding crime in hot spots through repeat address mapping. In V. Goldsmith, P. McGuire, J. Mollenkopf and T. Ross (Eds.), *Analyzing crime patterns: Frontiers of practice* (pp. 49–64). Thousand Oaks, CA: Sage.

Eck, John and Edward Maguire. (2000). Have changes in policing reduced violent crime? An assessment of the evidence. In A. Blumstein and J. Wallman (Eds.), *The crime drop in America* (pp. 207–265). Cambridge, England: Cambridge University Press.

Eck, John and Rob Guerette. (2012). "Own the place, own the crime" prevention: How evidence about place-based crime shifts the burden of prevention. In R. Loeber and B. Welsh (Eds.), *The future of criminology* (pp. 166–171). New York, NY: Oxford University Press.

Exum, Lyn. (2002). The application and robustness of the rational choice perspective in the study of intoxicated and angry intentions to aggress. *Criminology, 40,* 933–966.

Exum, Lyn, Joseph Kuhns, Brad Koch and Chuck Johnson. (2010). An examination of situational crime prevention strategies across convenience stores and fast-food restaurants. *Criminal Justice Policy Review, 21,* 269–295.

Fagan, Jeffrey and Alex Piquero. (2007). Rational choice and developmental influences on recidivism among adolescent felony offenders. *Journal of Empirical Legal Studies, 4,* 715–748.

Farrell, Graham. (1995). Preventing repeat victimization. In M. Tonry and D. Farrington, (Eds.), *Crime and justice: Strategic approaches to crime prevention, Vol. 19* (pp. 469–534). Chicago, IL: University of Chicago Press.

Felson, Marcus. (1986). Linking criminal choices, routine activities, informal control, and criminal outcomes. In D. Cornish and R. Clarke (Eds.), *The reasoning criminal: Rational choice perspectives on offending* (pp. 119–128). New York. NY: Springer-Verlag.

Felson, Marcus. (1994). *Crime and everyday life.* Thousand Oaks, CA: Pine Forge Press.

Felson, Marcus. (1998). *Crime and everyday life.* 2nd ed. Thousand Oaks, CA: Pine Forge Press.

Felson, Marcus. (2002). *Crime and everyday life.* 3rd ed. Thousand Oaks, CA: Sage.

Felson, Marcus and Roland Clarke. (2010). Routine precautions, criminology, and crime prevention. In H. Barlow and S. Decker (Eds.), *Criminology and public policy* (pp. 106–120). Philadelphia, PA: Temple University Press.

Frailing, Kelly. (2012). Fraud in the wake of disasters. In D.W. Harper and K. Frailing (Eds.), *Crime and criminal justice in disaster.* 2nd ed. (pp. 157–176). Durham, NC: Carolina Academic Press.

Frailing, Kelly and Dee Wood Harper. (2012). Fear, prosocial behavior and looting: The Katrina experience. In D.W. Harper and K. Frailing (Eds.), *Crime and criminal justice in disaster.* 2nd ed. (pp. 101–122). Durham, NC: Carolina Academic Press.

Frailing, Kelly and Dee Wood Harper. (2012a). Looking back to go forward: Toward a criminology of disaster. In D.W. Harper and K. Frailing (Eds.), *Crime and criminal justice in disaster.* 2nd ed. (pp. 7–36). Durham, NC: Carolina Academic Press.

FTC. (2013). FTC releases top 10 complaint categories for 2012. Retrieved from: http://ftc.gov/opa/2013/02/sentineltop.shtm.

Garofalo, James. (1987). Reassessing the life-style model of criminal victimization. In M. Gottfredson and T. Hirschi, (Eds.), *Positive criminology,* (pp. 23–42). Newbury Park, CA: Sage.

Grasmick, Harold and Robert Bursik. (1990). Conscience, significant others, and rational choice: Extending the deterrence model. *Law & Society Review, 24,* 837–862.

Green, Donald. (1989). Measures of illegal behavior in individual level research. *Journal of Research in Crime and Delinquency, 26,* 253–275.

Groff, Elizabeth. (2007). Simulation for theory testing and experimentation: An example using routine activity theory and street robbery. *Journal of Quantitative Criminology, 23,* 75–103.

Groff, Elizabeth. (2007a). Spatio-temporal aspects of routine activities and the distribution of street robbery. In L. Liu and J. Eck (Eds.), *Artificial crime analysis systems: Using computer simulations and geographic information systems* (pp. 226–251). Hershey, PA: Idea Group.

Groff, Elizabeth. (2008). Adding the temporal and spatial aspects of routine activities: A further test of routine activity theory. *Security Journal, 21*, 95–116.

Guidi, Sandro, Ross Homel and Michael Townsley. (1997). *Hot spots and repeat break and enter crimes: An analysis of police calls for service data.* Brisbane: Criminal Justice Commission, Research and Coordination Division.

Gurette, Rob and Kate Bowers. (2009). Assessing the extent of crime displacement and diffusion of benefits: A review of situational crime prevention evaluations. *Criminology, 47*, 1331–1368.

Hagan, Frank. (2013). *Introduction to criminology.* 8th ed. Thousand Oaks, CA: Sage.

Harcourt, Bernard. (2001*). Illusion of disorder: The false promise of Broken Windows policing.* Cambridge, MA: Harvard University Press.

Helfgott, Jacqueline. (2008). *Criminal behavior: Theories, typologies and criminal justice.* Thousand Oaks, CA: Sage.

Hendricks, Scott, Douglas Landsittel, Harlan Amandus, Jay Malcan, and Jennifer Bell. (1999). A matched case-control study of convenience store robbery risk factors. *Journal of Occupational and Environmental Medicine, 41*, 995–1004.

Hindelang, Michael, Michael Gottfredson and James Garofalo. (1978). *Victims of personal crime: An empirical foundation for a theory of personal victimization.* Cambridge, MA: Ballinger.

Holt, Thomas. (2010). Becoming a computer hacker: Examining the enculturation and development of computer deviants. In P. Cromwell (Ed.), *In their own words: Criminals on crime.* 5th ed. (pp. 109–123). New York, NY: Oxford University Press.

Huizinga, David, Anne Weiher, Rachele Espiritu and Finn Esbensen. (2003). Delinquency and crime: Some highlights from the Denver Youth Survey. In T. Thornberry and M. Krohn (Eds.), *Taking stock of delinquency* (pp. 47–91). New York, NY: Kluwer Academic.

Jeffery, C. Ray. (1977). *Crime prevention through environmental design.* 2nd ed. Beverly Hills, CA: Sage.

Jensen, Gary and David Brownfield. (1986). Gender, lifestyle, and victimization: Beyond routine activity. *Violence and Victims, 2*, 85–99.

Johnson, Elmer. (1990). Yakuza (criminal gangs) in Japan: Characteristics and management in prison. *Journal of Contemporary Criminal Justice, 6*, 113–126.

Kennedy, Leslie and David Forde. (1990). Routine activities and crime: An analysis of victimization in Canada. *Criminology, 28*, 137–152.

Kigerl, Alex. (2012). Routine activity theory and the determinants of high cybercrime countries. *Social Science Computer Review, 30*, 470–486.

Kleck, Gary, Brion Sever, Spenser Li and Marc Gertz. (2005). The missing link in general deterrence research. *Criminology, 43*, 623–660.

Knox, George and Leslie Fuller. (1995). Gang profile: The Gangster Disciples. *Journal of Gang Research, 3*, 58–76.

Kovandzic, Tomislav, John Sloan III and Lynne Vieraitis. (2004). "Striking out" as crime reduction policy: The impact of "three strikes" law on crime rates in U.S. cities. *Justice Quarterly, 21*, 207–239.

Kshetri, Nir. (2006). The simple economics of cybercrimes. *IEEE Security & Privacy*, 33–39.

Levitt, Steven. (2002). Deterrence. In J. Wilson and J. Petersilia (Eds.), *Crime* (pp. 435–450). Oakland, CA: ICS Press.

Logan, Samuel. (2009). *This is for Mara Salvatrucha*. New York, NY: Hyperion.

Lyman, Michael and Gary Potter. (2004). *Organized crime*. 3rd ed. Upper Saddle River, NJ: Prentice Hall.

Matsueda, Ross, Derek Keager and David Huizinga. (2006). Deterring delinquents: A rational choice model of theft and violence. *American Sociological Review, 71*, 95–122.

McCarthy, Bill. (1995). Not just "for the thrill of it:" An instrumentalist elaboration of Katz's explanation of sneaky thrill property crime. *Criminology, 33*, 519–538.

McCarthy, Bill. (2002). New economics of social criminology. *Annual Review of Sociology, 28*, 417–442.

McCarthy, Bill and John Hagan. (2005). Danger and the decision to offend. *Social Forces, 83*, 1065–1096.

McEvoy, Alan. (2013). Routine activities theory reconsidered: The case of inmate gambling. *ACJS Today, 28*, 1, 5, 7–9.

Meier, Robert and Terrence Miethe. (1993). Understanding theories of criminal victimization. In M. Tonry (Ed.), *Crime and justice, Vol. 17* (pp. 459–499). Chicago, IL: University of Chicago Press.

Miller, Joel. (2012). Individual offending, routine activities, and activity settings: Revisiting the routine activity theory of general deviance. *Journal of Research in Crime and Delinquency*. DOI:10.1177/0022427811432641.

Montgomery, Bill. (2012). Into the mind of Bill Montgomery. *The Arizona Republic*, May 26, B7.

Mustaine, Elizabeth and Richard Tewksbury. (1998). Predicting risks of larceny theft victimization: A routine activity analysis using refined lifestyle measures. *Criminology, 36*, 829–858.

Nagin, Daniel and Raymond Paternoster. (1993). Enduring individual differences and rational choice theories of crime. *Law & Society Review, 27*, 201–230.

Nagin, Daniel. (1998). General deterrence: A review of the empirical evidence. In M. Tonry (Ed.), *Crime and justice: A review of research, Vol. 23* (pp. 1–42). Chicago, IL: University of Chicago Press.

Newman, Oscar. (1972). *Defensible space: Crime prevention through urban design*. New York, NY: Macmillan.

Newman, Graeme, Ronald Clarke and S. Giora Shoman (Eds.). (1997). *Rational choice and situational crime prevention*. Aldershot, England: Ashgate.

Paternoster, Raymond. (1985). Assessments of risk and behavioral experience: An explanatory study of change. *Criminology, 23*, 417–436.

Paternoster, Raymond and Ronet Bachman (Eds.). (2001). Classical and neue classical schools of criminology: Deterrence, rational choice, and situational theories of crime. In *Explaining criminals and crime* (pp. 11–22). Los Angeles, CA: Roxbury.

Pease, Ken. (1998). *Repeat victimisation: Taking stock*. Police Research Group. Crime Detection and Prevention Series Paper 90. London, England: Home Office.

Pease, Ken and Gloria Laycock. (1996). *Reducing the heat on hot victims.* Research in Action. Washington, D.C.: National Institute of Justice.

Peek, Lori and Michelle Lueck. (2012). When hate *is* a crime: Temporal and geographic patterns of anti-Islamic hate crime after 9/11. In D.W. Harper and K. Frailing (Eds.), *Crime and criminal justice in disaster.* 2nd ed. (pp. 203–226). Durham, NC: Carolina Academic Press.

Piquero, Alex and Greg Pogarsky. (2002). Beyond Stafford and Warr's reconceptualization of deterrence: Personal and vicarious experiences, impulsivity, and offending behavior. *Journal of Research in Crime and Delinquency, 39,* 153–186.

Piquero, Alex and Stephen Tibbetts. (2002). *Rational choice and criminal behavior.* New York, NY: Routledge.

Pogarsky, Greg and Alex Piquero. (2003). Can punishment encourage offending? Investigating the "resetting" effect. *Journal of Research in Crime and Delinquency, 40,* 95–120.

Power, Richard. (2000). *Tangled web: Tales of digital crime from the shadows of cyberspace.* Indianapolis, IN: Que Books.

Pratt, Travis, Francis Cullen, Kristie Blevins, Leah Daigle and Tamara Madensen. (2006). The empirical status of deterrence theory: A meta-analysis. In F. Cullen J. Wright and K. Blevins (Eds.), *Taking stock: The status of criminological theory, Vol. 15.* New Brunswick, NJ: Transaction.

Reynolds, Morgan. (1995). *Crime and punishment in America.* National Center for Policy Analysis. Retrieved from: http://www.ncpa.org/pdfs/st193.pdf.

Reyns, Bradford. (2011). Online routines and identity theft victimization: Further expanding routine activity theory beyond direct-contact offenses. *Journal of Research in Crime and Delinquency.* DOI:10.1177/0022427811425539.

Roncek, Dennis. (2000). Schools and crime. In V. Goldsmith, P. McGuire, J. Mollenkopf and T. Ross (Eds.), *Analyzing crime patterns: Frontiers of practice* (pp. 153–166). Thousand Oaks, CA: Sage.

Rosoff, Steven, Henry Pontell and Robert Tillman. (1998). *Profit without honor: White-collar crime and the looting of America.* Upper Saddle River, NJ: Prentice-Hall.

Sanchez-Jankowski, Martin. (2003). Gangs and social change. *Theoretical Criminology, 7,* 191–216.

Sherman, L. (1995). Hot spots of crime and criminal careers of places. In J. Eck and D. Weisburd (Eds.), *Crime and place: Crime prevention studies, Vol. 1* (pp. 35–52). Monsey, NY: Criminal Justice Press.

Sherman, Lawrence. (2011). Democratic policing on the evidence. In J. Wilson and J. Petersilia (Eds.), *Crime and public policy* (pp. 589–618). New York, NY: Oxford University Press.

Sherman, Lawrence, Patrick Gartin and Michael Buerger. (1989). Hot spots of predatory crime: Routine activities and the criminology of place. *Criminology, 27,* 27–56.

Sherman, Lawrence and David Weisburd. (1995). General deterrent effects of police patrol in crime hot spots: A randomized, controlled trial. *Justice Quarterly, 12,* 635–648.

Sherman, Lawrence, Denise Gottfredson, Doris MacKenzie, John Eck, Peter Reuter and Shawn Bushway. (1998). *Preventing crime: What works, what doesn't, what's promising.* Retrieved from: https://www.ncjrs.gov/works/index.htm.

Shover, Neal and Heith Copes. (2010). Decision making by persistent thieves and crime control policy. In H. Barlow and S. Decker (Eds.), *Criminology and public policy* (pp. 128–149). Philadelphia, PA: Temple University Press.

Sorg, Evan, Cory Habermn, Jerry Ratcliffe and Elizabeth Groff. (2013). Foot patrol in violent crime hot spots: The longitudinal impact of deterrence and posttreatment effects of displacement. *Criminology, 51,* 65–102.

Stafford, Mark and Mark Warr. (2003). A reconceptualization of general and specific deterrence. *Journal of Research in Crime and Delinquency, 30,* 123–128, 133–135.

Sung, Hung-En. (2004). State failure, economic failure, and predatory organized crime: A comparative analysis. *Journal of Research in Crime and Delinquency, 41,* 111–129.

Sutherland, Edwin. (1940). White-collar criminality. *American Sociological Review, 5,* 1–12.

Thornton, William and Lydia Voigt. (2012). Disaster rape: Vulnerability of women to sexual assaults during Hurricane Katrina. In D.W. Harper and K. Frailing (Eds.), *Crime and criminal justice in disaster.* 2nd ed. (pp. 123–156). Durham, NC: Carolina Academic Press.

Thornton, William and Lydia Voigt. (2012a). Disaster phase analysis and crime facilitation patterns. In D.W. Harper and K. Frailing (Eds.), *Crime and criminal justice in disaster.* 2nd ed. (pp. 37–72). Durham, NC: Carolina Academic Press.

Tittle. Charles. (1995). *Control balance: Toward a general theory of deviance.* Boulder, CO: Westview.

Tittle, Charles and Ekaterina Botchkovar. (2005). Self-control, criminal motivation and deterrence: An investigation using Russian respondents. *Criminology, 43,* 307–354.

Tonry, Michael. (2008). Leaning from the limitations of deterrence research. *Crime & Justice, 37,* 279–308.

Trickett, Alan, Denise Osbom, Julie Seymour and Ken Pease. (1992). What is different about high crime areas? *British Journal of Criminology, 32,* 81–90.

Trickett, Alan, Denise Osborn, and Dan Ellingworth. (1995). Property crime victimization: The roles of individual and area influences. *International Review of Victimology, 3,* 273–295.

Tunnel, Kenneth. (1992). *Choosing crime.* Chicago, IL: Nelson-Hall.

Varin, Nadine and Eric Beauregard. (2010). Victims' routine activities and sex offenders' target selection scripts: A latent class analysis. *Sexual Abuse: A Journal of Research and Treatment, 22,* 315–342.

Voiskounsky, Alexander and Olga Smyslova. (2003). Flow-based model of computer hackers' motivation. *Cyberpsychology & Behavior, 6,* 171–180.

von Lampe, Klaus. (2011). The application of the framework of situational crime prevention to "organized crime." *Criminology & Criminal Justice, 11,* 145–163.

Walsh, Anthony and Craig Hemmens. (2011). *Introduction to criminology: A text/reader.* 2nd ed. Los Angeles, CA: Sage.

Ward, David, Mark Stafford and Louis Gray. (2006). Rational choice, deterrence, and theoretical integration. *Journal of Applied Social Psychology, 36,* 571–585.

Weisburd, David. (1997). *Reorienting crime prevention research and policy: From the causes of criminality to the context of crime.* National Institute of Justice Research Report. Washington, D.C.: U.S. Department of Justice.

Weisburd, David, Stanton Wheeler, Elin Waring and Nancy Bode. (1991). *Crimes of the middle class: White-collar offenders in the federal courts.* New Haven, CT: Yale University Press.

Weisburd, David and Lorraine Green. (1995). Policing drug hotspots: The Jersey City drug market analysis experiment. *Justice Quarterly, 12*, 711–735.

Weisburd, David, Shawn Bushway, Cynthia Lum and Su-Ming Yang. (2004). Trajectories of crime at places: A longitudinal studies of street segments in the city of Seattle. *Criminology, 42*, 283–320.

Weisburd, David, Tomar Einat and Matt Kowalski. (2008). The miracle of the cells: An experimental study of interventions to increase payment of court-ordered financial obligations. *Criminology & Public Policy, 7*, 9–36.

Weisel, Deborah, Ronald Clarke and John Stedman. (1999). *Hot dots in hot spots: Examining repeat victimization for residential burglary in three cities.* National Institute of Justice. Retrieved from: https://www.ncjrs.gov/pdffiles1/nij/grants/193808.pdf.

Wikstrom, Per-Olof. (2008). Deterrence and deterrence experiences: Preventing crime through the threat of punishment. In S. Shoham, O. Beck and M. Kett (Eds.), *International handbook of penology and criminal justice* (pp. 345–378). Boca Raton, FL: CRC Press.

Wikstrom, Per-Olof, Dietrich Oberwittler, Kyle Treiber and Beth Hardie. (2012). *Breaking rules: The social and situational dynamics of young people's urban crime.* Oxford, England: Oxford University Press.

Wilson, James and George Kelling. (1982). Broken windows. *The Atlantic Monthly, 249*, 29–38.

Wortley, Robert. (2002). *Situational prison control: Crime prevention in correctional institutions.* Cambridge, England: Cambridge University Press.

Yar, Majid. (2005). The novelty of "cybercrime:" An assessment in light of routine activity theory. *European Journal of Criminology, 2*, 407–427.

Zahran, Sammy, Tara Shelley, Lori Peek and Samuel Brody. (2009). Natural disasters and social order: Modeling crime outcomes in Florida. *International Journal of Mass Emergencies and Disasters, 27*, 26–52.

Zimring, Franklin. (2007). *The great American crime decline.* New York, NY: Oxford University Press

Chapter 10

The Victims of Crime

Introduction

In this chapter, we turn our attention temporarily away from offenders and toward the victims of crime. Victimology is the study of the victims of crime and victimologists focus on the characteristics of victims, theories of victimization and changes in the ways the victim is viewed by the criminal justice system and by society. We will focus on each of these areas in turn.

Who Is Victimized?

The 2011 NCVS provides a wealth of information on victims of crime. In that year, United States residents ages 12 and over experienced an estimated 5.8 million violent victimizations and an estimated 17.1 million property victimizations. The overall violent victimization crime rate increased 17 percent between 2010 and 2011, with increases in aggravated and simple assaults accounting for the jump. The rate of violent victimization has been on a general decline since 1993, from 79.8 per 1,000 to 22.5 per 1,000 in 2011. The rate of serious violent victimization has similarly declined in those 18 years (Truman and Planty, 2012). Table 10.1 reveals the demographic characteristics of violent and serious violent crime victims in 2011 and Table 10.2 reveals the percentage of victimizations reported to the police by type and seriousness of crime.

It is clear from Table 10.1 that victims of violent crime and serious violent crime in 2011 tended to be young unmarried males. In fact, the increase in the rate for all violent victimizations noted above was largely accounted for by increases in the rates of violent victimizations for younger people, males, whites and Hispanics. It is clear from Table 10.2 that generally speaking, the more serious the crime the more likely it would be reported to the police, though overall, less than half of violent victimizations

Table 10.1. Demographic characteristics of violent and
serious violent crime victims, 2011

Demographic Characteristics	Rate of Violent Victimization per 1,000	Rate of Serious Violent Victimization per 1,000
TOTAL	22.5	7.2
SEX		
Male	25.4	7.7
Female	19.8	6.7
RACE/ETHNICITY		
White	21.5	6.5
African American	26.4	10.8
Hispanic	23.8	7.2
Native American	45.4	12.6
Asian	11.2	2.5
AGE		
12–17 years	37.7	8.8
18–24 years	49.0	16.3
25–34 years	26.5	9.5
35–49 years	21.9	7.0
MARITAL STATUS		
Never married	35.5	11.7
Married	11.0	3.7
Divorced	37.8	9.2

Source: Adapted from Truman and Planty, 2012.

were reported to law enforcement. The relatively high rates of reporting for burglary and especially motor vehicle theft likely have to do with the need for a police report in order to make an insurance claim. Victims of crime may choose not to report to police for a number of reasons, including fear of retaliation by the perpetrator, belief that the police are ineffectual and belief that the victimization is a personal matter (Truman and Planty, 2012).

Of course, when we consider different types of crimes, we start to see different patterns emerge. For example, though males had greater rates of victimization than females overall, females had far higher rates of rape and sexual assault (2.1 per 1,000) than did males (0.1 per 1,000). About 78 percent of sexual violence victims knew their attacker in 2010 (Planty, Langton, Krebs, Berzofsky and Smiley-McDonald, 2013). More than half of robberies were committed by strangers between 2005 and 2010, compared to 42 percent of aggravated assaults and about a quarter of rapes and sexual

Table 10.2. Percentage of victimizations reported to the
police by type and seriousness of crime, 2011

Type of Crime	Percent Reported to the Police
VIOLENT CRIME	49
Rape/sexual assault	27
Robbery	66
Assault	48
— Aggravated assault	67
— Simple assault	43
Domestic violence	60
— Intimate partner violence	60
Violent crime resulting in injury	61
SERIOUS VIOLENT CRIME	61
Serious domestic violence	58
— Serious intimate partner violence	59
Serious violent crime involving weapons	67
Serious violent crime resulting in injury	66
PROPERTY CRIME	37
Burglary	52
Motor vehicle theft	83
Theft	30

Source: Adapted from Truman and Planty, 2012.

assaults. Men were violently victimized by strangers at a higher rate (9.5 per 1,000) than women (4.7 per 1,000) in 2010 (Harrell, 2012).

We may tend to think of offenders and victims as two distinct groups with no overlap, but research has shown the opposite to be the case. Remember that the NCVS does not gather information on offending, so the best source on victimization does not offer much in understanding this overlap. Shaffer and Ruback (2002) were interested in the relationship between violent victimization and violent offending among juveniles and they used Add Health data to create measures for both violent victimization and violent offending for over 5,000 juveniles at two points in time to investigate this relationship. They found that at time one, juveniles who had committed violent offenses were 5.3 times more likely to be violently victimized than those who had not. At time two, juveniles who had committed violent offenses were six times more likely to be violently victimized than those who had not. The data did not permit conclusions to be drawn about whether violent offending or victimization came first or how close in time the two occurred. Nevertheless, Shaffer and Ruback (2002) conclude that violent victimization is a risk factor for violent offending, that repeat offending is more common than repeat victimization and that violent victimization and offending share many of the same risk factors. These risk factors include use of intoxicants, being male, experiencing depression, being more physically developed and of course, previous violent victimization and offending. Loeber Kalb and Huizinga (2001) similarly found that low socioeconomic status, a single parent household, hyperactivity, drug use and impulsiveness predicted both offending and victimization.

Child Abuse

All 50 states, the District of Columbia and the U.S. territories have laws that mandate reporting suspected maltreatment of children to a child protective services (CPS) agency. Federal law provides the guidelines for the states to identify a set of acts or behaviors that define child abuse and neglect. At a minimum, child abuse and neglect is defined as "any recent act or failure to act on the part of a parent or caretaker which results in death, serious physical or emotional harm, sexual abuse or exploitation; or an act or failure to act, which presents an imminent risk of serious harm" (NCANDS, 2011, p. vii). States typically recognize four major categories of maltreatment, neglect, physical abuse, psychological maltreatment and sexual abuse. These forms of child maltreatment may occur separately or together.

The National Child Abuse and Neglect Data System is a federally sponsored annual data collection and analysis of child abuse and neglect that began in 1990. The 2011 Child Maltreatment report revealed there were 676,569 victims of child abuse and neglect during that year for a rate of 9.1 victims per 1,000 children. Nearly half of all children victims of abuse and neglect were ages five and under. Child victims were about equally male (49 percent) and female (51 percent). Twenty two percent of child victims were African American, 22 percent were Hispanic and 44 percent were white. Far more children, nearly 79 percent, suffered neglect than physical abuse (18 percent) or sexual abuse (nine percent). Twenty six percent of victims of sexual abuse were between the ages of 12 and 14 and 22 percent were between the ages of 15 and 17 (NCANDS, 2011). It is very difficult to estimate the number of victims of sexual abuse in large part because of the way the crime is defined and recorded, but a reasonably reliable estimate is that 25 percent of girls and 10 percent of boys experience sexual abuse at some point during their childhood (Knudsen, 1991).

Remember that the NCVS does not collect data on respondents under 12 years of age, so the sexual victimization of children under 12 is not captured by the NCVS. Similarly, the UCR does not collect data on sexual assaults that do not meet the narrow definition of forcible rape. The NCVS estimated about 307,000 rapes and sexual assaults in 1996 and the UCR indicates that only 31 percent, about 94,000, were reported to police that year. This discrepancy may indicate that many victims of sexual assault are under the age of 12.

In order to find out, Snyder (2000) turned to the comparatively rich NIBRS data but one of the problems with the use of NIBRS data at this time was the limited number of participating states; just 12 of the 50 provided data. Nevertheless, Snyder (2000) found nearly 61,000 victims of sexual assault and nearly 58,000 sexual assault offenders identified by victims in those data. The single age with the largest proportion of sexual assaults was 14. However, one out of every seven victims of sexual assault was under the age of six and for victims under age 12, the single age with the largest proportion of sexual assaults was four. Eighty six percent of all victims were female and 96 percent of offenders were male. The peak age for offending was 14. For both male and female victims, victimization by strangers was quite rare; about 60 percent of offenders were acquaintances of the victim and the bulk of the remainder were family members.

Using NIBRS data, it was also possible for Snyder (2000) to develop probability estimates about the characteristics of offenders given certain characteristics of the offense. For example, for a victim under six assaulted in a residence, the most likely offender is a juvenile acquaintance aged 12 to 17 (15.2 percent) or a family member aged 25 to 34 (15 percent). If the assault occurs outside the residence it is less likely to be a family member and the probability of the offender being a juvenile under age 12 increases significantly. When the victim is between six and 12, the likelihood of the offender being a juvenile acquaintance goes up to 41 percent.

Besides youth and relationship with offenders, what are some other risk factors for childhood and adolescent sexual victimization? As seen in Snyder's (2000) findings, females experience more sexual victimization than males. Females also have a different set of risk factors than males. For females, risk factors for victimization in childhood include living with a stepfather, living away from the biological mother, an emotionally distant mother, a mother who never completed high school, a mother who punishes sexual behavior or questions, little or no physical affection from the biological father, low family income and few friends. Females with none of these risk factors are in virtually no danger of victimization while females with five of these risk factors have an approximately 66 percent risk of victimization (Finkelhor, 1984). The strongest predictor of female victimization in childhood is having a stepfather; Glaser and Frosh (1993) found that stepfathers are five times more likely to sexually abuse their daughters than are biological fathers. The strongest predictor of male victimization in childhood, on the other hand, is absence of the biological father (Walsh, 1988); sexual offending is discussed in more detail in Chapter 15.

Box 10.1. What about Recurring Victimization?

All this talk about child molestation is sure to have sparked astute readers to think about recurring victimization. People who have been victimized are more likely to be victimized again in the future than those who have not and recurrent victims experience a large share of all victimization. For example, six percent of the respondents to the British Crime Survey over 10 years experienced nearly 70 percent of all the thefts that occurred during that time (Nicholas, Povey, Walker and Kershaw, 2005) and the seven percent of women on college campuses who had experienced two different sexual victimizations in the previous year experienced nearly three quarters of all the sexual victimizations that occurred (Daigle, Fisher and Cullen, 2008). Recurring victimizations tend to happen shortly after the first. Two competing explanations for recurring victimization are risk heterogeneity and state dependence. Risk heterogeneity says that the factors that put one at risk for being victimized in the first place persist after the initial victimization and that these risk factors will keep that person at risk for future victimization. State dependence says that how the victim and offender respond to the initial victimization impacts the likelihood of future victimization (Hagan, 2013).

Bullying

Though we may think of neglect, physical abuse and sexual abuse first when we think of childhood victimization, another form of victimization that children and adolescents are at risk for is bullying. The Centers for Disease Control and Prevention's Youth Risk Behavior Surveillance System indicates that 20 percent of children in ninth through twelfth grades experienced bullying in 2011 (CDC, 2012). The Department of Education's School Crime Supplement indicates that 28 percent of students in the sixth through twelfth grades experienced bullying between 2008 and 2009 (DeVoe, Bauer and Hill, 2011). Table 10.3 reveals the characteristics of those likely (but not guaranteed) to be bullied and to bully. Table 10.4 reveals some of the warning signs of both being bullied and bullying; similarly, these warning

There are three types of bullying into which much of bullying behavior falls, verbal, physical and social or relational. Verbal and physically bullying involve just what their designations imply, name calling, teasing and threats in the case of the former and hitting, pushing or kicking, spitting, tripping and damaging another's property in the case of the latter. Social or relational bullying involves deliberately excluding someone from a social group or activities, spreading rumors and instructing others not to be friends with that person. These types of bullying can happen at school or school events, on the way to or from school or school events or electronically. Approximately 16 percent of ninth through twelfth grades were electronically bullied, though e-mail, instant messages, chat rooms and texts, in 2011 (CDC, 2012).Sixty four percent of those who were bullied did not report it (Petrosino, Guckenberg, DeVoe, and Hanson 2010). More than half of bullying episodes

Table 10.3. Characteristics of those likely to be bullied and to bully

Those likely to be bullied	Those likely to bully
Perceived as different from their peers, including but not limited to physical, behavioral, emotional and cognitive differences	Some are popular and well connected to peers; like to dominate and be in charge of others
Perceived as weak and unable to defend themselves	Others are more isolated from peers, depressed or anxious with low self-esteem and less involved in school; may not be able to identify with others' feelings
Depressed or anxious; low self esteem	Aggressive and easily frustrated; view violence positively
Less popular and few friends	Issues at home and less parental involvement in their lives
Perceived as annoying and antagonistic	Think poorly of others
	Have a hard time following rules
	Have friends who bully others

Source: Adapted from Stopbullying.gov, 2013.

Table 10.4. Warning signs for bullying and being bullied

For bullying	For those being bullied
Inexplicable injuries	Getting into fights; getting into trouble at school
Missing or damaged property	Having friends who bully others
Headaches, stomachaches, feigning illness	Increasing aggression
Changes in eating habits	Have inexplicable new belongings or money
Difficulty sleeping	Blame others for their problems
Declining grades and loss of interest in school	Do not accept responsibility for actions
Sudden loss of friends	Competitive and worried about popularity
Decreased self-esteem; feeling helpless	
Self-destructive behaviors	

Source: Adapted from Stopbullying.gov, 2013.

cease when a peer intervenes on behalf of the student being bullied (Craig, Hawkins and Pepler, 2001). In fact, the notion that other children who witness bullying are in a potential position to stop it is a major piece of the government's current antibullying campaign.

Bullying has detrimental effects on its victims, including decreases in school performance and in self-esteem, self-confidence and self-worth. It can also produce negative physical symptoms, such as headaches and stomachaches and negative emotional symptoms such as anxiety and depression; they may also be at greater risk for suicide. Witnesses to bullying experience feelings of insecurity, helplessness and fear. In the school setting, strategies that hold students accountable for their bullying behavior but empower students to change that behavior can be effective at reducing bullying; efforts to increase bystander intercession are also important (PACER, 2012).

Workplace Violence

Violence in the workplace is not an uncommon occurrence, though it has been on the decline since 2003. There were approximately 572,000 nonfatal violent crimes against people ages 16 and older while they were at work in 2009. Workplace violence accounted for nearly a quarter of all nonfatal violence against employed people ages 16 and older. Law enforcement officers, security guards and bartenders had the highest rates of workplace violence; law enforcement officers made up only two percent of employed persons but experienced about 19 percent of all the workplace violence. Law enforcement officers, along with people working in custodial care and at technical/industrial schools had higher rates of workplace violence than non workplace violence. The opposite was true for nurses, those working in preschools and at colleges or universities as well as convenience or liquor store clerks. Males were the victims of 63 percent of workplace violence and whites were victims of 78 percent of workplace violence. Strangers committed the greatest proportion of workplace violence and firearms were less likely to be used in workplace violence than in non workplace violence (Harrell, 2011).

Box 10.2. Are Schools Safe Places?

It is very easy to draw to mind recent and tragic school shootings and conclude the answer to the above question is no. However, DeVoe, Peter, Kaufman, Miller, Noonan, Snyder and Baum (2004) note that there were 390 violent deaths on elementary, middle and high school campuses in the United States between 1992 and 2000. Two hundred forty three of these violent deaths were homicides and 43 were suicides. During that same time period, 24,406 school age children (i.e., children ages 5–19) were victims of homicide away from school and 16,735 school age children committed suicide away from school. Across the time period, school age children were at least 70 times more likely to be murdered away from school than at school.

Even though schools are low risk environments, efforts have been made to make schools and their occupants less vulnerable to violence. Among these efforts are locking doors during the school day and requiring all staff and visitors to wear identification. In addition, the Department of Homeland Security has issued active shooter guidelines. These guidelines describe what to do when an active shooter is present. The first action to take when an active shooter is present is to evacuate. If this is not possible, hiding out, preferably in a room, is recommended. The door should be locked and heavy furniture moved in front of it. Emergency help should be summoned by dialing 911 as soon as possible, but noise from cell phones and other sources should be reduced or eliminated. As a last resort and when no other action is an option, an attempt to incapacitate the shooter should be made (DHS, 2008).

During 2009, 521 people were victims of homicide in the workplace, about a third of whom had office or sales jobs. The majority of victims of workplace homicides were male and middle-aged and robbers and other assailants accounted for the majority of workplace homicide offenders (Harrell, 2011). However, taking a closer look at the relationship between victim and offender, we see that gender plays a role. For nearly 40 percent of women killed at work in 2011, their assailant was a relative or domestic partner, compared to just two percent of men killed at work that year. Sixty three percent of men killed at work in 2011 were killed by robbers or other assailants, compared to just 34 percent of women killed at work that year. The 458 homicides in the workplace in the United States in 2011 comprised 10 percent of all workplace fatalities that year (BLS, 2011).

Box 10.3. Going Postal?

Going postal is slang for perpetrating violence, including lethal violence in the workplace setting. The most notable and deadly shooting by an employee of the United States Postal Service (USPS) occurred in Edmond, Oklahoma on August 20, 1986 when Patrick Sherrill shot and killed 14 USPS employees, wounded six others then turned the gun on himself. Between 1986 and 2000, there were 15 incidents of homicide involving current or former USPS employees and there were 14 incidents of homicide perpetrated against USPS employees by non-employees. However, the USPS (2000) concluded that going postal is a myth. Postal workers are no more likely to physically assault, sexually harass or verbally abuse coworkers than employees in the national workforce as a whole and postal employees are only about a third as likely as the national workforce to be victims of homicide at work.

Hate Crime Victims

Victimizing people because of their membership or perceived membership in a group is probably as old as human history. However, it was not until 1990 that the U.S. Congress passed the Hate Crimes Statistics Act requiring that data on the prevalence of hate crime be gathered. Hate crimes are those motivated by biases based on race/ethnicity, religion, sexual orientation, national origin and disability.[1] In 2011, law enforcement agencies across the United States reported 6,222 hate crime incidents involving 7,254 offenses. Nearly half of hate crimes in 2011 were racially motivated, with nearly a quarter of those involving anti-African American or anti-Black bias. Twenty one percent of hate crimes in 2011 were motivated by sexual orientation bias and 58 percent of those involved anti-male homosexual bias. Twenty percent of hate crimes in 2011 were motivated by religious bias and 62 percent of those involved anti-Jewish bias while 13 percent involved anti-Islamic bias. Eleven percent of hate crimes in 2011 were motivated by ethnicity bias and 57 percent of those involved anti-Hispanic bias. Sixty four percent of hate crimes in 2011 were crimes against persons and 36 percent were crimes against property; intimidation, simple assault and aggravated assault were the most common types of hate crimes against persons and property damage, destruction and vandalism were the most common property crimes. Fifty nine percent of all hate crime offenders in 2011 were white and 21 percent were African American (FBI UCR, 2011).

Certain events may put certain groups at greater risk of experiencing hate crime. Just days after the 9/11 terrorist attacks, the U.S. Congress passed a resolution affirming the need to protect the civil liberties of all Americans and condemning bigotry against Arabs, Muslims and South Asians. Soon thereafter, the U.S. Commission on Civil Rights made a special hate crimes reporting hotline available, the U.S. Equal Employment Opportunity Commission introduced a new category designed to track instances of employment discrimination against Muslims, Arabs, Middle Easterners, South Asians and Sikhs, the U.S. Department of Education issued a call for tolerance and respect in the nation's schools and universities and the U.S. Department of Justice created the Initiative to Combat Post-9/11 Discriminatory Backlash, with the stated goals of reducing the incidence of bias-related attacks and ensuring that the perpetrators of hate crimes would be brought to justice (for a complete discussion of these initiatives, see Peek 2011).

While important, these efforts did little to stem hate crimes against Muslims and those thought to be Muslims. Peek and Lueck (2012) demonstrate that 9/11 provoked a sudden and dramatic increase in hate crime against Muslims and that the effect of 9/11 on hate crime against Muslims was enduring, with the of post-9/11 hate crime against Muslims remaining elevated over pre-9/11 rates for eight years. Moreover, anti-African American hate crime and anti-Jewish hate crime both declined in the year following 9/11, indicating that the rise in hate crimes agains Muslims after 9/11 was not part of a

---

1. Until 2009, sexual orientation and disability were not considered official categories of hate crime. The Matthew Shepard and James Byrd, Jr. Hate Crimes Prevention Act signed into law by President Obama in 2009 expanded federal hate crime definitions to include those crimes motivated by the perceived or actual gender, sexual orientation, gender identity or disability of the victim.

overall increase in hate crimes. The proportion of all hate crimes that were identified as anti-Islamic increased from just .5 percent in the year before 9/11 to over six percent of all such crimes in the year after 9/11.

> ### Box 10.4. Hate Crimes against the Amish. . . by the Amish
>
> As seen above, the majority of religiously motivated hate crimes are normally against Jews. However, they are far from the only group victimized. In 2011, a dissident Amish group in Ohio began assaulting other mainstream Amish by breaking into their homes, holding them down and forcibly removing their beards and head hair. Beards and head hair are particularly important symbols in the Amish faith. Sixteen people were convicted of hate crimes against eight members of the Amish faith and while the prosecutor asked for a life sentence, the ringleader of the dissident group was sentenced to 15 years in federal prison. The other defendants received sentences ranging in length from one to seven years. The penalty for their crimes was enhanced by the application of the hate crime statute (Gabriel, 2013).

Theories of Victimization

Just as there are theories of crime, there are theories of victimization. Each of the theoretical perspectives we will explore suggests that the victim may have less than a completely passive role in their victimization.

Victim Precipitation Theory

Victim precipitation theory was first proposed by Hans von Hentig (1948). Victim precipitation theory proposes that in the case of violent crimes, some victims act in ways that provoke the offender and set off a chain of events that lead to victimization. Marvin Wolfgang supported the notion that homicides could be initially precipitated by the ultimate victim. "The term victim-precipitated is applied to those criminal homicides in which the victim is a direct, positive precipitator in the crime. The role of the victim is characterized by his having been the first in the homicide drama to use physical force directed against his subsequent slayer" (1958, p. 252). About 25 percent of all of the cases in Wolfgang's Philadelphia study of nearly 600 homicides examined involved victim-precipitation. Moreover, as we have seen above, there is a great deal of overlap in offenders and victims, indicating that offending behavior and victimization are linked. Victim precipitation theory is most controversial when it is applied to the crime of rape. In 1971, Menachem Amir, a student of Wolfgang's, conducted a study of rapes in Philadelphia to try to determine what amount were victim precipitated. He concluded that about one in five were victim precipitated and he characterized them in this way because of the appearance and behavior of the victims. Victim precipitated rapes were likely to involve alcohol consumption, seductive behavior, language and dress and a bad reputation, all on the part of the victim. Amir (1971) concluded that the offender interprets the victim as acting inappropriately for a female and rapes her because she deserves it. As is easy to imagine, Amir's (1971) work garnered a great deal of criticism, most of which held that Amir (1971) was blaming women for their own rapes.

Routine Activity and Lifestyle Theories

As seen in Chapter 9, Lawrence Cohen and Marcus Felson (1979) proposed a theory of crime that placed emphasis on the routines of victims rather than on the characteristics of offenders, apart from assuming that offender motivation is a constant. Their thesis was that for a crime to occur, it required convergence of a potential offender, a suitable target and the absence of capable guardianship in time and space. Cohen and Felson (1979) found that a change in routine activities in the United States after World War II created greater numbers of suitable targets and reduced capable guardianship, thereby producing an increase in crime.

Some people's routine activities put them at little to no risk for victimization. However, some people have routine activities that put them at great risk for victimization. Routine activities that can increase the risk of victimization include drug and alcohol consumption outside of the home, being out late at night, associating with delinquents and gang involvement. These routine activities put people in situations that are criminogenic (Chapple and Hope, 2003).

In their lifestyle theory of victimization, Michael Hindelang, Michael Gottfredson and James Garofalo (1978) proposed that variations in lifestyle can account for variations in rates of personal victimization across various subgroups. They propose that variations in lifestyle, the characteristic way individuals allocate their time between work and leisure activities, cause differential probabilities of being in certain places at certain times and coming into contact with others who possess certain characteristics. Because criminal victimization is not randomly distributed across time and space and because potential offenders are not representative of the general population but are instead concentrated in high risk times and places, peoples' lifestyle differences correlate with differences in exposure to high risk situations. Again, some people's lifestyles put them at little to no risk for victimization while some people's lifestyles put them at great risk for victimization.

Box 10.5. Tourism: A Risky Lifestyle?

The opportunity for crime against tourists is largely created by the place in which tourists find themselves and by the choices they make while there. Harper (2005) found that tourists are typically victimized in areas adjacent to the main attractions of the tourist destination. Crimes against tourists tend to occur late at night or early in the morning after tourists are likely to have been drinking, further limiting their knowledge of their surroundings. Tourist robbers often work in groups, with one approaching the victim and asking for the time, for directions or for a lighter and when the tourist obliges, the other robbers subdue the victim and take (usually) his wallet and valuables, then quickly flee the scene. Moreover, tourist victims may play some role in their own victimization, particularly if they are in search of illicit drugs or sex. Advertising their willingness to involve themselves in illegal activity makes them easier targets for criminals, who may promise that drugs or sex are right around the corner, then rob the tourist of (usually) his wallet and valuables once they have lured the victim away from the guardianship provided by the main tourist attraction. Robbers in these scenarios are very knowledgeable about the layout and features of the physical location, which aids their escape.

The motivation on the part of the victim to involve (usually) himself in illicit activity may make him reticent to report his victimization to the police, as may his status as a tourist who is unwilling or unable to return again and again to the destination to follow through with prosecution of the offender (Harper, 2005).

Changing Perspectives on Victims of Crime

When a law is violated, the victim is the state. In criminal proceedings, the role of the prosecutor is to establish beyond a reasonable doubt that the accused has violated a state or federal statute. The actual victim of the crime is largely relegated to the role of a witness to the crime. The Constitution grants rights to defendants, which tends to marginalize victims in the process to the point where they have few defined rights and little or no input in the process; they are essentially ignored by the state. It was not until the mid 20th century in the United States that politicians and academics began to show interest in the victims of crime and their role (or lack thereof) in the criminal justice process. As the victim rights movement began to gain traction, it provided a catalyst for a variety of victim-centered legislation to be passed and take effect over the next few decades (Howley and Dorris, 2007); some of this legislation is discussed below.

The Problems of Crime Victims

At least until the middle of the 20th century, the conclusion of a criminal trial brought little to the victim of crime in terms of restitution, monetary or otherwise and if the victim chose to proceed against the perpetrator in a civil action, the likelihood of recovering some monetary compensation for being injured was slim. Even a ruling that the victim was wronged or the victim of a wrongful act did not always translate into compensation. There is also ample evidence that in addition to physical injury that victims of crime may experience, they also often feel emotional and psychological trauma, including shock, fear, confusion, guilt, shame, anxiety, depression, hostility, rage, posttraumatic stress disorder (PTSD) and suicidal ideation; these effects may continue for months and years after the victimization (Green and Roberts, 2008).

This list of problems for the victims of crime, both tangible and intangible, have monetary costs. McCollister, French and Fang (2010) collected data on the per offense cost for 13 different offenses, some violent and some property. Importantly, they tallied both the tangible costs, in terms of victim costs (direct economic losses for the victim), criminal justice system costs (police, court and corrections services) and crime career costs (opportunity costs associated with engaging in illegal behavior) and the intangible costs in terms of pain and suffering, which includes decreased quality of life and psychological distress and in term of risk of homicide, which refers to potential loss of lifetime earnings. Table 10.5 reveals the tangible, intangible and total costs per offense for each of 13 crimes in 2008 dollars. Clearly, predatory crimes including murder, rape and sexual assault, robbery and aggravated assault are the most costly to victims and to society, though non predatory crimes carry costs as well and even though the costs per offense are lower for property crimes than they are for violent crimes, we will see

Table 10.5. Tangible and intangible costs per offense for
each of 13 crimes in 2008 dollars

| Offense | Tangible Costs | | | Intangible Costs | | TOTAL COST PER OFFENSE |
	Victim Costs	CJS Costs	Crime Career Costs	Pain and Suffering	Risk of Homicide	
Murder	$737,517	$392,352	$148,555	$8,442,000	N/A	$9.720,424
Rape/Sexual Assault	$5,556	$26,479	$9,212	$198,212	$1,430	$240,889
Aggravated Assault	$8,700	$8,641	$2,126	$13,435	$81,588	$114,560
Robbery	$3,299	$13,827	$4,272	$4,976	$17,599	$43,973
Motor Vehicle Theft	$6,114	$3,867	$553	N/A	$262	$10,796
Arson	$11,452	$4,392	$584	N/A	$5,133	$21,561
Household Burglary	$1,362	$4,127	$681	N/A	$10	$6,491
Larceny/Theft	$480	$2,879	$163	N/A	N/A	$3,533
Stolen Property	N/A	$6,842	$1,132	N/A	N/A	$7,974
Vandalism	N/A	$4,160	$701	N/A	N/A	$4,860
Forgery and Counterfeiting	N/A	$4,605	$660	N/A	N/A	$5,265
Embezzlement	N/A	$4,820	$660	N/A	N/A	$5,480
Fraud	N/A	$4,372	$660	N/A	N/A	$5,032

Source: Adapted from McCollister, French and Fang, 2010.

in Chapter 12 that there are far more property than violent crimes committed in the United States each year.

Legislation and Services to Assist Victims

In 1984, Congress passed the Victims of Crime Act (VOCA), which led to the formation of the federal level Office of Victims of Crime. VOCA also established the Crime Victims Fund. The Crime Victims Fund is financed by fines and penalties paid by federal offenders and the money is used in two principal ways. First, it is used to compensate victims for losses, including payment of medical costs, funeral and burial costs, mental health counseling and lost wages or other financial support. Second, it is used to support organizations in their provision of victims' services, including crisis intervention, emergency shelters, emergency transportation, counseling and criminal justice advocacy (McCormick, 2000; OVC, 2012a). In 2004, the Senate passed a crime victim's bill of rights that gives victims in federal criminal cases a number of rights, including the right to be reasonably protected from the accused, the right to reasonable, accurate and timely notice of court or parole proceedings against the accused, the right not to be excluded from any such proceeding, the right to be reasonably heard during pleas, sentencing or parole proceeding, the right to confer with the attorney for the government in the case, the right to restitution, the right to unhindered proceedings and the right to be treated with fairness and respect (OVC, 2012).

Every state now has some form of victims' rights legislation; rights to compensation, notification of court appearances and submission of an impact statement before sentencing are provided in all states, though not necessarily to all victims. A majority of states provide restitution, attendance at sentencing hearings and the right to be consulted before pleas are offered or before release from custody (Davis and Mulford, 2008).

The right to notification of events in their case has been rated by victims as one of the most important rights and in fact, without notification, they will be unable to attend hearings, provide impact statements and be consulted about plea and release decisions as guaranteed by their other rights. Victim impact statements are the most common way victims participate in criminal justice system proceedings, but critics maintain victim impact statements reduce uniformity in sentencing and research shows that even judges and prosecutors who favor victim impact statements do not integrate them into their work (Davis and Mulford, 2008). Victims may recover some of their losses through restitution, which offenders may be ordered to pay by the judge or by corrections officials as a condition of parole. Victims may also receive compensation from programs such as the Crime Victims Funds that are administered at the state level. Receipt of compensation from victims' funds is limited to those victims who report their victimization to the police and help prosecute offenders. Only a minority of eligible victims, less than 20 percent, actually receive restitution or compensation (Davis and Mulford, 2008). As alluded to, the mere existence of rights for victims does not ensure their meaningful participation in the criminal justice system process.

Though not usually provided through the criminal justice system, there are a number of services available to victims of crime that can be useful in emergent situations. These services include rape crisis centers, hotlines and domestic violence shelters. These services, especially the shelters, may be helping women escape from situations in which lethal violence is more likely to occur, both against them and by them. When women do kill, it is usually in self-defense and usually in intimate relationships, so shelters that allow them to escape victimization may also allow them to avoid situations in which they engage in lethal violence (Thornton, Voigt and Harper, 2013; Benekos, 1995).

Box 10.6. Some Other Legislation Designed to Assist Victims

The VOCA and the crime victim's bill of rights may be among the most notable pieces of legislation designed to assist victims of crime, but they are not the only ones:

Child Abuse Prevention and Treatment Act (1974)
Victim and Witness Protection Act (1982)
Family Violence Prevention and Services Act (1984)
Victims of Child Abuse Act (1990)

Victims' Rights and Restitution Act (1990)
Child Sexual Abuse Registry Act (1993)
Violence Against Women Act (1994)
Mandatory Victims' Restitution Act (1996)
Crime Victims with Disabilities Awareness Act (1998)
Trafficking Victims Protection Act (2000)
Justice for All Act (2004)
Adam Walsh Child Protection and Safety Act (2006)
Matthew Shepard and James Byrd, Jr. Hate Crimes Prevention Act (2009)
Tribal Law and Order Act (2010)
Violence Against Women Act (2013 reauthorization despite conservative concerns about the reach of tribal courts and the provision of services to gay, lesbian, and transgendered victims of domestic violence)

Source: OVC, 2013.

Conclusion

In this chapter, we discussed the characteristics of those who become victims of crime, theories of victimization and the changing perceptions on victims of crime. Because there is overlap between offenders and victims in terms of characteristics and risk factors, we believe a better understanding of victims leads to a better understanding of crime. However, we do not wish to leave readers with the idea that criminals and victims are all the same or that all victims' lifestyles put them at risk for (and therefore precipitate their) victimization. We do not believe that victims are to blame for their victimization, not in the least. We do believe that the academic study of victimization can help us better prevent it in the future and may go a long way to helping us understand how better to approach crime prevention, as well.

Websites to Visit

National Center for Victims of Crime: http://www.victimsofcrime.org/
The Office for Victims of Crime: http://www.ojp.usdoj.gov/ovc/
Active Shooter Guidelines: http://www.dhs.gov/xlibrary/assets/active_shooter_booklet.pdf
Law Enforcement Officers Killed and Assaulted, 2011: http://www.fbi.gov/about-us/cjis/ucr/leoka/2011

Discussion Questions

1. How can you explain the overlap between offenders and victims?
2. Why do you think girls are at such great risk of victimization from their stepfathers but boys are not?

3. Does the estimated prevalence of bullying match what you would guess was the prevalence at your school? Why or why not?
4. Are there any groups of people whose victimization should be counted as a hate crime that are not currently on the list? If so, what group(s) and why? If not, why is the current list acceptable?
5. Which theory of victimization makes more sense to you and why? Is your answer crime-specific?
6. Should victims of crime who precipitate their victimization be allowed to collect money from the Crime Victims Fund? Why or why not?

References

Amir, Meachem. (1971). *Patterns in forcible rape*. Chicago, IL: University of Chicago Press.

Benekos, Peter. (1995). Women as victims and perpetrators of murder. In A. Merlo and J. Pollock (Eds.), *Women, law, and social control* (pp. 219–237). Boston, MA: Allyn & Bacon.

BLS. (2011). *Fatal work injuries*. Bureau of Labor Statistics. Retrieved from: http://www.bls.gov/iif/oshwc/cfoi/cfch0010.pdf.

CDC. (2012). *Youth risk behavior surveillance system: 2011 national overview*. Centers for Disease Control and Prevention. Retrieved from: http://www.cdc.gov/healthyyouth/yrbs/pdf/us_overview_yrbs.pdf.

Chapple, Constance and Trina Hope. (2003). An analysis of the self-control and criminal versatility of gang and dating violence offenders. *Violence and Victims, 18*, 671–690.

Cohen, Lawrence and Marcus Felson (1979). Social change and crime rate trends: A routine activity approach. *American Sociological Review, 44*, 588–608.

Craig, Wendy, Debra Pepler and Lynn Hawkins. (2001). Naturalistic observations of peer interventions in bullying. *Social Development, 10*, 512–527.

Daigle, Leah, Bonnie Fisher and Francis Cullen. (2008). The violent and sexual victimization of college women: Is repeat victimization a problem? *Journal of Interpersonal Violence, 23*, 1296–1313.

Davis, Robert and Carrie Mulford. (2008). Victim rights and new remedies: Finally getting victims their due. *Journal of Contemporary Criminal Justice, 24*, 198–208.

DeVoe, Jill, Lynn Bauer and Monica Hill. (2011). *Student victimization in U.S. schools*. U.S. Department of Education. Retrieved from: http://nces.ed.gov/pubs2012/2012314.pdf.

DeVoe, Jill, Katharin Peter, Phillip Kaufman, Amanda Miller, Margaret Noonan, Thomas Snyder and Katrina Baum. (2004). *Indicators of school crime and safety: 2004*. U.S. Department of Education. Retrieved from: http://www.eric.ed.gov/PDFS/ED483086.pdf.

DHS. (2008). *Active shooter: How to respond*. Department of Homeland Security. Retrieved from: http://www.dhs.gov/xlibrary/assets/active_shooter_booklet.pdf.

FBI UCR. (2011). Hate crime statistics 2011. Retrieved from: http://www.fbi.gov/about-us/cjis/ucr/hate-crime/2011/hate-crime.

Finkelhor, David. (1984). *Child sex abuse: New theory and research.* New York, NY: Free Press.

Gabriel, Trip. (2013). Amish sect leader sentenced to 15 years in hair-cutting attacks. *The New York Times*, February 8. Retrieved from: http://www.nytimes.com/2013/02/09/us/amish-sect-leader-gets-15-years-in-beard-cutting-attacks.html?ref=amish&_r=0.

Glaser, Danya and Steven Frosh. (1993). *Child sex abuse.* Toronto, Canada: University of Toronto Press.

Green, Diane and Albert Roberts. (2008). *Helping victims of violent crime: Assessment, treatment, and evidence-based practice.* New York, NY: Springer.

Hagan, Frank. (2013). *Introduction to criminology.* 8th ed. Thousand Oaks, CA: Sage.

Harper, Dee Wood. (2005). The tourist and his criminal: Pattern in street robbery. In Y. Mansfield and A. Piazam, (Eds.). *Tourism, security and safety: A case approach* (pp. 125–137). Burlington, MA: Butterworth-Heinemann.

Harrell, Erika. (2011). *Workplace Violence, 1993–2009.* Bureau of Justice Statistics. Retrieved from: http://bjs.gov/content/pub/pdf/wv09.pdf

Harrell, Erika. (2012). *Violent victimization committed by strangers, 1993–2010.* Bureau of Justice Statistics. Retrieved from: http://bjs.gov/content/pub/pdf/vvcs9310.pdf.

Hindelang, Michael, Michael Gottfredson and James Garofalo. (1978). *Victims of personal crime: An empirical foundation for a theory of personal victimization.* Cambridge, MA: Ballinger.

Howley, Susan and Carol Dorris. (2007). Legal rights for crime victims in the criminal justice system. In R. Davis, A. Lurigio and S. Herman, S. (Eds.), *Victims of crime*, 3rd ed (pp. 255–297). Los Angeles, CA: Sage.

Knudsen, Dean. (1991). Child sexual coercion. In E. Garuerholz and M. Koralewski (Eds.), *Sexual coercion: A sourcebook on its nature, causes, and prevention* (pp. 17–28). Lexington, MA: D.C. Health.

Loeber, Rolf, Larry Kalb and David Huizinga. (2001). *Juvenile delinquency and serious injury victimization.* U.S. Department of Justice. Retrieved from: https://www.ncjrs.gov/pdffiles1/ojjdp/188676.pdf.

McCollister, Kathryn, Michael French and Hai Fang. (2010). The cost of crime to society: New crime-specific estimates for policy and program evaluation. *Drug and Alcohol Dependence, 108*, 98–108.

McCormack, Robert. (2000). United States crime victim assistance: History, organization, and evaluation. In P. Tobolowsky (Ed.), *Understanding victimology* (pp. 247–260). Cincinnati, OH: Anderson Publishing Company.

NCANDS. (2011). *Child maltreatment 2011.* U.S. Department of Health and Human Services. Retrieved from: http://www.acf.hhs.gov/sites/default/files/cb/cm11.pdf.

Nicholas, Sian, David Povey, Allison Walker and Chris Kershaw. (2005). *Crime in England and Wales 2004/2005.* Home Office Research Development and Statistics Directorate. Retrieved from: http://news.bbc.co.uk/2/shared/bsp/hi/pdfs/home_office_crime_21_09_05.pdf.

OVC. (2012). Crime victims' rights. Office for Victims of Crime. Retrieved from: http://www.ojp.usdoj.gov/ovc/rights/legislation.html.

OVC. (2012a). Crime victims fund. Office for Victims of Crime. Retrieved from: Office for Victims of Crime.

OVC. (2013). Landmarks in victims' rights and services. Office for Victims of Crime. Retrieved from: http://ovc.ncjrs.gov/ncvrw2013/pdf/Landmarks.pdf.

PACER. (2012). Bullying: Fast facts. Retrieved from: http://www.pacer.org/bullying/about/media-kit/facts.asp.

Peek, Lori. (2011). *Behind the backlash: Muslim Americans after 9/11.* Philadelphia, PA: Temple University Press.

Peek, Lori and Michelle Meyer Lueck. (2012). When hate *is* a crime: Temporal and geographic patterns of anti-Islamic hate crime after 9/11. In D.W. Harper and K. Frailing (Eds.), *Crime and Criminal Justice in Disaster,* 2nd ed (pp. 203–225). Durham, NC: Carolina Academic Press.

Petrosino, Anthony, Sarah Guckenberg, Jill DeVoe, and Thomas Hanson. (2010). *What characteristics of bullying, bullying victims, and schools are associated with increased reporting of bullying to school officials?* Washington, D.C.: National Center for Education Evaluation and Regional Assistance.

Planty, Michael, Lynn Langton, Christopher Krebs, Marcus Berzofsky and Hope Smiley-McDonald. (2013). *Female victims of sexual violence, 1994–2010.* Bureau of Justice Statistics. Retrieved from: http://bjs.gov/content/pub/pdf/fvsv9410.pdf.

Shaffer, Jennifer and R. Barry Ruback. (2002). *Violent victimization as a risk factor for violent offending among juveniles.* U.S. Department of Justice. Retrieved from: https://www.ncjrs.gov/pdffiles1/ojjdp/195737.pdf.

Snyder, Howard. (2000). *Sexual assault of young children as reported to law enforcement: Victim, incident, and offender characteristics.* U.S. Department of Justice. Retrieved from: http://bjs.gov/content/pub/pdf/saycrle.pdf.

Stopbullying.gov. (2013). Who is at risk. Retrieved from: http://www.stopbullying.gov/at-risk/index.html.

Thornton, William, Lydia Voigt and Dee Wood Harper. (2013). *Why violence?* Durham, NC: Carolina Academic Press.

Truman, Jennifer and Michael Planty. (2012). *Criminal victimization, 2011.* Bureau of Justice Statistics. Retrieved from: http://www.bjs.gov/content/pub/pdf/cv11.pdf.

USPS. (2000). *Report of the United States Postal Service Commission on a safe and secure workplace.* The National Center on Addiction and Substance Abuse Recovery. Retrieved from: http://www.apwu.org/dept/ind-rel/sh/shirk/Hyperlinks/Report%20-%20 USPS%20Commission%20on%20a%20Safe%20Workplace.pdf.

Von Hentig, Hans. (1948). *The criminal and his victim: Studies in the sociobiology of crime.* New Haven, CT: Yale University Press.

Walsh, Anthony. (1988). Lessons and concerns from a case study of a "scientific" molester. *Corrective and Social Psychiatry, 34,* 18–23.

Wolfgang, Marvin. (1958). *Patterns in criminal homicide.* Philadelphia, PA: University of Pennsylvania Press.

Part IV

Explanation of Crime Types

Chapter 11

Violent Crime[1]

Introduction

When we talk about violent crime, we are talking about serious crimes against people. This chapter describes the major types of violent crime including murder, rape, robbery and aggravated assault. It also discusses some "new" forms of violence and concludes with some theoretical explanations for crimes of violence. Figure 11.1 illustrates the rates per 100,000 people of the four main categories of violent crime in the UCR from 1960 through 2011. It reveals that after ascending between 1960 and 1980, violent crime rates have been falling since the mid 1990s; this is true of overall crime rates for this time period.

Murder

Murder is "the willful (nonnegligent) killing of one human being by another" (FBI UCR, 2011f). Homicide and murder are often used interchangeably when in fact they are not. Homicide is a general term which includes murder but means simply to kill a human being. Homicide includes justifiably killing someone in self-defense, accidentally killing someone in an automobile accident or a hunting accident, killing someone who is a member of an enemy force and even killing someone in a legal, state sanctioned execution. The killing of someone who is terminally ill and even at their request remains a criminal homicide in the United States. In some jurisdictions in the United States, if a fetus is killed as a result of its mother being attacked and wounded, it is considered a criminal homicide even when the mother survives the attack.

The prohibition against taking a life has been around for millennia and the law recognizes different degrees of culpability for this crime. For example, the state of Louisiana

---

1. For a thorough treatment of violence that goes beyond what is possible in the scope of this book, see Thornton, Voigt and Harper (2013).

Figure 11.1. Murder, rape, robbery and aggravated assault
rates in the United States per 100K, 1960–2011

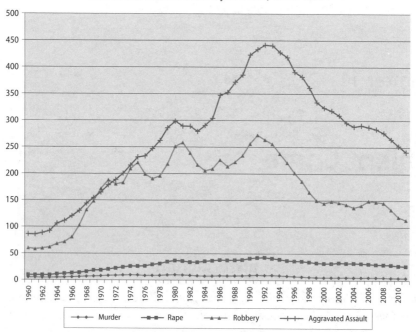

Source: FBI UCR, 2010, 2011.

recognizes five grades of homicide, first degree murder, second degree murder, manslaughter, negligent homicide and vehicular homicide. Each of these grades is subject to different punishments with first degree murder carrying a possible death sentence or life in prison without parole, second degree murder carrying a sentence of life in prison without parole, manslaughter carrying a sentence of 40 years in prison, negligent homicide carrying a sentence of five years in prison and vehicular homicide carrying a sentence of between five and 30 years (LSA RS 14:29–14:32.1). Louisiana also recognizes feticide in the first, second and third degrees, criminal abortion, aggravated criminal abortion by dismemberment, partial birth abortion and suicide as crimes (LSA RS 14:32.5–14:32.12).

As seen in Figure 11.2, the murder rate in the United States rose steadily from the mid 1960s to the mid 1970s, when it began a high fluctuating plateau with a peak of 10.2 murders per 100,000 people in 1980. It began to descend in the mid 1990s and today, the murder rate for the United States is about half of what it was at its all time high in 1980. Changes in crime rates are explored in much more detail in Chapter 15, but briefly, one of the reasons criminologists think the murder rate in particular has declined is the ubiquity of cell phones and better medical care. People that would have died as the result of a violent attack in the past survive today because help can summoned quickly.

Figure 11.2. Murder rate per 100,000 in the United States, 1960–2011

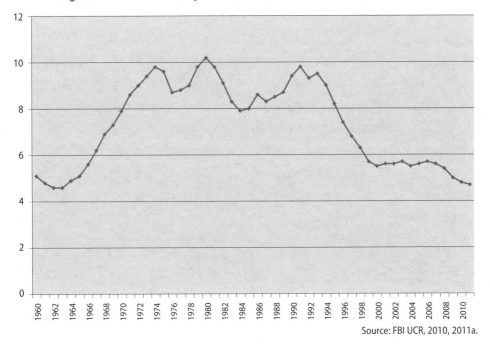

Source: FBI UCR, 2010, 2011a.

In 2011, there were 14,022 murders reported to the police for a rate of 4.8 per 100,000. Of course, this rate is for the entire country and not necessarily representative of one place. Some small cities go years or decades without a murder, so their rate is very low. Cities such as New Orleans, on the other hand, consistently have murder rates 10 or more times the national average.

There were 8,359 arrests for murder in 2011. Eighty eight percent of those arrested were male and 12 percent were female. Forty eight percent of those arrested were white and 50 percent were African American. Twelve percent of those arrested were under the age of 18 (FBI UCR, 2011a, 2011b). Figure 11.3 shows arrests for murder by age in the United States in 2011and makes it clear that murderers are quite young, with the peak ages for perpetrating this crime between 18 and 21. Figure 11.4 reveals that many murder victims and offenders know one another in some capacity.

What appears to be underlying many murders in the United States is an interpersonal dispute between young men that they attempt to resolve with violence. Firearms were used in 61 percent of murders in 2011 (FBI UCR, 2011a); as we have alluded to in Chapter 8 and as we will see in more detail in Chapter 15, guns are an important factor in the amount of lethal violence in the United States.

Figure 11.3. Number of arrests for murder by age in the United States, 2011

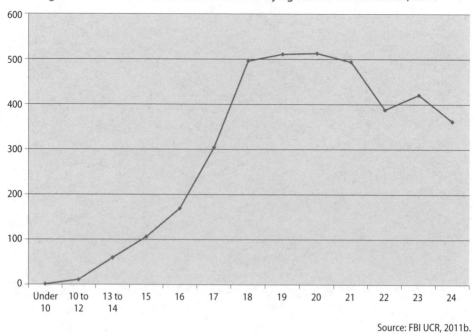

Source: FBI UCR, 2011b.

Figure 11.4. Percent of relationships between murder offenders and victims
(where the relationship is known, 56 percent of murders) in the United States, 2011

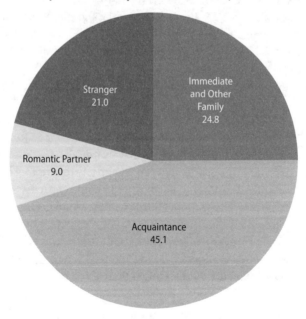

Source: FBI UCR, 2011a.

Multiple Murder[2]

There are a number of different types of multiple murder including mass murder, spree murder, serial murder and homicide-suicide. Table 11.1 summarizes the first three types of multiple murder and provides brief definitions and examples; it is clear that what differentiates types of multiple murderers from one another is time and location.

There were 31 multiple murder incidents in the United States between 1999 and 2012 (excluding serial murder), resulting in a total of 241 victims. We can probably easily draw some of these multiple murder events to mind—Columbine, Virginia Tech, Tuscon, Fort Hood, Aurora, Sandy Hook—but it may be surprising to learn that 11 of the multiple murder incidents took place in schools (Telegraph, 2012). In large part in response to the Columbine shooting, the U.S. Secret Service and the U.S. Department of Education collaborated on the Safe Schools Initiative. Informed by extensive analysis of 37 school shootings between 1974 and 2000, the Safe Schools Initiative provides information on characteristics of past school shooters to help us identify characteristics of potential future school shooters before they perpetrate their violence. Vossekuil, Fein, Reddy, Borum and Modzeleski (2002) found that all school shooters in the study were male with 85 percent between 13 and 18 years of age. Only two attackers were failing in school. Nearly two thirds had no school record or were rarely in trouble there. Nearly three quarters felt bullied, threatened, persecuted or attacked. Most school shooters had considered or attempted suicide and experienced depression, though few had been formally evaluated for mental health needs. Over half of school shooters had expressed an interest in violence and consumed violent media, but few had any criminal or violent behavior in their past. Many had demonstrated difficulty coping with loss or failure. The Safe Schools Initiative report on shooter characteristics does not have

Table 11.1. **Multiple murder types and definitions**

Type of multiple murder	Definition and example
Mass murder	Definition: Killing four or more people in one place with little time in between each kill (no cooling off period) Example: Eric Harris and Dylan Klebold (Columbine, 1999)
Spree murder	Definition: Killing several people over several locations over several hours or days Example: Adam Lanza (Sandy Hook, 2012)
Serial murder	Definition: Killing three or more people over time with a substantial cooling off period between each kill Examples: Jeffrey Dahmer, Ted Bundy, John Wayne Gacy

Source: Adapted from Walsh and Hemmens, 2011.

---

2. As we were writing this section, Tamerlan Tsarnaev, age 26, and his brother Dzhokar Tsarnaev, age 19, set off explosives near the finish line of the Boston Marathon, killing three and injuring over 170. They were identified through video camera footage. Tamerlan was killed during the ensuing manhunt and Dzhokar was taken into custody a couple of days later. The motives for their actions are unclear at this time. What is clear is that they committed multiple murder.

all the answers, and of course there is no guarantee that a child with the above characteristics will go on to perpetrate a mass shooting at a school, but it does help us understand what characteristics are common among school shooters and if this knowledge is used well, it may help us prevent future incidents.

Even though they constitute a type of multiple murderer, serial killers appear to be quite different than both mass and spree killers. A great deal of attention, both popular and academic, has been paid to these worst of the worst criminals. This attention has given rise to a number of myths about serial killers that the FBI (2005) has collected and debunked:

Myth: Serial killers are all dysfunctional loners. Fact: Many serial killers have jobs, families and connections to the community and their ability to appear normal can make them more difficult to apprehend.

Myth: Serial killers are all white males. Fact: Serial killers are overwhelmingly (though not always) male, but they are found in every racial and ethnic group. Failure to acknowledge African American serial killers in particular puts this community at greater risk (Walsh, 2005).

Myth: Serial killers are only motivated by sex. Fact: Many serial killers are motivated in part by sex, but there are other motivations, including anger, thrills, monetary gain and attention.

Myth: Serial killers travel and operate interstate. Fact: A few serial killers do travel and operate interstate, but many find and kill victims close to where they live and work. In fact, many criminals prefer to operate close to home, as being in their comfort zone increases their confidence.

Myth: Serial killers cannot stop killing. Fact: Some serial killers do stop killing because circumstances in their lives do not permit them to continue. When this happens, they typically substitute some variety of sexual activity for murder.

Myth: All serial killers are insane or evil geniuses. Fact: There is a great deal of variation in the intelligence of serial killers and very few of them are found to be legally insane (as seen in Chapter 1, this means unable to tell right from wrong and/or an inability to control one's actions).

Myth: Serial killers want to get caught. Fact: The reality is probably more that they feel they cannot get caught; by the time they meet the definition of a serial killer seen above, they have successfully killed at least three people without detection and this emboldens them to take chances with later victims that may eventually lead to their apprehension.

As we have seen, serial killers have different motivations for killing multiple victims over time. Holmes and DeBurger (1998) have developed a typology of serial killers based on different motivations. Table 11.2 provides details on the types and gives an example of each.

It is important to note that as with any typology, serial killers may not fit neatly into one category or another and moreover, this typology is based on known serial killers. It is possible that a future serial killer or killers will necessitate a new addition to the typology.

Table 11.2. Holmes and DeBurger's (1998) typology of serial killers with examples

Type	Characteristics	Example
Visionary	Respond to visions or voices in their heads, out of touch with reality, may be psychotic	Herb Mullin
Mission-oriented	Believe they have a mission to kill those who belong to certain groups, such as homosexuals or prostitutes	Gary Ridgway
Hedonistic	Kill for thrills and sexual satisfaction; this is the most common type of serial killer	Jeffrey Dahmer
Power/control	Take satisfaction in having complete control over victims, sex is almost always involved	Ted Bundy

Source: Adapted from Holmes and DeBurger, 1998.

Homicide-Suicide

Homicide followed by suicide is a rare event, with a rate of .05 to 1.55 per 100,000 (Liem, Barber, Markwalder, Killias and Nieuwbeerta, 2011). As seen in Table 11.3, homicide-suicide events overwhelmingly involving a male perpetrator and a female victim.

Homicide-suicide appears to be a planned event, where the perpetrator kills his victim and then himself. An overwhelming majority of homicide-suicides involve firearms and almost all take place in the home. These events seem to be explained by three patterns of structural and social psychological dynamics present in the event:

Table 11.3. The characteristics of homicide-suicides compared to homicides and suicides in the United States, 2004–2006

Characteristics	Homicide-Suicide N=461	Homicide Only N=11,480	Suicide Only N=22,569
Offender/Initiator — Gender — Mean Age	92% male, 8% female 45.1 years	90% male, 10% female 28.2 years	78% male, 22% female 45.3 years
Victim — Percent Female — Percent Multiple Victims	75 12	20 4	N/A N/A
Event — Percent Residential Location — Percent Firearms	81 87	49 66	75 51

Source: Adapted from Liem, Barber, Markwalder, Killias and Nieuwbeerta, 2011.

- Conflict intensity structures that include dependency, an unequal relationship, previous jealousy or hostility and immediate crisis such as loss of a job
- Social psychological stress or strain arising from blocked goals or needs, such as money, sex, autonomy or masculine status, from loss of nurturer and from loss of meaning
- Dominance and control expressed as part of a history of hostility, abuse, and violence and/or the explicit assertion of control such as the murder believing he is the only one who can take care of his family (Harper and Voigt, 2012).

Harper and Voigt (2012) conclude that any one or even two of the three patterns may be characteristic of a tumultuous relationship between perpetrator and victim that could and does sometimes lead to homicide. However, elements of these three patterns taken together are present in homicide followed by suicide cases, especially in cases of intimate partner homicide-suicide.

Rape

"Man's discovery that his genitalia could serve as a weapon to generate fear must rank as one of the most important discoveries of prehistoric times, along with the use of fire and the first crude stone axe. From prehistoric times to the present, I believe, rape has played a critical function. It is nothing more or less than a conscious process of intimidation by which *all* men keep *all* women in a state of fear" (Brownmiller, 1975. p. 14).

Historically speaking, rape is about ownership. The earliest form of a permanent conjugal accommodation, now called marriage, appears to have been institutionalized by men forcibly abducting and raping women — bride capture as it was later called existed in England as late as the fifteenth century. At least to men, forcible seizure was a perfectly acceptable way of acquiring a wife. "It seems eminently sensible to hypothesize that man's violent capture and rape of the female led first to the establishment of a rudimentary mate-protectorate and then sometime later to full blown male solidification of power, the patriarchy" (Brownmiller, 1975, p. 17). Man's first real property was woman and the extension of his property rights to include their offspring was the beginning of the concept of ownership. Concepts such as hierarchy, slavery and private property flowed from the initial subjugation of women.

The concept of rape as a crime initially enters the picture as a property crime of a man against another man. While abducting a woman from another tribe or in warfare was perfectly acceptable, doing so within your own tribe amounted to theft and violating a woman became criminalized as rape because if a woman was violated, it amounted to stealing a daughter at fair market price as a virgin. In the Code of Hammurabi, someone who steals and rapes a betrothed virgin would be seized and slain. Recognizing the power of the Patriarch, Hammurabi decreed that incest would result in banishment from the walls of the city. A married woman raped in Babylon shares the blame with her rapist. The crime was labeled adultery and both offender and victim were bound and thrown into the river. A husband could fish out this wife if he chose to and the

King could let the rapist go free. A married woman in Hebrew culture was treated even more harshly when victimized by rape—she along with her victimizer was stoned to death. The Hebraic idea of rape as a criminal act only involved the spoiling of a virgin. Virgins were property and were sold in marriage for fifty pieces of silver. If a man raped a virgin within the confines of the city, they were both put to death by stoning; had the virgin screamed, she would have been rescued. If she was raped outside of the walls of the city and her screams could not be heard, the rapist was ordered to pay the bride price to the father and marry the girl. If the girl was already promised to another man, the rapist was stoned to death and the girl went unpunished to be eventually sold as spoiled goods at a discounted price (Brownmiller, 1975, p. 20).

Fast-forward to 11th century England and it is still unclear whether rape is a crime against a woman's body or a crime against her estate. Before the Norman Conquest, rape was punished by death and dismemberment but that punishment was reserved for those who raped a highborn and propertied virgin under the protection of a powerful lord. After the conquest, William the Conqueror reduced the punishment for raping a virgin to castration and the loss of both eyes. Under Edward I at the end of the 13th century and the promulgation of the Statutes of Westminster in England, we begin to get a more modern legal notion of rape, with the Crown taking an active interest in all manner of rapes including what is now referred to as statutory rape—carnal knowledge of a child where consent was not an issue because the child could not legally give it. Moreover, no distinction was made between the rape of a virgin and the rape of a married woman. Edward I decreed that if a raped woman failed to institute a private suit within 40 days of the incident, the right to prosecute passed to the Crown and was no longer just treated as a family misfortune but became a public safety issue of the state. The penalty for rape in the Statutes is two years imprisonment plus a fine set at the King's pleasure. This lenient penalty was revised by Parliament in the Second Statute of Westminster. Any man who ravished a married woman, dame or damsel, without her consent was guilty of a felony and the penalty was death. There was little change in the law in England for the next 700 years (Brownmiller, 1975, p. 30).[3]

Defining and Measuring Rape

Rape is currently defined as "the carnal knowledge of a female forcibly and against her will" (FBI UCR, 2011f). However, in early 2012, Attorney General Eric Holder announced that the new definition of rape that will be used to count these crimes in the UCR is: "the penetration, no matter how slight, of the vagina or anus with any body part or object, or oral penetration by a sex organ of another person, without the consent of the victim." Under the new definition, males can also be raped and rape is not limited to penile penetration of the vagina. It also includes instances in which the victim could not give consent because of incapacitation or because of age. The new definition of rape reflects state criminal codes and will better capture victim experiences of rape and sexual assault. It should also provide us with a better understanding of how much rape

---

3. Astute readers will have imagined by now that some take umbrage with Brownmiller's claims about rape. For an easy to comprehend look at other perspectives on rape, see McElroy (n.d.).

Figure 11.5. Number of arrests for rape by age in the United States, 2011

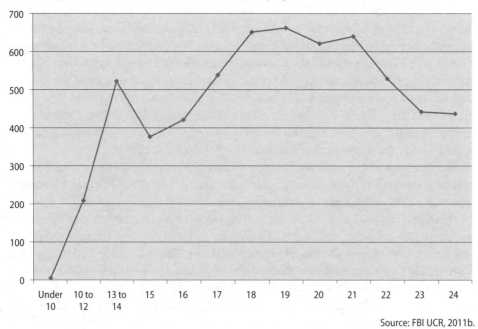

Source: FBI UCR, 2011b.

and sexual assault occurs. The UCR began defining and counting rape in this way in early 2013, meaning that in 2014, we will be able to see for the first time how the new definition affects rates. The FBI will continue to collect data based on the historical definition of rape, enabling law enforcement to track consistent trend data until the statistical differences between the old and new definitions are more fully understood (DOJ, 2012).

In 2011, there were 83,425 rapes reported to the police for a rate of 52.7 per 100,000. There were 14,679 arrests for rape. Ninety-nine percent of those arrested were male and one percent was female. Sixty five percent of those arrested were white and 33 percent were African American. Fourteen percent of those arrested were under the age of 18; as seen in Figure 11.5, arrests for rape peak between the ages of 18 and 21 and then start to decline (FBI UCR, 2011c, 2011b). As we know, the 2011 data excludes males as victims. Also, the UCR reports the rate as the number per 100,000 males and females, thus diluting the rate by not reporting it as a rate for 100,000 females. The new definition, which includes males as victims, will accommodate this flaw in the data in the near future.

The National Crime Victimization Survey (NCVS) reported 243,800 rapes and sexual assaults for 2011 which reflected a 30 percent decline from 2002 (Truman and Planty, 2012). However, this number compared to rapes and attempts known to the police from the UCR data indicates that rape and sexual assault are woefully underreported, which can put the public at risk for sexual and other victimization. Using NCVS and UCR data in tandem, it appears that only one in three rapes are reported to the police and slightly more than 17 percent result in an arrest. Based on a survey of adjudication outcomes in large urban counties in the United States, only 62 percent of those arrested for rape were convicted, with 12 percent of this number having pled guilty to a misdemeanor sexual offense Based on these data, it can be estimated that only one in ten rapes results in prison or jail time (Cohen and Kyckelhahn, 2006). Lisak and Miller (2002) found that of 1,882 men who were assessed for acts of interpersonal violence, 120 men who self-reported behaviors that met the legal definition of rape or attempted rape were never prosecuted (though it is unclear how many were arrested). A majority of the 120 were repeat rapists who averaged 5.8 rapes each. These 120 men were responsible for 1,225 separate acts of interpersonal violence including rape, battery and child physical and sexual abuse. As we saw in Chapter 10, victims of crime can be reluctant to report their victimization for a variety of reasons including fear and a desire for the matter to stay private. Fear of retaliation from the attacker may be a particularly salient reason that many rape victims do not report their victimization—about half of rape victims know their attacker (Walsh and Ellis, 2007)[4] and the fear of retaliation may be all the more intense if the victim has to see the attacker on a regular basis.

Statutory Rape

Statutory rape in the United States is generally described as an offense that takes place when an individual (regardless of age) has consensual sex with an individual not old enough to give consent. All states prohibit sex with a minor. In some states where the offender is three or more years older than the minor, the age difference establishes the crime. So the offender can be an adult or a juvenile. The age of consent varies from state to state as well as does the label of and the punishment for the crime.

To get at an estimate of how many statutory rapes occur in a given year Troup-Leasure and Snyder (2005) compared counts from the UCR and NIBRS data for 2000. In that year, the UCR reported 90,186 forcible rapes known to law enforcement. Law enforcement agencies in the 2000 NIBRS sample (21 states) reported 13,862 forcible rapes, consistent with the UCR definition of forcible rape. The agencies in NIBRS had 15 percent of all the forcible rapes in the United States in 2000. Assuming that they also had 15 percent of all the statutory rapes, the 2,414 statutory rapes in the 2000 NIBRS sample would imply there were about 15,700 statutory rapes reported to all law enforcement agencies in the United States in 2000, making the ratio of statutory to forcible rape about 1 to 3.

Motives for Rape: Sex or Power?

As alluded to above, Brownmiller (1975) believes that rape is about power, not sex. Rape is a way for men to oppress women and not a way for men to achieve sexual satisfaction, though that may occur. In this view, any man is a potential rapist. Groth and Birnbaum (1979) take a different view that is rooted in psychology rather than feminism. Their typology is based on a theoretical understanding of the role of displaced aggression, compensation and sexual diffusion in rape. In displaced aggression, the goal of the

---

4. Recall from Chapter 10 that about 78 percent of sexual violence victims knew their attacker in 2010 (Planty, Langton, Krebs, Berzofsky and Smiley-McDonald, 2013).

rapist is to physically harm and degrade the victim; there is little thought of sexual grat- ification and this type of rapist is known as an anger rapist. In compensation, sexual excitation is the key component and aggression is generally minimized; this type of rapist is the power rapist. Finally, sexual diffusion explains the sadistic rapist's behavior in terms of attempts to fulfill sexual fantasies (sexual sadism is an extreme example of this phenomenon). Evolutionary theorists view rape as an unfortunate and maladaptive form of what was once a very adaptive behavior, securing as many mates as possible in order to continue one's genetic line (Thornhill and Palmer, 2000).

Evolution of Rape Definitions and Laws

As we have seen, ideas about rape are slow to change. Think now about what con- stitutes a rape, then read the following scenarios from Anderson (2005, pp. 625–626):

(1) A fair young woman is walking home alone at night. Gray street lamps cast shadows from the figure she cuts through an urban landscape. She hurries along, unsure of her safety. Suddenly, perhaps from behind a dumpster, a strange, dark man lunges out at her, knife at her throat, and drags her into a dark alley where he threatens to kill her, and beats her until she bleeds. The young woman puts up a valiant fight to protect her sexual virtue, but the assailant overcomes her will and rapes her. Afterwards, she immediately calls the police to report the offense.

(2) A male and a female student meet at a party and begin to talk, drink, and flirt. Later, she wanders to a quiet place with him. Once there, he pushes her down, pins her, and begins kissing her aggressively. She does not want to be rude. He must have misunderstood, she thinks. The alcohol is getting to her, she feels dizzy, and she wonders if she is going to throw up. She says, "Ummm ... wait ... please ... I'm not sure that this is what we should do." He ignores her and begins taking off their clothes. She cannot seem to get away, and her panic rises. She cries as he penetrates her. Shamed by the experience, she does not tell anyone until three years later when she confides in a trusted friend. She never calls the police.

Which of these more closely matches the imagined scenario? It may very well be the first, but of course as we now know, the second scenario is far more typical of rapes in the United States today. The point is that ideas about what constitute rape as well as definitions of it are slow to change.

The FBI's definition of rape is finally changing after nearly eight decades, but states have been ahead of the curve on this one. Twenty-five states and the District of Columbia have removed the word rape from their criminal codes, opting instead to call these crimes sexual assaults. The impetus behind the change was a slow but steady reconcep- tualization of rape by society itself from being a crime about sex to a crime about violence. For states that do retain the word rape in their criminal codes, it varies whether penile penetration of the vagina is required to call a crime a rape. In a state with this requirement, such as New York, a woman who is orally and anally but not vaginally penetrated by a man's penis cannot be said to be raped. The definition of consent also differs from state to state. Some states require a rape victim to explicitly say no, while others take the inability or unwillingness to give consent, including through silence, as lack of consent. Changes in the law books both reflect society's perceptions and alter them, in this case causing us to rethink what rape is (Hughes, 2013).

Recall from Chapter 6 that it was legal for a husband to rape his wife within the context of their marriage in the United States until the 1980s under spousal exception laws. Every state has since amended spousal exception laws to make rape of a spouse a crime, but some states, such as Washington, still carry provisions that make spousal rape a lesser crime than rape of someone to whom the offender is not married (Williams, 2013). Rape shield laws were passed in a vast majority of states in the early 1980s. These laws were designed to make it more difficult for defense attorneys to introduce a rape victim's sexual history at trial and to use that sexual history to argue that the victim consented. Rape shield laws vary from state to state and some states do allow the introduction of a rape victim's sexual history at trial, particularly when the victim and the defendant had a prior consensual sexual relationship (Glaberson, 1992).

Box 11.1. Stalking: An Intimate Problem

Stalking "is a course of conduct directed at a specific person that involves repeated (two of more occasions) visual or physical proximity, nonconsensual communication, or verbal, written, or implied threats or a combination thereof, that would cause a reasonable person fear" (Tjaden and Thoennes, 1998). Stalking can be carried out in person, as it were, but is now enabled by a variety of electronic devices as well. Cyberstalking is similar to real life stalking because it involves the pursuit, harassment and unsolicited contact via the Internet. Even though this form of stalking does not involve direct contact, it is still a serious assault on a person's sense of self. The increasing ubiquity of social media and the easy availability of personal information have made this form of stalking ever more prevalent. Would be stalkers may find it easier to stalk through social media than to confront an actual person.

Approximately 1 in 6 women (16.2 percent) in the United States has experienced stalking at some point in her lifetime, according to the CDC's 2010 National Intimate Partner and Sexual Violence Survey. About 4 percent, or approximately 5.2 million women, were stalked in the 12 months prior to taking the survey. Two-thirds of the female victims of stalking reported stalking by a current or former intimate partner in their lifetime (Black, et al., 2011). Approximately 1 in 19 men (5.2 percent) in the United States has experienced stalking victimization at some point during his lifetime and 1.3 percent of men (about 1.4 million) reported being stalked in the 12 months prior to taking the survey. Approximately 41 percent reported that they had been stalked by an intimate partner in their lifetime (Black et al, 2011). Partner stalking is the largest category of stalking cases (Mohandie, Meloy, McGowan and Williams, 2006).

College women appear to experience partner stalking at high rates. Approximately 5.3 percent of female college students from a large national sample reported being stalked by an intimate partner in about a 7-month period (Fisher, Cullen and Turner, 2002). For this study, stalking was defined to include repeated following; waiting outside a classroom, residence, workplace, or other buildings or car, watching, telephoning, writing letters, cards, emails, et cetera and communicating with the respondent in other ways that seemed obsessive and made the respondent afraid or concerned for her safety. Another smaller study of college women found that 6.9 percent of the sample was stalked by a current or former partner (Buhi, Clayton and Surrency, 2009).

Robbery

Robbery is "the taking or attempting to take anything of value from the care, custody, or control of a person or persons by force or threat of force or violence and/or by putting the victim in fear" (FBI UCR, 2011f). A slightly different definition is used internationally; in the Tenth United Nations Survey on Crime Trends and the Operations of Criminal Justice Systems, robbery "may be understood to mean the theft of property from a person, overcoming resistance by force or threat of force" and should also include purse- or bag-snatching and theft by violence (UNDOC, 2008, p. 10). Robbery is classified as a violent crime because the act puts another person in fear of his or her life and it carries commensurately harsh penalties. Figure 11.6 reveals that robbery occurs most commonly on streets and highways in the United States followed by residences, businesses, gas station and convenience stores and finally banks. Bank robberies yielded a higher average return of $4,704, compared to the average for other types of robbery, $1,153 (FBI UCR, 2011d).

In 2011, there were 354,396 robberies reported to the police for a rate of 113.7 per 100,000. There were 82,557 arrests for robbery. Eighty-eight of those arrested were male and 12 percent were female. Forty three percent of those arrested were white and 56 percent were African American. Twenty two percent of those arrested were under the age of 18; as seen in Figure 11.7, 18 is the peak age for robbery, after which time it starts to decline (FBI UCR, 2011d, 2011b).

A now classic typology of robbers was proposed by John Conklin in 1972 based on his interviews with 67 incarcerated robbers and 90 victims of robbery. He classified

Figure 11.6. Percent of robberies committed by location in the United States, 2011

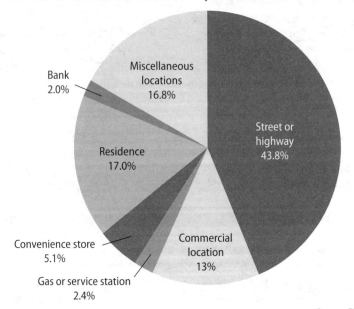

Source: FBI UCR, 2011d.

Figure 11.7. Number of arrests for robbery by age in the United States, 2011

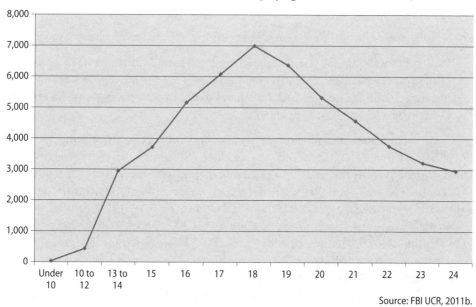

Source: FBI UCR, 2011b.

robbers into four types, the first of which the professional robber. The professional robber makes his living by robbing people and makes careful, rational decisions when it comes to victim selection. The second type is the opportunist robber. Opportunist robbers are the most common type of robber and have little commitment to robbery itself. Instead, they are equal opportunity offenders who engage in robbery if a suitable opportunity presents itself and they have a need to do so. Their robberies usually involve little planning. The third and fourth types, addict and alcoholic robbers, commit robberies to support their habits and are not interested in perpetrating violence so much as they are obtaining money to get their next fix.

As we saw in Chapter 8, Richard Wright and Scott Decker use interviews with active robbers as the basis of their conclusions. There may be important differences between incarcerated robbers and active robbers, i.e., those who got caught and those who did not, so their choice of methods is useful and leads to some enlightening conclusions. In interviews with 86 active robbers, Wright and Decker found that in addition for the need for fast cash due to heavy involvement in street life as we saw in Chapter 8, they commit their offenses in a specific way that allows them to maintain control over the situation. There is a four step process to committing robbery, approaching the victim, announcing the crime, transferring the goods and making the escape (Wright and Decker, 2010). In the first of these steps, approaching the victim, robbers usually do so in one of two ways. They may use speed and stealth to sneak up on their victims, as this robber did:

> I just come up on you. You could be going to your car. If you are facing this way, I want to be on your blind side. If you are going this way, I want to be on that side where I can get up on you and grab you: "This is a robbery,

motherfucker, don't make it no murder!" I kind of like shake you. That's my approach (Wright and Decker, 2010, pp. 159–160).

Robbers also use a normal interaction style in order to appear nonthreatening to victims:

> Well, if I'm walking, say you got something that I want, I might come up there [and say] "Do you have the time?" or "Can I get a light from you?" something like that. "Yeah, it's three o'clock." By then I'm up on you, getting what I want (Wright and Decker, 2010, p. 160).

In the second step, announcing the crime, most robbers do three things in short order. They demand that the victim stop and listen ("Just hold up right where you at! Don't move! Don't say nothing!"), they declare their intentions to rob ("It's a robbery! Don't nobody move!") and they warn of the consequences of not following orders ("It's a robbery! Don't make it a murder!" Wright and Decker, 2010, p. 161). Nearly all robbers in this study used guns, recognizing that a gun makes it less necessary to verbally interact with victims after the announcement of the crime. Many opted for medium sized or smaller guns, determining that they were threatening enough to compel victims' compliance but small enough to conceal.

The third step, transferring the goods, is the most difficult. In order to be successful, robbers must maintain complete control over their victims while ensuring that they have obtained all the money and valuables the victims have. Moreover, this must be done very quickly. Some robbers made the victims responsible for the transfer of goods:

> I tell [my victims], "Man, if you don't want to die, give me your money! If you want to survive, give me your money! I'm not bullshitting!" So he will either go in his back pocket and give me the wallet or the woman will give me her purse (Wright and Decker, 2010, p. 163).

It can be unclear when the full transfer of goods is complete, though, and many robbers become verbally and physically aggressive in order to hasten victim's transfer of the goods. Some robbers chose to take goods off of and away from victims themselves, believing that the victim would either shortchange them or surprise them with a weapon:

> I don't let nobody give me nothing. 'Cause if you let somebody go in they pockets, they pull out a gun, they could pull out anything. You make sure they are where you can see their hands at all times (Wright and Decker, 2010, p. 164).

During the transfer of goods, some robbers encountered resistance from their victims and in these instances, resorted to serious but not lethal violence. This violence typically involved hitting the victim in the head with their gun and was done to encourage speedy compliance with demands:

> It happened [that some of my victims initially refuse to hand over their money, but] you would be surprised how cooperative a person will be once he been smashed across the face with a 357 Magnum (Wright and Decker, 2010, p. 164).

Some robbers admitted that they would not resort to lethal violence if a victim refused to comply and would probably abandon the situation:

I really ain't gonna shoot nobody. I think a lot of people are like that. I wouldn't shoot nobody myself, if they gave me too much of a problem, I might just take off (Wright and Decker, 2010, p. 165).

The fourth step, making the escape, is more difficult than it might seem. During the first three steps, the robber is able to maintain control over the situation, but that becomes increasingly difficult to do when the physical distance between the two is increasing. Some robbers choose to make their escape before the victims:

I done left people in gangways and alley and I've told them, "If you come out of this alley, I'm gonna hurt you. Just give me 5 or 10 minutes to get away. If you come out of this alley in 3 or 4 minutes, I'm gonna shoot the shit out of you!" (Wright and Decker, 2010, p. 166).

Others prefer that victims depart the scene first:

I try not to have to run away. A very important thing that I have learned is that when you run away, too many things can happen running away. Police could just be cruising by and see you running down the street. I just prefer to be able to walk away, which is one of the reasons why I tend, rather than to make an exit, I tell the victim to walk and don't look back: "Walk away, and walk fast!" When they walk, I can make my exit walking (Wright and Decker, 2010, pp. 166–167).

Aggravated Assault

Aggravated assault is "an unlawful attack by one person upon another for the purpose of inflicting severe or aggravated bodily injury" (FBI UCR, 2011f). The difference between aggravated assault and murder may simply be a function of the distance between where the assault occurred and a hospital, or the location of a wound or whether a vital organ or artery was damaged by a bullet or knife. This is consistent with what we see in Figure 11.8. Notice how relatively few aggravated assaults are committed with firearms, just about one in five. It is likely that the use of guns turns aggravated assaults into murders most of the time.

In 2011, there were 751,131 aggravated assaults reported to the police for a rate of 241.1 per 100,000 people, making it by far the most prevalent form of violent crime. There were 305,939 arrests for aggravated assault. Seventy seven percent of those arrested were male and 23 percent were female. Sixty four percent of those arrested were white and 34 percent were African American. Ten percent of those arrested were under the age of 18; like the other crimes described in this chapter, aggravated assault is most frequently committed by young people, with a peak age of 21, as seen in Figure 11.9 (FBI UCR, 2011e, 2011b).

Figure 11.8. Percent of weapons used in aggravated assaults in the United States, 2011

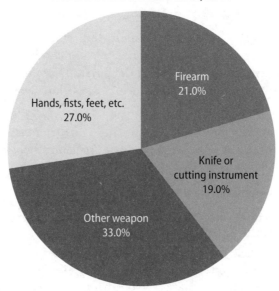

Source: FBI UCR, 2011e.

Figure 11.9. Number of arrests for aggravated assault by age in the United States, 2011

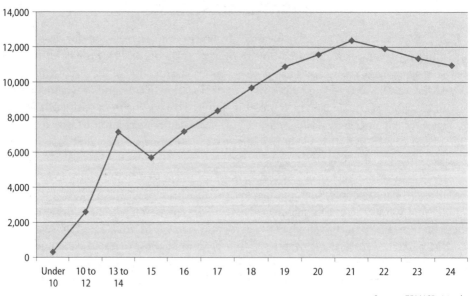

Source: FBI UCR, 2011b.

"New" Forms of Violence

"New" is justifiably set off in quotation marks because the forms of violence we will discuss here have been around for a long time but have only received considerable attention by the public, scholars and policy makers beginning in the second half of the twentieth century. We will cover domestic violence, human trafficking and terrorism.[5]

Domestic Violence

Domestic violence can be thought of a crimes committed by family members, intimates and cohabitants against one another. Domestic violence is widespread, with over 1.7 million domestic violence victimizations and over 1.1 million victimizations involving intimate partner violence in the United States in 2011 (Truman and Planty, 2012), though intimate partner violence has been on a steady decline since 1993. Women are much more likely to be victimized by domestic violence than men and men are more likely to be perpetrators. In fact, intimate partner violence represented over a fifth of all violent victimizations of women and 30 percent of all homicides of women between 2001 and 2005 (Catalano, 2007). Domestic violence also occurs in dating relationships (DeKeseredy and Schwartz, 1998) and among same sex couples (Merrill, 1998). No race, ethnicity, class or gender is immune from domestic violence, but it does appear to be more common in households with low incomes. Catalano (2007) found that households with an average annual income of less than $7,500 experienced the most domestic violence, while those with average annual incomes of $50,000 or more experienced the least. Why a low income is so strongly associated with intimate partner violence is as yet unclear, but it may be because a low income gives couples something to fight about, because a low income makes it harder for women to leave or because of other factors associated with low income, such as hopelessness (WHO, 2002).

In households where one adult partner perpetrates violence against the other, child abuse is more likely to occur (Gelles, 1974; Bergen, 1998) and experiencing physical abuse in childhood strongly predicts arrests for violent crime in adulthood (Widom, 1992; Brezina, 1998). Though most known instances of domestic violence do not result in serious physical injury for the victims (Felson and Cares, 2005), it appears that domestic violence incidents escalate in frequency and severity once they start (Crowell and Burgess, 1996). In interviews with 33 male, heterosexual domestic violence offenders, Anderson and Umberson (2010) found that these batterers describe their violence against their female partners as a rational response to provocation, a momentary loss of control or the escalation of a minor incident. They characterized their own violence as rational and violence committed by their partners as trivial or irrational:

---

5. Other forms of "new" violence, violence in the workplace and hate crimes, are covered in Chapter 10.

> I came out of the kitchen and then I got in her face and I shoved her. She shoved, she tried to push me a little bit, but it didn't matter much (Anderson and Umberson, 2010, p. 172).

and

> She has got no control. She sees something and she don't like it, she'll go and pull my hair, scratch me, and [act] paranoid, crazy, screaming loud, make everybody look at her, and call the police, you know. Just nuts (Anderson and Umberson, 2010, p. 173).

However, the batterers in this sample also cast themselves as victims, characterizing both their partners and the criminal justice system as having control over their lives:

> You ask the guy sitting next door to me, the guy that's down the hall. For years they all say, "Bill, man, reach down and grab your eggs. She wears the pants." Or maybe like, "Hey, man, we're going to go—oh, Bill can't go. He's got to ask his boss first." And they were right (Anderson and Umberson, 2010, p. 176).

and

> I'm going to jail for something I haven't even done because the woman is always the victim and the guy is always the bad guy. And O.J., I think, has made it even worse—that mentality. I know that there's a lot of bad, ignorant, violent guys out there that probably think that it's wonderful to batter their wife on a regular basis, but I think there's a lot of reverse mentality going on right now (Anderson and Umberson, 2010, p. 177).

As we saw in Chapter 10, only about 60 percent of those who are victimized by domestic violence report it to the police. A common reason victims give for why they choose not to report is the belief that domestic violence is a family matter.[6] The idea that what happens in the home is a private matter and that the male head of the household is free to do what he wants is at least as old as the Bible (Ephesians 5:23; Timothy 2:11–15). Similarly, there are reasons that victims of domestic violence do not leave the abusive environment. They may feel partially responsible for their own victimization, they may not want to risk criticism from family and friends and they may be simply unable to leave due to financial considerations. Especially lower class and unemployed women run a real risk of homelessness for themselves and their children if they leave an abusive environment (Crowell and Burgess, 1996; Waldrop and Resick, 2004), putting them in a very serious Catch 22.

Domestic violence has a long history as a private matter and that includes the desire of police to stay out of it. However, the Women's Movement helped spur changes in the way law enforcement responds to domestic violence. Sherman (1992) found that

---

6. For years, the typical admonishment by police in New Orleans, for example, was to tell the male, "Now you go stay by your mamas tonight and y'all get back together tomorrow and work this thing out." On another occasion, the second author confronted a man beating a woman in a car in a parking lot. When confronted the man explained, "It's okay, she's my wife."

people arrested for domestic violence were less likely during the subsequent six months to commit repeat domestic violence than those who were not arrested. These findings led some cities' law enforcement agencies to encourage their officers to make domestic violence arrests and some states even made arrests mandatory, though mandatory arrests do not appear to reduce recidivism. Mandatory arrest policies for domestic violence may even make victims more reluctant to call the police in a domestic violence incident (UK, 2011). Other criminal justice system approaches include special domestic violence prosecution units (Fagan, 1996) and hot spot policing for households with repeated calls for service for domestic violence issues (Goldstein, 1990). Gelsthorpe (2012) notes that restorative justice such as we covered in Chapters 5 and 6 can be a useful and effective way to address domestic violence, though there are cultural limits on this. Domestic violence courts may also be useful, but generally speaking, these courts are focused on victim safety and support over offender rehabilitation (Labriola, Bradley, O'Sullivan, Rempel and Moore, 2010).

Human Trafficking

Human trafficking is the general term that refers to the acquisition of people by force, deception or fraud for the purpose of exploiting them for labor and/or sex. Like many of our other forms of violent crime, trafficking has been around for a long time, but only recently was there an effort to quantify the problem and tackle it. The United Nations created a Trafficking Protocol in 2003, which spurred many countries to enact legislation that criminalizes human trafficking. Today, 124 countries have such laws on the books, though 32 percent of countries did not record any human trafficking prosecutions and 40 percent of countries did not record any human trafficking convictions between 2003 and 2007, due in part to the newness of the laws (UNODC, 2009).

There were 14,909 victims of human trafficking in 71 countries in 2006, up from 11,706 in 2003. Sixty-six percent of victims of trafficking in 61 countries in 2006 were women, followed by girls (13 percent), men (12 percent) and boys (9 percent). Children make up about 21 percent of those trafficked, but in some parts of the world, particularly in West Africa and the Mekong region of southeast Asia, children comprise up to 100 percent of those trafficked. The most common form of exploitation to which victims were subject in 2006 in 52 countries was sexual exploitation at 79 percent—not a huge surprise considering how many women and girls are victims of trafficking—followed by forced labor at 18 percent. Forced labor trafficking may be harder to detect than sexual exploitation trafficking because some countries' laws only include trafficking for sexual exploitation and not for labor, because of the popular conception that trafficking is for sexual exploitation only and because trafficking for sexual exploitation has a more visible outcome, prostitution, than forced labor, which is largely hidden from public view. In the 14 countries with at least one human trafficking conviction and where the gender of the offender was known, more women were convicted of this crime than men. This pattern was most evident in Eastern Europe and Central Asia, but observable elsewhere, including East Asia, Central America and the Caribbean (UNODC, 2009). As we have seen, women engage in crime much less often than men, which makes these findings all the more interesting.

In the United States, 103 people were charged and 89 were convicted of human trafficking in 2007, up from just 21 charged and 27 convicted in 2003. Most of the human trafficking victims in the United States in 2006 came from Latin America and the Caribbean (62 percent), but in 2007, they were more evenly split between Latin American and the Caribbean (41 percent) and Asia (41 percent)[7] (UNODC, 2009).

Terrorism

Terrorism is difficult to define because it has been used liberally in a variety of contexts. Terrorism expert Bruce Hoffman has pointed out that the term can include such "disparate acts as the bombing of a building, the assassination of a head of state, the massacre of civilians by a military unit, the poisoning of produce on supermarket shelves, or the deliberate contamination of over-the-counter medication in a drugstore" (2006, p. 1). The Department of Defense, the State Department, the FBI and the United Nations all have different definitions of terrorism. Though different, each incorporates elements of political groups targeting civilians with violence in order to intimidate an audience (Verma, 2012). A good working definition for our purposes is that provided by the FBI. Terrorism is "the unlawful use of force and violence against persons or property to intimidate or coerce a government, the civilian population, or any segment thereof, in furtherance of political or social objectives" (C.F.R., 2008). As with many of our violent crimes, terrorism and terrorist acts have been around for a long time.

Box 11.2. Terrorism: In the Eye of the Beholder?

It is fairly easy to draw to mind events we consider terrorism (think 9/11) and to ascribe objective bad guy status to those who perpetrate these events. However, terrorism is one of those crimes that is in the eye of the beholder. Think for just a moment about George Washington. The father of our country, the hero of democracy, the man responsible for the freedom and liberty we enjoy today was probably not viewed as such by Britons in the late 1700s. In fact, he and his men were described by the British as terrorists (Verma, 2012). Nevertheless, today we hail Washington as a hero.

There were over 63,000 terrorist incidents throughout the world between 1990 and 2011. Interestingly, incidents were on a downward trend from 1993 to 1998, at which time they hit a low plateau of between 900 and 1,800 per year. The number started increasing in 2005 and hit a modern all time high of about 5,200 in 2011. Most of these incidents involved bombs or explosives and many resulted in less than 10

---

7. It is important to note that the way human trafficking victims are measured in the United States is the possession of a certificate (for adults) or a letter (for children) from the Department of Health and Human Services (UNODC, 2009); it is likely that many victims of human trafficking in the United States have not been issued such a document.

fatalities (GTD, 2013). The FBI's National Counterterrorism Center maintains a list of 39 active and dangerous terrorist groups. While many of these groups originated in the Middle East and Africa, there are also active and dangerous terrorist groups in Central and Southeast Asia and South America. Though our current focus as a country is on Islamic fundamentalist groups, these are by no means the only groups involved in terrorism. They do stand out in one way, though. Terrorist organizations need funding and in order to obtain money for their cause, they often engage in rather ordinary criminal activity, such as drug, weapon and human trafficking, extortion and bank robbery. For many terrorist groups, the money they make from their illegal activities undermines or mutes their commitment to their goals as a terrorist group. In other words, money reorients their values (Albanese and Pursley, 1993; Dishman, 2001). This does not appear to be the case for many Islamic fundamentalist groups, however; these groups do not appear so easily distracted from their political and ideological goals.

Miller (2006) notes that modern terrorist activities appear to have several things in common, the first of which is the use of violence in order to intimidate and coerce others. Importantly, it appears that violence by terrorist groups is becoming less instrumental, with intimidation as the main goal, and more retributive, with taking revenge on the enemy as the main goal. The second commonality of modern terrorist activities is the choice of victims for maximum propaganda value. A great deal of thought usually goes into selecting targets that achieve maximum publicity at minimum risk. The third commonality is the use of unconventional military tactics including sneak attacks and attacks on civilians, including women and children and with this, terrorist groups are distinguished from guerilla groups. The fourth commonality is unshakable devotion and loyalty, which is a must if terrorist group members are expected to voluntarily give their lives for the cause. A fifth commonality is the new demographic composition of terrorist groups. In the 1960s and 1970s, many international terrorist groups consisted of educated, sophisticated members of the middle class who were well trained and widely traveled. Terrorism recruitment during this time was done in universities or urban cultural centers. From the 1990s forward, however, we can see a change. The typical international terrorist today is likely to be a poor, under- or uneducated and poorly trained refugee of Middle Eastern origin. They are indoctrinated with political and religious extremism, especially taught to hate the West and its material excesses. Especially for those groups that make frequent use of suicide bombings, little to no training is needed for the person who carries one out.

Miller (2006) contends that terrorism is at least partially motivated by legitimate and oftentimes longstanding grievances of a political and social nature. That being the case, a campaign of shock and awe is very unlikely to solve the terrorist problem, as it does little to address the reasons for terrorist group formation. Instead, Miller (2006) advocates meaningful dialogue between terrorist groups and those they perceive to be enemies so that some of the root causes of terrorism that lay in perceived injustices can be effectively addressed. Miller (2006) also endorses the provision of justice to victims of terror, noting that both Truth and Reconciliation Commissions and restorative justice principles may be useful in this regard.

Conclusion:
Theoretical Explanations of Violent Crime

Many of the theories developed to explain crime were developed to explain all types of crime, from violent to property to public order to white collar. Particularly the leading theories of crime, Hirschi's (1969) social control (social bond) theory, Gottfredson and Hirschi's (1990) self-control theory, Agnew's (2002) general strain theory and Akers' (1997, 2002) social learning theory, were developed to be able to explain all types of crime. The architects and proponents of these theories would argue that their theories are well able to explain violent (as well as other types of) crime.

However, it appears that other theories of crime may have particular utility in explaining violent crime, especially psychosocial and biosocial theories and subcultural theories of crime. As we saw in Chapter 3, psychosocial factors such as being high on the traits negative emotionality and impulsiveness and low on agreeableness and constraint may contribute to a wide variety of antisocial behavior, including violence. Biosocial factors including brain damage, inability to achieve psychological arousal, neurotransmitter dysfunction and genetics may all play a role in the development of violent behavior. In fact, we often turn to psychosocial or biosocial factors to explain the worst of the worst criminals such as serial killers, perhaps because we are uncomfortable with the notion that there is not something very different about them and us.

As seen in Chapter 4, subcultural theories of crime such as that advanced by Wolfgang and Ferracuti (1967) and supported by Anderson (1999) appear to have particular utility in the explanation of violence in the United States. Remember from Chapter 8 that a subculture of violence is a subculture in which the use of violence to solve conflicts is normative and even encouraged. The ability to use violence to successfully solve interpersonal conflicts allows members of the subculture to prove their manhood and earn the most desirable commodity of all, respect. Respect is so easily lost, though, that members of the subculture must be ready to engage in violence at even the slightest provocation, lest they lose respect and their self-esteem in the process.

The World Health Organization's risk factors for interpersonal violence draws on many of the theories of crime we have already discussed:

> The different forms of interpersonal violence share many common underlying risk factors. Some are psychological and behavioral characteristics such as poor behavioral control, low self-esteem, and personality and conduct disorders. Others are tied to experiences, such as lack of emotional bonding and support, early exposure to violence in the home (whether experiencing or witnessing family violence), and family or personal histories marked by divorce or separation. Abuse of drugs and alcohol is frequently associated with interpersonal violence, and poverty as well as income disparities and gender inequality stand out as important community and societal factors. (WHO, 2002, p. 18)

Websites to Visit

UCR Violent Crimes, 2011: http://www.fbi.gov/about-us/cjis/ucr/crime-in-the-u.s/
   2011/crime-in-the-u.s.-2011/violent-crime/violent-crime
Serial Killers: http://www.biography.com/people/groups/serial-killers/all
Human Trafficking: http://www.unodc.org/documents/Global_Report_on_TIP.pdf
Terrorism: http://www.nctc.gov/, http://www.start.umd.edu/gtd/

Discussion Questions

1. Describe the trends in violent crime in the United States in the last 50 years and comment on some possible reasons for changes in crime rates over time.
2. Does any of the information given in this chapter with regard to the characteristics of those who are arrested for violent crime change your conception of who is involved in crime? If so, how?
3. Can you think of a serial killer who does not appear to fit the typology given above? If so, what new category would you suggest and why?
4. Do you think rape is motivated by sex or power? Explain your answer.
5. What can be done to encourage rape victims to report their victimization to law enforcement?
6. Knowing what you do now about how robbers obtain and maintain control over a robbery interaction, what do you think you would do if ever confronted by a robber?
7. What are the pros and cons of mandatory arrest policies for domestic violence? Do you think the pros outweigh the cons or vice versa?
8. Do you think terrorism is in the eye of the beholder or are there some people who are universally exalted or condemned?
9. What are some terrorism reduction strategies according to Miller (2006)? How much if any effort should we devote to these strategies and why?

References

Agnew, Robert. (2002). Foundation for a general strain theory of crime. In S. Cote (Ed.), *Criminological theories: Bridging the past to the future* (pp. 113–124). Thousand Oaks, CA: Sage.

Akers, Ronald. (1997). *Criminological theories: Introduction and evaluation.* 2nd ed. Los Angeles, CA: Roxbury.

Akers, Ronald. (2002). A social learning theory of crime. In S. Cote (Ed.), *Criminological theories: Bridging the past to the future* (pp. 135–143). Thousand Oaks, CA: Sage.

Albanese, Jay and Robert Pursley. (1993). *Crime in America: Some existing and emerging issues.* Englewood Cliffs, NJ: Prentice Hall.

Anderson, Elijah. (1999). *Code of the streets: Decency, violence and the moral life of the inner city*. New York, NY: W.W. Norton and Company.

Anderson, Kristin and Debra Umberson. (2010). Masculinity and power in men's accounts of domestic violence. In P. Cromwell (Ed.), *In their own words: Criminals on crime*. 5th ed (pp. 168–186). New York, NY: Oxford University Press.

Anderson, Michelle. (2005). All-American rape. *St. John's Law Review, 79*, 625–633.

Bergen, Raquel. (1998). *Issues in intimate violence*. Thousand Oaks, CA: Sage.

Black, Michele, Kathleen Basile, Matthew Breiding, Sharon Smith, Mikel Walters, Melissa Merrick, Jieru Chen and Mark Stevens (2011). *The national intimate partner and sexual violence survey*. Centers for Disease Control and Prevention. Retrieved from: http://www.cdc.gov/ViolencePrevention/pdf/NISVS_Report2010-a.pdf.

Brezina, Timothy. (1998). Adolescent maltreatment and delinquency: The question of intervening processes. *Journal of Research in Crime and Delinquency, 35*, 71–89.

Brownmiller, Susan. (1975). *Against our will: Men, women and rape*. New York, NY: Simon and Schuster.

Buhi, Eric, Heather Clayton, and Heather Helper Surrency. (2009). Stalking victimization among college women and subsequent help-seeking behaviors. *Journal of American College Health, 57*, 419–425.

C.F.R. (2008). Code of Federal Regulations. 28 C.F.R. Section 0.85.

Catalano, Shannan. (2007). *Intimate partner violence in the United States*. Bureau of Justice Statistics. Retrieved from: http://bjs.gov/content/pub/pdf/ipvus.pdf.

Cohen, Thomas and Tracey Kyckelhahn. (2010). *Felony defendants in large urban counties, 2006*. Bureau of Justice Statistics. Retrieved from: http://bjs.gov/content/pub/pdf/fdluc06.pdf.

Conklin, John. (1972). *Robbery and the criminal justice system*. Philadelphia, PA: J.B. Lippincott Company.

Crowell, Nancy and Ann Burgess. (1996). *Understanding violence against women*. Washington, D.C.: National Academy Press.

DeKeseredy, Walter and Martin Schwartz. (1998). *Woman abuse on campus: Results from the Canadian national survey*. Thousand Oaks, CA: Sage.

Dishman, Chris. (2001). Terrorism, crime, and transformation. *Studies in Conflict & Terrorism, 24*, 43–58.

DOJ. (2012). Attorney General Eric Holder announces revisions to the Uniform Crime Report's definition of rape. U.S. Department of Justice. Retrieved from: http://www.justice.gov/opa/pr/2012/January/12-ag-018.html.

Fagan, Jeffrey. (1996). *The criminalization of domestic violence: Promises and limits*. Washington, D.C.: U.S. Department of Justice.

FBI. (2005). Serial murder. Retrieved from: http://www.fbi.gov/stats-services/publications/serial-murder.

FBI UCR. (2010). FBI UCR data tool. Retrieved from: http://www.ucrdatatool.gov/Search/Crime/State/TrendsInOneVar.cfm.

FBI UCR. (2011). Crime in the United States 2011: Violent crime. Retrieved from: http://www.fbi.gov/about-us/cjis/ucr/crime-in-the-u.s/2011/crime-in-the-u.s.-2011/violent-crime/violent-crime.

FBI UCR. (2011a). Crime in the United States 2011: Murder. Retrieved from: http://www.fbi.gov/about-us/cjis/ucr/crime-in-the-u.s/2011/crime-in-the-u.s.-2011/violent-crime/murder.

FBI UCR. (2011b). Crime in the United States 2011: Persons arrested. Retrieved from: http://www.fbi.gov/about-us/cjis/ucr/crime-in-the-u.s/2011/crime-in-the-u.s.-2011/persons-arrested/persons-arrested.

FBI UCR. (2011c). Crime in the United States 2011: Rape. Retrieved from: http://www.fbi.gov/about-us/cjis/ucr/crime-in-the-u.s/2011/crime-in-the-u.s.-2011/violent-crime/forcible-rape.

FBI UCR. (2011d). Crime in the United States 2011: Robbery. Retrieved from: http://www.fbi.gov/about-us/cjis/ucr/crime-in-the-u.s/2011/crime-in-the-u.s.-2011/violent-crime/robbery.

FBI UCR. (2011e). Crime in the United States 2011: Aggravated assault. Retrieved from: http://www.fbi.gov/about-us/cjis/ucr/crime-in-the-u.s/2011/crime-in-the-u.s.-2011/violent-crime/aggravated-assault.

FBI UCR. (2011f). Offense definitions. Retrieved from: http://www.fbi.gov/about-us/cjis/ucr/crime-in-the-u.s/2011/crime-in-the-u.s.-2011/offense-definitions.

Felson, Marcus and Alison Cares. (2005). Gender and the seriousness of assaults on intimate partners and other victims. *Journal of Marriage and Family, 67,* 1182–1195.

Fisher, Bonnie, Francis Cullen and Michael Turner. (2002). Being pursued: Stalking victimization in a national study of college women. *Criminology & Public Policy, 1,* 257–308.

Gelles, Richard. (1974). *The violent home: A study of physical aggression between husbands and wives.* Beverly Hills, CA: Sage Publications.

Gelsthorpe, Loraine. (2012). Violence against women: Repairing harm through kith and kin. In D. Harper, L. Voigt and W. Thornton (Eds.), *Violence: Do we know it when we see it?* (pp. 387–406). Durham, NC: Carolina Academic Press.

Glaberson, William. (1992). Assault case renews debate on rape shield law. *The New York Times,* November 2. Retrieved from: http://www.nytimes.com/1992/11/02/nyregion/assault-case-renews-debate-on-rape-shield-law.html?pagewanted=all&src=pm.

Goldstein, Herman. (1990). *Problem-oriented policing.* New York, NY: McGraw-Hill.

Gottfredson, Michael and Travis Hirschi (1990). *A general theory of crime.* Stanford, CA: Stanford University Press.

Groth, Nicholas and Jean Birnbaum. (1979). *Men who rape: The psychology of the offender.* New York, NY: Plenum Press.

GTD. (2013). *Global terrorism database.* Retrieved from: http://www.start.umd.edu/gtd/.

Harper, Dee Wood and Lydia Voigt (2012). Intimate partner homicide followed by suicide: A case of gendered violence. In D.W. Harper, L. Voigt and W. Thornton (Eds.), *Violence: Do we know it when we see it?* (pp. 45–88). Durham, NC: Carolina Academic Press.

Hirschi, Travis. (1969). *The causes of delinquency.* Berkeley, CA: University of California Press.

Hoffman, Bruce. (2006). *Inside terrorism.* New York, NY: Columbia University Press.

Holmes, Ronald and James DeBurger. (1998). Profiles in terror: The serial murder. In R. Holmes and A. Holmes (Eds.), *Contemporary perspectives on serial murder* (pp. 1–16). Thousand Oaks, CA: Sage.

Hughes, Stephanie. (2013). When the law won't call it rape. *Salon.com*, January 26. Retrieved from: http://www.salon.com/2013/01/26/when_the_law_wont_call_it_rape/.

Labriola, Melissa, Sarah Bardley, Chris O'Sullivan, Michael Rempel and Samantha Moore. (2010). *A national portrait of domestic violence courts.* Center for Court Innovation. Retrieved from: https://www.ncjrs.gov/pdffiles1/nij/grants/229659.pdf.

Liem, Marieke, Catherine Barber, Nora Markwalder, Martin Killias and Paul Nieuwbeerta (2011). Homicide-suicide and other violent deaths: An international comparison. *Forensic Science International, 207,* 70–76.

Lisak, David and Paul Miller (2002). Repeat rape and multiple offending among undetected rapists. *Violence and Victims, 17,* 73–84.

LSA RS. Louisiana Revised Statutes. RS 14:29 Homicide, RS 14:30 First degree murder, RS 14:30.1 Second degree murder, RS 14:31 Manslaughter, RS 14:32.1 Vehicular homicide. Retrieved from: http://www.legis.state.la.us/lss/lss.asp?folder=88.

LSA RS. Louisiana Revised Statutes. RS 14:32.5 Feticide, RS 14:32.6 First degree feticide, RS 14:32.7 Second degree feticide, RS 14:32.8 Third degree feticide, RS 14:32.9 Criminal abortion, RS 14:32.9.1 Aggravated criminal abortion by dismemberment, RS 14:32.10 Partial birth abortion, RS 14:32.11 Partial birth abortion, RS 14:32.12 Suicide. Retrieved from: http://www.legis.state.la.us/lss/lss.asp?folder=88

McElroy, Wendy. (N.d.). The new mythology of rape. Retrieved from: http://www.wendymcelroy.com/rape.htm.

Merrill, Gregory. (1998). Understanding domestic violence among gay and bisexual men. In R. Bergen (Ed.), *Issues in intimate violence* (pp. 129–141). Thousand Oaks, CA: Sage.

Miller, Laurence. (2006). The terrorist mind I: A psychological and political analysis. *International Journal of Offender Therapy and Comparative Criminology, 50,* 121–138.

Mohandie, Kris, J. Reid Meloy, Mila McGowan and Jenn Williams, (2006). The RECON typology of stalking: Reliability and validity based upon a large sample of North American stalkers. *Journal of Forensic Science, 51,* 147–155.

Planty, Michael, Lynn Langton, Christopher Krebs, Marcus Berzofsky and Hope Smiley-McDonald. (2013). *Female victims of sexual violence, 1994–2010.* Bureau of Justice Statistics. Retrieved from: http://bjs.gov/content/pub/pdf/fvsv9410.pdf.

Sherman, Lawrence. (1992). Attacking crime: Police and crime control. In M. Tonry and N Morris (Eds.), *Modern policing: Crime and Justice, Vol. 15* (pp. 159–230). Chicago, IL: University of Chicago Press.

Telegraph. (2012). A history of mass shootings in the US since Columbine. *The Telegraph,* August 24. Retrieved from: http://www.telegraph.co.uk/news/worldnews/northamerica/usa/9414540/A-history-of-mass-shootings-in-the-US-since-Columbine.html.

Thornhill, Randy and Craig Palmer. (2000). *A natural history of rape: Biological bases of sexual coercion.* Cambridge, MA: MIT Press.

Thornton, William, Lydia Voigt and Dee Wood Harper. (2013). *Why violence?* Durham, NC: Carolina Academic Press.

Truman, Jennifer and Michael Planty. (2012). *Criminal victimization, 2011.* Bureau of Justice Statistics. Retrieved from: http://www.bjs.gov/content/pub/pdf/cv11.pdf.

UK. (2011). *What is the impact of mandatory arrest laws on intimate partner violence victims and offenders?* Top Ten Series. Retrieved from: http://www.uky.edu/CRVAW/files/TopTen/05_Mandatory_Arrest.pdf.

UNODC. (2009). *UNODC global report on trafficking in persons.* United Nations Office on Drugs and Crime. Retrieved from: http://www.unodc.org/documents/Global_Report_on_TIP.pdf.

Verma, Arvind. (2012). Managing the aftermath of the Mumbai terrorist attacks. In D.W. Harper and K. Frailing (Eds.), *Crime and criminal justice in disaster.* 2nd ed. (pp. 263–284). Durham, NC: Carolina Academic Press.

Vossekuil, Brian, Robert Fein, Marisa Reddy, Randy Borum and William Modzeleski. (2002). *The final report and findings of the Safe School Initiative: Implications for the prevention of school attacks in the United States.* U.S. Secret Service and U.S. Department of Education. Retrieved from: http://www.secretservice.gov/ntac/ssi_final_report.pdf.

Waldrop, Angela and Patricia Resick. (2004). Coping among adult female victims of domestic violence. *Journal of Family Violence, 19,* 291–302.

Walsh, Anthony. (2005). African Americans and serial killing in the media: The myth and the reality. *Homicide Studies, 9,* 271–291.

Walsh, Anthony and Lee Ellis. (2007). *Criminology: An interdisciplinary approach.* Thousand Oaks, CA: Sage.

Walsh, Anthony and Craig Hemmens. (2011). *Introduction to criminology: A text/reader.* 2nd ed. Los Angeles, CA: Sage.

WHO. (2002). *World report on violence and health: Summary.* World Health Organization. Retrieved from: http://www.who.int/violence_injury_prevention/violence/world_report/en/summary_en.pdf.

Widom, Cathy. (1992). *The cycle of violence.* NIJ Research in Brief. October 1–6.

Williams, Mary Elizabeth. (2013). Why do rape laws still protect spouses? *Salon.com,* January 30. Retrieved from: http://www.salon.com/2013/01/30/why_do_rape_laws_still_protect_spouses/.

Wolfgang, Marvin and Ferracuti, Franco. (1967). *The subculture of violence: Towards an integrated theory in criminology.* London, England: Tavistock Publications.

Wright, Richard and Scott Decker. (2010). Creating the illusion of impending death: Armed robbers in action. In P. Cromwell (Ed.), *In their own words: Criminals on crime.* 5th ed. (pp. 158–167). New York, NY: Oxford University Press.

Chapter 12

Property Crime

Introduction

When we talk about property crime, we are talking primarily about the theft or destruction of property. This chapter begins with a brief discussion of the history of property crime and continues with an explanation of the wide variety of thefts, which include shoplifting, pocket picking and purse snatching, forgery, fraud, embezzlement and looting,[1] an explanation of burglary and related crimes, including fencing, an explanation of motor vehicle theft, an explanation of crimes that cause property damage, including arson and vandalism and an explanation of confidence games. The notion of professional criminals is woven into these explanations where relevant. The chapter concludes with an analysis of how the different theories of crime covered in this book are able to explain the different types of property crime.

A Brief History of Property Crime

The concept of property crime, especially theft, is nothing new. In fact, both the Code of Hammurabi from about 1772 B.C. and the Roman Law of the Twelve Tables from 449 B.C. contain laws against theft. These laws designate certain types of theft as more serious than others, with the Code of Hammurabi determining that theft from the church and from the state was worse than theft from ordinary citizens, and the Roman Law of the Twelve Tables determining that theft which occurred at night was

---

1. According to the FBI UCR (2011, 2011a), Part I property crimes are divided into larceny-theft, burglary, motor vehicle theft and arson. Larceny-theft includes offenses such as shoplifting, pocket picking and purse snatching, theft of bicycles, theft from (importantly, not of) motor vehicles and the taking of anything without the use of force or violence. Forgery, fraud and looting are excluded from this definition, but forgery, fraud and embezzlement are included among the UCR's Part II (i.e., less serious) property crimes (FBI UCR, 2004).

more serious than that which occurred during the day (Kauzlarich and Barlow, 2009). Of course, these laws against theft were in place long before what is probably the most famous prohibition against theft from the Christian Bible, thou shalt not steal.

Our modern day concept of what constitutes theft has its roots in English common law. The notion of possession rather than ownership was of the utmost importance in early England. Theft was predicated on unlawful possession of an item. To be considered theft, a thief had to be shown to be in unlawful possession of an item by the person who claimed to lawfully possess the item and who could prove that claim. Another important notion in English common law was trespass, which was conceived of as putting one's hands on another's property. Trespass is important to the concept of theft because it provides the first step in theft, i.e., putting hands on property. Theft[2] occurs when there is intent to steal and in this now-antiquated conception, there can be no theft without trespass (Turner, 1966; Kauzlarich and Barlow, 2009).[3] English common law was also concerned with what could be stolen and those things that could be most easily stolen were moveable goods. Certainly this includes goods that can be picked up and carried away without much effort, but it also includes farm animals. These animals were very valuable property and also served as currency in some instances, so their theft was a very serious matter. Interestingly, the monetary value of the goods stolen mattered little in English common law and still matters relatively little today, at least in determining whether an action is a theft or not. Stealing $30 headphones and stealing a $500 computer tablet are both acts of theft. Where the value of the goods matters is in the punishment meted out. Distinctions between less serious and more serious thefts have been observed for centuries and are present in our modern day laws, where petty and grand thefts carry different punishments (Kauzlarich and Barlow, 2009).

As discussed in Chapter 1, laws constantly undergo revision and restatement and laws surrounding theft are no exception. A very important development in theft law is the Carrier's Case from England in the 1400s. In this case, a man was tasked with transporting several bales of merchandise to the city of Southampton. Instead of transporting them, though, he forced open the bales and took what was inside. Of course, since the man was in lawful possession of the bales and the merchandise they contained at the time, he had not violated the law as it was written and applied then. Nevertheless, the case went before a panel of judges who concluded that the man had committed serious theft and with this decision, those judges extended the law to protect the property of merchants when it was not in their possession and introduced an element of ownership into the concept of the crime of theft (Kauzlarich and Barlow, 2009).

---

2. The legal term for theft is larceny and as seen above, the FBI uses the term larceny-theft to categorize certain property crimes.

3. Astute readers may be thinking back to the discussion of cybercrime in Chapter 9 and asking themselves if it is still necessary to physically put hands on another's property (i.e., trespass) in order to steal that property. Trespassing is not a necessary element of cybercrime.

**Figure 12.1. Property and violent crime rates in the
United States per 100K, 1960–2011**

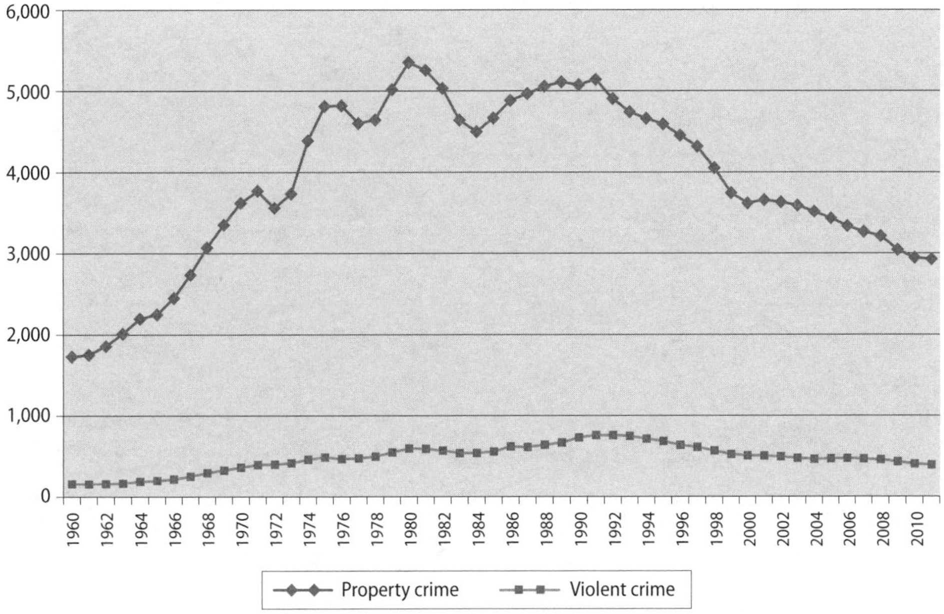

Source: FBI UCR, 2010, 2011, 2011c.

The Wide Variety of Theft

Figure 12.1 provides a graphic view of trends in property and violent crime in the United States from 1960 through 2011. It is clear from just a quick glance at the figure that property crime is much more common than violent crime. It is also true that property crime, which is defined by the FBI as including larceny-theft, burglary, motor vehicle theft and arson (FBI UCR, 2011), increased rather dramatically between 1960 and 1980 but by the early 1990s, was on a decline that continued for 20 years. These crime trends reflect the overall crime trends in the United States during this time.

Figure 12.2 shows the rates per 100,000 people of the four main categories of property crime in the UCR.

There were 9,063,173 property crimes in the United States in 2011 for a rate of 2,908.7 per 100,000 people (FBI UCR, 2011). Larceny-theft makes up the greatest number of property crimes, followed by burglaries and motor vehicle thefts in that order. Larceny-theft is defined by the FBI as "the unlawful taking, carrying, leading, or riding away of property from the possession or constructive possession of another" (FBI UCR, 2011a) and as noted above, examples of this crime include theft of bicycles, theft from motor vehicles, shoplifting, pocket picking and purse snatching. Larceny-theft made up 68 percent of all property crime in the United States in 2011. The average value of the property taken in larceny-theft was $987 in 2011, meaning that the loss to victims for all larceny-theft was more than $6 billion for that year alone (FBI UCR, 2011a).

Figure 12.2. Larceny-theft, burglary, motor vehicle theft and
arson rates in the United States per 100K, 1960–2011

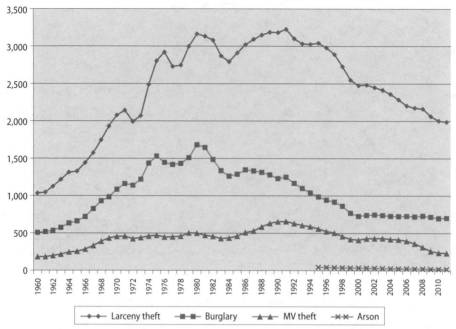

* Arson data only available from 1995–2011.   Source: FBI UCR, 2010, 2011, 2012.

Figure 12.3. Percent of different larceny-theft in the United States, 2011

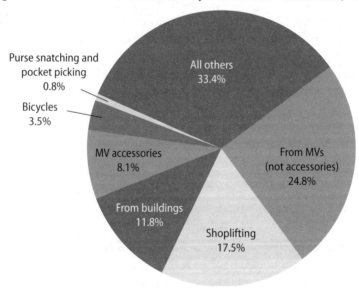

Source: FBI UCR, 2011a.

Figure 12.3 shows the percent of the different types of larceny-theft in the United States in 2011.

In 2011, there were over six million larceny-thefts reported to the police for a rate of 1,976.9 per 100,000 people. There were fewer than a million people, 981,116 to be exact, arrested in the United States for this crime in 2011. Fifty seven percent of those arrested were male and 43 percent were female. Sixty nine percent of those arrested were white and 29 percent were African American. Twenty percent of those arrested for larceny-theft in 2011 were under the age of 18 (FBI UCR, 2011a, 2011b). Figure 12.4 reveals that arrests for larceny-theft peak at age 18, after which time they start to drop.

Figure 12.4. Number of arrests for larceny-theft by age in the United States, 2011

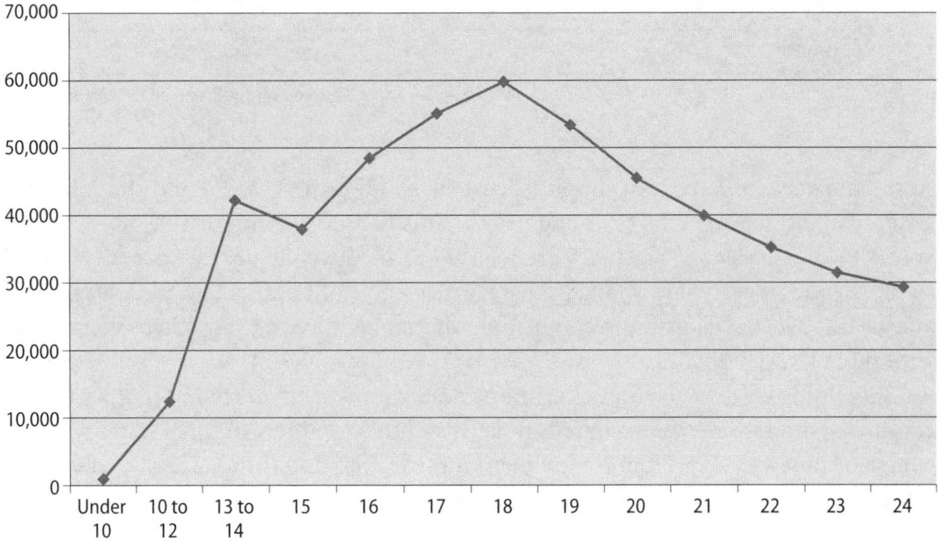

Source: FBI UCR, 2011b.

Types of UCR Larceny-Theft: Shoplifting

Shoplifting is defined as "the theft by a person (other than an employee) of goods or merchandise exposed for sale" (FBI UCR, 2004, p. 32). Shoplifting, or the five finger discount, has been of great interest to researchers in part because of its prevalence. More than $13 billion worth of goods are shoplifted each year, translating to more than $35 million per day. One in 11 people in the United States are shoplifters for a total of about 27 million. More than 10 million people were caught shoplifting over a recent five-year period (NASP, 2006).

Shoplifters come in all ages, races and genders and from all socioeconomic, educational and employment backgrounds. Though it was once thought that women shoplifted much more than men, empirical evidence reveals that men and women shoplift in about equal numbers and that men tend to shoplift more items per trip to the store than do women (Buckle and Farrington, 1984; Klemke, 1992; NASP, 2006).

Table 12.1. Shoplifters' motivations

Motivation	Percent of shoplifters reporting as primary
Wanted the item but did not want to pay for it	25.6
Peer pressure	15.3
Making a living by stealing	14.4
Wanted the item but unable to pay for it	12.8
Impulsive action	11.6
Intoxication at the time	5.3
Thrill, rush, excitement or danger of stealing	4.7
Coping with stress	4.1
Compulsion	3.1

Source: Adapted from Cromwell, Parker and Mobley, 2010.

Approximately 25 percent of shoplifters are juveniles (NASP, 2006) and shoplifting is a very common crime among young people. It is the most common reason for which young people under the age of 15 are referred to the juvenile justice system (Nimick, 1990). Nearly 90 percent of young people say they know other young people who shoplift and nearly two-thirds of the young people that know juvenile shoplifters spend time with them (NASP, 2006).

Shoplifting is far from always a crime of need. Cromwell, Parker and Mobley (2010) conducted interviews with hundreds of active adult shoplifters in three states over the course of nine years and found nine main motives for shoplifting. These motivations are summarized in Table 12.1.

In their interviews with active shoplifters, Cromwell, Parker and Mobley (2010) provide comments from the shoplifters themselves that illustrate these motivations. On wanting an item but not wanting to pay for it:

> "I did it because I didn't want to pay for anything. I've got better things to do with my money." and "I've got better things to spend my money on. Some things you can't lift ... everything that I can lift, I do" (p. 96).

On peer pressure:

> "My mom is a shoplifter. Both my sisters do it. I got it from them." and "These girls [in seventh grade] had a sorority and to get in you had to shoplift something" (p. 97).

Those who shoplift for a living are small in number. Only about three percent of shoplifters make their living from stealing, but they are responsible for 10 percent of the monetary losses (NASP, 2006). Those who shoplift for a living are commonly drug addicted and in need of money to support their habits. They tend to prefer shoplifting to other criminal activity because they perceive it as less dangerous in terms of both potential confrontations with a victim and criminal justice penalties. Some of Cromwell, Parker and Mobley's (2010) interview subjects put it thusly:

> I gotta have $200 every day—day in and day out. I gotta boost [shoplift] a $1,000, $1,500 worth to get it. I just do what I gotta do.... Do I feel bad about what I do? Not really. If I wasn't boosting, I'd be robbing people and maybe somebody would get hurt or killed." and "Taking stuff from stores is a lot easier than robbing people or burglary. Nobody ever shoots boosters. Even if I get caught, nothing much gonna happen. Probation—a few days in county. It's like my job (p. 98).

Wanting the item but not being able to pay for it was a much more common motivation for shoplifting among women than among men. In the words of some shoplifters:

> "I want nice things for my family but I can't afford to buy them." and "I stole a wallet from Sears for my boyfriend. I didn't have the money so I took it" (p. 99).

Though not commonly reported as the primary motivation by many active shoplifters, impulse was commonly reported as a motivation for the first shoplifting experience. In the words of some shoplifters:

> "It was a watch and I just wanted that watch then." and "I didn't really plan on it. It just kinda happened." and "I liked this shirt and on the spur of the moment I stuffed it in my purse" (pp. 99–100).

In most cases of shoplifting under the influence, interview subjects stole small items, including beer, cigarettes and candy:

> "We were sitting around drinking. My roommate bet me I couldn't go across the street and steal a pack of cigarettes." and "I picked up a pack of cigarettes and put them into my pocket. I forgot I had them there. I'd been drinking most of the afternoon" (p. 100).

On enjoyment of the thrill, rush, excitement or danger of shoplifting, interview subjects put it thusly:

> "I do it for the rush. Adrenaline rush, you know. You get all excited and you feel kinda crazy inside. I can't explain it. It's adrenaline." and "It's fun when you get away with it. It's scary in the store. Heart pumping—adrenaline pumping. It's exciting. Addicting" (pp. 100–101).

On compulsion:

> "I'm a kleptomaniac. I steal anything I can get in my purse. The other day I stole a key chain—can you believe it? Took a chance on going to jail with a stupid key chain." and "I tell myself I'm not going to do it again and then I see something I want and I lift it. I already have it in my purse before I think about it. It's like, you know, automatic pilot. I'm addicted—that's all I know" (p. 101).

Finally, on the effects of stress:

> "I was working long hours and not getting along with my wife and we had a lot of bills and some sickness. I don't know what happened to me. Next thing

I know I'm stealing things." and "I get depressed. Things start to pile up and I start shoplifting. Sometimes it's at finals or when I have a fight with my boyfriend. One time when I thought I was pregnant" (pp. 101–102).

Two of the motivations explored by Cromwell, Parker and Mobley (2010) deserve further explanation. The first of these is stealing for a living. As alluded to above, some people do make their living shoplifting. Professional shoplifters are called boosters, while amateur shoplifters are called snitches (Cameron, 1964); snitch is a term that has come to include other retail crimes as well, including gift card and receipt fraud and ticket switching (Finklea, 2010). Boosters are careful in their consideration of merchandise that they will steal. They typically take items that they are sure they can sell for a profit and they plan their stealing in advance, bringing containers that will help them conceal what they shoplift, carrying knives or razor blades to open packaging while in the store or wearing clothes that will allow them to hide stolen goods. Some boosters employ what is called a crotch walk, where they walk out of the store with items in between their legs.[4] Many boosters work in pairs or groups in which one member distracts store personnel and the other or others shoplifts the desired goods (Finklea, 2010). On the continuum of professional thieves, boosters fall on the low end because their activities are viewed as requiring less talent or skill than other types of theft (King, 1972; Adams, 1976).

The second of these motivations is the thrill, risk or danger of shoplifting. The person most famously associated with bringing attention to the notion of the thrill of shoplifting and other sneaky crimes such as vandalism and joyriding is Jack Katz. Katz (1988) gathered data on the shoplifting activities of college students and determined that what he called the sneaky thrill of shoplifting has three components. The first of these components is the sensual attraction to a specific object in the store. Katz's (1988) respondents often reported certain items in stores calling out to them to be taken. This notion is very much in accord with NASP (2006) research that reveals shoplifting is rarely a premeditated crime, especially for snitches. The second component is a return to reason, in which the shoplifter recognizes the importance of appearing to be and behaving as a normal shopper. Katz's (1998) respondents reported that they walked at the same pace as other shoppers, tried to spend the right amount of time in the store and busied themselves by looking at items they had no intention of taking, all in the interest of not attracting attention. The third component is the experience of euphoria upon getting away with shoplifting. Katz's (1988) respondents reported feeling invincible upon making a clean getaway and were able to re-experience the euphoria when remembering the crime or describing it to others. Taken together and especially considered

---

4. For a rather humorous depiction of shoplifting, including the crotch walk, see the video for the 1990 Jane's Addiction song Been Caught Stealing. Another humorous depiction of shoplifting with a particular focus on the influence of peer pressure can be seen in the episode of The Simpsons entitled Marge Be Not Proud, which originally aired in 1995.

5. The research on shoplifting discussed to this point relies on responses from shoplifters to investigators' questions. For research on shoplifting that involves observation of potential shoplifters in action, see Baumer and Rosenbaum (1982).

in conjunction with those from Cromwell, Parker and Mobley (2010), Katz's (1988) findings indicate that shoplifting is a more complicated crime than it might appear on the surface. It is rarely done strictly out of need and some of the many motivations for shoplifting contain a strong emotional component.[5]

What can be done to prevent shoplifting? It may be more effective to target the environmental features of stores and their goods rather than offenders' motivations because, as we have seen, there are so many motives to shoplift. Perhaps unsurprisingly, Ronald Clarke (2002), who we read about in Chapter 9, has weighed in on this question and his answers will come as little surprise to those who remember choice and opportunity theories of crime in detail. Clarke (2002) lists some of the highest risk items for shoplifting, among them small automobile parts and accessories, CDs, DVDs, video games, designer clothing, tools, shoes, jewelry and small toys. He notes that all these items have essential features that make them ripe for shoplifting. They are concealable, removable, available, valuable, enjoyable and disposable; these essential features can be remembered with the handy acronym CRAVED. Stores that carry CRAVED items are going to be at risk for shoplifting.

Clarke (2002) proposes four broad categories of changes that can be made to prevent shoplifting. The first of these categories is retail practices and changes here involve improving the store layout to facilitate surveillance of shoppers, upgrading security of items themselves, such as by locking some in cases, and posting warnings to potential shoplifters, especially on high value items. The second category is staffing and changes here involve better training for store staff about shoplifting, as well as hiring store detectives or other security. Having well trained employees is particularly effective in preventing shoplifting (Lindblom and Kajalo, 2011). The third category proposed by Clarke (2002) is shoplifting policies and changes here include instituting civil recovery programs that allow the store to recover losses due to theft directly from the shoplifters themselves, using informal police sanctions rather than just store sanctions because the former may be perceived by shoplifters as more serious, establishing early warning systems in which stores notify each other of shoplifting activity in the area, banning known shoplifters and instituting a public information campaign on the personal and social harms of shoplifting. The final category is technology and changes here include the installation of closed circuit television (CCTV) cameras, the application of electronic monitoring devices to items themselves and the use of ink tags, particularly with clothing. Electronic tags in particular appear to be an effective way to prevent shoplifting (Lindblom and Kajalo, 2011).

Types of UCR Larceny-Theft: Pocket Picking and Purse Snatching

Pocket picking and purse snatching accounted for nearly 50,000 of the over 6 million larceny-theft crimes reported to the police in the United States in 2011 (FBI UCR, 2011a). Pocket picking is defined as "the theft of articles from a person by stealth where the victim usually does not become immediately aware of the theft" (FBI UCR, 2004, p. 32). The greatest amount of scholarly attention has been devoted to professional pickpockets, who are also known as cannons, picks or dips. Professional pickpockets need to possess a great deal of dexterity to ply their trade, as it involves taking wallets or other valuables off the persons of unsuspecting victims. They also need to have a well-honed ability to determine who would make a good victim. Some professional pickpockets work in pairs or small groups in which one member distracts the potential victim by bumping into him or her and another member takes advantage of the victim's distraction by picking his or her pocket, at which time the stolen item or items may be handed off to a third member of the group (Inciardi, 1977, 1983, 1984).

A crime related to pocket picking but one that requires less skill is purse snatching. Purse snatching is defined as "the grabbing or snatching of a purse, handbag, etc., from the custody of an individual" (FBI UCR, 2004, p. 32). Purse snatchers may attempt to cut the straps of a purse or bag that someone is carrying in order to steal it. The person who engages in this variety of purse snatching is known as a cutpurse. When the potential victim resists the theft and the offender resorts to force, such as pushing, shoving or hitting, that offender has become a robber in the eyes of the law. Some purse snatchers attempt to avoid confrontation with a victim and confine their theft to what appear to be unattended purses and bags in public places; this variety of purse snatcher is known as a moll buzzer (Hagan, 2013).

Though there are many fewer professional pickpockets and purse snatchers than there were before World War II, they do still exist and any place in which crowds gather is ripe territory for both pocket picking and purse snatching. Crowds may gather for occasional events, such as a concert or sporting event; they may also gather more routinely at tourist destinations. Pocket pickers and to a lesser extent purse snatchers are always on the lookout for suitable victims at these crowded places. In fact, a habit that can betray the identity of a professional pickpocket or purse snatcher is watching people in the crowd instead of the event or attraction itself (Hagan, 2013). As seen in Chapter 9, people can help prevent their own victimization by pickpockets and purse snatchers by minimizing the amount of money and number of valuables they carry with them and by remaining alert and aware of their surroundings.

Not Part I UCR Property Crimes, but Theft Just the Same: Forgery, Fraud, Embezzlement and Looting

Forgery, fraud and embezzlement and looting are property crimes but are not included in the UCR's list of Part I offenses. Rather, the first three are Part II offenses (FBI UCR, 2004), meaning they are typically less serious than the Part I property crimes detailed throughout this chapter.[6]

The crime of forgery is coupled with counterfeiting in the UCR. Forgery and counterfeiting are defined as "the altering, copying, or imitating of something, without authority or right, with the intent to deceive or defraud by passing the copy or thing altered or imitated as that which is original or genuine; or the selling, buying, or possession of an altered, copied, or imitated thing with the intent to deceive or defraud" (FBI UCR, 2011d). In 2011, 53,983 people were arrested for forgery and counterfeiting. Sixty two

---

6. The FBI only collects arrest data on Part II offenses.

percent of those arrested for forgery and counterfeiting were male and 38 percent were female. Sixty six percent of those arrested for forgery and counterfeiting were white and 33 percent were African American. Those over 18 were arrested for forgery and counterfeiting more often than those 18 and younger and those between 20 and 29 were arrested for this crime more often than any other age group (FBI UCR, 2011b). Remember back to Chapter 7 and our discussion of crime as peaking in the teen years, then dropping off in early adulthood. Arrest data for crimes such as forgery and counterfeiting remind us that crime is usually but not always a youthful phenomenon.

A variety of documents may be forged, but perhaps the one most commonly thought of is the check. Edwin Lemert (1953), whose name we remember from Chapter 5 and the discussion of labeling theory, proposed a typology of check forgers. He called amateur check forgers naïve check forgers. Naïve check forgers make up the majority of check forgers and they write bad checks, which are checks that have no funds behind them, in order to cover all manner of debts, including those that result from gambling and drug addiction. For naïve check forgers, writing bad checks is a crime of last resort. In contrast to naïve check forgers are systematic check forgers (Lemert, 1958), who are otherwise known as paper hangers. Paper hangers make a living out of forging checks.[7]

Counterfeiting is a unique kind of forgery that involves creating or altering currency. Counterfeiters no longer need engravers' plates to make fake money; the proliferation of more sophisticated copy machines and related technology may have facilitated some recent notable attempts at large scale counterfeiting. In the early 1990s, fake $100 bills so authentic that they could fool equipment at the Federal Reserve began appearing around the world. An unfriendly government or terrorist organization is thought to be responsible for this attempt to destabilize the economy of the United States (Wartzman, 1992).[8] The U.S. Treasury has recently changed the design of paper currency in an effort to prevent counterfeiting and included more security features in each denomination of money. Three dimensional security ribbons in the center and a picture of the Liberty Bell inside the picture of the inkwell on $100 bills are examples of these new security features (U.S. Treasury, 2013).

Fraud is defined as "the intentional perversion of the truth for the purpose of inducing another person or other entity in reliance upon it to part with something of value or to surrender a legal right" (FBI UCR, 2011d). In 2011, 168, 217 people were arrested for fraud. Fifty nine percent of those arrested for fraud were male and 41 percent were female. Sixty seven percent of those arrested for fraud were white and 32 percent were African American. Those over 18 were arrested for fraud more often than those 18 and younger and those between 20 and 29 were arrested for this crime more often than any other age group (FBI UCR, 2011b). Just like with forgery and counterfeiting, arrest data for fraud remind us that crime is usually but not always a youthful phenomenon.

---

7. One of the most famous cinematic depictions of a paper hanger is seen in the 2002 movie *Catch Me If You Can*, which told the story of systematic check forger Frank Abagnale.

8. For a fascinating depiction of Nazi attempts to bring down the government of Great Britain by flooding the country with counterfeit money, see the 2007 movie *The Counterfeiters*.

There are a wide variety of frauds, including but not limited to insurance fraud, benefit fraud, personal fraud and contractor fraud; fraud also includes the confidence game. Insurance fraud involves filing false claims for exaggerated or nonexistent losses to insurance companies. Fraud against the travel, automotive, home or renter's, fire and flood insurance agencies is estimated to occur in one to five percent of claims. However, insurers have been reluctant in the past to investigate claims because insurers deal in a service business. They sell a protection that may never be claimed, so there is an incentive to act in good faith in the recruitment and retention of customers (Clarke, 1989). Another reason insurance fraud is thought to be so prevalent, especially in the United States where 10 percent of insurance claims are estimated to be fraudulent, is passing cases from adjuster to adjuster. Keeping cases with the same adjuster from start to finish may improve fraud detection and cut down on the number of fraudulent claims made (Morely, Ball and Omerod, 2006). Negative attitudes about the insurance industry may also promote fraudulent claim making. Insurance companies' efforts to improve their public images may then be useful in reducing fraud (Tennyson, 1997). Benefit fraud involves receiving or attempting to receive government benefits despite having no entitlement to do so. Benefit fraud recently received a great deal of attention in the United Kingdom, where an estimated 10 percent of the 90 billion pound (approximately $135 billion) budget is lost to fraud annually. Legislation was enacted there in an effort to reduce fraudulent claims on social security benefits, but the legislation required that every claim be treated as potentially fraudulent and it may have actually produced an increase in fraud. With the claims process already being quite difficult, what might have been innocent errors on claimants' parts were treated as fraud under the new legislation (McKeever, 1999).[9]

Personal fraud can be thought of as fraud perpetrated by one individual on another, including the promise of goods, services or financial benefits with no intent to deliver. One survey of over 1,000 adults places the personal fraud victimization rate at 15 percent. Interestingly, it was younger and more highly educated people who were more likely to be victims of personal fraud, perhaps because they have a wider range of interests and activities that put then in contact with potential fraudsters (Titus, Heinzelmann and Boyle, 1995). Finally, contractor fraud involves an agreement between two parties in which one pays the other to make repairs to his or her property, but those repairs are never done, are done shabbily or are worth less than the amount paid. Certainly contractor fraud exists during ordinary times, but natural disasters may facilitate the commission of contractor fraud because disasters can serve to disorganize the community and create opportunities for this crime to occur. Davila, Marquart and Mullings (2005) conducted a survey with just over 2,000 residents of two areas in Texas affected by severe flooding in 2001 and 2002. Nearly half reported hiring a contractor and of those who did, 17 reported being victims of contractor fraud. These 17 victims had an average age of 60 and most were white, married, educated females. The elderly are common targets for contractor fraud because they are believed to have cash on hand, they are

---

9. For a detailed discussion of benefit fraud in the context of disaster, see Chapter 9 as well as Harper and Frailing (2012).

vulnerable to sales pressure and they have a desire to help others. It is interesting how different the demographic profiles of personal and contractor fraud victims are.

Among the crimes included in the definition of fraud is the confidence game. Confidence games are so called because they involve winning the confidence of the victim in order to take his or her money. Because confidence games do not have their own distinct category in the UCR, it is difficult to determine how many people are victimized by them and victims may be too embarrassed to go to the police, which makes it nearly impossible to determine the full extent of this crime. There are two types of confidence games, small cons and big cons. Table 12.2 gives the names and details of some small and big cons.

Embezzlement is defined as "the unlawful misappropriation or misapplication by an offender to his/her own use or purpose of money, property, or some other thing of value entrusted to his/her care, custody, or control" (FBI UCR, 2011d). In 2011, 12,496 people were arrested for embezzlement. Fifty percent of those arrested for embezzlement were male and 50 percent were female. Sixty six percent of those arrested for fraud were white and 32 percent were African American. Nearly everyone who was arrested for embezzlement was over 18 and those between 20 and 29 were arrested for this crime more often than any other age group (FBI UCR, 2011b). While we tend to think of crime as an overwhelmingly male phenomenon, arrest data for embezzlement reminds us that is not always the case. We typically think of embezzlement happening in the work environment,[10] but embezzlement can be perpetrated by one individual on another. Consider for example the adult daughter who writes checks from an infirm parent's checkbook without permission to cover her expenses.

The arrest rate for embezzlement is low because this crime is difficult to detect and to prove. Williams (2006) identifies seven conditions that lead to embezzlement. First, a trusting relationship with the employer or beneficiary is necessary. Second, the potential offender must perceive a need. Third, awareness that a way to meet the need lies in the funds with which he/she is entrusted is necessary. Fourth, the potential offender must adjust his or her self-conception. Fifth, the potential offender must devise a plan to conceal his or her embezzlement. Sixth, the potential offender must have the fortitude or the desperation to put the plan into effect. Seventh, the potential offender becomes an actual offender when he or she tests the plan.

Looting is a special kind of property crime not included in the Uniform Crime Reports. The reason it is not included is because it is rare. Only six states have looting statutes (Hamrick, 2006) and by its very definition, the crime of looting is bound to disasters and riots. Consider the looting statute in Louisiana: "Looting is the intentional entry by a person without authorization into any dwelling or other structure belonging to another and used in whole or in part as a home or place of abode by a person, or any structure belonging to another and used in whole or in part as a place of business, or any vehicle, watercraft, building, plant, establishment, or other structure, movable

---

10. Embezzlement as a white collar crime is covered in more detail in Chapter 13.

11. This statute was enacted in 1993 after Hurricane Andrew devastated Florida and revised in 2005 and 2006, just after Hurricane Katrina.

Table 12.2. Some small and big cons

Small Con		Big Con	
Name	Details	Name	Details
Pigeon Drop	A con artist begins a conversation with a victim. A second con artist rushes over, claiming to have found a wallet full of cash. The second con artist makes a fake phone call to the police or an attorney and reports that all three can split the money if they each put up a small good faith deposit. The first con artist leaves with the wallet, the second takes the victim to get his or her deposit. After collecting the deposit from the victim, the second con artist gives the victim a fake time and place to meet and makes off with the money.	Ponzi Scheme	Named for Charles Ponzi, this scheme pays off early investors with the money from later investors. Paying off larger than expected dividends to the earlier investors keeps the later ones coming; Bernie Madoff was convicted of operating the largest Ponzi scheme in history and was sentenced to 150 years in prison in 2009.
Bank Examiner's Scam	A con artist pretends to be a government agent who needs the victim's help in finding a dishonest bank teller. The con artist tells the victim to with-draw a large sum of cash from the teller and give it to the con artist, who takes it, claiming he or she will mark it in order to investigate the bank teller. Victims of the pigeon drop and bank examiner's scam are typically white, unmarried women in their 60s and 70s.	Pyramid Scheme	The con artist approaches the victim with an investment opportunity, promising a large return if the victim recruits a number of other people to invest who then get other people to invest and so on. Usually the scheme breaks down with only the con artist, the person at the top of the pyramid, getting paid. The Friends' Network that was shut down in 1994 is one example.
Badger Game	A young woman pretends to be from a religious group and visits an older man a number of times. On one visit, a second con artists pretending to be the young woman's father bursts in, accusing the older man of having an inappropriate rela-tionship with his daughter. He tells the older man he will forget everything in exchange for the man's life savings.	Religious Cons	Religious cons involve the heads of churches and other religious organizations taking the money that was raised for the church for their personal use. The Praise the Lord (PTL) Ministry scandal of 1987 is one example.

Sources: Friedman, 1992; Kauzlarich and Barlow, 2009.

or immovable, in which normal security of property is not present by virtue of a hurricane, flood, fire, act of God, or force majeure of any kind, or by virtue of a riot, mob, or other human agency, and the obtaining or exerting control over or damaging or removing property of the owner" (LSA RS 14:62.5, 2006).[11] While scholars once believed that looting was common during riots and rare after natural disasters, recent work has demonstrated that post-disaster conditions can be ripe for looting, especially when the socioeconomic conditions of the location hit by the disaster are poor to begin with (Frailing and Harper, 2012). Looting in the wake of disasters, especially Hurricane Katrina, is discussed in more detail in Chapter 9.

Burglary and Related Crimes

Burglary is defined as "the unlawful entry of a structure to commit a felony or a theft" (FBI UCR, 2011e). Burglaries make up the second largest number of property crimes, behind larceny-theft and ahead of both motor vehicle theft and arson. Burglary made up 24 percent of all property crime in the United States in 2011. Three quarters of burglaries were residential and one quarter were commercial. The average value of the property taken or damaged in each burglary was $2,185 in 2011, meaning that the loss to victims for all burglary was nearly $5 billion for that year alone (FBI UCR, 2011e). Figure 12.5 shows the percent of daytime and nighttime residential and commercial burglaries.

In 2011, there were over 2 million burglaries reported to the police for a rate of 703.2 per 100,000 people (FBI UCR, 2011e). However, the NCVS (2011) reports a notably higher total of burglary victimizations for that year, 3,251,810, for a rate of 29.5 per 1,000 households. This discrepancy serves as a reminder that far from all crime is reported to the police and official statistics such as those in the UCR must be taken with a grain of

Figure 12.5. Percent of daytime and nighttime residential and commercial burglaries in the United States, 2011*

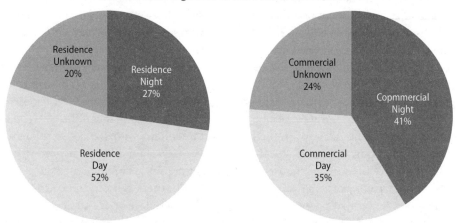

* Recent research by D'Alessio, Eitle and Stolzenberg (2012) found that unemployment was associated with a reduction in daytime residential burglary, ostensibly because of the provision of guardianship.

Source: FBI UCR, 2011.

Figure 12.6. Number of arrests for burglary by age in the United States, 2011

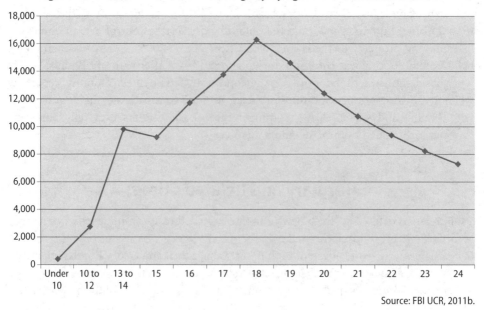

Source: FBI UCR, 2011b.

salt. There were 227, 899 people arrested in the United States for this crime in 2011. Eighty four percent of those arrested were male and 16 percent were female. Sixty seven percent of those arrested were white and 32 percent were African American. Twelve percent of those arrested for burglary in 2011 were under the age of 18 (FBI UCR, 2011b). Figure 12.6 reveals that arrests for burglary peak at age 18, after which time they start to drop.

It is clear from the above information that burglars are typically young males, but what else is known about them? Think back to Chapter 9 and some of the factors that go into burglars' decision making as described by Cromwell and Olson (2010). These factors are centered on the decision to burgle one house rather than another. Mawby (2001) notes that the four most important factors in choosing a burglary target are target exposure (how visible and accessible the home is), guardianship (how well the home is or appears to be protected), target attractiveness (indicators of valuable items in the house) and proximity (the distance between the target and the burglar's residence). All four of these considerations are important to the professional burglar, but guardianship seems to be the most important to the occasional burglar (Mawby, 2001; Wright and Decker, 1994).

Once a decision to burgle a specific house is made, the burglar continues to engage in a decision making calculus. In their in depth interviews with 105 active residential burglars in St. Louis, Missouri, Wright and Decker (1994) found that the first concern of burglars once they are in a house to ensure that no one is home. Some take a quick look in every room, others listen intently and still others call out. Once they have satisfied themselves that no one is home, burglars undertake a brief search of the home for valuables. They recognize that the longer they remain in the house, the greater the chances of apprehension or injury are and they start their search in the master bedroom, believing this is where valuables, cash and guns are likely to be. They search dressers, bedside tables, beds and closets in that order. Some burglars leave the home after finding valuables in the master bedroom, declining to search elsewhere. Others, though, take a cursory look around the rest of the house, especially the kitchen and bathroom, where they are trying to find cash and medication respectively. Few burglars take the time to search children's bedrooms, but some take a look at the living room as they are leaving. Most burglars do not seem to make a habit of taking more than will meet their immediate financial needs, but some burglars do take the time to engage in a leisurely search when they are certain that they can remain in the house undetected for some time. This leisurely search may involve cooking a meal and watching television in addition to burglary. Wright and Decker (1994) point out that while burglars have not been deterred by the threat of sanctions, the threat nevertheless impacts their decision to make a quick search of the home. A more thorough understanding of the ways burglars make decisions once in the house can help limit the losses during burglaries.

It is not uncommon for burglars to work together. Wright and Decker (1994) report that having an accomplice provided the burglars in their study with both practical and psychological advantages. Many burglars who work in groups point to the advantage of having one serve as a look out. Committing burglaries in a group also reduces the time needed to search the house and accomplices may come to the aid of their fellow burglars in the case of a physical attack. Having an accomplice also reduces the perceived level of risk for burglars, who believe that if they are working in a group, at least one can likely get away should the police or homeowners arrive unexpectedly. The lower perception of risk serves to bolster burglars' confidence.[12]

As alluded to above, there are occasional burglars, those who engage in burglary sometimes, and professional burglars, those who rely on burglary as their primary source of income. This is not to imply that once unemployed, people turn to burglary as a profession. On the contrary, some researchers contend that burglary leads to unemployment. Burglary not only provides material gain with little effort and skill; it also provides thrills and it does not require the time commitment that legitimate employment does, freeing up burglars to use their loot to pay for drugs, alcohol, sex and gambling (Rengert and Wasilchick, 2000; Wright and Decker, 1994).

Concern with all four of Mawby's (2001) target selection factors is one of the things that sets apart the professional from the occasional burglar. Another appears to be the honed ability to pick a lock. Professional burglars may be among the first to buy so-called "burglar proof" locks and practice picking them. They may take locksmith courses to aid them in this effort. At the top of the hierarchy of professional burglars are professional safecrackers, who are also referred to as box men. Much like professional burglars who practice on locks before trying to pick them during the course of a burglary, box men work to improve the methods they use to break into increasingly sophisticated safes without damaging the contents (King and Chambliss, 1984).

For both occasional and professional burglars alike, there is the question of what to do with the goods they have stolen. In the interest of converting the goods to cash, some

---

12. For more on the decision making processes of street offenders who work in groups, see Hochstetler (2010).

burglars turn to a fence. A fence is a person who buys and sells stolen property, usually with a legitimate business to cover this illegal activity. Fences deal primarily with professional burglars and are a major asset to these burglars, who do not want to hang on to stolen merchandise for any longer than they need to. Fencing is a Part II property crime in the UCR and in 2011, 71,727 people were arrested for buying, receiving or possessing stolen goods. Eighty percent of those arrested were male and 20 percent were female. Sixty six percent of those arrested for fencing were white and 32 percent were African American. Nearly 15 percent of those arrested for fencing were under the age of 18 (FBI UCR, 2011b). Burglars who do not have a fence may turn to pawn shops to get rid of their stolen (also called hot) merchandise, but because pawn shops ask for identification for transactions, these are not popular outlets. Some burglars prefer to trade their stolen goods for drugs and others sell to friends and family, knowing that others find it hard to resist the low prices they offer (Wright and Decker, 1994; Walsh and Hemmens, 2011).

In the same way as there are professional and occasional burglars, so too are there different types of fences. In their interviews with 30 active burglars, Cromwell and Olson (2010a) were able to develop a typology of fences. This typology extends that developed by Blakely and Goldsmith (1976), who identified the neighborhood, outlet, professional and master fence in ascending order of sophistication. Cromwell and Olson (2010a) identify six types of fences, the first of which is the professional fence. A professional fence buys and sells stolen property as his or her profession. The professional fence may have a legitimate business as a front for his or her fencing operation. The second type is the part-time fence. Part-time fences do not buy as much stolen merchandise or buy it as often as do professional fences. They may purchase stolen goods for personal use or for resale, but they do not derive their entire livelihood from fencing. The third type of fence is professionals who trade their services for stolen property. A number of professionals are in regular contact with burglars, including police officers, defense attorneys or bail bondsmen, and they may exchange their services for stolen property. In the case of defense attorneys and bail bondsmen especially, the only payment their clients may have is stolen goods. Refusal to take it might mean loss of a customer. The fourth type of fence is the neighborhood hustler, who buys and sells stolen property as one of many lower level crimes in which he or she engages. Few if any professional burglars would trust a neighborhood hustler to sell their merchandise. The fifth type of fence is the drug dealer who barters drugs for stolen property. One advantage to the drug dealer here is determining the value of the goods brought to him or her by the burglar. The burglar may bring thousands of dollars of merchandise to the drug dealer, only to leave with a small amount of drugs. The dealer then has more drugs than he or she would have had the burglar come with cash, as well as potentially lucrative stolen goods. The sixth and final type of fence is the amateur. Amateur fences attempt to sell their stolen goods directly to strangers with little success and are viewed with contempt by nearly all thieves.[13]

---

13. Cromwell and Olson (2010a) note that online sales sites such as eBay, Amazon and Craigslist, may have created new, unwitting cyberfences. For more on computer crime, see Chapter 9.

Box 12.1. Did My House Get Robbed While I Was at Work? Disentangling Robbery and Burglary

Are robbery and burglary really that different? In a word, yes. Just look at the definitions. As seen in Chapter 11, robbery is defined as "the taking or attempting to take anything of value from the care, custody, or control of a person or persons by force or threat of force or violence and/or by putting the victim in fear" (FBI UCR, 2011d). And as seen in this chapter, burglary is defined as "the unlawful entry of a structure to commit a felony or a theft" (FBI UCR, 2011d). A key, probably the key, element of burglary is entry into a structure. Of course, entry into a structure is not necessary for robbery to occur and when we think of robbery (or a mugging, a colloquial way to refer to robbery), we probably think of stickups on the street, outside the confines of a structure. Can a robbery take place in a home? Yes it can, if the home is occupied at the time of the entry. In that case, both burglary (entry into a structure to commit a felony or theft) and robbery (taking something of value from the care of another by force, violence or threat thereof) have been committed. Can an unoccupied house be robbed? No, by definition, it cannot. It is a misnomer to say that an unoccupied house was robbed. Instead, it is accurate to say it was burgled.

Motor Vehicle Theft

Motor vehicle theft is defined as "the theft or attempted theft of a motor vehicle. A motor vehicle is self-propelled and runs on land surface and not on rails" (FBI UCR, 2011d). Motor vehicle thefts make up the third largest number of property crimes, behind larceny-theft and burglary and ahead of arson. Motor vehicle theft made up 8 percent of all property crime in the United States in 2011 (FBI UCR, 2011). Nearly three quarters of the motor vehicles stolen in 2011 were automobiles. The average dollar loss per stolen vehicle in 2011 was $6,089, meaning that the loss to victims for all motor vehicle theft was about $4.3 million for that year alone (FBI UCR, 2011f).

Table 12.3. **Motor vehicle theft top ten cities and cars**

City and State	Rank	Make and Model
Fresno, CA	1	1994 Honda Accord
Modesto, CA	2	1998 Honda Civic
Bakersfield, CA	3	2006 Ford Pickup
Spokane, WA	4	1991 Toyota Camry
Yakima, WA	5	2000 Dodge Caravan
San Francisco, CA	6	1994 Acura Integra
Stockton, CA	7	1999 Chevrolet Pickup
Anderson, SC	8	2004 Dodge Pickup
Vallejo, CA	9	2002 Ford Explorer
Visalia, CA	10	1994 Nissan Sentra

Source: NICB, 2011.

The National Insurance Crime Bureau (NICB) keeps track of the cities with the most motor vehicle theft and the makes and models of the cars that are stolen most often. Table 12.3 reveals the top ten cities and top ten makes and models for auto theft in 2011.

There are several commonalities in Table 12.3. First, it is obvious that California tops the list for cities with high rates of motor vehicle theft. Second, many of the cars that are stolen most often are older, with six made before the year 2000. Older cars tend to have fewer security measures, such as smart keys, alarms, kill switches and tracking systems, that are more common among newer cars and this may make them more attractive targets for auto thieves.

In 2011, there were 715,373 motor vehicle thefts reported for a rate of 233.8 per 100,000 people (FBI UCR, 2011f). However, as was the case with burglary, the NCVS (2011) reports a notably higher total of motor vehicle theft victimizations for that year, 1,018,690, for a rate of 9.2 per 1,000 households. There were 51,027 arrests for motor vehicle theft made in the United States in 2011. Eighty two percent of those arrested were male and 18 percent were female. Sixty four percent of those arrested were white and 34 percent were African American. Twenty one percent of those arrested for motor vehicle theft in 2011 were under the age of 18 (FBI UCR, 2011b). Figure 12.7 reveals that arrests for motor vehicle theft peak at ages 17 and 18 and then begin to drop.

Most cars are stolen by juveniles for the purposes of joyriding. A young person or group of young people happen upon a car with the keys in the ignition, hop in and drive around until they run out of gas, at which time they abandon the car. Some juvenile joyriders appear to take pleasure in purposely damaging the car before deserting

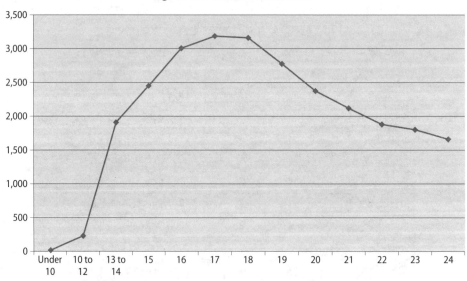

Figure 12.7. Number of arrests for motor vehicle theft by age in the United States, 2011

Source: FBI UCR, 2011b.

it (Rice and Smith, 2002). Nearly two thirds of stolen vehicles are recovered,[14] which indicates that most motor vehicle thefts have expressive (i.e., psychological) rather than instrumental motives behind them (Linden and Chaturvedi, 2005). Cars stolen for instrumental (i.e., financial) reasons typically end up in pieces in chop shops or intact on a boat headed overseas.

Motor vehicle theft is also committed for profit.[15] Vehicles may be stolen and sold to chop shops, where mechanics dismantle the car for its parts and sell those parts to auto repair shops, auto supply stores and directly to individuals more quickly and at lower cost than parts obtained legitimately; this is especially true for older cars, including the ones on the list in Table 12.3. Newer and higher value cars may be stolen in order to be sold overseas, where luxury cars from the States fetch a high price. Professional car thieves, known as jockeys, may even steal certain cars at the request of a professional auto theft ring to meet customer demand in other countries (Walsh and Hemmens, 2011).

In interviews with 100 car thieves in Great Britain, Light, Nee and Ingham (1993) found that many car thieves began stealing cars in their mid to late teens under the guidance of a more experienced auto thief. Excitement, peer pressure and boredom were the main reasons the thieves cited for their entry into car theft, but over time, the opportunity to make money kept them stealing cars. More than half of the sample described themselves as auto thieves and for the most part, did not engage in other crime. They recognized that auto theft was morally wrong, but did not consider it a very serious violation of the law. Nearly all of the car thieves in this study were not deterred from auto theft by the threat of criminal justice sanctions. Rather, the excitement of stealing cars in combination with the financial gain was sufficient to keep car thieves in the trade. Those who did stop stealing cars attributed their desistance to maturity and not to the threat of sanctions. Car alarms did serve to deter about a third of the car thieves in this sample.

Copes and Cherbonneau (2010) used a similar method to determine how car thieves obtain keys in order to steal cars. They interviewed two groups, 42 people in community corrections in Tennessee and 12 incarcerated auto thieves in Louisiana. Some of the car thieves simply took advantage of opportunities for car theft that presented themselves, such as encountering a car with the keys left inside. Importantly, these opportunities resonate much more with car thieves than with law abiding citizens. In the words of one car thief:

> I went off up in this neighborhood by General Hospital. They had this convertible Benz, it was parked up under the garage, you know. And I kind of found that funny. The top down in the garage with the door open. So I waited for a little while and I ain't seen nobody come out. So I went in and the keys were just sitting right there. I was like damn. So I cranked it up and I pulled out (Copes and Cherbonneau, 2010, p. 72).

---

14. Note: this is not the same as the arrest rate for motor vehicle theft, which is much lower than the recovery rate of the cars themselves.

15. While fun and profit are the main motivations for car theft, Fleming (1999) mentions two other practical ones, personal use and transportation to other crimes.

Participation in street life that includes commission of other crimes also precipitated car theft.[16] In the words of another car thief:

> I broke into like a rent-a-car place and stoke the keys to a Lexus.... I remember it was so easy. I went in there looking for money but I didn't find any. I found these keys, so I took the keys. I went and tried it out in the front that night to see which car it was for. It opened up a black Lexus (Copes and Cherbonneau, 2010, p. 73).

While some of the car thieves in the sample were simply opportunists, taking advantage of easy opportunities to obtain car keys and therefore cars, some engaged in a more active search for keys. They actively tried to take advantage of the carelessness of others. In the words of one New Orleans car thief:

> During [holidays] is the best time you know because all the cars are lined up in the street.... That be the best days because New Orleans is a main attraction for the tourists and stuff, and tourists they get drunk, they might leave the keys in the car. Hell, the door might be open! All we got to do is open it up [and] go up in there, you know (Copes and Cherbonneau, 2010, p. 75).

Many of the car thieves in this sample disliked using force to obtain car keys. However, force may become an action of last resort when car thieves only know how to steal cars using keys. In that case, they may have to resort to carjacking, in which they use force to obtain the keys in order to steal the car.

The most skilled auto thieves in this sample used manipulation to obtain keys. For these car thieves, many of whom targeted car dealerships, remaining in control of the interaction with the victim is crucial and a large part of control over the interaction is derived from control over the conversation; physical appearance at the dealership is also important. Once these car thieves had talked their way into a test drive, they used one of two techniques to obtain the car key. The first is slight of hand:

> But you get the key and the key ring is nothing but a little, old, thin piece of wire with a couple of keys on it. You know how easy it is to take the key off? When you finish your test drive you park the car back and when you are getting out of the car you switch the keys. Give him a new key. Then you got a key to that car, you know.... Then you can go back [at night] and just drive off because you got the keys (Copes and Cherbonneau, 2010, p. 78).

The second is to make a mould of the key:

> I would sit and talk to them [the car salesman] like they was an associate, you know. Like we fixing to do business. I would like more or less take advantage of the conversation.... I would have a lot of play-dough in my pocket and I was getting in the car to start it and test drive it, I would make a copy of it in the play-dough and I bring it to a locksmith friend of mine and he would make keys (Copes and Cherbonneau, 2010, pp. 78–79).

---

16. The burglary of a home or business for the sole purpose of obtaining car keys has been referred to as car key burglary (Shaw, Smith and Bond, 2010).

Some of the manipulative car thieves in this sample chose to target individuals rather than dealerships and drug users make particularly good targets. Crack users are willing to rent out their vehicles for small amounts of crack (this is called rock renting) and are reluctant to go to the police should a thief steal their car.

Some of the car thieves in this sample relied on the existence of master keys and close-cousin keys. Master keys are made with universal grooves that are designed to work with a number of different models in a certain make of car. They are more common among older than newer cars. Close-cousin keys can be made by modifying existing keys so that, for example, a key for a Honda would work with a Toyota and vice versa. Though master keys have been sold online, few of the car thieves in this sample obtained their master keys in this way, getting them instead from acquaintances or friends. In the words of one car thief:

> In the gang we was in, everybody had [a master key]. There were so many of us and everybody had one. You put it on your key chain and as soon as you see a Toyota, you can break into it. Like an '89 or '90. You can start them up right there (Copes and Cherbonneau, 2010, p. 80).

Copes and Cherbonneau (2010) conclude by noting that as long as keys are needed to open and drive cars, car thieves will target car keys. Importantly, as keyless entry and keyless ignition become more common in newer models, the cars, especially older cars, that do not have these features are likely to be targeted for theft, especially by car thieves who engage in active searches and manipulation to obtain keys. Copes and Cherbonneau (2010) point to the importance of guarding car keys at all times, for both ordinary citizens and car salespeople, in the effort to reduce motor vehicle theft.

Box 12.2. What about Carjacking?

Most if not all readers have heard of carjacking, which amounts to robbing someone for their automobile. Carjacking is a violent rather than a property crime. Jacobs, Topalli and Wright (2003) interviewed 28 active carjackers and found that their motivations appeared to mirror those of robbers more than those of auto thieves. The decision to commit a carjacking was rooted in perceived needs and opportunities to do so, but was also shaped by participation in street culture. Carjacking rates in the United States have fluctuated in recent years, from 21 per 100,000 in the mid-1990s to 13 per 100,000 in the late 1990s and early 2000s (Klaus, 2004).[17] Because of the potential for physical harm, the penalties for carjacking are harsh, from three to 99 years of hard labor and, at the federal level, the death penalty; these severe penalties may be partially responsible for the recent drop in carjacking seen above.

Carjacking is distinct from other types of robbery because victims are in their cars and therefore mobile, the opportunity for carjacking is transitory based on the mobility of the car, it occurs in public rather than private and it requires great attention to the victim because the car is both the target and the victim's means of escape. Because of these differences, offenders

---

17. For a brief review of the literature on carjacking, including in South Africa, see Harper and Frailing (2013).

must establish and exploit fear in their victims and do it quickly if they are going to be successful in their carjacking (Copes, Hochstetler and Cherbonneau, 2012). In interviews with 24 active carjackers, Wright (2013) found that carjackers chiefly use verbal threats and the display of firearms to increase victims' level of fear to the point that it compels compliance, but that others use gentler techniques, such as reminding victims that a car is not worth their lives or reassuring them that the only item of interest is the car in order to get them to comply.

Crimes that Cause Property Damage: Arson and Vandalism

Arson is defined as "any willful or malicious burning or attempt to burn, with or without intent to defraud, a dwelling house, public building, motor vehicle or aircraft, personal property of another, etc." (FBI UCR, 2011d). Only those fires that can be determined to be "willful or malicious" are counted as arson by the FBI, but because of the inherent difficulty in determining whether a fire was accidentally or purposefully started, it is difficult to determine the true extent of arson.[18] Nevertheless, the FBI reported the total number of arsons for 2011 as 15,640 for a rate of 18.2 per 100,000. The average dollar loss per arson was $13,196 for a total loss of over $572 million (FBI UCR, 2011g). Figure 12.8 reveals the percent of arson offenses involving structures, mobile and other property.

In 2011, 8,994 people were arrested for arson. Eighty two percent of those arrested were male and 18 percent were female. Seventy two percent of those arrested were white

Figure 12.8. Percent of arson offenses involving structures, mobile and other property

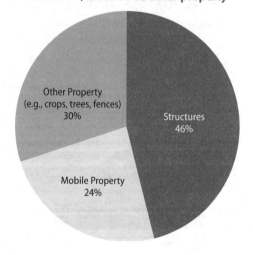

Other Property (e.g., crops, trees, fences) 30%

Structures 46%

Mobile Property 24%

Source: FBI UCR, 2011g.

---

18. For a fascinating look at the real life consequences of arson investigations, see the PBS Frontline documentary, *Death By Fire*.

Figure 12.9. Number of arrests for arson by age in the United States, 2011

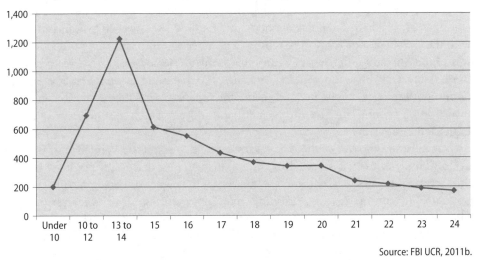

Source: FBI UCR, 2011b.

and 26 percent were African American. Sixty two percent of all those arrested for arson were ages 24 and under and 42 percent of those arrested for arson were under the age of 18. Figure 12.9 reveals that arrests for arson peak much earlier than they do for other crimes, between the ages of 13–14, and then begin to decline.

Motivations for arson can be either instrumental or expressive and both motivations are captured in the typology developed by McCaghy (1980). The first type of arson is profit-motivated arson, which is nicely illustrated by the crime of insurance fraud. The owner of a failing business may try to burn it down him or herself or hire a professional arsonist (a torch) to do the job in the hopes of collecting on the insurance money. The second type of arson, revenge arson, may be done out of spite, jealousy or to get even, such as burning down the office building one was fired from or the house of an ex-wife's new boyfriend. The third type of arson, vandalism arson, is done to damage the property of and in so doing express hatred toward a certain individual or group. The fourth type of arson, crime concealment arson, is used as a way to cover up commission of another crime or to distract law enforcement from other criminal activity. The fifth type of arson, sabotage arson, refers to fires set during riots or other tumultuous situations. The sixth type of arson, excitement arson, is that committed by those fascinated with fire; these arsonists may have psychopathological issues. McCaghy's (1980) typology sets the stage for that developed by Kocsis (2002), who contends there are six motivations for arson, profit, animosity, vandalism, crime concealment, political objectives and psychopathology.

Juveniles ages 5–17 only make up 17.3 percent of the United States population (U.S. Census, 2011), yet 42 percent of those arrested for arson in 2011 fell within this age group. For this reason, the expressive rather than the instrumental motivations for arson have been of greater interest to researchers, especially excitement arson. For many juvenile fire setters, arson may be a matter of curiosity. If the arson is detected and dealt with appropriately, it is likely not to be repeated. For a small group of juvenile fire setters, though, higher levels of antisocial behavior, hostility and impulsiveness along with lower levels of sociability and assertiveness facilitate persistence in fire setting (Brett, 2004; Hakkanen, Puolakka and Santilla, 2004). Kocsis (2002) points out that with the variety of motives for fire setting, a number of approaches are needed to curb this crime, including harsher penalties for profit-motivated arsonists, treatment for those arsonists with psychopathological issues, fire safety education for children, more rigorous screening for firefighters, who are sometimes arsonists themselves, better arson investigation training for law enforcement and more research that helps us to better understand this crime.

Vandalism is another crime that causes damage to property. Vandalism is defined as "to willfully or maliciously destroy, injure, disfigure, or deface any public or private property, real or personal, without the consent of the owner or person having custody or control by cutting, tearing, breaking, marking, painting, drawing, covering with filth, or any other such means as may be specified by local law" (FBI UCR, 2011d). In 2011, 183,203 people were arrested for vandalism. Eighty-one percent of those arrested were male and 19 percent were female. Seventy-three percent of those arrested were white and 25 percent were African American. Twenty-nine percent of those arrested for vandalism were under the age of 18 (FBI UCR, 2011b). Figure 12.10 reveals that arrests for vandalism, like those for arson, peak much earlier than they do for other crimes, between the ages of 13 and 14, after which they begin a slow decline.

Wade (1967) proposed three basic types of vandalism, wanton, predatory and vindictive. Wanton vandalism is senseless vandalism usually but not always undertaken by juveniles for fun. Predatory vandalism involves deliberate destruction of property for gain, such as damaging or destroying an automated teller machine (ATM) to try to get the cash inside. Vindictive vandalism is done out of hatred for a group and can

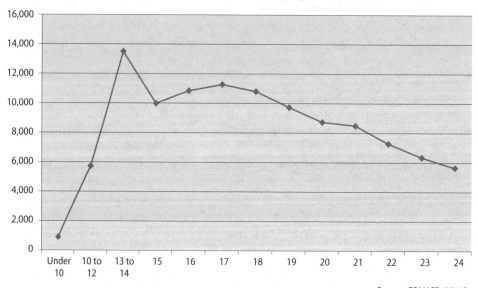

Figure 12.10. Number of arrests for vandalism by age in the United States, 2011

Source: FBI UCR, 2011b.

include the painting of swastikas on synagogues. Later, Cohen (1973) described five types of vandalism. Acquisitive vandalism involves looting or petty theft, tactical or ideological vandalism is done to draw attention to an issue or to oneself, vindictive vandalism is done for revenge, play vandalism is done to overcome boredom and malicious vandalism is done to diffuse anger and usually in a public setting.

One well-known kind of vandalism is graffiti. According to Weisel (2002), there are several different types of graffiti, each with its own underlying motives. Gang graffiti is primarily communicative—it can mark the gang's turf, brag about achievements, honor those who have died and insult other gangs. Common tagging, putting graffiti in highly visible and hard to reach locations, is done in the interest of gaining prestige or notoriety or to defy authority. Artistic tagging, creating colorful and complex pictures, is done out of the need for artistic prestige or recognition. Conventional graffiti may be done as a rite of passage or for the excitement, or it may be done out of more negative emotions, such as anger and despair. Finally, ideological graffiti involves the use of offensive symbols and is done out of hatred toward a group.

Weisel (2002) points out a number of ways in which graffiti may be reduced. Some readers may be wondering why is such a concerted effort needed to combat what is essentially extra paint on the walls. Remember from Chapter 9 and the discussion of broken windows that graffiti may be seen as a sign of disorder and part of an invitation for predatory criminals to set up shop in certain areas. The first and most important graffiti reducing strategy is rapid removal. Rapid removal reduces the psychological rewards to the offender and reduces the reoccurrence of graffiti. Increasing the risk of detection is another useful graffiti prevention strategy, as is increasing the difficulty of offending. These three strategies are thought to be responsible for the dramatic decrease in subway car graffiti in New York in the 1980s. Weisel (2002) notes that a number of responses to graffiti that have been tried before have been met with limited success, in large part because they do not take offender motivations into account; these include controlling access to spray paint and other graffiti tools, providing prosocial activities for youth, expanding graffiti laws and sanctions, holding parents accountable and applying new technologies.

Of course, graffiti is not the only type of vandalism. Other types include the property destruction that sometimes occurs after a sports team wins or loses an important game, usually the championship. Interestingly, destruction of property following a win seems to be a uniquely American phenomenon. Some notable and recent wins that led to massive property destruction were the Denver Broncos' Super Bowl victory in 1998, the Philadelphia Phillies' clinch of the World Series in 2008 and the Los Angeles Lakers winning the NBA championship in 2010. Massive property destruction that follows losses in other countries, such as Argentina and Canada to give just two notable and recent examples, may be due in part to the dominance of one sport over all others in those countries (soccer in Argentina and hockey in Canada); losses may mean a great deal more in this case (Assael, 2011).

Box 12.3. Cyber Vandalism: Is That Even a Thing?

In a word, yes. As seen in Chapter 9, computer use presents new opportunities for crime, particularly cybercrime. One form of cybercrime that has not been fully explored is cyber vandalism, which can be of two types. Cyber vandalism is defined as "the defacement or destruction of commercial, government or personal websites" but it also encompasses the defacement or destruction of virtual property in online communities (Williams, 2004, p. 1). If and when we think of cyber vandalism, we probably think of the first type, that aimed at websites. In this case, cyber vandalism involves hacking into websites and then altering them in a way which is sometimes intended to be humorous, but may also be malicious or even politically motivated (Burden and Palmer, 2003). Although such acts are likely to fall within the scope of Section 3 of the Computer Misuse Act of 1990, which covers any intentional act which causes an unauthorized modification of the contents of any computer (Burden and Palmer, 2003), cyber vandalism remains a grey area in crime because it is very difficult to prosecute and because cyber vandalism may be somewhat in the eye of the beholder; what one person considers destruction or defacement of a website might be considered freedom of expression by another. The second type of cyber vandalism, the defacement or destruction of virtual property in an online community, can actually serve to degrade the online community for which that virtual property has become an important part, just as vandalism in the real world might (Williams, 2004).

Conclusion:
Theoretical Explanations of Property Crime

As seen in the conclusion of Chapter 11, many of the theories developed to explain crime were developed with just that purpose in mind—to explain all types of crime, from violent to property to public order to white collar. Particularly the leading theories of crime, Hirschi's (1969) social control (social bond) theory, Gottfredson and Hirschi's (1990) self-control theory, Agnew's (2002) general strain theory and Akers' (1997, 2002) social learning theory, were developed to be able to explain all types of crime. The architects and proponents of these theories would argue that their theories are well able to explain property (as well as other types of) crime. Social learning theory might be very well suited to explain professional criminals of different types, as professional criminals spend appreciable amounts of time learning techniques and values from other criminals and getting reinforced in different ways for their success.

However, it seems as though both choice and environmental theories have particular resonance with and utility for property crime as a whole. As seen in Chapter 9 and above, burglars engage in rational decision making when they choose to burgle a particular house and what they do once they are inside, consistent with Cornish and Clarke's (1986) rational choice theory. Target suitability and the absence of capable guardianship, consistent with Cohen and Felson's (1979) routine activity theory appear to be particularly relevant to shoplifting, burglary, motor vehicle theft and vandalism, especially graffiti. Reducing target suitability and introducing or improving capable guardianship across these settings can be effective at reducing these crimes. As we have seen, many of the crimes described in this chapter have both instrumental and expressive motivations and may fill a variety of different needs for offenders. Though it is easy to associate choice and opportunity theories with crimes that are instrumentally (e.g., financially) motivated, these theories appear to have at least some applicability for expressively (e.g., psychologically) motivated crimes as well.

Importantly, research has shown that property crime offenders do not generally take the threat of punishment by the criminal justice system into account when deciding whether to commit a specific criminal action. Moreover, the experience of incarceration may diminish its harshness, reaffirm that a stay in prison can be endured and give the property crime offender time to perfect his or her techniques (Shover and Copes, 2010), so total reliance on deterrence theory (see Chapter 9) to solve the problem of property crime would be a serious error.

Websites to Visit

UCR Property Crimes, 2011: http://www.fbi.gov/about-us/cjis/ucr/crime-in-the-u.s/ 2011/crime-in-the-u.s.-2011/property-crime/property-crime

National Association for Shoplifting Prevention: http://www.shopliftingprevention.org/ main.asp

Fraud Prevention Tips: http://www.stopfraud.gov/

Burglary Prevention Tips: http://www.memphispolice.org/Burglary%20Prevention%20 Tips.htm

Motor Vehicle Theft Prevention Tips: http://www.nhtsa.gov/Vehicle+Safety/Vehicle-Related+Theft/Motor+Vehicle+Theft+Prevention+Precautions

Graffiti: http://www.d.umn.edu/~schi0456/5230/glocal/styles.html, http://www.graffiti 911.com/types.php

Discussion Questions

1. Describe the trends in property crime in the United States in the last 50 years and comment on some possible reasons for changes in crime rates over time.
2. Comparing the information in Chapter 11 to that in Chapter 12, it is obvious that the clearance rate for violent crimes is much higher than that for property crimes. Why do you think this is the case?
3. Does any of the information given in this chapter with regard to the characteristics of those who are arrested for property crime change your conception of who is involved in crime? If so, how?
4. How do you reconcile the findings of Katz (1988) on the one hand and those of Cromwell, Parker and Mobley (2010) on the other with regard to shoplifting?
5. What are some explanations for the fact that residential burglaries occur more often during the day and commercial burglaries occur more often at night?
6. Knowing what you do now about the way burglars search homes, will you change the way in which you secure your valuables in your residence? If so, why? If not, why not?

7. Who bears more responsibility for lowering the rate of motor vehicle thefts, individual citizens or the criminal justice system?

8. Do you or have you ever owned one of the cars on the list in Table 12.3? If so, did you take any precautions to prevent the theft of your car?

9. Do McCaghy's (1980) or Kocsis' (2002) typologies of arson need updating, considering what we know about juvenile involvement in this crime? If so, in what ways? How about Wade's (1967) and Cohen's (1973) typologies of vandalism?

10. When does graffiti cross the line from crime into art (or vice versa)?

11. Which do you think are more important in the commission of property crime, instrumental motives or expressive motives? Which type of motive should we focus our attention on when it comes to preventing property crime?

12. Many of the crimes discussed in this chapter are committed in pairs or groups. What are some of the advantages to committing property crime in a group?

13. Do you agree that the theories of crime named in the conclusion of this chapter well explain property crime, or are other perspectives needed?

References

Adams, Virginia. (1976). *Crime.* New York, NY: Time-Life Books.

Agnew, Robert. (2002). Foundation for a general strain theory of crime. In S. Cote (Ed.), *Criminological theories: Bridging the past to the future* (pp. 113–124). Thousand Oaks, CA: Sage.

Akers, Ronald. (1997). *Criminological theories: Introduction and evaluation.* 2nd ed. Los Angeles, CA: Roxbury.

Akers, Ronald. (2002). A social learning theory of crime. In S. Cote (Ed.), *Criminological theories: Bridging the past to the future* (pp. 135–143). Thousand Oaks, CA: Sage.

Assael, Shaun. (2011). Why do fans riot? *ESPN Magazine.* Retrieved from: http://espn.go.com/espn/story/_/id/6823745/shaun-assael-why-americans-riot-big-wins.

Baumer, Terry and Dennis Rosenbaum. (1982). *Combatting retail theft: Programs and strategies.* Boston, MA: Butterworth.

Blakely, G. Robert and Michael Goldsmith. (1976). Criminal redistribution of stolen property: The need for law reform. *Michigan Law Review, 71,* 1518–1545.

Brett, Adam. (2004). "Kindling theory" in arson: How dangerous are firesetters? *Australian and New Zealand Journal of Psychiatry, 38,* 419–425.

Buckle, Abigail and David Farrington. (1984). An observational study of shoplifting. *British Journal of Criminology, 24,* 63–72.

Burden, Kit and Creole Palmer. (2003). Internet crime: Cyber crime—A new breed of criminal? *Computer Law & Security Review, 19,* 222–227.

Cameron, Mary Owen. (1964). *The booster and the snitch: Department store shoplifting.* New York, NY: Free Press.

Clarke, Michael. (1989). Insurance fraud. *The British Journal of Criminology, 29,* 1–20.

Clarke, Ronald. (2002). Shoplifting: Guide no. 11. Retrieved from: http://www.popcenter.org/problems/shoplifting/print/.

Cohen, Lawrence and Marcus Felson. (1979). Social change and crime rate trends: A routine activity approach. *American Sociological Review, 44*, 588–607.

Cohen, Stan. (1973). Property destruction: Motives and meanings. In C. Ward (Ed.), *Vandalism* (pp. 23–53). London, England: The Architectural Press.

Copes, Heith and Michael Cherbonneau. (2010). The key to auto theft: Emerging methods of auto theft from the offenders' perspective. In P. Cromwell (Ed.), *In their own words: Criminals on crime*. 5th ed. (pp. 69–89). New York, NY: Oxford University Press.

Copes, Heith, Andy Hochstetler and Michael Cherbonneau. (2012). Getting the upper hand: Scripts for managing victim resistance in carjackings. *Journal of Research in Crime and Delinquency, 49*, 249–268.

Cornish, Derek and Ronald Clarke. (1986). *The reasoning criminal*. New York, NY: Springer-Verlag.

Cromwell, Paul, Lee Parker and Shawna Mobley. (2010). The five-finger discount: An analysis of motivations for shoplifting. In P. Cromwell (Ed.), *In their own words: Criminals on crime*. 5th ed. (pp. 90–108). New York, NY: Oxford University Press.

Cromwell, Paul and James Olson. (2010). The reasoning offender: Motives and decision-making strategies. In P. Cromwell (Ed.), *In their own words: Criminals on crime*. 5th ed (pp. 22–45). New York, NY: Oxford University Press.

Cromwell, Paul and James Olson. (2010a). Fencing: Avenues for redistribution of stolen property. In P. Cromwell (Ed.), *In their own words: Criminals on crime*. 5th ed. (pp. 265–282). New York, NY: Oxford University Press.

D'Alessio, Stewart, David Eitle and Lisa Stolzenberg. (2012). Unemployment, guardianship, and weekday residential burglary. *Justice Quarterly, 29*, 919–932.

Davila, Mario, James Marquart and Janet Mullings. (2005). Beyond mother nature: Contractor fraud in the wake of natural disasters. *Deviant Behavior, 26*, 271–293.

FBI UCR. (2004). UCR handbook. Retrieved from: http://www.fbi.gov/about-us/cjis/ucr/additional-ucr-publications/ucr_handbook.pdf/view.

FBI UCR. (2010). FBI UCR data tool. Retrieved from: http://www.ucrdatatool.gov/Search/Crime/State/TrendsInOneVar.cfm.

FBI UCR. (2011). Crime in the United States 2011: Property crime. Retrieved from: http://www.fbi.gov/about-us/cjis/ucr/crime-in-the-u.s/2011/crime-in-the-u.s.-2011/property-crime/property-crime.

FBI UCR. (2011a). Crime in the United States 2011: Larceny-theft. Retrieved from: http://www.fbi.gov/about-us/cjis/ucr/crime-in-the-u.s/2011/crime-in-the-u.s.-2011/property-crime/larceny-theft.

FBI UCR. (2011b). Crime in the United States 2011: Persons arrested. Retrieved from: http://www.fbi.gov/about-us/cjis/ucr/crime-in-the-u.s/2011/crime-in-the-u.s.-2011/persons-arrested/persons-arrested.

FBI UCR. (2011c). Crime in the United States 2011: Violent crime. Retrieved from: http://www.fbi.gov/about-us/cjis/ucr/crime-in-the-u.s/2011/crime-in-the-u.s.-2011/violent-crime/violent-crime.

FBI UCR. (2011d). Offense definitions. Retrieved from: http://www.fbi.gov/about-us/cjis/ucr/crime-in-the-u.s/2011/crime-in-the-u.s.-2011/offense-definitions.

FBI UCR. (2011e). Crime in the United States 2011: Burglary. Retrieved from: http://www.fbi.gov/about-us/cjis/ucr/crime-in-the-u.s/2011/crime-in-the-u.s.-2011/property-crime/burglary.

FBI UCR (2011f). Crime in the United States 2011: Motor vehicle theft. Retrieved from: http://www.fbi.gov/about-us/cjis/ucr/crime-in-the-u.s/2011/crime-in-the-u.s.-2011/property-crime/motor-vehicle-theft.

FBI UCR (2011g). Crime in the United States 2011: Arson. Retrieved from: http://www.fbi.gov/about-us/cjis/ucr/crime-in-the-u.s/2011/crime-in-the-u.s.-2011/property-crime/arson.

FBI UCR (2012). Uniform Crime Reports. Arson data available for each year from 1995–2011. Retrieved from: http://www.fbi.gov/about-us/cjis/ucr.

Finklea, Kristin. (2010). *Organized retail crime.* Congressional Research Service. Retrieved from: http://assets.opencrs.com/rpts/R41118_20100616.pdf.

Fleming, Zachary. (1999). The thrill of it all: Youthful offenders and auto theft. In P. Cromwell (Ed.), *In their own words: Criminals on crime.* 2nd ed. (pp. 71–79). Los Angeles, CA: Roxbury Publishing Company.

Frailing, Kelly and Dee Wood Harper. (2012). Fear, prosocial behavior and looting: The Katrina experience. In D.W. Harper and K. Frailing (Eds.), *Crime and criminal justice in disaster.* 2nd ed. (pp. 101–122). Durham, NC: Carolina Academic Press.

Friedman, Monroe. (1992). Confidence swindles of older consumers. *Journal of Consumer Affairs, 26,* 20–46.

Gottfredson, Michael and Travis Hirschi. (1990). *A general theory of crime.* Palo Alto, CA: Stanford University Press.

Hagan, Frank. (2013). *Introduction to criminology.* 8th ed. Thousand Oaks, CA: Sage.

Hakkanen, Helina, Pia Puolakka and Pekka Santilla. (2004). Crime scene actions and offender characteristics in arsons. *Legal and Criminal Psychology, 9,* 197–214.

Hamrick, Stephanie. (2006). Is looting ever justified? An analysis of looting laws and the applicability of the necessity defense during natural disasters and states of emergency. *Nevada Law Journal, 7,* 182–211.

Harper, Dee Wood and Kelly Frailing (Eds.). (2012). *Crime and criminal justice in disaster.* 2nd ed. Durham, NC: Carolina Academic Press.

Harper, Dee Wood and Kelly Frailing. (2013). Robbery. In A. Thio. T. Calhoun and A. Conyers (Eds.), *Deviance today* (pp. 49–62). Boston, MA: Pearson.

Hirschi, Travis. (1969). *The causes of delinquency.* Berkeley, CA: University of California Press.

Hochstetler, Andy. (2010). Opportunities and decisions: Interactional dynamics in robbery and burglary groups. In P. Cromwell (Ed.), *In their own words: Criminals on crime.* 5th ed. (pp. 46–66). New York, NY: Oxford University Press.

Inciardi, James. (1977). In search of the class cannon: A field study of professional pickpockets. IN R. Weppner (Ed.), *Street ethnography* (pp. 55–78). Beverly Hills, CA: Sage.

Inciardi, James. (1983). On grift at the Super Bowl: Professional pickpockets and the NFL. In G. Waldo (Ed.), *Career criminals* (pp. 31–41). Beverly Hills, CA: Sage.

Inciardi, James. (1984). Professional theft. In R. Meier (Ed.), *Major forms of crime* (pp. 221–243). Beverly Hills, CA: Sage.

Jacobs, Bruce, Volkan Topalli and Richard Wright. (2003). Carjacking, street life and offender motivation. *British Journal of Criminology, 43*, 673–678.

Katz, Jack. (1988). *Seductions of crime: Moral and sensual attractions of doing evil.* New York, NY: Basic Books.

Kauzlarich, David and Hugh Barlow. (2009). *Introduction to criminology.* 9th ed. Lanham, MD: Rowman and Littlefield.

King, Harry. (1972). *Boxman: A professional thief's journey.* W. Chambliss (Ed.). New York, NY: Harper and Row.

King, Harry and William Chambliss. (1984). *Harry King: A professional thief's journal.* New York, NY: Wiley.

Klaus, Patsy. (2004). *Carjacking, 1993–2002.* Bureau of Justice Statistics Crime Data Brief. Retrieved from: http://bjs.ojp.usdoj.gov/content/pub/pdf/c02.pdf.

Klemke, Lloyd. (1992). *The sociology of shoplifting: Boosters and snitches today.* New York, NY: Praeger.

Kocsis, Richard. (2002). *Arson: Explaining motives and possible solutions.* AIC Trends and Issues in Crime and Criminal Justice. Retrieved from: http://www.aic.gov.au/documents/A/1/8/%7BA18209AF-C67E-4E5E-9FCD-D5413DCA4686%7Dti236.pdf.

Lemert, Edwin. (1953). An isolation and closure theory of naïve check forgery. *Journal of Criminal Law, Criminology, and Political Science, 44*, 296–307.

Lemert, Edwin. (1958). The behavior of the systematic check forger. *Social Problems, 6*, 141–149.

Light, Roy, Claire Nee and Helen Ingham. (1993). *Car theft: The offender's perspective.* London, England: HMSO.

Lindblom, Arto and Sami Kajalo. (2011). The use and effectiveness of formal and informal surveillance in reducing shoplifting: A survey in Sweden, Norway and Finland. *The International Review of Retail, Distribution and Consumer Research, 21*, 111–128.

Linden, Rick and Renuka Chaturvedi. (2005). The need for comprehensive crime prevention planning: The case of motor vehicle theft. *Canadian Journal of Criminology and Criminal Justice, 47*, 251–270.

LSA RS 14:62.5. (2006). §62.5. Looting. Retrieved from: http://www.legis.state.la.us/lss/lss.asp?doc=78582.

Mawby, Robert. (2001). *Burglary.* Devon, England: Willan.

McCaghy, Charles. (1980). *Crime in American society.* New York, NY: Macmillan.

McKeever, Grainne. (1999). Detecting, prosecuting and punishing benefit fraud: The social security administration (fraud) act of 1997. *Modern Law Review, 62*, 261–270.

Morley, Nicola, Linden Ball and Thomas Omerod. (2006). How the detection of insurance fraud succeeds and fails. *Psychology, Crime & Law, 12*, 163–180.

NASP. (2006). National Association for Shoplifting Prevention: Shoplifting statistics. Retrieved from: http://www.shopliftingprevention.org/WhatNASPOffers/NRC/PublicEducStats.htm.

NCVS. (2011). *Criminal Victimization, 2011.* Retrieved from: http://bjs.ojp.usdoj.gov/content/pub/pdf/cv11.pdf.

NICB. (2011). National Insurance Crime Bureau. Hot spots and hot wheels. Retrieved from: https://www.nicb.org/newsroom/nicb_campaigns/hot_spots and https://www.nicb.org/newsroom/nicb_campaigns/hot-wheels.

Nimick, Ellen. (1990). *Juvenile court property cases: OJJDP update on statistics.* Washington, D.C.: U.S. Department of Justice.

Rengert, George and John Wasilchick. (2000). *Suburban burglary: A tale of two suburbs.* Springfield, IL: Charles C. Thomas.

Rice, Kennon and William Smith. (2002). Socioecological models of automotive theft: Integrating routine activity and social disorganization approaches. *Journal of Research in Crime and Delinquency, 39*, 304–336.

Shaw, Sophia, Lisa Smith and John Bond. (2010). Examining the factors that differentiate a car key burglary from a regular domestic burglary. *International Journal of Police Science & Management, 12*, 450–459.

Shover, Neal and Heith Copes. (2010). Decision making by persistent thieves and crime control policy. In H. Barlow and S. Decker (Eds.), *Criminology and public policy* (pp. 128–149). Philadelphia, PA: Temple University Press.

Tennyson, Sharon. (1997). Economic institutions and individual ethics: A study of consumer attitudes toward insurance fraud. *Journal of Economic Behavior & Organization, 32*, 247–265.

Titus, Richard, Fred Heinzelmann and John Boyle. (1995). Victimization of persons by fraud. *Crime & Delinquency, 41*, 54–72.

Turner, J. W. Cecil (Ed.). (1966). *Kennedy's outlines of criminal law.* 19th ed. Cambridge, England: Cambridge University Press.

U.S. Census. (2011). American FactFinder: Age and Sex. Retrieved from: http://fact finder2.census.gov/faces/tableservices/jsf/pages/productview.xhtml?pid=ACS_11_1YR_S0101&prodType=table.

U.S. Treasury. (2013). The New $100 Note. Retrieved from: http://www.newmoney.gov/currency/100.htm.

Wade, Andrew. (1967). Social processes in the act of juvenile vandalism. In M. Clinard and R. Quinney (Eds.), *Criminal behavior systems: A typology* (pp. 94–109). New York, NY: Holt, Rinehart and Winston.

Walsh, Anthony and Craig Hemmens. (2011). *Introduction to criminology: A text/reader.* 2nd ed. Los Angeles, CA: Sage.

Wartzman, Rick. (1992). Counterfeit bills confound detectors at the Fed, sleuths at the Secret Service. *The Wall Street Journal,* July 2.

Wiesel, Deborah. (2002). Graffiti: Guide no. 9. Retrieved from: http://www.popcenter.org/problems/graffiti/print/.

Williams, Matthew. (2004). Understanding King Punisher and his Order: Vandalism in an online community—motives, meanings and possible solutions. *Internet Journal of Criminology.* Retrieved from: http://www.internetjournalofcriminology.com/Williams%20-%20Understanding%20King%20Punisher%20and%20his%20Order.pdf.

Wright, Richard. (2013). The manipulation of fear in carjacking. *Journal of Contemporary Ethnography.* DOI: 10.1177/0891241612474934.

Wright, Richard and Scott Decker. (1994). *Burglars on the job: Streetlife and residential break-ins.* Boston, MA: Northeastern University Press.

Chapter 13

White and Other Collar Crime

Introduction

In Chapters 11, 12 and 14, the topics of violent, property and public order crimes are explained in some detail. Offenses against people, property and the public order are probably what we bring to mind most readily when we are asked to think about crime. Violent, property and public order offenses are traditional street crimes and importantly, these are the crimes around which the theories of crime covered in Chapters 3–7 and in Chapter 9 were developed. However, there is another type of crime that requires full description if we are to understand criminal activity in all its forms and that is white collar crime. This chapter introduces the concept of white collar crime, describes examples of the different types of white collar crime and provides some theoretical explanations. This chapter also discusses the concepts of pink and khaki collar crime.

White Collar Crime[1]

We can thank Edwin Sutherland,[2] who used it for the first time in an address in 1939, for the term white collar crime. Sutherland wanted to draw attention to the fact that until then, much of criminologists' focus had been on traditional street crime to the exclusion of crime committed by corporations and the people in them. In this day and age, the notion of white collar crime is a part of life, but 75 years ago when Sutherland made his now famous address, this was not the case and the audience and the wider

---

1. Interestingly, the use of the term blue collar crime to describe traditional street crimes committed by people of lower social statuses is relatively rare in the literature (but see O'Hear, 2001; Shover, 2010). This may be due in part to our common conception of crime; if everyone means the same thing when they talk about crime, there is little need to designate it as blue collar.

2. This is the same Edwin Sutherland who devised differential association theory; see Chapter 5.

academic community was shocked at the idea that people in business occupations might be violating the law (Cullen and Agnew, 2011). At the time, Sutherland defined white collar crime as "a crime committed by a person of respectability and high social status in the course of his occupation" (1983, p. 7). Two parts of this definition are potentially problematic. First, what constitutes a person of respectability and high social status? Does just being employed in a business environment earn one enough respect and status to potentially qualify as a white collar offender? Put another way, is there a difference between the bank teller who embezzles and the bank president who does the same? Second, what constitutes a crime in this context? On this point, Sutherland (1940) argued that what he termed convictability was central to determining whether some action was a crime. If an action could be prosecuted under the criminal law, it should be viewed as a crime (Cullen and Agnew, 2011).

In 1949, Sutherland published his famous work on the subject, entitled *White Collar Crime.* He used the book to detail the many legal violations of the 70 largest corporations over the course of their existence, which averaged nearly 50 years. Every one of the corporations that Sutherland studied had at least one violation, 98 percent had two and the average across all 70 corporations was 14. When he eliminated civil judgments against the corporations from his analysis and just focused on criminal convictions, he found that 60 percent of the corporations were convicted in criminal courts and had an average of four convictions each. Sutherland sagely noted that an individual with such a criminal history would be called a recidivist.[3]

In addition to detailing the extent of crime committed by corporations, Sutherland (1940) used his work in this area to discuss the importance of studying white collar crime. The first reason he pointed to was financial cost. Sutherland (1940) noted that a single white collar offense can cost millions of dollars and that the cost of white collar crime is several times greater than all the traditional street crime in a given time period. The second reason he highlighted was social cost. Corporations provide us with goods and services we use every day and Sutherland (1940) believed that corporations erode the trust citizens place in them when they commit criminal acts. The third reason Sutherland (1940) believed it was important to study white collar crime is that it challenged existing theories of crime that had been developed around traditional street crimes. He was particularly critical of the notion that poverty could be associated with all crime, including white collar crime. In his mind, white collar crime could not be explained by an impoverished background. He did believe that his differential association theory was useful in explaining white collar and traditional street crime, maintaining that the process of learning the techniques and attitudes necessary to violate the law happened on the streets as well as in the boardroom (Cullen and Agnew, 2011).

A new and more precise definition of white collar crime was offered by Congress in 1979. Congress defined white collar crime as "an illegal act or series of acts committed by non-physical means and by concealment or guile, to obtain money or property, or to obtain business or personal advantage" (Weisburd, Wheeler, Waring and Bode, 1991).

---

3. Sutherland's publisher made him remove the names of the corporations from his book for its initial publication; the names are included in the 1983 reissue (Cullen and Agnew, 2011). And kudos to Sutherland for collecting all this data the old fashioned way long before the advent of the Internet.

The acts described below fit this definition, but it is important to distinguish between crime committed in the business context for one's personal gain and crime committed in the business context for the benefit of the corporation. Per Clinard and Quinney's (1973) and Rosoff, Pontell and Tillman's (1998) distinction mentioned in Chapter 9, occupational crime is that committed in the business context for one's personal gain and corporate crime is that committed in the business context for the benefit of the corporation.

Types and Examples of White Collar Crime: Occupational and Professional Occupational Crime

Occupational crime is that committed by individuals in the course of their jobs for their own personal gain. One example of occupational crime that is easily brought to mind is embezzlement. Embezzlement can range from the theft of pens and paper from the office to sophisticated schemes that involve siphoning money out of accounts. The ubiquity of computers may have increased the amount of embezzlement because they make it easier to commit; arrests for embezzlement in banking rose 56 percent as computers became the way to do business in that industry. A preferred way to embezzle using computer technology is the salami technique, so named because it involves slicing off a few cents from a number of different accounts and funneling that money into a phantom account the embezzler can access (Rosoff, Pontell and Tillman, 1988).[4] Embezzlement is an unusual crime in that, unlike most other crimes, it is committed almost equally by men and women. Figure 13.1 shows the percent of men and women arrested for embezzlement from 1995 through 2011.

Pink Collar Crime

The fact that women engage in embezzlement as frequently or more frequently than men has encouraged some scholars to devise and investigate the concept of pink collar crime. Pink collar crime was a term introduced by Daly (1989) in her study of gender and different types of white collar crime. She found that women who engaged in any behavior that could qualify as white collar crime were likely to be nonwhite clerical workers who did not finish college and did not own many assets. Men who engaged in white collar crime, on the other hand, were more likely to be managers or administrators and to work in groups, using organizational resources to attempt to steal greater amounts of money. Moreover, men and women had different rationalizations for committing white collar crime. Women were much more likely to claim family need as the reason for their crime while men were more likely to claim greed or self-interest as their motive. Daly (1989) concludes that the white collar crimes committed by men and women are different and that occupational marginality, including having a low rank at one's job,

---

4. The salami technique is rather humorously illustrated in the 1999 movie *Office Space*.

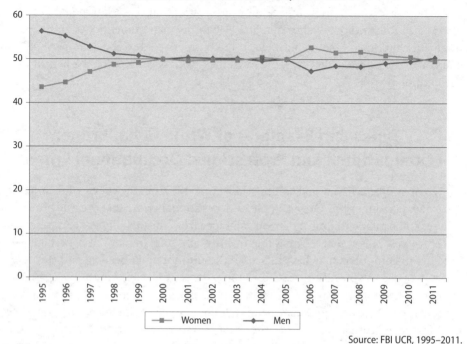

Figure 13.1. Percent of men and women arrested for
embezzlement in the United States, 1995–2011

Source: FBI UCR, 1995–2011.

explains the type of white collar crime that women engage in. The term pink collar crime applies specifically to the kind of white collar crime committed by the women in her study. More recently, Gottschalk (2013) contends that women are less involved in white collar crime because they cannot justify it as easily as men. Women appear to be more fearful of apprehension than men and perceive the consequences of incarceration as worse than men do.

However, Dodge (2007)[5] contends that when women are provided with the opportunity to commit this crime, their embezzlement schemes can rival those of men. She points to the high profile cases of Leona Helmsley, Dede Brooks and Martha Stewart as evidence for this notion and she includes some lesser-known names of women who embezzled thousands and sometimes tens and hundreds of thousands of dollars during the course of their employment as further support. Dodge (2007) notes that women have more opportunities in the current day and age to rise to the highest levels of corporations. For women in the corporate inner circle, saying no to crime may be difficult. These women may wish to fit in with their male counterparts and they likely feel the same pressure to perform as do men.

Recent media attention to pink collar criminals has focused for the most part on embezzlement and it is clear that women are not only capable of but do embezzle large

---

5. The handbook in which this work is found provides a fuller recitation of white collar and corporate crime than is possible in a chapter of this length and is recommended to the reader.

Table 13.1. Some pink collar criminals

Name	Age	Amount Embezzled	Sentence
Rita Crundwell	60	$53,000,000	20 years in prison
Harriette Walters	52	$48,000,000	16½ years in prison
Judy Del Galdo*	66	$16,000,000	Four to 12 years in prison, restitution
Linda Speaks Tribby*	42	$14,170,000	Seven years in prison
Patricia Smith*	58	$10,200,000	78 months in prison
Susan Curtis*	50	$6,200,000	Eight and a half years in prison
Kinde Durkee*	59	$5,844,000	Eight years in prison, restitution
Georgia Engelhart*	67	$4,800,000	46 months in prison, restitution
Connie Stills	56	$1,300,000	41 months in prison, three years supervised release after
Donna Gregor	42	$1,000,000	42 months in prison, restitution
Sarah Johnson	42	$986,481	4 years in prison, supervised release after, restitution
Mary Ann Williams	48	$500,000	Three and a half years in prison, seven years supervised release after
Kham Sisaleumsak	45	$300,000	Five years in prison, five years supervised release after
Barbara Ann Paulson	40	$170,000	70 months in prison, three years supervised release after, restitution
Julie Phillips	39	$100,000	366 days in jail

* On the list of the top ten worst embezzlers for the year 2011 (see Marquet, 2012).

Sources: Adapted from Pope, 2013; Paxton, 2013; Marquet, 2012.

amounts of money from their places of work. Table 13.1 gives the details of some of these cases.

A specific type of occupational crime is professional occupational crime. Professional occupational crime involves crime committed by professionals, such as lawyers, lawmakers or doctors, in the course of their jobs; their professions provide opportunities for very specific occupational crime. Lawyers might encourage their clients to pursue frivolous lawsuits or bill them for hours not worked. Lawmakers might accept bribes or kickbacks from those trying to influence their decisions on proposed changes to the law. Doctors might steer patients to specialists or laboratories in which they have a financial interest or bill insurance companies, including Medicare and Medicaid, for procedures not performed (Walsh and Hemmens, 2011). Doctors are not the only members of the medical field who might engage in professional occupational crime. Dabney's (2010) study of supply theft by nurses found that nurses routinely engage in theft of supplies such as scrubs and over the counter and nonnarcotic medicines. The nurses in this study neutralized their theft by defining it as a perk of the job. However, the nurses drew a clear line between the theft of over the counter and nonnarcotic medicine and narcotic medicine, with the latter not being tolerated by the group of nurses in this study. Dabney (2010) concludes that two sets of norms guide nurses' conduct, official hospital policy and group norms. When the two are at odds, group norms appear to win out and define what is acceptable behavior.

Types and Examples of White Collar Corporate Crime

Corporate Theft and Fraud

Corporate crime, that committed by individuals or groups in a corporation for the benefit of the corporation, comes in two varieties. The first of these is corporate theft and fraud and one type of corporate theft and fraud is restraint of trade. To understand restraint of fair trade, it is important to understand a bit about the Sherman Antitrust Act of 1890. This Act made it a misdemeanor for companies to restrain trade by forming monopolies and engaging in both price fixing and price discrimination. In 1974, Congress made restraint of trade a felony, meaning that those convicted of it could go to prison. The most common restraint of trade crime is price fixing (Kauzlarich and Barlow, 2009).

Price fixing involves the collusion of competing companies to raise or lower prices for goods; ostensibly, this price fixing benefits the companies and hurts the consumer.[6] One example of price fixing was seen in 1961, when 21 companies, including giants General Electric and Westinghouse, and 45 executives in the heavy electrical equipment industry were successfully prosecuted for price fixing. They were very careful to cover their tracks, holding secret meetings and using assumed names, but they were discovered when two of the companies submitted identical bids for equipment to the Tennessee Valley Authority. The cost to the consumer of their decade-long price fixing was estimated at $3 billion, much more than was stolen in all the thefts, burglaries and robberies in the United States during that time combined (Geis, 1978; Kauzlarich and Barlow, 2009). One of the largest price fixing cases in the history of the United States involved the grain company Archer Daniels Midland. Archer Daniels Midland executives conspired with executives at other agricultural companies in order to fix the price of the lysine, an animal food additive; this price fixing drove up the price of corn, which benefited a number of companies, including Coca Cola, Pepsi, Kellogg's and Tyson Foods. Evidence of the price fixing was collected and turned over to the FBI by Mark Whitacre, an Archer Daniels Midland executive. The company pled guilty to price fixing in 1997 and was ordered to pay a fine of $100 million; it later paid $400 million to settle a class action lawsuit by consumers. In an interesting twist, Whitacre was found guilty of embezzling $9 million from the company between 1991 and 1995. Because of his embezzlement, he lost his whistleblower's immunity and spent eight

---

6. For an overview of criminal enforcement of antitrust cases, see Griffin (2003).

and a half years in federal prison (Cohn, 2012).[7] Six of the 10 worst corporate crimes of the 1990s, of which Archer Daniels Midland was one, involved antitrust violations such as price fixing (Mokhiber, 1999).

Corporate theft and fraud can also come in the form of money laundering. The Bank of Credit and Commerce International (BCCI) was started by Agha Hassan Abedi in 1972 and was the first international bank to originate in the developing world. By 1990, it had more than $20 billion in assets in 75 countries. BCCI was famous for accepting large deposits and asking no questions. It became apparent to officials in many countries where BCCI operated that the bank was involved in questionable dealings. Instead of tackling the problem, those officials found a way to use the bank to their own ends. In 1988, BCCI was indicted for laundering million dollars of drug money. It pled guilty two years later and was fined $14 billion (Kauzlarich and Barlow, 2009). Banks originating in the developing world are not the only ones involved in shady dealings such as these. The British banking giant HSBC routinely accepted huge deposits from drug cartel members in Mexico, who were permitted to deposit hundreds of thousands of dollars in cash into the same bank on the same day with no questions asked. HSBC executives also worked to cover up the fact that transactions from Iran, a country with which the United States does not do business, were disguised and funneled through its U.S. branches. HSBC agreed to pay a nearly $2 billion settlement for these violations of the law, which included but were not limited to money laundering, and prosecutors in the United States retain the power to prosecute if HSBC does not follow through on payment and mandatory reforms. Avoiding a criminal conviction with this settlement allows HSBC to continue operating in the United States (McCoy, 2012a).

Another example of corporate theft and fraud was seen in the savings and loan crisis of the 1980s. Savings and loan associations accept savings deposits and make a variety of personal loans to its members. Savings and loans were freed up to engage in riskier investing of their depositors' money due to Reagan-era deregulation of the industry. Some of these riskier investments included ultimately unsound real estate ventures as well as junk bonds. The government, which insured deposits at savings and loan associations, began to get nervous that such risky investments were putting their insured deposits in jeopardy. The Federal Home Loan Bank Board (FHLBB) set a limit on the amount of savings and loans' deposits that could be invested in risky ventures. Many savings and loans invested more than the allowed amount in risky ventures, the most famous example of which was the Lincoln Savings and Loan Association; Lincoln went over the limit set by the FHLBB by $615 million. Lincoln Savings and Loan was headed by Charles Keating. Keating was part of the push for deregulation and gave generously to politicians who supported his position and his projects. In fact, these politicians, the so-called Keating Five, came to his aid when the FHLBB discovered Lincoln's violations, suggesting the savings and loan be spared charges. The politicians' intervention allowed Lincoln to operate for two more years, during which time Keating skimmed money from Lincoln Savings and Loan to his own real estate firm and sold his junk

---

7. The price fixing and embezzlement at Archer Daniels Midland is semi-fictionally portrayed in the 2009 movie *The Informant!*

bonds to Michael Milken for quick cash. Lincoln Savings and Loan was eventually seized by FHLBB, leaving tens of thousands with worthless bonds and their life savings gone. The total cost of the savings and loan scandal was approximately $500 billion. Keating was convicted on 73 counts of fraud and spent four years in prison (Fetini, 2008). Calavita and Pontell (1991) coined the term collective embezzlement in the wake of the savings and loan crisis to describe company executives looting their own companies and rendering them insolvent.

Younger readers may not remember the savings and loan crisis but some of the details of it described above are likely to sound very familiar, especially deregulation and risky investments, when thinking about the global economic meltdown of 2008. To fully understand the meltdown, it is necessary to first go back to 1999, when then President Clinton signed the Financial Services Modernization Act (FSMA) into law. The Act overturned a key piece of legislation, the Glass-Steagall Act of 1933, which made it a felony for banks and other financial institutions to take deposits and engage in securities activities simultaneously. With Clinton's signature, the separation between investment and commercial banks evaporated, creating something of an anything goes environment. Banks that took deposits were now free to gamble with those deposits in the securities market. This is exactly what Wall Street giants AIG, Countrywide, Lehman Brothers and Bear Stearns did for years following the passage of the FSMA. Their accounting books were bursting with securities that contained subprime mortgages, which were issued to homebuyers who were very unlikely to be able to make their payments. As homes were foreclosed upon in record numbers and home values plummeted, those who had investments comprised of loans and debt sustained heavy losses and the financial institutions named above failed, were bought out or were bailed out with taxpayer money, facilitating a worldwide economic depression that began in 2008 (Barak, 2012: Pontell and Black, 2012). These failures occurred in tandem with theretofore unheard of salaries and bonuses for corporate CEOs, even the CEOs of insolvent institutions. CEOs now earn about 500 times what their employees do and the richest one percent of Americans now holds as much wealth as the bottom 99 percent (Pontell and Black, 2012). These disparities are unheard of and Rosoff (2007) notes that today's corporate cultures facilitate aspirations to what he terms psychopathic wealth.

Among others, criminologists have asked themselves how this could have happened, especially when there were two preventive measures in place. The first of these was the Sarbanes-Oxley Act (SOX), which was passed in 2002 and the second was the creation of the Corporate Fraud Task Force, also in 2002. The Sarbanes-Oxley Act was designed to ensure oversight of corporations, transparency of their books and independence of auditors as well as to provide resources necessary to the Securities and Exchange Commission (SEC) to regulate financial institutions. The Corporate Fraud Task Force (CFTF) was designed to bring the power of multiple federal level law enforcement agencies to the problem of corporate crime, to deter said crime and to try to restore the confidence of investors. Both of these measures were created after a spate of particularly egregious corporate crime in the late 1990s and early 2000s, which included that perpetrated by the likes of Enron, Arthur Andersen, Adelphia Communications, Tyco and WorldCom (Barak, 2012); the text box below explains the crimes of these corporate entities in more detail.

Box 13.1. Corporate Theft and Fraud in the Late 1990s and Early 2000s

Enron: The energy giant seriously misrepresented its financial position by concealing debts and inflating profits in order to obscure its inevitable bankruptcy. Enron routinely encouraged shareholders and employees to buy more Enron stock and invest more in their pension plans and executives Kenneth Lay and Jeffrey Skilling took bonuses out for themselves from Enron's subsidiaries to fund their extravagant lifestyles, further diminishing the company's profitability. Lay and Skilling were convicted of multiple counts of securities and wire fraud. Lay died of a heart attack shortly after the verdicts, but Skilling was sentenced to 24 years in prison. Enron's corporate fraud is estimated to have cost $2 billion in pension plans and $60 billion in lost market shares (Friedrichs, 2004; Kauzlarich and Barlow, 2009).[8]

Arthur Andersen: Former accounting giant Arthur Andersen cooked Enron's books, creating a second set that reflected the aforementioned and inaccurate profitability. Executives at Arthur Andersen were convicted of obstruction of justice for shredding Enron's financial documents and the company is now defunct (Kauzlarich and Barlow, 2009).

Adelphia Communications: Adelphia used to be one of America's largest cable providers and appeared very profitable until news surfaced that the cable giant's finances were in shambles. In large part, this was due to $2.3 billion in loans made to business partnerships owned or operated by family members of Adelphia CEO John Rigas. These loans were not included in the company's balance sheet and Adelphia filed for bankruptcy in 2002 (Gutman, 2002).

Tyco International: Once one of the world's largest conglomerates, questions were raised about how Tyco was able to acquire so many small companies in such a short time that facilitated its massive growth. The CEO of Tyco, Dennis Kozlowski, and another executive, Mark Swartz, were convicted in 2005 of securities fraud, falsifying business records and grand larceny after it was discovered that they took unauthorized bonuses to the tune of $600 million while lying about Tyco's finances. Kozlowski was sentenced to 8 1/3 to 25 years in prison and was denied parole in 2012 (Gutman, 2002; NBC, 2005; McCoy, 2012).

WorldCom: The telecommunications giant engaged in fraudulent accounting that hid at least $3.8 billion from investors and shareholders. WorldCom made it a practice to record costs as capital expenditures, which allowed it to obscure a huge operating loss and demonstrate a large but ultimately false profit (Gutman, 2002).

With the SOX and the CFTF in place, there were 357 corporate fraud indictments between 2002 and 2005, but just 14 in 2006 and 12 in 2007. What accounted for the decline? Was it spectacular success at finding and prosecuting corporate fraud? Probably not. Rather, it appears that the CFTF was not targeting mortgage and securities fraud, the kinds of fraud that were at the root of Wall Street institutions' ultimate failure. President Obama created the Fraud Enforcement and Recovery Act (FERA) of 2009 and its enforcement arm, the Financial Fraud Enforcement Network, in part to target these frauds specifically, but by 2012, not a single case of fraud involving any of the six largest banks in the United States had been prosecuted. The greatest successes of the

---

8. For a fascinating and more detailed look at Enron, see the 2005 documentary *Enron: The Smartest Guys in the Room*.

Financial Fraud Enforcement Network involved prosecuting lower level mortgage fraudsters; that may be due in part to the fact that there were a maximum of 55 people assigned to the Financial Fraud Enforcement Network at the federal level. For each of these 55, there were $100 billion of lost home equity to investigate. In comparison, there were about a thousand FBI agents assigned to investigate the much simpler savings and loan crisis detailed above (Barak, 2012).[9]

Corporate Violence

Up to this point, readers may be thinking that corporate theft and fraud, while despicable, is not so serious that it leads to injury or death. However, there are examples of what can be called corporate violence. Perhaps the most well-known example is that of the Ford Pinto. In the late 1960s, Ford was trying to break into the small car market and devised the Pinto, primarily to compete with the Volkswagen. As Pintos were first manufactured and tested, a major problem became apparent: the gas tank was six inches from the rear bumper. In collisions as slow as 30 miles an hour, the bumper could push the gas tank forward into bolts that would pierce the tank, releasing gasoline and causing the car to explode in flames (Cullen, Cavender, Maakestad and Benson, 2006). This problem had an easy fix, namely, covering the gas tank with a rubber casing or moving the gas tank to a less dangerous place in the car. However, Ford rejected both of these easy fixes because the assembly line was ready for production and to stop and reset it would have cost the company millions of dollars. At this point, readers may be wondering if one can get to be an executive at Ford without thinking ahead to possible lawsuits from the families of those injured or killed in the Pinto due to its faulty design. Indeed, Ford executives did think ahead to these possible lawsuits and decided it would be cheaper to pay them out than to retool the assembly line and make the Pinto safer. In more detail, Ford calculated they would have to pay $200,000 per death and about $67,000 per injury, but would have to pay almost $50 million to retool the assembly line and decided to take the chance on releasing the dangerous cars for sale. Dozens of people were ultimately killed or seriously burned as a result of the faulty design of the Pinto (Cullen, Makkestad and Cavender, 1987; Kauzlarich and Barlow, 2009).

Another famous example of corporate violence against consumers is that perpetrated by the German drug company Chermie Grunenthal. Chermie Grunenthal manufactured and sold the drug thalidomide, which was marketed as a tranquilizer and as relief for morning sickness for pregnant women in the late 1950s and the 1960s. Chermie Grunenthal had evidence that the drug was dangerous for expectant mothers and their fetuses but downplayed those dangers in the interest of sales. The company could no longer deny the hazards of the drug when over 8,000 babies who were exposed to thalidomide in the womb were born with deformities of their eyes, ears, genitals and limbs as well as brain damage. Chermie Grunenthal avoided criminal prosecution,

---

9. For more on why it has proved so difficult to date to prosecute Wall Street executives for causing the recent global economic meltdown, see the PBS Frontline documentary entitled *The Untouchables*; this is in great contrast to the savings and loan crisis, after which there were more than a thousand major criminal prosecutions (Calavita, Pontell and Tillman, 1997; Black, 2005; Pontell, 2005).

but a company called Distillers Ltd. that distributed thalidomide in England was forced to pay victims of the drug in that country and in Germany (Mokhiber, 1988; Kauzlarich and Barlow, 2009).

Ford Pintos and Thalidomide are not the only products for which the manufacturers knew there was a danger to the public but decided to release them anyway. In fact, the list of these products is quite long and includes defibrillators, heart valves, intrauterine devices (IUDs), tampons, contact lens solution, bullet proof vests, magnet toys, cribs, peanuts, pistachios, poultry, beef, tires, automobiles, asbestos, fungicide, pesticides and of course a variety of pharmaceutical products including Propulsid, Trasylol, Avandia, Zyprexa, Seroquel, Ortho Evra, Prozac, Paxil and Zoloft. In all of these cases, the manufacturers of the products knew that they posed a danger to consumers but made them available to the public anyway in what appears to be rather flagrant disregard for customer safety (AAJ, 2010).

Corporate violence may be perpetrated against consumers and it may be perpetrated against workers. Readers may already be familiar with the Triangle Waist Factory fire of 1911, in which 146 people were killed in a fire at a shirtwaist factory in New York in just 18 minutes. Escape from the factory, which was located on the ninth floor of its building, was rendered impossible after the fire broke out because the owners had locked the doors in order to keep workers from stealing materials. Those hoping for rescue soon discovered that firefighters' ladders were too short to reach their floor and water from the fire hoses fell well short of the fire, as well. Many leaped to their deaths rather than burn alive. The owners of the Triangle Waist Factory, Blanck and Harris, were acquitted of criminal wrongdoing and were only forced to pay $75 per life lost in a civil suit (Cornell, 2011). The 1991 fire at Imperial Food Products resulted in the deaths of 24 workers. Again, the owner of the company had locked the doors of the plant to prevent employees from stealing chicken parts and when the fire broke out, they could not escape. The owner served over four years in prison for his role in the deaths, but Aulette and Michalowski (1993) contend this is more than example of corporate violence against workers; it can be considered state-corporate crime because the state and its agents allowed a clearly unsafe plant to keep operating. It was over a century old, it had no sprinklers and it lacked a sufficient number of escape routes. The government of North Carolina where the plant was located enacted business friendly legislation that did not require strict adherence to worker safety regulations.

Corporate violence against workers is hardly a thing of the past. Just this year (2013), nearly 1,200 garment workers were killed in Bangladesh when a building housing several garment factories collapsed. The owner of the building added floors to it that reduced its structural integrity and the factories were permitted to bring in heavy equipment that the building could not support, resulting in its collapse. The frantic search for survivors in the rubble lasted almost two weeks. The owners have been arrested and garment worker advocates in Bangladesh are using the tragedy to push for unionization rights and safer working conditions (AP, 2013). Two particularly egregious offenders in the United States in recent years are the McWayne and Massey Energy companies. McWayne is a sewer and water pipe manufacturing company headquartered in Alabama. It has what can only be described as a terrible safety record; nine workers were killed while on the job between 1995 and 2004 and three of those deaths were the result of deliberate violations of safety protocols. More than 4,600 injuries were documented among the company's 5,000 employees. That is not a typo: 4,600 injuries were documented among the company's 5,000 employees. When safety inspectors would come to the factory, McWayne higher ups would stall them at the gates while defective equipment was hidden from view. Moreover, when accidents and deaths did occur at McWayne as they often did, the sites were altered before they could be inspected by government officials in violation of federal law. The punishment that was meted out for the most serious safety violations was so minor that McWayne had no incentive to change its ways and continued to view injuries, deaths and related fines as a cost of doing business (Mokhiber and Weissman, 2005).[10] Massey Energy operates a number of coal mines in the United States. In 2010, an explosion in the Upper Big Branch mine in West Virginia killed 29 miners in the worst mining accident in the United States since 1970. It soon came to light that the Mine Safety and Health Administration (MSHA) had issued 557 safety violations to Massey in the year before the explosion, forcing the shutdown of portions of the mine 48 times. Again, no typo: 557 safety violations in the year before the explosion. The mine was allowed to stay open even with such a dismal safety record because proving a pattern of violation is very hard to do under current law and the difficulty is deliberate, with the mining industry itself helping to write the law (Sheppard, 2011). A former Massey Energy executive, David Hughart, pled guilty in 2013 to conspiring to violate mining safety regulations; during his plea, he implicated the former Massey Energy CEO Don Blankenship in the conspiracy as well (Berkes, 2013). Because the mining industry had so much influence in writing the regulations to which they were subject, the Massey Energy mine explosion might also be considered an example of state-corporate crime.

Corporate violence is not limited to that perpetrated against consumers or workers. The environment itself may also be a victim of corporate violence. Two well-known instances of corporate violence against the environment include Love Canal and the *Exxon Valdez* oil spill. In the 1940s, Hooker Chemical and Plastics Corporation purchased Love Canal in Niagara Falls, New York. They used the land to dump and bury dangerous chemicals from their production process. In a move that appeared to be quite generous but was actually quite nefarious, Hooker sold the land where it had been dumping and burying toxins to the local school board for $1 in the mid 1950s. Hooker neglected to inform the school board of the hundreds of toxic chemicals it had been dumping and burying for the last few years on their recently purchased land. The school board used the land to develop a playground and recreation center for local residents, but soon, people began complaining of the smell emanating from the playground and from the center. Moreover, residents experienced higher than normal rates of miscarriages, emotional problems and other illnesses and several died due to exposure to the buried toxins. Hooker initially claimed it was not responsible for the many problems plaguing local residents, but it was eventually forced to pay millions to victims as well as to the federal government for proper cleanup of the area (Mokhiber, 1988; Kauzlarich and Barlow, 2009).

---

10. For more on McWayne, see the PBS Frontline documentary *A Dangerous Business Revisited*. A warning: The documentary contains disturbing stories and imagery.

In 1989, the oil tanker *Exxon Valdez* ran aground in Prince William Sound, Alaska. The ship spilled between 11 and 33 million gallons of oil into what had been a pristine environment. The captain of the *Exxon Valdez*, Joseph Hazelwood, was known to have a drinking problem and his blood alcohol content was still high 11 hours after running the ship aground. Oil spill plans in place at the time were completely inadequate for the magnitude of the spill. Nevertheless, action during the first two days after the spill may have ameliorated it somewhat, but no action was taken and on the third day, a severe storm dispersed the oil across 44,000 square kilometers, including coastline. Of course, hundreds of thousands of animals were killed in the immediate aftermath, but the destruction of the way of life for those people who were part of renewable resource fishing communities was particularly devastating. Making things worse is the extended litigation process against Exxon that has taken decades, in large part because Exxon continues to appeal the amount the courts determine it owes plaintiffs. This interminable process prevents victims of this corporate violence from repairing the damage to the social fabric caused by the spill (Gil, Picou and Ritchie, 2012). Again, younger readers may not remember the *Exxon Valdez* oil spill of 1989, but they likely remember the BP oil spill of 2010. In April of that year, the *Deepwater Horizon* oil rig in the Gulf of Mexico exploded and sank, killing 11 workers. The explosion broke open an underwater oil pipeline owned by BP (formerly British Petroleum) and oil flooded the Gulf until July when the leak was finally stopped. During those four months, nearly 4.5 million barrels of oil spewed into the Gulf, fouling the water, beaches and wildlife. The spill severely diminished the ability of those dependent on the Gulf for their livelihoods, from fishermen to shrimpers to oystermen to hoteliers to those in the related professions, to make a living. BP was directed by the federal government to establish a $20 billion compensation fund to pay those whose businesses or properties were damaged by the spill (Frailing, 2012). Gill, Picou and Ritchie (2012) point out that the BP oil spill damaged the social fabric of Gulf Coast communities and that protracted legal wrangling is likely to prevent its full repair.

Theories of White Collar Crime

What causes white collar crime? Even though many of the theories discussed throughout this book purport to be general in nature, that is, able to explain all types of crime equally well. Consider for example Gottfredson and Hirschi's (1990) self-control theory. Remember it is one of the most well-supported theories of crime causation (e.g., Pratt and Cullen, 2000; Moffitt, 2012). Hirschi and Gottfredson (1989) themselves contend that self-control theory can explain lower level white collar crime, such as passing bad checks and other petty offenses. However, it may have little utility when it comes to explaining high level white collar crime such as that detailed above in the sections on corporate theft and fraud and corporate violence. In fact, some researchers contend it is not a lack of self-control but an excess of it that allows high level white collar offenders to rise to the positions in which they commit their crimes (Steffensmeier, 1989; Benson and Moore, 1992; Reed and Yeager, 1996).

Rational choice theory in the corporate context has also been subjected to empirical research. Paternoster and Simpson (1996) presented vignettes describing various types of white collar crime to 96 participants and found that the intentions to commit price fixing, bribery, manipulation of sales statistics or Environmental Protection Agency (EPA) violations were influenced by the threat of both formal and informal sanctions, moral evaluations of the behavior and organizational factors. Moral evaluations are particularly important because they can narrow the range of acceptable behaviors to exclude white collar crimes. When morals are lax, the range of acceptable behaviors widens to possibly include white collar crime and the calculation of costs and benefits to the individual and to the corporation becomes more instrumental in nature.

Agnew's (1992) General Strain Theory has also been tested as an explanatory theory of white collar crime. Langton and Piquero (2007) extracted data from the presentencing investigations of 1,910 convicted white collar offenders in order to determine if general strain was a useful explanation for their crimes. They found that strain relates to negative emotions for white collar offenders the same way it does for traditional street offenders, but the negative emotions experienced by white collar offenders are different from those of traditional street offenders. In particular, white collar offenders experience financial and business concerns as negative emotions more than do street offenders. Strain appears to work through financial concerns to facilitate the commission of both embezzlement and credit fraud, but strain did not appear to explain bribery, mail or wire fraud or false claims. Strain appears to work through business concerns to facilitate the commission of securities violations but not antitrust offenses. Langton and Piquero (2007) point out that embezzlement and credit fraud are low level white collar crimes and are usually committed by people of lower social statuses, while bribery, mail or wire fraud and false claims are middle level white collar crimes that are usually committed by people of higher social statuses. While there is some support for GST as an explanatory theory of white collar crime, its utility appears to be limited to lower level white collar crime; higher level white collar crimes such as corporate crime may be best explained by organizational theories.

Because even the strongest traditional theories of crime were created with traditional street crimes in mind and because, as seen above, their empirical support for explaining white collar crime is limited, other explanations of white collar crime have been put forth. Cullen and Agnew (2011) contend that most alternative explanations of white collar crime incorporate one or more of four elements. The first of these elements is exposure to a criminal culture. As alluded to above, Sutherland (1983) was one of the first to recognize that corporations could be organized for criminal activity the same way some neighborhoods could be. Within corporations organized for crime and in accord with differential association theory, long term employees teach newcomers not only the techniques of crime, but the definitions that favor it, as well. New employees who resist engaging in criminal activity may be derided by coworkers and denied perks and promotions, while those who engage in criminal activity are rewarded with friendships and advancement. Piquero, Tibbetts and Blankenship (2005) examined the ability of differential association and neutralization theories to explain white collar crime. They gave a vignette describing the sale of a drug known to be dangerous to 133 MBA students. The strongest predictors of releasing the drug were belief that the board of directors and closest coworkers agree with the decision, consistent with differential association theory, and the beliefs that the government exaggerates safety concerns and that profit is most important, consistent with neutralization theory. Importantly, the perceived beliefs of those outside the corporation, respondents' friends, family and professors, did not predict what respondents decided and this is evidence for the powerful effects of the corporate culture on decision making within it.

Research has shown that corporate cultures are formed in large part by the ethical orientations of upper level management (Clinard and Yeager, 1980; Clinard, 1983) and that the extent of law breaking by executives and other higher ups sets the tone for the rest of the employees in the corporation. In this conceptualization, white collar crime can be said to be not the result of a few rotten apples, but of a rotten barrel. Gottschalk (2012) found support for the existence of both rotten apples and rotten barrels among white collar criminals in Norway, with rotten barrels committing more costly crime and receiving shorter jail sentences than rotten apples. A related explanation has surfaced for corporate cultures that encourage or permit reckless decisions, such as Ford's decision to release the Pinto knowing it was dangerous. Vaughan (1992, 1996) notes that when corporations are under pressure to deliver, values can develop that allow for what she terms the normalization of deviance. In this case, risks begin to be viewed as technical problems that can be dealt with or safely ignored. A 2011 report contended that Massey Energy, the coal mining company described above, valued the production of coal over worker safety and as a result, violation of safety regulations became routine, eventually leading to an explosion that killed 29 miners (Berkes, 2011).

The second element of alternative explanations for white collar crime identified by Cullen and Agnew (2011) is the competitive financial world. Though it is unlikely that white collar offenders, especially those committing the highest level crimes, are disadvantaged in any way, they still may experience financial woes. Cressey (1953) proposed that embezzlers steal money from their places of work because they have what he called a non-shareable problem such as gambling debts that only embezzlement can solve. However, not all white collar offenders are driven to theft by perceived deprivation (Dodge, 2009; Agnew, Piquero and Cullen, 2009); some steal to fund extravagant lifestyles. The competitive financial world may also create an exclusive focus on making money within some corporations. This exclusive focus creates a situation in which morals and norms that constrain criminal behavior are weakened, consistent with both Merton's (1938) anomie theory and Messner and Rosenfeld's (2012) institutional anomie theory covered in more detail in Chapter 4. When these norms are weak, corporations may engage in practices such as price fixing or endangering the safety of workers in furtherance of profit.

Cullen and Agnew's (2011) third element of alternative explanations of white collar crime is opportunities to offend. We think of meaningful employment as insulating against crime, but the workplace is often replete with opportunities for criminal activity. Our economic system can only function with trust at its foundation. We trust that our money is being wisely invested, that the drugs we take will benefit us and that the automobiles we drive are safe. The opportunity to violate this trust is at the heart of white collar crime. Benson and Simpson (2009) point out that three conditions are part of most white collar crime. First, the offender has legitimate access to the workplace and hence the location of the crime, second, the offender is separated from the victim and third, the offender's actions appear on the surface to be legitimate ones. These conditions provide many opportunities to violate the trust we put in corporations. According to

Shover and Hochstetler (2006), the opportunity to offend (the lure, in their terms) is not sufficient for white collar crime to occur. Credible oversight must be lacking as well. As alluded to in many of the examples above, the oversight that is supposed to be provided by regulatory agencies and even the criminal justice system at the federal level is often absent or seriously deficient. Astute readers may be thinking back to Cohen and Felson's (1979) routine activity theory described in Chapter 9. Their concept of the absence of capable guardianship is similar to Shover and Hochstetler's (2006) concept of lack of credible oversight. Moreover, the concept of target suitability from routine activity theory is similar to the lure or opportunity to offend. So why not stop there and say white collar crime is well explained by routine activity theory? Shover and Hochstetler (2006) claim that offenders are not equally motivated to engage in crime. In their terms, offenders are not equally responsive to lures. Some are predisposed because of their experiences in childhood and in adulthood to be more susceptible to lures; susceptibility to lures is also predicated on the level of self-control or self-restraint. For Shover and Hochstetler (2006), white collar and indeed all crime is shaped by lures, predisposition for susceptibility to lures, the level of self-restraint and oversight or lack thereof.

The fourth element of Cullen and Agnew's (2011) alternative explanations of white collar crime is decision making by respectable offenders. If white collar offenders are indeed respectable (and this is certainly a point of contention), how do they handle the cognitive dissonance that must come with committing a crime? Benson (2010) proposes a version of neutralization that he terms denying the guilty mind. When white collar offenders break the law, they use justifications (accounts in Benson's terms) that allow them to mitigate the seriousness of their actions and therefore their guilt. This is very similar to Sykes and Matza's (1957) techniques of neutralization theory. However, the reason that Benson (2010) does not adopt techniques of neutralization wholesale as an explanatory theory for white collar crime is that the context is important. White collar offenders' accounts are tied firmly to the corporate context, so for example, employees may deny their guilty minds by saying that their white collar crime was necessary to improve the image of the firm and draw more investors.

In a sample of 30 convicted white collar offenders, Benson (2010) found that the most consistent pattern was denial of criminal intent rather than denial that a crime had occurred. The conviction process elicited a number of emotions in offenders, including embarrassment, anger and a desire for the process to be over. Benson (2010) describes denials of different kinds of white collar offenders, beginning with antitrust offenders. Antitrust offenders frequently noted that antitrust activities were necessary for their businesses to survive. They often reduced their crimes to technical violations and were quick to compare their crimes to those of traditional street offenders in an effort to deny or at least mitigate their guilt. Tax violators frequently claimed that everyone cheats on their taxes and they were just the unlucky ones who got caught. They denied criminal intent by claiming ignorance or altruistic motives. Financial trust violators, all embezzlers, were unusual among this group in that they acknowledged that their actions were criminal. Antitrust offenders can deny their guilt by claiming the best interests of the business were at stake and tax violators can claim ignorance or altruism, but embezzlers can claim neither account because this is an individual crime that solely benefits the offender. Some embezzlers denied their guilt by claiming that if they were truly criminal, they would have stolen much more and done it much faster than they did. Those convicted of fraud and false statements often claimed that while a crime had occurred, they personally did not commit it. They claimed to have been set up by business associates or railroaded by the criminal justice system and utilize a scapegoating strategy to deny their guilt. The nature of fraud makes it possible to shift the blame to another and deny not just culpability but any involvement in crime. Implied in Benson's (2010) description of convicted white collar offenders is resistance to adopting and internalizing a criminal label. Dhami (2013) interviewed 19 convicted white collar criminals and found that their views of their criminal activities as neutral or even positive, plus enduring support from their families who identified them as law abiders, created circumstances in which they did not adopt and internalize a criminal label.

What can be done about white collar crime? As it does for other types of crime, the answer to that question depends on what we believe causes white collar crime. Paternoster and Simpson (1996) contend that attempts to strengthen the ethics of corporate managers may prove useful in curbing white collar crime because their research shows ethical orientations are important in causing white collar crime. This strengthening may best be started at the university level; Tang, Chen and Sutarso (2008) found that business students, long before they are managers, are less ethical than those in other areas of study. Piquero and Schoepfer (2010) note that some companies take a proactive approach to white collar crime and screen job applicants using a personality test that is focused on work ethic. Shover and Hochstetler (2006) say more enforcement efforts are necessary to curb white collar crime (see also Benson and Cullen, 1998; Cullen, Cavender, Maakestad and Benson, 2006). The threat of punishment is currently weak for white collar offenders and making punishment more certain will raise the risk of engaging in this crime. Moreover, many white collar offenders have social bonds to family, work and the community that they probably do not wish to jeopardize with a prison sentence. Of course, the certainty of punishment is predicated on credible oversight in the form of both regulatory agencies and law enforcement at the federal level. Benson (2010) and to a larger extent Dhami (2013) suggest that white collar offenders enroll in programs that help them to accept the criminal nature of their actions, to take responsibility for their actions and their consequences and to show remorse. Perhaps the most prudent approach to solving the white collar crime problem is to attack it from all sides, enhancing ethical training for students and managers, thoroughly screening job applicants, increasing the threat of punishment through the provision of credible oversight and showing convicted white collar offenders the harm caused by their actions.

Khaki Collar Crime

The seminal work on khaki collar crime is by Clifton Byrant (1979). In this book, he draws on studies of military crime from different countries and different time periods to develop two different typologies for understanding military crime. The first typology classifies military crimes by type and includes crimes against property, crimes against persons and crimes against performance; the latter type had theretofore never been utilized to understand military or any type of crime. The activities Bryant (1979) called crimes against performance include malingering, dereliction of duty, mutiny, fraternization with the enemy, cowardice, desertion, conduct unbecoming, fragging, substance addiction and black marketeering. Bryant (1979) contends that there are three military contexts in which crimes against property, people and performance may be committed, intraoccupational (involving other military members), extraoccupational (involving civilians) and interoccupational (involving enemy soldiers).

A number of factors facilitate khaki collar crime of all types. The most important of these factors are the makeup of the armed forces and the large number of rules and regulations that characterize military life. Bryant (1979) contends that many rank and file members of the armed forces are young, single, lower class males for whom social control is less effective; this group appears to be more prone to rule breaking. That in combination with the sheer number of rules and regulations governing life in the military means that rules are going to be violated. It is impossible to detect and punish every rule violation and Bryant (1979) maintains that a certain amount of deviance is tolerated by the military, especially crimes against property or people. He views these crimes as part and parcel of military service within the intraoccupational context. Interestingly, Bryant (1979) intimates that crimes against performance are viewed as more serious by the military than crimes against property or people. Within the extraoccupational context, violent crimes against civilians are more common than crimes against property and Bryant (1979) attributes this to the makeup of the armed forces in combination with the stress of wartime service. Within the interoccupational crime context, Bryant (1979) notes that there are strict rules and regulations governing comportment when engaged with the enemy, but that the number of these rules coupled with the fact that they can change from conflict to conflict makes their violation likely.

Writing shortly after the end of the Vietnam War, Bryant (1979) concludes his book with a series of questions that need to be answered before we can fully understand khaki collar crime. Among these questions were whether a host of changes in the military, including the composition of military members in terms of race and gender, the increased sophistication and value of equipment and the ability to kill from a great distance, would foster various forms of deviance.

Moore (1981) points out that one of the lingering questions of Bryant's (1979) work has to do with situational definitions of deviance. What is deviant in one setting may not be deviant in another, so it can be difficult to tell when behavior has deviated from the norm and to what extent it has. One recent example of the apparent normalization of seriously deviant behavior in the extraoccupational context was seen in the Iraqi prison Abu Ghraib. Anyone who watched television in 2004 is likely to have seen graphic pictures of prisoner abuse. The abuse included but was not limited to forcing prisoners to simulate sex with one another, to masturbate themselves in front of other prisoners, to remain naked for days at a time, to form a pile with other prisoners while naked, to wear a leash, to wear hoods for extended periods of time and to wear women's underwear;[11] other abuses included punching, slapping and kicking prisoners, beating prisoners with a broom

---

11. In Arab culture, homosexual acts are forbidden and it is very humiliating for a man to be naked in front of another man; forcing any of these activities on an Arab man amounts to torture (Hersh, 2004).

handle, pouring cold water on prisoners, threatening male prisoners with rape, threatening them with guns, threatening them with dogs, pouring the chemicals from broken lights on prisoners and sodomizing them (Hersh, 2004; Taguba, 2004).

How could such widespread abuse become a matter of practice among members of the military? How could such seriously deviant behavior have become so routine, so normal? Two of the seven offenders most directly involved in the abuse of prisoners, Chip Frederick and Charles Graner, actually had experience as civilian prison guards before arriving at Abu Ghraib, but their military unit as a whole was trained for traffic and police duties, not for prison security. Moreover, the prison was often overcrowded and understaffed, compounding the problem. Frederick maintained that he was following orders and in torturing prisoners, was just doing things the way that the dominant forces inside the prison—military intelligence comprised of CIA officers and private interrogations specialists—wanted them done. While his claims are self-serving, there may be some truth to them. The torture at Abu Ghraib had a purpose beyond humiliation, namely breaking prisoners' spirits so they would reveal information useful in the war on terror. Military intelligence instructed the military police in charge of guarding the prison to treat prisoners in a way that would make them more likely to give up information when interrogated and the military police, including Frederick, Graner and others, went along with these orders. In fact, General Taguba, charged with investigating abuse at Abu Ghraib, contends that high ranking military intelligence rather than low ranking military police are ultimately to blame for the torture of prisoners there (Hersh, 2004; Taguba, 2004).

It turns out that Bryant's (1979) question about how the changing demographics of the military might foster deviance was rather prescient. One of the intraoccupational military crimes that has received a great deal attention in recent years is the rape and sexual assault of those in uniform by others in uniform.[12] A recent study reveals that over 16,000 service members per year are estimated to have been raped or sexually assaulted while serving in the military.[13] There are a wide range of serious life consequences for the many female military members who have been raped during their service, including high rates of homelessness after discharge and even higher rates of post-traumatic stress disorder (Dick, 2012).

While serving, many female military members are actively discouraged from reporting rapes to their superior officers when they happen. When they try to report, they are reminded of the legal repercussions of filing a false report, which include loss of rank and a possible charge of adultery if either the offender or the victim is married. Compounding the problem is that victims and offenders are usually in very close quarters due to their shared military service and continue to encounter one another after the

---

12. Much of the material for this subsection is taken from the recent documentary *The Invisible War* (Dick, 2012).

13. Rape, sexual assault and sexual harassment are nothing new in the military. Consider the U.S. Navy's Tailhook scandal of 1991, the U.S. Army's rape and sexual harassment scandal at Aberdeen Proving Ground in 1996 and the U.S. Air Force's rape and sexual assault scandal at the Air Force Academy in 2003. In the present day, the elite Marine Barracks in Washington, D.C. tolerates a great deal of sexual harassment of female Marines, which has been shown to facilitate the occurrence of rape (Dick, 2012).

initial assault; offenders' repeated assaults of the same victim or assaults of a number of different victims are not uncommon. Offenders may also be highly regarded by and even friends with the senior officers to whom a report of rape or sexual assault is made; in this case, the victim of the rape may be investigated or even punished. In the worst case, the person to whom victims are supposed to report rapes is the rapist himself (Dick, 2012).

Rape and sexual assault allegations made within the military are not investigated by the civilian criminal justice system, where there are professionals with law enforcement, legal and correctional training and expertise. Rather, the military maintains its own justice system and investigative, prosecutorial and sentencing duties are centered in the unit's commanding officer. The commanding officer has total authority when deciding whether to investigate a claim of rape or sexual assault and if so, whether to adjudicate it himself or whether to pass it along to a senior officer; the latter is a very rare occurrence. Should the case get to a point where the accused is tried before a military panel, the commanding officer chooses the panel members himself. The accused is permitted to introduce evidence of his good character during the panel. Moreover, the commanding officer has wide discretion in deciding whether to bring charges against the accuser (Natelson, 2012). For the over 3,200 offenders who were found to have committed rape or sexual assault while in the military in just one year, less than 200 were incarcerated for any length of time. After seeing the aforementioned documentary on rape in the military, Secretary of Defense Leon Panetta took the decision to prosecute away from commanding officers (Dick, 2012).

Conclusion

In this chapter, we have seen that a variety of traditional theories of crime have been put forth to try to explain white (and to a lesser extent pink and khaki) collar crime. These theories include self-control, rational choice and differential association, as well as variations on routine activity and neutralization. However, there is little agreement on what the best explanatory theory is for white collar crime and even those who claim that their theory is useful struggle to some degree to demonstrate that it explains all types of white collar crime, from the lowest level embezzlement to the highest level destruction of the American housing market, which facilitated the recent global economic meltdown. Perhaps the best reason to continue our study of white collar crime has its roots in the one specified by Sutherland (1940) nearly three quarters of a century ago; it reminds us that the ways we might be victimized are not limited to street crimes. Moreover, because white collar crime broadens our definition of the very concept of crime, it calls into question what we know about crime's correlates and causes and encourages us to reach a more comprehensive understanding of this phenomenon. A better understanding of white collar crime and criminals is also essential if we are to formulate effective, proactive policies for its prevention.

Websites to Visit

White Collar Crime: http://www.fbi.gov/about-us/investigate/white_collar/whitecollar
  crime, http://www.nw3c.org/
Pink Collar Crime: http://www.pinkcollarcrime.com/
Corporate Crime Task Forces: http://www.justice.gov/archive/dag/cftf/, http://
  www.sec.gov/news/press/2009/2009-249.htm

Discussion Questions

1. What do you think is worse, traditional street crime or white collar crime? Why
    do you think this?
2. What is the worse cost of white collar crime in your estimation, the financial cost
    or the social cost? Why do you think this?
3. What is the appropriate punishment for a serious white collar offender?
4. Are there any traditional theories of crime that are useful in understanding white
    collar crime, or do we need new theoretical perspectives?
5. How do you explain the fact that women are commonly involved in low level white
    collar crime but rarely involved in high level white collar crime?
6. What is the value of the military maintaining its own justice system?

References

AAJ. (2010). *They knew and failed to.* American Association for Justice. Retrieved from:
  http://www.justice.org/clips/theyknewandfailedto.pdf.
Agnew, Robert. (1992). Foundation for a general strain theory of crime and delinquency.
  Criminology, 30, 47–87.
Agnew, Robert, Nicole Leeper Piquero and Francis Cullen. (2009). General strain theory
  and white-collar crime. In S. Simpson and D. Weisburd (Eds.), *The criminology of
  white-collar crime* (pp. 35–60). New York, NY: Elsevier/JAI Press.
AP. (2013). Search for dead in Bangladesh collapse over; 1,127 killed in worst garment
  industry disaster. The Washington Post, May 13. Retrieved from: http://www.wash-
  ingtonpost.com/world/asia_pacific/bangladesh-plans-to-raise-wages-for-garment-
  workers-after-factory-collapse-raises-scrutiny/2013/05/12/41942dfe-bb72-11e2-b537-ab47
  f0325f7c_story.html.
Aulette, Judy and Raymond Michalowski. (1993). Fire in the hamlet: A case study of
  state-corporate crime. In K. Tunnell (Ed.), *Political crime in contemporary America:
  A critical approach* (pp. 171–206). New York, NY: Garland.
Barak, Gregg. (2012). On the rhetoric and reality of fighting financial fraud on Wall
  Street. *The Criminologist, 37,* 1, 3–7.

Benson, Michael and Elizabeth Moore. (1992). Are white-collar and common criminals the same? An empirical and theoretical critique of a recently proposed general theory of crime. *Journal of Research in Crime and Delinquency, 29,* 25–72.

Berkes, Howard. (2011). Report blasts Massey for "deviance" in safety culture. *NPR,* May 19. Retrieved from: http://www.npr.org/2011/05/19/136426906/report-blasts-massey-for-deviance-in-safety-culture.

Berkes, Howard. (2013). Former Massey CEO accused of conspiracy in court hearing. *NPR,* February 28. Retrieved from: http://www.npr.org/blogs/thetwo-way/2013/02/28/173178951/former-massey-ceo-accused-of-conspiracy-in-court-hearing.

Benson, Michael. (2010). Denying the guilty mind. In P. Cromwell (Ed.), *In their own words: Criminals on crime.* 5th ed. (pp. 224–234). New York, NY: Oxford University Press.

Benson, Michael and Francis Cullen. (1988). *Combating corporate crime: Local prosecutors at work.* Boston, MA: Northeastern University Press.

Benson, Michael and Sally Simpson. (2009). *White-collar crime: An opportunity perspective.* New York, NY: Routledge.

Black, William. (2005). *The best way to rob a bank is to own one: How corporate executives and politicians looted the S&L industry.* Austin, TX: University of Texas Press.

Bryant, Clifton. (1979). *Khaki collar crime: Deviant behavior in the military context.* New York, NY: Free Press.

Calavita, Kitty and Henry Pontell. (1991). "Other's people's money" revisited: Collective embezzlement in the savings and loan and insurance industries. *Social Problems, 38,* 94–112.

Calavita, Kitty, Henry Pontell and Robert Tillman. (1997). *Big money crime: Fraud and politics in the savings and loan crisis.* Berkeley, CA: University of California Press.

Clinard, Marshall. (1983). *Corporate ethics and crime: The role of middle management.* Beverly Hills, CA: Sage.

Clinard, Marshall and Richard Quinney. (1973). Reflections of a typologic, corporate, comparative criminologist. *The Criminologist, 14,* 1, 6, 11, 14–15.

Clinard, Marshall and Peter Yeager. (1980). *Corporate crime.* New York, NY: Free Press.

Cohen, Lawrence and Marcus Felson. (1979). Social change and crime rate trends: A routine activity approach. *American Sociological Review, 44,* 588–607.

Cohn, Michael. (2012). Informant blew the whistle on price fixing at ADM. *Accounting Today,* June 21. Retrieved from: http://www.accountingtoday.com/debits_credits/informant-mark-whitacre-price-fixing-adm-acfe-63051-1.html.

Cornell. (2011). Remembering the 1911 Triangle Factory fire. Retrieved from: http://www.ilr.cornell.edu/trianglefire/story/introduction.html.

Cressey, Donald. (1953). *Other people's money: A study in the social psychology of embezzlement.* New York, NY: Free Press.

Cullen, Francis, William Maakestad and Gray Cavender. (1987). *Corporate crime under attack: The Ford Pinto case.* Cincinnati, OH: Anderson.

Cullen, Francis, Gray Cavender, William Maakestad and Michael Benson. (2006). *Corporate crime under attack: The fight to criminalize business violence.* 2nd ed. Cincinnati, OH: Anderson/LexisNexis.

Cullen, Francis T. and Robert Agnew. (2011). *Criminological theory: Past to present.* 4th ed. New York, NY: Oxford University Press.

Dabney, Dean. (2010). Neutralization and deviance in the workplace: Theft of supplies and medicines by hospital nurses. In P. Cromwell (Ed.), *In their own words: Criminals on crime.* 5th ed. (pp. 235–250). New York, NY: Oxford University Press.

Daly, Kathleen. (1989). Gender and varieties of white-collar crime. *Criminology, 27,* 769–794.

Dhami, Mandeep. (2013). White-collar crime. In A. Thio, T. Calhoun and A. Conyers (Eds.), *Deviance today* (pp. 169–178). Boston, MA: Pearson.

Dick, Kirby. (2012). Director, *The Invisible War.*

Dodge, Mary. (2007). From pink to white with various shades of embezzlement: Women who commit white-collar crimes. In H. Pontell and G. Geis (Eds.), *International handbook of white-collar and corporate crime* (pp. 379–404). New York, NY: Springer.

Dodge, Mary. (2009). *Women and white-collar crime.* Upper Saddle River, NJ: Prentice.

FBI UCR. (2011). Persons arrested, 1995–2011. Retrieved for each year from: http://www.fbi.gov/about-us/cjis/ucr/ucr-publications#Crime.

Fetini, Alyssa. (2008). A brief history of the Keating Five. *Time,* October 8. Retrieved from: http://www.time.com/time/business/article/0,8599,1848150,00.html.

Frailing, Kelly. (2012). Fraud in the wake of disasters. In D.W. Harper and K. Frailing (Eds.), *Crime and criminal justice in disaster.* 2nd ed. (pp. 157–176). Durham, NC: Carolina Academic Press.

Friedrichs, David. (2004). *Trusted criminals: White collar crime in contemporary society.* 2nd ed. Belmont, CA: Thomson/Wadsworth.

Geis, Gilbert. (1978). Deterring corporate crime. In M. Ermann and R. Lundman (Eds.), *Corporate and governmental deviance* (pp. 251–261). New York, NY: Oxford University Press.

Gill, Duane, J. Steven Picou and Liesel Ritchie. (2012). When the disaster is a crime: Legal issues and the Exxon Valdez oil spill. In D.W. Harper and K. Frailing (Eds.), *Crime and criminal justice in disaster.* 2nd ed. (pp. 73–96). Durham, NC: Carolina Academic Press.

Gottfredson, Michael and Travis Hirschi. (1990). *A general theory of crime.* Palo Alto, CA: Stanford University Press.

Gottschalk, Peter. (2012). Rotten apples versus rotten barrels in white collar crime: A qualitative analysis of white collar offenders in Norway. *International Journal of Criminal Justice Sciences, 7,* 575–590.

Gottschalk, Peter. (2013). Women's justification of white-collar crime. *International Journal of Contemporary Business Studies, 4,* 24–32.

Griffin, James. (2003). *The modern lenience program after ten years: A summary overview of the antitrust division's criminal enforcement program.* Retrieved from: http://www.justice.gov/atr/public/speeches/201477.htm.

Gutman, Huck. (2002). Dishonesty, greed and hypocrisy in corporate America. *The Statesman,* July 14. Retrieved from: http://www.commondreams.org/views02/0712-02.htm.

Hersh, Seymour. (2004). Torture at Abu Ghraib. *The New Yorker,* May 10. Retrieved from: http://www.newyorker.com/archive/2004/05/10/040510fa_fact?currentPage=all.

Hirschi, Travis and Michael Gottfredson. (1989). The significance of white-collar crime for a general theory of crime. *Criminology, 27*, 359–371.

Kauzlarich, David and Hugh Barlow. (2009). *Introduction to criminology*. 9th ed. Lantham, MD: Rowman and Littlefield.

Langton, Lynn and Nicole Leeper Piquero. (2007). Can general strain theory explain white-collar crime? A preliminary investigation of the relationship between strain and select white-collar offenses. *Journal of Criminal Justice, 35*, 1–15.

Marquet. (2012). *Marquet International 2011 report on embezzlement*. Retrieved from: http://www.marquetinternational.com/pdf/the_2011_marquet_report_on_ embezzlement.pdf.

McCoy, Kevin. (2012). Ex-Tyco CEO Dennis Kozlowski begged parole board for mercy. *USA Today*, April 12. Retrieved from: http://usatoday30.usatoday.com/money/ companies/management/story/2012-04-11/dennis-kozlowski-parole-hearing/ 54180674/1.

McCoy, Kevin. (2012a). HSBC will pay $1.9 billion for money laundering. *USA Today*, December 11. Retrieved from: http://www.usatoday.com/story/money/business/ 2012/12/11/hsbc-laundering-probe/1760351/.

Merton, Robert K. (1938). Social structure and anomie. *American Sociological Review, 3*, 672–682.

Messner, Steven F. and Richard Rosenfeld. (2012). *Crime and the American dream*. Independence, KY: Cengage Learning.

Moffitt, Terrie. (2012). Self-control, then and now. In R. Loeber and B. Welsh (Eds.), *The future of criminology* (pp. 40–45). New York, NY: Oxford University Press.

Mokhiber, Russell. (1988). *Corporate crime and corporate violence*. San Francisco, CA: Sierra Club.

Mokhiber, Russell. (1999). Top 100 corporate criminals of the decade. Retrieved from: http://www.corporatecrimereporter.com/top100.html.

Mokhiber, Russell and Robert Weissman. (2005). The 10 worst corporations of 2004. Retrieved from: http://www.commondreams.org/views05/0124-21.htm.

Moore, J. Malcolm. (1981). Khaki-collar crime: Deviant behavior in the military context book review. *Journal of Criminal Law and Criminology, 72*, 864–866.

Natelson, Rachel. (2012). In military justice system, an all-powerful arbiter. *The New York Times*, June 29. Retrieved from: http://atwar.blogs.nytimes.com/2012/06/29/ in-military-justice-system-an-all-powerful-arbiter/.

NBC. (2005). Ex-Tyco CEO Dennis Kozlowski found guilty. *NBC News*, June 17. Retrieved from: http://www.nbcnews.com/id/8258729/.

O'Hear, Michael. (2001). Blue-collar crimes/white-collar criminals: Sentencing elite athletes who commit violent crimes. *Marquette Sports Law Review, 12*, 427–447.

Paxton, Kelly. (2013). Pink collar crime website. Retrieved from: http://www.pinkcollar crime.com/category/the-ladies-of-pcc/.

Paternoster, Raymond and Sally Simpson. (1996). Sanction threats and appeals to morality: Testing a rational choice model of corporate crime. *Law & Society Review, 30*, 549–584.

PBS. (2002). Criminal prosecutions of workplace fatalities. Retrieved from: http://www.pbs.org/wgbh/pages/frontline/shows/workplace/osha/referrals.html.

Piquero, Nicole Leeper, Stephen Tibbetts and Michael Blankenship. (2005). Examining the role of differential association and techniques of neutralization in explaining corporate crime. *Deviant Behavior, 26,* 159–188.

Piquero, Nicole Leeper and Andrea Schoepfer. (2010). Theories of white-collar crime and public policy. In H. Barlow and S. Decker (Eds.), *Criminology and public policy* (pp. 188–200). Philadelphia, PA: Temple University Press.

Pontell, Henry. (2005). Control fraud, gambling for resurrection, and moral hazard: Accounting for white-collar crime in the savings and loan crisis. *Journal of Socio-Economics, 34,* 756–770.

Pontell, Henry and William Black. (2012). White-collar criminology and the Occupy Wall Street movement. *The Criminologist, 37,* 1, 3–6.

Pope, Kelly. (2013). Most notorious "pink-collar" criminal to be sentenced for $53 million theft. *The Daily Beast,* February 14. Retrieved from: http://www.thedailybeast.com/articles/2013/02/14/most-notorious-pink-collar-criminal-to-be-sentenced-for-53-million-theft.html

Pratt, Travis and Francis Cullen. (2000). The empirical status of Gottfredson and Hirschi's general theory of crime: A meta-analysis. *Criminology, 38,* 931–964.

Reed, Gary and Peter Yeager. (1996). Organizational offending and neo-classical criminology: Challenging the reach of a general theory of crime. *Criminology, 34,* 357–382.

Rosoff, Steven. (2007). The role of the mass media in the Enron fraud: Cause or cure? In H. Pontell and G. Geis (Eds.), *International handbook of white-collar and corporate crime* (pp. 513–522). New York, NY: Springer.

Rosoff, Steven, Henry Pontell and Robert Tillman. (1998). *Profit without honor: White-collar crime and the looting of America.* Upper Saddle River, NJ: Prentice-Hall.

Sheppard, Kate. (2011). How to rack up 557 safety violations and not get shut down. *Mother Jones,* January 21. Retrieved from: http://www.motherjones.com/environment/2011/01/mine-safety-massey-msha.

Shover, Neal. (2010). Blue-collar, white-collar: Crimes and mistakes. In W. Bernasco (Ed.), *Offenders on offending: Learning about crime from criminals* (pp. 205–227). Portland, OR: Willan.

Shover, Neal and Andy Hochstetler. (2006). *Choosing white-collar crime.* New York, NY: Cambridge University Press.

Steffensmeier, Darrell. (1989). On the causes of white-collar crime: An assessment of Hirschi and Gottfredson's claims. *Criminology, 27,* 345–358.

Sutherland, Edwin. (1940). White collar criminality. *American Sociological Review, 5,* 1–12.

Sutherland, Edwin. (1983 [1949]). *White collar crime: The uncut version.* New Haven, CT: Yale University Press.

Sykes, Gresham and David Matza. (1957). Techniques of neutralization: A theory of delinquency. *American Sociological Review, 22,* 664–670.

Taguba, Antonio. (2004). Article 15-6 investigation of the 800th military police brigade. Retrieved from: http://www.npr.org/iraq/2004/prison_abuse_report.pdf.

Tang, Thomas, Yuh-Jia Chen and Toto Sutarso. (2008). Bad apples in bad (business) barrels: The love of money, Machiavellianism, risk tolerance, and unethical behavior. *Management Decision, 46,* 243–263.

Vaughan, Diane. (1992). The macro-micro connection in white-collar crime theory. In K. Schlegel and D. Weisburd (Eds.), *White-collar crime reconsidered* (pp. 124–145). Boston, MA: Northeastern University Press.

Vaughan, Diane. (1996). *The Challenger launch decision: Risky technology, culture, and deviance at NASA.* Chicago, IL: University of Chicago Press.

Walsh, Anthony and Craig Hemmens. (2011). *Introduction to criminology: A text/reader.* 2nd ed. Los Angeles, CA: Sage.

Weisburd, David, Stanton Wheeler, Elin Waring and Nancy Bode. (1991). *Crimes of the middle classes: White-collar offenders in the federal courts.* New Haven, CT: Yale University Press.

Chapter 14

Public Order Crime and Criminalized Lifestyles

Introduction

When we talk about public order crimes, we are talking primarily about alcohol, drug and prostitution offenses. These crimes are *mala prohibita* crimes—they are bad because we say they are bad. We see the notion of making something a crime by calling it a crime and calling the people who do it criminals illustrated in a classic work by Howard Becker (1963). He contended that it is not the quality of the act that makes it deviant but rather the consequence of the application of rules and sanctions on the person who has committed the act or broken the rule. The deviant then is one to whom the label deviant has been successfully applied. The successful application of a deviant label, according to Becker (1963), reflects the work of two types of moral entrepreneurs: rule makers and rule enforcers. "Before an act can be viewed as deviant, and before any class of people can be labeled and treated as outsiders for committing the act, someone must have made the rule which defines the act as deviant" (Becker, 1963, p. 162).[1] We also consider lifestyles that have been criminalized to varying degrees, including homosexuality, pedophilia and child pornography, homelessness and mental illness.

The Extent of Public Order Crime

Table 14.1 shows the number of arrests and characteristics of arrestees for a number of different public order crimes for 2011.

---

1. Astute readers should be thinking back to labeling theory in Chapter 5.

Table 14.1. Number of arrests and arrestee characteristics for public order crimes in the U.S., 2011

Crime	Number of Arrests and % of Total Arrests (12,408,899)	% White Arrested	% African American Arrested	% Male Arrested	% Female Arrested	% Under 18 Arrested	% Under 25 Arrested
Alcohol offenses total	2,248,943, 18.1%	83.1	13.7	75.8	24.2	7	42.9
—DUI	1,215,077, 10%	85.3	12.1	75.4	24.6	.8	26.2
—Liquor laws	500,648, 4%	82	13.5	70.3	29.7	18.2	75.9
—Drunkenness	534,218, 4.3%	81.9	15.5	81.8	18.2	2.1	26.7
Drug abuse violations	1,531,251, 12.3%	66.9	31.7	80.2	19.8	9.6	45.5
Prostitution/ commercialized vice	57,345, .46%	53.4	43.6	31.2	68.8	1.7	29.9
Disorderly conduct	582,158, 4.7%	63	34.4	72	28	23.6	50.8
Gambling	8,596, <.01%	29.8	66.9	87.9	12.1	11.8	47.1
Vagrancy	29,203, .24%	58.1	39.3	80.6	19.4	6.2	29.5

Source: FBI UCR, 2011.

Table 14.1 clearly shows that together, alcohol and drug offense arrests made up 30.4 percent of all arrests in 2011. African Americans were overrepresented in arrests for drug abuse violations, prostitution, disorderly conduct, gambling and vagrancy. Men were arrested far more often for all of these crimes except prostitution. Many of these crimes are youthful crimes, with people under age 25 overrepresented in arrests for alcohol offenses, drug abuse violations, disorderly conduct and gambling.

Alcohol

As we saw in Chapter 8, drug use and crime are linked. But what about alcohol and crime? Here, the link may be even stronger. Of all the mind and mood altering substances out there, the link between alcohol and crime, including and especially violent crime, is the strongest and most direct. Alcohol is a factor in more than half of homicides and assaults and forty percent of offenders incarcerated for a violent offense reported drinking at the time of their offense (Martin, 2001). What explains this connection? Part of the answer lies in the pharmacological properties of alcohol itself. Alcohol's effects on the neurotransmitter GABA reduce anxiety about the consequences of aggressive behavior. Alcohol also increases dopamine in the brain and lowers the amount of serotonin, the neurotransmitter responsible for inhibiting behavior. When serotonin is reduced, the effects of dopamine are even more pronounced and aggressive behavior is more likely to occur, especially for males (Martin, 2001).[2] However, social context also plays a role in the production of aggressive behavior. Violence is more likely at bars where groups of young men gather to drink, for example. With their inhibitions lowered and aggression more likely, what might otherwise be innocuous encounters between these young men, bumping into one another or prolonged eye contact, for example, can result in physical confrontations that turn violent (Martin, 2001).

A special kind of alcohol offense is drunk driving. The National Highway Traffic Safety Administration reports 9,878 alcohol impaired driving fatalities in 2011. Vermont had the fewest with 18, while Texas had the most with 1,213 (Century Council, 2012). Drunk driving deaths used to be thought of as accidents, but the founding of Mothers Against Drunk Driving in the early 1980s and their lobbying power resulted in harsher penalties for drunk drivers, the nationwide increase in the legal drinking age to 21 and the lowering of the legal limit for operating a motor vehicle to a blood alcohol content (BAC) of 0.10 to 0.08 grams per deciliter of blood.[3] In fact, MADD's efforts and their outcomes appear to have helped change the very way we conceive of drunk driving.

---

2. Just because aggression is more likely to occur when drinking does not mean it is a foregone conclusion. People have a number of different reactions to alcohol ingestion, including becoming more amorous, maudlin or silly. The authors of this book largely limit their uninhibited-by-alcohol behavior to toneless singing. The first author prefers The Gambler or In the Ghetto while the second author's usual choice is This World Is Not My Home.

3. Maruschak (1999) found the average BAC of a person arrested for DUI was 0.24, three times the legal limit.

Where we once thought of deaths resulting from drunk driving as accidents, we now consider them criminal (Walsh and Hemmens, 2011).[4]

Box 14.1. The Evolution of Blue Laws

We bring up blue laws (so called because they were originally written on blue paper) here to illustrate the ready compunction found in our society to design laws to essentially support and enforce religious standards and single out and punish those who would dare to violate the law. Every state in the United States continues to have blue laws on the books. Largely growing out of the Temperance movement of the 19th and early 20th centuries, the most common blue laws focused on the control and sale of alcoholic beverages either all day Sunday or the part of the day that coincided with religious services. In earlier times, blue laws also controlled other retail sales occurring on Sundays such as the sale of automobiles.

The earliest known example of a blue law dates back to 1610 in the colony of Virginia. In Virginia, it was mandatory for people to go to church service on Sundays and to close businesses. Mandating the closure of business gave people less reason to miss church. Astute readers may be wondering how a law mandating church attendance could be permitted in the United States were such a high premium is placed on the separation of church and state. The issue came before the Supreme Court in *McGowan* v. *Maryland* in 1961. Maryland's blue laws only permitted the sale of drugs, tobacco, newspapers and some food items on Sundays. The law was challenged by retailers as violating both their First and Fourteenth Amendment Rights, but the Supreme Court found that even though shop closures on Sundays had their roots in colonial law mandating church attendance on the day most important to Christians, the modern purpose of these laws is secular, to promote citizens' health and safety. The Court held that Maryland's blue law did not violate either amendment.

Drugs

To understand drug offenses, we need to understand more about the complicated relationship the United States has had with mind and mood altering substances. Using the common descriptor War on Drugs conjures up an image of going toe-to-toe with an enemy who will destroy us if we fail to fight it to our last breath but the truth of the matter is that the drugs we are warring against have only been our enemy in any real sense for a little more than 100 years. Prior to the Harrison Act, drugs were largely unregulated within the United States. So-called patent medicines often contained cocaine and heroin derivatives and were sold without prescription. Addicts in the late 19th century were for the most part middle-class women treating female problems with laudanum and paregoric (tincture of opium) and disabled Union veterans of the American Civil War (Ball, 1965; O'Donnell and Ball, 1966). These conventional usages were undertaken primarily to control pain and not necessarily for the euphoric effect.

---

4. Though we may think of risking the lives of the general public as criminal, that does not stop people from attempting to excuse drunk driving or other impaired driving behavior. For a fascinating list of excuses and challenges of them, see NHTSA (2013).

The Harrison Narcotic Tax Act of 1914 was the opening salvo on the part of the federal government to restrict the sale of opium or coca leaves. The Act initially provided for "the registration of, with collectors of internal revenue, and to impose a special tax on all persons who produce, import, manufacture, compound, deal in, dispense, sell, distribute, or give away opium or coca leaves, their salts, derivatives, or preparations, and for other purposes" (Harrison Narcotics Tax Act, 1914). At first blush, this appears to be just a tax on heroin and cocaine; importers, manufacturers, physicians and pharmacists could still bring in and use opium and coca leaves for a moderate fee. However, physicians were only permitted to prescribe heroin and cocaine "in the course of his professional practice only," which was interpreted by law enforcement officials to mean that physicians could not prescribe heroin or cocaine to addicts to treat their addiction. The reasoning went that addiction was not a disease, so the addict was not a patient so the physician could not lawfully prescribe drugs "in the course of his professional practice." Physicians were arrested en masse under this interpretation and quickly stopped writing prescriptions for heroin and cocaine (Brecher, 1972). Media stories around this time depicting southern African Americans as cocaine addicted madmen bent on raping white women and Chinese opium den operators using their drugs to seduce white women no doubt helped the passage of the Act (Jarecki, 2012).

Box 14.2. Before the Harrison Act

This excerpt from a newspaper in New Orleans from 1912 provides insight into local drug ordinances on the books before the Harrison Act took effect. The writing is colorful, though it is unclear why the two in the story are (already) called inmates:

> Sergeant John M. Dunn and Corporal Jackson, with two patrolmen, raided an opium joint at No. 1326 Gravier Street and found Dude Calvin and Ida Fisher smoking 'hop' in the place. The two inmates were arrested, and charged with having poisonous drugs in their possession.

Source: The New Orleans Daily Picayune, 1912.

Current drug policy in the United States owes much to the pioneering efforts at suppression by the first Director of the Federal Bureau of Narcotics (FBN) Harry Anslinger (McWilliams, 1990). The FBN came into existence in 1930 as an agency of the United States Department of the Treasury. It consolidated two older bureaucracies, the Narcotic Control Board and the Narcotic Division, which had enforcement responsibility for the Harrison Act and the Narcotic Drugs Import and Export Act of 1922. Anslinger remained at the helm of the FBN from 1930 until 1962 when he was forced into retirement by President Kennedy (McWilliams, 1990).

The period of Anslinger's tenure was marked by a number of social changes that apparently allowed him to almost single-handedly shape drug policy in the direction of criminalization. After the Harrison Act was passed, effectively creating illicit drug markets where they had not existed before, it changed the face of addiction. Thanks to the migration of rural southern African Americans to the urban centers of the North and the American public's fear and anxiety over the presence of immigrants (Asians on the West Coast, Italians and Eastern Europeans in the urban areas of the Midwest and East), the communist threat and the expanding role of the federal government during the Great Depression of the 1930s, Anslinger was able to link drugs to minorities and enjoyed a great deal of political power. This moral crusader was also a nimble bureaucrat who protected the FBN from budget cuts and controlled information on drug addiction quite successfully. He effectively created in the minds of the public the image of the drug addict as a crazed dope fiend (who was most likely a racial or ethnic minority group member) and who must be punished for their addiction (Galliher, Keys and Elsner, 1998). Or, to put it another way, the crime was euphoria and experiencing euphoria was not something a truly moral person would seek out.[5]

Anslinger used his position in the FBN to both define the drug problem and shape the response through legislative initiatives and the implementation of a law enforcement plan. For over 30 years, Anslinger largely shaped the United States government's war on drugs, though the moniker had not yet been attached. One of the few academics that spoke out against the way in which addicts were dealt with was Indiana University sociologist Alfred Lindesmith (1948), who advocated for treatment of addicts. Essentially he proposed that the narcotics problem be removed from the hands of police and prisons and turned over to treatment professionals. While this proposal does not sound particularly radical today, Lindesmith rightly anticipated criticism from those vested in the status quo. He stated:

> Unfortunately these same persons who sometimes seem to assume that they have a monopoly on all legitimate opinions and information in the field, have not provided the interested public with adequate data concerning the practices of other countries. Vested interests cannot, of course, be expected to examine critically the basic scheme of treatment on which their existence depends (1948, p. 25).

In the same publication containing Lindesmith's article, Dr. Victor Vogel, then the Medical Officer in charge of the U.S. Public Health Service (USPHS) Hospital in Lexington, Kentucky, provided a paper with data evaluating how addicts were treated by the United States Public Health Service (Vogel, 1948). At the time of publication, the hospital had been treating addicts for 13 years and the official position of the USPHS was that "drug addiction is a symptom of an emotional disorder more in need of treatment than of punishment" (Vogel, 1948, p. 45).

One of Vogel's (1948) interesting observations had to do with the reasons provided for the decline in admissions during the war years. The combined count for both Lexington and the Fort Worth hospitals was 1,350 on January 1, 1940, falling to a low of 822 during World War II. Vogel (1948) asserted that the decrease in addiction and the consequent decrease in need for treatment during the war years was due to strict government control over foreign shipping, which effectively reduced the movement of narcotics into the United States. However, he makes no mention of the fact that the market probably had constricted because of the military draft; this would run counter to his thesis that addicts are emotionally disturbed.

---

5. Unless of course that euphoria was religious in origin such as the ecstasy of St. Teresa.

According to Vogel (1948), an addict patient is not cured until he has regained self-control with regard to the use of drugs. This involves not just kicking the habit but also being rid of physical dependence, being able to experience regular living without drugs and psychiatric treatment and to build resistance to the emotional desire for drugs. This desire may persist for months, therefore, under the best prognosis, a treatment period of four months, an average of six months and a maximum of nine to 12 months is desirable. The voluntary patients who made up the bulk of the cases at USPHS hospital at Lexington proved difficult to deal with. While volunteers signed affidavits agreeing to remain under treatment until medical staff deemed them cured, if they changed their mind and decided to leave they could not be detained. Ninety percent of volunteer admits left prematurely and against medical advice. Vogel (1948) contended that there are two times when volunteer patients' desire to leave is not in their best interest; first, during the period of physical withdrawal when they are likely to become physically ill and desire to self-medicate to relieve the symptoms of withdrawal and second when they feel after only two or three months that they are recovered and are anxious to prove themselves clean and sober. Less than one percent of those leaving before 30 days stayed off drugs whereas 24 percent stayed off if they remained for the recommended treatment period (Vogel, 1948).

Lindesmith's (1948) and Vogel's (1948) calls for change notwithstanding, drug addiction remained a criminal justice system problem and two other important pieces of federal legislation that were designed to further control and punish drug users were passed in the 1950s. The Boggs Amendment of 1951 enacted mandatory sentences for narcotics violations, with no suspended sentence or parole for repeat offenders, and made prosecution for users and dealers easier. The Narcotic Control Act of 1956 extended the Boggs law, eliminating parole for all but first offenders and mandating minimum sentences for the first conviction (Conrad and Schneider, 1992). In terms of punishment, these pieces of legislation tended to cloud the distinction between marijuana and narcotics because marijuana was viewed as a gateway drug (with absolutely no research supporting this assertion). One experience with marijuana and the next step is heroin addiction![6]

The phrase War on Drugs first came into common use after President Richard Nixon uttered it in a press conference on June 17, 1971, during which he described illegal drugs as "public enemy number one in the United States" (Payan, 2006). In the same year, Nixon appointed Pennsylvania Governor Raymond P. Shafer to chair a national commission to report on the effects of marijuana and other drugs and to recommend appropriate drug policies. The results of the Shafer Commission were in stark contrast to federal drug policies leading up to the commission report and were not to President Nixon's liking. Specifically, the Shafer Commission report declared that marijuana use posed little physical or psychological harm, that marijuana use did not lead to crime and that the harm caused by marijuana use could not justify intrusion of the law into private behavior, recommending a discouragement of use policy rather than one of criminalization (Zeese, 2002). The Shafer Commission report had little impact on

---

6. For a hilarious and wholly unrealistic depiction of marijuana users, see the 1936 classic *Reefer Madness*.

Table 14.2. DEA's drug schedules

Schedule	Definition	Level of Dangerousness	Examples
Schedule I	No currently accepted medical use, high potential for abuse, potentially severe psychological or physical dependence	Extreme	Heroin, LSD, marijuana, ecstasy, methaqualone and peyote
Schedule II	High potential for abuse and severe psychological or physical dependence	Very High	Cocaine, methamphetamine, methadone, Dilaudid, Demerol, OxyContin, fentanyl, Dexedrine, Adderall and Ritalin
Schedule III	Moderate to low potential for abuse and psychological or physical dependence	High	Vicodin, Tylenol with codeine, ketamine, anabolic steroids, testosterone
Schedule IV	Low potential for abuse and psychological or physical dependence	Moderate	Xanaz, Soma, Darvon, Darvocet, Valium, Activan, Talwin, Ambien
Schedule V	Lowest potential for abuse and psychological or physical dependence	Low	Robitussin, Lomotil, Mototfen, Lyrica, Parepectolin

Source: Adapted from DEA, n.d.

national drug policy and this became more evident when in 1973, President Nixon created by executive order the Drug Enforcement Administration, a single unified command in the Department of Justice (DEA, 2010).

The DEA provides us with one of the best known ways of classifying drugs. Its famous schedules classify drugs by their medical use and their potential for abuse. Table 14.2 summarizes the schedules.

What exactly is the nature of the crime when someone takes an illicit or banned substance? In 2010, the DEA made notice of intent to place five synthetic cannabinoids in Schedule I, saying "the popularity of these THC-like synthetic cannabinoids has greatly increased in the United States and they are being abused for their psychoactive properties" (Federal Register, 2010, p. 71637). Now let us return to 1937 when Harry Anslinger provided testimony in Congressional hearings prior to the passage of the Marijuana Tax Act of 1937 in which he described the toxic effect of marijuana:

> The drug produces first an exaltation with a feeling of well-being; a happy, jovial mood, usually; and increased feeling of physical strength and power; and a general euphoria is experienced. Accompanying this exaltation is a stimulation of the imagination, followed by a more-or-less delirious state characterized by vivid

kaleidoscopic visions, sometimes of a pleasing sensual kind, but occasionally of a gruesome nature. Accompanying this delirious state is a remarkable loss in spatial and time relations; persons and things in the environment look small; time is interminable; seconds seem like minutes and hours like days. Let us think, for instance, of what might happen if a person under its influence were driving a high-powered automobile (Quoted in Schaffer Library, n.d.).

It appears from a federal law enforcement perspective, even after 73 years, what is at the root of the crime of taking banned drugs is enjoying the psychoactive properties of the drug—a feeling of general euphoria. Policy makers are perhaps more sophisticated in their claims making now than they were seven decades ago, but it appears that a good deal of effort goes into managing information about the drug problem in a manner to perpetuate a permanent war on drugs and, concomitantly, a self-serving drug enforcement bureaucracy. Currently, as illustrated below, the trend in the United States is toward legalization. Even in states where it is still illegal, penalties for simple possession of marijuana have been reduced to a citation, a municipal charge not requiring a trip to jail but a fine instead, which has the effect of keeping the money flowing without the expense of incarceration.

The effects and costs of the War on Drugs are serious and wide ranging. Since Nixon first uttered the phrase 42 years ago, the War on Drugs has resulted in the creation of a permanent underclass of ex-convicts who, besides having a criminal record, have few

Box 14.3. Where Is Marijuana Legalized?

As seen in the table below, different countries and different states within the United States take different approaches to the decriminalization and legalization of marijuana.

Country and status	United States' states and status
Argentina, decriminalized	Alaska, decriminalized and medical use
Australia, decriminalized in some states	California, decriminalized and medical use
Belgium, decriminalized	Colorado, legal
Cambodia, de facto legal	District of Columbia, medical use
Canada, legal for medical and industrial use with a license	Hawaii, medical use
Columbia, decriminalized	Maine, medical use
Costa Rica, decriminalized	Massachusetts, medical use
Croatia, decriminalized	Michigan, medical use
Netherlands, decriminalized and sold openly in coffee shops with a license	Montana, medical use
Portugal,* decriminalized	Nevada, medical use
	New Jersey, medical use
	Oregon, medical use
	Vermont, medical use
	Washington, legal

* Portugal has decriminalized all drugs as long as the amount possessed is a 10 day supply or less. For marijuana, a 10 day supply is 25 grams or less. Portugal treats drug addicts as medically sick people, though those who are found in possession several times may be arrested or mandated to go to rehabilitation.

Source: Adapted from Reuter, 2010.

educational or job skills and opportunities. Many of these individuals were involved in drug offenses because dealing drugs is an attractive way to earn a living when other opportunities are limited due to low levels of education and job skills. As we saw above, there were 1.5 million drug arrests in the United States in 2011, 17 percent of those serving sentences in state prisons that year were serving time for drug convictions and 56 percent of those serving sentences in federal prisons that year were serving time for drug convictions (Carson and Sabol, 2012). As we will see in Chapter 15, sentences for drug crimes drive the U.S. prison population up to the highest in the world.[7]

Current spending on the War on Drugs can only be described as astronomical. Forty billion (billion with a b, no typo) taxpayer dollars are spent per year on law enforcement, courts and corrections for drug offenses and offenders. Moreover, it appears that the more warlike the War on Drugs becomes, the greater the benefit to major traffickers. When drug traffickers are caught and punished harshly, drug prices go up to compensate for the risk that other traffickers take. Large scale traffickers who avoid apprehension and have few competitors are therefore very profitable and traffickers are actually benefiting from the War on Drugs, especially the current version that seems to target low to mid level dealers and personal use offenders (Becker and Murphy, 2013). We can also look to the many lost lives in Mexico, approximately 50,000 since 2006 and former President Calderon's antidrug campaign was initiated as a cost; another is the bitterness Mexico probably feels toward the United States and the way our War on Drugs has intruded into their country. Transnational operation makes these cartels stronger; Mexican drug cartels are so profitable and powerful and are able to wreak their violence and corruption in Mexico because they operate in the United States. The illegality of drugs also makes it more difficult for addicts who need help to seek it and obtain it out of fear of their drug use being detected and reported to law enforcement (Becker and Murphy, 2013).

Becker and Murphy (2013) advocate decriminalization of drugs in the United States for several reasons. They believe decriminalization would reduce the prison population and point to research that shows the prison population in Portugal has decreased since it instituted a policy of decriminalization. Moreover, more people are seeking help for addiction and there have been fewer opiate related deaths in Portugal since decriminalization; the increase in drug use by young people has been modest at best. However, decriminalization would not reduce the cost of the war on drugs unless selling drugs was also decriminalized. Decriminalizing drug sales as well as drug use would have many beneficial effects, not the least of which are cost savings from the freeing up of criminal justice system resources, revenue generation from taxing legal production of drugs and the reduction in violence associated with a criminal market. Becker and Murphy (2013) note that violent gangsters abandoned the alcohol market after Prohibition ended and alcohol was made legal again and believe the same thing would happen with decriminalized drug sales and use. We return to the issue of the effects of wider legalization of drugs in Chapter 15.

---

7. For an enlightening look at the War on Drugs, see the 2012 documentary *The House I Live In*.

Prostitution

The FBI defines prostitution and commercialized vice as "the unlawful promotion of or participation in sexual activities for profit, including attempts to solicit customers or transport persons for prostitution purposes; to own, manage, or operate a dwelling or other establishment for the purpose of providing a place where prostitution is performed; or to otherwise assist or promote prostitution" (FBI UCR, 2011a). This definition covers all the major players in prostitution, including the prostitute her or himself, the customer, the pimp and the madam operating the brothel. As we saw above, women are disproportionately arrested for prostitution and other commercialized vice, which might seem right at first blush (more women than men are prostitutes, after all) but it begs the question of how many male customers are not being arrested when they solicit the services of a prostitute, or sex worker, as many prefer to be called.[8]

The exchange of sexual services for something of value is as old as humankind and the conception of prostitution is different from place to place and over time. Table 14.3 shows the legal status of prostitution in a sample of 100 countries chosen to be inclusive of major religions, geographical regions and prostitution policies.

There are a number of different routes through which women get involved in prostitution and these routes depend in part on the type of sex work at issue. Street prostitutes are more likely to be runaways who have no other way to survive other than to engage in prostitution (for astute readers, this should call to mind the discussion of the patriarchy in feminist criminology in Chapter 6). Street prostitutes are more likely to use drugs and engage in unsafe sex and they are at greater risk for victimization than prostitutes who work indoors, in part because they cannot afford to turn away potential customers. Those who work indoors, either independently or as a member of a brothel, come to prostitution through other routes, including exotic dancing, and while there is an economic motivation for their foray into sex work, it is not survival in nature so much as a desire for more money. Indoor sex workers can also amass a client list, which lowers their risk of victimization. The types of activities street and indoor prostitutes engage in are different, as well, with street prostitutes typically engaging in quick, customer-focused encounters and with indoor prostitutes typically having more sexually satisfying and emotionally enriching experiences with customers (Weitzer, 2007).

Prostitution is a dangerous profession. James Alan Fox, a noted expert on serial killers, has written that prostitutes are the most frequent victims targeted by serial killers mainly because they are easily assessable and the perpetrator can in most instances count on a slow response from the police and little attention from the public. According to Fox (2011), marginal and vulnerable victims are recurring themes in serial murder cases. Quinet (2007) reported that although most homicides of prostitutes are not committed by serial killers, there are many serial murder cases documented in the literature with prostitute victims. For example, Quinet (2007) cites the case of Gary Ridgway,

---

8. There is an opposite arrangement in Sweden, where selling sex is legal but buying it is not (Ritter, 2008).

Table 14.3. The legal status of prostitution around the world*

ILLEGAL (N=39)		LIMITED LEGALITY (N=11)	LEGAL (N=50)		
Afghanistan	North Korea	Australia	Argentina	France	Poland
Albania	South Korea	Bangladesh	Armenia	Germany	Portugal
Angola	Liberia	Bulgaria	Austria	Greece	Senegal
Antigua and Barbuda	Lithuania	Iceland	Belgium	Guatemala	Singapore
Bahamas	Malta	India	Belize	Honduras	Slovakia
Barbados	Philippines	Japan	Bolivia	Hungary	Switzerland
Cambodia	Romania	Malaysia	Brazil	Indonesia	Turkey
China (includes Taiwan)	Rwanda	Norway	Canada	Ireland	United Kingdom (includes Scotland)
Croatia	Saint Kitts and Nevis	Spain	Chile	Israel	Uruguay
Cuba	Saint Lucia	Sweden	Colombia	Italy	Venezuela
Dominica	Saint Vincent and Grenadines	United States (legal in brothels in some counties in Nevada only)	Costa Rica	Kyrgyzstan	
Egypt	Saudi Arabia		Cyprus	Latvia	
Grenada	Slovenia		Czech Republic	Luxembourg	
Guyana	South Africa		Denmark	Mexico	
Haiti	Suriname		Dominican Republic	Netherlands	
Iran	Thailand		Ecuador	New Zealand	
Iraq	Trinidad and Tobago		El Salvador	Nicaragua	
Jamaica	Uganda		Estonia	Panama	
Jordan	United Arab Emirates		Ethiopia	Paraguay	
Kenya			Finland	Peru	

* Around the world is a slang term within the context of prostitution for oral, vaginal and anal sex in a single encounter.

Source: Adapted from Procon.org, 2013.

the Green River killer in Washington, who murdered 48 prostitutes. One third of this group was never reported as missing. In a study of mortality in a long-term open cohort of prostitute women, Potterat, et al. (2004) found the Crude Mortality Rate (CMR) for death by homicide among active prostitutes was an astounding 229 per 100,000; in contrast, the murder rate in the United States in 2011 was 4.8 per 100,000. This easily makes homicide the leading cause of death among prostitutes.

Though we may think of the two as similar or the same, there is a difference between sex work and sex trafficking. Remember in Chapter 10, we saw that the driving force behind human trafficking in the vast majority of cases is the purposes of sexual exploitation. The United Nations distinguishes sex work from sex trafficking based in large part on voluntary entry into each:

> Sex work and sex trafficking are not the same. The difference is that the former is consensual whereas the latter coercive. Sex worker organizations understand sex work as a contractual arrangement where sexual services are negotiated between consenting adults. Sex work is not always a desperate or irrational act; it is a realistic choice to sell sex—in order to support a family, an education or maybe a drug habit. It is an act of agency. By contrast, trafficking in persons, as defined by international and local treaties, is 'the recruitment, transportation, transfer, harbouring or receipt of persons, by means of the threat or use of force or other forms of coercion, of abduction, of fraud, of deception, of the abuse of power or of a position of vulnerability or of the giving or receiving of payments or benefits to achieve the consent of a person having control over another person, for the purpose of exploitation.' Such exploitation can include many forms of forced labour or slavery—in factories, fields, homes or brothels. Trafficking for the purposes of commercial sexual exploitation involves adults or children providing sexual services against their will, either through force or deception. A denial of agency, trafficking violates their fundamental freedoms (GCHIVL, 2012).

We discuss the consequences that wider legalization of prostitution could have on human trafficking in Chapter 15. Arguments for wider legalization that do not necessarily include considerations of trafficking include state regulation in the interest of public health and safety as well as the opportunity for taxation and revenue generation; decriminalization would similarly result in criminal justice system savings. However, moral arguments against wider legalization and decriminalization remain part of the debate.

The Criminalization of Some Lifestyles

In this section of the chapter, we will consider the notion that some lifestyles are criminalized and in so doing, discuss homosexuality, pedophilia, child pornography, homelessness and mental illness. We want to take this opportunity to make two things clear. First, pedophilia and child pornography result in direct harm to children and they should be criminalized for that reason. Causing harm to others distinguishes pedophilia and child pornography from the other lifestyles in this section and these activities should have criminal consequences as a result. Second, lifestyle is a bit of a misnomer, as it implies a choice, in the same way the phrase active lifestyle might. We do not believe that homosexuality, homelessness or mental illness are choices over some alternative. The use of the term lifestyle does allow us to discuss the criminalization of certain activities that are part of being homosexual, homeless or mentally ill.

Homosexuality

The gradual liberalization of attitudes and sexual mores in the 20th century has led to most states eliminating their laws against sodomy, which includes any copulation-like act such as oral and anal sex that is not actual copulation, i.e., vaginal sex. The landmark sodomy case in the United States is *Lawrence* v. *Texas*, decided in a 6–3 ruling in 2003. In 1998, John Lawrence, for whom the case is named, was entertaining two friends in his apartment, Garner and Eubanks. Garner and Eubanks were in a relationship, but Garner and Lawrence had been flirting all evening. Upset, Eubanks left to get a soda from the apartment complex's vending machine and called the police while doing so to make a false report of an armed individual on complex grounds. When the police arrived and entered Lawrence's apartment, they found Lawrence and Garner engaged in either anal or oral sex, which under Texas law was sodomy. In fact, what was termed deviate sexual intercourse with an individual of the same sex was illegal in Texas even in the privacy of one's own home. In *Lawrence*, the Supreme Court struck down the sodomy law in Texas and effectively invalidated it in 13 other states because the law violated the equal protection clause of the Fourteenth Amendment, which holds that laws must apply equally to everyone in the United States. Sodomy laws were viewed as unfairly and illegally criminalizing the activities of same sex couples. *Lawrence* overturned the ruling in *Bowers* v. *Hardwick* from 1986.

Sodomy was categorized as a felony in all states until 1962 and punishments for this crime were harsh. Idaho's punishment was particularly severe, a five year prison sentence for a crime against nature with a person or an animal. One of the best treatments of laws against sodomy in the United States is by Eskridge (2008).[9] He recounts the evolution of sodomy laws going back to the colonial era and discusses sodomy in a way that makes it fundamentally about homosexuality. Sodomy technically is not about homosexuality exclusively. Rather, it is about sex without the possibility of procreation, which of course can be both heterosexual and homosexual. The connection of sodomy with homosexuality in the United States has served to blur the line between the two. Eskridge (2008) recounts that sodomy laws in the 17th century (called buggery then to include anal sex) were rarely enforced but when they were, the penalty was often death. These laws were maintained into the 19th century, when they were used in cases in which the sexual activity was either violent or extremely public. Immigrants and men of African descent were most commonly charged with the crime. But the general pattern in the 19th century was non enforcement, though things began to change in the 20th century.

Canaday (2008) points out that changes in sexual mores prompted the enactment of expanded sodomy laws that included fellatio, which most states did by the 1920s. With more behaviors counting as sodomy, more people became violators of the law and more aggressive law enforcement ensued. Both men and women were prosecuted for fellatio, for example, and a few states also included cunnilingus under the umbrella of crimes against nature. While sodomy arrests during the first part of the 20th century

---

9. Eskridge also wrote an amicus brief that was cited extensively by the majority opinion in *Lawrence* v. *Kansas*.

increased tenfold as compared with the late 19th century, the policing of sodomy was still modest relative to other sexual offenses. Prostitution, rape, fornication and adultery were the sexual crimes for which the greatest amount of police resources was used.

By the time the legal regime was expanded and enforcement was becoming more aggressive, interest in sodomy as a criminal activity began to wane, not because of a vocal gay rights movement but rather, the legal community began to pull back, largely influenced by the Kinsey report on what Americans were doing in bed besides sleeping. Generalizing from the Kinsey report (discussed below), it appeared that some 95 percent of Americans were technically lawbreakers. When the American Law Institute approved its Model Penal Code (MPC) in 1962, it eliminated consensual sodomy as a crime. Public solicitation for sodomy, however, was criminalized, in what appeared to be a compromise with those who were firmly convinced that homosexuals were out to seduce non homosexuals, particularly young boys. The state of Illinois became the first to decriminalize consensual sodomy in the mid 1960s (Canaday, 2008).

The related debate about the inherent nature of heterosexuality and homosexuality was sparked by the research of Alfred Kinsey and his associates and their two reports, Sexual Behavior in the Human Male (1948) and Sexual Behavior in the Human Female (1953). The significant findings of these two reports on the topic of same sex behavior were:

- 37 percent of males and 13 percent of females had at least some overt homosexual experience to orgasm.
- Ten percent of males were more or less exclusively homosexual and eight percent of males were exclusively homosexual for at least three years between the ages of 16 and 55. For females, Kinsey reported a range of two to six percent for more or less exclusively homosexual experience/response.
- Four percent of males and one to three percent of females had been exclusively homosexual after the onset of adolescence up to the time of the interview.

In spite of the fact that both reports contained lengthy tables and charts and were written in the scientific style of the time, they spent several weeks on the New York Times bestseller list (Emilio, 1998). The implications for defining a whole segment of the United States population as criminal or deviant considering that those who were not exclusively heterosexual made up a significant portion of the population raised significant arguments against discrimination of homosexuals. Kinsey's definitions of sexual orientation were not based on identity but on behavior and he concluded that sense same sex behavior was normal sexual behavior among a significant number of white Americans[10] and that it should not be criminalized (Kinsey, 1953).

The Kinsey reports became a benchmark in the 1970s for an estimate of how many gay men and lesbians lived in the United States to highlight discrimination based on sexual orientation. While Kinsey (1948, 1953) concluded that sexual behavior was not based on a binary notion of sexuality but ranged along a continuum, it was important for those engaged in fighting sexual orientation discrimination to view sexuality as innate with a few folks in the bisexual middle. It was important to the gay and lesbian

---

10. Kinsey's samples were all white.

movement for homosexuals to be viewed as a politically substantial minority deserving of their place at the political table.

Their claims garnered additional support in 1973 when the board of trustees of the American Psychological Association agreed to redefine mental illness in a way that eliminated homosexuality. Previously, disorders had been determined by deviations from an objective norm, but this redefinition held that the norm should be more subjective and that people should not be considered disordered if they did not experience distress over their condition and if they showed no major impairment in social functioning. With this redefinition, homosexuality was removed as a presenting disorder from the *Diagnostic and Statistical Manual of Mental Disorders III (DSM III)*. This decision by the board struck many at the time to be rather strange. A profession committed to clinical observation and scientific rigor made a significant change in di-agnostics by a vote of a board which did not at the time represent the professional judgments of its members. Many practitioners were particularly disturbed by not having an objective measure instead relying on the subjective feelings (of normality) by the homosexual. Of course, it is easy to understand why many homosexuals were disturbed by the first edition of the DSM (1952), which listed homosexuality as a mental disorder and a severe form of psychopathology.

Box 14.4. Is There an Epigenetic Basis for Homosexuality?

Rice, Friberg and Gavrilets (2012) propose that epigenetic influences acting on androgen signaling in the brain may underlie sexual orientation. They point to the fact that no gay gene has as of yet been discovered and the fact that homosexuality runs in families as evidence for their idea that epigenetic factors could be responsible for sexual orientation. Epigentics, which are changes in genotype due to factors other than DNA, could play a role in shaping how cells respond to androgen signaling while a fetus is in the womb. Androgens strongly determine gonad development and Rice, Friberg and Gavrilets (2012) believe it may also influence sexual orientation. They cite the example of girls with congenital adrenal hyperplasia (CAH), who pro-duce very high levels of testosterone, have masculinized genitalia and have high rates of same sex attraction as evidence for the idea of differential sensitivity to androgens caused by epige-netic factors as evidence for their theory. However, it remains unclear if less testosterone than it takes to masculinize female genitalia is sufficient for the development of same sex attraction and some question the need to find an epigenetic basis for homosexuality. Homosexuality is not some harmful disease, it is a perfectly normal variation of human behavior. Perhaps efforts to explore the role of epigenetics in disease causation would be better concentrated on cancer or mental illness (Richards, 2013).

Today it is clear that casting homosexuality as deviant or homosexual behavior is criminal is quickly becoming a thing of the past. As we write this section, the Supreme Court has heard oral arguments on and will rule on the constitutionality of the Defense of Marriage Act, which restricts federal level marriage benefits and interstate recognition of same sex marriages and Proposition 8 from California, which limited legally recognized marriages to only include those between one man and one woman. In April of 2013, Washington Wizards center Jason Collins came out and in so doing, became the first openly gay male active player in a major American sport. His actions were heralded as courageous by the public, his fellow players and the President of the United States. Though many religions may continue to condemn homosexuality, homosexuality is fast becoming legitimate from a legal standpoint.

Pedophilia

Adult-child sexual contact is against the law in every state in the United States. State criminal codes spell out an age of consent, usually between 16 and 18 years of age, meaning that we as a society presume younger persons have neither the intellectual nor the emotional capacity to deal with sex and its consequences and to consent to enter into sexual activity or relationships. Moreover, state law considers age differentials in the severity of the event and culpability if it involves a juvenile offender and generally speaking, the younger the child, the more harshly the sexually abusing adult may be punished. Pedophilia has not always been viewed as deviant or criminal. Most famously, the Athenian Greeks promoted a formal bond between an adult man and an adolescent boy outside of the immediate family. In addition to being a loving and sexual relationship, it was an upper class activity that involved teaching and conveying to the younger one the importance of certain cultural values that were important in ancient Greek society (Yates, 2005).

McCaghy (1967) produced the seminal work on child molestation and he concluded that the nature of the offenses of child molesters were typically nonviolent, non coital acts between lower status adult males and underage girls with whom they were acquainted. In spite of the above conclusion, the typical molester is difficult to describe. They vary considerably in their characteristics, motivations and the way they select victims; the circumstances of their offenses also vary, as McCaghy's (1967) six item typology illustrates:

- Incestuous Molester: Incest goes beyond molestation. The concept of incest is used to set limits within the extended family on who may marry whom and between whom sexual intercourse may occur.[11] Incest also refers to any activities of a sexual nature between close relatives without benefit of marriage especially when one is an adult and the other is a child. Sex between father and daughter is the most common form and while this violates the incest taboo, there are apparently some people who feel that the taboo does not apply to them (Bagley, 1969).
- High-Interaction Molester: These molesters are unrelated to their victims but occupy positions that bring them into frequent interaction with children outside the home either through their occupations or hobbies that involve children. Athletic coaches, scout masters and assistants, dance instructors, school teachers,

---

11. All states in the United States have statutes that prohibit incest. Usually prohibited are relationships between ascendants and descendants (brother and sister, uncle or niece, aunt or nephew). Some states specify aggravated incest if the victim is under 18 years of age and is related to the offender as any of the following biological, step, or adoptive relatives: child , grandchild of any degree, brother, sister, half brother, half sister, uncle, aunt, nephew or niece. The prohibited acts include sexual intercourse, sexual battery, indecent behavior with juveniles, pornography involving juveniles, molestation, crimes against nature, cruelty, parents enticing a child into prostitution and lewd fondling or touching by either with the intent to arouse or satisfy sexual desire of either party or both.

choir directors, ministers and priests and all other occupations that bring adults into close contact with children. High interaction molesters' victims are usually those whom the molester holds in special regard and the relationship that evolves is based on affection with the child. As a result, these offenses may go undetected and occur frequently and often over long periods of time. Because of their social position and often enjoying considerable prestige in the community for their apparent commitment to good works, high interaction molesters may continue with impunity and may never be detected.

Box 14.5. Jerry Sandusky

One recent and famous example of the high interaction molester is Jerry Sandusky a long time assistant football coach at Pennsylvania State University under legendary head coach Joe Paterno. In a highly publicized trial, he was convicted of 45 counts of child abuse and was sentenced to 30 to 60 years in October, 2012. During the sentencing hearing, the prosecutor in the case spoke of Sandusky's "rampant degradation of children." He called Sandusky's Second Mile Charity "a victim factory" from which he chose his prey. "He [Sandusky] was cruel beyond imagination. It went from touching, to washing, to grabbing, to anal penetration. He used them as his sexual property ... he damaged their families as well." Sandusky's defense attorney described him as "a gentleman, who, by many accounts was a generous, kind, giving person who always only wanted to help people." Sandusky himself called the first of his victims to come forward in 2008 "a young man who was dramatic, a veteran accuser [who] always sought attention." Sandusky further called the victim "a disturbed boy" and declared a conspiracy: "The media, investigators, the system, Penn State, psychologists, and other accusers" concocted terrible stories about him. He also took care to note that his wife Dottie has been his only sexual partner and they did not begin a sexual relationship until after they were wed (Diamond, 2012).

- Asocial molester: This type usually has a criminal record other than molestation, the lowest socioeconomic status and is divorced or never married. Molestation is not a pattern for them; their molestation offenses seem to be opportunistic and spontaneous and usually involve drunkenness.

- Aged molester: The name implies the outstanding feature of these molesters. The children are rarely coerced and the aged molester is likely to have several non coital sexual contacts with neighborhood children before he is discovered. Age does not imply that the offense is linked to senility or any age related physical impairment. It is likely in the absence of adult friends the offender becomes attached to children.

- Career Molester: These are the offenders that come closest to the stereotype of the dirty old man that frequent playgrounds to prey on children. They typically have long records of molestation and seek their victims in a deliberate and systematic way. These molesters tend to be strangers to their victims and are indiscriminate in terms of the victim's gender. They do not use force but rely on the gullibility of the victim and their powers of persuasion, sometimes resorting to using baits such as a puppy or candy to lure the victim to an isolated location. They have no affectionate interest in the child except as a sex object.

- Spontaneous-Aggressive Molester: What these molesters do is usually defined in the law as forcible rape. There is little or no attempt at persuasion and the victim and perpetrator have no prior relationship. The offender pulls the child into a car or an isolated location and proceeds to rape them. The selection of a victim is a matter of opportunity and circumstance and not necessarily preference.

McCaghy's (1967) typology is probably not exhaustive nor should it be construed to suggest that the types are discreet categories. Instead, there is likely overlap in victim, offender and motivation. Two things are clear throughout, however: it is about sex and the perpetrator is almost always male. Recent sex scandals within the Catholic Church have shed new light on the context in which the crime of adult-child sex can occur and organizational factors that can facilitate ongoing abuse. Some officials within the Church through their actions of moving offending priests to other parishes rather than bringing them to the attention of law enforcement, tacitly decriminalized what the offending priests had done (Vollman, 2012).

Remember at the heart of pedophilia is an inability on the part of the victim to be able to consent. The roots of this inability are legal and emotional in nature. However, there are those that contend that childhood sexuality is real and that children should have a right to be sexual and the right to experience what has been called intergenerational sexual contact. Nelson (1989) recommends a change in the terms we use to describe consensual intergenerational sexual contact. "Non-condemnatory terms are recommended to reduce cognitive confusion and, it is hoped, to protect those who can be exploited without resorting to unscientific and puritanical hysteria. In each individual case, until abuse is clearly established, three specific non-condemnatory terms are recommended" (Nelson, 1989). These terms are intergenerational sexuality, sexual experience and participant. Intergenerational sexuality should be used in place of incest and sexual abuse, sexual experience should be used in place of abuse, victimization, molestation, assault and exploitation and participant should be used in place of perpetrator, victim or consenting partner until the nature and circumstances of the contact can be established and the most accurate terms chosen to describe it. Nelson (1989) hopes the use of these terms "will distinguish problems caused by social condemnation from problems caused by exploitation and abuse." This, of course, minimizes or overlooks the legal (and psychiatric and medical) theory that below a certain age one cannot consent, but it also raises the valid point that being labeled a victim in itself can be unhelpful at best and permanently traumatizing at worse.

Box 14.6. The North American Man/Boy Love Association (NAMBLA)

One organization that believes consensual sexual relationships between adults and children are possible and that actively supports the decriminalization of consensual relationships between men and boys is the North American Man/Boy Love Association (NAMBLA). Founded in 1978, it has as its stated goal the end of oppression of men and boys in mutual consensual relationships by:

- building understanding and support for such relationships
- educating the general public on the benevolent nature of man/boy love

- cooperating with lesbian, gay, feminist and other liberation movements and
- supporting the liberation of persons of all ages from sexual prejudice and oppression

Their webpage claims that they do not encourage, refer or assist people seeking sexual contacts, nor do they engage in illegal activities or advocate that anyone else should (NAMBLA, 2013). They portray themselves as a political, civil rights and educational organization that promotes the positive benefits of man/boy love.

Child Pornography

The erotic depiction of children has been around for some time. Pornography as we presently know it began with the invention of the camera in the early part of the 19th century. Child pornography and pornography in general largely went undetected because those engaged in it were quite secretive in collecting it and sharing it among trustworthy friends. The 1970s saw a veritable explosion of child pornography in the United States in the form of magazines. With the advent of the Internet in the last decade of the 20th century, the scale and nature of child pornography took a dramatic change that required new approaches to investigation and control (Wortley and Smallbone, 2006). Child pornography in photograph, audio and video forms can now be shared by a user in the United States with a user in Japan, for example, in a matter of seconds with just the click of a mouse with very little expense and relatively little risk of detection.

The first federal level law against child pornography was not passed until 1978 and since then, a handful of major legal decisions and laws have been enacted that give us an understanding of what child pornography is, at least from the point of view of the law, and who is a criminal under these laws. In *New York v. Ferber* in 1982, the Supreme Court ruled that child pornography was not protected free speech because of the harm it causes children. In 1984, the Child Protection Act raised the age of children covered by child pornography legislation from 16 to 18. In 1988, the Child Protection and Obscenity Enforcement Act made it illegal to use a computer to depict or advertise child pornography. In *Osborne v. Ohio* in 1990, the private possession of child pornography was deemed illegal. The Child Protector and Sexual Predator Punishment Act required Internet Service Providers (ISPs) to report known incidents of child pornography. In *Ashcroft v. Free Speech Coalition* in 2002, virtual images in which adults are made to look like children though digital modification was determined not to be child pornography. Around 1,000 people a year in the United States are arrested for child pornography offenses (Wortley and Smallbone, 2006).

Of course the content of child pornographic images can vary widely. Taylor, Holland and Quayle (2001) have proposed a ten item severity scale of child pornographic images and videos:

1. Indicative: Non-sexualized pictures collected from legitimate sources (e.g., magazines, catalogs)
2. Nudist: Naked or semi-naked pictures of children in appropriate settings collected from legitimate sources

3. Erotica: Pictures taken secretly of children in which they reveal varying degrees of nakedness
4. Posing: Posed pictures of children in varying degrees of nakedness
5. Erotic posing: Pictures of children in sexualized poses and in varying degrees of nakedness
6. Explicit erotic posing: Pictures emphasizing the genitals
7. Explicit sexual activity: Record of sexual activity involving children but not involving adults
8. Assault: Record of children subjected to sexual abuse involving digital touching with adults
9. Gross assault: Record of children subjected to sexual abuse involving penetrative sex, masturbation or oral sex with adults
10. Sadistic/bestiality: Record of children subjected to pain, or engaging in sexual activity with an animal

According to Taylor, Holland and Quayle (2001), pictures or videos in levels 8–10 with either an animal or an adult present are pictures of a sexual assault or rape in process and they clearly fall within all contemporary legal definitions of child pornography. Level 7 would also rise to the level of child pornography even when an adult is not pictured but with an adult directing the activity off camera. Though the images or videos that rise to a 7 or above are clearly child pornography, Taylor, Holland and Quayle (2001) point out that determining whether less severely rated pictures or videos are child pornography requires investigation of context. The way in which the images and videos are organized and stored can be helpful in determining whether the less severely rated images and videos rise to the level of child pornography. Consider images or videos of nude toddlers in the tub. A few pictures of one's own children in the tub adorned with shampoo mohawks and scattered across a hard drive or displayed on a bookshelf would not qualify as child pornography, but an extensive and highly organized collection of many different toddlers at bath time that is used for fantasizing probably would.

It has proven difficult to devise a typology of those who use Internet child pornography. The only two commonalities they seem to have is that they are not necessarily involved in the sexual abuse of children and that they come from all walks of life and show few warning signs, though many are white males between 26 and 40 years of age who make frequent use of the Internet (Wortley and Smallbone, 2006). However, Krone (2004) has proposed a more detailed typology of childhood pornography offending behavior. Table 14.4 describes each type of child pornography offender in the typology.

Table 14.4. A typology of child pornography offenders

Type of Offender	Activity	Networks with Others?	Employs Security Strategy?	Level of Abuse of Children?
Browsers	Offenders who stumble across child pornography but knowingly save the images	No	No	Indirect
Private fantasizers	Offenders who create digital images (e.g., through morphing) for private use to satisfy personal sexual desires	No	No	Indirect
Trawlers	Offenders who seek child pornography on the web through open browsers	Yes, minimal	Yes, minimal	Indirect
Non secure collectors	Offenders who seek child pornography in non-secure chat rooms (i.e., chat rooms that do not employ security barriers such as passwords) and other open levels of the Internet	Yes, relatively high	No	Indirect
Secure collectors	Offenders who are members of a closed newsgroup or other secret pedophile ring	Yes, high	Yes, sophisticated	Indirect
Groomers	Offenders who develop online relationships with children and send pornography to children as part of the grooming process	Yes	Security depends on child's silence	Direct
Physical abusers	Offenders who sexually abuse children and for whom an interest in child pornography is just part of their pedophilic interests. They may record their own abuse behaviors for their personal use, in which case, from a legal standpoint, the possession of pornography is secondary to the evidence of their abusive behavior that it records	Maybe	Security depends on child's silence	Direct
Producers	Offenders who record the sexual abuse of children for the purpose of disseminating it to others	Maybe	Security depends on child's silence	Direct
Distributors	Offenders involved in disseminating abuse images. In some cases they have a purely financial interest in child pornography. More often, offenders at any of the above levels who share images may be classified as distributors	Depends on other level classification	Depends on other level classification	Direct

Source: Adapted from Krone, 2004.

Homelessness

Homelessness is not a crime. This is both a fact and a rallying cry for advocates for the homeless. Nevertheless, many homeless people have contact with the criminal justice system. There are approximately 1.6 million homeless people in the United States, nearly 110,000 of whom are chronically homeless. The chronically homeless are largely racial and ethnic minority males, about 30 percent of whom have mental health conditions and about half of whom have substance abuse problems. Moreover, nearly half of all homeless people report spending five or more days in jail and over 15 percent of jail inmates report at least some homelessness in the year before their incarceration. (Paquette, 2011). People who are homeless have relatively frequent contact with the criminal justice system for a number of reasons. First, their behavior is much more public than that of people who have places to live, which means their behavior is much more detectable. It is not uncommon for the homeless to be reported to or detected by police for the most minor crimes such as public urination and loitering. The techniques used by the homeless to acquire money, goods and sometimes drugs and alcohol, including panhandling and shoplifting, are often crimes, as well. The related condition of mental illness may also increase criminalization. Mental illness can have a profound effect on behavior and strange or odd behavior that results from symptoms of mental illness may be deemed disturbing the peace. It is not that being homeless is a crime. Rather, it is that the behaviors in which many homeless must engage in to survive are criminal.

Homelessness is dangerous for those who experience it. Using census data from 1991–2001, Canadian researchers identified and tracked 15,000 homeless and marginally housed people across Canada for 11 years. Death rates among homeless and marginally housed people were substantially higher than rates in the poorest income groups who were housed, with the highest death rates observed for younger homeless people. Among those who were homeless and marginally housed, the probability of survival to age 75 was 32 percent for men and 60 percent for women, compared to 51percent of men and 72 percent of women in the lowest income group in the general population. Remaining life expectancy at age 25 among homeless and marginally housed men was just 17 years, 10 years less than the general population and six years less than the poorest income group. For homeless and marginally housed women, remaining life expectancy at age 25 was 27 years, seven years lower than the general population and five years lower than the poorest income group.

A large part of this premature mortality is potentially avoidable because many deaths were attributable to alcohol and smoking-related diseases and to violence and injuries, much of which is likely implicated in drug abuse. There were also deaths related to suicide and mental illness. This study substantiates that homelessness and marginally housed people in shelters, rooming houses and hotels have much higher mortality and shorter life expectancy than could be expected on the basis of low income alone.

Box 14.7. A Police Initiative to Aid the Homeless

In 2003 the second author was involved in a police initiative to keep the homeless out of the criminal justice system in New Orleans. At first, we were greeted with skepticism by the homeless advocate community, who had always presumptively assumed that the police were out to throw homeless people in jail. Homeless people do in fact get arrested but arrest creates more costs (the city was billed by the jail a per diem of about $22) and problems for the homeless (e.g., losing access to medications). And while it was never spoken as a part of the agenda of the New Orleans Police Department (NOPD), New Orleans is a tourist attraction and having hundreds of homeless folks swarming the French Quarter was not desirable. For homeless persons, the French Quarter and the parks in the adjacent area present wonderful panhandling opportunities. The police did not want tourists, a huge source of revenue for the city, to feel harassed or endangered so they needed a strategy to reduce, without harassment, the homeless populations in and around the city's tourist attractions.

In the early stages of this grant supported program, the second author conducted a series of focus groups with homeless persons and the police. One of the police main concerns was how to deal with homeless folks that were mentally ill. This was a legitimate concern, with perhaps 10 to 15 percent of chronic homeless on the streets with mental health issues and another 10 percent or so who were ex-military and had service related mental health issues. Most of the balance of the chronic homeless were drug and alcohol involved. The research team quickly arranged for additional training for police to assist them in dealing with mentally ill homeless persons.

The homeless came to our focus groups with another set of problems which fit well within a rubric of victimhood. The shelters imposed hours — residents had to be out by a certain time in the morning and could not get back in until that evening. They resented the discipline imposed by the shelters. They were convinced that the police actually had an arrest quota of homeless persons and that they could be arrested with no probable cause at any time. The job here for the NOPD was to disabuse them of these sentiments.

With the aid of some foundation support, the NOPD purchased a van outfitted with uniformed civilian personnel but with clear markings that the van was NOPD Homeless Assistance. The purpose of the van was to transport homeless to locations where they could receive a variety of services including outpatient medical attention and housing acquisition assistance. If they were found sleeping on the street, they were offered transportation to shelters. Arrests of homeless persons dropped dramatically in the areas patrolled by the homeless van. Part of the drop was a declining population of homeless persons in the area because the van was active in moving many of these people to the shelters. While the homeless assistance van is still in operation at this writing (spring of 2013), the larger program which would have included the development of a homeless court in New Orleans was brought to a standstill by Hurricane Katrina, like so many other human service initiatives (e.g., Jenkins, Brown and Mosby 2012).

Mental Illness

The criminalization of people with mental illness occurs in much the same way it does for the homeless and for that, we can thank the process of deinstitutionalization. As we saw in Chapter 8, deinstitutionalization was the practice of emptying out psychiatric hospitals. This occurred for a variety of reasons, not the least of which were belief in the efficacy of community based psychiatry, the advent of psychotropic medication and desire for cost savings. Increasing concern for the rights of people with mental illness beginning in the middle of the 1900s also played a role. Buoyed by the Civil Rights Movement, advocates for the rights of the mentally ill began to demand a change in institutionalization practices to require more stringent admission criteria. However, the utopia of accessible and effective community based care was not to be realized because funding for community based services was inadequate and the staff at centers that were built were not trained or equipped to care for people with such profound mental illness. The result of deinstitutionalization was thousands of people with severe mental illness being turned out into the community with few or no treatment options, weak if any family connections and bleak job, education and housing prospects (Slate and Johnson, 2008). As we saw in Chapter 8, people with mental illness are far more likely to be victimized by violence while in the community than they are to perpetrate violence against others.

As this large group of people with mental illness returned to the community, many ended up homeless or addicted to drugs or alcohol or both and unable to find any relief through mental health treatment and related services. The only system to which many people with mental illness did have access was the criminal justice system, which has become the de facto mental health system in the United States (Slate and Johnson, 2008). In much the same way as the homeless (and as alluded to, the homeless and people with mental illness are far from always distinct groups), the behaviors in which they have to engage to survive are criminal, so people with mental illness became offenders with mental illness. There are currently about half a million people in jail and prison who have serious mental illnesses, making prisons the new asylums in the United States (PBS, 2005). The Los Angeles County Jail is the largest single provider of mental health services in the United States and people with mental illness face dangers while they are incarcerated as well as when they are on the street. Their strange behavior may result in victimization by other inmates, they may have difficulty following institution rules due to their symptoms that results in sanctions, including solitary confinement, and they are nine times more likely to commit suicide while incarcerated than those without mental illness (Slate and Johnson, 2008). The criminal justice system is poorly equipped to help people with mental illness, especially in the prison setting, but because it has been charged with doing so, a number of initiatives have been employed to better address the many challenges that offenders with mental illness bring to bear on the system,[12] including crisis intervention teams within police departments that connect people with mental illness who are in acute crisis to treatment and services (for an overview of the research on crisis intervention teams, see Compton, Bahora, Watson and Oliva, 2008) and mental health courts that provide mental health treatment and other services in lieu of incarceration with the hope that engagement in treatment will reduce or eliminate future contact with the criminal justice system (for an overview on the research on mental health courts, see Frailing, 2012).

---

12. One might argue that the criminal justice system should not be trying to meet these challenges because the provision of treatment and services to people with mental illness is the responsibility of and can ostensibly be done better by the mental health system. However, finding criminal justice system solutions for offenders with mental illness is very much a practical matter and one dictated by current circumstances.

Conclusion

Theoretical Explanations of Public Order Crime

Which of our theories of crime explain involvement in public order crime, including alcohol, drunk driving, drug and prostitution offenses? As we saw with violent and property crimes, our leading theories of crime contend that they can explain public order crimes as well. In fact, it is relatively easy to understand how the tenets of the leading theories of crime including Hirschi's (1969) social control (social bond) theory, Gottfredson and Hirschi's (1990) self-control theory, Agnew's (2002) general strain theory and Akers' (1997, 2002) social learning theory can explain involvement in alcohol and drug use and in prostitution. Both Agnew's (2002) general strain theory and Gottfredson and Hirschi's (1990) self-control theory explicitly consider the use of drugs in the tenets of the theory, with Gottfredson and Hirschi (1990) maintaining that drug and alcohol use are symptomatic of low self-control and manifest themselves when no criminal opportunities are available and with Agnew (2002) noting that drug and alcohol use may result from strain or it may be a cause of strain. However, these are not the only theories that can explain involvement in public order crimes. As we saw in Chapter 6, radical feminist criminology maintains that women's path to offending, including offending with the crime of prostitution is paved with past victimization. And as we saw in Chapter 9, drunk driving is surprisingly well explained by Cornish and Clarke's (1986) rational choice theory, indicating that even when people are inebriated, they engage in some sort of calculated decision making before choosing to offend.

Criminalized Lifestyles

On the other hand, our theories of crime are rather poor at explaining criminalized lifestyles. Instead, what appears to explain criminalized lifestyles is the combination of our level of empirical understanding, public sentiment and legal machinations. No label of deviance appears to be inextricably attached to any mode of comportment forever. Prohibition belongs to the distant past, attitudes on drug use are relaxing, homosexuality is gaining wider acceptance than ever and both the homeless and the mentally ill are increasingly recognized as treatable conditions rather than bizarre, frightening and immutable afflictions. These changes are encouraging but slow to occur and some groups have to carry the deviant label as a result, at least for a while.

Websites to Visit

Alcohol and Crime: http://bjs.gov/index.cfm?ty=pbdetail&iid=2313, http://bjs.gov/content/pub/pdf/ac.pdf
Shaffer Library of Drug Policy: http://www.druglibrary.org/schaffer/
Sex Workers Project: http://www.sexworkersproject.org/
Biologic Explanation for Homosexuality: http://borngay.procon.org/
Bishop Accountability: http://www.bishop-accountability.org/

National Alliance to End Homelessness: http://www.naeh.org/
National Alliance on Mental Illness: http://www.nami.org/

Discussion Questions

1. Is it appropriate to restrict alcohol consumption by setting bar closing and sales stoppage times? Is it appropriate to do so if these measures reduce alcohol related violence?
2. Why do you think blue laws are still on the books in many states?
3. How do you see the misuse of legal prescription drugs fitting into the current debate surrounding the legalization of drugs?
4. Describe the benefits of legalized prostitution from the point of view of a sex worker, a customer, a pimp or madam and the criminal justice system. Are the benefits a convincing case for legalization?
5. Can you think of any other lifestyles that were criminalized but are gradually gaining acceptance, similar to homosexuality?
6. Is pedophilia an illness that can be treated? If so, how? If not, what should be done with those who sexually abuse children?
7. Do you think that consuming child pornography leads to the sexual abuse of children?
8. What are some ways to reduce the criminalization of homelessness and mental illness?

References

Agnew, Robert. (2002). Foundation for a general strain theory of crime. In S. Cote (Ed.), *Criminological theories: Bridging the past to the future* (pp. 113–124). Thousand Oaks, CA: Sage.

Akers, Ronald. (1997). *Criminological theories: Introduction and evaluation.* 2nd ed. Los Angeles, CA: Roxbury.

Akers, Ronald. (2002). A social learning theory of crime. In S. Cote (Ed.), *Criminological theories: Bridging the past to the future* (pp. 135–143). Thousand Oaks, CA: Sage.

Ashcroft v. *Free Speech Coalition.* 535 U.S. 234 (2002).

Bagley, Christopher. (1969). Incest behavior and incest taboo. *Social Problems, 16,* 505–519.

Ball, John. (1965). Two patterns of narcotic addiction in the United States. *Journal of Criminal Law, Criminology and Police Science, 56,* 203–211.

Becker, Howard. (1963). *Outsiders: Studies in the sociology of deviance.* New York, NY: The Free Press.

Becker, Howard and Kevin Murphy. (2013). Have we lost the war on drugs? *The Wall Street Journal,* January 4. Retrieved from: http://online.wsj.com/article/SB10001424127887324374004578217682305605070.html.

Bowers v. *Hardwick.* 478 U.S. 186 (1986).

Brecher, Edward. (1972). The consumers union report on licit and illicit drugs. Retrieved from: http://www.druglibrary.org/schaffer/library/studies/cu/cu8.html.

Canaday, Margot. (2008). We colonials: Sodomy laws in America. *The Nation,* September 22. Retrieved from: http://www.thenation.com/article/we-colonials-sodomy-laws-america?page=0,0#.

Carson, E. Ann and William Sabol. (2012). *Prisoners in 2011.* Bureau of Justice Statistics. Retrieved from: http://bjs.gov/content/pub/pdf/p11.pdf.

Century Council. (2012). *State of drunk driving fatalities in America 2011.* Retrieved from: http://www.centurycouncil.org/sites/default/files/materials/SODDFIA.pdf.

Compton, Michael, Masuma Bahora, Amy Watson and Janet Oliva. (2008). A comprehensive review of extant research on crisis intervention team (CIT) programs. *Journal of the American Academy of Psychiatry and the Law, 36*(1), 47–55.

Conrad, Peter, and Joseph Schneider. (1992). *Deviance and medicalization: From badness to sickness.* Philadelphia, PA: Temple University Press.

Cornish, Derek and Ronald Clarke. (1986). *The reasoning criminal.* New York, NY: Springer-Verlag.

D'Emilio, John. (1998). *Sexual politics, sexual communities: The making of a homosexual minority in the United States, 1940–1970.* Chicago, IL: University of Chicago Press.

DEA. (N.d.). Drug schedules. Retrieved from: http://www.justice.gov/dea/druginfo/ds.shtml.

DEA. (2010). Drug Enforcement Administration, 1970–1975. Retrieved from: http://www.justice.gov/dea/pubs/history/1970-1975.pdf.

Diamond, Diane. (2012). Sandusky sentenced to 30 to 60 years. *The Daily Beast,* October 9. Retrieved from: http://www.thedailybeast.com/articles/2012/10/09/sandusky-sentenced-to-30-to-60-years-inside-the-courtroom.html.

Eskridge, William. (2008). *Dishonorable passions: Sodomy laws in America, 1861–2003.* New York, NY: Viking Adult.

FBI UCR. (2011). Crime in the United States 2011: Persons arrested. Retrieved from: http://www.fbi.gov/about-us/cjis/ucr/crime-in-the-u.s/2011/crime-in-the-u.s.-2011/persons-arrested/persons-arrested.

FBI UCR. (2011a). Crime in the United States 2011: Offense definitions. Retrieved from: http://www.fbi.gov/about-us/cjis/ucr/crime-in-the-u.s/2011/crime-in-the-u.s.-2011/offense-definitions.

Federal Register. (2010). Proposed Rules, Volume 75, Number 226, November 24, 71635–71638. Retrieved from: http://www.justice.gov/dea/pr/micrograms/2011/mg0111.pdf

Fox, James. (2011). Why killers target prostitutes. *Crime and Punishment,* April 15. Retrieved from: http://boston.com/community/blogs/crime_punishment/2011/04/why_killers_target_prostitutes.html.

Frailing, Kelly. (2012). Mental health courts. In A. Columbus (Ed.), *Advances in psychology research, Vol. 95* (pp. 1–26). Hauppague, NY: Nova Science Publishers.

Galliher, John, David Keys and Michael Elsner. (1998). Lindesmith v. Anslinger: An early government victory in the failed war on drugs. *Journal of Criminal Law and Criminology, 88,* 661–682.

GCHIVL. (2012*). Global commission on HIV and the law.* Retrieved from: http://www.hivlawcommission.org/resources/report/FinalReport-Risks,Rights&Health-EN.pdf.

Gottfredson, Michael and Travis Hirschi. (1990). *A general theory of crime*. Palo Alto, CA: Stanford University Press.

Harrison Narcotics Tax Act. (1914). Harrison Narcotics Tax Act. Retrieved from: http://www.druglibrary.org/Schaffer/history/e1910/harrisonact.htm.

Hirschi, Travis. (1969). *The causes of delinquency*. Berkeley, CA: University of California Press.

Jarecki, Eugene. (2012). Director, *The House I Live In*.

Jenkins, Pamela, Bethany Brown and Kimberly Mosby. (2012). Rebuilding and reframing: Non-profit organizations respond to Hurricane Katrina. In D.W. Harper and K. Frailing (Eds.), *Crime and Criminal Justice in Disaster*. 2nd ed (pp. 339–357). Durham, NC: Carolina Academic Press.

Kinsey, Alfred, Wardell Pomeroy and Clyde Martin. (1948). *Sexual behavior in the human male*. Philadelphia: W.B. Saunders.

Kinsey, Alfred, Wardell Pomeroy, Clyde Martin and Paul Gebhard (1953). *Sexual behavior in the human female*. Philadelphia: W.B. Saunders.

Lawrence v. *Texas*. 539 U.S. 558 (2003).

Lindesmith, Alfred. (1948). Handling the opiate problem. *Federal Probation, 12*, 23–25.

Maruschak, Laura. (1999). *DWI offenders under correctional supervision*. Bureau of Justice Statistics. Retrieved from: http://bjs.gov/content/pub/pdf/dwiocs.pdf.

Martin, Susan. (2001). The links between alcohol, crime and the criminal justice system: Explanations, evidence and interventions. *The American Journal on Addictions, 10*, 136–158.

McCaghy, Charles Henry. (1967). Child molesters: A study of their careers as deviants. In M. Clinard and R. Quinney (Eds.), *Criminal behavior systems: A typology* (pp. 75–88). New York, NY: Holt, Rinehart and Winston.

McGowan v. *Maryland* 366 U.S. 420 (1961).

McWilliams, John C. (1990). *The protectors: Harry J. Anslinger and the Federal Bureau of Narcotics, 1930–1962*. Newark, NJ: University of Delaware Press.

Nelson, Joan. (1989). Intergenerational sexual contact: A continuum model of participants and experiences. *Journal of Sex Education & Therapy, 15*, 3–12. Retrieved from: http://www.ipce.info/ipceweb/Library/nelson.htm.

New Orleans Daily Picayune. (1912). An opium raid. *The New Orleans Daily Picayune*, February 24.

New York v. *Ferber*. 458 U.S. 747 (1982).

NHTSA. (2013). *Challenges and defenses II*. U.S. Department of Transportation. Retrieved from: http://www.nhtsa.gov/Impaired (Challenges and Defenses II link).

NAMBLA. (2013). North American Man Boy Love Association home page. Retrieved from: www.nambla.org.

O'Donnell, John and John Ball. (1966). *Narcotic addiction*. New York, NY: Harper and Row.

Osborne v. *Ohio*. 495 U.S. 103 (1990).

Paquette, Kristen. (2011). *Current statistics on the prevalence and characteristics of people experiencing homelessness in the United States*. Substance Abuse and Mental Health Services Administration (SAMHSA). Retrieved from: http://homeless.samhsa.gov/ResourceFiles/hrc_factsheet.pdf.

Payan, Tony. (2006). *The three U.S.-Mexico border wars: Drugs, immigration, and homeland security.* Westport, CT: Praeger.

PBS. (2005). *The New Asylums,* Frontline documentary.

Potterat, John, Devon Brewer, Stephen Muth, Richard Rothenberg, Donald Woodhouse, John Muth, Heather Stites and Stuart Brody. (2004). Mortality in a long-term open cohort of prostitute women. *American Journal of Epidemiology, 159,* 778–785.

Procon.org. (2013). 100 countries and their prostitution policies. Retrieved from: http://prostitution.procon.org/view.resource.php?resourceID=000772.

Reuter, Peter. (2010). *Marijuana legalization: What can be learned from other countries?* RAND Working Paper. Retrieved from: http://192.5.14.43/content/dam/rand/pubs/working_papers/2010/RAND_WR771.pdf.

Rice, William, Urban Friberg and Sergey Gavrilets (2012). Homosexuality as a consequence of epigenetically canalized sexual development. *The Quarterly Review of Biology, 87,* 343–368.

Richards, Sabrina. (2013). Can epigenetics explain homosexuality? *The Scientist,* January 1. Retrieved from: http://www.the-scientist.com/?articles.view/articleNo/33773/title/Can-Epigenetics-Explain-Homosexuality-//.

Ritter, Karl (2008). Sweden prostitution law attracts interest. *USA Today,* March 16. Retrieved from: http://usatoday30.usatoday.com/news/world/2008-03-16-sweden-prostitution_N.htm.

Schaffer Library. (N.d.). The marihuana tax act of 1937: Additional statement of H.J. Ansligner, Commissioner of Narcotics. Shaffer Library of Drug Policy. Retrieved from: http://druglibrary.net/schaffer/hemp/taxact/t10a.htm.

Slate, Risdon and Wesley Johnson. (2008). *The criminalization of mental illness.* Durham, NC: Carolina Academic Press.

Taylor, Max, Gemma Holland and Ethel Quayle. (2001). Typology of paedophile picture collections. *Police Journal, 74,* 97–107.

Vogel, Victor. (1948). Treatment of the narcotic addict by the U. S. Public Health Service. *Federal Probation, 12,* 45–50.

Vollman, Brenda. (2012). Pedophilia and the U.S. Catholic Church: Victimization and its effects. In D. Harper, L. Voigt and W. Thornton (Eds.), *Violence: Do We Know It When We See It?* (pp. 345–367). Durham, NC: Carolina Academic Press.

Walsh, Anthony and Craig Hemmens. (2011). *Introduction to criminology: A text/reader.* 2nd ed. Los Angeles, CA: Sage.

Weitzer, Ronald. (2007). Prostitution as a form of work. *Sociology Compass, 1,* 143–155.

Wortley, Richard and Stephen Smallbone. (2006). Child pornography on the internet. Center for Problem Oriented Policing. Retrieved from: http://www.popcenter.org/problems/child_pornography/print/.

Yates, Velvet. (2005). Anterastai: Competition in Eros and politics in classical Athens. *Arethusa, 38,* 33–47.

Zeese, Kevin. (2002). *Nixon tapes show roots of marijuana prohibition: Misinformation, culture wars and prejudice.* Common Sense Drug Policy Research Report. Retrieved from: http://www.csdp.org/research/shafernixon.pdf.

Part V

Connecting Criminology and Criminal Justice

Chapter 15

What Criminology Means for Criminal Justice Now and in the Future

Introduction

Those readers who are criminal justice majors and may be required to take a criminology course for the major may be mystified at this point, asking themselves how criminology is connected to criminal justice and why they spent an entire semester learning about theories of crime and crime types if there is little association between the ideas from criminology and the practical application of criminal justice. In this chapter, we aim to allay confusion by explaining the application of criminology to criminal justice policymaking in different areas, including punishment, crime prevention and rehabilitation. We then discuss a number of lingering issues for both criminology and criminal justice; these issues include changing crime rates in the United States, gun control, the legalization of both prostitution and drugs, sex offender policies and the death penalty.

Criminology and Criminal Justice Policymaking: Punishment

For well over a century, the guiding principle of the American criminal justice system was rehabilitation. From the 1800s through the 1970s, the criminal justice system operated under the stated goal of solving the problems that brought offenders to its attention in the first place. This is not to say that the criminal justice system was efficient and effective at addressing the problems that can lead to offending. In fact, the opposite is true. There is little evidence that offenders received much in the way of meaningful rehabilitation that helped to solve underlying problems during this long period (Cullen and Agnew, 2011). Moreover, there was little focus during this time on preventing crime. One might think that if the focus of the criminal justice system was rehabilitation, it would be natural to incorporate a prevention perspective as well, one that identified risk factors for crime and worked to ameliorate those risk factors early in life before they could lead to crime. However, with the exception of President Lyndon Johnson's War on Poverty in the mid-1960s, there was almost no focus on preventing crime during this time. The War on Poverty was largely rooted in Merton's (1938) ideas about an inability to achieve monetary goals through legitimate means and is the collective name for a group of programs that provided education and employment acquisition assistance to people in disadvantaged communities. War on Poverty programs have fallen away over the ensuing decades, with the notable exceptions of Head Start and Job Corps (Cullen and Agnew, 2011).

The goal for the criminal justice system of rehabilitation started to undergo major reconsideration beginning in the mid-1970s. There are a number of reasons for this, two of the most important of which were the increasing crime rate and the Martinson Report. The increase in crime during this period is covered in much more detail below. Suffice it to say here that both violent and property crime were on the rise in the mid-1970s and the increase in crime would not abate until the 1990s. The Martinson Report was a comprehensive review of rehabilitative programs written by sociologist Robert Martinson in 1974. He concluded that rehabilitative programs had no noticeable effect on recidivism and that the criminal justice system had proven ineffective at addressing the reasons offenders commit crime. Though Martinson (1974) never said as much, the report quickly became known as the Nothing Works report[1] and it was so widely read that its conclusions set the stage for a massive overhaul of the very goals of the criminal justice system (Cullen and Agnew, 2011).

Moreover, the United States started to undergo a turn toward conservatism in the early 1980s, most noticeably in the election of Republican presidential candidate Ronald Reagan for the first time in 1980. Reagan won 91 percent of the electoral votes possible that year and Republicans won the Senate for the first time in 28 years, ushering in a new conservative era (Shirley, 2009). The increase in crime, the Martinson Report and the newly conservative orientation of the United States culminated in the reorientation of the criminal justice system away from rehabilitation and toward deterrence. Remember from Chapter 9 that deterrence is concerned with utilizing punishment to increase the costs of crime and reduce the likelihood that a criminal action will be taken. In order to be effective, punishment must be swift, severe and above all, certain. But remember also from Chapter 9 that punishment in the United States is notoriously uncertain. Given the nature of our criminal justice system, making punishment more certain is a Herculean task and making it swifter is no easy feat, either. The aspect of punishment that is most easily adjusted is its severity and punishments in the United States started

---

1. As reported in Sarre (1999), Martinson believed that his report would have the effect of emptying out prisons. Because he had shown that rehabilitation does not work and that prisons cannot be reformed, he surmised that policymakers would rethink the very value of imprisonment. As we will see, his report had the opposite effect.

to get much more severe in the 1980s because it was believed harsher punishments would have both a specific and a general deterrent effect. Harsh punishments should prevent recidivism by current offenders because the experience of punishment is so unpleasant, they should not engage in further crime that risks a similar punishment. Harsh punishments should also prevent crime among members of the general public, who should not want to risk such punishment by engaging in crime. Moreover, harsh punishments that include lengthy incarcerations would also have an incapacitation effect, keeping offenders locked up and unable to commit crime (Cullen and Agnew, 2011).

Increasing the severity of punishment did have a profound effect on the United States and that effect was most easily seen in the prison population. The change in prison population is explained in more detail below. Suffice it to say here that the prison population exploded beginning in the 1970s and reached epic proportions by the early 2000s. The United States incarcerates more people in terms of both raw numbers and rates than any other country. The increase in the harshness of punishment was not limited to longer prison terms. Many states started to adopt intermediate sanctions during this time. Intermediate sanctions can be thought of as falling on the continuum between probation on the one hand and prison on the other; they are more expensive than the former but much less costly than the latter. Intermediate sanctions include measures such as house arrest coupled with electronic monitoring, boot camps and intensive probation that requires closer supervision in the form of more meetings with the probation officer and frequent drug tests. However, it appears these intermediate sanctions did not serve the purpose of driving down prison costs because they were routinely used instead of probation and not instead of prison (Cullen and Agnew, 2011). Moreover, some research shows that intermediate sanctions have no reductive effect on recidivism (Gendreau, Goggin, Cullen and Andrews, 2000).

Criminologists turned their collective attention to evaluating this get tough on crime approach that took hold in the United States beginning in the 1980s. The most robust research reveals there is little evidence that increasing the severity of punishment reduces crime. For example, MacKenzie (2006) found that boot camps and intensive probation are no more effective at reducing recidivism than regular probation. Redding (2008) found that trying juveniles as adults and thereby subjecting them to the harsher punishments of the adult criminal justice system is no more effective at reducing recidivism than keeping them in the juvenile justice system. Chen and Shapiro (2007) found that harsh prison conditions are not more effective at reducing recidivism than less harsh conditions. Finally, Nagin, Cullen and Jonson (2009) found that imprisonment is no

Box 15.1. Three Strikes and You're Out Laws

Perhaps no legal development is more closely associated with the application of harsh punishment than three strikes and you're out laws. Three strikes laws are designed to provide a lengthy prison sentence for a third offense so that repeat offenders can be effectively incapacitated. Three strikes laws caught fire in the 1990s and by 2000, 24 states had them. As seen in the table, the states with three strikes laws vary in what they consider a strike and what it means to be out.

State	Year	What is a Strike?	How Many Strikes to be Out?	What Does it Mean to be Out?
Arkansas	1995	Murder, kidnapping, robbery, rape, terrorism AND	Two	40+ years in prison, no parole Range of no parole sentences
		First degree battery, firing a gun from a vehicle, use of a prohibited weapon, conspiracy to commit murder, kidnapping, robbery, rape, first degree battery, first degree sexual abuse	Three	
California	1994	Murder, voluntary manslaughter, rape, lewd act on a child under 14, continual sexual abuse of a child, forcible penetration by foreign object, sexual penetration by force,	Two	Mandatory sentence of twice the sentence for the offense committed
		forcible sodomy, forcible oral copulation, robbery, assault with a deadly weapon on a peace officer, assault with a deadly weapon by an inmate, assault with intent to rape or rob, any felony resulting in bodily harm, arson causing bodily injury, exploding device with intent to injure or murder, kidnapping, mayhem, arson, residential burglary, grand theft with firearm, drug sales to minors, any felony with a deadly weapon, any felony where a firearm is used, attempt to commit any of these offenses	Three	Mandatory indeterminate life sentence with no parole for 25+ years
Colorado	1994	Any Class 1 or 2 felony or any Class 3 felony that is violent	Three	Mandatory life with no parole for 40+ years
Connecticut	1994	Murder, attempted murder, assault with intent to kill, manslaughter, arson, kidnapping, aggravated sexual assault, robbery, first degree assault	Three	Up to life in prison
Florida	1995	Any forcible felony, aggravated stalking, aggravated child abuse, lewd or indecent conduct, escape	Three	Life if the third strike involved a first degree felony, 30–40 years if it was a second degree felony, 10–15 years if it was a third degree felony
Georgia	1995	Murder, armed robbery, kidnapping, rape, aggravated child molesting, aggravated sodomy, aggravated sexual battery AND	Two	Mandatory life without parole
		Any felony	Four	Mandatory maximum sentence for the offense
Indiana	1994	Murder, rape, sexual battery with a weapon, child molesting, arson, robbery, burglary with a weapon or resulting in serious injury, drug dealing	Three	Mandatory life without parole

State	Year	Offenses	Strikes	Penalty
Kansas	1994	Any felony against a person	Two	Court may double specified sentence for the offense
			Three	Court may triple specified sentence for the offense
Louisiana	1994	Murder, attempted murder, manslaughter, rape, armed robbery, kidnapping, any drug offense punishable by more than five years, any felony punishable by more than 12 years AND	Three	Mandatory life without parole
		Any four felony convictions if at least one was on the above list	Four	Mandatory life without parole
Maryland	1994	Murder, rape, robbery, first or second degree sexual offense, arson, burglary, kidnapping, carjacking, manslaughter, use of a firearm in a felony, assault with intent to murder, rape, rob or commit a sexual offense	Four with separate prison terms served for first three strikes	Mandatory life without parole
Montana	1995	Deliberate homicide, aggravated kidnapping, sexual intercourse without consent, ritual abuse of a minor AND	Two	Mandatory life without parole
		Mitigated deliberate homicide, aggravated assault, kidnapping, robbery	Three	Mandatory life without parole
Nevada	1995	Murder, robbery, kidnapping, battery, abuse of children, arson, home invasion	Three	Life without parole, life with parole in 10+ years, 25 years with parole in 10+ years
New Jersey	1995	Murder, robbery, carjacking	Three	Mandatory life without parole
New Mexico	1994	Murder, shooting at or from a vehicle and causing harm, kidnapping, criminal sexual penetration, armed robbery resulting in harm	Three	Mandatory life with no parole for 40+ years
North Carolina	1994	47 violent felonies; separate indictment required that the offender is habitual	Three	Mandatory life without parole
North Dakota	1995	Any Class A, B or C felony	Two	If second strike was for a Class A felony, up to life in prison possible, up to 20 years for Class B, up to 10 years for Class C
Pennsylvania	1995	Murder, voluntary manslaughter, rape, involuntary deviate sexual intercourse, arson, kidnapping, robbery, aggravated assault	Two	Sentence enhancement of up to 10 years
			Three	Sentence enhancement of up to 25 years

State	Year	What is a Strike?	How Many Strikes to be Out?	What Does it Mean to be Out?
South Carolina	1995	Murder, voluntary manslaughter, homicide by child abuse, rape, kidnapping, armed robbery, drug trafficking, embezzlement, bribery, accessory and attempt offenses	Two	Mandatory life without parole
Tennessee	1995	Murder, especially aggravated kidnapping, especially aggravated robbery, aggravated rape, rape of a child, aggravated arson AND	Two if a prison term was served for the first strike	Mandatory life without parole
		Same as above, plus rape and aggravated sexual battery	Three if separate prison terms served	Mandatory life without parole for the first two strikes
Utah	1995	Any first or second degree felony	Three	From five years to life
Vermont	1995	Murder, manslaughter, arson causing death, assault and robbery with weapon or causing bodily injury, aggravated assault, kidnapping, maiming, aggravated sexual assault, aggravated domestic assault, lewd conduct with a child	Three	Up to life
Virginia	1994	Murder, kidnapping, robbery, carjacking, sexual assault, conspiracy to commit any of these	Three	Mandatory life without parole
Washington	1993	Any Class A felony, conspiracy or solicitation to commit a class A felony, extortion, manslaughter, promoting prostitution all in the first degree, assault, child molestation, kidnapping, manslaughter, robbery all in the second degree, rape in the third degree, controlled substance homicide, incest against a child under 14, indecent liberties, leading organized crime, sexual exploitation, vehicular assault, vehicular homicide by impaired or reckless driver, any other Class B felony with sexual motivation, any other felony with deadly weapon	Three	Mandatory life without parole
Wisconsin	1994	Murder, manslaughter, vehicular homicide, aggravated battery, abuse of children, robbery, sexual assault, taking hostages, kidnapping, arson, burglary	Three	Mandatory life without parole

Source: Adapted from Austin, Clark, Hardyman and Henry, 2000.

California's three strikes laws have received the greatest scholarly attention to date. Despite the laundry list of crimes that can constitute third strikes, this law did not deliver the promised reductions in crime rates in California. Six years after the law went into effect, it had no demonstrable effect on crime rates in that state (Austin, Clark, Hardyman and Henry, 2000). California recently softened its three strikes law to include a life sentence only when the third felony is serious or violent. Up until that reform, though, the three strikes law in California appeared to disproportionately affect offenders with mental illness, who made up about 40 percent of three strikes inmates in 2011 (Staples, 2012). These offenders often pose little to no danger to the public in terms of violence, which begs the question of whether three strikes laws in general and California's three strikes law in particular is effectively incapacitating those who pose the greatest risk to the population at large.

more effective than less severe punishments at reducing recidivism. How could these findings be accurate, when it makes so much intuitive sense that raising the cost of crime through punishment should drive future crime down? Cullen and Agnew (2011) note that harsh punishment does little to address the underlying causes of crime that we have explored throughout this book. It does not minimize strain, diminish the social learning of crime or increase control and it may even make these root causes worse. It may increase strain, it may promote the social learning of crime and it may decrease control so much so that harsh punishment may actually increase future criminal involvement. As seen in Chapters 5 and 9, the application of a criminal label may also make leading a law abiding life very difficult and as seen in Chapter 9, the likelihood that one will be punished for a crime is quite low, so the most important aspect of deterrence, making punishment certain, is rarely practiced. In fact, increasing the certainty or even the perceived certainty of punishment could make punishment a more effective general deterrent, but it is so difficult to increase actual or perceived certainty given the nature of our criminal justice system that lawmakers have opted instead to increase severity.

Criminology and Criminal Justice Policymaking: Prevention

With the value of the get tough on crime approach clearly in question, what other ways have we tried to respond to the crime problem? One answer to this question is prevention techniques and programs that are rooted in the theories of crime described in this book. A whole host of crime prevention techniques are detailed in Chapter 9 and for the most part, these involve making changes to the environment that make crime harder to commit. For individuals, these changes include locking doors, safeguarding valuables, installing alarm systems, window bars and outdoor lighting, avoiding unsafe areas, avoiding excessive intoxication and getting a dog. For businesses, these changes include installing closed circuit television cameras (CCTV), limiting the number of entry and exit ways, keeping lines of sight clear and limiting the amount of cash on hand. Eck and Eck (2012) remind us that we know a great deal about the concentration of crime in a few places, the stability of crime in these places, that crime prevention benefits often outweigh displacement efforts at these places and the owners of high crime places can be held accountable for the crime there. With this knowledge, we are in a good position to go beyond individual efforts at crime reduction based on place and to utilize regulation and regulatory practices to reduce crime at places. However, Cullen and Agnew (2011) remind us that we should not stop at environmental crime prevention techniques and try to incorporate those programs that have been shown to successfully address the root causes of crime. This two-pronged approach is the only way we can hope to eliminate most crime.

We may associate prevention most closely with Farrington and Welsh (2007) and the myriad programs detailed in Chapter 7 that aim to address known risk factors for crime at an early age. These programs include the Perry Preschool Project, the Montreal Longitudinal-Experimental Study, the Nurse-Family Partnership, the Syracuse University Family Development Research Project, the Responding in Peaceful and Positive Ways (RIPP) program, the Positive Action Through Holistic Education (PATHE) program, the Boys and Girls Club of America (BGC) and Big Brothers Big Sisters (BBBS).

However, we can also think of some of the other programs described elsewhere in this book as preventive. As described in Chapter 4, the Chicago Area Project was designed to ameliorate the criminogenic effects of social disorganization. The War on Poverty was designed to help those in disadvantaged communities access legitimate means to success, consistent with strain theory. Programs that attempt to eliminate child abuse and bullying, that help to provide education and lucrative work, that improve problem solving skills, the level of self-control and the ability to manage anger and that assist with increasing social support and resisting peer pressure are all crime prevention initiatives consistent with General Strain Theory. The Buddy Systems includes a mentoring component and the Oregon Social Learning Center has several programs, including the Adolescent Transition Program (ATP), the Multidimensional Treatment Foster Care (MTFC) program and the Linking the Interests of Families and Teachers (LIFT) program designed to connect youth with prosocial others inside and outside the home, in accord with both differential association and social learning theories. The Social Development Model combines social learning and social bond principles in its efforts to strengthen bonds to school and family, to teach prosocial skills and attitudes and to help young people avoid delinquent learning patterns. Finally, programs that assist parents with helping their children develop self-control as well as those that foster the development of self-control in school and other settings are consistent with self-control theory.[2] All of these initiatives are designed to address the root causes of crime and many have been empirically shown to be effective at doing so. These initiatives are probably most valuable in preventing crime when they

---

2. Before reading this book, we would hazard to guess that most readers had not heard of a single one of these theory-based crime prevention programs. However, we strongly suspect that many readers have heard of G.R.E.A.T. and that all or nearly all readers have heard of and perhaps participated in D.A.R.E. Remember from Chapter 4 that there is no evidence the D.A.R.E. program reduces drug use among young people. Pity the poor criminologist who spends his or her entire career gathering, analyzing and disseminating evidence that a program works only to have it overshadowed by and underfunded due to its unsupported brethren! For more on this issue, see Berman and Fox (2009) as a starting point.

are widely implemented together as part of a multifaceted approach to crime prevention; Greenwood and Welsh (2012) detail the challenges of implementing these evidence-based practices and suggest ways states can promote, support and adopt these programs.

Criminology and Criminal Justice Policymaking: Rehabilitation

Prevention is a noble goal for those at risk of offending but who have not yet done so, but what about those who have offended? What can be done to reduce their risk of recidivism? There has been a good deal of research devoted to rehabilitation programs since the Martinson Report concluded in 1974 that these programs are ineffective at reducing recidivism for offenders. Moreover, this research has included more sophisticated analyses of rehabilitation programs, including meta-analysis.[3] Meta-analysis involves taking a number of studies on the same topic and reviewing them in tandem. The findings of each study are coded to determine the relationship between the independent and dependent variable (in this case, rehabilitative program and recidivism, respectively), which is known as an effect size. The effect sizes are averaged across studies and the average effect size reveals the degree to which rehabilitative programs are effective at reducing recidivism. More recent research using meta-analyses has attempted to differentiate findings by program success. In other words, meta-analyses can now be used to determine what programs are associated with reduced recidivism and what the features of those programs are (Cullen and Jonson, 2011).

There are two types of programs found in many prisons throughout the United States, education and work programs and drug treatment programs, and studies on these programs have been subjected to meta-analyses. Wilson, Gallagher and MacKenzie (2000) reviewed 33 studies on educational, vocational and work programs and found that participants in those programs recidivated at a rate of 39 percent, versus 50 percent for those not participating in these programs. Steurer, Tracy and Smith (2001) found that participation in educational programs on their own were associated with less recidivism for over 3,100 inmates across three states. Educational program participants were arrested at a lower rate than nonparticipants (48 versus 57 percent), they were convicted at a lower rate than nonparticipants (27 versus 35 percent) and they were reincarcerated at a lower rate (21 versus 31 percent). Bouffard, MacKenzie and Hickman (2000) note that multifaceted programs such as those that combine vocational education with job search assistance and community employment opportunities are effective at reducing recidivism. Latessa (2012) contends that those programs which target and improve offenders' attitudes about work as well as help them learn marketable skills are likely to be the most effective at reducing recidivism.

Drug treatment programs in prisons take on several forms, including narcotic maintenance programs, boot camps for drug offenders, group counseling, residential substance

---

3. The meta-analysis as a data gathering technique is discussed in more detail in Chapter 2.

abuse treatment and therapeutic communities, which are residential units devoted exclusively to drug treatment and the promotion of prosocial behavior and attitudes. All five types have the shared goals of reducing drug use and recidivism. Mitchell, Wilson and MacKenzie (2007) performed a meta-analysis of 66 evaluations of these different types of drug treatment programs and found that overall, drug treatment programs produced an eight percent reduction in recidivism, though no appreciable effect on drug use. Involvement in therapeutic communities significantly reduced recidivism and future drug use (Pearson and Lipton (1999) found the same thing). Counseling and residential programs produced a reduction in recidivism but not in drug use. Neither boot camps nor narcotic maintenance programs had an effect on recidivism or drug use. Thanks to these meta-analyses, it is clearer which programs are the most effective at rehabilitating offenders and where resources should be allocated.[4]

Box 15.2. What about Drug Courts?

Drug courts are a type of specialty court. Specialty courts, also called problem solving courts, are designed to address the issues that keep offenders coming back into contact with the criminal justice system with the hope that once these issues are solved, a reduction or elimination in criminal justice system involvement will occur. Specialty courts typically voluntarily enrolled participants with treatment and other services designed to address their major issues; this treatment is provided in lieu of incarceration. There are a variety of specialty courts, including but not limited to drug courts, mental health courts, homeless courts, community courts, domestic violence courts, DUI courts and veterans' courts. Research has shown that these courts are able to reduce recidivism among participants (see e.g., Roman, Rossman and Rempel (2011) for an overview of the drug court literature and Frailing (2012) for an overview of the mental health court literature). However, before we put all our eggs in the specialty court basket, it is important to consider that drug courts cannot possibly serve all drug users who come into contact with the criminal justice system. According to Boyum, Caulkins and Kleiman (2011), there are 30 times as many seriously drug involved offenders (2,100,000) as there are drug court participants (about 70,000) in the United States today. Trying to serve even a third of seriously drug involved offenders through drug courts would require more than half of all the judges in the United States to serve as drug court judges and would probably overload existing community based treatment and services.

Drug courts, then, are only part of the answer. Another program designed to provide treatment to drug offenders is HOPE, which stands for Hawaii's Opportunity Probation with Enforcement. In 2004, a judge in Honolulu decided to start giving random and frequent drug tests to

---

4. In the 1980s, military-style boot camps became increasingly popular in the criminal justice system. The idea was that offenders could be transformed into law abiding citizens through discipline and tough physical work. Boot camps retained their level of popularity despite no empirical evidence for their success at reducing recidivism. That failed intervention certainly diverted badly needed resources away from effective rehabilitation programs (Cullen and Jonson, 2011).

a group of 35 felony probationers who had been noncompliant with the conditions of their probation in the past. Instead of scheduling drug tests for some future date, the judge helped institute a practice in which these probationers had to call in every day and find out if they were scheduled for a random drug test. Those who tested positive or who failed to show when required had a warrant issued and were jailed during the short wait until their hearing before the judge. At that hearing, the judge imposed a sanction for failure to comply with the conditions of probation; this sanction usually took the form of a few days in jail. After serving time for noncompliance, probationers in HOPE could resume their attempts to meet the conditions of their probation. That is, they did not automatically have their probation revoked for instances of noncompliance. HOPE increases the certainty of sanctions for noncompliance and it may be unsurprising to learn that only half of the original group of 35 received an actual sanction for noncompliant behavior. For the other half, the threat of sanction was enough to discourage their law breaking behavior. HOPE also appears to be quite cost effective, especially when compared to prison, and it is a model for managing drug involved felony offenders in the community ((Boyum, Caulkins and Kleiman, 2011; Kleiman, Caulkins and Hawken, 2011).

Based on their meta-analysis of the meta-analyses on offender rehabilitation programs, Lipsey and Cullen (2007) point out well designed rehabilitation programs have several things in common. First, they address the known causes of crime and to do so, they use cognitive behavioral interventions, the preferred treatment method (Smith, Gendreau and Swartz, 2009). Cognitive behavioral programs are based on the idea that our thoughts (cognitions) are learned and that they affect our behaviors. These programs include cognitive restructuring components that challenge what offenders believe about why crime is acceptable and cognitive skills programs that restructure the way offenders reason and ultimately behave (Van Voorhis and Lester, 2004). Second, Lipsey and Cullen (2007) note that successful rehabilitation programs are intensive and long lasting and that they incorporate a number of techniques in their provision of cognitive behavioral treatment. Third, these programs focus on high risk offenders, making the most efficient use of resources. Fourth, they are administered in the community where possible, as administration in prison comes with its own difficulties. For example, the massive prison population makes the provision of rehabilitation programs difficult and prisoners are less likely now than in the past to participate in programs designed to address the root causes of offending while they are incarcerated (Useem and Piehl, 2008; Vieraitis, Kovandzic and Marvell, 2007). Petersilia (2008) found that in California, which has the largest prison population of any state, less than half of prisoners released in 2006 participated in any rehabilitation program.

Rehabilitation programs appear to be quite cost effective, especially when compared to incarceration (Greenwood, 2006). It is cheaper to prevent crime through a prevention or rehabilitative program than it is to prevent crime through imprisonment. Moreover, rehabilitative programs have a good deal of public support these days. That is not to say people favor rehabilitation to the exclusion of punishment. Rather, the public seems to favor both rehabilitation and punishment for offenders (Cullen and Agnew, 2011; Cullen and Jonson, 2011).

Some Lingering Issues for
Criminology and Criminal Justice[5]

Changing Crime Rates in the United States

One of the issues that criminological and criminal justice researchers have tried to shed some light on is the changing crime rate in the United States over the past 50 years. As we saw in Chapters 11 and 12, there was a dramatic increase in crime in the United States beginning in the 1960s and continuing through the 1980s. Crime rates started to fall precipitously in the early 1990s and these trends were observed with both violent and property crime. Figures 15.1 and 15.2 graphically depict the changing crime rates in the United States.

Figure 15.1. Violent crime rate in the United States per 100K, 1960–2011

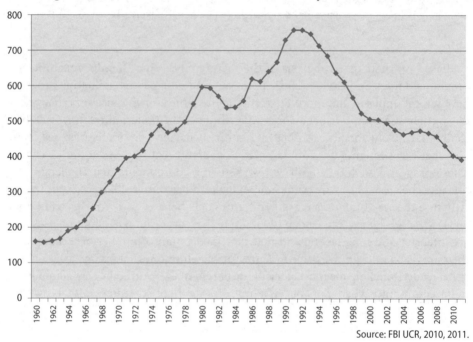

Source: FBI UCR, 2010, 2011.

But what can account for these changes, both the increase in earlier years and the decrease in more recent years? Rosenfeld (2011) cautions that to more fully understand these changes, it is crucial to disaggregate crime rates by groups and he points to homicide trends as seen in the Uniform Crime Reports to illustrate the importance of doing so. Importantly, few homicides are likely to go unreported to the police, so these data reflect the actual rate of homicide per year. Figure 15.3 shows the homicide rate in the United States over the last 50 years.

---

5. The issues described here are a handful of those that are currently important to both criminological and criminal justice researchers. For a longer list, see the National Conference of State Legislatures website at http://www.ncsl.org/issues-research.aspx?tabs=951,62,94.

Figure 15.2. Property crime rate in the United States per 100K, 1960–2011

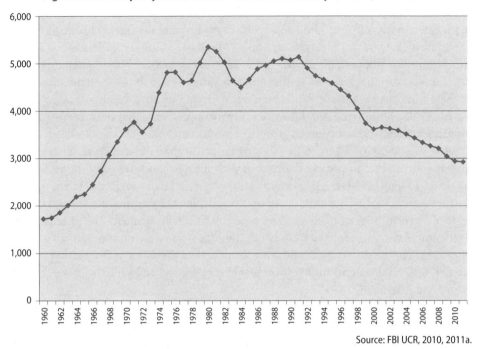

Source: FBI UCR, 2010, 2011a.

Figure 15.3. Homicide rate in the United States per 100K, 1960–2011

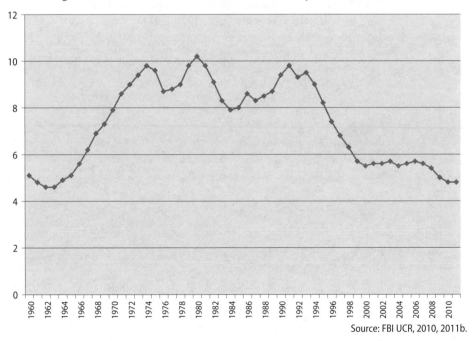

Source: FBI UCR, 2010, 2011b.

The homicide rate increased from about eight to 10 per 100,000 between 1984 and 1991. But during that time, youth homicides accounted for almost the entire increase in the rate as a whole (Cook and Laub, 1998; Blumstein and Rosenfeld, 1998). Moreover, the homicide rate increase was concentrated in minority youth, especially young African American men (Blumstein, 2006). If we want to better understand changing crime rates, it is crucial that we look at how different groups contribute or do not contribute to these rates. In the case of youth homicides driving up the overall homicide rate in the late 1980s, Blumstein (2006) provides convincing evidence that the increase in youth homicides resulted from younger people's recruitment into the crack trade as dealers because they were less likely to be targeted for arrest than older dealers. These young dealers soon started to protect themselves with firearms and the youth homicide rate escalated. Rosenfeld (2011) makes a similar claim about the change in the rate of intimate partner homicides. The intimate partner homicide rate declined for both men and women between 1976 and 2005, but more for men than for women. This change points to the importance of shelters and restraining orders in reducing the intimate partner homicide rate, somewhat ironically more for men than for women because they provide women with nonlethal means to escape an abuser (Browne and Williams, 1989; Dugan, Nagin and Rosenfeld, 1999).

Another example we believe illustrates Rosenfeld's (2011) point about the importance of disaggregating the homicide rate in order to better understand changes in it is the city of New Orleans. Figure 15.4 shows New Orleans' homicide rate in comparison to the national homicide rate.

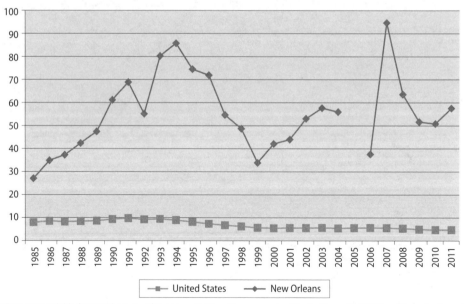

Figure 15.4. Homicide rate for New Orleans, LA and the United States per 100K, 1985–2011

* Data not available for 2005 because of Hurricane Katrina; the pronounced fluctuations after 2005 are likely due in part to the sudden and dramatic decrease in population post-storm followed by its slow increase in subsequent years

Source: FBI UCR, 2010, 2011c.

The homicide rate in New Orleans is and has been several times higher than the national homicide rate for quite a long time. Importantly, while the homicide rate was declining for the country as a whole in the early 2000s, it was climbing again in New Orleans. Disaggregating the homicide rate by city, the same as disaggregating it by age or by type, is instructive in better understanding it. In the case of New Orleans, it is likely a combination of intergenerational impoverishment, limited school and work opportunities and subcultures comprised of young, often criminally involved men that support violent and even lethal solutions to interpersonal conflicts that account at least in part for its nation-leading homicide rate.

When asked to provide an explanation for the most recent dramatic drop in crime, the one that began in the 1990s, criminologists point to five likely factors. As Rosenfeld (2011) details, the first of these is a demographic change. As baby boomers born in the 1940s and 1950s began to age into adolescence, there was a corresponding increase in the crime rate (Steffensmeier and Harer, 1991; Fox, 2006; Blumstein and Rosenfeld, 2008); it is a commonly observed phenomenon in criminology that crime increases as children age into adolescence and decreases as adolescents age into adulthood (Hirschi and Gottfredson, 1983; see also Chapter 7). The second factor is drug markets. While the increase in the number of young people is likely important in the increase in crime in the 1960s and 1970s, it cannot well explain the dramatic increase in violent crime among youth in the 1980s. As we have seen, Blumstein (2006) attributes this increase to expanding crack markets and an increased number of young males with firearms.

The third factor that may explain the drop in the crime rate in the 1990s is imprisonment. The drop in the crime rate in the 1990s coincided with the greatest expansion in imprisonment in the history of the United States. Between 1987 and 2007, in just 20 years, the prison population in the United States nearly tripled to nearly 1.6 million. Adding the approximately 723,000 people in jail means that 2.3 million people in the United States are behind bars, for a rate of one per 100 (Pew Center on the States, 2008). Moreover, people are serving longer prison sentences than in the past. Those released from prison in 2009 served 36 percent more time (an average of nine months more) than those released from prison in 1990. Nine months may not seem like very much time, but the extra time served cost the states approximately $10 billion and about half of that was spent to incarcerate nonviolent offenders (Pew Center on the States, 2012).

Box 15.3. The United States' Imprisonment Rate: How and Why?

The United States incarcerates a lot of people, sure, but how does it stack up against other Western countries? The following table reveals that the United States has far and away the highest rate of imprisonment in the world.

There are three huge drivers in the United States' incarceration rate. The first is the higher levels of serious violence in this country. The second is sentencing policy and rooted in sentencing policy is the United States' tendency, far greater than that in any other country in the world, to incarcerate drug offenders. According to Lynch and Pridemore (2011), the United States is not unique in the commission of drug offenses or police detection of drug crime.

Country	Prison Population Rate (per 100K) in 2008 for selected countries
United States	756
Russian Federation	629
South Africa	335
Mexico	207
Saudi Arabia	132
United Kingdom	131
Australia	129
China	119
Canada	116
The Netherlands	100
Germany	89
Egypt	87
Japan	63
India	33

Source: Adapted from Walmsley, 2009.

Where the United States stands alone is in the use of incarceration for drug offenses and the length of those sentences; prison and jail are imposed in 67 percent of drug cases in the United States, followed most closely yet distantly by the Netherlands at 46 percent of cases. The average length of incarceration for a drug crime in the United States is 23 months followed most closely yet distantly by England and Wales at 12 months. Moreover, the amount of time served for drug crimes is growing at the same rate as that for violent crimes in the United States (Pew Center on the States, 2012).

Astute readers may be asking themselves if every state contributes equally to the world-leading prison population in the United States. The simple and clear answer is no. Louisiana, the adopted home of the authors of this book, has far and away the highest rate of incarceration of all the states at 867 per 100,000 people. In fact, Louisiana leads the world in incarceration rates. The prison population there has undergone a six fold increase since 1977.[6] There are several reasons for this increase and for the frankly astonishing number of people in prison in the Pelican State, the first of which is tough sentencing laws. Tough sentences mean more prison inmates and more inmates remaining incarcerated for longer periods of time. The second reason is money. In the 1990s, Louisiana had a serious prison overcrowding problem

---

6. This massive incarceration has not served to drive down Louisiana's violent or property crime rates, though; the state has some of the highest violent and property crime rates in the country (Chang, 2012).

and it had two choices to solve it, change sentencing laws to allow more people to be released from prison or build more prisons. Louisiana chose the latter and offered local sheriffs great incentives to build prisons in rural areas of the state. Sheriffs were rewarded for their compliance with inmates, who each bring about $25 per day of state money into local coffers. Sheriffs can use the profits from this arrangement to beef up local law enforcement (Chang, 2012).

Ironically, the more than 160 local prisons in Louisiana house less dangerous offenders who might stand a good shot at rehabilitation, but rehabilitative and reentry services are only found in the 12 state prisons, which house more dangerous offenders, including those who might never be released. Sentencing reform, which might help to ameliorate part of the root of this incarceration crisis, is hard to come by in Louisiana; there is a great deal of opposition to softening sentencing laws, even for drug and nonviolent offenses, from both district attorneys and — no surprises here — sheriffs (Moller and Chang, 2012). The effects of incarceration are evident not only for inmates but for the families and neighborhoods they leave behind, as well. A full eight percent of those who are incarcerated in Louisiana and call New Orleans home come from a neighborhood known as Central City. Less than one in five children in this neighborhood are growing up in a two parent household; about half are growing up with a single mother. These children regularly see adults from their neighborhood go to prison and some believe this contributes to a sense of hopelessness and a mentality among the youth in Central City that the future holds little promise (Simerman, 2012).

Imprisonment disproportionately affects men and minorities, so much so that the imprisonment rate for African American men ages 20 to 34 is one in nine (Pew Center on the States, 2008). That is no typo, one in nine African American men ages 20–34 in the United States is in prison. How could this be? Early research on this subject pointed to differential involvement in crime (Blumstein, 1982; Langan, 1985). That is, African Americans were shown to be more involved in crime than those of other races and therefore sent to prison more often. However, more recent research has revealed that involvement in drug markets and residence in high density urban neighborhoods may also be factors. Tonry and Melewski (2008) note that African Americans involved in the drug trade are typically easier to arrest because of the nature of the drug market in which they are involved, which includes open air and street dealing. Combine that with high density neighborhoods that practically guarantee these markets exist in drug free zones that provide for increased penalties (Brownsberger and Aromaa, 2001; NJ Sentencing Commission, 2007) and the stage is set for higher incarceration rates for African Americans.

Why did the prison population explode the way it did? To answer that question, we need to investigate the ascendance of the get tough approach on crime. As seen above, the United States took a conservative turn in the 1980s and with that turn was greater adherence to the idea that people did not engage in crime because of some disadvantage but because they chose to. With that very classical school idea taking hold, new measures were taken to increase the severity of punishment, such prison terms for nonviolent drug offenders, three strikes laws and mandatory minimum sentences laws. These had a dramatic effect on the prison population because they sent more people to prison for longer periods of time (Cullen and Agnew, 2011). But did the explosion of the prison population have an effect on the crime rate? The short answer is yes. Both Levitt (2004) and Spelman (2008) found that about 25 percent of the drop in violent crime in the 1980s is attributable to the increase in imprisonment rates. However, Piehl and Useem (2011) point out that there is a limit to the crime reducing effects of prison. Now that there is such a large prison population, imprisoning more people does not have the same reductive effect as it did when the prison population was smaller. In fact, more recent estimates of the crime reducing effect of imprisonment appear more modest. For every 10 percent increase in incarceration, there appears to be a one percent drop in crime rates. Piehl and Useem (2011) point out that as a society, we must decide if such small returns in terms of crime reduction are worth their financial and social costs of prison, including the disruption of communities from which many young men are sent to prison. Mass imprisonment from these usually minority communities can lead to disorganization through the removal of residents and that disorganization can lead to an increase in crime rates rather than a decrease (Rose and Clear, 1998; Clear, 2007).

The fourth factor that may explain the drop in the crime rate in the 1990s is policing. Studies on whether policing reduces crime and whether it was partially responsible for the reduction in crime in the 1990s usually take one of two types; either they focus on the size of the police force or the activity of the police force. Levitt (1996) found that increasing the size of the police force does reduce crime, but those results have been disputed for failing to disentangle the effects of police activity from police size on the crime rate (Skogan and Frydl, 2004). Some police activities that have been shown to reduce crime are hot spots and broken windows policing; these two police activities were covered in Chapter 9. There is a fair amount of agreement that hot spots policing leads to a reduction in crime in the hot spots with very little displacement (Skogan and Frydl, 2004; Sherman, 2011), but the evidence is more mixed on broken windows policing. Recall from Chapter 9 that New York experienced an astonishing drop in crime in the 1990s. Kelling and Sousa (2001)[7] found that New York's drop in crime came as a result of the police making more misdemeanor arrests, but Harcourt and Ludwig (2006) found that more misdemeanor arrests had no effect on the crime drop. Further confusing the issue is that both Messner, et al. (2007) and Rosenfeld, Fornango and Rengifo (2007) found that making misdemeanor arrests had a modest but significant reductive effect on the violent crime rate, but that the crime drop would have happened anyway with no changes in police activity.

The fifth factor that may explain the drop in the crime rate in the 1990s is the economy. It is logical to believe that as unemployment rates rise, so too with the crime rate. Those now out of work will turn to crime in its various forms in order to survive. However, this logical assumption finds little empirical support in the literature in large part because unemployment is a rather poor measure of the strength of the economy. The unemployment rate only includes those actively looking for work and excludes those not participating in the labor force. Moreover, there is a lag effect of unemployment on crime. For example, someone who finds themselves suddenly unemployed should not have to turn to crime for a while, until his or her severance package and savings

---

7. Recall that George Kelling helped to develop broken windows theory with James Wilson.

are exhausted. Moreover, that person likely spends more time at home, removing him or herself from situations in which he or she is more likely to offend or to be offended against (Rosenfeld, 2011). More recent research that focuses on better indicators for the strength of the economy than unemployment, such as per capita growth and consumer sentiment reveals that crime rates increase during economic slumps and they decrease during economic expansions (Arvanites and Devin, 2006; Rosenfeld and Fornango, 2007). Rosenfeld and Messner (2009) conclude that the economic upturn of the 1990s can explain a considerable portion of the drop in both property and violent crime throughout the United States and Europe during this time, though Rosenfeld (2009) notes that the improved economy's effect on violent crime is largely mediated through its effect on violent crime. Bushway (2011) adds the important concept of workforce attachment to this issue, noting that when workforce attachment is low, particularly among crime prone groups such as young men, crime will increase. Workforce attachment among young men hit historic lows during the recent (2008) recession and this criminogenic detachment that has its roots in the recession is compounded by the detachment that comes as a result of a stint in prison. Of course being in prison prevents one from holding gainful employment at that time, but a prison stay has a lingering effect on workforce attachment, making it more difficult to find work after release (Bushway, 2011).

Rosenfeld (2011) notes that even if these five factors, demographic changes, drug markets, imprisonment, policing and the economy, can explain the drop in crime rates in the United States as a whole beginning in the 1990s when taken together, this does not necessarily mean that these factors are responsible for the drop in crime in a given single location. Baumer (2008) looked at crime rates in cities in the United States during both the increase and decrease in crime rates and found that changes in drug markets, imprisonment and the size of the 15–24-year-old population was associated in the expected directions with changing crime rates. Baumer (2008) also found other factors to be important in crime rate changes, including the proportion of children born to teenage mothers and the proportion of households with cohabitating but unmarried couples. He further found that these factors did not contribute equally to the increase and the subsequent decrease in crime rates. For example, changes in the drug market, including greater use of firearms and the increase in the number of youth homicides, contributed greatly to the crime rate increase, but not the decrease. The economy, on the other hand, contributed to the decrease in crime rates in later years, but not the increase in earlier years. Rosenfeld (2011) notes that findings such as these make it difficult to predict coming crime rate trends, but encourages us to take advantage of advances in econometric forecasting to try.

Gun Control

In the wake of the Sandy Hook Elementary School shootings of December 2012, the issue of gun control came once again to national attention. In order to better understand this issue, we need to understand three things, the patterns in gun ownership and use, the connection between guns and crime and both current and suggested gun control policies (Cook, Braga and Moore, 2011). Understanding gun ownership and use is predicated first on knowing the extent of gun ownership. In their nationwide survey utilizing a representative sample, Hepburn, Miller, Azrael and Hemenway (2007) found that 60 percent of firearms owned by Americans are long guns, primarily shotguns and rifles, and the remaining 40 percent are handguns. The single most prevalent type of gun is the rifle. Thirty eight percent of households and 26 percent of individuals reported owning at least one gun, which equals out to 42 million households and 57 million individuals who own guns. The average number of guns owned by each of these 42 million households is 5.2, for a total of 218 million firearms. The average number of guns owned by each of these 57 million individuals is five, for a total of 283 million firearms. Nearly half of respondents said the most important reason for their gun ownership was self-protection. Firearm owners are most likely to be white, middle aged men with high incomes who live in rural areas in the Midwest or South and who grew up with guns in the home.

Many Americans die by firearm. Over 28,000 Americans were killed by guns in suicides, homicides and accidents in every year between 1978 and 2006. In 2006, there were more gun suicides than homicides, but guns are still used in 70 percent of homicides; the gun used most often in homicides is the handgun. Both victims and perpetrators of gun homicides tend to be young, African American males. Guns are used in non-lethal acts of violence as well. According to the 2006 National Crime Victimization Survey (NCVS), there were about 500,000 non-lethal but violent gun crimes spread over robberies, aggravated assaults and rapes (Cook, Braga and Moore, 2011). There is some disagreement about how often firearms are used in self defense. Cook (1991) found that three percent of victims were able to use a firearm against an intruder, but Kleck and Gertz (1995) reported millions of self defense uses of firearms per year. This discrepancy may be due in part to methods employed in various studies and it may be due in part to many acts of self defense occurring not between an innocent homeowner and predatory robber, but among drug dealers and serious criminals, as the latter two groups have a very high risk of being assaulted (Levitt and Venkatesh, 2000; Cook and Ludwig, 2000). The Kleck-Gertz number has also been reported as an outright myth (Cook, Ludwig and Hemenway, 1997).

Box 15.4. Conceal Carry Laws and Crime

Do conceal carry laws serve to increase or decrease crime? This question has been the subject of spirited academic debate, with lauded scholars taking positions on either side. At issue are concealed carry laws, which require law enforcement to issue permits to those who qualify to carry concealed firearms. Lott and Mustard (1997) examined changes in crime in 10 states that passed concealed carry (also called shall issue) laws between 1977 and 1992 and compared them to changes in crime in 10 states that did not pass concealed carry laws during that time and concluded that concealed carry laws reduce crime; in other words, more guns means less crime. However, Donohue (2003) describes problems in the data and analyses used to come to this bold conclusion, noting that states that passed concealed carry laws were less likely to have their crime rates driven up independently by the crack epidemic of the late 1980s. Those states that did not pass concealed carry laws were more likely to have serious crack epidemics in their poor, urban areas, so the fact that states that passed concealed carry laws had less crime than those that did not may not be fully attributable to the passage of concealed carry laws. Moreover, those states that were likely to pass concealed carry laws in the first place may have been experiencing increases in crime that led to the passage of the law, after which time crime decreased; it is not accurate in this case to attribute the decrease in crime to the passage of the law. Donohue (2003) also points to the importance of disaggregating states and time periods in data analysis such as this. For example, some concealed carry law states experienced increases rather than decreases in crime during the time period in question. It appears as though massive changes in the crime rate in the 1980s and the 1990s happened to coincide with the passage of concealed carry laws in some states and that concealed carry laws have a very minor influence on the crime rate. Nevertheless, it is likely the debate, academic and otherwise, on this contentious issue will continue.

The connection between guns and crime has long been fraught with contention, not because there is disagreement about the use of guns in criminal activity, but because of the importance attached to the American right of gun ownership. So do guns kill people or do people kill people? As seen above, Blumstein (2006) cites the recruitment of young dealers into the crack trade and their eventual use of firearms to protect themselves from rival dealers as a key reason for the increase in homicide in the United States in the 1980s. Evidence shows robberies and assaults committed with guns are more likely to be fatal to the victim than robberies or assaults carried out with other weapons (Cook, 1987; Kleck and McElrath, 1991). Some have argued that those motivated to kill will choose the more lethal gun and that guns indicate the intent of the offender (Wolfgang, 1958; Wright, Rossi and Daly, 1983), but Zimring (1968, 1972) counters this argument by noting the high amount of overlap between robberies and robbery murders as well as between aggravated assaults and assaultive murders and that whether the victim survives the attack is not indicative of the offender's intent. Robbers who use guns are less likely to experience resistance from victims and less likely to resort to physical attacks on victims (Conklin, 1972; Cook, 1976, 1980); the same is true for assaults (Kleck and McElrath, 1991). A logical explanation for these findings is that guns are intimidating enough to secure compliance from victims. Guns also allow offenders to execute more lucrative robberies because the intimidation of a gun allows the offenders to select targets that appear to be more lucrative; in fact, the value of the material robbed when a gun is used is about double that when another weapon is used. When robbers who use guns do resort to physical attacks, these attacks are far more lethal than attacks with other weapons (Cook, Braga and Moore, 2011).

There are substantial difficulties when determining whether the number of guns available leads to more crime. The most robust research that addresses many of the methodological issues that arise when studying this topic, such as comparing states that differ not just on gun ownership but on sociodemographics and values systems as well, has found that a greater number of guns leads to a greater number of homicides. Moreover, this relationship is driven by the connection between the prevalence of guns and homicides by guns; there is little connection between the number of guns and non-gun homicides or other crimes (Duggan, 2001; Cook and Ludwig, 2006). However, it appears that gun prevalence has little effect on robbery and assault rates (Cook,

1979; Kleck and Patterson, 1993), so the amount of violence in the United States cannot be fully explained by guns, but the fact that so many violent crimes in the United States are lethal has a great deal to do with the availability of guns (Zimring and Hawkins, 1997).

Current gun laws do not appear to have facilitated a low enough gun violence rate, so what reforms can be undertaken in order to reduce gun violence? There are three broad categories of gun control measures (Zimring, 1991; Wintemute, 2000), the first of which involves raising the price of guns to restrict availability. If the monetary cost of obtaining a gun goes up, those effects should ripple all the way to the black market and may keep guns out of the hands of those prone to violence (Cook and Leitzel, 1996). One of the ways suggested to raise prices is an increase on federal taxes; another is to require more safety features on guns such as childproofing, trigger locks and loaded chamber warnings that will make them more expensive to produce and sell (Cook and Leitzel, 1996). However, the counterargument here is that these more expensive safety features will make guns unaffordable to the poorest households that may be at greatest risk of victimization (Cook, Braga and Moore, 2011).

The second broad category of gun control measures is restricting access to guns. One way to restrict access to guns is to treat gun ownership not as a right but as a privilege that requires proof of competence the same way driving does. Even if there is a move to treat gun ownership in this fashion, there is still the considerable problem of preventing the transfer of legal guns into criminal hands. This considerable problem is caused by disreputable gun dealers, screening difficulties and the unregulated secondary market (Cook, Braga and Moore, 2011). When the police confiscate guns, they give the guns to the Bureau of Alcohol, Tobacco and Firearms (ATF) for tracing. Just 1.2 percent of gun dealers were connected back to 57 percent of the firearms traced (ATF, 2000), indicating that a small number of disreputable gun dealers are responsible for many guns reaching the black market. In 1994, the Brady Handgun Violence Protection Act[8] mandated that anyone wanting to purchase a handgun from a gun dealer had to submit to a criminal background check. In the first four years after the passage of the Brady Act, 320,000 people seeking to buy handguns from dealers were rejected on the basis of the background check, nearly 70 percent of them due to their criminal histories (BJS, 1999). However, it appears the Brady Act had a negligible effect on homicide rates (Ludwig and Cook, 2000).

Box 15.5. What about Gun Marketing?

Does the marketing of guns by manufacturers have any connection with crime? While there has been little academic investigation of this idea, there has been some popular discussion, most of which is focused on Intratec, the company that manufactures the assault pistol known as the TEC-9. The Violent Crime Control and Law Enforcement Act of 1994, also known as the

---

8. Then press secretary James Brady was shot in the head by John Hinckley, Jr. in 1981 during the attempted assassination of President Ronald Reagan. He was left partially and permanently paralyzed by the shooting.

Crime Bill, banned the TEC-9 and its cousin the TEC-DC9 by name. Adhering to the letter but not the spirit of the new law, Intratec began manufacturing a modified version of the TEC-9 after the ban, calling it the AB-10, which was technically legal after passage of the Crime Bill (in fact, AB stands for after ban).

There is little doubt to whom these assault weapons are marketed: Intratec catalog copy from the mid 1990s calls their guns "as tough as your toughest customers" and notes "only your imagination limits your fun!" The California Court of Appeals ruled in 1999 that Intratec could be held liable for damages that occurred during a 1993 mass shooting in San Francisco because firearms manufacturers have a duty not to increase the killing power of their weapons. The Court noted that Intratec's marketing of the TEC-DC9 as having high firepower, an easily attached silencer and "excellent resistance to fingerprints" as well as Intratec's knowledge of a report by the Bureau of Alcohol, Tobacco and Firearms that concluded the TEC-DC9 is a popular weapon of choice among criminals influenced its decision on this matter (Violence Policy Center, 2000).

The secondary gun market is surprisingly unregulated. It is completely legal for one person to sell a gun or a couple of guns to another person as long as that other person is not restricted from owning one, for example by being a convicted felon or a juvenile and these transactions account for 30 to 40 percent of all gun transactions (Cook and Ludwig, 1996); the Internet has made these transactions all the easier. Requiring transactions to go through licensed dealers may be a step in the right direction, but as seen above, licensed dealers are not always above reproach. The aforementioned gun traces have revealed that many guns used in criminal activity are newly gotten from dealers through straw purchases, so limiting the number of guns that can be purchased at one time by one person from a licensed dealer and/or requiring that multiple purchases are tracked may be useful measures (Cook, Braga and Moore, 2011). Guns that are stolen commonly end up on the secondary market and there is some evidence that larger scale thefts of guns are organized (Braga, Cook, Kennedy and Moore, 2002), so a useful tactic here may be for law enforcement to infiltrate or otherwise disrupt this source of guns. Using technological advancements to personalize guns, especially if depersonalization were only possible at a specialized dealer might also reduce the theft of guns and their addition to the unregulated secondary market (Cook and Leitzel, 2002).

The third broad category of gun control measures is controlling the criminal use of guns. One way to do this is to focus on places where gun crime is known to occur and gun crime is known to occur in hot spots (Sherman, Gartin and Buerger, 1989; see also Chapter 9). Research on hot spots in Boston has shown that 53 percent of shootings were concentrated in just five percent of Boston's square mileage in 2006 (Braga, Hureau and Winship, 2008) and that just five percent of street corners and blocks in Boston accounted for nearly three quarters of all shootings between 1980 and 2008 (Braga, Papachristos and Hureau, 2010). This knowledge makes it fairly easy for police to target areas where gun crime is known to occur. The police could also target the people known to commit gun crime in order to control the criminal use of guns. The Boston Gun Project is the most well known effort in this area. Most of the gun crime in Boston in the 1990s was being committed by gang members. The police reached out to the gangs and informed them that gun violence by one member of the gang would lead to massive legal problems for all members of the gang, thereby encouraging the gang to self-police. The Boston Gun Project was associated with significant drops in youth homicide, assaults in which guns were used and shots fired (Braga, Kennedy, Waring and Piehl, 2001; Piehl, Cooper, Braga and Kennedy, 2003); other cities are currently experimenting with the Boston model.[9]

Wider Legalization of Prostitution and Drugs

There are a number of different issues we could consider when discussing the wider legalization of prostitution (as we saw in Chapter 14, prostitution is legal in some countries and stateside, has limited legality in Nevada), including moral and financial considerations. However, this discussion focuses most closely on the criminogenic effects that the legalization of prostitution might have on human trafficking. Though there are deeply held and defended positions on both sides of this issue, there is little empirical evidence on whether the legalization of prostitution would increase human trafficking. Cho, Dreher and Neumayer (2013) begin by noting that there are two possible effects of the legalization of prostitution on human trafficking. The first is the scale effect, in which legalized prostitution increases the demand for prostitutes and trafficking increases as a result. The second is the substitution effect, in which legalized prostitution creates a demand for legal prostitutes (as opposed to those brought in from other countries) and reduces trafficking as a result. Cho, Dreher and Neumayer (2013) used United Nations data on human trafficking in 161 countries to test which of these two effects was more prominent and found that on average, countries with legalized prostitution have larger human trafficking flows.

However, with so many countries in the analysis, it is difficult to control for differences from country to country, so the quantitative results are supplemented with case studies from Sweden, Denmark and Germany. Sweden criminalized prostitution in 1999 while Denmark decriminalized self-employed prostitution in the same year. Cho, Dreher and Neumayer (2013) report that the number of prostitutes in Sweden shrank from 2,500 in 1999 to 1,500 in 2002 as a result of criminalization, with between 200–600 human trafficking victims recorded by the country between 2002 and 2003. In Denmark, on the other hand, there were about 6,000 prostitutes in 2004, five years after prostitution was decriminalized, and an estimated 2,250 victims of human trafficking. Sweden and Denmark are socioeconomically similar and Sweden's population is about 40 percent larger than Denmark's; Cho, Dreher and Neumayer (2013) maintain neither of these factors can explain the difference in the number of human trafficking victims and that the difference is very likely due to the legal status of prostitution in each of these

---

9. However, we suggest that cities adopting the Operation Ceasefire in the future do so with caution. It makes sense that for the program to be successful, a city's gang structure must mirror that of Boston's. We point specifically to New Orleans as a city with a very different gang structure that should exercise care before embracing this program as a panacea for its homicide and violence problems.

countries. In Germany, prostitution is treated like any other form of work, taxed and highly regulated. Germany has about 150,000 people employed as prostitutes (60 times the number in Sweden where prostitution is illegal) and about 32,800 human trafficking victims (62 times the number in Sweden). Moreover, the full legalization of prostitution in Germany in 2002 coincided with a dramatic increase in the number of recorded human trafficking victims.

As with prostitution, there are a number of different issues to consider when broaching the subject of the wider legalization of drugs, including moral and financial concerns. Because we are interested in exploring the possible effects on crime that wider legalization would have, we begin our discussion with (and largely limit it to) a consideration of how the legalization of various drugs would affect crime. If marijuana were legalized to the same degree that alcohol is legal, we could expect a major decline in violence in the marijuana market and a substantial reduction in law enforcement and corrections resources currently devoted to marijuana. However, marijuana causes little violence within the United States (outside the United States is a different story, as alluded to above) and marijuana offenders do not occupy prisons and jails in great numbers; they make up perhaps one percent of those incarcerated (Boyum, Caulkins and Kleiman, 2011). Marijuana is affordable enough that many users are not compelled to engage in economic-compulsive crime to obtain it (see Chapter 8 for an explanation of Goldstein's (1985) framework for drug-related violence) so legalization would not lead to a reduction in this type of crime, but it would not lead to an increase in pharmacological violence, as marijuana intoxication is not associated with aggression. On that note, if marijuana were legal and users ingested marijuana instead of alcohol, there could be a great reduction in pharmacological crime. A number of studies indicate that marijuana serves as a substitute for alcohol among some users (DiNardo, 1991; Chaloupka and Laixuthia, 1997; Cameron and Williams, 2001), but other studies find that marijuana and alcohol are used simultaneously (Pacula, 1998; Pacula, Grossman, Chaloupka, O'Malley, Johnston and Farrelly, 2001; Farrelly, Bray, Zarkin, Wendling and Pacula, 1999; Williams, Pacula, Chaloupka and Wechsler, 2004), so if marijuana were made legal, alcohol consumption might increase and lead to more pharmacological violence. In sum, marijuana legalization would likely have a small effect on crime, but it would eliminate more than half of all drug arrests in the United States and probably a considerable amount of violence in Mexico; the question that follows is whether these benefits offset the costs of wider marijuana use (Boyum, Caulkins and Kleiman, 2011).

It is more difficult to predict what would happen if cocaine were legalized. The bulk of cocaine is purchased by heavy users, so if cocaine were legal to the point where heavy users could buy as much cocaine as they wanted (similar to alcohol), cocaine dealers would go out of business. These dealers might turn to other types of crime in lieu of an honest living or, if other drugs remained illegal while cocaine was made legal, they might try to deal other illegal drugs and might have to use violence to find a place in that market. Less lucrative illegal cocaine markets would mean less crime associated with those markets and increased participation in legal activities for former illegal market participants. Approximately a fifth of the nation's criminal justice system resources would be freed up if cocaine was legalized (Boyum, Caulkins and Kleiman, 2011). However, it is crucial to consider the price of legal cocaine when making these predictions.

If legal cocaine cost the same as illegal cocaine does now (approximately $100 per gram), an illegal market would likely thrive right alongside the legal one, with the illegal market offering cocaine at lower prices. It would be impossible to amass the resources necessary to police this illegal market (Caulkins, 2000) and crime in furtherance of cocaine purchases would likely persist. If cocaine were made legal and priced at its free market value ($1–5 per gram of power or about 25 cents per crack rock), people would probably commit less crime to be able to afford cocaine (Boyum, Caulkins and Kleiman, 2011). Though the number of people who might try legal and cheap cocaine cannot be accurately estimated, nor can the number of those who might become dependent on or addicted to it, it is still reasonable to assume that there would be an increase in crime that is linked to cocaine use. Moreover, the simultaneous use of alcohol and cocaine would likely lead to an increase in pharmacological violence. Much like with marijuana, the question then becomes whether the decrease in economic compulsive and systemic violence at home and abroad is worth an increase in pharmacological violence plus the devastation cocaine addiction can cause users and their friends and families (Boyum, Caulkins and Kleiman, 2011). In sum, Kleiman, Caulkins and Hawken (2011) claim that legalizing drugs would likely have two main effects, the worsening of the drug abuse problem and the amelioration of the crime problem, but note it is difficult to predict the extent of these effects.

Sex Offender Policies

The term sex offender is likely to stir some visceral reactions and sex offenders have been treated differently by the criminal justice system than other offenders for decades. Beauregard and Lieb (2011) point out that two arguments fuel the exceptional treatment of sex offenders by the criminal justice system, first the degree to which sex offenses impact victims and second the high rates of recidivism among sex offenders. As for the first argument, understanding the prevalence of rapes and sexual assaults is difficult because these crimes are subject to serious underreporting (see e.g., Rand, 2009). Nevertheless, a fairly reliable estimate of the prevalence of rape over the lifetime is 1 in 6 women and 1 in 33 men; more than half the female victims and nearly three quarters of the male victims were under 18 when they were raped (Tjaden and Thoennes, 2000). Almost all rape victims experience symptoms of posttraumatic stress disorder (PTSD) immediately after and even three months after their rapes (Rothbaum, Foa, Riggs, Murdock and Walsh, 1992) and for children, sexual abuse is more likely than nonsexual abuse to cause lingering PTSD symptoms (Deblinger, Steer, and Lippmann, 1999); moreover, the negative effects of sexual abuse in childhood persist and manifest themselves in anxiety, depression, withdrawal, anger, aggression and substance abuse (Kendall-Tackett, Williams and Finkelhor, 1993; Kendler, Bulik, Silberg, Hettema, Myers and Prescott, 2000).

As for the second argument, determining the rate at which sex offenders recidivate is difficult because results are highly dependent on methods used. Langan, Schmitt and Durose (2003) found that five percent of sex offenders in their study recidivated with sexual crimes, while just one percent of nonsexual offenders recidivated with sexual crimes. Forty three percent of sex offenders recidivated with any crime while 68 percent of nonsexual offenders recidivated with any crime; 75 percent of sex offenders were rearrested for a felony crime compared to 86 percent of nonsexual offenders. Sample and Bray (2003) found similar results, with sex offenders recidivating with sexual offenses more often than nonsexual offenders. Recidivism rates differ further when considering victims; those who offended against women had a 23 percent sexual reconviction rate while heterosexual child molesters had an 18 percent sexual reconviction rate and homosexual child molesters had a 35 percent sexual reconviction rate (Quinsey, Lalumiere, Rice and Harris, 1995). Clearly not all sex offenders are certain to reoffend and moreover, different types of sex offenders appear to be at higher risk of reoffending. The risk assessment tool known as STATIC-99 has been shown to be useful in predicting which sex offenders are likely to recidivate (see Doren, 2004 for a meta-analysis of studies on this tool).

Thanks to studies with apprehended sex offenders, a fair amount is known about how they select their targets. Not surprisingly, these selection methods differ based on preferred victim, age of victim and relationship with the victim. For example, male sex offenders who primarily offend against children usually know their victims (Snyder, 2000) and they gradually desensitize victims to sexual contact through a process known as grooming (Berliner and Conte, 1990; Elliot, Browne and Kilcoyne, 1995). Older sex offenders who offend against children make less use of coercion than younger (including adolescent) offenders who offend against children and this may be due in part to manipulation skills that older sex offenders develop as well as older offenders' relationship with the victim (e.g., a parent or relative); in this circumstance, violence is likely less necessary (Kaufman, et al., 1998). Moreover, sex offenders appear to follow one of three scripts when committing their crimes. When places and targets are familiar, offenders employ the manipulative script and often refrain from using violence, instead opting for gifts, money or drugs and alcohol to entice victims to the place of the assault. When targets are unfamiliar, offenders employ either the coercive or non-persuasive scripts and are likely to use violence or aggression to lead the victim to the place of the attack; the difference between the coercive script and the non-persuasive script is that the former involves attacks in the victims' home or an outdoor place while the latter involves attacks in places such as bars or malls (Beauregard and Leclerc, 2007; Beauregard, Proulx, Rossmo, Leclerc and Allaire, 2007; Beauregard, Rossmo and Proulx, 2007). Beauregard and Lieb (2011) point out that as valuable as this information is, it is all collected from convicted sex offenders, meaning they have been caught and may not be representative of sex offenders whose law breaking has gone undetected.

Even though the number of sexual victimizations dropped by 53 percent between 1998 and 2008 and substantiated cases of sexual abuse in the child welfare system declined by 52 percent during the same period (Rand, 2009; Jones and Finkelhor, 2007), public concern about sex offending has been on the rise and a number of different policies have been employed to deal with sex offenders, including longer prison sentences, indefinite civil commitment after imprisonment, electronic monitoring, registration with law enforcement upon release from prison and public notification of the presence of a sex offender in the community, residency restrictions and treatment (Beauregard and Lieb, 2011). The latter three deserve further consideration here.

Registration and notification: Sex offenders have been required to register with states since 1994, thanks to the Jacob Wetterling Crimes Against Children and Sexually

Violent Offender Registration Act and in1996, public notification about sex offenders was made mandatory thanks to Megan's Law. In 2007, a national sex offender registry was created thanks to the Adam Walsh Child Protection and Safety Act (Prescott and Rockoff, 2011). Registration and notification laws may appease the public, but do they have any effect on sex offenses? A meta-analysis of studies on whether registration and notification have a specific deterrent effect found no clear evidence one way or the other (Drake and Aos, 2009). Studies on the general deterrent effect revealed more consistent results. Prescott and Rockoff (2011) and Letourneau, Levenson, Bandyopadhyay, Sinha and Armstrong (2010) found that sex offender registration appears to reduce the frequency of sex offenses. Shao and Li (2006) found that registration of sex offenders resulted in a two percent reduction in rapes reported to the police (importantly, this is not necessarily the same as rapes committed). However, a number of studies have found that while notification laws appeared to serve as a deterrent for first time sex offenders, they had no effect on recidivism rates (Schram and Milloy, 1995; Adkins, Huff and Stageberg, 2000; Zevitz, 2006; Sandler, Freeman and Socia, 2008; Zgoba, Witt, Dalessandro and Veysey, 2008; Letourneau, Levenson, Bandyopadhyay, Sinha and Armstrong, 2010). Prescott and Rockoff (2011) found that notification laws appeared to increase recidivism (of all kinds) for those on the registry, presumably because being on the registry has detrimental social and financial effects on the life of the sex offender; ultimately, registration of sex offenders has a greater reductive effect on sex offenses than notification.[10]

Residency restrictions: Many recently passed laws determine where sex offenders can and cannot reside. Typically, sex offenders are prohibited from living near schools, playgrounds, parks and other places where children are known to congregate (Nieto and Jung, 2006) note that this restriction usually applies to all sex offenders whether they offended against children or not. It is unclear whether restricting where sex offenders can live has had a reductive effect on sex offenses but it has definitely increased the rate of homelessness among sex offenders and homelessness is likely to diminish opportunities to successfully reintegrate into the community as a law abiding citizen (Petersilia, 2003).

Treatment: The debate about whether treatment for sex offenders works is characterized by strong opinions on both sides. A meta-analysis of studies on effective treatments for sex offenders by MacKenzie (2006) revealed that the treatment programs most effective at reducing recidivism for sex offenders are those that employ a cognitive behavioral component; chemical or pharmaceutical castration are also among the most effective treatments (see also Losel and Schmuker, 2005). Moreover, treatment provided in the hospital setting appears to be more effective than that provided in prison.

---

10. However, Duwe and Donnay (2008) found that notification reduced sexual recidivism in Minnesota. The authors believe this is because Minnesota targets high risk sex offenders with what is known as broad notification. Broad notification of sex offender status reduce the ability of these high risk offenders to form relationships that are often precursors to offending.

Box 15.6. Confinement of Sexually Violent Predators

Several states have implemented laws that permit sex offenders who have served their criminal sentence but are deemed dangerous to be civilly committed for an indefinite period of time. The table reveals a number of details about states with sexually violent predator laws, including the year of implementation, the number of people civilly confined under these laws, the cost per person per year and treatment providers.

State	Year	Number Confined (as of 2006)	Cost per person per year	Treatment Providers
Arizona	1996	414	$110,000	State
California	1996	558	$166,000	State
Florida	1999	942	$41,845	State contracts with providers
Illinois	1988	307	$88,000	State contracts with providers
Iowa	1998	69	$71,000	State
Kansas	1994	161	$69,070	State
Massachusetts	1998	121	$73,197	State contracts with providers
Minnesota	1999	342	$141,255	State
Missouri	1994	143	$75,920	State
Nebraska	2006	18	$93,325	State
New Jersey	1994	342	$67,000	State
North Dakota	1997	75	$94,728	State
Pennsylvania	2003	12	$150,000	State
South Carolina	1998	119	$41,176	State
Texas	1999	69	$17,391	State contracts with providers
Virginia	2003	37	$140,000	State
Washington	1990	305	$149,904	State
Wisconsin	1994	500	$102,500	State

Source: Adapted from Gookin, 2007.

In *Kansas* v. *Hendricks*, the Supreme Court delineated the necessary procedures for the indefinite civil commitment of sex offenders who are nearing the end of their criminal sentence and have been deemed dangerous due to a mental abnormality. At issue in this 1997 case was the definition of mental abnormality as a basis for indefinite civil commitment. The state of Kansas relied on diagnoses from psychiatrists and testimony from offenders to determine whether someone was a dangerous sexual predator or not. In Hendricks' case, he was diagnosed with pedophilia and agreed that he would be very likely to molest children again in the future. The Court ruled that the way the state of Kansas made this determination did not violate due process or double jeopardy and that it was acceptable to indefinitely civilly confine someone deemed to be a dangerous sexual predator.

Besides extant policies, Wortley and Smallbone (2006; see also Smallbone, Marshall and Wortley, 2008) suggest a number of techniques for the prevention of sex offenses against children that are rooted in situational crime prevention (described in Chapter 9). Increasing the effort needed to commit sex offenses involves teaching children self-protective behaviors in school-based programs. A meta-analysis on studies of self-protection programs delivered to children found that in simulated situations, those children who had participated in such a program were six times more likely to demonstrate self-protective behavior than those who had not participated (Zwi, 2007), but it is unknown whether these programs prevent actual victimization (Finkelhor, 2009). Increasing the effort needed to commit a sex offense also involves controlling access to facilities where children are likely to congregate, such as parks and schools. Increasing the risk of committing a sex offense involves improved surveillance of children in various forms, including accompaniment of children by parents or other trusted adults, a police and security guard presence, training for lifeguards and other place managers to recognize behavior that might precede a sex offense and sufficient lighting. Finally, reducing permissibility involves challenging the justifications or dismissals some sex offenders provide for their actions and includes public education campaigns and posting explicit codes of acceptable and unacceptable conduct, especially where adults spend time with children such as in a school setting (see also Leclerc, Proulx and Beauregard, 2009).

Beauregard and Lieb (2011) point out that sex offending prevention resources are necessarily limited and instead of applying a one size fits all approach such as the kind created by recent policy changes, it would be to our collective benefit to use what we know about sex offenders to make educated decisions about the use of those resources. They suggest devoting the majority of resources to those who have been shown to be most at risk for reoffending.

The Death Penalty

As with prostitution and drugs, there are a number of issues we could address in a discussion of the death penalty, including moral and financial concerns. We are most interested in whether the death penalty is an effective crime deterrent and there is a vigorous debate on this issue, with scholars taking positions on both sides. In 1972, the Supreme Court decided in *Furman* v. *Georgia* that the death penalty was unconstitutional because it violated the Eighth Amendment's prohibition on cruel and unusual punishment in some circumstances. The Court was concerned with the arbitrary application of the death penalty, particularly against African American defendants.

Furman created a de facto moratorium on the death penalty in the United States. The Court reversed its earlier ruling in *Gregg* v. *Georgia* in 1976, when it decided that the death penalty was not cruel and unusual in all cases. The ruling in *Gregg* permitted states to resume application of the death penalty.

A number of researchers have found a deterrent effect for the death penalty, meaning that the application of the death penalty deters future crime, especially murder. Ehrlich and Liu (1999), Liu (2004) and Zimmerman (2009) all found deterrent effects for the death penalty, as did other empirical work. Ehrlich (1975) found that in the 1950s and 1960s, each execution prevented eight murders. Cloninger and Marchesini (2001) found that in Texas, there is a larger number of homicides when there is a lower number of executions and vice versa. Dezhbakhsh, Rubin and Shepherd (2003) found that each execution results in an average of 18 fewer murders with a margin of error of plus or minus 10. Mocan and Gittings (2003) found that each additional execution decreases the number of homicides by about five, while each commuted sentence increases the number of homicides by five and each removal of an inmate from death row increases the number of homicides by one. Zimmerman (2004) found that each execution deters about 14 murders per year. Shepherd (2004) found that each execution results in three fewer murders, that capital punishment can even deter crime of passion and intimate partner homicides and that longer waits on death row are associated with more murders; there is one less murder for every 2.75 year reduction in time spent on death row. Cloninger and Marchesini (2006) found that a moratorium on executions in Illinois in 2003 put residents there at greater risk for homicide in the 48 subsequent months and that the moratorium produced 150 additional homicides. Dezhbakhsh and Shepherd (2006) found that actual executions, not just instatement or reinstatement of the death penalty have a deterrent effect. Land, Teske and Zheng (2009) found a small short term deterrent effect for the death penalty in Texas. There were 4.5 fewer homicides in the first and fourth month after each execution, for a .5 total reduction in homicides per year.

However, a host of other researchers have come to the complete opposite conclusion. Leamer (1983), McManus (1985), Sorensen, Wrinkle, Brewer and Marquart (1999), Katz, Levitt and Shustorovich (2003), Berk (2005), Donohue and Wolfers (2005), Cohen-Cole, Durlauf, Fagan and Nagin (2009), Hjalmarsson (2009) and Nagin and Pepper (2012) all found that the death penalty does not have a deterrent effect on homicides. How could it be that lauded economic and legal scholars have come to (and continue to come to) such diametrically opposed conclusions?[11] Yang and Lester (2008) point out that whether a study on the death penalty finds a deterrent effect is determined in very large part by the methods used in that study. For example, in their meta-analysis of 104 death penalty deterrent studies, Yang and Lester (2008) found that the deterrent effect of the death penalty on homicides was more pronounced in studies that used time series and panel data designs and weaker in those that utilized cross sectional

---

11. Part of the answer may lie in the very different orientations of economists and legal scholars. They usually work on different problems with different data sets and take different approaches, so perhaps disparate findings are not all that surprising (Liptak, 2007).

studies. Indeed, some of the harshest criticisms researchers in this area level at one another regards their choice of data and methods; see for example Dezhbakhsh and Rubin (2011) and Cloninger and Marchesini (2009), who take great issue with the work of Donohue and Wolfers (2005). Donohue and Wolfers (2005) concluded that no matter what research design is used and what statistical techniques are employed, there are simply too few executions to be able to observe their deterrent effect on homicides, the number of which is affected by a whole host of factors. Cloninger and Marchesini (2009, p. 1709) note that Donohue and Wolfers' (2005) work was published in a law review, not a peer reviewed journal and that it "contains elements that undoubtedly would not have survived peer review." Similarly, Dezhbakahsh and Rubin (2011, p. 3655) claim that Donohue and Wolfers' (2005) "work has serious flaws and their reporting appears to be selective."[12] Other factors that may confound research on the death penalty's deterrent effect include whether potential murderers are aware of the death penalty and the certainty of its application (Donohue and Wolfers, 2009), the methods of executions used (Zimmerman, 2006), the inclusion of guns and other crime variables (Narayan and Smyth, 2006), the number of states that actually execute people (Berk, 2005), the inclusion of the high execution rate state Texas in any analysis (Weisberg, 2005), prison conditions (Katz, Levitt and Shustorovich, 2003 and whether national or state level data are used (Yunker, 2002).

The current last word on whether the death penalty is a deterrent comes from Nagin and Pepper (2012), who reviewed three decades' worth of research on the deterrent effect of the death penalty and found three major flaws in the body of work as a whole. First, there is little consideration of the effects of serious but noncapital punishments. Second, the ways potential murderers' perceptions of the death penalty are modeled are inadequate. Third, the estimates of the effects of capital punishment are based on inadequate models. Nagin and Pepper (2012) note these concerns are sufficient to cease use of studies that claim to show a deterrent effect of the death penalty as justification for retaining or increasing the use of the death penalty. Debate on this issue is very likely to continue.[13]

Conclusion

Throughout this book, we have focused on the issues that are most important to criminologists and to criminology. These issues include theories of crime causation,[14] the factors that increase the likelihood of involvement in crime, the different types of crime, the efficacy of existing theories in explaining these different types, the measurement of crime and the effect of crime on victims. In this chapter, we tied some of these issues together with criminal justice in order to demonstrate how ideas from criminology

---

12. This is academic trash talk.

13. For more, see the special issue of the *Journal of Quantitative Criminology* on deterrence and capital punishment (volume 29, issue 1, 2013).

14. See the Appendix for a tabular summary of the major theories of crime.

inform (or do not inform) the practice of justice provision in the United States. With this multidimensional focus, that included a number of new dimensions of criminology rarely if ever found in other texts, our goal was to provide readers with a thorough and rich understanding of criminology and to provide them with the foundation necessary to be able to critically assess the main ideas in the discipline. To be sure, there are many unresolved issues in criminology and we are hopeful readers are now interested in posing and testing some of their own answers to these lingering questions.

Websites to Visit

Louisiana's Prisons: http://www.nola.com/prisons/
Drug Courts: http://www.nadcp.org/learn/what-are-drug-courts, http://www.court innovation.org/multi-site-adult-drug-court-evaluation
International Centre for Prison Studies: http://www.prisonstudies.org/
Law Enforcement Against Prohibition (LEAP): http://www.leap.cc/
Coalition Against Trafficking in Women: http://www.catwinternational.org/
National Sex Offender Public Website: http://www.nsopw.gov/en-US
Death Penalty Information Center: http://www.deathpenaltyinfo.org/

Discussion Questions

1. Which do you think is the preferred approach for solving the crime problem, getting tough, prevention or rehabilitation? Why?
2. Is there any value in three strikes laws? If so, what? If not, why not?
3. What amount of criminal justice resources should be used for prevention and for rehabilitation?
4. Which approach to prevention do you think is more valuable, trying to change the environment or trying to change people? Why?
5. Which of the factors described above do you think was the single most important in the reduction in the crime rate beginning in the 1990s?
6. What factors are most useful in explaining the crime rate in the first decade of the 2000s and why?
7. How might the prison population be reduced in a way that preserves public safety?
8. How could the small number of gun dealers who are responsible for a majority of guns reaching the black market be identified and dealt with before their guns fall into criminal hands?
9. Should drugs that are currently illegal in the United States be legalized? Why or why not?
10. Should funding for sex offender registration and notification programs be continued, even though the research has shown that these programs are not effective at reducing sex offenders' sexual recidivism?
11. In your mind, is there sufficient evidence to conclude that the death penalty is a homicide deterrent? What about the arguments from the other side?

References

Adkins, Geneva, David Huff and Paul Stageberg. (2000). *The Iowa sex offender registry and recidivism*. Des Moines: Iowa Department of Human Rights.

Arvanites, Thomas and Robert Defina. (2006). Business cycles and street crime. *Criminology, 44*, 139–164.

ATF. (2000). *Commerce in firearms in the United States*. U.S. Department of the Treasury. Retrieved from: http://permanent.access.gpo.gov/lps4006/020400report.pdf.

Austin, James, John Clark, Patricia Hardyman and Alan Henry. (2000). *Three strikes and you're out: The implementation and impact of strike laws*. U.S. Department of Justice. Retrieved from: https://www.ncjrs.gov/pdffiles1/nij/grants/181297.pdf.

Baumer, Eric. (2008). An empirical assessment of the contemporary crime trends puzzle: A modest step toward a more comprehensive research agenda. In A. Goldberger and R. Rosenfeld (Eds.), *Understanding crime trends* (Chapter 4). Washington, D.C.: National Academies Press.

Beauregard, Eric and Benoit Leclerc. (2007). An application of the rational choice approach to the offending process of sex offenders: A closer look at the decision-making. *Sexual Abuse: A Journal of Research and Treatment, 19*, 115–133.

Beauregard, Eric, Kim Rossmo and Jean Proulx. (2007). A descriptive model of the hunting process of serial sex offenders: A rational choice perspective. *Journal of Family Violence, 22*, 449–463.

Beauregard, Eric, Jean Proulx, Kim Rossmo, Benoit Leclerc and Jean Francois Allaire. (2007). Script analysis of hunting process in serial sex offenders. *Criminal Justice and Behavior, 34*, 1069–1084.

Beauregard, Eric and Roxanne Lieb. (2011). Sex offenders and sex offender policy. In J. Wilson and J. Petersilia (Eds.), *Crime and public policy* (pp. 345–367). New York, NY: Oxford University Press.

Berk, Richard. (2005). New claims about execution and general deterrence: Déjà vu all over again? *Journal of Empirical Legal Studies, 2*, 303–330.

Berman, Greg and Aubrey Fox. (2009). *Lessons from the battle over D.A.R.E.* Center for Court Innovation. Retrieved from: http://www.courtinnovation.org/sites/default/files/DARE.pdf.

BJS. (1999). *Presale handgun checks, the Brady interim period, 1994–1998*. Bureau of Justice Statistics, U.S. Department of Justice.

Blumstein, Alfred. (1982). On racial disproportionality of the United States' prison populations. *Journal of Criminal Law and Criminology, 73*, 1259–1281.

Blumstein, Alfred. (2006). Disaggregating the violence trends. In A. Blumstein and J. Wallman (Eds.), *The crime drop in America*. Revised ed. (pp. 13–44). New York, NY: Cambridge University Press.

Blumstein, Alfred and Richard Rosenfeld. (1998). Explaining recent trends in U.S. homicide rates. *Journal of Criminal Law and Criminology, 88*, 1175–1216.

Blumstein, Alfred and Richard Rosenfeld. (2008). Factors contributing to U.S. crime trends. In A. Goldberger and R. Rosenfeld (Eds.), *Understanding crime trends* (Chapter 1). Washington, D.C.: National Academies Press.

Bouffard, Jeffrey, Doris MacKenzie and Laura Hickman. (2000). Effectiveness of vocational education and employment programs for adult offenders: A methodology-based analysis of the literature. *Journal of Offender Rehabilitation, 31*, 1–41.

Boyum, David, Jonathan Caulkins and Mark Kleiman. (2011). Drugs, crime, and public policy. In J. Wilson and J. Petersilia (Eds.), *Crime and public policy* (pp. 368–410). New York, NY: Oxford University Press.

Braga, Anthony, David Kennedy, Elin Waring and Anne Piehl. (2001). Problem-oriented policing, deterrence, and youth violence. An evaluation of Boston's Operation Ceasefire. *Journal of Research in Crime and Delinquency, 38*, 195–225.

Braga, Anthony, Philip Cook, David Kennedy and Mark Moore. (2002). The illegal supply of firearms. In M. Tonry (Ed.), *Crime and justice: A review of research, Vol. 29* (pp. 229–262). Chicago, IL: University of Chicago Press.

Braga, Anthony, David Hureau and Christopher Winship. (2008). Losing faith? Police, black churches, and the resurgence of youth violence in Boston. *Ohio State Journal of Criminal Law, 6*, 141–172.

Braga, Anthony, Andrew Papacrhistos and David Hureau. (2010). The concentration and stability of gun violence at micro-places in Boston, 1980–2008. *Journal of Quantitative Criminology, 26*, 33–53.

Browne, Angela and Kirk Williams. (1989). Exploring the effect of resource availability and the likelihood of female-perpetrated homicides. *Law & Society Review, 23*, 75–94.

Brownsberger, William and Susan Aromaa. (2001). *An empirical study of the school zone law in three cities in Massachusetts.* Boston, MA: Join Together. Retrieved from: http://willbrownsberger.com/wp-content/uploads/2011/02/school_zone.pdf.

Bushway, Shawn. (2011). Labor markets and crime. In J. Wilson and J. Petersilia (Eds.), *Crime and public policy* (pp. 183–209). New York, NY: Oxford University Press.

Cameron, Lisa and Jenny Williams. (2001). Substitutes or compliments? Alcohol, cannabis and tobacco. *Economic Record, 77*, 19–34.

Caulkins, Jonathan. (2000). *Do drug prohibition and enforcement work?* White paper in the What Works series. Arlington, VA: Lexington Institute.

Chaloupka, Frank and Adit Laixuthai. (1997). Do youths substitute alcohol and marijuana? Some econometric evidence. *Eastern Economic Journal, 23*, 253–276.

Chang, Cindy. (2012). Sheriffs and politicians have financial incentives to keep people locked up; Some rural parishes' economies hinge on keeping their prisons full. *The Times-Picayune*, May 13.

Chen, M. Keith and Jesse Shapiro. (2007). Do harsher prison conditions reduce recidivism? *American Law and Economic Review, 9*, 1–29.

Cho, Seo-Young, Axel Dreher and Eric Neumayer. (2013). Does legalized prostitution increase human trafficking? *World Development, 41*, 67–82.

Clear, Todd. (2007). *Imprisoning communities: How mass incarceration makes disadvantaged neighborhoods worse.* New York, NY: Oxford University Press.

Cloninger, Dale and Roberto Marchesini. (2001). Execution and deterrence: A quasi controlled group experiment. *Applied Economics, 33*, 569–576.

Cloninger, Dale and Roberto Marchesini. (2006). Execution moratoriums, commutations and deterrence: The case of Illinois. *Applied Economics, 38*, 967–973.

Cloninger, Dale and Roberto Marchesini. (2009). Reflections on a critique. *Applied Economics Letters, 16,* 1709–1711.

Cohen-Cole, Ethan, Steven Durlauf, Jeffrey Fagan and Daniel Nagin. (2009). Model uncertainty and the deterrent effect of capital punishment. *American Law and Economics Review, 11,* 335–369.

Conklin, John. (1972). *Robbery and the criminal justice system.* Philadelphia, PA: Lippincott.

Cook, Philip. (1976). A strategic choice analysis of robbery. In W. Skogan (Ed.), *Sample surveys of the victims of crimes* (pp. 173–187). Cambridge, MA: Ballinger.

Cook, Philip. (1979). The effect of gun availability on robbery and robbery murder: A cross-section study of fifty cities. In R. Haverman and B. Zellner (Eds.), *Policy Studies Review Annual, Vol. 3* (pp. 743–781). Beverly Hills, CA: Sage.

Cook, Philip. (1980). Reducing injury and death rates in robbery. *Policy Analysis* (Winter), 21–45.

Cook, Philip. (1991). The technology of personal violence. In M. Tonry (Ed.), *Crime and justice: A review of research, Vol. 14* (pp. 1–72). Chicago, IL: University of Chicago Press.

Cook, Philip and James Leitzel. (1996). Perversity, futility, jeopardy: An economic analysis of the attack on gun control. *Law and Contemporary Problems, 59,* 91–118.

Cook, Philip and James Leitzel. (2002). "Smart guns:" A technological fix for regulating the secondary gun market. *Contemporary Economic Problems, 20,* 38–49.

Cook, Philip and John Laub. (1998). The unprecedented epidemic in youth violence. *Crime and Justice, 24,* 27–64.

Cook, Philip, Jens Ludwig and David Hemenway. (1997). The gun debate's new mythical number: How many defensive uses per year? *Journal of Policy Analysis and Management, 16,* 463–469.

Cook, Philip and Jens Ludwig. (2000). *Gun violence: The real costs.* New York, NY: Oxford University Press.

Cook, Philip and Jens Ludwig. (2006). Aiming for evidence-based gun policy. *Journal of Policy Analysis and Management, 25,* 691–735.

Cook, Philip, Anthony Braga and Mark Moore. (2011). Gun control. In J. Wilson and J. Petersilia (Eds.), *Crime and public policy* (pp. 257–292). New York, NY: Oxford University Press.

Cullen, Francis and Robert Agnew. (2011). *Criminological theory: Past to present.* 4th ed. New York, NY: Oxford University Press.

Cullen, Francis and Cheryl Jonson. (2011). Rehabilitation and treatment programs. In J. Wilson and J. Petersilia (Eds.), *Crime and public policy* (pp. 293–344). New York, NY: Oxford University Press.

Deblinger, Esther, Robert Steer and Julie Lippmann. (1999). Two-year follow-up study of cognitive behavioral therapy for sexually abused children suffering post-traumatic stress symptoms. *Child Abuse and Neglect, 12,* 1371–1378.

Dezhbakhsh, Hashem, Paul Rubin and Joanna Shepherd. (2003). Does capital punishment have a deterrent effect? New evidence from post moratorium panel data. *American Law & Economics Review, 5,* 344–376.

Dezhbakhsh, Hashem and Joanna Shepherd. (2006). The deterrent effect of capital punishment: Evidence from a "judicial experiment." *Economic Inquiry, 44*, 512–535.

Dezhbakhsh, Hashem and Paul Rubin. (2011). From the "econometrics of capital punishment" to the "capital punishment" of econometrics: On the use and abuse of sensitivity analysis. *Applied Economics, 43*, 3655–3670.

DiNardo, John. (1991). *Are marijuana and alcohol substitutes? The effect of state drinking age laws on the marijuana consumption of high school seniors.* Santa Monica, CA: RAND.

Doren, Dennis. (2004). *Bibliography of published works relative to risk assessment for sexual offenders.* Retrieved from: http://www.atsa.com/sites/default/files/riskAssessment Biblio.pdf.

Donohue, John. (2003). The impact of concealed-carry laws. In P. Cook and J. Ludwig (Eds.), *Evaluating gun policy: Effects on crime and violence* (pp. 287–341). Washington, D.C.: Brookings Institution Press.

Donohue, John and Justin Wolfers. (2005). Uses and abuses of empirical evidence in the death penalty debate. *Stanford Law Review, 58*, 791–846.

Donohue, John and Justin Wolfers. (2009). Estimating the impact of the death penalty on murder. *American Law and Economics Review, 11*, 249–309.

Drake, Elizabeth and Steven Aos. (2009). *Does sex offender registration and notification reduce crime? A systematic review of the research literature.* Washington State Institute for Public Policy. Retrieved from: http://www.wsipp.wa.gov/rptfiles/09-06-1101.pdf.

Dugan, Laura, Daniel Nagin and Richard Rosenfeld. (1999). Explaining the decline in intimate partner homicide: The effects of changing domesticity, women's status, and domestic violence resources. *Homicide Studies, 3*, 187–214.

Duggan, Mark. (1991). More guns, more crime. *Journal of Political Economy, 109*, 1086–1114.

Duwe, Grant and William Donnay. (2008). The impact of Megan's Law on sex offender recidivism: The Minnesota experience. *Criminology, 46*, 411–446.

Eck, John and Emily Eck. (2012). Crime, place and pollution: Expanding crime reduction options through a regulatory approach. *Criminology & Public Policy, 11*, 279–316.

Ehrlich, Isaac. (1975). The deterrent effect of capital punishment: A question of life and death. *American Economic Review, 65*, 397–417.

Ehrlich, Isaac and Liu Zhiqiang. (1999). Sensitivity analysis of the deterrence hypothesis: Let's keep the econ in econometrics. *Journal of Law and Economics, 42*, 455–487.

Elliott, Michele, Kevin Browne and Jennifer Kilcoyne. (1995). Child sexual abuse prevention: What offenders tell us. *Child Abuse and Neglect, 19*, 579–584.

Farrelly, Matthew, Jeremy Bray, Gary Zarkin, Brett Wendling and Rosalie Pacula. (1999). *The effects of prices and policies on the demand for marijuana: Evidence from the National Household Surveys on Drug Abuse.* National Bureau of Economic Research. Retrieved from: http://www.nber.org/papers/w6940.pdf?new_window=1.

Farrington, David and Brandon Welsh. (2007). *Saving children from a life of crime.* New York: Oxford University Press.

FBI UCR. (2010). FBI UCR data tool. Retrieved from: http://www.ucrdatatool.gov/Search/Crime/State/TrendsInOneVar.cfm.

FBI UCR. (2011). Crime in the United States 2011: Violent crime. Retrieved from: http://www.fbi.gov/about-us/cjis/ucr/crime-in-the-u.s/2011/crime-in-the-u.s.-2011/violent-crime/violent-crime.

FBI UCR. (2011a). Crime in the United States 2011: Property crime. Retrieved from: http://www.fbi.gov/about-us/cjis/ucr/crime-in-the-u.s/2011/crime-in-the-u.s.-2011/property-crime/property-crime.

FBI UCR. (2011b). Crime in the United States 2011: Murder. Retrieved from: http://www.fbi.gov/about-us/cjis/ucr/crime-in-the-u.s/2011/crime-in-the-u.s.-2011/violent-crime/murder.

FBI UCR. (2011c). Offenses known to law enforcement: Louisiana by city. Retrieved from: http://www.fbi.gov/about-us/cjis/ucr/crime-in-the-u.s/2011/crime-in-the-u.s.-2011/tables/table8statecuts/table_8_offenses_known_to_law_enforcement_louisiana_by_city_2011.xls.

Finkelhor, David. (2009). The prevention of childhood sexual abuse. *The Future of Children, 19*, 53–78. Retrieved from: http://futureofchildren.org/futureofchildren/publications/docs/19_02_08.pdf.

Fox, James. (2006). Demographics and U.S. homicide. In A. Blumstein and J. Wallman (Eds.), *The crime drop in America*. Revised ed. (pp. 288–318). New York, NY: Cambridge University Press.

Frailing, Kelly. (2012). Mental health courts. In A. Columbus (Ed.), *Advances in psychology research, Vol. 95*. Hauppague, NY: Nova Science Publishers.

Furman v. Georgia. 408 U.S. 238 (1972).

Gendreau, Paul, Claire Goggin, Francis Cullen and D. Andrews. (2000). The effects of community sanctions and incarceration on recidivism. *Forum on Corrections Research, 12*, 10–13.

Goldstein, Paul. (1985). The drugs/violence nexus: A tripartite conceptual framework. *Journal of Drug Issues, 15*, 493–506.

Gookin, Kathy. (2007). *Comparison of state laws authorizing involuntary commitment of sexually violent predators: 2006 update, revised*. Washington State Institute for Public Policy. Retrieved from: http://www.wsipp.wa.gov/rptfiles/07-08-1101.pdf.

Greenwood, Peter. (2006). *Changing lives: Delinquency prevention as crime control policy*. Chicago, IL: University of Chicago Press.

Greenwood, Peter and Brandon Welsh. (2012). Promoting evidence-based practice in delinquency prevention at the state level. *Criminology & Public Policy, 11*, 493–513.

Gregg v. Georgia. 428 U.S. 153 (1976).

Harcourt, Bernard and Jens Ludwig. (2006). Broken windows: New evidence from New York City and a five-city social experiment. *University of Chicago Law Review, 73*, 271–320.

Hepburn, Lisa, Matthew Miller, Deborah Arazel and David Hemenway. (2007). The U.S. gun stock: Results from the 2004 National Firearms Survey. *Injury Prevention, 13*, 15–19.

Hirschi, Travis and Michael Gottfredson. (1983). Age and the explanation of crime. *American Journal of Sociology, 89*, 552–584.

Hjalmarsson, Randi. (2009). Does capital punishment have a "local" deterrent effect on homicides? *American Law and Economics Review, 11*, 310–334.

Jones, Lisa and David Finkelhor. (2007). *Updated trends in child maltreatment, 2007.* Crimes against Children Research Center. Retrieved from: http://www.unh.edu/ccrc/pdf/Updated%20Trends%20in%20Child%20Maltreatment%202007.pdf.

Kansas v. *Hendricks.* 521 U.S. 346 (1997).

Katz, Lawrence, Steven Levitt and Ellen Shustorovich. (2003). Prison conditions, capital punishment, and deterrence. *American Law and Economics Review, 5,* 318–343.

Kaufman, Keith, Jennifer Holmberg, Karen Orts, Fara McCrady, Andrea Rotzien, Eric Daleiden and Daniel Hilliker. (1998). Factors influencing sexual offenders' modus operandi: An examination of victim-related relatedness and age. *Child Maltreatment, 4,* 349–361.

Kelling, George and William Sousa. (2001). *Do police matter? An analysis of the impact of New York City's police reforms.* Manhattan Institute Civic Report. Retrieved from: http://www.manhattan-institute.org/html/cr_22.htm.

Kendall-Tackett, Kathleen, Linda Williams and David Finkelhor. (1993). The impact of sexual abuse on children: A review and synthesis of recent empirical studies. *Psychological Bulletin, 113,* 164–180.

Kendler, Kenneth, Cynthia Bulik, Judy Silberg, John Hettema, John Myers and Carol Prescott. (2000). Childhood sexual abuse and adult psychiatric and substance use disorders in women: An epidemiological and cotwin control analysis. *Archives of General Psychiatry, 57,* 953–959.

Kleck, Gary and Karen McElrath. (1991). The effect of weaponry on human violence. *Social Forces, 69,* 669–692.

Kleck, Gary and E. Britt Patterson. (1993). The impact of gun control and gun ownership levels on violence rates. *Journal of Quantitative Criminology, 9,* 249–287.

Kleck, Gary and Marc Gertz. (1995). Armed resistance to crime: The prevalence and nature of self-defense with a gun. *Journal of Criminal Law and Criminology, 86,* 150–187.

Kleiman, Mark, Jonathan Caulkins and Angela Hawken. (2011). *Drugs and drug policy.* New York, NY: Oxford University Press.

Land, Kenneth, Raymond Teske and Hui Zheng. (2009). The short-term effects of executions on homicides: Deterrence, displacement, or both? *Criminology, 47,* 1009–1043.

Langan, Patrick. (1985). Racism on trial: New evidence to explain the racial composition of prisons in the United States. *Journal of Criminal Law and Criminology, 76,* 666–683.

Langan, Patrick (1985), Erica Schmitt and Matthew Durose. (2003). *Recidivism of sex offenders released from prison, 1994.* Bureau of Justice Statistics. Retrieved from: http://bjs.gov/content/pub/pdf/rsorp94.pdf.

Latessa, Edward. (2012). Why work is important and how to improve the effectiveness of correctional reentry programs that target employment. *Criminology & Public Policy, 11,* 87–91.

Leamer, Edward. (1983). Let's take the con out of econometrics. *American Economic Review, 73,* 31–43.

Leclerc, Benoit, Jean Proulx and Eric Beauregard. (2009). Examining the modus operandi of sexual offenders against children and its practical implications. *Aggression and Violent Behavior, 14,* 5–12.

Levitt, Steven. (1996). The effect of prison population size on crime rates: Evidence from prison overcrowding litigation. *Quarterly Journal of Economics, 111,* 319–352.

Levitt, Steven. (2004). Understanding why crime fell in the 1990s: Four factors that explain the decline and six that do not. *Journal of Economic Perspectives, 18,* 163–190.

Levitt, Steven and Sudhir Venkatesh. (2000). An economic analysis of a drug-selling gang's finances. *Quarterly Journal of Economics, 115,* 755–790.

Letourneau, Elizabeth, Jill Levenson, Dipankar Bandyopadhyay, Debajyoti Sinha and Kevin Armstrong. (2010). *Evaluating the effectiveness of sex offender registration and notification policies for reducing sexual violence against women.* U.S. Department of Justice. Retrieved from: https://www.ncjrs.gov/pdffiles1/nij/grants/231989.pdf.

Lipsey, Mark and Francis Cullen. (2007). The effectiveness of correctional rehabilitation: A review of systematic reviews. *Annual Review of Law and Social Science, 3,* 297–320.

Liptak, Adam. (2007). Does death penalty save lives? A new debate. *The New York Times,* November 18. Retrieved from: http://www.nytimes.com/2007/11/18/us/18deter.html?pagewanted=all&_r=1&.

Liu, Zhiqiang. (2004). Capital punishment and the deterrence hypothesis: Some new insights and empirical evidence. *Eastern Economic Journal, 30,* 237–258.

Losel, Friedrich and Martin Schmucker. (2005). The effectiveness of treatment for sexual offenders: A comprehensive meta-analysis. *Journal of Experimental Criminology, 1,* 117–146.

Lott, John and David Mustard. (1997). Crime, deterrence, and right-to-carry concealed handguns. *Journal of Legal Studies, 26,* 1–68.

Ludwig, Jens and Philip Cook. (2000). Homicide and suicide rates associated with implementation of the Brady Handgun Violence Prevention Act. *JAMA: Journal of the American Medical Association, 284,* 585–591.

Lynch, James and William Pridemore. (2011). Crime in international perspective. In J. Wilson and J. Petersilia (Eds.), *Crime and public policy* (pp. 5–52). New York, NY: Oxford University Press.

MacKenzie, Doris. (2006). *What works in corrections: Reducing the criminal activities of offenders and delinquents.* New York, NY: Cambridge University Press.

Martinson, Robert. (1974). What works? Questions and answers about prison reform. *Public Interest, 35,* 22–54.

McManus, Walter. (1985). Estimates of the deterrent effect of capital punishment: The importance of the researcher's prior beliefs. *Journal of Political Economy, 93,* 417–425.

Merton, Robert K. (1938). Social structure and anomie. *American Sociological Review, 3,* 672–682.

Messner, Steven, Sandro Galea, Kenneth Tardiff, Melissa Tracy, Angela Bucciarelli, Tinka Markham Piper, Victoria Frye and David Vlahov. (2007). Policing, drugs, and the homicide decline in New York City in the 1990s. *Criminology, 45,* 385–413.

Mitchell, Ojmarrh, David Wilson and Doris MacKenzie. (2007). Does incarceration-based drug treatment reduce recidivism? A meta-analytic synthesis. *Journal of Experimental Criminology, 3,* 353–375.

Mocan, H. Naci and Kaj Gittings. (2003). Getting off death row: Commuted sentences and the deterrent effect of capital punishment. *Journal of Law and Economics, 46,* 453–478.

Moller, Jan and Cindy Chang. (2012). Attempts at sentencing reform face tough opposition in the legislature. *The Times-Picayune,* May 16.

Nagin, Daniel, Francis Cullen and Cheryl Jonson. (2009). Imprisonment and reoffending. In M. Tonry (Ed.), *Crime and justice: A review of research, Vol. 38* (pp. 115–200). Chicago, IL: University of Chicago Press.

Nagin, Daniel and John Pepper. (2012). *Deterrence and the death penalty.* National Research Council, Committee on Law and Justice.

Narayan, Paresh and Russell Smith. (2006). Dead man walking: An empirical reassessment of the deterrent effect of capital punishment using the bounds testing approach to cointegration. *Applied Economics, 38,* 1975–1989.

Nieto, Marcus and David Jung. (2006). *The impact of residency restrictions on sex offender and correctional management practices: A literature review.* Sacramento: California Research Bureau. Retrieved from: http://www.library.ca.gov/crb/06/08/06-008.pdf

NJ Sentencing Commission. (2007). *Supplemental report on New Jersey's drug free zone crimes & proposal for reform.* Retrieved from: http://sentencing.nj.gov/downloads/supplemental%20schoolzonereport.pdf.

Pacula, Rosalie. (1998). Does increasing the beer tax reduce marijuana consumption? *Journal of Health Economics, 17,* 557–586.

Pacula, Rosalie, Michael Grossman, Frank Chaloupka, Patrick O'Malley, Lloyd Johnston and Matthew Farrelly (2001). Marijuana and youth. In J. Gruber (Ed.), *Risky behavior among youths: An economic analysis* (Chapter 6). Chicago, IL: University of Chicago Press.

Pearson, Frank and Douglas Lipton. (1999). A meta-analytic review of the effectiveness of corrections-based treatment for drug abuse. *The Prison Journal, 79,* 384–410.

Petersilia, Joan. (2003). *When prisoners come home: Parole and prisoner reentry.* New York, NY: Oxford University Press.

Petersilia, Joan. (2008). Influencing public policy: An embedded criminologist reflects on California prison reform. *Journal of Experimental Criminology, 4,* 335–356.

Pew Center on the States. (2008). *One in 100: Behind bars in America 2008.* Retrieved from: http://www.pewtrusts.org/uploadedFiles/wwwpewtrustsorg/Reports/sentencing_and_corrections/one_in_100.pdf.

Pew Center on the States. (2012). *Time served: The high cost, low return of longer prison terms.* Retrieved from: http://www.pewstates.org/uploadedFiles/PCS_Assets/2012/Pew_Time_Served_report.pdf.

Piehl, Anne, Suzanne Cooper, Anthony Braga and David Kennedy. (2003). Testing for structural breaks in the evaluation of programs. *Review of Economics and Statistics, 85,* 550–558.

Piehl, Anne and Bert Useem. (2011). Prisons. In J. Wilson and J. Petersilia (Eds.), *Crime and public policy* (pp. 532–558). New York, NY: Oxford University Press.

Prescott, J. J. and Jonah Rockoff. (2011). Do sex offender registration and notification laws affect criminal behavior? *Journal of Law and Economics, 54,* 161–206.

Quinsey, Vernon, Martin Lalumiere, Marnie Rice and Grant Harris. (1995) Predicting sexual offenses. In J. Campbell (Ed.), *Assessing dangerousness: Violence by sexual offenders, batterers, and child abusers* (pp. 114–137). Thousand Oaks, CA: Sage.

Rand, Michael. (2009). *Criminal victimization, 2008.* Bureau of Justice Statistics. Retrieved from: http://bjs.gov/content/pub/pdf/cv08.pdf.

Redding, Richard. (2008). *Juvenile transfer laws: An effective deterrent to delinquency?* U.S. Department of Justice. Retrieved from: https://www.ncjrs.gov/pdffiles1/ojjdp/220595.pdf.

Roman, John, Shelly Rossman and Michael Rempel. (2011). *The multi-site adult drug court evaluation. Volume 1, chapter 2: Review of the literature.* Retrieved from: http://www.courtinnovation.org/sites/default/files/documents/MADCE_1.pdf.

Rose, Dina and Todd Clear. (1998). Incarceration, social capital, and crime: Examining the unintended consequences of incarceration. *Criminology, 36,* 441–479.

Rosenfeld, Richard and Robert Fornango. (2007). The impact of economic conditions on robbery and property crime: The role of consumer sentiment. *Criminology, 45,* 735–769.

Rosenfeld, Richard, Robert Fornango and Andres Rengifo. (2007). The impact of order-maintenance policing on New York City robbery and homicide rates: 1988–2001. *Criminology, 45,* 355–383.

Rosenfeld, Richard. (2009). Crime is the problem: Homicide, acquisitive crime, and economic conditions. *Journal of Quantitative Criminology, 25,* 287–306.

Rosenfeld, Richard and Steven Messner. (2009). The crime drop in comparative perspective: The impact of the economy and imprisonment on American and European burglary rates. *British Journal of Sociology, 60,* 445–471.

Rosenfeld, Richard. (2011). Changing crime rates. In J. Wilson and J. Petersilia (Eds.), *Crime and public policy* (pp. 559–588). New York, NY: Oxford University Press.

Rothbaum, Barbara, Edna Foa, David Riggs, Tamera Murdock and William Walsh. (1992). A prospective examination of post-traumatic stress disorder in rape victims. *Journal of Traumatic Stress, 5,* 455–475.

Sample, Lisa and Timothy Bray. (2003). Are sex offenders dangerous? *Criminology & Public Policy, 3,* 59–82.

Sandler, Jeffrey, Naomi Freeman and Kelly Socia. (2008). Does a watched pot boil? A time-series analysis of New York State's sex offender registration and notification law. *Psychology, Public Policy, and Law, 14,* 284–302.

Sarre, Rick. (2009). *Beyond "what works?" A 25 year jubilee retrospective on Robert Martinson.* Presentation at the Australian Institute of Criminology meeting in Canberra. Retrieved from: http://www.aic.gov.au/media_library/conferences/hcpp/sarre.pdf.

Schram, Donna and Cheryl Milloy. (1995). *Community notification: A study of offender characteristics and recidivism.* Olympia, WA: Washington Institute for Public Policy.

Shao, Ling and Jing Li. (2006). *The effect of sex offender registration laws on rape victimization.* Unpublished manuscript. University of Alabama, Department of Economics, Tuscaloosa.

Shepherd, Joanna. (2004). Murders of passion, execution delays, and the deterrence of capital punishment. *Journal of Legal Studies, 33,* 283–322.

Sherman, Lawrence. (2011). Democratic policing on the evidence. In J. Wilson and J. Petersilia (Eds.), *Crime and public policy* (pp. 589–618). New York, NY: Oxford University Press.

Sherman, Lawrence, Patrick Gartin and Michael Buerger. (1989). Hot spots of predatory crime: Routine activities and the criminology of place. *Criminology, 27,* 27–56.

Shirley, Craig (2009). *Rendezvous with destiny: Ronald Reagan and the campaign that changed America.* Wilmington, DE: Intercollegiate Studies Institute.

Simerman, John. (2012). Incarceration tears apart families and entire communities and in some neighborhoods, doing time in prison has become commonplace. *The Times-Picayune,* May 18.

Skogan, Wesley and Kathleen Frydl (Eds.). (2004). *Fairness and effectiveness in policing: The evidence.* Washington, D.C.: National Academies Press.

Smallbone, Steven, William Marshall and Richard Wortley. (2008). *Preventing child sexual abuse: Evidence, policy and practice.* Portland, OR: Willan.

Smith, Paula, Paul Gendreau and Kristin Swartz. (2009). Validating the principles of effective intervention: A systematic review of the contributions of meta-analysis in the field of corrections. *Victims and Offenders, 4,* 148–169.

Snyder, Howard. (2000). *Sexual assault of young children as reported to law enforcement: Victim, incident, and offender characteristics.* Bureau of Justice Statistics, U.S Department of Justice. Retrieved from: http://bjs.gov/content/pub/pdf/saycrle.pdf.

Sorensen, Jon, Robert Wrinkle, Victoria Brewer and James Marquart. (1999). Capital punishment and deterrence: Examining the effect of executions on murder in Texas. *Crime and Delinquency, 45,* 481–493.

Spelman, William. (2008). Specifying the relationship between crime and prisons. *Journal of Quantitative Criminology, 24,* 149–178.

Staples, Brent. (2012). California horror stories and the 3-strikes law. *The New York Times,* November 24. Retrieved from: http://www.nytimes.com/2012/11/25/opinion/sunday/california-horror-stories-and-the-3-strikes-law.html.

Steffensmeier, Darrell and Miles Harer. (1991). Did crime rates rise or fall during the Reagan presidency? The effects of an "aging" U.S. population on the nation's crime rate. *Journal of Research in Crime and Delinquency, 28,* 330–359.

Steurer, Stephen, Linda Smith and Alice Tracy. (2001). *Three state recidivism study.* U.S. Department of Education. Retrieved from: http://www.gpo.gov/fdsys/pkg/ERIC-ED465886/pdf/ERIC-ED465886.pdf.

Tjaden, Patricia and Nancy Thoennes. (2000). *Full report of the prevalence, incidence, and consequences of violence against women.* National Institute of Justice. Retrieved from: https://www.ncjrs.gov/pdffiles1/nij/183781.pdf.

Tonry, Michael and Matthew Melewski. (2008). The malign effect of drug and crime control policies on Black Americans. In M. Tonry (Ed.), *Crime and justice: A review of research* (pp. 1–44). Chicago, IL: University of Chicago Press.

Useem, Bert and Anne M. Piehl. (2008). *Prison state: The challenge of mass incarceration.* New York, NY: Oxford University Press.

Van Voorhis, Patricia and David Lester. (2004). Cognitive therapies. In P. Van Voorhis, M. Braswell and D. Lester (Eds.), *Correctional counseling and rehabilitation.* 5th ed (pp. 183–208). Cincinnati, OH: Anderson.

Vieraitis, Lynne, Tomislav Kovandzic and Thomas Marvell. (2007). The criminogenic effect of imprisonment: Evidence from state panel data, 1974–2002. *Criminology & Public Policy,* 6, 589–622.

Violence Policy Center. (2000). Intratec (Navegar). Retrieved from: http://www.vpc.org/studies/deadint.htm.

Walmsley, Roy. (2009). *World prison population list.* KCL International Centre for Prison Studies. Retrieved from: http://www.prisonstudies.org/info/downloads/wppl-8th_41.pdf.

Weisberg, Robert. (2005). The death penalty meets social science: Deterrence and jury behavior under new scrutiny. *Annual Review of Law and Social Science, 1,* 151–170.

Williams, Jenny, Rosalie Pacula, Frank Chaloupka and Wechsler. (2004). Alcohol and marijuana use among college students: Economic complements or substitutes? *Health Economics, 13,* 825–843.

Wilson, David, Catherine Gallagher and Doris MacKenzie. (2000). A meta-analysis of corrections-based education, vocation, and work programs for adult offenders. *Journal of Research in Crime and Delinquency, 37,* 347–368.

Wintemute, Garen. (2000). Guns and gun violence. In A. Blumstein and J. Wallman (Eds.), *The Crime Drop in America* (pp. 45–96). New York, NY: Cambridge University Press.

Wolfgang, Marvin. (1958). *Patterns in criminal homicide.* Philadelphia, PA: University of Pennsylvania.

Wortley, Richard and Steven Smallbone. (2006). Applying situational principles to sexual offenses against children. In R. Wortley and S. Smallbone (Eds.), *Situational prevention of child sexual abuse, Crime prevention studies, Vol. 19* (pp. 7–36). Monsey, NY: Criminal Justice Press.

Wright, Richard, Peter Rossi and Kathleen Daly. (1983). *Under the gun: Weapons, crime, and violence in America.* Hawthorne, NY: Aldine de Gruyter.

Yang, Bijou and David Lester. (2008). The deterrent effect of executions: A meta-analysis thirty years after Ehrlich. *Journal of Criminal Justice, 36,* 453–460.

Yunker, James. (2002). A new statistical analysis of capital punishment incorporating U.S. post moratorium data. *Social Science Quarterly, 82,* 297–311.

Zevitz, Richard. (2006). Sex offender community notification: Its role in recidivism and offender reintegration. *Criminal Justice Studies, 19,* 193–208.

Zgoba, Kristen, Philip Witt, Melissa Dalessandro and Bonita Veysey. (2008). *Megan's Law: Assessing the practical and monetary efficacy.* U.S. Department of Justice. Retrieved from: http://www.ncjrs.gov/pdffiles1/nij/grants/225370.pdf.

Zimmerman, Paul. (2004). State executions, deterrence and the incidence of murder. *Journal of Applied Economics, 7,* 163–193.

Zimmerman, Paul. (2006). Estimates of the deterrent effect of alternative execution methods in the United States: 1978–2000. *American Journal of Economics and Sociology,* 65, 909–941.

Zimmerman, Paul. (2009). Statistical variability and the deterrent effect of the death penalty. *American Law and Economic Review, 11,* 370–398.

Zimring, Franklin. (1968). Is gun control likely to reduce violent killings? *University of Chicago Law Review, 35,* 21–37.

Zimring, Franklin. (1972). The medium is the message: Firearm caliber as a determinant of death from assault. *Journal of Legal Studies, 1,* 97–124.

Zimring, Franklin. (1991). Firearms, violence, and public policy. *Scientific American, 265,* 48–54.

Zimring, Franklin and Gordon Hawkins. (1997). *Crime is not the problem: Lethal violence in the United States.* New York, NY: Oxford University Press.

Zwi, Karen. (2007). School-based education programs for the prevention of child sexual abuse. *Cochrane Database for Systematic Reviews, 2,* 1–44.

Details of the Major Theories of Crime Causation

Theory and Chapter	Tenets	Theorists	Strengths	Weaknesses	Policy Implications
Psychosocial Theories Chapter 3	Certain traits, especially high levels of negative emotionality and impulsiveness and low levels of constraint and agreeableness are associated with crime; trait development is influenced by both biologic and environmental factors	Caspi, et al. (1994); Miller and Lynam (2001), Ellis and Walsh (2000)	Can explain why some individuals in aversive environments refrain from crime, especially violence, and why some in supportive environments commit it	Do not take social structural or social process variables into account, cannot explain desistance or changes in crime rate over time	Programs that utilize cognitive behavioral therapy
Biosocial Theories Chapter 3	Crime may be rooted in a number of biological factors, such as brain dysfunction, deficits in arousal, problems with neurochemistry and genetics; biological factors interact with environmental factors to produce crime	Bufkin and Luttrell (2005); Raine, Venables and Williams (1990); Day and Carelli (2007); Seo and Patrick (2008); Beaver, Wright and Walsh (2008); Caspi, et al. (2002)	Can explain why some individuals in aversive environments refrain from crime, especially violence, and why some in supportive environments commit it	Do not take social structural or social process variables into account, cannot explain desistance or changes in crime rate over time	Pharmacological treatment, positive changes in the environment, support for parents, social skills training, diet changes, school and community programs
Social Disorganization Chapter 4	Poverty, residential mobility, heterogeneity and family disruption lead to inability to exert informal social control, which leads to crime; collective efficacy insulates against crime	Shaw and McKay (1942), Sampson (1989, 1987), Wilson (1995)	Explains the existence of high crime neighborhoods and the intergenerational transmission of crime	Cannot explain middle class crime or white collar crime	Programs like the Chicago Area Project designed to provide opportunities for young people and opportunities for adults to guide young people, building up collective efficacy
Anomie Chapter 4	Normlessness and an unclear sense of what is right and wrong leads to crime	Durkheim (1895)	Shows the power of norms and solidarity in constraining crime, shows how weakening norms can facilitate crime	Focuses on whole societies and not any segments thereof that may be culturally distinct	No direct, see Classic Strain Theory for indirect
Institutional Anomie Chapter 4	Subjugation of all other social institutions to the economy means those social institutions cannot regulate criminal behavior, especially that done in pursuit of money	Messner and Rosenfeld (1995)	Explains why crime rates are higher in the U.S. than other capitalist countries	Concentrates on just one cause of and solution for crime that ignores known correlates of crime (strain, control, learning)	Decommodification, including more maternity and paternity leave, downplaying competition for young children in schools

Theory	Description	Key author(s)	Strengths	Weaknesses	Policy implications
Classic Strain Chapter 4	Belief in culturally accepted goals but rejection of legitimate means to attain them leads to innovation (criminal adaptation to strain)	Merton (1938)	Explains how crime is related to an inability to achieve goals	Does not explain how people choose different adaptations	Any program designed to alleviate the strain of not achieving the American Dream, e.g. the War on Poverty
General Strain Chapter 4	Failure to achieve positively valued goals, removal of positively valued stimuli and presentation of negatively valued stimuli lead to a negative view of others leads to negative emotions, especially anger, leads to criminal coping	Agnew (1992)	Expands the types of strain, explains the role of emotion in crime, substantial empirical support	Still somewhat unclear what strains are most relevant for whom and why, ignores structural features that may create strain in the first place	Programs that reduce strains and especially enhance ability to cope with strain in a non-criminal way
Subcultural Theories Chapter 4	Criminal groups reject middle class values and develop their own, easier to attain goals; there are limits to criminal as well as legitimate opportunities	Cohen (1955), Miller (1958), Cloward and Ohlin (1960), Anderson (1994, 1999)	Explains crime among deviant subcultures, explains how values are created among the lower class (especially Miller, Anderson), explains violence	Only explains crime among deviant subcultures	Provide legitimate opportunities that meet all the needs of a subculture (belonging, protection, education, employment)
Differential Association Chapter 5	Association with delinquent others leads to crime	Sutherland (1947)	Brings attention to the idea that crime is learned from others, emphasizes the importance of human interaction in learning crime	Does not explain how people actually learn crime, implies that once people learn an excess of definitions favorable to violating the law, they will always violate the law	Surround young people with prosocial peers through mentoring programs (e.g. BBBS)
Social Learning Chapter 5	Imitation of delinquent peers leads to initial crime, differential reinforcement for criminal activity leads to persistence in crime	Akers (1997, 2002)	Explains how people actually learn crime, one of the most empirically well supported theories of crime	Association with delinquent peers may amplify delinquency but not cause it (birds of a feather problem)	Surround young people with prosocial peers through mentoring programs (e.g. BBBS)
Social Control Chapter 5	The strength of bonds to social institutions and the people in them determines criminal involvement; the stronger the bond, the less criminal involvement	Hirschi (1969)	Answers the question why do people refrain from committing crime most of the time, substantial empirical support	Predicts that only friendless loners will engage in delinquency, empirical research shows the opposite	Programs that help young people bond to their families and to schools

Theory and Chapter	Tenets	Theorists	Strengths	Weaknesses	Policy Implications
Self-Control Chapter 5	Low self-control causes crime and is a result of ineffective parenting	Gottfredson and Hirschi (1990)	Very parsimonious, one of the most if not the most empirically well supported theory of crime	Recent evidence of a genetic basis of self-control and its malleability after age 10 undermine tenets of the theory	Programs that help parents, especially young, first time parents monitor, recognize and appropriately punish deviant behavior
Labeling Chapter 5	Formal labeling by the criminal justice system leads to an increase in crime (secondary deviance)	Tannenbaum (1938), Lemert (1952)	Shows how a label from the CJS may change self-identity and cut off opportunities for legitimate living	Does not explain initial delinquent act	Avoid labeling where possible, especially with juveniles
Neutralization Chapter 5	Offenders use a variety of techniques to ameliorate their guilty feelings and thereby engage in crime	Sykes and Matza (1957)	Shows how people can be delinquent without fully committing to law breaking attitudes	Unclear whether delinquents use neutralization before or after crime	Challenge neutralizations so that delinquents cannot commit to these excuses for crime
Marxist Criminology Chapter 6	Crime is the result of the struggle between the classes; the harsh capitalism in the United States is particularly criminogenic	Marx (N/A), Bonger (1905), Currie (1997), Colvin (2000)	Shows how capitalism, especially the U.S. version, may contribute to crime	Cannot explain crime in non-capitalist countries	Overthrow capitalism or failing that, a shift to a more compassionate capitalism
Conflict Criminology Chapter 6	Crime is an inevitable result of conflict among groups vying for power; the groups with more power will criminalize the actions of those with less	Weber (N/A), Vold (1958)	Draws attention to the power disparity between groups and how those with more power keep the activities of those with less power criminal	Ignores known correlates of crime, especially at the individual level (strain, control, learning)	Programs/policies that help spread power around more equitably (e.g., a higher minimum wage, et cetera)
Peacemaking Criminology Chapter 6	Harsh punishments beget violence; restorative justice is the solution to crime	Quinney (1991), Braithwaite (2002)	Focuses on the detrimental effects of involvement in the CJS	It is unclear what is meant by peacemaking or how to measure it	Restorative justice

Theory	Citations	Strengths	Weaknesses	Policy Implications
Feminist Criminology Chapter 6	Adler (1975), Simon (1975), Chesney-Lind (1989), Messerschmidt (1993)	Shows how girls' and women's victimization can lead to their criminal involvement (especially Chesney-Lind), explains the connection between masculinity and crime (especially Messerschmidt)	Predictions about women engaging in more crime as they leave the home have not been borne out	Recognition of victimization as a path to criminality and implement treatment and rehabilitation programs
Rational Choice Theory Chapter 9	Cornish and Clarke (1986)	Differentiates between crime and a specific criminal activity, contains prescriptions for how crime can be made less of a rational choice beyond adjusting punishment	Assumes that offenders are rational, much research shows they are not (e.g., many are intoxicated at the time of the criminal act)	Make crime less of a rational choice by increasing the certainty of punishment, but especially by locking doors, installing alarms, et cetera
Routine Activity Theory Chapter 9	Cohen and Felson (1979)	Explains the increase in crime in the U.S. after WWII. Focuses on the features of the environment that may create suitable targets, recognizes that capable guardians come in the form of ordinary citizens more often than law enforcement	Is not concerned with offender motivation	Ordinary citizens can reduce their target suitability by locking their doors, staying out of bad neighborhoods and so on
General Theory of Crime and Delinquency Chapter 7	Agnew (2005)	Focuses on risk factors across life domains and across the lifetime to paint a more comprehensive picture of crime causation	Unclear which risk factors in which life domains have the greatest influence on crime, limited empirical support to date	Programs that target those with risk factors especially in childhood with preventive programs
Integrated Cognitive Antisocial Potential (ICAP) Theory Chapter 7	Farrington (2003)	Considers short and long term risk factors, can explain empirically known facts about crime and individual differences in offending	Cannot explain differences in crime by neighborhood, region or country	Programs that target those with risk factors especially in childhood with preventive programs

Theory and Chapter	Tenets	Theorists	Strengths	Weaknesses	Policy Implications
Dual Pathway Developmental Theory Chapter 7	Offenders are either adolescent limited or life course persistent offenders; the latter start life with a host of risk factors while the former age out of offending in adulthood	Moffitt (1993)	Explains why the rate of offending is so high in adolescence, clear about who will become which type of offender	There may be more than two different groups of offenders, offenders may be able to change trajectories	Programs that target those with risk factors especially in childhood with preventive programs
Life-Course Theory Chapter 7	Even offenders who persist in crime well into adulthood can lead legitimate lives if they encounter and choose important turning points, such as marriage and jobs that allow them to build up social capital	Sampson and Laub (1993, 2005)	It extends social bond theory and explains how people desist from crime, a refreshing focus on human agency in desistance	It is more of a desistance theory, and it does not explain what causes crime	Programs to help ex-offenders get meaningful, good paying, jobs (assisting with good marriages is probably outside the realm of policy)

About the Authors

Kelly Frailing, Ph.D. is an assistant professor of criminal justice at Texas A&M International University. Though her research interests are wide ranging, her scholarship is starting to coalesce around offenders with mental illness on the one hand and crime and disasters on the other. She has authored a number of journal articles and book chapters on these topics and co-edited both the first and second editions of *Crime and Criminal Justice in Disaster* with Dee Wood Harper.

Dee Wood Harper, Ph.D. is professor emeritus of sociology and criminology and justice at Loyola University New Orleans. His research interests have varied over his 53-year (and counting) career; he is presently concentrating on violence, particularly murder and robbery, and also crime within the context of disaster. He is the co-author or co-editor of three recent books: *Violence: Do we know it when we see it? A Reader* (January 2012), the second edition of *Crime, Criminal Justice and Disaster* (August 2012) and *Why Violence? Leading Questions Regarding the Conceptualization and Reality of Violence in Society* (March 2013).

Index